2nd Edition

TIME FOR BUSINESS

Junior Cycle Business Studies

Joe Stafford
Siobhan O'Sullivan
Ultan Henry
James Cumiskey

Edco

Published 2020

The Educational Company of Ireland
Ballymount Road
Walkinstown
Dublin 12
www.edco.ie
A member of the Smurfit Kappa Group plc

© Joe Stafford, Siobhan O'Sullivan, Ultan Henry, James Cumiskey 2020

All rights reserved. No part of this publication may be reproduced, stored in a retrieval system, or transmitted in any form or by any means, electronic, mechanical, photocopying, recording or otherwise, without either the prior permission of the publishers or a licence permitting restricted copying in Ireland issued by the Irish Copyright Licensing Agency, 63 Patrick Street, Dún Laoghaire, Co. Dublin.

ISBN 978-1-84536-918-7

Project editor: Kristin Jensen
Copy editor and indexer: Jane Rogers
Design and layout: Design Image
Illustrations: ShelkyBean

While every care has been taken to trace and acknowledge copyright, the publishers tender their apologies for any accidental infringement where copyright has proved untraceable. They would be pleased to come to a suitable arrangement with the rightful owner in each case. Web references in this book are intended as a guide for teachers. At the time of going to press, all web addresses were active and contained information relevant to the topics in this book. However, The Educational Company of Ireland and the authors do not accept responsibility for the views or information contained on these websites. Content and addresses may change beyond our control and pupils should be supervised when investigating websites.

Introduction

For the student

Welcome to secondary school and your newly revised business textbook, *Time for Business*. This textbook comes with a **Student Activity Book** that has a wide range of **activities** for you to work on at home and in school. This book aims to develop your knowledge of business in everyday life – at a local, national and international level.

For the teacher

This newly revised book has been written for the Junior Cycle and aims to foster students' interest in business. It is based on the **learning outcomes** from the NCCA specification and develops students' knowledge of business through the three strands of **Personal Finance**, **Enterprise** and **Our Economy**.

Key aspects of *Time for Business*

- **Learning outcomes** from the specification are highlighted at the beginning of each chapter.
- **Learning intentions** for each chapter are stated in student-friendly language.
- **Key terms** are listed to allow students to become familiar with important new terms and to improve subject-specific vocabulary.
- **Key skills** are identified for each activity in the chapter:

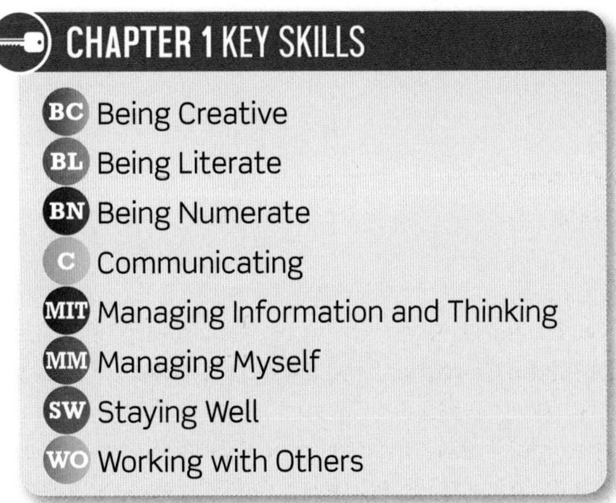

- The **language** used is clear and simple to suit students of varying reading levels.
- Simple and helpful **icons** are designed to aid understanding:
  - Key terms are explained
  - Reflection activity
  - Activity to be completed in your copy
  - Activity to be completed in your Student Activity Book
- **Special features** include chapter links, Did You Know?, In the News and Enterprise in Action.
- **Digital resources** are referenced throughout the chapters.
- **Assessment** supports include a comprehensive standalone chapter and exam questions at the end of chapters, included where relevant.

Contents

Strand 3: Our Economy

Your Guide to *Time for Business*

Study Business Studies with the *Time for Business* textbook and complete the exercises and questions in your Student Activity Book.

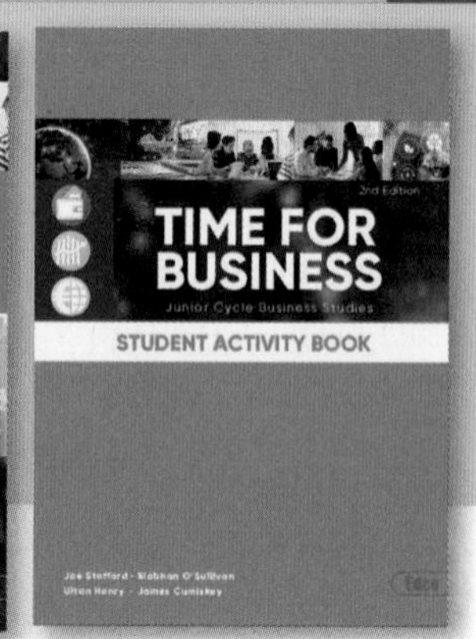

Textbook

Each chapter begins with learning outcomes, learning intentions, key terms and key skills and includes activities, Did You Know?, In the News and Enterprise in Action sections.

LEARNING OUTCOMES

Describe the knowledge, understanding, skills and values you will gain after covering the learning outcomes

KEY TERMS

Important words you will need to learn to master the material covered in each chapter

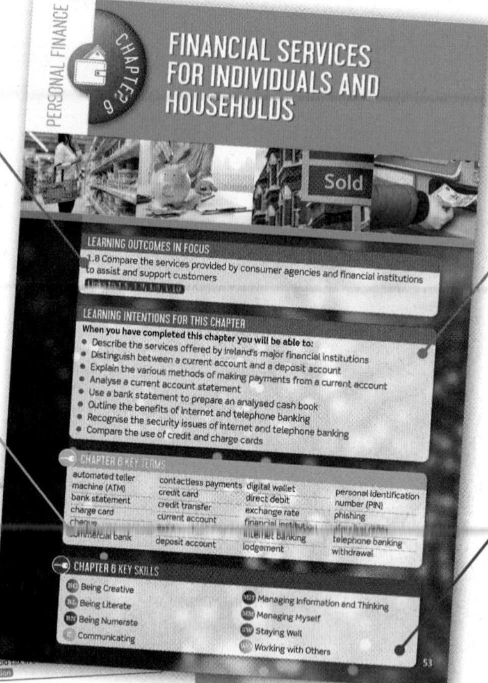
PERSONAL FINANCE

CHAPTER 6

FINANCIAL SERVICES FOR INDIVIDUALS AND HOUSEHOLDS

LEARNING OUTCOMES IN FOCUS

1.8 Compare the services provided by consumer agencies and financial institutions to assist and support customers

LEARNING INTENTIONS FOR THIS CHAPTER

When you have completed this chapter you will be able to:
- Describe the services offered by Ireland's major financial institutions
- Distinguish between a current account and a deposit account
- Explain the various methods of making payments from a current account
- Analyse a current account statement
- Use a bank statement to prepare an analysed cash book
- Outline the benefits of internet and telephone banking
- Recognise the security issues of internet and telephone banking
- Compare the use of credit and charge cards

CHAPTER 6 KEY TERMS

automated teller machine (ATM), bank statement, charge card, cheque, commercial bank, contactless payments, credit card, credit transfer, current account, deposit account, digital wallet, direct debit, exchange rate, financial institution, internet banking, lodgement, personal identification number (PIN), phishing, telephone banking, withdrawal

CHAPTER 6 KEY SKILLS

Being Creative, Being Literate, Being Numerate, Communicating, Managing Information and Thinking, Managing Myself, Staying Well, Working with Others

53

LEARNING INTENTIONS

What this chapter will help you to learn about relating to each topic

KEY SKILLS

Junior Cycle key skills that you will develop through carefully designed activities

ASSESSMENT

Questions from past Junior Cycle Business Studies exam papers are included as well as a dedicated assessment chapter

Student Activity Book

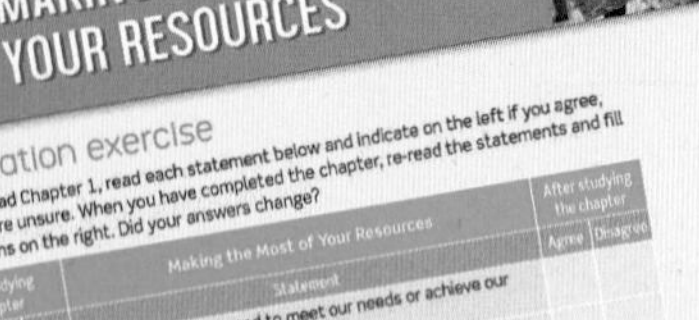

STUDENT ACTIVITY BOOK

Each chapter includes anticipation exercises, activities, self-assessment and reflection

Digital resources

The *Time for Business* digital resources will enhance classroom learning by encouraging student participation and engagement. They support the Junior Cycle specification's emphasis on the use of modern technology in the classroom.

To provide for the integration of digital resources in the classroom and aid lesson planning, they are referenced throughout the textbook using the following icons:

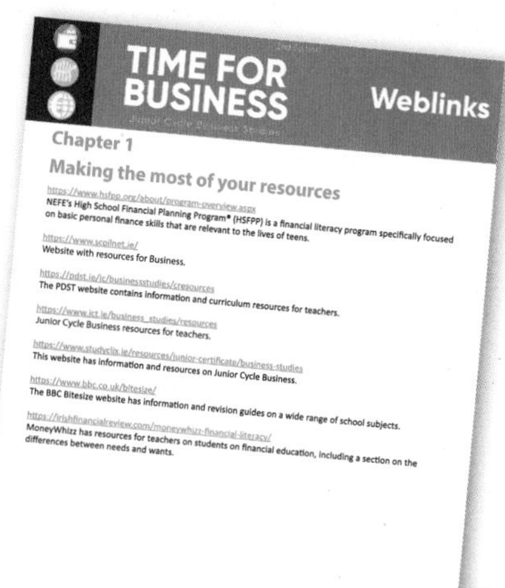
TIME FOR BUSINESS — Weblinks

Chapter 1

Making the most of your resources

https://www.hsfpp.org/about/program-overview.aspx
NEFE's High School Financial Planning Program® (HSFPP) is a financial literacy program specifically focused on basic personal finance skills that are relevant to the lives of teens.

https://www.scoilnet.ie/
Website with resources for Business.

https://pdst.ie/jc/businessstudies/cresources
The PDST website contains information and curriculum resources for teachers.

https://www.jct.ie/business_studies/resources
Junior Cycle Business resources for teachers.

https://www.studyclix.ie/resources/junior-certificate/business-studies
This website has information and resources on Junior Cycle Business.

https://www.bbc.co.uk/bitesize/
The BBC Bitesize website has information and revision guides on a wide range of school subjects.

https://irishfinancialreview.com/moneywhizz-financial-literacy/
MoneyWhizz has resources for teachers on students on financial education, including a section on the differences between needs and wants.

PowerPoint Summary

Editable PowerPoint presentations

Provide chapter summaries, highlighting key themes and topics in the textbook

Weblinks

Useful weblinks

Documents provide links to additional material

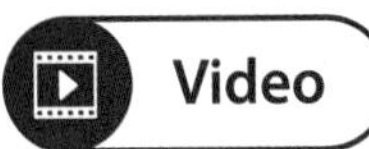

Video

Engaging videos

Linked to topics covered in the textbook

Excel template

Editable Excel templates

Can be used to draft final accounts

Step-by-step accounts

Step-by-step accounts

Demonstrations of accounting exercises

TIME FOR BUSINESS — Step-by-step account

General Ledger

(DR) VAT A/C (CR)

Date	Details	F	Total	Date	Details	F	Total
2022			€	2022			€
07/01	Cash purchases	ACB	500	03/01	Cash sales	GL	4,600
	Balance c/d		4,100				
			4,600				4,600
				07/01	Balance b/d		4,100

Joe Stafford · Siobhan O'Sullivan · Ultan Henry · James Cumiskey — Edco

Teachers and students can access the *Time for Business* digital resources via the *Time for Business* interactive e-book, which is available online at **www.edcolearning.ie**.

Acknowledgements

The authors and publisher would like to thank the following for permission to reproduce articles, graphs and data:
Page 13, 'EU report suggests living wage in Ireland is €11.90 per hour, 25% higher than existing minimum wage', *Irish Examiner* (30 November 2018); page 28, information from Central Statistics Office (cso.ie); page 35, 'Easy steps to keep your family budget on track', *Irish Independent* (15 January 2016); page 68, 'Majority of people don't know what interest rate is on their credit cards', Charlie Weston, *Irish Independent* (6 March 2019); page 87, information from Competition and Consumer Protection Commission (ccpc.ie); page 88, Citizens Information (citizensinformation.ie); page 91, 'Students beware gimmicks and lure of easy credit', Fiona Reddan, *Irish Times* (18 August 2015); page 109, 'Banks failing to deliver home insurance value', John Hearne, *Irish Examiner* (6 June 2019); page 111, '"Ghost brokers" leave thousands of motorists uninsured', RTÉ News (21 November 2019); page 131, 'Elder financial abuse: Demands from family members for money among issues – survey', *Irish Independent* (15 June 2015); page 141, 'Major retailers fined over breaches of consumer legislation', Elaine Edwards, *Irish Times* (6 March 2017); page 153, 'Ireland ranked worst in EU for performance on climate action', *Irish Times* (10 December 2018); page 154, RTÉ News (9 May 2019); page 158, quotation by Klaus Toepfer, former Executive Director, UNEP; page 159, 'Fast fashion is hard to escape, but it is damaging our environment', Saoirse McHugh, TheJournal.ie (October 2019); page 162, information from ReCreate (recreate.ie/about); page 164, quote from 'Regional campaign highlights the need to shop local', Ciara Whooley, *ISME* (11 December 2018); page 165, 'Older Irish consumers "care less about the ethics of businesses"', Conor Pope, *Irish Times* (17 December 2018); page 189, statistics from 'Top 1000 companies that spend the most on research and development' (data sources: Strategy&'s 2018 Global Innovation 1000 study, 2018 EU Industrial R&D Investment Scoreboard), Nick Skillicorn (ideastovalue.com); page 207, 'Tayto Park owner confident screams from proposed new €15.5 m rollercoaster won't impact residents', Gordon Deegan, BreakingNews.ie (3 March 2019); page 208, 'Peat didn't just keep our homes warm, it fuelled our economy', Kevin Doyle, *Irish Independent* (12 November 2019); page 232, 'McDonald's to buy Israel's Dynamic Yield', *Hospitality Ireland* (1 April 2019); page 237, 'A tweet from Kendall Jenner can be worth more than a €500k marketing budget', TheJournal.ie (2 October 2016); page 249, 'Brexit blamed for drop in new cars sale', TheJournal.ie (1 February 2019); page 253, 'IKEA launches kitchen made from recycled plastic bottles', Alice Morby, *Dezeen* magazine (24 January 2017); page 263, 'Cocoa Brown sold out in 24 hours after Kylie's tweet', RTÉ Lifestyle (18 August 2017); page 281, 'Businesses here raise €165m in venture capital funding', *Irish Independent* (4 November 2019); page 282, 'Easons launches Munster sale and leaseback deals worth over €4m', *Irish Independent* (27 August 2019); page 367, 'Rising cost of national children's hospital a scandal in the making', Paul Cullen and Martin Wall, *Irish Times* (22 December 2018); 'Individuals may be held accountable over cost of children's hospital', Paul Cullen and Pat Leahy, *Irish Times* (4 February 2019); page 400, graph from 'Budget 2019: Economic and Fiscal Policy', Department of Finance; page 401, 'Can carbon tax be used to change behaviour while also protecting the less well-off?', Kevin O'Sullivan, *Irish Times* (6 June 2019); page 420, 'Annual report on public debt in Ireland', Department of Finance (September 2018); page 421, 'Ireland still paying €14m a day in interest on national debt', Eoin Burke-Kennedy, *Irish Times* (15 April 2019); page 426, 'Everything you need to know about Ireland's economy', World Economic Forum (19 March 2019); page 433, '"Sugar tax" on fizzy drinks raises €32m, but none of it goes on tackling obesity', Douglas Broom, *Irish Independent* (8 July 2019); page 434, statistic from Safefood (safefood.eu), statistic from *Irish Times*; page 438, 'World on track to lose two-thirds of wild animals by 2020, major report warns', *The Guardian* (27 October 2016); page 441, 'Irish Sustainable Development Goal "champions" to be recognised', Kevin O'Sullivan, *Irish Times* (31 January 2019); page 444, 'Japan resumes commercial whaling', RTÉ News (1 July 2019); page 455, 'EU/Mercosur trade deal – what do you need to know', RTÉ News (28 June 2019); page 458, from a speech by Paschal Donohoe to the Valentia Transatlantic Cable Foundation, 'Globalisation – our interconnected and independent World' (12 July 2019).

The authors and publisher would like to acknowledge the following for logos and photographs:
Abbey Theatre, Advertising Standards Authority for Ireland, Alamy, An Post, Bank of Ireland, Cartoon Stock, Cocoa Brown Tan, Comhaltas, Competition and Consumer Protection Commission, ComReg, Consumers' Association of Ireland, Department of Finance, Directorate-General for Agriculture and Rural Development, DSC, EBS, Electric Picnic, Enterprise Ireland, FoodCloud, Getty Images, GOAL, Greenpeace, Industrial Development Authority, Irish League of Credit Unions, iStock, Jack and Jill Foundation, Lily O'Brien's Chocolates, Mairéad Finnegan, Médecins Sans Frontières, Money Advice and Budgeting Service, Office of the Ombudsman, Office of the Revenue Commissioners, Pixabay, ReCreate, Shutterstock, Social Entrepreneurs Ireland, Society of St Vincent de Paul, Stira Folding Attic Stairs, The Donkey Sanctuary, Tidy Towns, Ulster Bank, United Nations Development Programme.

The authors and publisher would also like to acknowledge the following for digital use:
Animated Explainer (What does the Central Bank of Ireland do?) featured with the permission of Central Bank of Ireland. © Central Bank of Ireland, 2019; CCPC Online Shopping Know your Rights © Competition and Consumer Protection Commission (CCPC), 2016; What is Fairtrade? © Fairtrade 2015; Let's Talk Future of Trade © World Trade Organization, 2019; Food Waste © European Union, 2016; Retail 2020 | 5 Technologies that will change the way you shop © Lifelong Learners I www.youtube.com; Discover a customs union... © European Union, 2018/Source: EC – Audiovisual Service; 25 years of the single market © European Union, 2019.

Author acknowledgements

To Sharon, Emily and Rachel – my heartfelt thanks for your endless patience and support.
– *Joe Stafford*

I'd like to thank my parents, Brian (RIP) and Moira, for instilling in me a love of reading, an appreciation of the value of education and a strong interest in business. Thanks to all my family and friends for their endless patience, love, support and guidance. – *Siobhan O'Sullivan*

I would like to thank my family for their support and understanding. I would also like to thank my parents, who have always been my inspiration in life. – *Ultan Henry*

I would like to thank my wife, Roisín, and my children, Ryan and Charlotte, for all their help, support and patience. I would also like to thank my parents, John and Phyllis. – *James Cumiskey*

STRAND ONE

PERSONAL FINANCE

CHAPTER 1

MAKING THE MOST OF YOUR RESOURCES

LEARNING OUTCOMES IN FOCUS

1.1 Review the personal resources available to them to realise their needs and wants and analyse the extent to which realising their needs and wants may impact on individuals and society

Links to 1.2, 1.3, 1.5, 1.9, 3.1, 3.4, 3.5

LEARNING INTENTIONS FOR THIS CHAPTER

When you have completed this chapter you will be able to:

- Explain what resources are
- Identify the main resources available to you
- Explain and illustrate the difference between needs and wants
- Match your resources to your needs and wants
- Illustrate how your needs and wants are likely to change over time
- Outline the difference between financial cost and opportunity cost
- Appreciate the impact of your use of resources on the lives of other people.

CHAPTER 1 KEY TERMS

- financial cost
- money
- needs
- opportunity cost
- priorities
- resources
- wants

CHAPTER 1 KEY SKILLS

- BC Being Creative
- BL Being Literate
- BN Being Numerate
- C Communicating
- MIT Managing Information and Thinking
- MM Managing Myself
- SW Staying Well
- WO Working with Others

What is a resource?

KEY TERM

A **resource** is anything we can use in order to meet our needs or help us to achieve our goals. Resources include your textbook, pens, computers, people, knowledge, money and time.

Resources:

- Are useful and valuable
- Help us to achieve things
- May be limited or scarce.

It doesn't matter how many resources you have – if you don't know how to use them, you will never have enough.

Types of resources

Households and individuals have a variety of resources available to them, such as:

- Physical/capital resources
- Natural resources
- Financial resources
- Human resources
- Time resources.

See Chapters 31 and 32 for economic resources

KEY SKILLS

1.1 Using resources

What does the image of the man trying to climb the wall make you think? How is it relevant to you and your life? #Reflect

Physical/capital resources

These are goods made by people and used to make other goods and provide services. They enable people to meet their day-to-day needs for food, clothing and shelter, but also help us to travel, communicate and enjoy our leisure time.

Examples of physical or capital resources are:

- Buildings or property
- Computers
- Family car
- Smartphone.

Natural resources

A person may have access to resources provided by nature, such as land and water.

Financial resources

This category includes all types and sources of money. Financial resources allow people to buy goods and services.

Examples of financial resources include:

- Income from employment
- Income from benefits (e.g. Child Benefit, pensions, Jobseeker's Benefit)
- Savings
- Borrowed money.

KEY SKILLS

1.2 Goods vs. services

What, do you think, are the main differences between *goods* and *services*? After you've listed them, think of three examples of goods and three examples of services that you or your parents have recently paid for. #Reflect #Think #Contrast

MIT BL MM

Human resources

This refers not only to your own personal skills, abilities and experience, but all the people available to help you. For example, your school counsellor or a librarian are valuable resources whose skills and knowledge can be used to help you.

Examples of human resources are:

- An ability to read and write
- Problem-solving abilities
- Skills in music, sport, technology, etc.
- Family and friends
- Librarians
- Teachers and coaches
- Community leaders.

Time resources

Time is a valuable and limited resource, so it is important to use it wisely. Unlike many physical and financial resources, you cannot earn, borrow or buy more time. However, if you make the best use of it, time will allow you to gather other resources, like education and skills, to achieve your goals. Time also allows you to work in order to earn the money needed to support your lifestyle.

'My favourite things in life don't cost any money. It's really clear that the most precious resource we all have is TIME.'

Steve Jobs, co-founder of Apple

PERSONAL FINANCE

KEY SKILLS

1.3 How do you use your time?

MM SW MIT BN BC

(a) Do you think Steve Jobs was right in saying that time is more valuable than money? Why/why not? #WhatDoYouThink #Reflect

(b) Next weekend, record how long you spend doing different activities, such as homework, chores, playing games, time spent online, sleeping and so on.

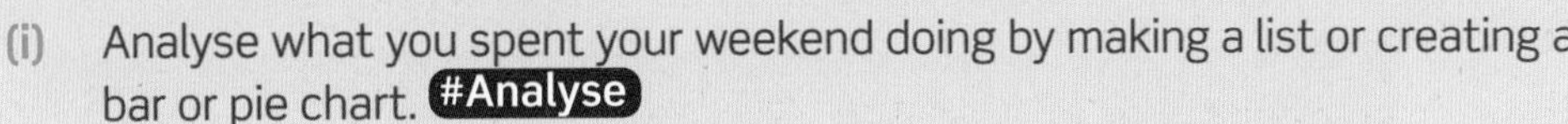

(i) Analyse what you spent your weekend doing by making a list or creating a bar or pie chart. #Analyse

(ii) Was there any time you could have spent doing something more useful? Were you happy with the amount of time you spent on 'work' and 'leisure'? Explain the reason for your answer. #Reflect

Access to resources

Having access to resources is more important than owning them. If you can use a resource, it is valuable to you. For example, you may not own the computers in your school or the books in the library, but you have access to these resources and can use them to help with your education.

KEY SKILLS

1.4 Your access to resources

WO MM MIT C

List five resources that you have access to besides those of your home and family. List the resources on your own, then share them with your partner and compare your lists. #ThinkPairShare

Needs vs. wants

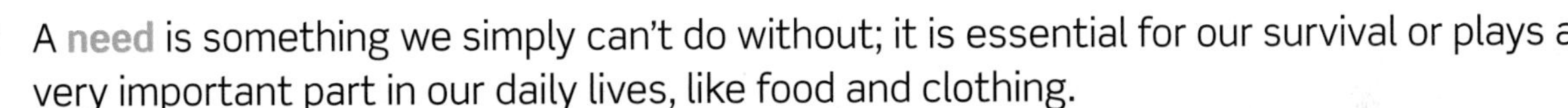

A **need** is something we simply can't do without; it is essential for our survival or plays a very important part in our daily lives, like food and clothing.

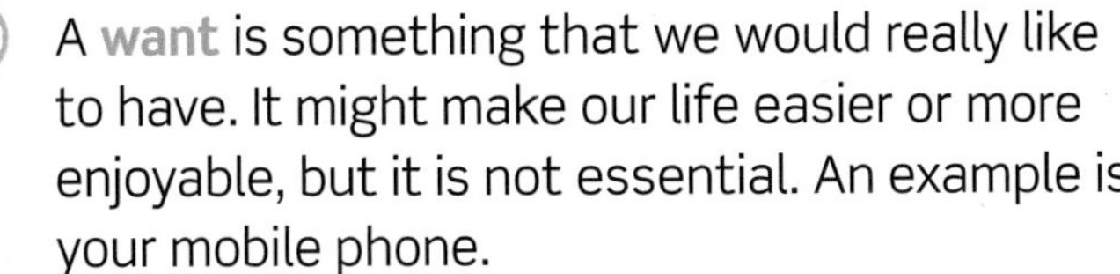

A **want** is something that we would really like to have. It might make our life easier or more enjoyable, but it is not essential. An example is your mobile phone.

Some needs, such as food, clothing and shelter, are essential at every stage of our lives. Other important needs change as we grow and develop. Most of us could think of many things we would love to buy if only we could! Everyone wants an expensive car, but we might only have the money to buy a small second-hand car. In this example, our financial resource (money) is able to satisfy our basic need for transport, but not the expensive sports car we might want.

While our list of wants may be endless, resources available are limited, so we're forced to make choices. Our choices and our use of resources affect other people too. For example, inexpensive clothing requires workers to earn low wages and possibly suffer poor working conditions. As the lowest wages will be in countries far away, goods will be transported long distances, which will impact all those people involved in transporting the goods and will require the use of petrol and vehicles.

See Chapter 13 for the impact of consumer choices

See Chapter 3 for expenditure

KEY SKILLS

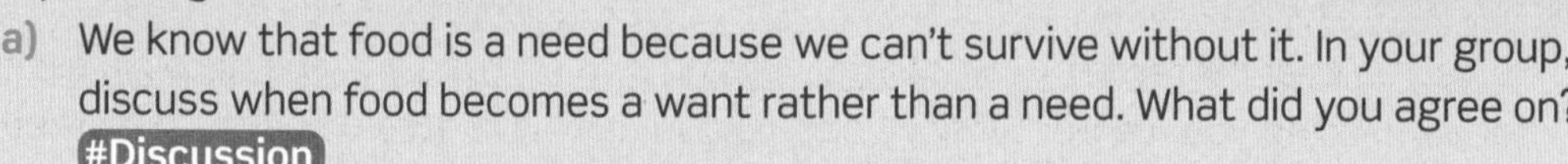

SW MM

1.5 Reflecting on our choices

(a) We know that food is a need because we can't survive without it. In your group, discuss when food becomes a want rather than a need. What did you agree on? #Discussion

(b) We will discuss the issue of global resources and the impact of our individual choices in later chapters, but for now it's important to understand that our planet has limited resources, so the choices we make about how to use them will have consequences for ourselves and for others. Can you think of any other examples where your use of resources might impact on the lives of others? #Reflect

KEY SKILLS

MM SW MIT

1.6 Your needs and wants

(a) Make two lists:
- Five items that you currently need
- Five items that you currently want.

Do you think that your needs and wants will stay the same as you get older? Write down the reason for your answer. #WhatDoYouThink

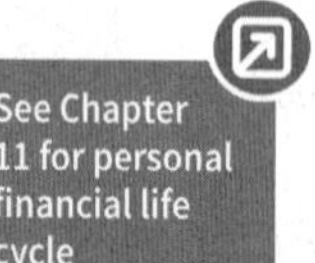

See Chapter 11 for personal financial life cycle

(b) List one example of a need and one example of a want that you think are relevant for people at the following stages of their lives: #List
- People in their late teens
- Adults in their 20s and 30s
- Adults in their 40s and 50s
- Retired people.

(c) Mary is growing out of her clothes, so she and her friends go shopping. Mary has saved up €150 to spend on new clothes. She falls in love with a designer dress that costs €125 and thinks about buying it. Joan says they should go to the department store, where Mary could buy a dress for €30. How does this illustrate the difference between a need and a want? #Illustrate

(d) Meeting your needs means that you will need to make use of resources. Make a list of four possible ways you could get the resources required to meet your current needs. #List

Making use of financial resources

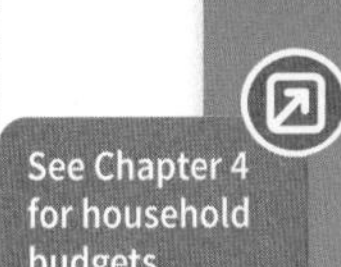

Managing our personal finances means learning how to buy the things we need and want with the money available to us. Knowing how to prioritise (rank in order of importance) our spending helps us to make informed and balanced spending decisions.

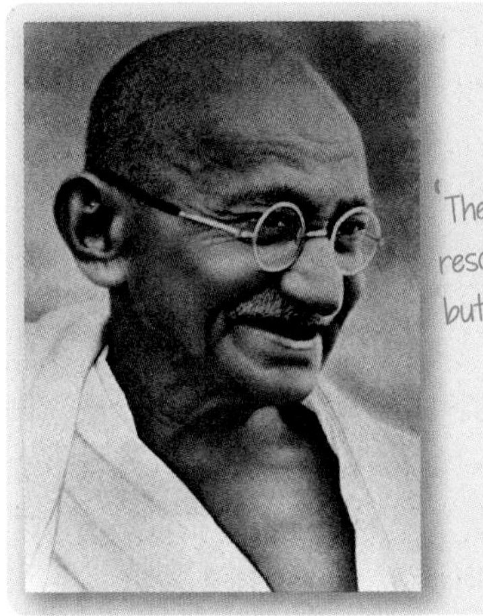

'The earth has enough resources for our need, but not for our greed.'
Mahatma Gandhi

See Chapter 4 for household budgets

As a rule, money should be spent on essential items first. When we look at household budgeting, you will examine these priorities in greater detail so that you can plan your spending and manage your money more carefully.

KEY TERM

Money is anything of value that is accepted by people in exchange for goods and services.

KEY TERM

A **priority** is something that is more important than other options.

KEY SKILLS WO MIT

1.7 Bartering resources

Have you ever bartered by swapping anything other than coins and notes in exchange for something you wanted? If so, what did you use? Compare your list with others in your class. #Discussion #Compare

Whatever we buy has a cost. In fact, everything we consume actually has two costs: a financial cost and an opportunity cost.

KEY TERM

Financial cost is the money cost or price of the items we choose to buy.

We often have to make choices about what to buy based on the financial cost, or price, of goods, such as a €10 shirt. This gives rise to an opportunity cost. We measure opportunity cost in terms of the other things we could have done with our money. When we decide to use our money for one thing, we lose the opportunity to use it on something else.

KEY TERM

The **opportunity cost** is the item we must go without when we have to make a choice.

For example, if you have €10 and choose to spend it on a shirt, you will not be able to use that money for phone credit. The financial cost of the shirt is €10 and the opportunity cost is the phone credit you now cannot buy.

Considering opportunity cost helps us to get the best value for money.

1.8 Financial and opportunity costs

(a) Looking back to question 1.6 (c), where Mary wanted to buy a designer dress instead of a department store dress, what was the financial cost and the opportunity cost of buying the designer dress? #Reflect

(b) Think of a recent example when you had only a certain amount of money and you had to make a decision on how to spend it. What was the financial cost and what was the opportunity cost? #Think #Reflect

See Chapter 32 for distribution of economic resources
See Chapter 37 for government economic policy

Your parents, business owners and even the government have to make these kinds of choices too. Just like you, they don't have enough resources to do all the things they would like to do. When we look at economics, we will examine the impact of these choices on local, national and global communities.

Money doesn't grow on trees!

Think about the last time you needed money to buy something. Where did you get the money from?

- Was it money you had saved?
- Was it money you had to earn by doing jobs for friends and family?
- Or was it money you had to borrow from your parents or other family members?

BANK OF MUM & DAD
9876 5432 1234 5678
01/00 12/99
A STUDENT

If you asked your parents or other family members for the money, what was their response? Did they ask you what you wanted it for? Did they remind you that money doesn't grow on trees?

1.9 Your money

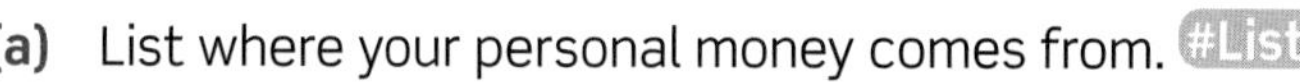

(a) List where your personal money comes from. #List

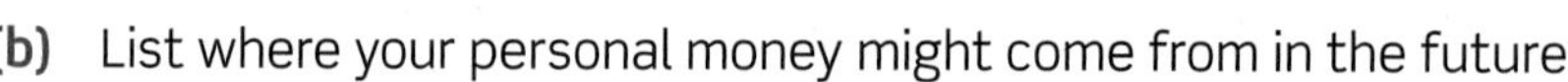

(b) List where your personal money might come from in the future:
- While you are at school and college
- When you have started working. #List

(c) How would you explain the phrase 'Money doesn't grow on trees'? #Explain

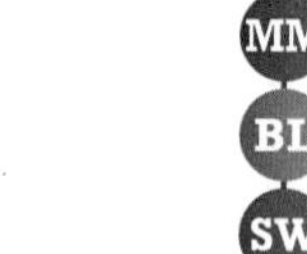

Being money smart

Money is a resource because it allows us to buy things that we need or want. As you grow older, your need for money will increase greatly and you may have to provide for the financial needs of others as well as for yourself. While money isn't the most essential thing in life, it is still important to manage your money well to get the most value and benefit from it. Financial problems can be very stressful, but a lot of money problems can be avoided by good planning.

When you have completed this strand on personal finance, you should have a set of skills that will help you to manage your money with realistic planning. This is a big part of being money smart, but it also involves:

- Thinking about where your money comes from and where it goes
- Being able to live within your means
- Being able to plan for future spending needs
- Being able to save regularly
- Understanding the consequences of overspending and borrowing
- Being able to evaluate different sources of finance and make informed decisions about managing personal finances
- Understanding what a personal financial life cycle is and being able to prepare one for yourself
- Using your money wisely.

See Chapter 11 for personal financial life cycle

We will discuss these issues in the following chapters.

PowerPoint Summary

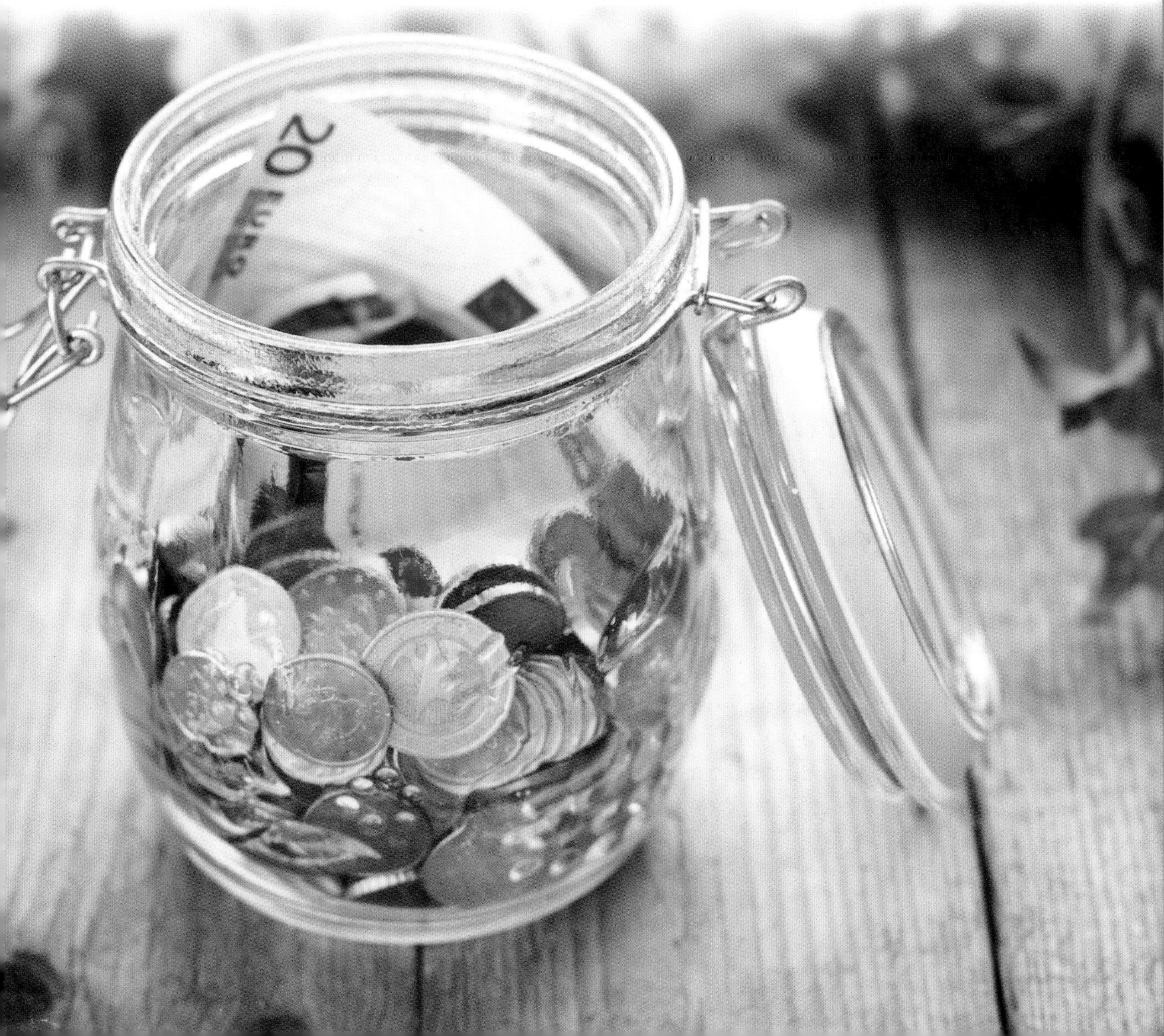

PERSONAL FINANCE

CHAPTER 2

HOUSEHOLD INCOME

LEARNING OUTCOMES IN FOCUS

1.2 Identify and classify sources of income and expenditure, compare options available to best manage financial resources, evaluating the risks associated with each option and making informed and responsible judgements

Links to 1.1, 1.3, 1.5, 1.6, 1.9, 1.11, 1.12, 1.13, 2.10, 2.11, 2.12, 3.1, 3.2, 3.4, 3.10, 3.11

1.11 Interpret a wage slip and calculate personal tax liability arising from employment Links to 1.2, 1.4, 1.6, 2.3, 3.4, 3.5

LEARNING INTENTIONS FOR THIS CHAPTER

When you have completed this chapter you will be able to:

- State the main sources of household income
- Distinguish between regular and irregular sources of income
- Explain 'benefit in kind' income
- Explain why tax must be paid on income
- Interpret a payslip
- Calculate gross and net income
- Differentiate between statutory and voluntary deductions from income
- Differentiate between disposable and discretionary income
- Prepare and evaluate a household income plan.

CHAPTER 2 KEY TERMS

basic pay	employee	net pay	salary
benefit in kind	employer	overtime	statutory deductions
bonus payments	grant	PAYE	time rate
commission	gross pay	payslip	USC
deductions	income	pension	voluntary deductions
discretionary income	income plan	piece rate	wage
disposable income	interest	PRSI	
dividend	irregular income	regular income	

CHAPTER 2 KEY SKILLS

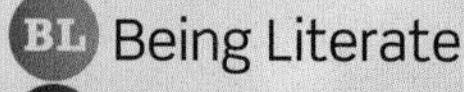
BL Being Literate

BN Being Numerate

C Communicating

MIT Managing Information and Thinking

MM Managing Myself

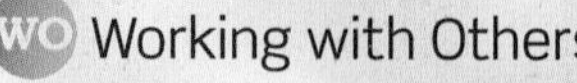
WO Working with Others

PERSONAL FINANCE

What is income?

In Chapter 1, when we looked at the differences between needs and wants, we saw that everyone requires a certain amount of money in order to satisfy them. We'll now look at where that money comes from.

KEY TERM

Income is money received by a person or coming into a household.
Employees are people who work for employers in return for a payment.
An **employer** is someone who pays another person to work for them.

Income comes in a variety of types and from various sources. Every household's income reflects the age and status of the people who live there. For example, most households will receive income from employment (wages and salaries), while others may rely on retirement income (pensions). All households with young children receive some income from the government in the form of Child Benefit.

The following are some of the most common sources of household income:

Wages and salaries	Income received as a reward for work.
Pensions	A **pension** is income paid to people who have retired.
Child Benefit	A payment made to parents/guardians of children.
Jobseeker's Benefit	A payment to people who are unable to find employment.
Working Family Payment (WFP)	A payment available to workers with children. It gives extra financial support to people on low pay. To qualify for the payment, the average weekly family income must be below a certain amount based on the family size.
Income from grants	A **grant** is a sum of money paid to someone for a specific purpose. Unlike a loan, it does not need to be repaid. Farm households may receive grants from the government and the European Union depending on how they use or upgrade their land. All households can apply for grants to carry out certain improvements, such as making their home more energy efficient.
Interest on savings	Banks, building societies, the post office and credit unions reward those who save money with them by paying **interest** on their savings.
Dividends on shares	A **dividend** is the portion of company profits paid to shareholders. Anyone who buys shares in a company is called a shareholder. Shareholders are the owners of a company and may be rewarded for their investment by receiving a dividend.
Windfall income	This is income that you don't expect, such as a win on the National Lottery or gifts and inheritances.

See Chapter 40 for the European Union Common Agricultural Policy

See Chapter 7 for saving and investing

KEY SKILLS

MIT MM WO C

2.1 Your household income

(a) Make a list of all the possible income sources for teenagers. #List

(b) On your own, make a list of all the ways households might receive income. #List

(c) Compare your lists with the person sitting next to you. #ThinkPairShare

(d) Share your combined answers with the pair sitting behind you/in front of you. #Discussion

(e) Compare your lists of household income with the items listed in the text below. Did you miss any that apply to your household? #Compare

Some household income may also come from rent or the sale of goods. If, for example, a householder rents out part of their property to students or on Airbnb, they will earn rental income.

Households might also generate extra income by selling items they no longer need, for example at car boot sales, via websites such as eBay and DoneDeal or by advertising in local papers, etc.

MIT

2.2 Government assistance for workers

Why is the government willing to support low-income workers with a top-up payment like the WFP, do you think? Consider the possible benefits for those households and for the wider society. Share your thoughts with the class.

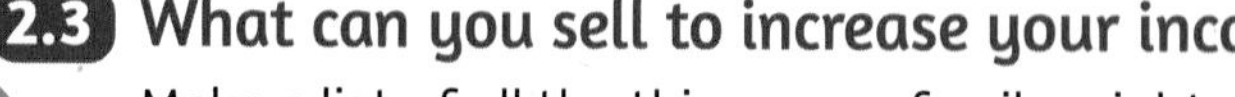

MIT

2.3 What can you sell to increase your income?

Make a list of all the things your family might consider selling, such as the family car when you want to buy a newer one, old school textbooks or birthday cards that you have made. Can you think of any others? #List

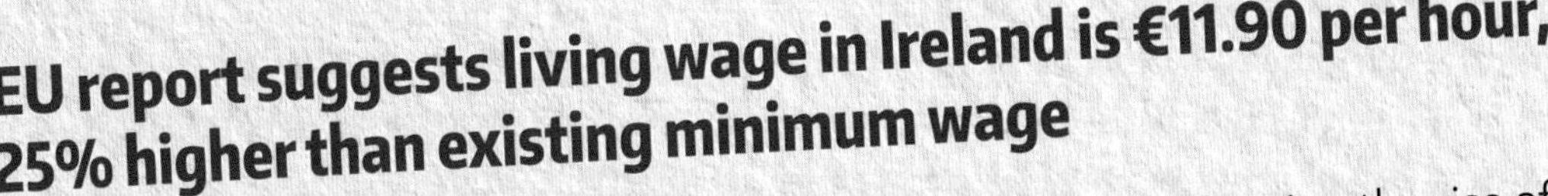

EU report suggests living wage in Ireland is €11.90 per hour, 25% higher than existing minimum wage

Implementing a living wage could play a significant role in offsetting the rise of in-work poverty across the European Union, according to a new report.

The living wage is a measure of income calculated to afford an employee a basic but socially acceptable standard of living. The living wage takes into account the costs of important aspects of daily life such as housing, transport, childcare and basic goods and services.

Campaigns around the living wage are often based on the premise that statutory minimum wages result in inadequate income for many workers, and that work should pay enough to allow workers to have a basic but decent standard of living.

For Ireland, the report highlights that the Irish living wage rate, based on a single adult with no dependants, is €11.90 per hour in 2018. This is 25% higher than the statutory minimum wage (€9.55 per hour*).

The report suggests that due to regional differentials in cost of living, the living wage rate for a single adult with no dependants in Dublin would be €14.45 per hour, 37% higher than the equivalent rate for those living in rural Ireland.

The report highlights findings from Living Wage Ireland that the main factor driving the most recent increases in the living wage has been the rapid increase in private rental housing costs. This, it suggests, was notably the case in Dublin, where housing costs for single workers were nearly 60% higher than outside the capital.

* The national minimum wage was increased to €10.10 from 1 February 2020.

Source: Irish Examiner, 30 November 2018

Lidl Ireland made the following commitment on Twitter on 19 November 2019:

Lidl Ireland @lidl_ireland · 4h

We are pleased to be the first supermarket in Ireland to commit to a €12.30 minimum hourly rate for our employees, in line with the latest Living Wage!

The change will benefit 800 employees in Ireland, while all other employees in Lidl already earn in excess of the Living Wage.

2.4 Minimum wage and living wage

(a) What is your understanding of the term 'in-work poverty'? What do you think causes it? #Think

(b) Research the difference between minimum wage and living wage.

- Which would a worker prefer to earn, do you think?
- Which would an employer prefer to pay?

Explain your answers. #Research #Think

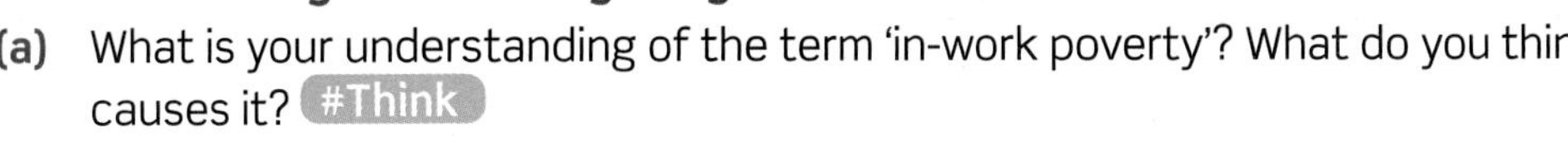

Regular and irregular income

Some sources of income are received on a regular or ongoing basis, such as weekly or monthly. The amounts received may be the same each time. Other types of income are less predictable and may be received only irregularly. The timing and amount of this income are less predictable and cannot be guaranteed. This difference is very important for household planning. Why, do you think, is this the case?

Examples of regular income	Examples of irregular income
› Wages › Salaries › Child Benefit › Pensions › Jobseeker's Benefit	› Overtime (from working extra hours) › Bonus (reward for meeting work targets) › Windfall (unexpected income)

2.5 Your income

Thinking about your own money, what types of regular income (if any) do you receive? On what occasions or from what sources might you receive irregular income? How do you think these income sources might change as you get older? #Reflect #Think

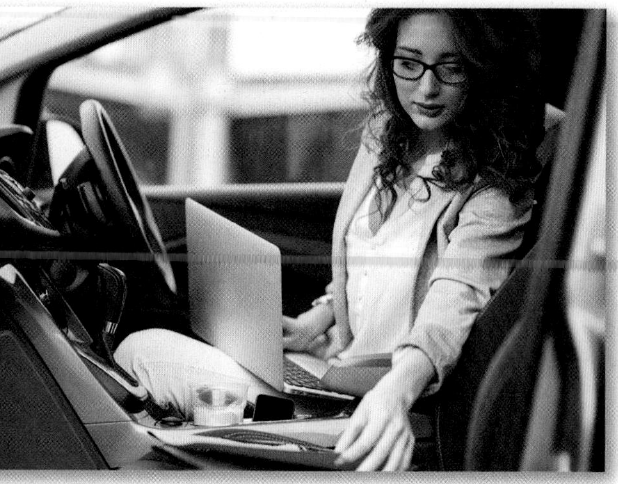

Benefit in kind income

Non-money income in the form of **benefits in kind** (BIK), also known as 'perks', may be received when the household is provided with goods or services that have a money value. For example, an employee may get a company car or mobile phone, or have their health insurance paid for by their employer.

Benefits in kind can also be provided by the state. These include certain social protection payments, such as free travel and medical cards.

Income from employment

Salary

A **salary** is a fixed annual payment made to an employee no matter how many hours they work (above an agreed minimum). For example, a job may carry an annual salary of €40,000, usually paid in equal monthly instalments. Employees who are paid a salary do not normally receive overtime payments for extra hours worked.

KEY SKILLS

2.6 Salary

Managers are often paid an annual salary. Can you think of any other employees who are paid a salary? #Think

Sal is Latin for salt and the word *salary* comes from the Latin *salarium*. This was a payment given to Roman soldiers so that they could buy salt, a valuable commodity at the time. It was generally given as extra payment on top of their wages. Someone who is 'worth their salt' is considered to be deserving of their pay.

PERSONAL FINANCE

Wage

A **wage** is a payment received for work done, normally calculated on the basis of actual work completed or on the amount of time spent working. Unlike the fixed payments of a salary, wages are more likely to vary from one week to the next. Wages may be calculated using a number of different methods, including:

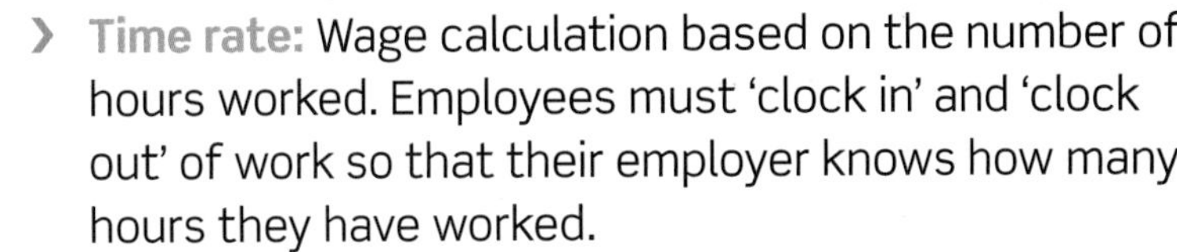

- **Time rate:** Wage calculation based on the number of hours worked. Employees must 'clock in' and 'clock out' of work so that their employer knows how many hours they have worked.
  Example: A 40-hour working week for an employee who is paid €15 per hour would generate a wage of €600 per week (40 hours × €15 per hour = €600).

A 'clocking-in' machine

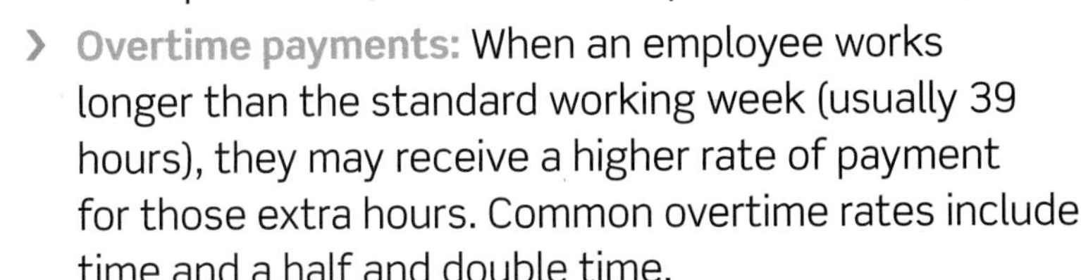

- **Overtime payments:** When an employee works longer than the standard working week (usually 39 hours), they may receive a higher rate of payment for those extra hours. Common overtime rates include time and a half and double time.
  Example: Erin is normally paid €10 an hour for a standard 40-hour working week. If she works more hours during the week, she is paid at time and a half for those extra hours and receives €15 for each extra hour (€10 × 1.5); if she works extra hours at the weekend, she is paid at double time and receives €20 per overtime hour (€10 × 2).

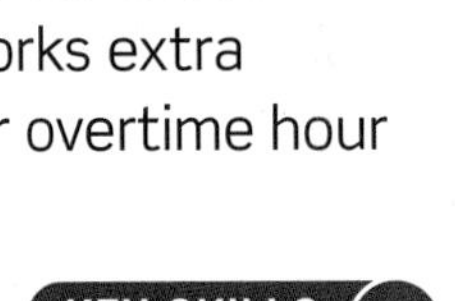

KEY SKILLS

2.7 Using time rate to calculate wages BN

If Erin, from the example above, worked 43 hours one week, including 2 hours at the weekend, calculate how much she would earn for that week. Show your workings clearly. #Calculate

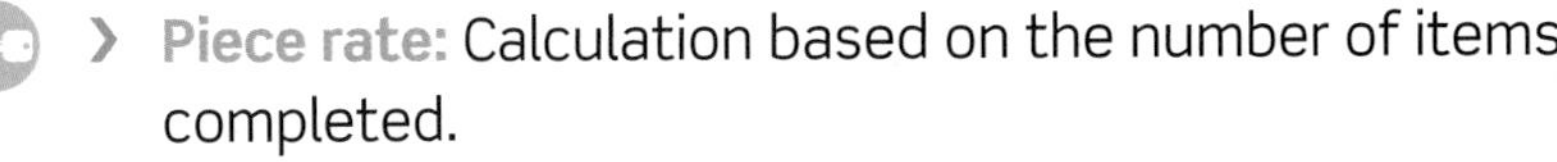

- **Piece rate:** Calculation based on the number of items completed.
  Example: A machinist in a clothing factory receives €3 for each garment made. A worker who successfully completes 200 garments will earn a wage of €600 (200 × €3 = €600).

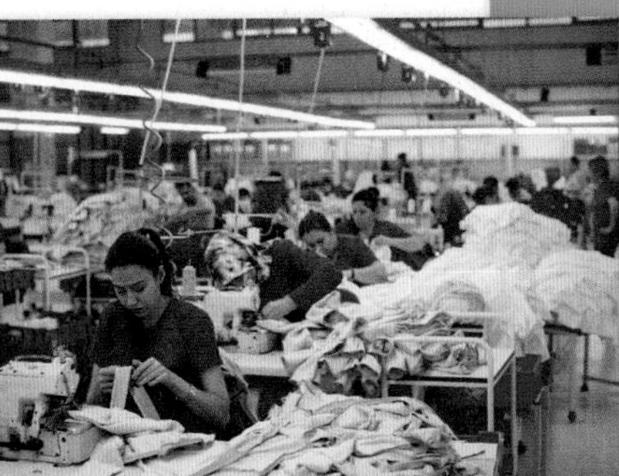

- **Commission:** Some workers, especially sales staff, receive a payment based on the value of the goods or services they have sold. This type of payment system motivates staff to sell more.
  Example: A car salesperson might earn 10% commission on each car sold. Therefore, a car sold for €30,000 will earn the seller a commission payment of €3,000 (€30,000 × 10% = €3,000).
- **Bonus payments:** Some employers reward their staff with extra payments for meeting performance targets or deadlines.
  Example: If a job completion deadline is met, the employee will receive a €100 bonus; if the job runs past the deadline, they won't get the bonus.

KEY TERM

Basic pay is the amount earned before any extra payments (overtime and bonuses) are added.

Payment received

Gross pay

Gross pay is the total pay before any **deductions**. It is the sum of basic pay plus any extra income earned from overtime, bonuses or commission.

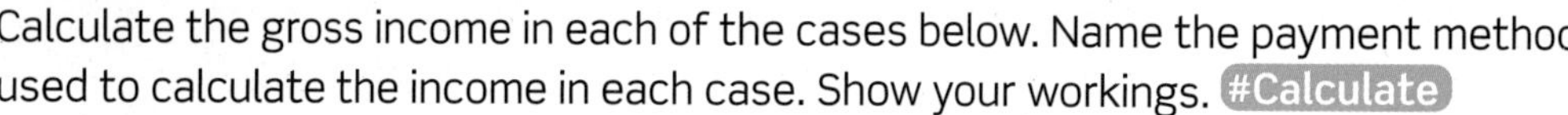

KEY SKILLS

BN

2.8 Calculating gross income

Calculate the gross income in each of the cases below. Name the payment method used to calculate the income in each case. Show your workings. #Calculate

(a) Calculate the gross pay for Cian, who is paid €15 an hour for a 39-hour working week.

(b) Calculate the gross pay for Charlotte, who is paid €18 an hour for a 37-hour working week.

(c) Calculate the gross pay for Niamh, who is employed to pick fruit. She picked 73 kilograms of fruit last week and is paid €3.50 per kilogram.

(d) Calculate the gross pay for Ryan, who is employed to pick apples. He picked 84 kilograms of fruit last week and is paid €2.90 per kilogram.

(e) Calculate the gross pay earned by Hisoka, who sold a €37,000 car and who receives 5% of the value of all car sales made.

(f) Calculate the gross pay earned by Gavin, who sold a €1,200 mobile phone and who receives 12% of the value of all mobile phone sales made.

(g) Calculate the gross pay earned by Thomas, who packs boxes for €9 an hour in a 39-hour week. Last week he also did overtime of 8 hours at time and a half and earned a bonus of €75 for reaching his packing target.

(h) Calculate the gross pay earned by Mason, who packs boxes for €12 an hour for a 40-hour week. Last week he also did overtime of 10 hours at time and a half and earned a bonus of €90 for reaching his packing target.

(i) Calculate the gross monthly income of Bríd, who earns a monthly salary of €1,750 and commission on monthly sales of 5% of sales of insurance. Last month she sold €15,000 worth of insurance.

(j) Calculate the gross monthly income of Breda, who earns a monthly salary of €1,900 and commission on monthly sales of 10% of sales of furniture. Last month she sold €10,000 worth of furniture.

Net pay

Net pay, also called take-home pay, is the amount left after all deductions from gross pay have been made.

Net pay = Gross pay – Total deductions

Deductions

There are two main types of deduction from pay:

- **Statutory deductions** are compulsory. Every worker is required by law to pay.

- **Voluntary deductions** are not compulsory, but workers may choose to pay them.

Statutory deductions

See Chapters 10 and 34 for taxation

Workers must pay tax on most kinds of earned income. This means that a certain percentage of our income must be paid over to the government. Governments use tax revenue to pay for state services such as healthcare and education as well as to redistribute wealth across the economy. Every citizen has a responsibility to pay their fair share of taxes.

2.9 Paying taxes: What's a fair share?

MIT C

(a) What is your understanding of the phrase 'fair share of taxes'? #ThinkPairShare #WhatDoYouThink

(b) Do you agree that we all have a responsibility to pay our fair share of taxes? Why/why not? Explain your reason(s). #Discuss #Think #Reflect

(c) What, do you think, should be considered when deciding how much tax each person should pay? Do you think it should be the same for everybody? Why/why not? #WhatDoYouThink

Most employees in Ireland are subject to the **Pay As You Earn (PAYE)** income tax system. Under this system, tax is paid on income as it is earned (weekly, fortnightly, monthly, etc.). Usually, the employer calculates the tax due on behalf of the employee and sends it directly to the Office of the Revenue Commissioners, the government agency responsible for taxation in Ireland.

Workers in Ireland also contribute to a system of **Pay Related Social Insurance (PRSI)**, which allows them to claim certain benefits in the future, if needed. These benefits include a state pension, Jobseeker's Benefit, Maternity Benefit, Carer's Benefit and some treatment benefits for dental and eye-care needs.

Another tax, called the **Universal Social Charge (USC)**, applies to all workers whose income is above a certain limit. At present, taxpayers get no specific benefit from paying the USC, as it is used to fund general government spending.

Voluntary deductions

Some workers may also choose to have extra money deducted from their gross pay in order to provide for pensions, savings, loan repayments, private health insurance or trade union membership.

DID YOU KNOW...

A *trade union* is an organisation that represents the views and interests of a group of workers. It tries to ensure that workers receive good pay and conditions and are not exploited by their employers.

See Chapter 19 for employee rights

After all deductions have been made, the remaining figure is the employee's take-home pay, also known as net pay.

Disposable income

The remaining income after all income taxes and statutory payments have been made is called **disposable income**. This is the amount of money available for all types of spending or saving.

Disposable income = Gross income – Statutory deductions

For example, Paula Dunne earns €2,000 gross pay per month but has to pay €450 in statutory deductions (PAYE, PRSI and USC). This leaves Paula with a monthly disposable income of €1,550 (€2,000 – €450 = €1,550).

KEY SKILLS

MIT

2.10 Voluntary deductions

In our Paula Dunne example, why, do you think, are voluntary deductions not included in the calculation for disposable income?

#WhatDoYouThink

Discretionary income

The income left over after taxes and essential spending on items such as the mortgage/rent, food and bills is called **discretionary income**, and you can choose how to spend it. Spending of discretionary income includes, for example, a family holiday or a trip to the cinema.

Discretionary income = Gross income – Statutory deductions – Essential payments (bills)

For example, Paula Dunne makes €1,000 essential payments from her income. This leaves Paula with €550 discretionary income from her salary (€2,000 – €450 – €1,000 = €550). Since Paula has paid all her taxes and accounted for all essential payments, she can now spend her discretionary income however she wants.

If you receive pocket money, it is likely that almost all of it is discretionary income and you have freedom over how you spend it. Your parents, on the other hand, despite receiving a larger amount of total income, may have very little discretionary income remaining after meeting all essential household costs.

Income calculation

Colm Kavanagh is paid €22 per hour for a standard 39-hour week. Overtime is paid at time and a half for the first 5 hours and double time for each additional hour after that. In week 27, he worked 48 hours and had the following deductions from his gross pay: PAYE €275, PRSI €48, USC €52, health insurance €50, trade union dues €25, savings €75.

By law, employers must provide employees with a **payslip**, either on paper or electronically, to show the amounts earned and deducted. These should be checked and kept in a safe place for future reference.

Colm's payslip for Week 27 is as follows:

Employee No. 15	Colm Kavanagh		Week 27	Date: 5 July 2020
PAY:	€	DEDUCTIONS:		
BASIC	€858	PAYE	€275	
OVERTIME	€341	PRSI	€48	
		USC	€52	
		HEALTH INSURANCE	€50	
		TRADE UNION DUES	€25	
		SAVINGS	€75	NET PAY
GROSS PAY	€1,199	TOTAL DEDUCTIONS	€525	€674

Workings

Basic pay: 39 hrs × €22 = €858

Overtime: 5 hrs × €33 = €165 (time and a half pays €33 per hour: €22 + €11)
plus 4 hrs × €44 = €176 (double time pays €44 per hour: €22 × 2)
Total overtime pay = €341

Net pay: €1,199 (gross pay) – €525 (total deductions) = €674

KEY SKILLS BN MIT

2.11 Calculating gross and net pay

16

Assuming a standard working week of 40 hours, for each of the following situations in week 31, calculate the gross pay earned, then complete the blank payslips in the Student Activity Book and calculate the net pay. #Calculate

(a) Daria Tchoryk worked 48 hours last week. She earns €10 per hour for her standard week and overtime is paid at time and a half. Her deductions were income tax €36.50, PRSI €20.80, USC €15.00.

(b) Peter Hogan worked 47 hours last week. He earns €12 per hour for his standard week. Overtime is paid at time and a half for the first 5 hours and at double time for any additional hours worked. His deductions were income tax €41.25, PRSI €24.72, USC €20.40, health insurance €20.

(c) Aoife Regan received €340 for working a standard week. Her payslip also showed 5 overtime hours paid at double time. Her deductions were income tax €12.87, PRSI €17.00, USC €9.78, union fee €3.07.

Planning and recording income

Households can use a cash book to keep and analyse records of actual income received. Whether in a record book, spreadsheet or other computer program, income records are useful for planning purposes, especially for regular income, as the household can see the source and amount of recurring income.

Income records help a household to estimate their future income and ensure that they live within their means and don't spend more money than they earn each month.

Here is an **income plan** for the Wilson household for three months. James and Louise Wilson both work outside the home. They have three school-aged children.

PLANNED INCOME	JANUARY	FEBRUARY	MARCH	TOTAL
	€	€	€	€
James Wilson - Salary	1,700	1,700	1,700	
Louise Wilson - Salary	1,900	1,900	1,900	
Child Benefit	500	500	500	
TOTAL INCOME				

The columns will be added up at the end of each month and the rows added at the end of the chosen time period.

KEY SKILLS

BN

MIT

2.12 Wilson household income plan

16

Complete the Total column and Total Income row in the Wilson household income plan in the Student Activity Book. Alternatively, copy the income plan into your Record Book 1, your copy or a spreadsheet. #Calculate

2.13 Your income plan

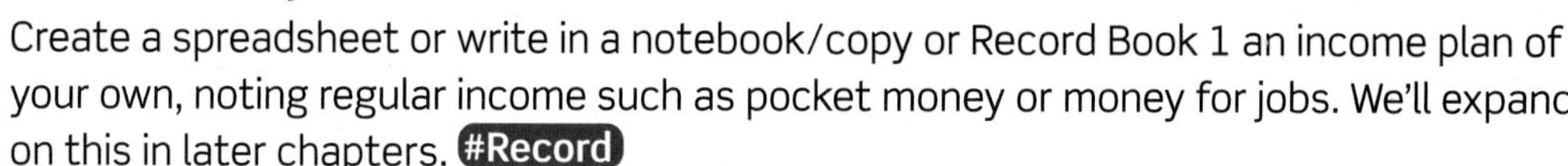

Create a spreadsheet or write in a notebook/copy or Record Book 1 an income plan of your own, noting regular income such as pocket money or money for jobs. We'll expand on this in later chapters. #Record

2.14 Job perks

(a) Have you heard the phrase 'a perk of the job'? Explain what this means and list some examples. #List

(b) Steven takes a packet of paper from the office stationery cupboard and puts it in his backpack. When his colleague Josie sees him, Steven justifies taking the paper by saying, 'I've run out of printer paper at home. It's just a perk of the job. The company buys enough and won't miss it.' Josie is shocked and considers it stealing. What do you think? In light of your discussion, define what you consider to be 'a perk of the job'. Give some examples of perks. #WhatDoYouThink

EXAM QUESTION

Junior Cycle 2019

Question 12

Name a source of income associated with each of the following people:

- Retired person
- Employed person
- Unemployed person.

Weblinks

PowerPoint Summary

HOUSEHOLD EXPENDITURE

LEARNING OUTCOMES IN FOCUS

1.2 Identify and classify sources of income and expenditure, compare options available to best manage financial resources, evaluating the risks associated with each option and making informed and responsible judgements

Links to 1.1, 1.3, 1.5, 1.6, 1.9, 1.11, 1.12, 1.13, 2.10, 2.11, 2.12, 3.1, 3.2, 3.4, 3.10, 3.11

LEARNING INTENTIONS FOR THIS CHAPTER

When you have completed this chapter you will be able to:

- Explain the difference between fixed, irregular and discretionary spending
- Appreciate the need to prioritise expenditure
- Explain the difference between current and capital expenditure
- Define the terms 'impulse buying' and 'false economy'
- Prepare a household expenditure plan.

CHAPTER 3 KEY TERMS

- analysed cash book
- budget
- capital expenditure
- cash flow
- current expenditure
- discretionary expenditure
- expenditure
- false economy
- fixed expenditure
- impulse buying
- invoice
- irregular expenditure

CHAPTER 3 KEY SKILLS

- BC Being Creative
- BL Being Literate
- BN Being Numerate
- C Communicating
- MIT Managing Information and Thinking
- MM Managing Myself
- SW Staying Well
- WO Working with Others

What is expenditure?

KEY TERM

Expenditure refers to the way people spend their income in order to satisfy various needs and wants.

Types of expenditure

Fixed expenditure

Fixed expenditure means that the same amount of money is spent on a regular basis (weekly, monthly or annually). Since the expenditure is fixed, the payment does not depend on usage. For example, car tax is an item of fixed expenditure, but the amount paid each year does not depend on how often the car is used. The tax paid covers a specific period of time and it doesn't matter if the car is driven every day or just one day a week – the amount paid remains the same (fixed).

Other examples of fixed expenditure are:

- Mortgage repayments
- Rent
- Local Property Tax
- TV licence
- Insurance costs.

Irregular expenditure

Items of **irregular expenditure** occur on a less regular basis or the amounts involved may vary with usage. Since both the timing and the amount of these payments are less predictable, irregular spending is harder to plan for. Fuel costs for a car are one example of irregular expenditure. The costs will change from week to week depending on how often the car is used. Higher mileage will mean higher expenditure. Other examples of irregular expenditure are:

- Groceries
- Clothing
- Light and heat
- Waste/recycling charges
- Telephone bills
- Education costs
- Repairs.

KEY SKILLS

3.1 Why does expenditure vary? MIT

For each of the examples listed above, can you explain why the amount of expenditure may vary over time? #Reflect

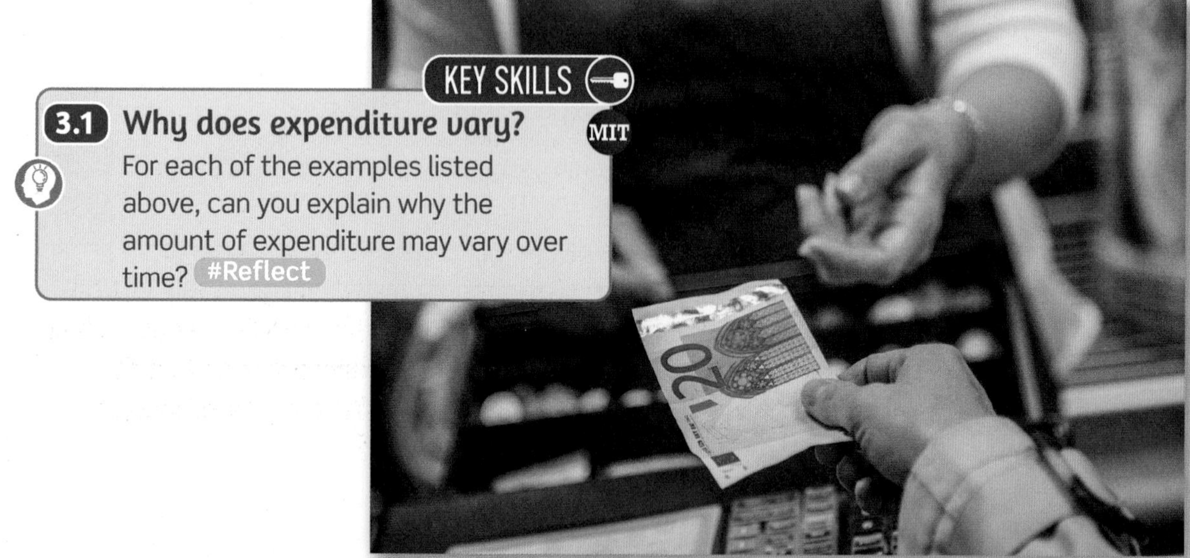

Discretionary expenditure

Discretionary expenditure is spending on non-essential items that we choose to buy. This type of spending tries to satisfy our wants rather than our needs. For that reason, money should be spent on discretionary items only after all essential items or needs have been paid for. Examples of discretionary expenditure are:

- Entertainment
- Holidays
- Gifts
- Upgrades to expensive items such as cars, furniture and household electronics
- Premium sports channels/movie channels.

KEY SKILLS

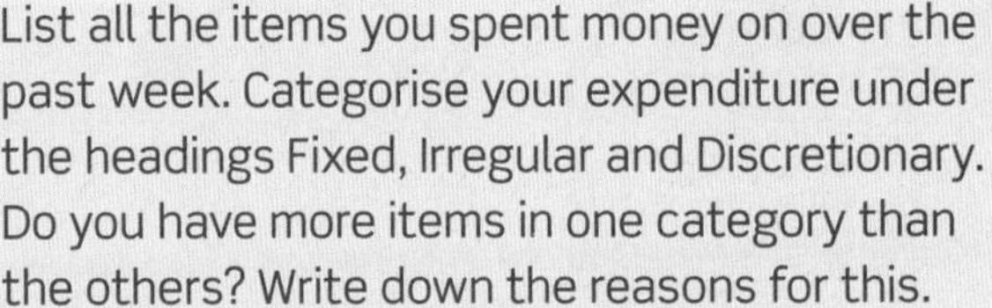

3.2 Your expenditure

List all the items you spent money on over the past week. Categorise your expenditure under the headings Fixed, Irregular and Discretionary. Do you have more items in one category than the others? Write down the reasons for this.

#List #Reflect

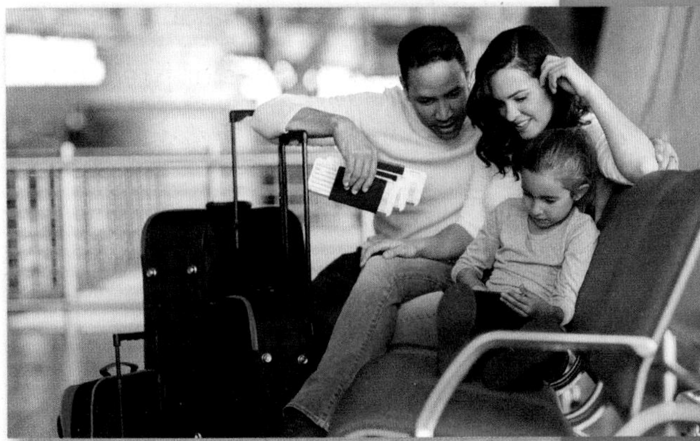

Current expenditure vs. capital expenditure

KEY TERM

Current expenditure is repeated or ongoing day-to-day spending.

Some expenditure is regular and ongoing. This type of repeated short-term spending is called **current expenditure**. Groceries are an example of current expenditure – we need to spend money on them week after week, month after month. Other examples of current expenditure are:

- Utility bills, such as gas and electricity
- Rent/mortgage payments
- Education
- Travel.

KEY TERM

Capital expenditure is once-off or long-term spending.

Once-off spending on something you will use for years to come is called **capital expenditure**. This type of expenditure happens less regularly and will generally not be repeated for a long time. For example, a household may install a new dishwasher in their home. This is a large item of expenditure, but the dishwasher is expected to last for several years. Other examples of household capital expenditure are the purchase of:

- A new car
- Furniture
- A laptop
- A TV.

KEY SKILLS

MIT

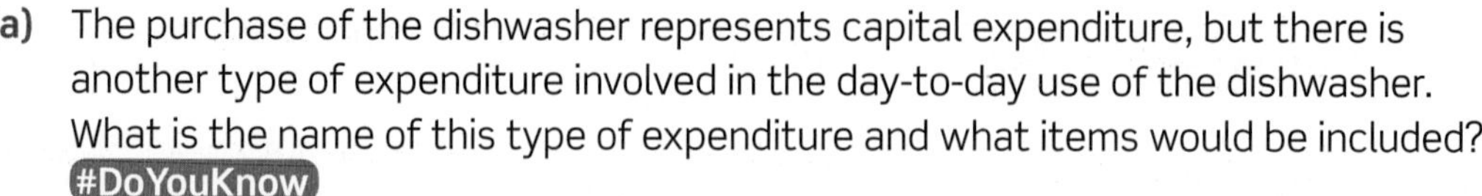

3.3 Household expenditure

(a) The purchase of the dishwasher represents capital expenditure, but there is another type of expenditure involved in the day-to-day use of the dishwasher. What is the name of this type of expenditure and what items would be included? #DoYouKnow

(b) Can you think of two other examples of household capital expenditure that will also create a need for extra current expenditure for a household? #CreativeThinking

Guidelines for effective spending

Households should look at all areas of spending to ensure that they live within their means. Here are some tips on how to do that.

1. Prepare a budget.
2. Prioritise expenditure.
3. Avoid impulse buying.
4. Beware of false economies.
5. Consider opportunity cost.
6. Check bills, invoices and interest rates.

1 Prepare a budget

The best way to make sure that a household spends effectively is to prepare a budget based on expected income and future household spending needs.

See Chapter 4 for household budgets

See Chapter 35 for national budget

KEY TERM

A **budget** is a financial plan for expected future income and expenditure.

2 Prioritise expenditure

Spend money on the most important items first. Examine the household's needs and wants and decide which are the most important and urgent items. Needs should get priority over wants. For example, food, heat and rent/mortgage payments must take priority over a TV subscription or a holiday.

3 Avoid impulse buying

Impulse buying is when we buy things in an unplanned way or 'on the spur of the moment'. This creates a risk of buying items that are not needed and may turn out to be wasteful or just poor value for money. It can also mean that the household does not have enough money available for essential or urgent spending. Making a shopping list, and sticking to it, can help people to avoid impulse buying.

KEY SKILLS

WO MIT SW MM C BC

3.4 Impulse buys

(a) How do supermarkets try to get their customers to impulse buy? #CreativeThinking

(b) How do magazine publishers persuade people to impulse buy their magazines? #CreativeThinking

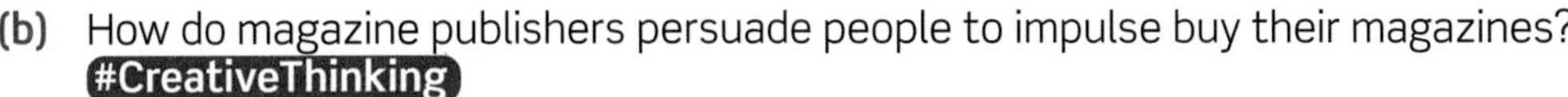

(c) What might small grocery shops do to persuade customers to impulse buy? #CreativeThinking

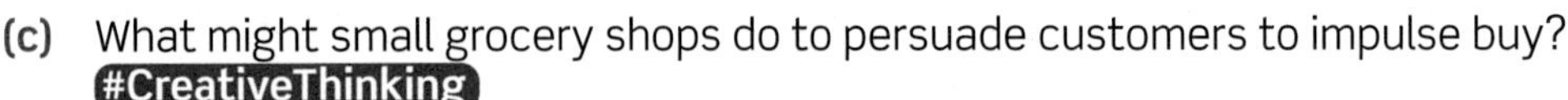

3.5 Your impulse buying

Think of a recent time when you bought something on impulse and answer the following questions:

(a) What was the item? #Record

(b) Can you think of what it was that persuaded you to buy that item? #Think

(c) Did you later regret spending your money on that item? Could you have put the money towards something you wanted more? #Evaluate #Reflect

(d) How could you prevent yourself impulse buying? Share your idea with your group, note what others would do and think about whether that would work for you too. #Discussion #GroupWork

3.6 Impulse buying – always bad?

Think of an occasion when impulse buying might be a good thing. Share your thoughts in pairs or small groups and see who agrees that this might be an occasion when impulse buying is not so bad. #Discussion #GroupWork

4 Beware of false economies

A **false economy** is a purchase that appears to be good value for money at first, but in the longer term turns out to be more expensive or poor value for money. You think you have made a saving, but you end up paying more. For example:

- A decision to purchase inexpensive, low-quality shoes that may need to be replaced at least once during the school year results in a higher overall cost.
- A decision to postpone a routine car service may result in major engine faults later. The cost of fixing these major faults is likely to be far greater than the routine service that could have prevented them.

KEY SKILLS

MIT

3.7 False economies

Can you think of any other false economies from your own experience? #Reflect

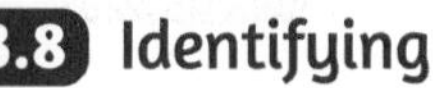

3.8 Identifying false economies

(a) Which of these would you consider to be a false economy and which are sensible? #Identify #Investigate

- Margaret buys two rolls of kitchen towel for €2; each roll has 200 sheets of one layer of tissue. She chooses this over one roll costing €1.50, which has 175 sheets of two-ply. When she uses it, she finds that she has to use two sheets instead of one as it doesn't soak up liquids very well.
- Roland buys a pack of five cereal bars for €3, when normally each bar costs €1.20, and takes one bar for a morning snack at school each day for a week.
- John buys the same pack of bars as Roland, but has no willpower and eats them all on the day he bought them. He has to buy more for his morning snacks for the rest of the week.
- Deirdre goes to the supermarket to buy an evening meal. She looks at meat and vegetables to make a stew, which will cost €4.50 and make a huge pot with at least six servings. Then she sees a pre-packaged stew for one meal that costs €2.50 and decides to buy that as it doesn't cost as much.
- Hettie goes to the farmers' market at the end of the day to buy a punnet of tomatoes and finds two huge boxes of tomatoes on offer for just three times what one punnet would cost. Since she has space in her freezer and loves making tomato sauce, she buys the lot.

(b) Which of the examples in the above list is an impulse buy? On this occasion, is it worth it? #Identify #Evaluate

(c) Which of the examples in the above list could be considered a calculated risk? On this occasion, is it worth it? #Identify #Evaluate

5 Consider opportunity cost

Before making a decision on spending, households need to consider alternative uses for their money. Opportunity cost is measured in terms of the 'next best thing' we could have done with our money. When we decide to use our money for one particular purpose, we lose the chance (opportunity) to do something else with that money. Remember also that saving is an alternative to spending.

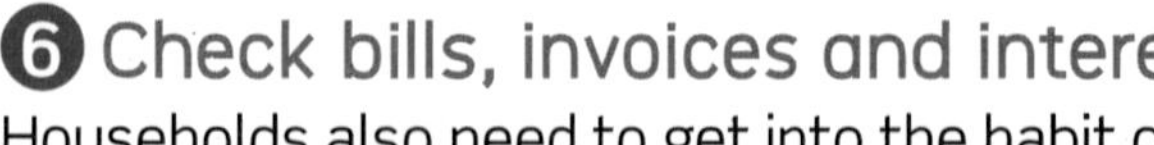

6 Check bills, invoices and interest rates

Households also need to get into the habit of checking all bills and invoices. An **invoice** is a type of bill received whenever goods or services are bought on credit. In this case, credit means 'buy now, pay later'. For example, households use electricity and receive a bill (or invoice) requesting payment for the units of electricity consumed during the previous two months.

In addition to making sure that the bills are accurate, checking bills should give the householders a better understanding of how much and why they are being charged. This will help the household to find ways of cutting back on unnecessary or excessive expenditure. For example, interest rates on credit cards, mortgages and loans vary enormously and switching to a different lender can help to save money.

See Chapter 8 for borrowing

KEY SKILLS BN MIT

3.9 Charges on an electricity bill

Grace's electricity bill included the following information:

Current reading	Previous reading	Units used	Unit price	Amount €
10,518 units	8,332 units	2,186	0.1659	362.66
Standing charge	59 days @ €0.4493 / day			26.51
PSO levy Jul/Aug				10.72
				399.89
VAT @ 13.5%				53.99
Amount due				453.88

(a) What is:

(i) A standing charge? #Research

(ii) The PSO levy? #Research

(b) Why do we have to pay these charges on our electricity bills? #CreativeThinking

(c) Grace takes her own readings and phones the electricity company, which makes a note of them and sends a new bill. Write out what the new bill will look like, using Grace's reading of 8,846 units. #Calculate #Record

KEY SKILLS BN

3.10 Chewing on the pizza bill

Kate and Ella go out for a pizza. The menu is on the right.

Menu	**Prices**
Basic pizza	€4.35
Each topping	75c (chorizo €1)
Large drink	€2.75
Small drink	€2.00
Desserts	€4.50
Shared dessert	€6.00

Kate has a pizza with mushrooms, sweetcorn, onion and olives, and a large orange drink. Ella has a pizza with ham, pineapple and chorizo, and a small lemonade. They share a large dessert. At the end of the meal they receive the bill on the right. Luckily, Kate and Ella checked the bill.

Bill

Thank you for your order!

Pizza + 4 toppings	€7.35
Pizza + 3 toppings + chorizo	€7.90
2 large drinks	€5.50
2 desserts	€9.00
Total	**€35.75**

Write out what it should look like and include a 10% tip (because the pizzas were lovely and the service was great, despite the bill being incorrect). #ProblemSolving #Calculate

KEY SKILLS WO BC MIT MM

3.11 The power of small changes

Energy bills (gas, electricity, oil, coal and wood, etc.) can be a huge cost for households, but even tiny changes to the way you use energy will help to save money. Think of all the ways you could save on energy at home, then create an **infographic** or poster that will inform others about how they can save energy (and money!) too. #CreativeThinking #Presentation

Here is an infographic showing how households spend their money. An infographic is a chart or diagram that represents information in a visual way.

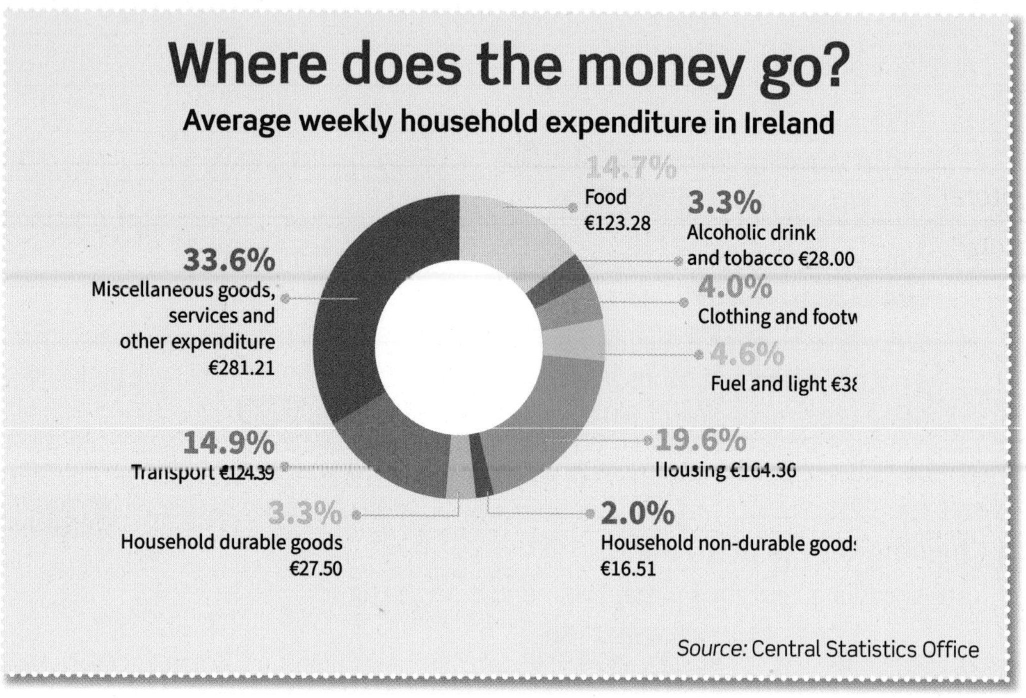

KEY SKILLS MIT BL BN

3.12 Interpreting infographics

Use the infographic above to identify one item each of **(a)** fixed expenditure **(b)** irregular expenditure and **(c)** discretionary expenditure. #Think

Recording and planning household expenditure

See Chapter 5 for recording household income and expenditure

Householders who are in the habit of recording ongoing expenditure and planning for future spending will have better control of their spending.

Both income and expenditure can be recorded in an **analysed cash book**, in a spreadsheet or in another accounting program on a computer. Income and expenditure records should help the household to plan future spending and household budgets.

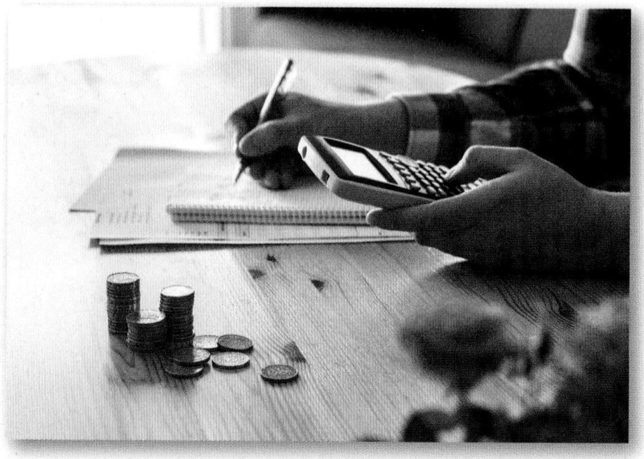

PERSONAL FINANCE

Planning expenditure

Planning is based on the best information you have available at the time. If something unexpected happens, you may need to review and change your plan.

Here is a three-month expenditure record for the Wilson household.

	JANUARY	FEBRUARY	MARCH	TOTAL
PLANNED EXPENDITURE	€	€	€	€
Fixed				
Mortgage	1,100	1,100	1,100	
House insurance		640		
Motor tax	140			
Motor insurance	60	60	60	
Subtotal				
Irregular				
Household costs	850	850	850	
Light and heat	210		190	
Telephone	70	110	70	
Car running costs	140	140	140	
Subtotal				
Discretionary				
Entertainment	120	120	120	
Presents	40		80	
Holidays			1,750	
Subtotal				
TOTAL EXPENDITURE				

KEY SKILLS BN MIT

3.13 Wilson family expenditure plan

22

On the copy of the Wilson expenditure plan in the Student Activity Book or using a spreadsheet, complete the Total column and the Subtotal and Total Expenditure rows. #Calculate

Charts

You can present the Wilson budget in chart format, as follows.

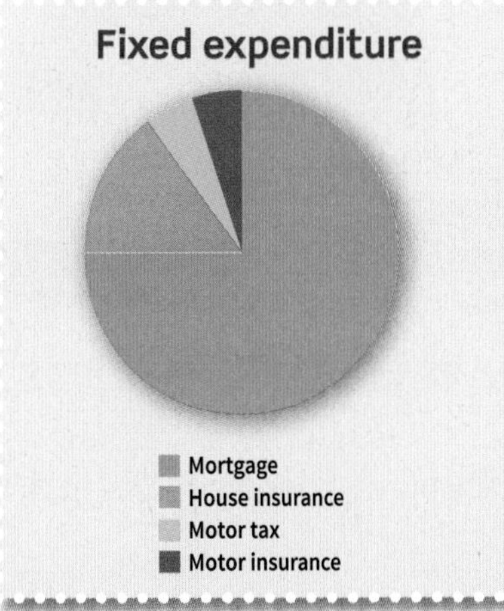

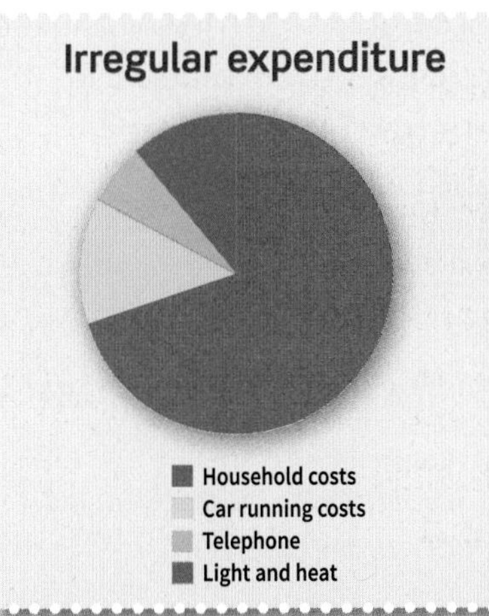

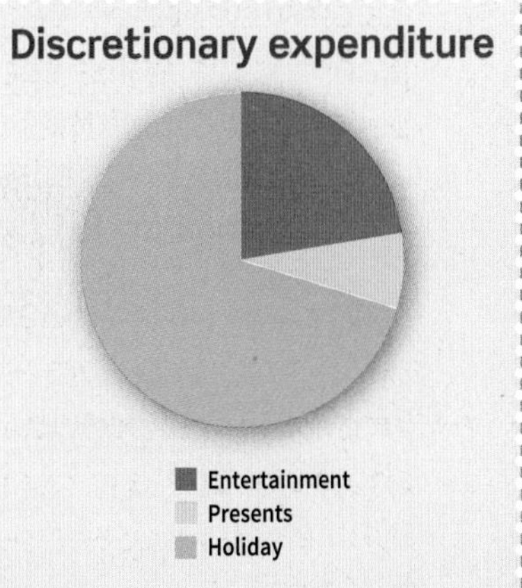

KEY SILLS 

3.14 Creating charts

Create bar charts using the information from the completed plan on page 23 of the Student Activity Book. #Presentation

3.15 Pie chart vs. bar chart

Do you think the pie charts or the bar charts are better for analysing and examining spending? Give a reason for your answer. #Compare #Opinion

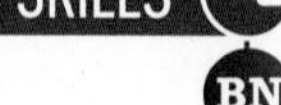

3.16 Your expenditure plan

Open the personal income plan you created in Activity 2.12 in Chapter 2. Add an expenditure plan of your own. You might include spending such as phone credit, games or an amount to put aside for buying birthday presents for family and friends. It might change later, but this will get you thinking about what you spend your money on. Present your personal expenditure in chart format. #Presentation #CreativeThinking

Solutions to overspending

If you keep detailed and up-to-date records of your actual spending and check them against planned spending, you can put measures in place to prevent overspending. When it comes to managing your financial resources, there isn't only one solution. You will need to consider each option carefully and take account of the costs, benefits and risks associated with each before choosing the option(s) best suited to your financial circumstances. Possible solutions include:

1. Cut back on spending.
2. Postpone non-essential spending.
3. Spread large payments over a longer period of time.
4. Use savings or surplus money from previous months.
5. Generate extra income.
6. Borrow money.

1 Cut back on spending

- Since discretionary spending is the least essential, spending cuts should be made here first.
- Some items of irregular spending are based on usage, so these should be looked at to make sure the household is getting good value for money. For example, it may be possible to save money on energy bills by turning off lights when you don't need them or turning down radiator thermostats slightly.
- It is also important to shop around for the best value available. Are there cost savings to be made by switching service providers from time to time? Shopping comparison websites are useful for choosing current best deals.

KEY SKILLS

3.17 Comparison websites

(a) Find three comparison websites and record each website name/address. #Research

(b) Choose one of the websites and create an advert to encourage people to use it. Display the adverts on your classroom wall or in a school corridor. #GroupWork

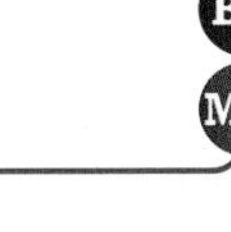

KEY SKILLS MIT BN MM

3.18 Reducing spending

(a) List other ways a household can cut back on spending. #List

(b) Write about the benefits of making savings on household expenditure. #Wellbeing

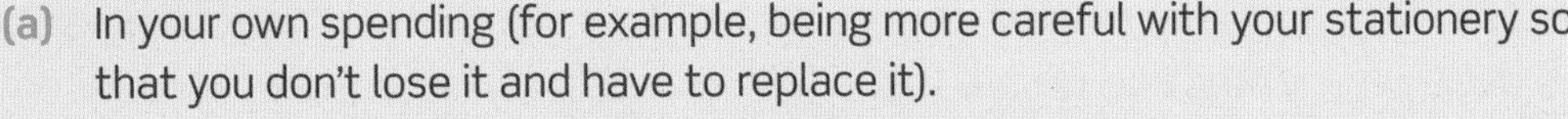

KEY SKILLS MIT MM

3.19 Reducing your own spending

On your own, think about ways you personally can help to save money: #Investigate #Reflect

(a) In your own spending (for example, being more careful with your stationery so that you don't lose it and have to replace it).

(b) In your household (for example, turning lights off when they are not needed).

2 Postpone non-essential spending

It may be possible to get better value for money by planning your purchase for a different time, such as buying plane tickets when airlines have a sale.

3 Spread large payments over a longer period of time

For example, it may be possible to pay a €570 annual house insurance bill over a 10-month period at a monthly cost of €57. In general it is more affordable to make a number of small payments rather than one large payment in a single month.

In some instances it may cost a bit more to spread the payments out, but it still remains the best option from a **cash flow** point of view. For example, a household has the option to pay its annual car tax with a once-off payment of €400 or four quarterly payments of €105. Despite the extra cost involved in spreading the payment across the entire year, it may be easier to manage four smaller payments rather than take one big hit to monthly household income.

KEY TERM

Cash flow is the day-to-day money coming into and going out of a household.

You may be owed a big sum of money that won't be paid to you for another month. In the meantime, your cash flow will be affected because you still have payments going out. Preparing a budget (or cash flow forecast) will put you in a better position to match income and expenditure cash flows.

4 Use savings or surplus money from previous months

If it is not possible to reduce or postpone the spending, the extra cost involved might be covered by using money that has been saved in previous months.

5 Generate extra income

While this may not be possible for everyone and is not a direct solution to the problem of overspending, the ability to generate extra income helps to reduce the negative effects of excessive spending.

Extra income can be earned by working overtime, taking on a part-time job or selling items you no longer need.

KEY SKILLS 

MIT MM C WO SW

3.20 Earning extra money

Working in a group, consider the following. #GroupWork #CreativeThinking

(a) Think of ways you could earn extra money as a teenager. Is it possible for you to earn money by working? You may have to wait until you are older.

(b) Consider ways an older student might be able to earn money.

(c) Consider how an adult might be able to increase their income.

See Chapter 15 for the skills, characteristics and role of the entrepreneur

6 Borrow money

Borrowing as a solution to overspending should only ever be used as a last resort and only for essential and unavoidable expenditure. The problem with borrowing is that it creates debt, which must be repaid (usually with interest), so borrowing reduces future disposable income.

See Chapter 8 for borrowing for individuals and households

When borrowing money, it's important to avail of the services of banks, building societies and credit unions. Avoid moneylenders, as their rates of interest can be very high.

KEY SKILLS

WO

3.21 Your attitude towards money

Discuss the people and things that influence our attitudes towards money and expenditure (such as parents and family, friends and peers, influencers, media and culture, access to money). #Discussion

KEY SKILLS

MIT

3.22 Evaluate the overspending solutions

Make a list of each of the solutions to overspending set out above. For each possible solution, write down one cost (financial or opportunity), one benefit and one risk. #List

EXAM QUESTION

Junior Cycle 2019

Question 15

The following items were identified as the main areas of expenditure for Irish consumers in 2018.

In your copy, classify each item of expenditure as a need or a want:

- Food
- Holidays
- Clothing and footwear.

Weblinks

PowerPoint Summary

HOUSEHOLD BUDGETS

LEARNING OUTCOMES IN FOCUS

1.2 Identify and classify sources of income and expenditure, compare options available to best manage financial resources, evaluating the risks associated with each option and making informed and responsible judgements

Links to 1.1, 1.3, 1.5, 1.6, 1.9, 1.11, 1.12, 1.13, 2.10, 2.11, 2.12, 3.1, 3.2, 3.4, 3.10, 3.11

1.12 Prepare and analyse a budget, determine the financial position, recommend appropriate action and present the analysis in tabular and graphic formats

Links to 1.2, 1.5, 1.6, 1.13, 2.11, 3.4

LEARNING INTENTIONS FOR THIS CHAPTER

When you have completed this chapter you will be able to:

- Explain what a budget is and outline the benefits of preparing household budgets
- Prepare a household budget
- Differentiate between net cash, opening cash and closing cash
- Identify a balanced budget, a budget deficit and a budget surplus
- Explain the financial consequences of budget deficits and budget surpluses
- Outline measures to deal with a budget deficit or surplus
- Use tables and graphs to illustrate key elements and trends in a household budget.

CHAPTER 4 KEY TERMS

- balanced budget
- budget
- budget deficit
- budget surplus
- closing cash
- net cash
- opening cash

CHAPTER 4 KEY SKILLS

- BC Being Creative
- BL Being Literate
- BN Being Numerate
- C Communicating
- MIT Managing Information and Thinking
- MM Managing Myself

Step-by-step accounts

Excel template

What is a household budget?

KEY TERM

A **budget** is a financial plan of expected future income and expenditure.

A household budget combines the income and expenditure plans we looked at in Chapters 2 and 3 and helps a household to see if they are living within their means for a given period of time.

Why prepare a budget?

There are many benefits of budgeting:

- Budgets help people to **live within their means**. For example, if income is expected to be €1,800 for the coming month, this sets the maximum amount you should spend in the month.
- A budget encourages people to **think about their spending**. They will need to consider the type, the timing and the amount of that spending.
- Budgets allow households to **identify months when there are a lot of bills and expenses**. They can then try to take steps to spread these payments out over several months or borrow the necessary funds.
- Budgets allow people to **plan for large items** of future expenditure (such as special occasions, holidays, family events, a new car) and help them to save for these items.
- When completed, a budget will show how much cash the household expects to have **left over** at the end of each time period. This is called their **net cash** and is the difference between planned income and planned expenditure.

KEY TERM

A **balanced budget** refers to a situation where income exactly equals expenditure.

A **budget surplus** occurs when income is greater than expenditure.

A **budget deficit** occurs when income is less than expenditure.

The budget allows a household to plan for expected deficits or surpluses.

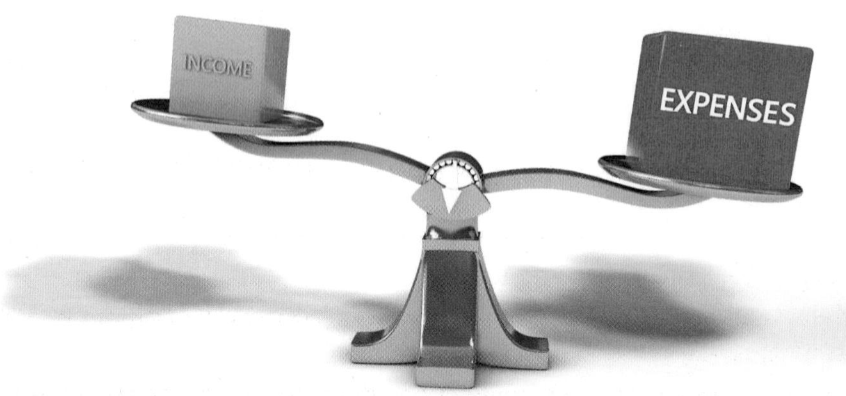

Figure 4.1 Does this image represent a balanced, surplus or deficit budget?

PERSONAL FINANCE

IN THE NEWS

Easy steps to keep your family budget on track

Most people simply run out of money at the end of the month and think they have no choice. Acknowledging your outgoings, understanding them and reorganising them can make all the difference. It is the unexpected that usually catches us out – the broken dishwasher, the emergency dental visit, an unplanned trip you have to take. Having money set aside to plot out even what you don't think will happen makes life easier when it does.

While we can all account for our weekly spending (e.g. groceries, petrol) and we may be able to remember some monthly outgoings (insurance, mortgage), we can get a little fuzzy with items that are less frequent, such as back to school, birthday costs, NCT tests, bin charges and the TV licence. They creep up on us and we end up scrambling.

A budget planner is where you start. The first thing to realise is that things change – circumstances vary and so should your budget. Use it as a template rather than a rule. Don't worry if it needs to be changed along the way; keeping it as accurate as possible is the key.

Start your budget planner with expenses you definitely know – those that are fixed. Add in those you can easily estimate – your weekly food shop, bus ticket or petrol fill. Estimate others with actual experience by keeping receipts for a few weeks and write those down.

Then, with the less frequent spenders, such as those that appear once a year, it's important to budget for them as you go. This means something as simple as setting up separate deposit accounts for different expenses:

- Car account
- Holiday account
- Household account (this one looks after things like Christmas costs, back-to-school expenses, doctors' and dentists' visits and things like annual bills for the TV licence, residents' association fees and a contingency if something breaks or needs repair).

The best way to start is add up all these expenses from your planner and divide them by 12 (or 52 if that's how you're paid). That's the amount you need to put by. But for many people that's simply not affordable, so another way is to work out how much you can afford each month and split it between your named accounts. Pay these accounts on payday, when you have the money.

Finally, do include a little for luxuries – we live in a family, not an economic unit. It's important to be able to eat out occasionally or go to a movie or the theatre. But budget for it and you'll enjoy it all the more!

Source: Irish Independent, 15 January 2016

KEY SKILLS

4.1 Plan, plan, plan!

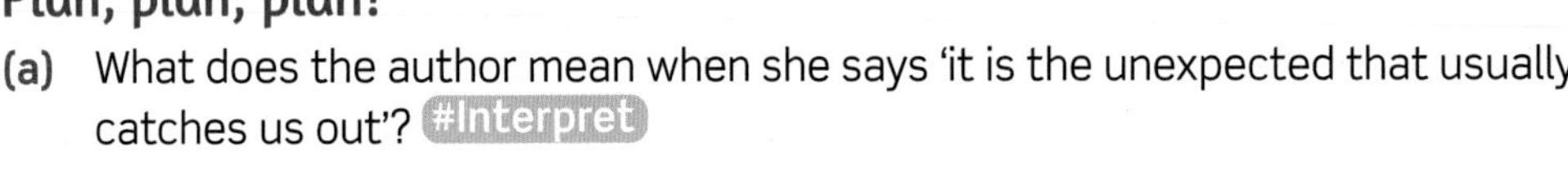
(a) What does the author mean when she says 'it is the unexpected that usually catches us out'? #Interpret

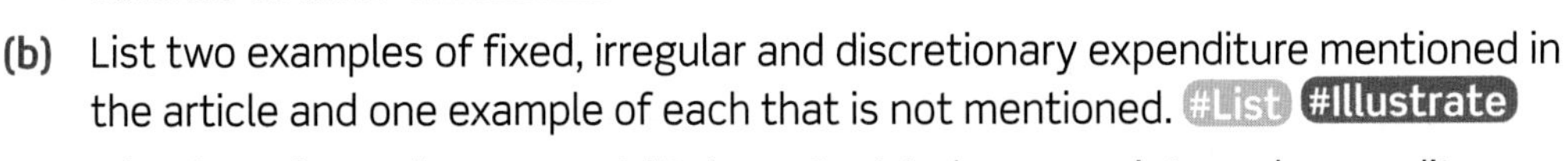
(b) List two examples of fixed, irregular and discretionary expenditure mentioned in the article and one example of each that is not mentioned. #List #Illustrate

(c) Why does the author suggest it's important to keep receipts and expenditure records? #Interpret

Creating the household budget

We will look again at the Wilson family, whose income and expenditure we examined in Chapters 2 and 3. They are preparing a household budget for the first three months of the year. They do this by combining their planned income (see page 20) and planned expenditure (see page 29) and then calculating the **net cash**, **opening cash** and **closing cash** for each month.

WILSON HOUSEHOLD BUDGET				
	JANUARY	FEBRUARY	MARCH	TOTAL
PLANNED INCOME	€	€	€	€
James Wilson – Salary	1,700	1,700	1,700	5,100
Louise Wilson – Salary	1,900	1,900	1,900	5,700
Child Benefit	500	500	500	1,500
A. TOTAL INCOME	**4,100**	**4,100**	**4,100**	**12,300**
PLANNED EXPENDITURE				
Fixed				
Mortgage	1,100	1,100	1,100	3,300
House insurance		640		640
Motor tax	140			140
Motor insurance	60	60	60	180
Subtotal	1,300	1,800	1,160	4,260
Irregular				
Household costs	850	850	850	2,550
Light and heat	210		190	400
Telephone	70	110	70	250
Car running costs	140	140	140	420
Subtotal	1,270	1,100	1,250	3,620
Discretionary				
Entertainment	120	120	120	360
Presents	40		80	120
Holidays			1,750	1,750
Subtotal	160	120	1,950	2,230
B. TOTAL EXPENDITURE	**2,730**	**3,020**	**4,360**	**10,110**
Net cash (A – B)	1,370	1,080	(260)	2,190
Opening cash	150	1,520	2,600	150
Closing cash	1,520	2,600	2,340	2,340

Once you have noted your income and expenditure, you need to calculate the difference to see whether your plan will show a surplus or a deficit at the end of the month.

- **Step 1:** Subtract total expenditure from total income to calculate net cash.
- **Step 2:** Add opening cash to net cash to calculate closing cash.
- **Step 3:** Closing cash for one month becomes the opening cash for the next month.

This is how you do the calculation:

		January		February		March
		€		€		€
Income (A)		€1,600		€2,000		€1,400
Expenditure (B)		– €950		– €2,100		– €2,150
Net cash (A – B)	=	€650	=	(€100)	=	(€750)
Opening cash		€3,200		€3,850		€3,750
Closing cash	=	€3,850	=	€3,750	=	€3,000

Deficits are negative amounts and are usually shown in brackets, e.g –€159 is shown as (€159).

–€159	(€159)

KEY SKILLS BN MIT

4.2 Looking at the Wilson family budget

(a) How did the Wilsons calculate their figures?

In January, the Wilsons calculated their total monthly expenditure by adding the three expenditure subtotals for that month:

	Fixed expenditure subtotal	€1,300
+	Irregular expenditure subtotal	€1,270
+	Discretionary expenditure subtotal	€160
=	Total expenditure	€2,730

The same method can be used to calculate the total expenditure for any given month.

Write this example into your copy, then see if you can work out what figures were added or subtracted in order to calculate the following key figures. Show your workings and write out your calculations: #Calculate

(i) Net cash of €1,370 in January.

(ii) Closing cash of €1,520 in January.

(b) How do they know what the opening cash figure is for February? #Investigate

(c) Where would the figure of €150 for the opening cash figure for January have come from? #Investigate

(d) Why is the opening cash figure of €150 for January the same as the opening cash in the total column? #Investigate

(e) Why is the closing cash for March the same as the total closing cash for the period January to March? #Investigate

Complete the household budget activities (questions 7–16) in your Student Activity Book.

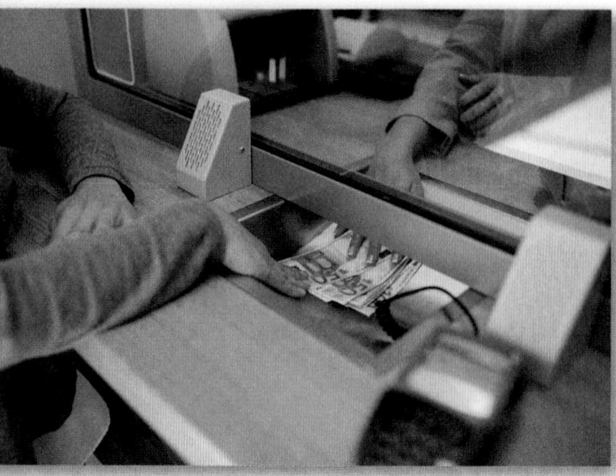

Dealing with a budget surplus

When a household predicts that it will have a large surplus, it may consider how to make the best use of that money. For example:

1. Save or invest it until it is needed.
2. Use it to repay a loan.
3. Use it to fund some extra expenditure, such as a family holiday.

Dealing with a budget deficit

Budget deficits can be resolved using one or more of these solutions:

1. **Increase income:** For example, taking on overtime or an extra part-time job.
2. **Make changes to expenditure:** When cutting back on expenditure, it's important to reduce non-essential discretionary spending before making cuts to essential fixed and irregular spending. This will ensure that there is enough money for the family's most important needs. For example, it's better to cut back on entertainment than on food for the family! It may also be possible to change the payment dates for some expenses or spread large payments over a longer time period. For example, annual car tax can be made as one single payment or as a number of smaller payments throughout the year. Spreading out the payments will help to avoid having this very large item of expenditure in just one month.
3. **Avail of borrowing:** Take out a loan and borrow the money needed to make up the shortfall.

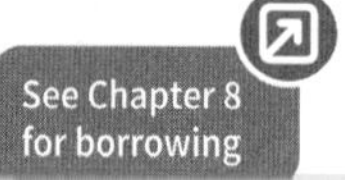
See Chapter 8 for borrowing

Quite often, the solution will involve a combination of two or more of these strategies, for example work some overtime and also cut some discretionary spending.

Remember!

Balanced budget:	Income = Expenditure
Budget surplus:	Income > Expenditure
Budget deficit:	Income < Expenditure

Analysing budgets

There is little point in preparing a household budget if you don't take the time to analyse it. This means looking at it closely to understand the key trends and patterns in the budget. Once you have done the analysis, you may need to revise spending patterns or perhaps even the entire budget. You will also need to deal with any surplus or deficit highlighted by the budget.

Analysis of the Wilson household budget

- The Wilsons expect to have a net cash surplus in both January and February but expect to have a small net cash deficit in March.
- This deficit is largely down to the decision to spend €1,750 on a family holiday in March.
- They can afford the small overspend in March because they can cover that deficit by using money left over from previous months. The budget clearly shows that they should begin March with opening cash of €2,600, which is more than enough to cover that month's deficit of (€260). This will leave them with a healthy closing cash surplus of €2,340 at the end of the three-month period.
- The total income for the three-month period is €12,300, while the total planned expenditure is €10,110. Overall, this is a good budget and will ensure that the Wilson household live within their means.

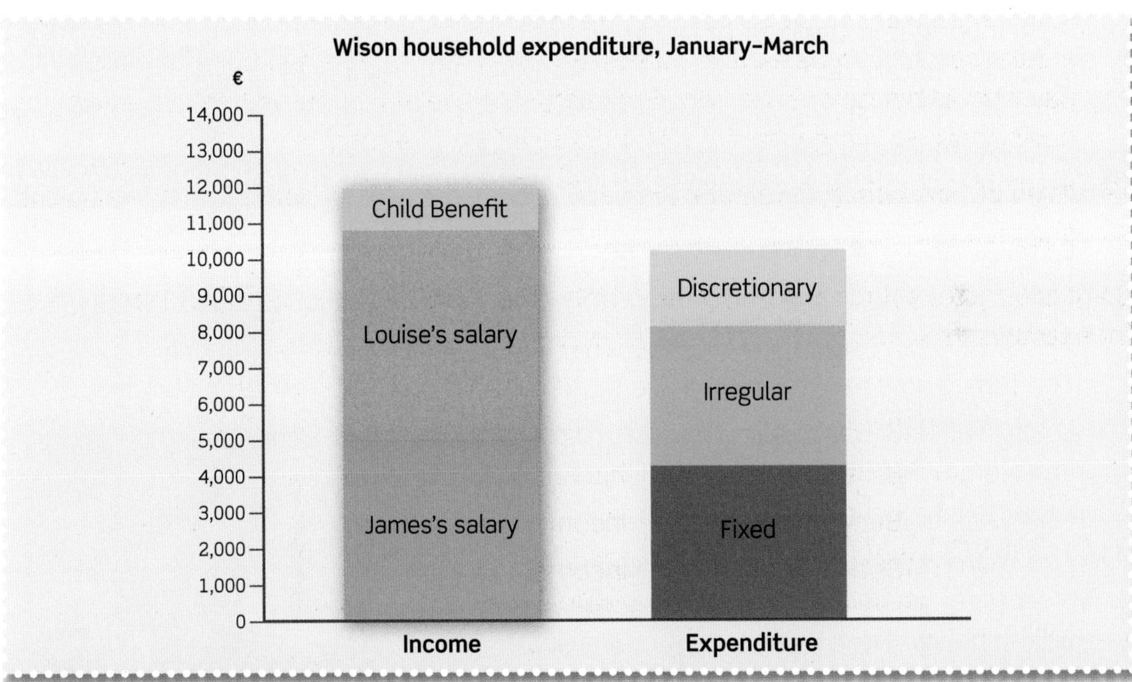

Figure 4.2 Breakdown of income and expenditure for the Wilson household for January–March

KEY SKILLS

BN

MIT

4.3 The Wilson household's total expenditure

Showing your workings, calculate what percentage of the Wilsons' total expenditure is:

(a) Fixed

(b) Irregular

(c) Discretionary. #Calculate

The Wilson family's irregular expenditure can be shown in a bar chart. Bar charts clearly show a household's expenditure over a period of time.

	January	February	March	Total
Irregular expenditure	€1,270	€1,100	€1,250	€3,620

KEY SKILLS

4.4 The Wilson household's fixed expenditure BN BC

Create a bar chart showing the Wilson household's fixed expenditure for January to March. #Presentation

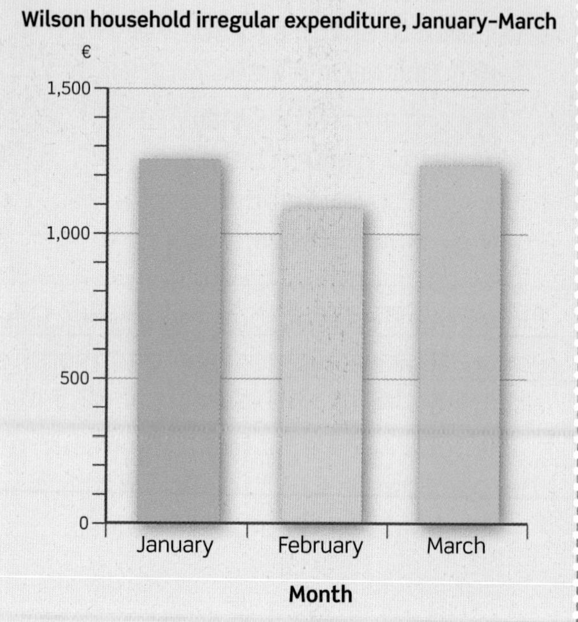

Figure 4.3 Bar chart of irregular expenditure for the Wilson household, January–March

Revised budget

After the Wilson household had prepared their original budget for January to March, Louise Wilson's work changed to part-time. To help make up for the reduction in her income, James increased his working hours and salary. The Wilsons decided to revise their budget in the light of these changed circumstances.

Example: Create a revised budget for the Wilson family

- James's salary increases by €200 per month from February.
- Louise works part time and her monthly salary will be reduced to €800 from January.
- The family now expects to receive €120 interest on their savings in March.
- Louise will now use public transport to travel to and from work. She intends to sell her car and expects to receive €3,200 in February.
- The Wilsons change to a different type of mortgage, which means their monthly payments will be halved from the beginning of January.
- Motor tax will be reduced by 50%.
- Motor insurance will be reduced because of the sale of Louise's car. James will now pay his annual car insurance with a single payment of €420 in February.
- Household costs will increase to €950 per month.
- Car running costs will be reduced to €100 per month from January.
- Louise will spend €80 per month on public transport.
- Entertainment costs will increase to €220 per month.
- The Wilson household decides to increase spending on their family holiday to €4,000 in March.
- The Wilsons plan to redecorate the house in February at a cost of €1,800.

All other income and expenditure remain unchanged.

Analysis of the Wilson household's revised budget

WILSON HOUSEHOLD REVISED BUDGET								
	ORIGINAL BUDGET				REVISED BUDGET			
	JAN	FEB	MAR	TOTAL	JAN	FEB	MAR	TOTAL
PLANNED INCOME	**€**	**€**	**€**	**€**	**€**	**€**	**€**	**€**
James Wilson – Salary	1,700	1,700	1,700	5,100	1,700	1,900	1,900	5,500
Louise Wilson – Salary	1,900	1,900	1,900	5,700	800	800	800	2,400
Child Benefit	500	500	500	1,500	500	500	500	1,500
Interest on savings							120	120
Sale of car						3,200		3,200
A. TOTAL INCOME	**4,100**	**4,100**	**4,100**	**12,300**	**3,000**	**6,400**	**3,320**	**12,720**
PLANNED EXPENDITURE								
Fixed								
Mortgage	1,100	1,100	1,100	3,300	550	550	550	1,650
House insurance		640		640		640		640
Motor tax	140			140	70			70
Motor insurance	60	60	60	180		420		420
Subtotal	1,300	1,800	1,160	4,260	620	1,610	550	2,780
Irregular								
Household costs	850	850	850	2,550	950	950	950	2,850
Light and heat	210		190	400	210		190	400
Telephone	70	110	70	250	70	110	70	250
Car running costs	140	140	140	420	100	100	100	300
Public transport					80	80	80	240
Subtotal	1,270	1,100	1,250	3,620	1,410	1,240	1,390	4,040
Discretionary								
Entertainment	120	120	120	360	220	220	220	660
Presents	40		80	120	40		80	120
Holidays			1,750	1,750			4,000	4,000
Decorating						1,800		1,800
Subtotal	160	120	1,950	2,230	260	2,020	4,300	6,580
B. TOTAL EXPENDITURE	**2,730**	**3,020**	**4,360**	**10,110**	**2,290**	**4,870**	**6,240**	**13,400**
Net cash (A – B)	1,370	1,080	(260)	2,190	710	1,530	(2,920)	(680)
Opening cash	150	1,520	2,600	150	150	860	2,390	150
Closing cash	1,520	2,600	2,340	2,340	860	2,390	(530)	(530)

The Wilsons' total income in the revised budget is slightly higher than it was in the original. This is mainly because of the income received from the sale of the car. In the future their spending plans will need to be adjusted downwards in order to reflect the lower level of *regular* income. The levels of both fixed and irregular expenditure are mostly unchanged, with reductions in motor tax and car running costs due to the sale of the vehicle. The mortgage payment has been halved and this will reduce monthly spending. There is a small increase in household costs. The Wilsons have taken the unusual step of increasing their planned discretionary spending even though future regular income will decrease. This will give rise to a large net cash deficit in March.

This revised budget illustrates that for the three months in question, the Wilsons will not be living within their means. Total planned income for the three-month period is €12,720, while total planned expenditure is €13,400. They can expect a large net cash deficit in March and an overall closing cash deficit of €530 for the three-month period.

Overall, the revised budget is not a good one for the family, taking into account the changed circumstances. Once-off discretionary spending has increased (holiday and decorating), but this cannot be fully financed from once-off increases in income (interest and sale of car). Looking to the future, the family will need to keep their spending under control because of reduced regular income.

KEY SKILLS

4.5 Solving the Wilsons' budget problem

What three solutions could the Wilsons use to resolve the budget problem highlighted by the revised budget? #CreativeThinking

MIT

4.6 Creating your own personal budget

In Chapters 2 and 3, you started a spreadsheet or a notebook for your own income and expenditure planning. Go back to these now and create a budget similar to the ones here, but relating to your own personal circumstances. It will, of course, not contain most of the headings that a household's would, but it will act as an excellent introduction to taking control of your own finances. #Calculate #Strategise

BC

KEY SKILLS MM C

4.7 Make do or buy new?

Your friend says to you, 'Everyone else has the latest tablet, but my dad says mine is fine and we can't afford a new one. My mum says she will buy me one, but she will have to borrow the money from the credit union. I really want the new tablet, but I don't know what to do.' What advice would you give to your friend? #Discussion

MM C

4.8 Getting out of debt

Debt can cause a lot of stress for individuals and families. Living beyond your means can get out of control and you can end up working just to pay the interest on loans. To get out of debt, some people have to minimise spending on birthday presents, going out or having a holiday and they have to make do with old possessions they'd rather replace. Answer the following questions:

(a) What could you/your family cut back on if you faced debts? #Strategise #Reflect

(b) What steps could you take to avoid getting into debt in the first place? #Strategise #Reflect

See Chapter 8 for borrowing

EXAM QUESTION

Junior Cycle 2019

Question 1

The graph below shows Joan Murphy's monthly budget:

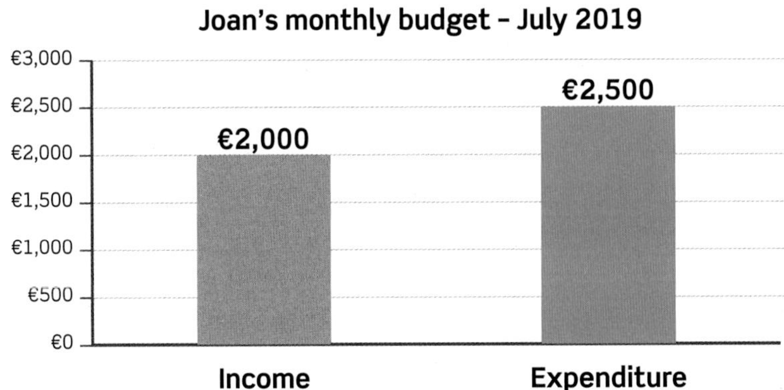

(i) Calculate the difference between Joan's income and expenditure. State if it is a surplus/deficit.

(ii) What advice would you give Joan based on your answer?

Weblinks

PowerPoint Summary

PERSONAL FINANCE

CHAPTER 5

RECORDING HOUSEHOLD INCOME AND EXPENDITURE

LEARNING OUTCOMES IN FOCUS

1.13 Monitor and calculate income and expenditure data, determine the financial position, recommend appropriate action and present the analysis in tabular and graphic formats

Links to 1.2, 1.5, 1.6, 1.12, 2.12, 2.13

LEARNING INTENTIONS FOR THIS CHAPTER

When you have completed this chapter you will be able to:

- Explain why households and businesses keep financial records
- Outline and demonstrate the rules that apply to cash book entries
- Complete an analysed cash book
- Balance and total an analysed cash book
- Explain the difference between opening and closing balances in an analysed cash book
- Interpret and evaluate an analysed cash book
- Account for opening and closing bank overdrafts in an analysed cash book.

CHAPTER 5 KEY TERMS

analysed cash book
balance
balance b/d
balance c/d
bank overdraft
closing balance
credit side
debit side
opening balance
T-account
transaction

CHAPTER 5 KEY SKILLS

BL Being Literate
BN Being Numerate
MIT Managing Information and Thinking

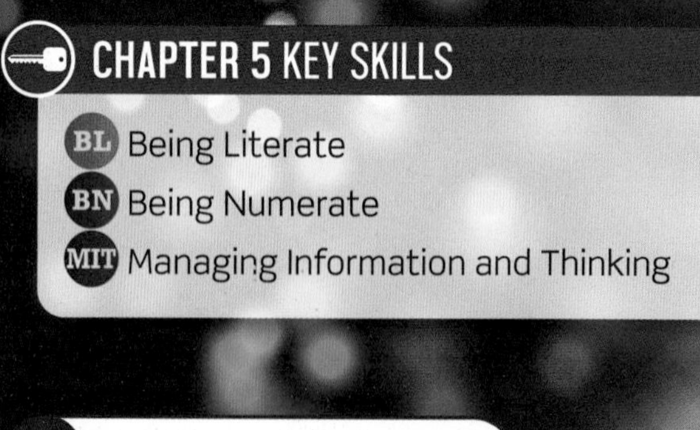

Step-by-step accounts

Excel template

PERSONAL FINANCE

Why keep income and expenditure records?

Everyone benefits from keeping accurate records of all the money they receive and spend. Not only does this help to keep track of actual income and expenditure, it also helps with financial planning and budgeting.

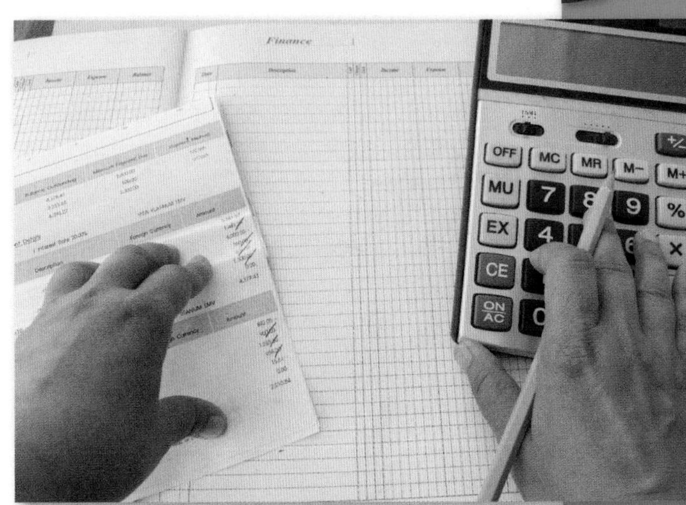

For businesses, these records are used to monitor its activity and calculate its profitability. Since businesses pay taxes on their profits, there is a legal requirement for all businesses to keep accurate financial records. While households are not legally required to keep such records, it can be a very useful activity and certainly helps householders to manage their money.

The analysed cash book

The **analysed cash book** is used to record all money actually received and spent.

See Chapter 4 for household budgets

See Chapter 26 for double entry bookkeeping

KEY SKILLS MIT

5.1 Analysed cash book vs. budget

How does the analysed cash book differ from a budget? #Compare #Contrast

It is called an *analysed* cash book (ACB) because all items of income and expenditure are recorded under suitable headings. This provides a clear record of where money comes from and what it gets spent on. You can then identify patterns of spending and highlight areas of overspending.

Sources of information

TESCO IRELAND

PASSATA	EURO.49
SOYA DRINK	EUR1.25
PASSATA	EURO.49
GARLIC GRNULS	EURO.49
LETTUCE I/BERG	EURO.89
WHITE GRAPES	EUR1.99
ORGANIC VEG	EUR2.29
QUORN STEAKS	EUR4.00
SUB-TOTAL	EUR27.89
MULTIBUY SAVINGS	
ANY 3 FOR 6.00	-6.00
TOTAL SAVINGS	-6.00
TOTAL TO PAY	21.89
VISA DEBIT SALE	21.89

Visa contactless
AID : A0000000031010
NUMBER : ************8250 ICC
PAN SEQ NO : 01
AUTH CODE : 290759
MERCHANT : 46359622
CHANGE DUE EURO.00

In order to write up an analysed cash book, the household needs to have accurate information about all the money it receives and spends. In the case of cash (notes and coins), there are few records, so it's important that income and expenditure is recorded in the analysed cash book as soon as the money is received or spent to ensure that the accounts are accurate and up to date. In the case of expenditure, the household may be able to rely on receipts as a reminder of how and where they have spent their money.

See Chapter 6 for bank statements

Nowadays, most income and expenditure for households takes place through their bank account. For example, most people's wages are paid directly into their bank account by their employer using the PayPath system. Many household bills are paid directly from a bank account or with a debit card. In the case of all bank transactions, we can rely on bank statements as a regular source of information about income and expenditure patterns.

The rules

Accounting rules help everyone using accounts to understand them.

- The analysed cash book is divided into a **debit (Dr)** side and a **credit (Cr)** side.
- A **debit is money received** (income/receipts).
- A **credit is money spent** (expenditure/payments).

This is the basic rule for all cash and bank transactions. A **transaction** occurs whenever money is received or spent. Each transaction requires a separate entry in the analysed cash book.

Here is a very simple two-sided account (sometimes called a **T-account**), which shows the basic accounting rules for all cash book entries. The cash book is used to record **all money** received and paid out.

Cash book rule	
DEBIT (Dr):	**CREDIT (Cr):**
Money in/money received	Money out/money spent

What the analysed cash book looks like

The analysed cash book takes the concept of the T-account and expands on it, using columns to record detailed information about each transaction. Here is a more detailed layout for an analysed cash book. This could be completed on paper, on a spreadsheet or using a specialised computer program. You can also use Business Studies Record Book 1 to prepare an analysed cash book.

ANALYSED CASH BOOK													
DEBIT SIDE													**CREDIT SIDE**
Date	Details	Cash	Bank	Wages	Child Benefit	Date	Details	Chq no.	Cash	Bank	Grocery	Light & Heat	Travel
2020		€	€	€	€	2020			€	€	€	€	€

The columns of the analysed cash book

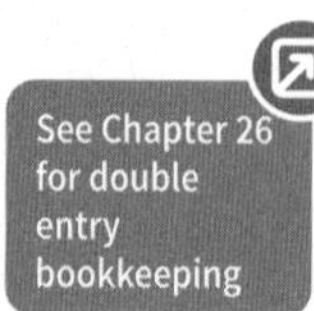
See Chapter 26 for double entry bookkeeping

- **Date:** The date (day, month and year) of each transaction.
- **Details:** The reason the money was received or paid.
- **Chq no.:** If a payment is made by cheque, the number of the cheque is recorded.
- **Cash:** The actual amount of cash (notes and coins) received or spent.
- **Bank:** This column records all amounts received or paid through a bank account.
- **Analysis columns:** These columns are used for recording exactly where the income came from (e.g. wages) and what it was spent on (e.g. groceries, electricity bill). These column names will vary according to what is most relevant to the household or business.

Example 1: Cash transactions

For our first example, we will assume that all transactions are in cash.

Cash only

On 1 March 2020 the Owen household had €280 cash on hand. This is money left over from previous months and will be shown as an opening balance in their cash book.

Opening balances are labelled '**Balance b/d**' (b/d = brought down) in the account. Since this is money that the household already owns, it is treated as income ('money in') and will appear on the debit side of the cash book.

The following is a list of all the cash received or spent by the Owen household for the first week of March 2020.

1 March: Cash on hand €280
2 March: Received Child Benefit €270
2 March: Grocery shopping €158
4 March: Petrol for family car €40
4 March: Paid school expenses €30
5 March: Received wages €800
5 March: Paid rent €320
6 March: Bought clothes €75
7 March: Bought cinema tickets €27

Figure 5.1 below shows how the above transactions would be recorded in the analysed cash book.

KEY SKILLS

5.2 Debit or credit?

48

The list of entries above is duplicated in your Student Activity Book. On that list, indicate which entries are debit (money in) and which are credit (money out).
#Activity

MIT BL

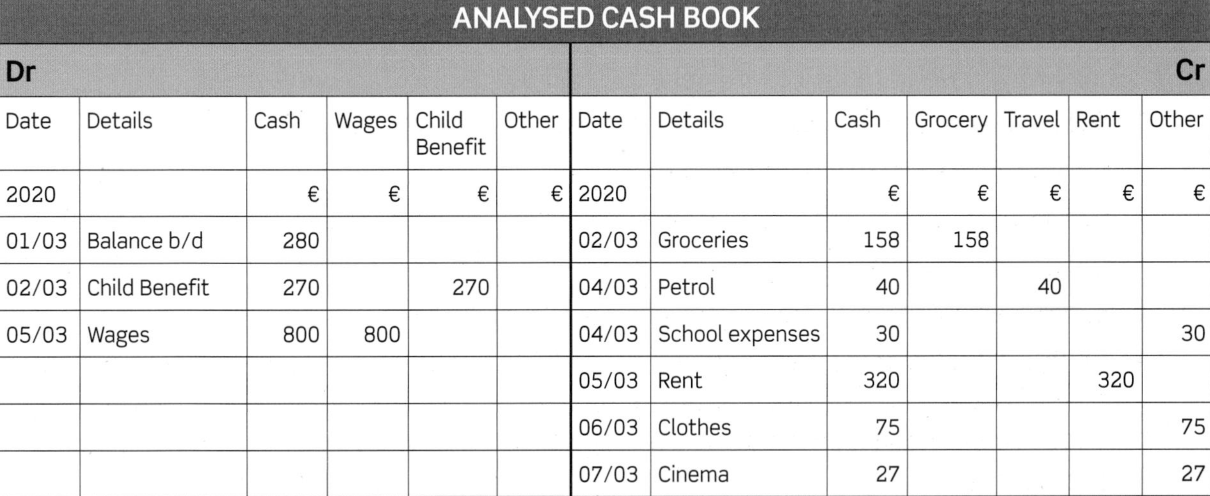

ANALYSED CASH BOOK

Dr												Cr
Date	Details	Cash	Wages	Child Benefit	Other	Date	Details	Cash	Grocery	Travel	Rent	Other
2020		€	€	€	€	2020		€	€	€	€	€
01/03	Balance b/d	280				02/03	Groceries	158	158			
02/03	Child Benefit	270		270		04/03	Petrol	40		40		
05/03	Wages	800	800			04/03	School expenses	30				30
						05/03	Rent	320			320	
						06/03	Clothes	75				75
						07/03	Cinema	27				27

Figure 5.1 Owen household income and expenditure

Notice that the opening balance appears on the **debit side** because the Owen family had cash on hand.

Each of the other transactions appears in the cash columns on either the debit or credit side as well as in the appropriate analysis column. For example, on 2 March the €158 entry on the credit side records the fact that the household spent €158 in cash. The entry information in the details and analysis columns tells us that the €158 was spent on groceries.

The Owen family has a column for 'Other' that is used to record any payments that cannot be categorised as 'grocery, 'travel' or 'rent'.

Balancing and totalling accounts

One of the benefits of preparing cash accounts is that it allows us to work out how much money we have at the end of each day, week, month, etc. When we **balance** our cash account we are really just working out the difference between the amount of money we received and the amount we spent.

This is our **closing balance** on the account. Closing balances are labelled '**Balance c/d**' (c/d = carried down). This also tells us the amount of cash we will have available at the start of the next accounting period (e.g. week, month). So the balance carried down (c/d) for one period becomes the balance brought down (b/d) (i.e. the opening balance) for the next accounting period.

If you think back to your work on household budgets, you will realise that this is very similar to the way in which the closing cash for one month becomes the opening cash for the next month.

KEY TERM

The **balance** is the *difference* between the amounts of money on the debit and credit sides of an account.

Balancing an account is very similar to balancing a weighing scales. For the scales (or account) to balance, both sides must total up to the same amount. For example, if you place a 10 kg weight on one side of a pair of scales and 7 kg on the other, you will need to add 3 kg to the lighter side to get the scales to balance. You balance an account in a similar way.

If you received €100 in cash and then spent a total of €70 during the week, you would have €30 remaining at the end of the week. This €30 is your closing balance at the end of the week and your opening balance at the beginning of the next week. We can show this on a T-account like this:

48 Complete question 3 in your Student Activity Book.

Dr		CASH BOOK			Cr
Date	**Details**	**Cash**	**Date**	**Details**	**Cash**
2020		€	2020		€
01/03	Cash received	100	06/03	Expenditure	70
			07/03	Balance c/d	30
		100			100
08/03	Balance b/d	30			

Figure 5.2 How to balance and total an account

Look at the income and expenditure for the Owen household in Figure 5.1. They received €1,350 (debit side) and their total spending (credit side) was €650. From these figures, we calculate the balance of €700 and insert it on the smaller side, then total both sides and carry the balance down. This is shown below in Figure 5.3.

ANALYSED CASH BOOK												
Dr												Cr
Date	Details	Cash	Wages	Child Benefit	Other	Date	Details	Cash	Grocery	Travel	Rent	Other
2020		€	€	€	€	2020		€	€	€	€	€
01/03	Balance b/d	280				02/03	Groceries	158	158			
02/03	Child Benefit	270		270		04/03	Petrol	40		40		
05/03	Wages	800	800			04/03	School expenses	30				30
						05/03	Rent	320			320	
						06/03	Clothes	75				75
						07/03	Cinema	27				27
						07/03	Balance c/d	700				
		1,350	800	270				1,350	158	40	320	132
08/03	Balance b/d	700										

Figure 5.3 The balanced account of the Owen household

Follow these steps to balance and total the cash accounts:

Step		Our example
1	Add up the amounts on each side and work out which has the biggest total. Write this amount in the total boxes on both sides. Underline all totals with a double line.	*The debit side total of €1,350 is the bigger amount and therefore appears as the total on both sides of the cash account in the ACB.*
2	Calculate how much we need to add to the smaller side to make it equal to the total. Subtract the smaller figure from the bigger one.	*The credit side entries add up to just €650. This means we will need to add €700 to this side in order to match the total of €1,350. (1,350 – 650 = 700)*
3	Show the balance c/d on the smaller side.	*The balance c/d of €700 appears on the credit side. Note that it appears above the total box.*
4	Bring this balance across to the other side of the account. It appears as a balance b/d on the opposite side. This represents the amount of money available at the start of the next accounting period.	*A balance b/d of €700 appears on the debit side. Note that it appears below the total box.*

In the analysed cash book, only the cash and bank columns require balancing before being totalled. The analysis columns are simply totalled in order to show the amount of money received or spent under each heading.

Example 2: Cash and bank transactions

In our second example, we will look at an analysed cash book that involves both cash and bank transactions.

Direct debits, standing orders, payments by debit card and withdrawals from an ATM all involve money being taken out of a current account. A current account is used for day-to-day banking needs. Lodging money means paying it into an account.

We'll look at current account transactions in more detail in Chapter 6.

Cash and bank transactions

The Walsh household had the following transactions in the week beginning 1 February 2020:

1 February	Cash on hand	€120
1 February	Cash in bank	€370
2 February	Wages lodged	€1,300
2 February	Paid mortgage by direct debit	€900
3 February	Bought groceries, debit card transaction	€180
3 February	Paid for petrol with cash	€40
4 February	Cash lottery win	€25
5 February	Child Benefit lodged	€270
6 February	Paid mobile phone bill by direct debit	€45
7 February	Paid school fees (cheque number 103)	€60

KEY SKILLS BN

5.3 Identifying debits and credits

50

The list of entries above is duplicated in your Student Activity Book. On that list, tick which entries should appear as debit and which should appear as credit. #Activity

Figure 5.4 below shows how the above transactions would be recorded in the analysed cash book of the Walsh family.

ANALYSED CASH BOOK

Dr																Cr
Date	Details	Cash	Bank	Wages	Child Benefit	Other	Date	Details	Chq no.	Cash	Bank	Grocery	Household	Travel	Other	
2020		€	€	€	€	€	2020			€	€	€	€	€	€	
01/02	Balance b/d	120	370				02/02	Mortgage			900		900			
02/02	Wages		1,300	1,300			03/02	Groceries			180	180				
04/02	Lottery win	25				25	03/02	Petrol		40				40		
05/02	Child Benefit		270		270		06/02	Mobile phone			45				45	
							07/02	School fees	103		60				60	
							07/02	Balance c/d		105	755					
		145	1,940	1,300	270	25				145	1,940	180	900	40	105	
08/02	Balance b/d	105	755													

Figure 5.4 The Walsh family's analysed cash book

Note that the cash and bank accounts have been balanced and totalled separately. This means that the cash column on the debit side is balanced against the cash column on the credit side, just as it was in Figure 5.2. The same process is then repeated for the bank columns. We do not combine the cash and bank amounts. This shows that the Walsh family will begin next week with €105 cash and €755 in the bank.

KEY SKILLS MIT BN

5.4 Cash vs. bank balance

Why do we balance the cash and bank accounts separately, do you think?

#Discussion

The benefits of keeping an analysed cash book

- You have a record of all income and expenditure.
- This record can be compared against your budget to make sure you are on track and can see where you might have to revise (or change) your budget to make it more realistic.
- You can see where you might be overspending (by looking at the totals of the analysis columns) and adjust your habits to make sure that you stay within your budget.
- You can check your bank and credit card statements against what you have recorded to make sure that no mistakes have been made and that all payments from your account were made by you (or with your approval).

Bank overdrafts

KEY TERM

A **bank overdraft** is an arrangement with the bank that allows an account holder to withdraw or spend more money than they actually have in their current account.

See Chapter 8 for overdrafts

The overdraft must be arranged in advance and the bank will set a limit on the amount that can be overdrawn. It is a useful way of getting a short-term loan if, for example, you have an emergency repair that costs more than you have available. You will be able to spend up to this overdraft limit – the money is available if you need it, but you don't have to use the full amount.

An overdraft means that you will have a minus balance in your current account, representing the amount that you owe the bank. Remember, this is only the amount of the overdraft you have used; it is not necessarily the full amount available to you.

If an account holder is overdrawn at the start of an accounting period, we show this as a balance b/d on the **credit side** of their bank account, as shown below in Figure 5.5. It is treated as 'money out' of the account.

ANALYSED CASH BOOK							
Dr							**Cr**
Date	Details	Cash	Bank	Date	Details	Cash	Bank
2020		€	€	2020		€	€
				01/03	Balance b/d		300

Figure 5.5 How an opening bank overdraft appears in the analysed cash book

Example 3: Bank overdraft

Bank overdraft

The Duggan household had the following weekly transactions:

1 April	Cash on hand	€180
1 April	Bank overdraft	€370
2 April	Wages lodged	€1,100
2 April	Paid mortgage by direct debit	€900
3 April	Bought groceries by debit card	€210
4 April	Bought petrol using cash	€50
5 April	Child Benefit lodged	€270
6 April	Paid mobile phone bill by direct debit	€65
7 April	Paid school fees by cheque no. 108	€150

Figure 5.6 below shows how the above transactions would be recorded in the analysed cash book of the Duggan household.

ANALYSED CASH BOOK

Dr														Cr
Date	Details	Cash	Bank	Wages	Child Benefit	Date	Details	Chq no.	Cash	Bank	Grocery	Household	Travel	Other
2020		€	€	€	€	2020			€	€	€	€	€	€
01/04	Balance b/d	180				01/04	Balance			370				
02/04	Wages		1,100	1,100		02/04	Mortgage			900		900		
05/04	Child Benefit		270		270	03/04	Groceries			210	210			
						04/04	Petrol		50				50	
						06/04	Mobile phone			65				65
						07/04	School fees	108		150				150
07/04	Balance c/d		325			07/04	Balance c/d		130					
		180	1,695	1,100	270				180	1,695	210	900	50	215
08/04	Balance b/d	130				08/04	Balance b/d			325				

Figure 5.6 The Duggan household's analysed cash book

Weblinks

PowerPoint Summary

FINANCIAL SERVICES FOR INDIVIDUALS AND HOUSEHOLDS

LEARNING OUTCOMES IN FOCUS

1.8 Compare the services provided by consumer agencies and financial institutions to assist and support customers

Links to 1.5, 1.7, 1.9, 1.10

LEARNING INTENTIONS FOR THIS CHAPTER

When you have completed this chapter you will be able to:

- Describe the services offered by Ireland's major financial institutions
- Distinguish between a current account and a deposit account
- Explain the various methods of making payments from a current account
- Analyse a current account statement
- Use a bank statement to prepare an analysed cash book
- Outline the benefits of internet and telephone banking
- Recognise the security issues of internet and telephone banking
- Compare the use of credit and charge cards

CHAPTER 6 KEY TERMS

automated teller machine (ATM)	contactless payments	digital wallet	personal identification number (PIN)
bank statement	credit card	direct debit	phishing
charge card	credit transfer	exchange rate	standing order
cheque	current account	financial institution	telephone banking
commercial bank	debit card	internet banking	withdrawal
	deposit account	lodgement	

CHAPTER 6 KEY SKILLS

- BC Being Creative
- BL Being Literate
- BN Being Numerate
- C Communicating
- MIT Managing Information and Thinking
- MM Managing Myself
- SW Staying Well
- WO Working with Others

What is a financial institution?

A **financial institution** provides financial services for its customers, including storing their money, managing payments and providing loans.

A number of different types of financial institutions operate in Ireland, including:

- Commercial banks
- Credit unions
- Building societies
- The post office (An Post).

KEY SKILLS

6.1 Local financial institutions

Can you identify any of these financial institutions in your local area? Make a list and share it with the class. #List #Discussion

C

A **commercial bank** is a bank that offers financial services to the general public and to businesses.

Financial institutions offer the following services to customers to help them manage their financial resources:

- Current accounts
- Deposit accounts
- Bill payment and money transfers
- Internet and telephone banking
- Credit cards
- Foreign exchange services
- Loans.

See Chapters 1, 7 and 8 for resources, saving and borrowing

Each institution tries to attract more customers by offering competitive rates on savings and loans.

Types of account available to customers

Most of the financial institutions in Ireland provide two main types of account:

1. **Current accounts** are offered by the commercial banks, credit unions and building societies. They are used for day-to-day banking needs.
2. **Deposit/savings accounts** are offered by the commercial banks, building societies, An Post and the credit unions. They are used to save money.

Many people have both types, as they serve different needs.

Current accounts

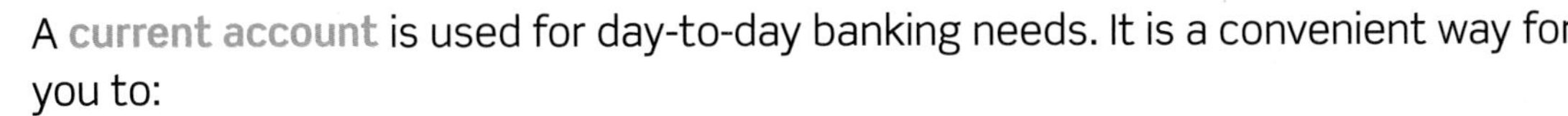

A **current account** is used for day-to-day banking needs. It is a convenient way for you to:

- Receive your income
- Store money safely
- Pay for goods and services
- Pay bills and transfer money to other people.

An account holder should keep their own records of all transactions in an analysed cash book and check these against their bank statements.

How current accounts are used

Current account holders receive regular **statements** detailing all transactions.

KEY TERM

Amounts paid into the account are known as **lodgements**.

DID YOU KNOW...

The term **lodge** means to leave money or a valuable item in a safe place.

KEY TERM

Withdrawals are amounts paid out of the account.

Example: Michael

Michael works for a medical company. His wages are paid directly into his bank account and each week he withdraws cash for spending.

Most of his bills are paid by direct debit, which means they are taken straight from his bank account by the companies he owes money to, such as his electricity provider, mobile phone provider, etc.

He buys his groceries, petrol, etc. using a debit card, so the money goes straight from his account to the shop without Michael having to use cash. He has set up a regular bank transfer to his landlord for the rent on his apartment and he makes manual transfers from his account to other people's accounts for less regular payments, such as sending his niece some birthday money.

Example: Holly

Holly is a self-employed translator. Her clients usually pay by electronic transfer, so the funds move from their bank account to hers. Occasionally a client pays her in cash, so she lodges this in her account to keep it so her other earnings. She pays some bills, such as advertising for her business, by direct debit, and she manually transfers money every month to her personal current account as spending money.

Opening a current account

There are several different financial institutions you could open a current account with, so it is worth shopping around and looking at what each has to offer. You can always change to a different institution at a later date, if you wish.

KEY SKILLS: MM, MIT, C

6.2 When is the right time for a current account?

Discuss what age or stage of your life you think is a good time to open a current account. #Discussion #Reflect

6.3 What's in it for the bank?

Discuss why banks provide incentives and rewards to young people who open an account with them. After all, a young person doesn't normally have enough money to make it worthwhile for a bank to look after it. #Discussion

Once you have chosen a financial institution, you will have to fill out an application form and supply documents to prove your identity and address. The following are required to open a current or deposit account:

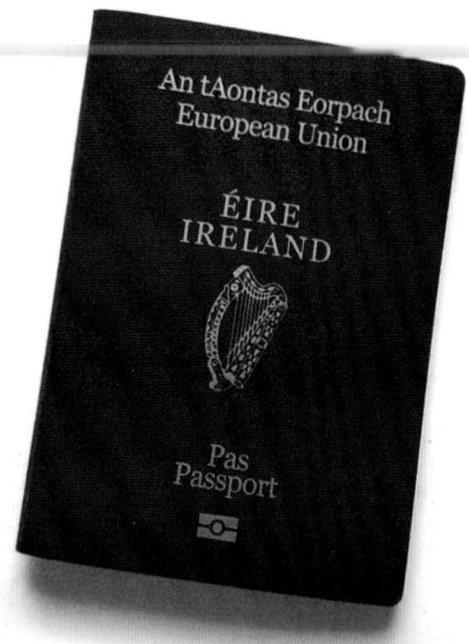

1. **Photographic proof of identity** – passport, driving licence or EU National Identity Card.
2. **Proof of address** – a (recent) utility bill, such as an electricity, gas or telephone bill, or correspondence from a financial institution or government organisation addressed to the person who is opening the account.
3. **Personal Public Service Number (PPSN)** – the government provides this number to everyone who needs to access social welfare benefits, public services and information in Ireland.

KEY SKILLS: MIT

6.4 The reasoning behind the documents

Why does a person have to provide photographic evidence and proof of address when opening a current account? #WhatDoYouThink

6.5 Documents for opening a joint account

If two (or more) people are opening an account together, do you think both/all of them will have to supply the proofs necessary? Why? #WhatDoYouThink

The application form will ask for further information about you and your circumstances. If you are under 16, you will need a parent's or guardian's signature on the application form.

KEY SKILLS

6.6 Find an application form

View or download an application form for a current account from the website of a financial institution of your choice. Keep it in your file as an example of what an application form looks like. #Research

When the customer's application has been approved by the financial institution, he or she will be given an account number.

WO

6.7 Why open a separate account for a business?

Jonathan has a small business called Jon's Jewellery. Jonathan has a personal current account and a business current account, even though all the money in both accounts belongs to him. Discuss why he has two current accounts instead of just one. #Discussion #Opinion

Lodging money into an account

Money is lodged to an account in various ways:

- The account holder lodges money (cash or cheques) over the counter, using an automated teller machine (ATM) (see page 58) or a self-service machine in the bank branch. A lodgement slip (see Figure 6.1) may be used.
- An employer transfers wages or salary directly into the account (via a system called PayPath).
- Pensions or benefits are paid directly into a current account.
- A third party transfers money electronically from their account to the recipient's account.

Memorandum only Lodgement
Branch
Name
Account Number
€
Note: Cheques, etc., are accepted subject to examination and verification and are transmitted for collection at customer's risk. Though credited to account, cheques should not be drawn against uncleared
Brand/Initials
Allied Irish Banks, p.l.c. Subject to verification AIB/F308EURO 03/13

AIB
Current Deposit
Tick Account applicable
Brand/Initials

Lodgement/Bank Giro Credit Transfer
Bank use only N B T M
National Sorting Code 93
AIB Bank
Branch
Account Name
Address
Paid in by
Narrative

Account Number
Notes Large
€20
€10
€5
TOTAL NOTES
TOTAL COINS
TOTAL CASH
Cheques, POs
€
euro euro euro

Figure 6.1 Sample lodgement slip

Withdrawing money from an account

Money can be withdrawn from your account in a number of ways:

- Withdrawing cash at a bank using a withdrawal slip (see Figure 6.2); you will sometimes need photo ID for this
- Using an ATM (see below) to withdraw cash with an ATM card or a debit card
- Paying for items using a debit card (see page 59)
- Using a digital wallet (see page 60)
- Direct debit (see page 60)
- Standing order (see page 60)
- Credit transfer (see page 60)
- Cheque (a personal cheque or a bank cheque, known as a bank draft) (see page 61)
- Fees and charges.

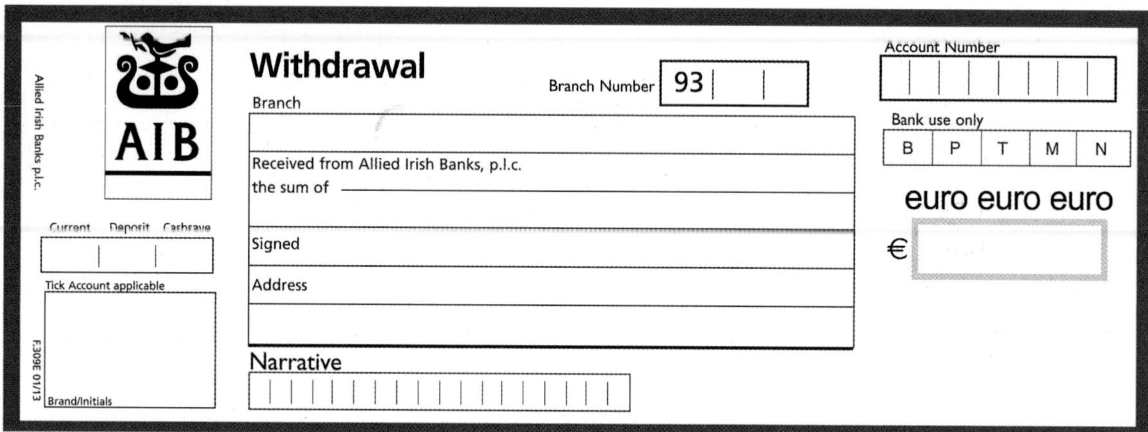

Allied Irish Banks p.l.c.

AIB

Withdrawal

Branch Number 93

Branch

Received from Allied Irish Banks, p.l.c.
the sum of

Signed

Address

Narrative

Current Deposit Cashsave

Tick Account applicable

Brand/Initials

F309E 01/13

Account Number

Bank use only

B	P	T	M	N

euro euro euro

€

Figure 6.2 Sample withdrawal slip

ATMs

ATM stands for **automated teller machine**. Current account holders are given an ATM card with a **personal identification number (PIN)**. This is a four-digit number linked to your ATM card that you type into the ATM to prove that the card is yours. When you order an ATM card, it is sent to you in the post and then a few days later you will receive a note containing your PIN. The ATM card can be used to withdraw cash and for other banking services.

DID YOU KNOW...

Bank counter clerks are called **tellers**. This comes from an Old English word, *tellan*, which means 'person who counts'.

KEY SKILLS WO BC BL MIT

6.8 How do you use ATM services?

Use a financial institution's website to find out the services that are available via ATMs. In pairs or small groups, prepare a poster or leaflet to let others know how they can make use of an ATM. Include step-by-step instructions on how to use the machine. Display the posters around the classroom. #Research #GroupWork

6.9 Why should you keep your PIN private?

PINs should never be given to anyone else because if someone has your card and PIN, they have access to the money in your current account. In pairs or small groups, create a poster warning of the need to keep your PIN secure and explaining how to do so. There is plenty of information online to help you. #Research

Debit cards

- **Debit cards** allow consumers to pay for goods and services without using cash.
- They provide electronic access to the money in your bank account.
- If there isn't enough money in the account to pay the requested amount, the shopkeeper will be told that the payment has been declined.

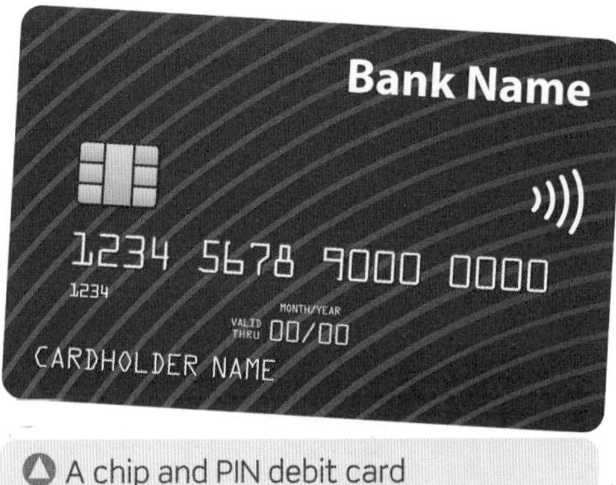

A chip and PIN debit card

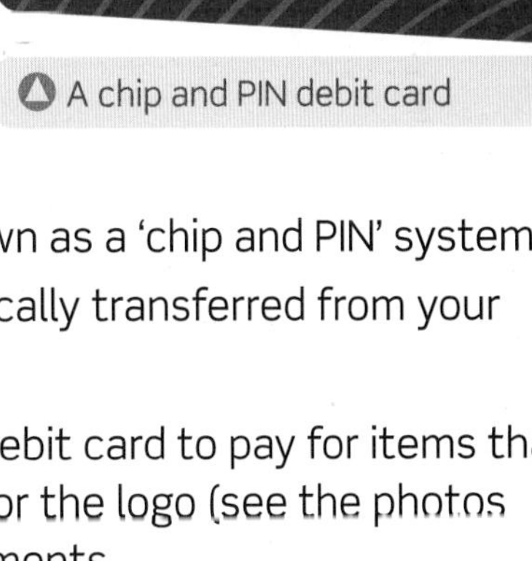

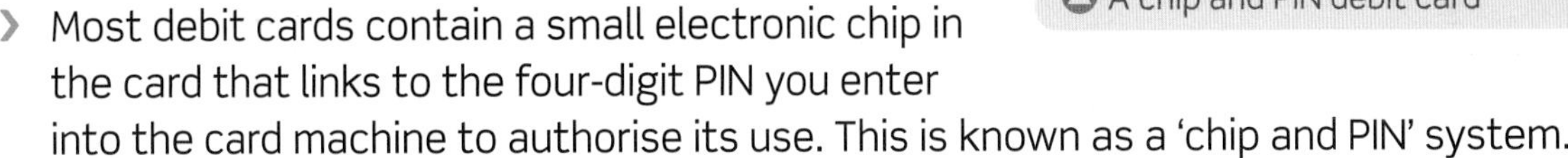

- Most debit cards contain a small electronic chip in the card that links to the four-digit PIN you enter into the card machine to authorise its use. This is known as a 'chip and PIN' system.

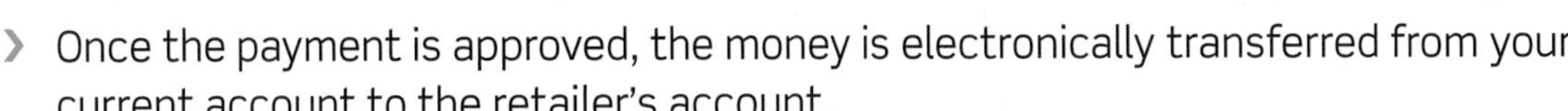

- Once the payment is approved, the money is electronically transferred from your current account to the retailer's account.

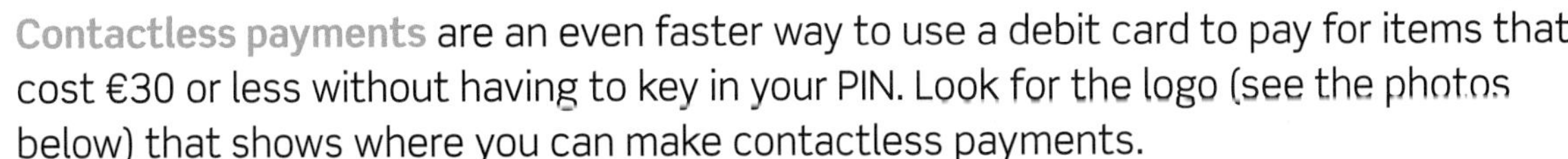

Contactless payments are an even faster way to use a debit card to pay for items that cost €30 or less without having to key in your PIN. Look for the logo (see the photos below) that shows where you can make contactless payments.

Advantages/benefits of using contactless payments:

- It is safer as it eliminates the need to carry cash.
- It is quicker and more convenient than going to an ATM or using cash.
- It is easier to use as you just tap your card against the reader to pay in seconds.

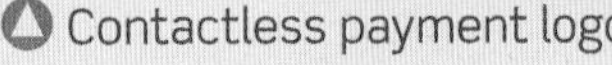

Contactless payment logo

Disadvantages/risks of contactless payments:

- If the card is stolen there is a risk that it can be used without the PIN.
- It can only be used for purchases up to €30.
- There may be an extra cost for each transaction.

Digital wallet

A **digital wallet** is an online service that allows you to make electronic transactions. This can include using your computer to buy items online or using your smartphone to buy something in a shop. Your bank account can be linked to the digital wallet.

Apple Pay and Google Pay are examples of digital wallets and they can be used to replace credit and debit card transactions at a contactless point-of-sale terminal. Consumers can use them to transfer funds to friends or tap to pay for items in shops.

Direct debit (DD)

A current account holder gives permission to another person or business to withdraw **variable** amounts from their account. **Direct debit** is used when the amount to be paid and/or the payment date are likely to change. The person or business who is owed money by the current account holder is called a creditor.

6.10 When would you use direct debit? KEY SKILLS MIT BC C WO

(a) On your own, think about and make a list of which payments are suitable for paying by direct debit. #CreativeThinking

(b) Compare your list with the person sitting next to you. #ThinkPairShare

(c) Share your combined answers with the pair sitting behind you/in front of you. #GroupWork

Standing order (SO)

A **standing order** is an instruction to a financial institution to pay a **fixed** amount to a **specific** person or organisation on a certain date.

Both standing orders and direct debits are used for ongoing or repeated payments from a bank account. Once they are set up, the bank will keep making payments until the account holder changes or cancels them.

6.11 When would you use a standing order? KEY SKILLS MIT BL

List three examples of when a standing order would be used rather than a direct debit. #List

Credit transfer

A **credit transfer** is a *once-off* instruction from a current account holder to their bank to transfer an amount of money to another account. A credit transfer can be made by phone, on paper or over the internet.

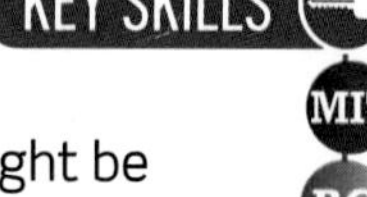

6.12 When might you send or receive a credit transfer?

(a) On your own, think of and record a situation when a credit transfer might be used. #CreativeThinking

(b) Compare your example with the person sitting next to you. #ThinkPairShare

(c) Share your combined answers with the pair sitting behind you/in front of you. #GroupWork

Cheques

Current account holders may request a chequebook. A **cheque** is a written instruction from an account holder to their bank to pay a specific amount of money to a named person or business. For hundreds of years cheques were the main way of paying via a bank account, but in recent years cheques have rapidly been taken over by electronic payments.

Figure 6.3 A completed cheque

Bank draft

This is like a cheque, but it is written on a bank's own account rather than a customer's account. The customer must pay for the draft using money in their current account. The bank then writes a draft made payable to whoever the customer specifies.

KEY SKILLS

6.13 Why use a bank draft? MIT

Why, do you think, do people use bank drafts rather than personal cheques to pay for some goods and services? #Discussion

Bank fees and charges

Some financial institutions charge customers for their services. Some accounts have annual fees and charges per transaction. The amount charged will depend on the transaction type.

KEY SKILLS

6.14 What do banks charge for transactions? MIT

(a) Search online to find the current charges/fees for one particular financial institution (make a note of which one) for the following transactions:
- A debit card purchase
- A direct debit
- An ATM withdrawal
- A lodgement over the counter
- A lodgement using a lodgement machine
- The maintenance fee for the account for one quarter (three months) #Research

(b) Why, do you think, is the charge for making a lodgement using a lodgement machine lower than the charge for making a lodgement over the counter? #CreativeThinking

(c) Which type of financial institution would you recommend opening an account with, based on the transactions above? Explain your answer. #Evaluate #Justify

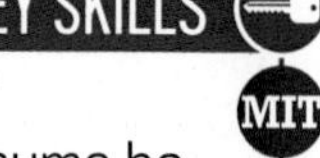

6.15 Terry's bank fees

MIT BN

Terry used his account in the following ways between January and March. Assume he uses the bank you researched in Activity 6.14. #Research

(a) Calculate Terry's fees at the end of the quarter.

- He used his debit card 35 times.
- He has two direct debits every week and another one once a month.
- He withdraws cash from an ATM once a week.
- He lodged money into his account twice over the counter.
- He lodged money using the lodgement machine three times.
- He had to pay a maintenance fee for the quarter.

(b) If Terry continues to use his current account in the same way for the rest of the year, how much will he have paid in bank charges for the whole year? #Calculate

6.16 Comparing bank charges

WO

(a) Compare the fees and charges from the bank you chose in Activity 6.14 with those of a student who chose a different bank. #ThinkPairShare

(b) Share your combined answers with the pair sitting behind you/in front of you. #GroupWork

Bank statements

A current account holder receives a statement from their bank on a regular (monthly or quarterly) basis. This might be on paper or electronically. Electronic statements (e-statements) are shown when they log in to their internet banking.

The statement shows all transactions that have taken place during that time period (i.e. all money going into and out of the account). Because the statement is written from the bank's point of view, the entries are on the opposite side to the bank records prepared by the account holder in their analysed cash book.

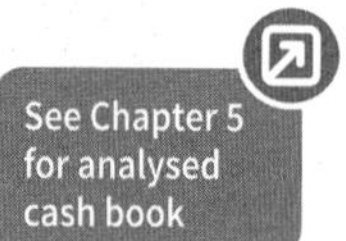

See Chapter 5 for analysed cash book

In the analysed cash book, the account holder will debit money in and credit money out of their bank account.

On the bank statement, the bank will credit money in and debit money out of the customer's account.

The *balance* column of the statement shows a continuous balance and it changes after each transaction. It increases when there are lodgements (credit) and decreases when payments are made (debit). This provides the customer with an up-to-date bank balance at all times.

Sample layout of a typical bank statement					
DATE	DETAILS	DEBIT €	CREDIT €	BALANCE €	EXPLANATION
01/03/20	Balance			400	*Opening balance. Customer starts with €400 in their account.*
01/03/20	Lodgement: PayPath		900	1,300	*Wages lodged to account. Balance increases (400 + 900 = 1,300).*
02/03/20	Standing order: Mortgage	700		600	*Mortgage paid. Balance decreases (1,300 – 700 = 600).*
05/03/20	Withdrawal: ATM	60		540	*Withdrew money from ATM. Balance decreases (600 – 60 = 540).*
06/03/20	Groceries: Debit card	200		340	*Paid for groceries with debit card. Balance decreases (540 – 200 = 340).*
07/03/20	Lodgement		150	490	*Money lodged to account. Balance increases. Closing balance at end of week is €490 = (340 + 150).*

Below is a bank statement for Gerry Duffy, who has an account with AIB in Carrickmacross, Co. Monaghan. He received his bank statement on 4 June 2020.

CURRENT ACCOUNT

AIB
Main Street Branch,
Carrickmacross, Co. Monaghan
Tel: 042–123456

National Sort Code: 93-12-34
Statement of Account

Account Name: Gerry Duffy
Account Number: 123456789

Mr Gerry Duffy
Farney Street
Carrickmacross
Co. Monaghan

Date of Statement: 31 May 2020
Page Number: 121

IBAN: IE25 AIBK 9312 3412 3456 78 (BIC: AIBKIE2D)
Authorised Limit at Date of Statement €550

Date	Details	Debit €	Credit €	Balance €
01 May 2020	Balance Forward			260.00
04 May 2020	SO Mortgage	590.00		330.00 DR
07 May 2020	DD Electricity	178.00		508.00 DR
12 May 2020	Hendy & Co PayPath		1200.00	692.00
14 May 2020	ATM Francis Street	100.00		592.00
15 May 2020	INET-AIB Visa	340.00		252.00
17 May 2020	Cheque 113456	122.00		130.00
21 May 2020	Credit Transfer – Deposit Account		175.00	305.00
24 May 2020	ATM Francis Street	100.00		205.00
27 May 2020	Bernie Duffy	30.00		175.00
29 May 2020	Bank Charges	14.50		160.50
29 May 2020	Bank Interest	3.50		157.00
31 May 2020	POS McGrath's Garage	50.00		107.00

An example of a bank statement

66 Complete question 8 in your Student Activity Book.

You should check your bank statement against your analysed cash book. It's important to file your statements and keep them safely because you might need them to prove that you have paid for something or received payment. The usual advice is to keep bank statements for six years, but if you have the space, it would be wise to keep them for even longer.

KEY SKILLS 

6.17 Checking your bank statement

(a) Why is it so important to check your bank statement against your analysed cash book? #Think

(b) Unless you regularly log on to your bank account on the internet, what unpleasant surprises might you get when you receive your bank statement? #Identify

KEY SKILLS

6.18 Analysing the bank statement

Discuss and answer these questions relating to the bank statement on the previous page. You can find some answers by looking at the bank statement; others you will have to research. #Research #Discussion #Analyse #Identify

(a) What do the following abbreviations stand for? (All but the last one are on the statement.) What do they mean in banking terms? What is their function?

(i) BIC	(iv) SO	(vii) ATM
(ii) IBAN	(v) POS	(viii) DR
(iii) DD	(vi) INET	(Ix) SEPA

(b) What is a sort code and what is the sort code of Gerry's bank?

(c) What is Gerry's account number?

(d) What method of payment does Gerry use for his electricity bill?

(e) On what date is Gerry's mortgage paid and what method of payment is used?

(f) On what date is Gerry paid and what is his employer's name?

(g) What method of payment did Gerry use to buy his petrol?

(h) How many times did Gerry withdraw cash during this month and which cash machine location did he use?

(i) Explain why 'bank interest' appears on the statement on 29 May.

(j) Does Gerry have any other bank accounts? How do you know?

(k) Does Gerry have a credit card? How do you know?

(l) Does Gerry ever use a chequebook? How do you know?

(m) How big is Gerry's overdraft facility?

(n) Gerry's sister lives in Cork. It was her birthday this month and Gerry sent her some money. How did he send it and how much did he give her?

KEY SKILLS 

6.19 Your changing banking needs

See Chapter 11 for financial life cycle

How do you predict your banking needs will change as you get older? #CreativeThinking #Reflect

Internet and telephone banking

Internet banking (also known as online banking) and **telephone banking** are useful and convenient ways for customers to pay bills, check their account balance, order statements and transfer money to other accounts. These services allow account holders to access their accounts 24 hours a day, seven days a week and every day of

the year. The financial institution issues customers with a registration number and personal access code (PAC) for accessing their accounts online and over the telephone. Some financial institutions provide telephone and internet access in their branches.

Advantages and drawbacks of internet and telephone banking to the account holder

Advantages:

- **Convenience** – banking when it suits the customer, 24 hours a day, 365 days a year.
- **Higher interest rates** – because online banks have fewer expenses, such as wage bills and costs associated with premises, they can afford to offer higher interest rates to people saving money.

Drawbacks:

- **Lack of access** – lack of high-quality Wi-Fi/ broadband in some parts of the country can limit customers' access to the service.
- **Security risks** – someone might hack into your account.

Be secure when using online banking

When you log in to your bank account, check that you see the little padlock to the left-hand side of the web address, as shown in the photo to the right. The address will start with **https://** – the 's' stands for 'secure'. You will see these security alerts on payment sites for retail websites, too.

Make sure you can see the little padlock and https:// in the address when you log in to your bank account.

Criminals use fake emails and fake websites as a way of tricking people into giving away passwords and bank details. This is known as **phishing**.

You may receive an email that looks as if it comes from your bank. Look out for emails that:

- Just don't look right. They might have an odd email address or include an odd web address.
- Are poorly designed and have typing mistakes or poor spelling or grammar.
- Ask you to log in to your bank account or send back personal information – your bank will never ask you to do this.

If you receive a call from someone claiming to be from your bank, never give the caller your log-in details.

ALWAYS IGNORE AND DELETE THESE EMAILS.

KEY SKILLS WO MM

For the following activities:

(a) Work on your own first and write the answers in your copy.

(b) Compare your answers with the person sitting next to you. #ThinkPairShare

(c) Share your combined answers with the pair sitting behind you/in front of you. #Discussion #GroupWork

6.20 Keeping your account safe

Although online banking is very safe and secure, there are always people who will try to find ways into your account. What steps can you take to keep your online account secure? #Wellbeing

6.21 Mobile banking safety

Are there extra security measures you can take if you use a smartphone for your banking rather than a laptop? #CreativeThinking

6.22 Your security top tips

An elderly relative has been nervous about doing online banking, but has now decided to try it. Write down some security tips for them to keep by their laptop to remind them how to be safe. #List #Wellbeing

DID YOU KNOW...

Some banks are exclusively online and have no physical branches, such as Revolut and N26.

KEY SKILLS C

6.23 Why open a current account?

Discuss the advantages of using a current account rather than using notes and coins for all transactions. #Discussion

KEY SKILLS C

6.24 Making use of current accounts

Ask your parents/guardians or other adults how they use their current account. You don't need to know about actual amounts, just whether they pay bills by direct debit, cheque, electronic transfer and so on, and what other services they use via their current account. #Research #Investigate

Deposit accounts

- **Deposit accounts** offer a way of saving while earning interest.
- Money in deposit accounts is safe and secure.
- You can choose from a range of deposit accounts, depending on how much money you want to save and how much access you want to your money.
- Many accounts can be opened with as little as €10, after which you can save either regular amounts or lump sums.

See Chapter 7 for saving

- These accounts, which are available from banks, building societies, An Post and credit unions, usually have no transaction fees or maintenance charges.
- Opening a deposit account is similar to opening a current account.

KEY SKILLS MIT BN MM

6.25 Shop around for interest rates

Research the current rates of interest that financial institutions offer customers for saving their money. #Research

PERSONAL FINANCE

Credit cards

Buying on credit means 'buy now, pay later' and **credit cards**, e.g. Visa and Mastercard, are designed to be used in this way. Each credit card has a spending limit, which is set by the bank and is based on the customer's income and ability to repay. The credit card company issues a bill (or statement) to the customer at the end of each month.

The benefit to the cardholder is that they do not need the money available to pay for goods and services at the time of purchase. The cardholder enters their PIN at the point of sale, just as with a debit card.

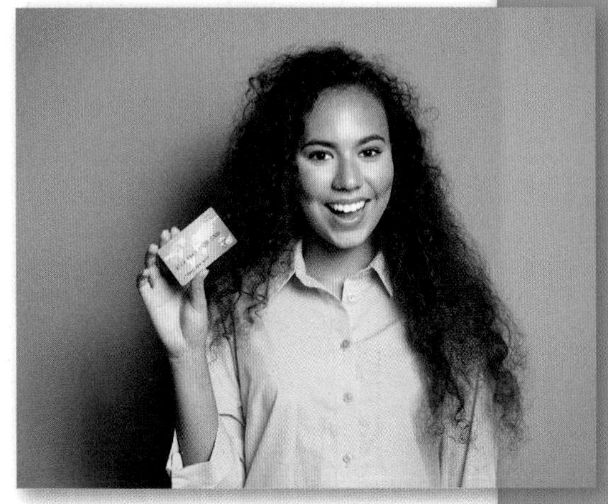

Credit cards are particularly useful for making online purchases. If you buy online using a credit card, you will be asked for the card's security number (also known as a CVC – card verification code – or a CVV – card verification value). This is three numbers on the back of the card, above the signature strip. This is to prove that you actually have the card and haven't copied the card number from somewhere.

The credit card statement

The statement sets out all the items purchased during the month as well as any balance due from previous months. If the bill is paid in full by its due date, no interest is charged. If the amount due is not paid in full, the bank will charge the cardholder interest on the outstanding amount. Interest rates on credit card debt are much higher than on bank overdrafts or loans, which makes a credit card an expensive source of finance.

Credit card interest

The credit card companies give a figure on the statement for the minimum amount due, which is the amount that covers that month's interest plus a small fraction of the amount owed. It can be tempting to pay only the minimum amount, but if you do, you will end up paying a large amount in interest.

Since you do not need any money (either in cash or in a bank account) to make a purchase with a credit card, people are often tempted to use it when they're short of cash. As a result, they may run up large debts that they will struggle to pay off. Banks also tend to offer generous credit limits and low interest rates to new customers, which makes it easier to build up debt.

DID YOU KNOW...

You have debt of €3,000 on a credit card that charges 18% interest. If you pay the minimum each month (about €46) and the interest rate stays the same, it will take you over 21 years to repay and thousands of euros in interest payments!

The golden rule with credit cards is not to spend more than you can afford to repay at the end of each month. If you clear the balance each month, you will in effect be able to use the bank's money 'interest free' for one month. If you don't clear the balance, you'll pay a high rate of interest.

It is best to set up a direct debit to pay off your card in full each month so that you won't be tempted to pay just part of it when you make the payment yourself.

6.26 Credit cards – good or bad?

In years gone by, people didn't have the option of 'buy now, pay later'. Discuss whether credit cards are a good thing, a bad thing or a mixture of both. What are the pros and cons of having a credit card?

#Discussion

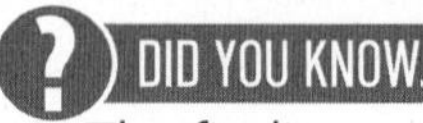

The findings contained in the first Central Statistics Office (CSO) Household Finance and Consumption Survey showed the financial state of Irish people in 2013. The survey found that many Irish people were relying on credit cards to make ends meet. The average amount of debt on a credit card in 2013 was €1,400.

Majority of people 'don't know what interest rate is on their credit cards'

According to a survey commissioned by the Irish League of Credit Unions and carried out by iReach, most people do not know what interest rate they are paying on their credit cards. Despite the fact that a majority of people say they rely on a credit card for making purchases, almost six out of ten card users say they are not aware of the interest they pay on an outstanding balance.

When people said they were aware of the interest, many got it wrong. Some 20% of people thought they were paying between 6% and 10%. However, card interest rates in this country typically range between 13% and 23%.

Consumers were also completely at sea when it comes to how interest is applied. Four out of ten incorrectly said they would have no interest imposed if they pay the minimum monthly amount. One in eight had no idea how much interest they would pay after paying the minimum amount due.

Most people feel that credit card companies do not put enough effort into explaining their interest rates. Some 68% agreed that people lack an understanding of how the interest works.

The vast majority of credit card owners said they will use their card for monthly ad-hoc purchases this year. Based on their previous credit card habits, two-thirds said they would clear the entire balance every month.

Source: Irish Independent, 23 September 2019

6.27 Get interested in interest

(a) Are you shocked by the finding that most people don't know how much interest they pay on their credit card? #Opinion

(b) In your opinion, why is it important to always know how much interest you are paying? #Opinion

C

Charge cards

A **charge card** is similar to a credit card – it involves buying goods now but paying later. Unlike a credit card, the account must be settled when the statement arrives. Since the bill must be cleared each month, no interest is charged to the customer. Instead, the customer pays an annual fee to the card provider for use of the charge card. Examples include American Express and Diners Club.

KEY SKILLS MIT

6.28 Charge cards vs. credit and debit cards

(a) What is the difference between a debit card and a credit card? #Identify

(b) What are the benefits and drawbacks of a charge card over a credit card? #Identify

Foreign exchange

When you visit countries outside the euro area, you need to get the currency that is accepted in that country. For example, before a trip to the USA, you would need to get US dollars. You can buy foreign currency from the commercial banks, building societies, An Post and credit unions. When you buy foreign currency, you must pay the current price or 'rate of exchange'.

An **exchange rate** is the price at which one currency can be exchanged for another.

Rule for calculating exchange rates:
Converting **from** euro – **multiply** by the bank **sells** rate.
Converting **to** euro – **divide** by the bank **buys** rate.

Below are the bank sells and bank buys rates for four currencies.

Bureau de change			
Country	**Currency**	**Bank sells**	**Bank buys**
UK	Pound sterling (GBP£)	0.85	0.88
USA	Dollar (USD$)	1.12	1.17
Australia	Australian dollar (AUD$)	1.63	1.74
Japan	Yen (JPY¥)	122	125

For each €1 we would receive £0.85, USD$1.12, AUD$1.63, or ¥122.

Using the information from the table, to convert €400 to sterling, multiply 400 by the 'bank sells' sterling rate, i.e.

400 × 0.85 = £340

To convert 1,552 yen into euro, we divide 1,552 by the 'bank buys' yen rate, i.e.

1,552 ÷ 125 = €12.42

KEY SKILLS

BN

6.29 Calculating exchange rates

(a) Using the table on the previous page, how many Australian dollars would you receive if you changed €650? #Calculate

(b) Using the table above, how many euros would you receive if you changed £345? #Calculate

Loans

Individuals and households sometimes use loans from financial institutions. A number of different types of loan are available to individuals and households, including:

- Short-term loans – repaid within one year (e.g. bank overdraft)
- Medium-term loans – repaid between one and five years
- Long-term loans – repaid over longer than five years (e.g. a mortgage).

See Chapter 8 for borrowing

The amount of interest you pay on loans can vary enormously, so it is worth shopping around the different lenders for the best rates and terms.

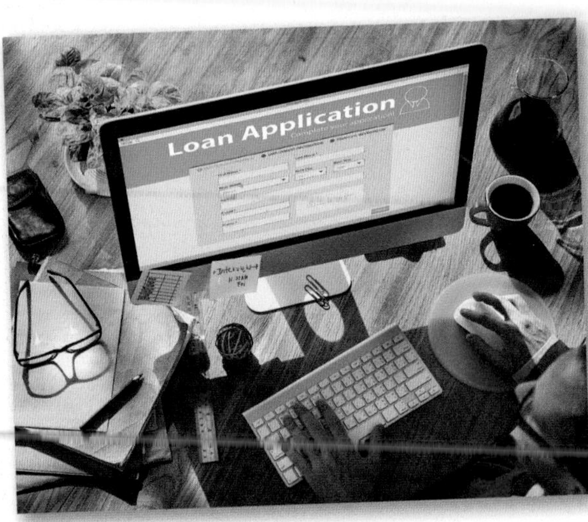

Wherever possible, try to save up for things and buy them when you have enough money rather than taking out a loan. Sometimes this isn't possible, of course, such as if you are buying a house or if you need a car to enable you to work, but a loan shouldn't be seen as an easy way of getting what you want now. There are financial penalties for having loans and if you have too many loans you may find it difficult to get a mortgage. Remember, borrowing money has a financial cost and an opportunity cost.

Banks invest the money that people have in their accounts in order to make money that they can lend to other people. Sometimes the lending may be to an organisation that you do not find acceptable. For example, the company might make weapons, use animal testing or use cheap labour in poor countries. Usually, customers of the bank don't know how or where their money is being used.

KEY SKILLS

WO

C

6.30 How should banks use your money?

A bank called Triodos, which operates in the Netherlands, Belgium, the UK, Spain and Germany, says on its website:

> *Do you know what your bank does with your money? We believe banks should be open, which is why we publish details of every organisation we lend to on our website. By lending exclusively to organisations that put people and the planet before profits, our savers' money works to create a positive impact and real returns.*

(a) Do you think all banks should operate ethically (for the good of others), as Triodos does? Write down the reasons for your opinion. #Discussion

(b) Does it bother you if banks lend to organisations that some people might find unethical? Or do you think that the bank's purpose is to make as much money as possible? #Discussion

Weblinks

PowerPoint Summary

SAVING AND INVESTING MONEY

LEARNING OUTCOMES IN FOCUS

1.5 Identify reasons for saving and borrowing money, relate the reasons to determining appropriate sources of finance with respect to their purpose, costs and risks

Links to 1.1, 1.2, 1.3, 1.8, 1.12, 1.13, 2.11, 3.2, 3.5

1.8 Compare the services provided by consumer agencies and financial institutions to assist and support customers

Links to 1.5, 1.7, 1.9 , 1.10

LEARNING INTENTIONS FOR THIS CHAPTER

When you have completed this chapter you will be able to:

- Outline the main reasons for saving money
- Consider where to save money
- List the major savings products offered by financial institutions in Ireland
- Outline the tax implications of saving
- Differentiate between saving and investing.

CHAPTER 7 KEY TERMS

An Post	deposit account	notice deposit account
annual equivalent rate (AER)	Deposit Interest Retention Tax (DIRT)	principal
building society	dividend	risk
commercial bank	flat rate of interest	savings
compound interest	interest	simple interest
credit rating	investing	term deposit
credit union	liquidity	
demand deposit account		

CHAPTER 7 KEY SKILLS

- BC Being Creative
- BL Being Literate
- BN Being Numerate
- C Communicating
- MIT Managing Information and Thinking
- MM Managing Myself
- WO Working with Others

What is saving?

When we refer to our **savings**, we mean the part of our income we choose not to spend. Savings could also be seen as **deferred (or postponed) spending** because we are making a decision to put this money aside with the intention of spending it at some point in the future.

See Chapter 11 for personal financial life cycle

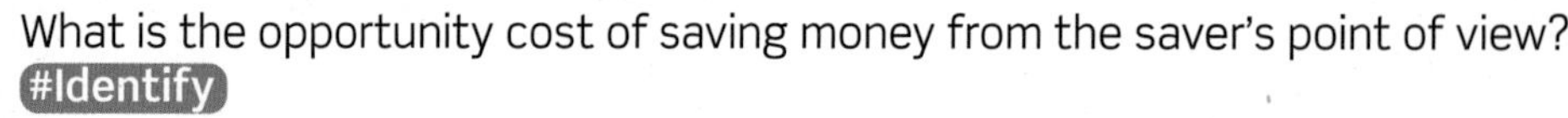

KEY SKILLS

WO C

7.1 The opportunity cost of saving

What is the opportunity cost of saving money from the saver's point of view? #Identify

7.2 What if you don't save?

Do you think there are any current or future costs for people who don't save any of their income? #Identify

7.3 Your reasons for saving over time

Do you think the reasons you save now will be the same reasons you save in the future? Discuss how your saving patterns might change as you reach different stages of your life. #Discussion

Reasons for saving money

Here are some reasons for saving money:

See Chapter 11 for financial planning for your future

1. For future planned expenditure, e.g. a new car, holiday, home extension
2. For emergencies: to have money available in case something goes wrong, for example a washing machine breaks and needs to be replaced
3. For major family events, e.g. a wedding
4. For retirement, when our income level will reduce
5. To improve our credit rating: lenders like to see that a person is saving money regularly.

A person's **credit rating**, or creditworthiness, reflects how likely they are to repay a loan. If they have a good track record of saving and of repaying previous loans, their credit rating will improve and they are more likely to get a loan in the future. Some financial institutions will only lend money to existing customers who have a proven track record of savings.

Factors to consider when saving

There are various places where you can save your money. Here are some factors you should consider before deciding where to save your money:

- Risk
- Reward
- Liquidity
- Taxation
- Convenience
- Future benefits
- Terms and conditions.

Risk

Will your savings be safe? Money saved in a licensed financial institution (e.g. bank, building society, post office, credit union) is far safer than money kept in a drawer or even in a safe at home.

Savings with **An Post** are 'state guaranteed', which means they are 100% secure and will definitely be repaid by the government.

Funds held in all financial institutions authorised by the Central Bank of Ireland are protected by the **Deposit Guarantee Scheme (DGS)** if the bank, building society or credit union can't repay deposits. Every customer is covered up to €100,000.

Reward

Will the savings earn interest?

Interest is a reward for saving your money with a financial institution. It is extra money you will receive on top of the money you have saved.

All financial institutions offer slightly different rates of interest. Savers may have to shop around to get the best deal. The rate quoted by the financial institutions is the **annual equivalent rate (AER)**. This tells the saver the full rate of interest if all of the money is left in a savings account for a full year.

Liquidity

Is it easy to withdraw or access your savings should you need to, i.e. how quickly can your savings be turned back into cash? Some savings accounts require you to give the financial institution written notice and penalties may apply if you withdraw earlier than the terms agreed. For example, a 14-day notice deposit account requires the saver to give the bank 14 days' notice of their intention to withdraw money.

An Post Savings Bonds offer a higher rate of interest than most savings schemes, but this is greatly reduced if the money is withdrawn within three years. In this case, there is a trade-off between the reward on offer and the liquidity.

Taxation

Will you have to pay tax on your interest? **Deposit Interest Retention Tax (DIRT)** is a tax on interest earned on savings. Some savings products offered by An Post, such as Savings Certificates and savings bonds, are not subject to DIRT.

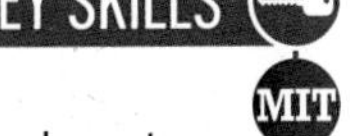

7.4 Digging the DIRT

Research and record the current rate of DIRT. Who decides the DIRT rate and when to change it? #Research

MIT BN

Convenience

Is the account convenient for making regular lodgements and withdrawals? For example, is the financial institution located conveniently? What are its opening hours?

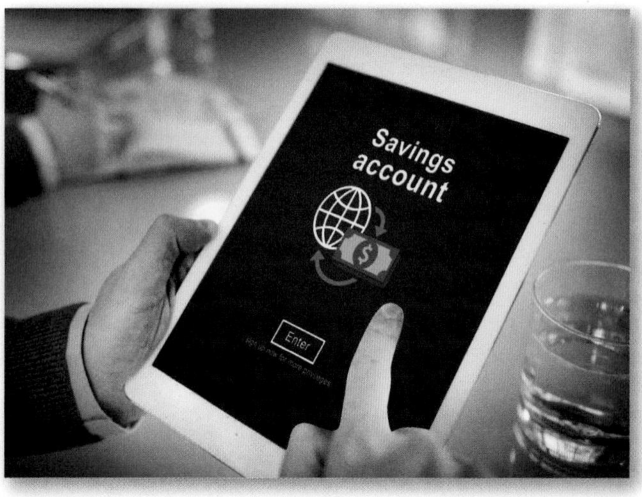

Many banks provide online savings accounts for customers, which makes it easy to transfer money into them. Once the savings account is opened, setting up a standing order might be the most convenient way to regularly transfer money into it.

7.5 Opening hours

Research and record the opening hours of a local bank, credit union, post office and building society. #Research

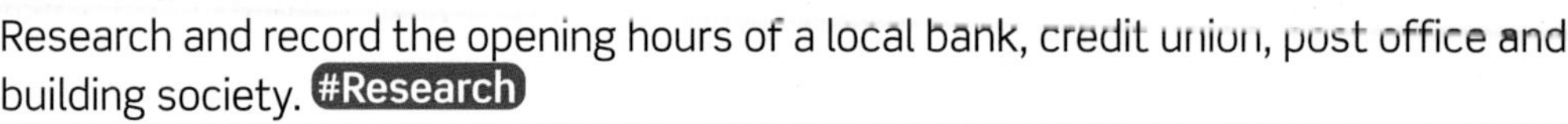

Future benefits

Will you qualify for future benefits, including loans or bonus interest payments? If you save in a financial institution that you may want to borrow from in the future, you will have a history of saving with them. This might make it easier for you to get a loan.

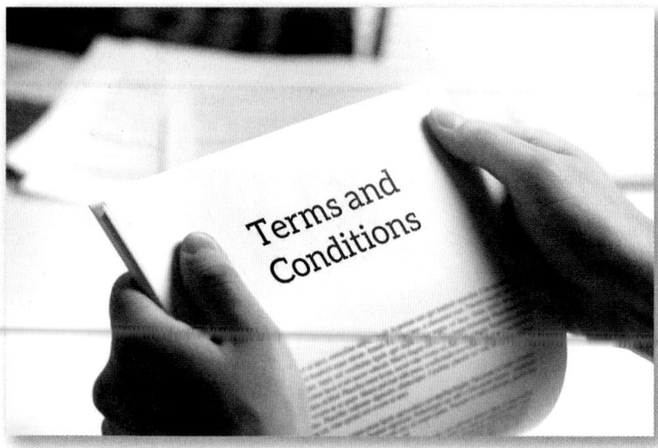

Terms and conditions

Are there fees and banking charges involved in operating a deposit account? Is there a minimum/maximum deposit required? Will you be penalised for withdrawing money early?

7.6 Deciding where to put your money

In pairs, role play an interviewer and a financial expert. Create a podcast or video of questions and answers for the factors you need to think about when deciding where to save your money. Alternatively, you can create a poster or infographic. #ThinkPairShare

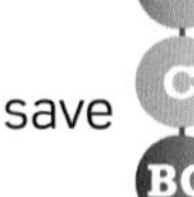

Where to save

Money can be saved in the following financial institutions in Ireland:

- Commercial banks
- An Post
- Credit unions
- Building societies.

Commercial banks

Commercial banks are banks that households and individuals deal with. They offer their customers a range of financial services, including deposit accounts.

Opening a savings account

You looked at how to open a current account in Chapter 6. Opening a savings account is very similar, so you will need to provide proof of identity and address.

KEY SKILLS MM MIT

7.7 Proving yourself

What proof of identity and address do you need to provide to open an account with a financial institution? #Research

Types of deposit account offered by commercial banks

You can choose from a wide range of savings accounts depending on how much you want to save and how soon you want to access your money. The interest earned on all deposit accounts is subject to DIRT.

- **Demand deposits** allow you to withdraw (or demand) your money when you choose to. You do not have to give the bank any notice. Demand deposit accounts typically pay a very low rate of interest.
- **Term deposits** require you to leave your money in the account for a certain length of time. The agreed timeframe (or term) could be anything from seven days to five years. Term deposits carry a higher rate of interest than demand deposits. It may be possible to withdraw money early, but there will be a penalty for doing so – a lower rate of interest will be applied.
- **Notice deposits** require you to give the bank advance notice of your intention to withdraw money. For example, a 10-day notice deposit account means that the saver must notify the bank 10 banking days in advance of a withdrawal.

As a general rule, *the greater the liquidity, the lower the rate of interest paid.* This means that savers who leave their money in the bank for long periods of time will be able to get the highest rates of interest.

KEY SKILLS WO C

7.8 Highly interested

Why, do you think, are financial institutions willing to pay higher rates of interest to those who agree to leave their savings in a deposit account for longer? #Discussion

An Post

An Post offers a range of savings products. These offer competitive rates of interest and are state-guaranteed. In some cases, the interest earned is not subject to DIRT. An Post also offers **Prize Bonds**. Thousands of weekly prizes can be won, including a €1 million tax-free prize four times a year. Prize Bonds do not earn interest, but are eligible to win prizes every week. You may get lucky with a Prize Bond, or you may not!

Credit unions

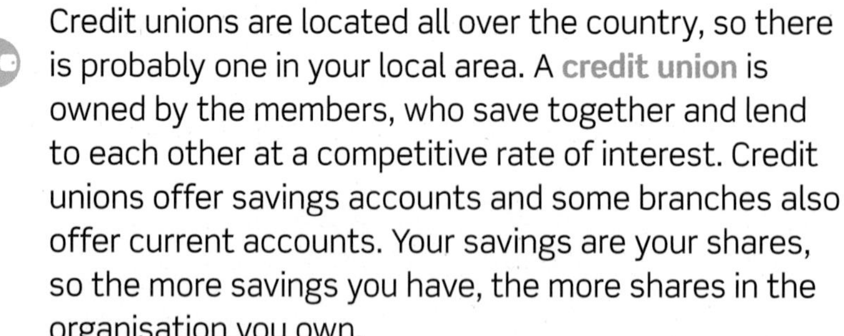

Credit unions are located all over the country, so there is probably one in your local area. A **credit union** is owned by the members, who save together and lend to each other at a competitive rate of interest. Credit unions offer savings accounts and some branches also offer current accounts. Your savings are your shares, so the more savings you have, the more shares in the organisation you own.

Savings accounts: Saving in this type of account may give you a dividend at the end of the year. The dividend will not be the same amount every payout, as the amount will depend on the available money and the number of people between whom it has to be shared. Money can be lodged to this account at any time.

> KEY TERM
>
> A **dividend** is a payment to shareholders based on the number of shares owned.

Deposit accounts: As credit unions are community based, you will be helping your community by being a member. If you save with a credit union, you can apply for a personal loan for many things, including buying a car, improving your home or going on holiday.

You will receive a competitive rate of interest from a deposit account, but interest on deposits in credit unions is subject to DIRT.

Building societies

The main reason for saving in a building society is to get a mortgage or a loan for upgrading property. However, a building society does pay interest on savings. They offer a wide range of services (similar to banks), a competitive rate of interest on savings and they have branches located all over the country. An example of a building society in Ireland is the Educational Building Society (EBS).

> KEY SKILLS
>
> 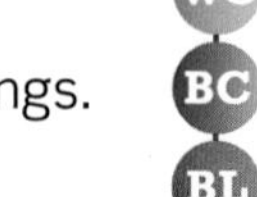
>
>
> **7.9 Compare savings options**
>
> In small groups, compare savings options in each of the following type of financial institution: credit union, building society, commercial bank and An Post. In your group, choose one type of financial institution and create a group poster to display your findings.
>
> #Research #GroupWork
>
> MIT WO BC BL BN

Calculating interest on savings

Interest is a reward for saving money with a financial institution. There are two ways to calculate interest you receive on your savings:

- Simple interest
- Compound interest.

Simple interest

Simple interest (also known as **flat rate of interest**) is money you can earn by saving money (the **principal**).

The interest, which is a percentage of the principal, is added to the principal, making your money grow.

The simple interest formula is:
Interest = Principal × Time × Rate

Example
Megan saves €1,000 at a rate of 2% for two years:
Interest = 1,000 × 2 × 2% = €40

Compound interest

Compound interest is when interest is added to the savings and then that added interest also earns interest from then on. This means that the saver is earning interest on their principal as well as getting interest on their interest. For this reason, compound interest will reward savers with more interest than simple interest savings schemes.

What is the difference between simple interest and compound interest?

Example
Mary Daly has €2,000 saved in her deposit account. Interest is calculated at 5% per annum. How much will she receive into her account after (a) one year (b) two years and (c) three years with (i) simple interest and (ii) compound interest?

Solution

Interest earned at simple interest rate (5%)			Interest earned at compound interest rate (5%)		
	Amount	Interest		Amount	Interest
Year 1	€2,000	€100	Year 1	€2,000	€100.00
Year 2	€2,000	€100	Year 2	€2,100	€105.00
Year 3	€2,000	€100	Year 3	€2,205	€110.25
Total interest		€300.00	Total interest		€315.25
Note: Interest earned is based on the original amount deposited; therefore, the annual interest payment will not change.			**Note:** The interest from the previous year is added to the principal before the current year's interest is calculated, so interest is paid on a higher amount each year, increasing the amount of interest paid.		

Annual equivalent rate (AER)

AER is the rate of interest you could earn on your savings in a full year with a compound interest rate. That doesn't mean you have to keep your money in the account for a year, but this is what you would earn if you did. AER is usually given without taking DIRT into account.

It is standard practice in Ireland for financial institutions to show the AER, which makes it easier for savers to compare different financial institutions.

Deposit Interest Retention Tax (DIRT)

DIRT is a tax on the interest earned on deposit accounts. It is deducted by the bank at source and transferred to the Office of the Revenue Commissioners, which collects all tax in Ireland. The account holder is credited with the net interest, i.e. interest minus DIRT.

Example

Louise Hughes has €2,000 saved in a bank. Simple interest is 5% per annum and Louise must pay 35% DIRT on interest earned. How much DIRT does she pay and how much does she have in her account after one year?

Solution

Calculate interest	€2,000 @ 5% = €100 interest
Calculate DIRT	€100 @ 35% = €35 DIRT
Interest received	= €65 net

Louise now has €2,000 + €65 = €2,065 in her account.

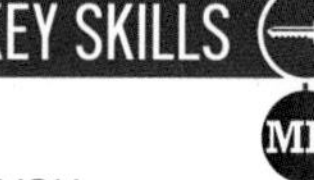

7.10 Where would you save?

Assume you have €2,000 that you want to save for two years. Where would you place your money and why? #CreativeThinking

7.11 Choose a savings option

You work out that you can afford to save €20 a month, every month. What type of account would you open? Give reasons for your answer. #Research

7.12 When should you start?

Discuss at what age or time of life you think people should start to save. Give a reason for your answer. #Discussion

Investing

Investing is often seen as putting money aside in order to get a better return on it in the future. This is very similar to saving, but we expect to get some sort of extra reward for investing our money.

Savings are generally low-risk, low-reward schemes that provide easy access to your money when required. This applies to savings in both piggy banks and commercial banks.

Investing often involves greater risk to the money invested and it may not be possible to get it back immediately. However, investments may offer greater potential for rewards. Examples of investments include buying property, art or company shares. Investing in company shares, art or property does not guarantee a positive return, as values may go up or down. In the longer term property prices may rise, but you might have to keep the property for 10 or more years in order to cover the costs involved in buying and selling it and then benefit from the price rises.

See Chapter 11 for personal financial life cycle

Most people don't focus on the difference between saving and investing as it relates to their everyday lives, but the distinction becomes more important when it comes to longer-term financial planning. For example, when you put together a personal financial life cycle, you will identify both short-term and longer-term financial needs. You may choose to meet these needs in different ways. You may decide to save some money in low-risk, low-reward savings accounts, while investing some of it in other options that carry a higher level of risk but also offer the potential for higher long-term rewards. In this situation, it is sensible to look at exactly when you are likely to need your money and also what type of return you are expecting. You should also consider the level of risk you can afford to take with your money.

PERSONAL FINANCE

CHAPTER 8

BORROWING FOR INDIVIDUALS AND HOUSEHOLDS

LEARNING OUTCOMES IN FOCUS

1.5 Identify reasons for saving and borrowing money, relate the reasons to determining appropriate sources of finance with respect to their purpose, costs and risks

Links to 1.1, 1.2, 1.3, 1.8, 1.12, 1.13, 2.11, 3.2, 3.5

1.8 Compare the services provided by consumer agencies and financial institutions to assist and support customers

Links to 1.5, 1.7, 1.9 , 1.10

LEARNING INTENTIONS FOR THIS CHAPTER

When you have completed this chapter you will be able to:

- Explain the role of borrowing in both personal and household finance
- Outline the reasons for borrowing
- Compare the major sources of finance for individuals and households
- Outline the different types of loan available to individuals and households
- Explain the factors a lender will consider before agreeing to give out a loan
- Examine the costs and consequences of borrowing
- Outline the rights and responsibilities of borrowers.

CHAPTER 8 KEY TERMS

annual percentage rate (APR)	guarantor	matching principle
asset	hire purchase	medium-term loan
borrowing	Insolvency Service of Ireland (ISI)	Money Advice and Budgeting Service (MABS)
collateral	insolvent	moneylender
cooling-off period	instalment	mortgage
cost of credit	interest	responsible borrowing
credit rating	Irish Credit Bureau (ICB)	security
creditworthiness	leasing	stress test
declining principal		

CHAPTER 8 KEY SKILLS

BL Being Literate

BN Being Numerate

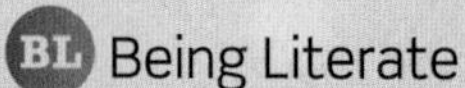
C Communicating

MIT Managing Information and Thinking

MM Managing Myself

SW Staying Well

WO Working with Others

PERSONAL FINANCE

Should we borrow money?

It may not always be possible to buy everything we need (or want) with the money available to us. In Chapter 4, we saw that households sometimes have budget deficits because their planned expenditure is greater than the money they can earn and save. One solution to this cash shortfall is to borrow.

KEY SKILLS

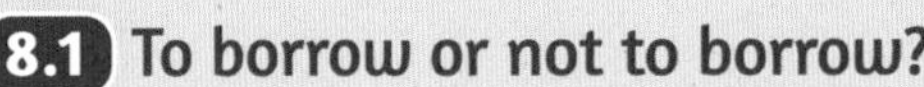

8.1 To borrow or not to borrow?

BL C MIT

'Neither a borrower nor a lender be
For loan oft loses both itself and friend.'
Hamlet, William Shakespeare

What does the quotation from *Hamlet* mean? Do you think it is good advice? Give one reason to support your point of view. #Opinion #Reflect

KEY TERM

Borrowing means getting money from a person or financial institution and agreeing to pay it back at a later date. The borrower will usually have to pay an extra amount to the lender for the use of their money. This extra charge is called interest.

KEY TERM

Interest is the **financial cost** of borrowing money.

KEY SKILLS

8.2 The opportunity cost of borrowing

MIT

Borrowing also has an opportunity cost. What could that be? #Think

Since borrowing money has costs, it needs to be considered very carefully. The borrower must understand all the costs and consequences involved. These are some sensible questions to ask before borrowing:

- ***Do I really need the item?*** If it is not essential, it might be better to do without it or to save for it and buy it when you can afford to pay for it. The more you save, the less you will have to borrow and repay.
- ***How much will it cost?*** If you have to borrow money to buy an item, it will add to the price because you will be charged interest on the loan. For example, if you have to borrow the money to buy a car costing €20,000, the real cost to you may be €23,000 when you add on the interest.
- ***Can I afford the repayments?*** You will need to pay back an amount of money each week or month. Your income must be enough to cover this ongoing cost. If you don't make the repayments, your credit rating will suffer and you will find it hard to get loans in the future.

KEY SKILLS

8.3 Risks of borrowing for the borrower

WO MIT

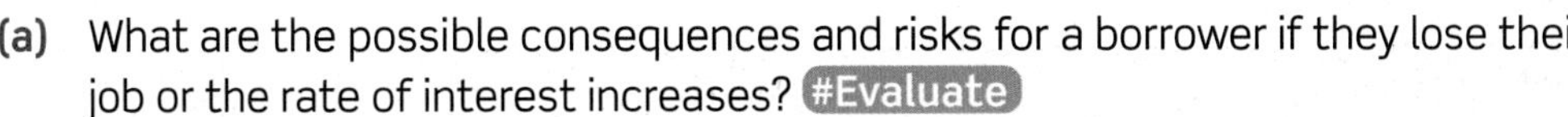

(a) What are the possible consequences and risks for a borrower if they lose their job or the rate of interest increases? #Evaluate

(b) Compare your answer with the person sitting next to you. #ThinkPairShare

(c) Share your combined answers with the pair sitting behind you/in front of you. #GroupWork

KEY SKILLS C MIT MM SW

8.4 What would you do?

If there is something you really want to buy that costs €150, but you don't have any savings at the moment, which of the following options would you choose? Give reasons for your answer. #CreativeThinking

(a) Save up for it by not spending any money you didn't need to (e.g. no treats) in order to save the money in the shortest possible time

(b) Save up for it, but still allow yourself to spend a little money on treats, even though it would take a little longer to save the full amount

(c) Borrow the money so you could have the item now, but you will be paying back the loan for two years and end up paying €225 because of the interest

Reasons for (household) borrowing

Although it is nearly always best if you don't have to borrow, sometimes it is necessary, for example in the following situations:

- **To pay for very expensive items:** It is very difficult for most people to pay cash for a high-cost item such as a car or house. A loan or mortgage may be your only realistic option to raise the finance needed. You will have to repay the money over a number of years, but you will eventually own a valuable asset.

KEY TERM

An asset is something of value that you own.

See Chapters 7 and 9 for savings and insurance

- **To deal with short-term deficits:** If a household is facing a budget deficit and doesn't have enough savings to make up the difference, they may have no option but to look for short-term finance.
- **For emergencies:** From time to time, things will go wrong or break down and households may need to borrow money to pay for repairs or unexpected costs. Savings and insurance cover can also be useful to deal with some of these unexpected problems.

Write down which of the following are *not* good reasons to borrow money and discuss why not: #Discussion

WO C MIT MM SW

(a) To buy a home
(b) To buy a second house
(c) To go on holiday
(d) To pay for special occasions (Christmas, birthdays, etc.)
(e) To pay for college fees
(f) To pay household/utility bills
(g) To buy a new TV
(h) To pay for your wedding
(i) To pay for an emergency operation
(j) To provide money until the next payday
(k) To pay a tax bill
(l) To pay off another loan or credit card bill

Borrowers should match the type of loan with the type of need they have. The **matching principle** ensures that short-, medium- and long-term needs are matched with suitable short-, medium- and long-term sources of finance. These sources are explained in Table 8.1.

A person's financial needs often depend on their personal financial life cycle. People at different ages and stages are likely to have different needs.

See Chapter 11 for personal financial life cycle

Need	Example	Repayment period	Source of finance
Short-term	Budget deficit	Within one year	Bank overdraft, credit card, etc.
Medium-term	Purchase of a new car	One to five years	Medium-term loan, hire purchase, leasing
Long-term	Purchase of a house	More than five years	Mortgage, etc.

Table 8.1 The matching principle

Before you can be approved for a loan with a financial institution, you will agree a time limit for repayment. You will need to work out **how much you can afford to pay back each month**.

Since interest will continue to be charged until the loan is repaid, **the longer the repayment period, the greater the overall cost will be**. On the other hand, **if the repayment period is short, the monthly repayments will be high**, which may have a major impact on household cash flow.

For example, a €20,000 car loan will have monthly repayments of around €410 if repaid in five years, but may be about €630 per month if repaid in just three years. The shorter repayment term will reduce overall cost, but the larger monthly repayment may have a negative impact on the household budget by increasing monthly expenditure.

Make sure you will be able to keep up the monthly amounts for the full term of the loan before agreeing to it. This is responsible borrowing.

Responsible borrowing means that you do not borrow more than you are able to pay back.

KEY SKILLS

8.6 What is a sun holiday worth?

The Murphy family wanted to go on a sun holiday for two weeks. The only way they could afford it was to take out a loan that would take three years to pay off. Discuss the following questions and write down your conclusions:

(a) How do you think the Murphys might feel when they are still paying off the loan long after the suntan and the holiday memories have faded? #Opinion

(b) What do you think would be a better timeframe for paying off a loan for a holiday? #Opinion

(c) Is a holiday a good reason for taking out a loan? Briefly explain the reason(s) for your answer. #Discussion

KEY SKILLS

8.7 Responsible borrowing

How can you ensure that you can afford to repay a loan? #Plan

KEY SKILLS

WO SW MM

8.8 What is a reasonable loan payment?

Ben wants to renovate his kitchen. He has had a quote from a kitchen company for €7,000. Ben has worked out that his disposable income will enable him to repay a loan for this amount in one year as long as he goes out less, doesn't take a holiday and spends the minimum on household bills for the year. Discuss the danger of Ben using up all his spare income on loan repayments. #Discussion

Types of borrowing for individuals and households

Short-term sources of finance

Bank overdraft

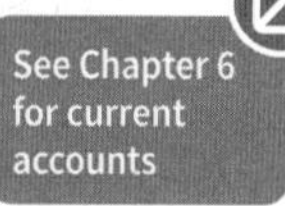
See Chapter 6 for current accounts

A current account holder with a bank overdraft has permission to withdraw more money from their account than they actually have in it. Borrowing is allowed up to a specific limit.

DID YOU KNOW...

According to the Central Statistics Office (CSO) Household Finance and Consumption Survey, which offered an insight into the financial state of Irish homes in 2013, the average amount of debt on an overdraft in 2013 was €1,000. Around 10% of households had an overdraft, but this rose to 18% for self-employed people. The average overdraft for a self-employed person was €4,000, compared to €700 for an unemployed person.

KEY SKILLS

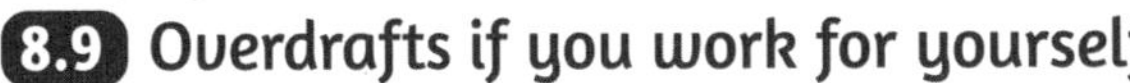

8.9 Overdrafts if you work for yourself

MIT

(a) Write down the reasons why self-employed people are more likely to need an overdraft than people in regular employment. #List

(b) Compare your answers with the person sitting next to you. #ThinkPairShare

(c) Share your combined answers with the pair sitting behind you/in front of you. #Discussion

Credit card

Cardholders can buy items now and pay for them at a later date. Interest rates on credit card debt can be very high, which makes this an expensive source of short-term finance.

See Chapter 6 for credit cards

KEY SKILLS

8.10 The pros and cons of a credit card

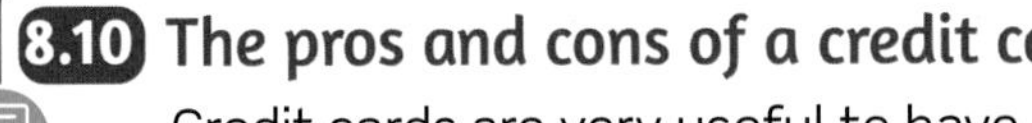

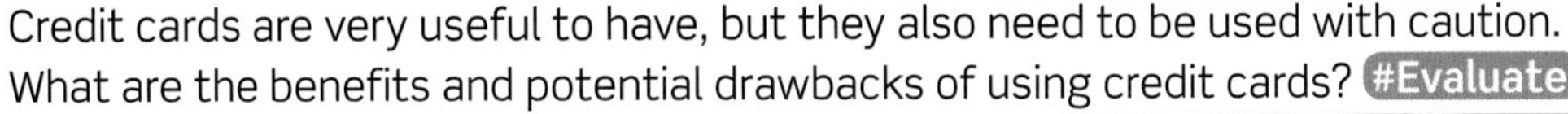

MIT MM BN SW

Credit cards are very useful to have, but they also need to be used with caution. What are the benefits and potential drawbacks of using credit cards? #Evaluate

Medium-term sources of finance

Medium-term loan

This source of finance is available from a range of financial institutions, including banks, building societies and credit unions. Borrowers make fixed monthly repayments over an agreed time period. These monthly payments cover repayment of the loan plus interest.

Leasing

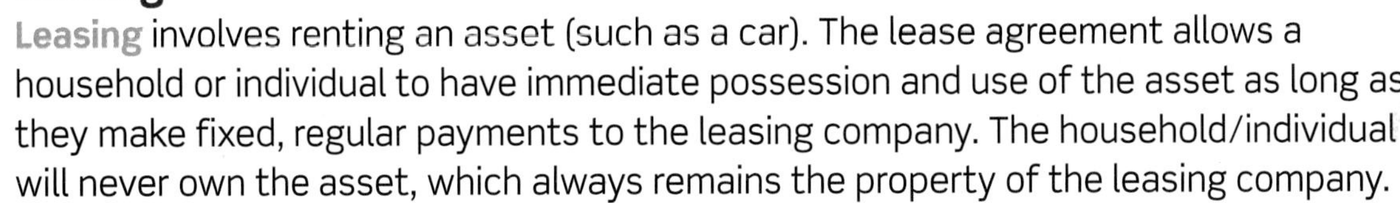

Leasing involves renting an asset (such as a car). The lease agreement allows a household or individual to have immediate possession and use of the asset as long as they make fixed, regular payments to the leasing company. The household/individual will never own the asset, which always remains the property of the leasing company.

Hire purchase (HP)

Hire purchase is a medium-term source of finance used to purchase an asset. The purchaser pays a deposit followed by an agreed number of regular instalments.

KEY TERM

An **instalment** is a fixed sum of money due as one of a number of payments spread over an agreed period of time.

Ownership of the asset will eventually pass to the hirer, but not until the last instalment has been paid. No security or **collateral** is required, but the interest charges are very high (often more than 20%). For that reason, HP is often used as a last resort by those who cannot get a medium-term loan.

KEY TERM

Collateral is something used as **security** for repayment of a loan. If you cannot pay back the loan, the lender can take the asset, such as your property, and sell it to recover the money owed by you.

Hire purchase example

The Hanlons want to buy a washing machine from Kitchen Electrics Ltd under a hire purchase arrangement. A finance company will pay Kitchen Electrics Ltd the full price of the washing machine and the Hanlons will then repay the finance company in regular instalments over a fixed period of time.

The washing machine belongs to the finance company until the Hanlons pay the last instalment.

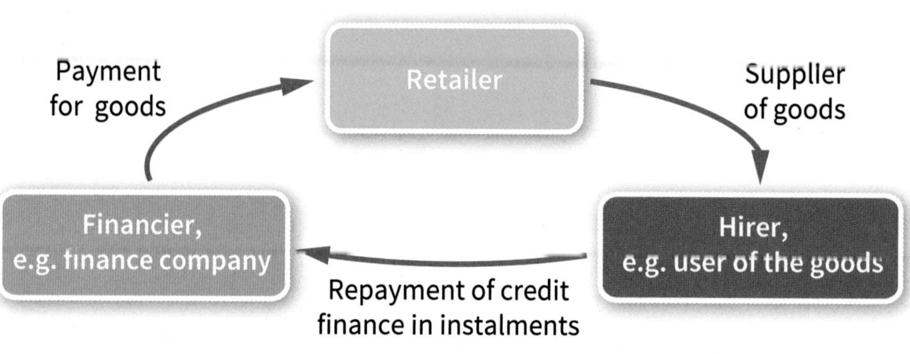

Figure 8.1 How hire purchase works

The hirer has the right to withdraw from the agreement within 10 days of receiving a copy of the agreement. This is known as a **cooling-off period**.

Personal contract plans (PCP finance)

PCP finance is a very popular option for financing vehicles and is often arranged through the motor dealer or their finance company. It appears attractive because car buyers only need a relatively small deposit and the monthly repayments are low. This is because the buyer is only financing part of the vehicle's cost. At the end of an agreed period (usually three to five years), the car buyer will not have paid the full purchase price of the vehicle and has a number of options:

- Pay the outstanding balance needed to buy the car outright, either from savings or by taking out a new loan.
- Return the car to the dealer and owe no more money. In other words, the buyer has really just been leasing the vehicle up to this point.
- Return to the dealer and use the vehicle as a deposit against a new vehicle. This often involves entering into a new PCP agreement. Most customers choose this option and benefit from upgrading to a new vehicle at regular intervals. Car dealers also benefit from this arrangement because customers return to buy new vehicles more often.

As with all sources of finance, there are lots of terms and conditions, so it's very important to do some research and understand what exactly is involved before entering into any financial contract.

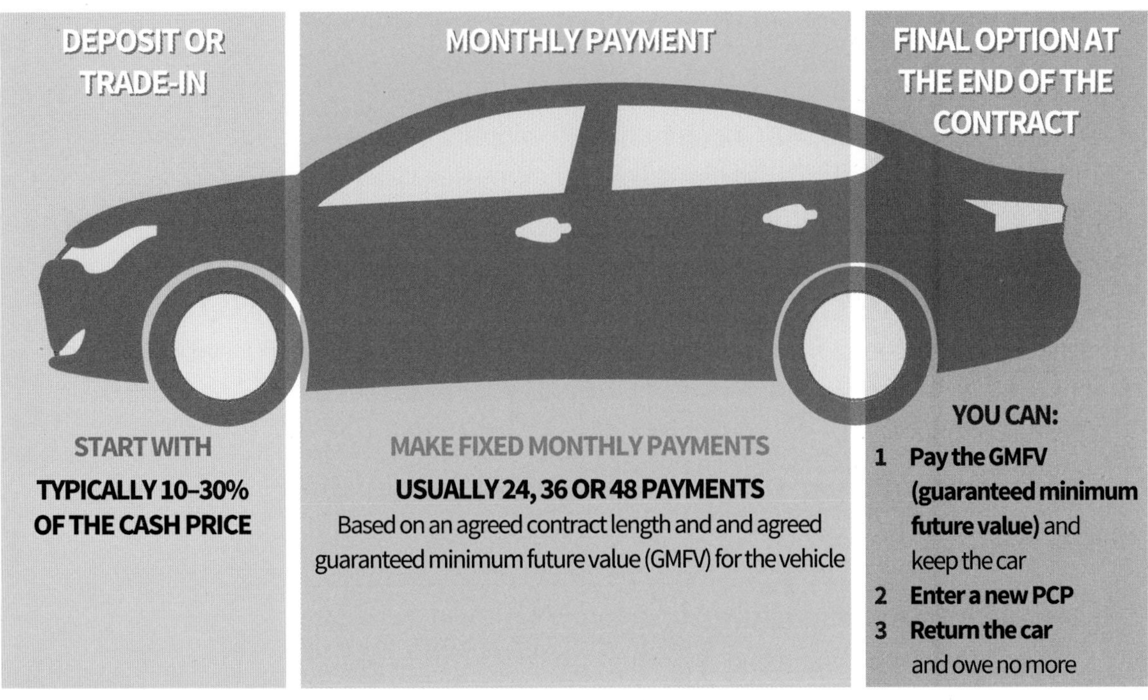

Figure 8.2 PCP explained (*Source:* Competition and Consumer Protection Commission)

KEY SKILLS 

8.11 Mary's new television

Mary wants to buy a new television that will cost €2,000. She does not have the money saved, so she has two options to get the television.

Option 1: Hire purchase – pay a deposit of €400 and then pay €150 per month for one year.

Option 2: Rent the TV for €50 per week.

(a) What is the total cost of hire purchase? #Calculate

(b) What is the total rent for a year? #Calculate

(c) Which option would you choose? Explain your choice and show your workings. #Opinion #Discussion

Long-term borrowing

Long-term loan/mortgage

Households and individuals generally use a special long-term loan called a **mortgage** for buying property. Mortgages are available from commercial banks, building societies and some credit unions.

When a borrower takes out a mortgage, they enter into a contract with a lender to repay the loan plus interest. They are also agreeing to use their home as collateral (security) for the loan. If they don't repay the debt, the lender can sell the property to recover the money owed.

Mortgages usually have repayment periods of between 15 and 30 years. Loan rates on mortgages are lower than on medium-term loans, but the total cost of the mortgage will be much higher because the repayment period is so long.

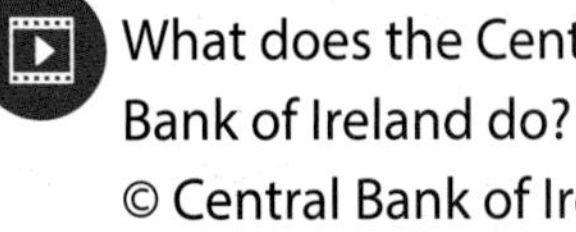

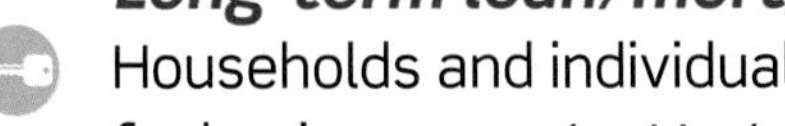

According to figures from the CSO's Household Finance and Consumption Survey 2018, just over one in four households (25.8%) have a mortgage on their main residence. The median value of the outstanding balance of the mortgage is €119,400.

Borrowing from moneylenders

Moneylenders are individuals or companies (excluding banks, building societies and credit unions) whose main business is to lend money. In Ireland, moneylenders must have a licence to lend money. Licensed moneylenders have to obey strict rules and regulations.

Moneylenders without a licence (unlicensed moneylenders) are breaking the law. Unlicensed moneylenders are not regulated and may charge very high rates of interest (up to 188% APR) and place borrowers under a lot of pressure to repay debts quickly. For these reasons, avoid unlicensed lenders.

As the regulator of the industry, the Central Bank of Ireland issues moneylending licences in Ireland.

KEY SKILLS BN

8.12 How long to repay a loan?

Research moneylenders and the rates of interest they charge. Choose one of the moneylenders you identified. If you borrowed €1,000 from them, how much would it cost you to repay it within (a) one year (b) two years and (c) five years? #Consider

IN THE NEWS

It Makes Sense loans

In 2015, a microcredit scheme was launched in over 30 credit unions to reduce dependence on moneylenders. This proved so successful that the scheme was extended to all credit unions that sign up for it. It Makes Sense loans are available to people receiving social welfare payments who may not be able to get credit from other sources. Loan values are between €100 and €2,000 and the maximum interest rate is 1% per month, or 12% per year (12.68% APR).

Source: Citizens Information website

MIT

8.13 Microcredit

Why, do you think, is this source of finance specifically targeted at people receiving social welfare payments? #Opinion #Consider

Applying for a loan from a financial institution

Money can be borrowed from the following financial institutions in Ireland:

- Commercial banks
- Credit unions
- Building societies.

It is important not to borrow on impulse. Take time to consider the answers to the following important questions:

- How much money do I need to borrow?
- What can I afford to pay back each week or month?
- How long do I have to repay the money?
- Where can I get the best rates of interest?

You will need to contact the financial institution from which you are hoping to get a loan, either in person or online.

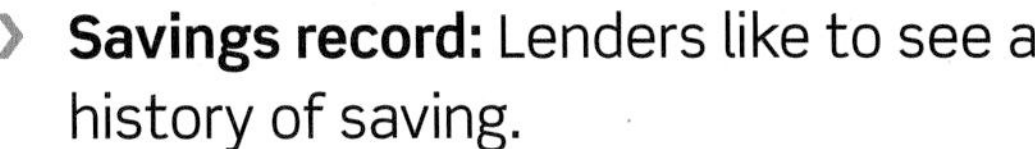

You will need to fill out a loan application form and provide the following information:

- **Personal details:** Name, address, date of birth, etc. A person under 18 cannot borrow money from a financial institution.
- **Residential details:** Your address; whether you rent or have a mortgage.
- **Employment details:** You will be asked for your most recent payslips to see how much you earn. You may also need to provide an employment detail summary, which shows your annual earnings for the last year.

See Chapter 10 for taxation

- **Savings record:** Lenders like to see a history of saving.
- **Borrowing history:** Lenders want to know if you have other debts and like to see evidence that you have repaid previous loans on time and in full.
- **Purpose of the loan:** You may have to provide details and costings, for example if you are building a house, carrying out home improvements or buying a car. If a loan is taken out by more than one person, each person will have to provide the above information.

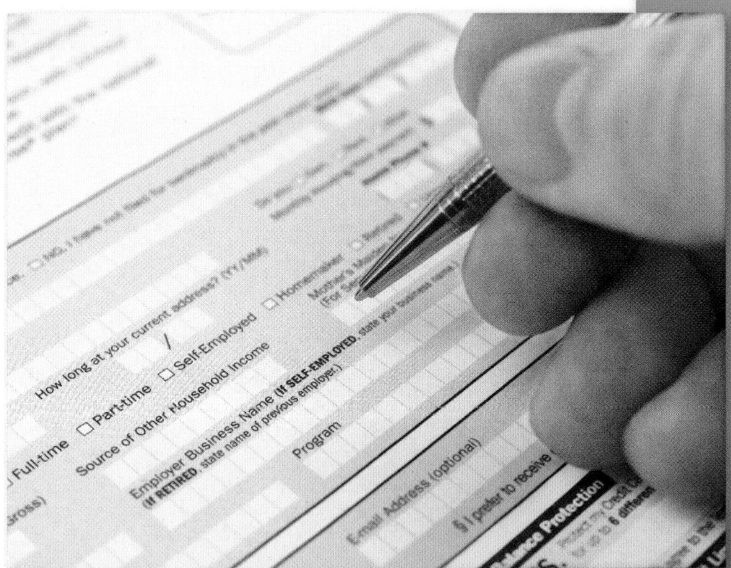

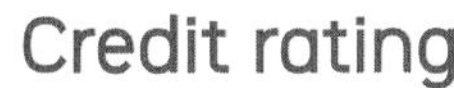

Credit rating

Before granting a loan, the financial institution will check your **credit rating** or **creditworthiness**.

> **KEY TERM**
>
> **Creditworthiness** is an estimate of a person's ability to pay off a loan, based on their saving and borrowing history with financial institutions.

A person who is creditworthy is seen as having a reliable source of income and can be trusted to repay a loan. Your creditworthiness will also be examined if you apply for a credit card or a hire purchase agreement. Your creditworthiness can be proved from your bank statements and also by a report from the **Irish Credit Bureau (ICB)**.

Your creditworthiness: Information from the Irish Credit Bureau (ICB)

1 ***What affects whether my loan is approved?***

Most lenders look for information about your income, employment, living costs and existing loan repayments to help them decide whether you can afford to repay a loan. Most lenders also want to look at your creditworthiness. It can be a good indication of how likely you are to pay back the money. You are likely to have a positive creditworthiness record if you have a good history of repayment on previous loans. Your credit record may be poor if you missed repayments on a regular basis or failed to pay off a loan in the past.

2 ***How do lenders know about my previous loans?***

Most lenders in Ireland send information about borrowers and their repayments to a central agency, the Irish Credit Bureau (ICB). The ICB holds information about borrowers and their loans for five years after the loan is concluded. This information is held in an individual credit report that is kept by the ICB about each borrower.

Your credit report includes:

- Your name, date of birth, address(es) used by you in relation to financial transactions
- The names of lenders and account numbers of loans you currently hold or that were active within the last five years
- Repayments made or missed for each month on each loan
- The failure to clear off any loan
- Loans that were settled for less than you owed
- Legal actions your lender took against you.

The ICB's information reflects a full picture of your credit history, good and/or bad.

3 ***Is my lender allowed to check my credit history?***

When you sign a mortgage or loan application, you also give your lender permission to send information about your repayments to a credit reference agency such as the ICB and to seek information about your credit history. If your credit history is poor, a lender is unlikely to give you a loan even if you have the income to repay it. However, even if your credit history is excellent, you still may not be given a loan if, in the view of the lender, you have reached your repayment limit.

Source: Irish Credit Bureau website

If the lender is unhappy with your credit history or your ability to repay, you may be asked to get a guarantor.

KEY TERM

A **guarantor** is a person who agrees to repay a loan for you should you be unable or unwilling to do so.

For example, if you need to get a loan for college but do not have a regular source of income, the bank may allow your parents to sign as guarantors for the loan. This means your parents are now liable for your debt if you default on repayments. To become guarantors, your parents would have to prove their creditworthiness. The financial institution may also ask for collateral when you are getting a loan.

Students beware gimmicks and lure of easy credit

IN THE NEWS

Many students take out loans to cover fees and living costs, but sooner or later it's payback time. Banks are often far more generous in their lending practices with students than they are with people who actually have an income. But if you're a student looking for access to credit, remember that while it may be easy to come by, it can be a lot more difficult to repay. If you fall behind on repayments during your student years, this may affect your credit rating in later years and your ability to get a mortgage or car loan.

Consider the example of a student who applies for the loan for each year of their undergraduate degree. While monthly payments will come to just under €150 a month over eight years, the cost of credit will come to a significant €2,271.32. So, those €12,000 contribution charges have now turned into a €14,271 charge.

Source: Irish Times, 18 August 2015

8.14 Generous lending

Why are banks more generous in their lending practices with students than they are with people who have a regular income? #Opinion

Financial institutions are more likely to lend to households if the risk is shared. This usually requires the borrower to part-finance the project with some of their own money. For example, the O'Donoghues want to build an extension on their house that costs €22,000; the bank agrees to lend them €18,000 if the O'Donoghues use €4,000 of their own money for the balance of the cost.

Lenders often **stress test** each client's ability to repay the proposed loan. Stress testing a loan application looks at how an increase in interest rates will impact on a borrower's ability to repay a loan. If the borrower can afford the loan based on current income and interest rates, the lender will check to see if they could still afford it if interest rates were to rise before the loan is repaid. If a very large amount of disposable income is committed to loan repayments, the lender may decide that a smaller loan or longer time period is more appropriate.

8.15 Loans from the lender's point of view

There is a house for sale for €200,000. Three parties are interested in it, but they all need a loan. All of them are first-time buyers, which means they need at least a 10% deposit to buy the house.

1. Pat has a good job and can easily afford the mortgage repayments each month. At the moment he is living rent-free with his parents and has no savings, but his parents have offered to give him €20,000 as a deposit.
2. Enda and Siobhan have savings of €25,000 for a deposit. Only Siobhan is bringing home a salary at the moment, a third of which goes towards paying rent on the couple's apartment. Enda has not yet paid off a loan that should have finished five years ago and he has credit card debt of €16,500. Siobhan has two credit cards with a total debt of €8,950 and she was late with repayments for three months earlier this year.
3. Julie and Rachel have savings of €20,000. Julie had a loan in the past that was paid regularly every month and completely paid off a year ago. Rachel has a credit card with €600 owing on it, but no charges for late payments. Rachel is renting an apartment and Julie is currently living with her parents, paying them €300 a month rent.

If you were the lender, how would you view the three loan applications based on the above information? Give reasons for your answer in each case. #Compare #Opinion

8.16 Why stress test?

Can you think of any benefits to (a) the lender and (b) the borrower of stress testing a loan? #CreativeThinking #Reflect

How to calculate interest

Interest on loans is shown as an annual percentage rate (APR).

The **annual percentage rate (APR)** is a calculation of the overall cost of a loan and represents the actual yearly cost of the amount borrowed. It takes into account all the costs during the term of the loan, including any set-up charges and the interest rate. The APR represents the true cost of borrowing.

The higher the APR, the more it will cost you to borrow money. The APR is calculated each year on the **declining principal** of a loan.

The **declining principal** (or reducing balance) is the amount you still owe at any point during the loan. It gets lower every month because of repayments.

The reducing balance means that you pay interest only on the amount still owed each year rather than on the original amount borrowed. For example, if you borrow €20,000 and repay €5,000 during the first year, you will be charged interest on only €15,000 during the second year of the loan.

You can use the APR to compare loans for the *same amount* and the *same term*. For example, a loan of €20,000 over 15 years with an APR of 17% will cost more than it would with an APR of 12%. APR is not suitable for comparing loans of different terms. If the terms are different, you should look at the cost of credit.

The **cost of credit** is the real cost of borrowing, i.e. the difference between the amount you borrow and the total you repay.

Example 1: Calculating APR

You want to take out a credit union education loan for €600 at 8.5% APR over four years, with the loan amount to reduce by €150 each year (i.e. the repayments must reduce the loan by this much as well as pay the interest). Calculate the total cost of the loan.

Solution

		Interest
Year 1	€600 × 8.5%	€51.00
Year 2	€600 – €150 = €450 × 8.5%	€38.25
Year 3	€450 – €150 = €300 × 8.5%	€25.50
Year 4	€300 – €150 = €150 × 8.5%	€12.75
Total paid = €600 + €51.00 + €38.25 + €25.50 + €12.75 = €727.50		
Cost of credit = €127.50 (€727.50 – €600)		

Example 2: Hire purchase vs. loan

Mary decides to buy a car for €6,000. She has the following options:

- Option 1: Hire purchase – €400 deposit and 35 instalments of €240 each.
- Option 2: Loan – €6,000 at 9.5% APR over four years, with the loan amount to reduce by €1,500 each year.
  - (a) Calculate the total cost of each option. #Calculate
  - (b) Which option is better? #Identify

Solution

Option 1 – hire purchase (€6,000)		***Option 2 – loan (€6,000)***		
Deposit	€400.00	Year 1	€6,000 × 10.5%	€630.00
35 instalments × €240	€8,400.00	Year 2	€4,500 × 10.5%	€472.50
Total paid	€8,800.00	Year 3	€3,000 × 10.5%	€315.00
		Year 4	€1,500 × 10.5%	€157.50
		Total interest		€1,575.00
		Payments per year	4 x €1,500	€6,000.00
		Total paid		€7,575.00
Cost of credit = €2,800		**Cost of credit = €1,575**		

Option 2 (the loan) is the better option, as the total cost of borrowing is lower.

KEY SKILLS

BN

8.17 Donal's new car

Donal needs to borrow €16,000 to buy a new car. He is looking at two options and wants to calculate how much each would cost him before choosing which to apply for. The options are:

1. 9.75% APR over four years
2. 8.5% APR over five years

(a) What is the cost of credit in each case? #Identify

(b) If repayments were evenly distributed over the loan term, in each case how much would Donal pay each month (to the nearest cent)? #Calculate

(c) If Donal could afford no more than €360 each month, which option will he have to apply for? #Identify

(d) How much extra is it going to cost him to apply for this loan rather than the other? #Calculate

Rights of a borrower

A borrower has the right to:

- Written details of the agreement
- A cooling-off period of 10 days
- Be informed of the APR
- Know what the cash price and total credit price are for the product (such as a car)
- Know the number of instalments and the amount of each one
- Be made aware of any fees or penalties for paying off the loan early.

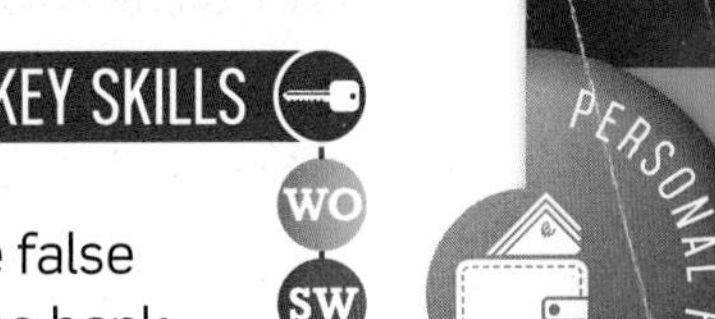

KEY SKILLS

8.18 An ethical question about proof of earnings

WO SW MIT C

Mark's friend Nysa runs a payroll service. Mark asks Nysa if she will print out some false payslips that he can show the bank when he is applying for a long-term loan, as the bank will consider that he doesn't earn enough to lend him the money on his real salary.

Discuss whether or not Mark is right to do this. How do you think Nysa might feel about being asked? #Discussion

Risks of borrowing

You may not be able to repay the amount borrowed (plus interest) due to a change in circumstances. If this occurs:

- You may lose the item you used as collateral
- You may be taken to court and risk a fine or prison sentence
- Your creditworthiness will be affected, which will reduce your ability to get future loans.

Money Advice and Budgeting Service (MABS)

MABS is the state's free and confidential money advice service. It guides people through dealing with problems in paying money they owe and helps them manage their money. The MABS website contains a useful budgeting tool to help manage your finances and avoid getting into debt. Money advisers for the organisation provide practical help to people in debt.

Insolvency Service of Ireland (ISI)

The **ISI** is an independent statutory body that was set up by the Personal Insolvency Act 2012. It is responsible for all matters concerning personal insolvency.

KEY TERM

Being **insolvent** means being unable to pay your debts as they fall due.

KEY SKILLS

8.19 'Neither a borrower nor a lender be.'

Write a speech arguing either for or against borrowing. #Debate

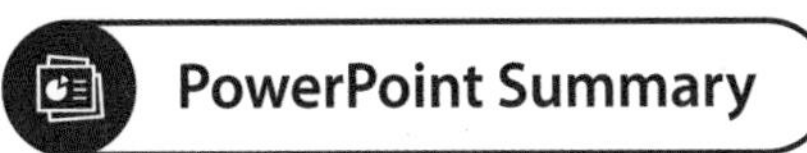

PERSONAL FINANCE

CHAPTER 9

INSURANCE

LEARNING OUTCOMES IN FOCUS

1.6 Identify appropriate types of insurance for particular personal needs and consider costs, benefits and risks

Links to 1.2, 1.3, 1.11, 1.12, 1.13, 2.1, 3.1

LEARNING INTENTIONS FOR THIS CHAPTER

When you have completed this chapter you will be able to:

- Explain what insurance is
- Outline the principles of insurance
- Determine the types of household/personal insurance that you may need at different times
- Identify jobs in the insurance industry
- Identify the costs, benefits and risks associated with both insurance and non-insurance
- Complete insurance documentation
- Calculate a premium.

CHAPTER 9 KEY TERMS

actuary
agent
average clause
claim form
compensation
comprehensive insurance
contribution
critical illness cover
endowment policy
excess
exclusions
health insurance
holiday/travel insurance
home insurance (buildings cover)
home insurance (contents cover)
income protection insurance
indemnity
insurable interest
insurance
insurance broker
insurance policy
life assurance
loading
loss adjuster
material fact
mortgage protection insurance
motor insurance
no-claims bonus
PRSI
payment protection insurance
personal accident insurance
premium
proposal form
renewal notice
risk
subrogation
term policy
third party insurance
third party, fire and theft insurance
underinsurance
uninsurable risk
utmost good faith
whole-life policy
write-off

CHAPTER 9 KEY SKILLS

BC Being Creative
BL Being Literate
BN Being Numerate
C Communicating
MIT Managing Information and Thinking

MM Managing Myself
SW Staying Well
WO Working with Others

What is insurance?

KEY TERM

Insurance offers **(financial) protection against possible loss** and tries to put the insured person back in the same financial position that they were in before the loss occurred.

Insurance can only ever provide *financial* compensation for losses. Sadly, it may not always be possible to restore people's lives to the way they were before an accident or loss.

Insurance is based on sharing (or pooling) risk. A large number of people each pay a small amount of money, called a **premium**, into a fund to cover a specific risk. This fund is managed by an insurance company and is used to pay **compensation** when a loss occurs. It is also used to cover insurance company expenses. Any remaining money is profit for the insurance company.

Figure 9.1 How insurance works

KEY TERM

An **insurance policy** sets out details of the types of losses covered and the amount of compensation to be paid.

KEY TERM

Compensation is a financial payment made to an insured person if they suffer an insured loss.

KEY TERM

A **premium** is the amount paid by the insured person to an insurer in return for providing insurance cover for a particular risk.

9.1 The effect of false claims on pooling risk

Consider the concept of pooling risk. If people were to falsely claim on their insurance, what effect would this have on all the other people who are insured? #Discussion

Principles of insurance

All insurance is based on the following five basic rules or principles:

1. Insurable interest
2. Utmost good faith
3. Indemnity
4. Subrogation
5. Contribution.

1 Insurable interest

To insure something, you must benefit from its existence and suffer (financially) from its loss.

For example, a householder can insure their own property and possessions because they have an insurable interest in those items. They will suffer a financial loss if they are stolen or damaged. The householder does not, however, have the same insurable interest in their neighbour's property and will not be able to insure it against loss or damage.

2 Utmost good faith

You must answer all questions truthfully and reveal all relevant information when completing a **proposal form** (application form) or **claim form** (for compensation).

When applying for insurance, all **material facts** relating to the policy must be made known to the insurance company.

KEY TERM

A material fact is anything that is likely to change the decision to grant insurance or to affect the level of premium charged.

For example, when you are applying for motor insurance, you should report any penalty points. If you don't, the insurance company will not pay out on an insurance claim, as you have not been truthful about all relevant information.

3 Indemnity

The insured person should not profit from insurance. This is the most important rule of insurance because insurance exists to put the insured person back in the same financial position that they were in before suffering the loss, not a better one. For example, if a car valued at €10,000 is stolen, the maximum amount of compensation that will be paid is €10,000.

4 Subrogation

Once an insurance company has paid compensation for any insured item, the right of ownership of that item passes to the insurance company. The insurance company is entitled to any scrap or salvage value that remains. For example, if the insurance company pays €10,000 compensation for a vehicle that is a write-off, the insurance company takes ownership of the damaged vehicle.

The insured person is now in the same financial position as before the accident and can use the compensation payment to replace the damaged vehicle. The insurance

company owns the damaged vehicle and may be able to sell it for its scrap value – say, €800 – thereby reducing the cost of the claim.

Note that if the original owner of the vehicle got this €800 in addition to the €10,000 compensation, they would have received a total of €10,800 for a vehicle that was worth only €10,000. This would represent a profit on the claim and would breach the principle of indemnity.

KEY TERM

An insurance **write-off** means that the cost of repairing the damaged item is greater than the item's replacement value.

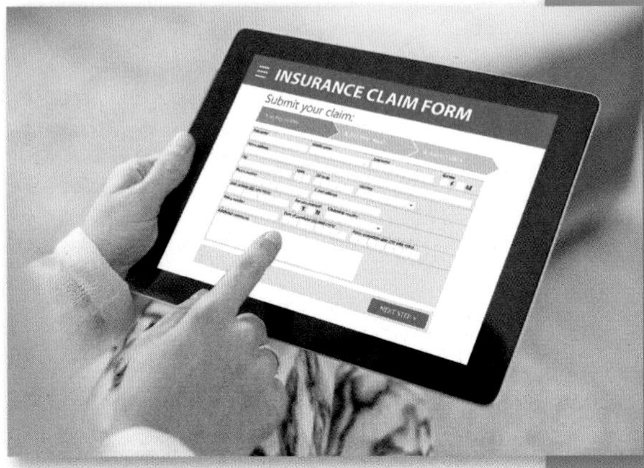

The insurance company is also entitled to sue any third party responsible for the loss in order to recover any compensation paid. For example, an electrician rewires a house that burns down a short time later. An investigation finds that the wiring was faulty and that the electrician is to blame for the fire. The householder's insurance company will settle the compensation claim with the homeowner, but will take legal action against the electrician to recover the money paid out.

5 Contribution

Where the same risk is insured with more than one insurer, they will divide the cost of the claim between them.

The total compensation paid cannot be greater than the replacement value of the item (the principle of indemnity). The amount paid by each insurance company will be in proportion to the risk insured by each of them. For example, a homeowner insures their house for €350,000 with two different insurance companies. In the event that the house is completely destroyed by fire, the homeowner may claim the entire €350,000 compensation from one insurer, or may claim half the money (€175,000) from each insurance company.

9.2 Insurance principles case studies

BL MIT

In each case below, identify which principle has been breached. #Identify

- **(a)** Derek's car is written off in a car accident. He expects to receive the full amount of its worth of €4,500, but he removes some parts and makes another €1,000 by selling them before the insurance company sends someone to collect the vehicle.
- **(b)** Kylie's antique vase was valued at €5,750. On the insurance form, she says it is worth €9,000. When it is stolen, she expects to receive €9,000 from her insurance company.
- **(c)** Paddy's friend Jack parks his car in front of Paddy's house every day. As this is very close to a junction, Paddy is sure the car will be hit by another vehicle one day and sees an opportunity to try to make a few euro, so he insures Jack's car.
- **(d)** Gwen has insured her engagement ring, which is worth €8,000. When it is stolen from her fiancé's house, she makes a claim with her insurance company for €8,000. Her fiancé also makes a claim for the ring on his household insurance.
- **(e)** Collette takes her dog Bobby for his annual check-up. After examining him, the vet says that it is likely that in a few months' time Bobby will need to take heart tablets. Collette thinks this could be expensive, so she takes out pet insurance but doesn't say on the form that Bobby has been diagnosed with a heart complaint.

Types of household and personal insurance

A person's insurance needs will change over time. For cost reasons, a household or individual can't take out all available types of insurance. Each person has to decide which types of policies meet their needs and financial resources. Here, we look at the most common types of insurance for individuals and households.

See Chapter 11 for personal financial life cycle

Motor insurance

Motor insurance is compulsory in Ireland. This means that it is required by law and it is a criminal offence to drive without motor insurance.

There are three types of motor insurance, as shown in Table 9.1. Policies, benefits and costs can vary widely, so it is worth shopping around for the right policy for you.

Type of motor insurance	What it covers
Third party *The minimum legal requirement for driving any motorised vehicle on a public road*	Injury to another person or damage to another person's car or property caused by the insured driver. It does **not** cover the policy holder or their vehicle.
Third party, fire and theft	As per third party, plus compensation for the insured person if their vehicle catches fire or is stolen.
Comprehensive	This benefits all parties and vehicles that suffer loss or injury in an incident, including the insured person and their vehicle.

Table 9.1 Types of motor insurance (from the least expensive to the most expensive)

DID YOU KNOW...

Who's who?

The **first party** is the person who takes out the insurance.

The **second party** is the insurance company that the first party is insured with.

The **third party** is any person or item (vehicle, property, etc.) that suffers a loss caused by the first party.

The insurance company of the person who caused an incident pays compensation.

KEY SKILLS MIT

9.3 Who's at fault here?

In each of the following situations, who might receive compensation and whose insurance company would pay it? #Identify

	First party	Type of insurance	Third party	Incident
(a)	Máire	Third party, fire and theft	Jakob	Máire reversed into Jakob's van in a car park; both vehicles were damaged.
(b)	Steven	Third party	Unknown	Steven's car was stolen from its parking place.
(c)	Bernard	Third party	Renée	Bernard scraped Renée's car door as he passed her on the road; both vehicles were damaged.
(d)	John	Comprehensive	Margaret	John drove into the back of Margaret's jeep as she waited at traffic lights; both vehicles were damaged.
(e)	Conor	Comprehensive	None	Conor drove into a pillar in his driveway and damaged the front of his pick-up.

If the insured driver does not make a claim on their insurance during the year, they will receive a no-claims bonus that will make next year's premium cheaper.

KEY TERM

A **no-claims bonus** is a discount on an insurance premium. It rewards the insured party for not making any claims on the policy.

Sometimes a person may have to pay a **loading** on their premium. For example, motor insurance may be more expensive if a person does not have a full driving licence or has penalty points on their licence.

KEY TERM

Loading is an extra amount added to the basic premium to cover increased risk.

KEY SKILLS WO MIT

9.4 Why is driving inexperience driving up the price?

When you start driving, you will have to pay quite a high premium to insure your car. Discuss why you think insurers raise the price and whether you think it is fair. #Discussion #Opinion

KEY SKILLS BC SW MM MIT

9.5 How to put the brakes on rising insurance costs

Young drivers represent a high risk for insurers because statistics show that they cost the insurance companies more than other categories of driver. There are things you can do to reduce the cost of your motor insurance as a young person. Find out what these things are, then create a newspaper advert from an insurance company listing these things and saying that your company will provide cheaper insurance for young people that do them. #Research #Presentation

Home insurance (buildings cover)

This covers the building in the event of fire, flood, storm or accidental damage. It provides compensation if the structure of the building is damaged.

Home insurance (contents cover)

This covers all the contents of the house from accidental damage such as fire, flood, burst pipes, etc. It also covers against burglary. Most home insurance policies cover the buildings themselves as well as their contents, e.g. furniture and personal belongings.

KEY SKILLS WO BC MIT

9.6 Reducing risk and insurance premiums

In pairs or small groups, research what you can do around your house to help reduce the risk of loss due to fire, flooding from burst pipes and theft. These precautions are also likely to reduce your insurance premiums because you can show that your risk is reduced because of them. Create a poster, leaflet or podcast informing householders of the precautions they can take and why they should take them. #Research #GroupWork

KEY SKILLS MIT

9.7 Insurance for renters

How do you think your insurance needs will be different if you rent a property rather than live in a property you own? #Compare #Research

Personal accident insurance

The insured person is covered in the event of an accident, for example falling and breaking your tooth. In this case the insurance company may pay compensation to cover emergency dental treatment. Every year, students in many Irish schools are given the option of taking out personal accident insurance.

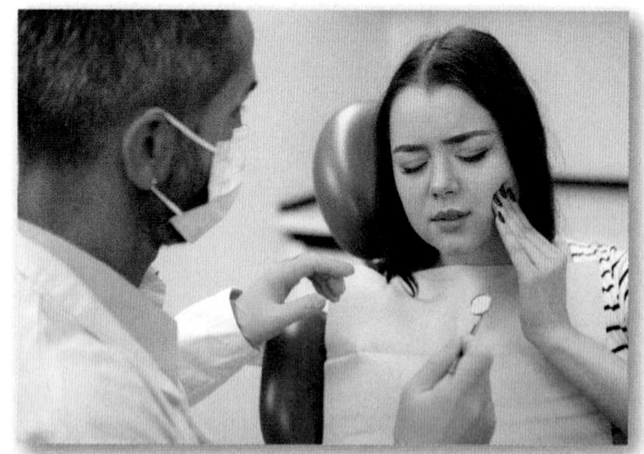

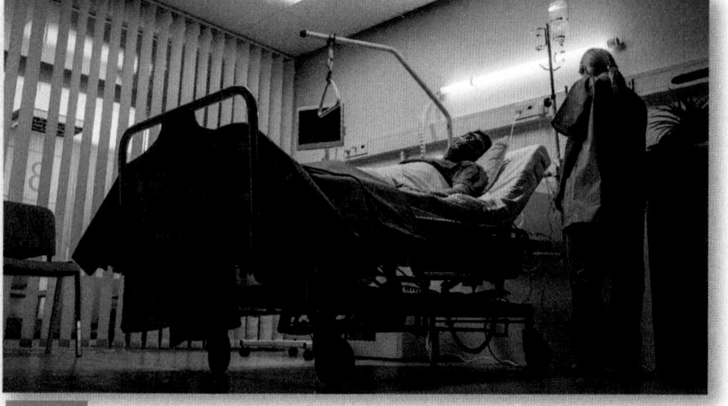

Health insurance

In the event of serious illness or accident, health insurance covers the cost of hospital care and some medical bills. It can provide cover for a hospital stay and operations.

Critical illness cover

In the event of a serious illness, this cover pays out a tax-free lump sum if you are medically diagnosed with one of the serious illnesses or disabilities that your policy covers. Examples include heart attack, stroke, cancer and loss of limbs.

Holiday/travel insurance

If something unfortunate happens to the insured person while they are on holiday or travelling, they will be covered – for example, if their belongings are stolen or they have an accident, cancelled flights, delayed or missed departure, loss or theft of passport or money, and illness or injury.

Mortgage protection insurance

In the event of the death of the insured during a mortgage repayment term, this type of life insurance policy repays their mortgage. The cover lasts until the mortgage is paid off.

Payment protection insurance (PPI)

Your repayments on a loan for a certain period of time (usually one year) will be covered with PPI if you suffer from an accident, illness, death or compulsory redundancy.

Income/salary protection insurance

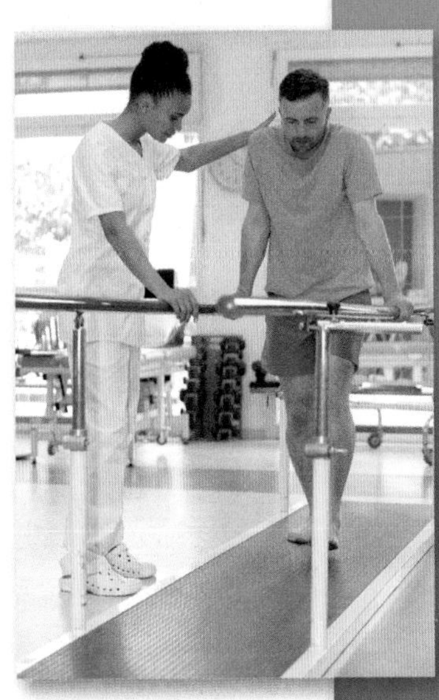

If you have to take time off work or lose your employment due to disability, illness or injury, this insurance will pay part of your income. The benefit is paid out for a certain period of time, usually until the policyholder gets better or reaches retirement age.

Mobile phone insurance

You can take out insurance in case your mobile phone is lost or stolen. Gadget insurance can also be used to insure other devices, such as laptops and tablet computers.

Pay Related Social Insurance (PRSI)

By law, all employees must pay employee PRSI. It entitles the worker to Illness, Disability, Maternity or Jobseeker's Benefit, should they require them. This payment is deducted at source by employers. Unlike other forms of insurance, this is paid to the government instead of an insurance company.

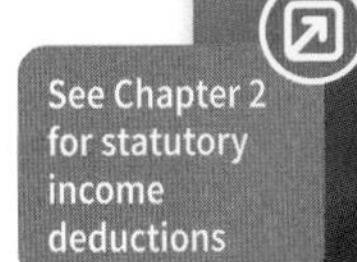

See Chapter 2 for statutory income deductions

Life assurance

Assurance is protection against a guaranteed future loss; in the case of life assurance, this means death. A **life assurance** policy pays out *when* the insured person dies, not *if* they die.

There are three main types of life assurance cover:

- **Whole-life policy:** Pays compensation on the death of the insured person.
- **Term policy:** For a fixed time period – usually the duration of a loan or mortgage. If the insured person dies during the term of the loan or mortgage, any outstanding amount is paid off. The premiums and cover finish at the end of the mortgage repayment term.
- **Endowment policy:** Pays a guaranteed amount on a specified date or, if it occurs sooner, on the death of the insured person.

KEY SKILLS

MIT MM SW

9.8 Why bother with life assurance?

Why might someone take out a life assurance policy? #Discussion

9.9 When should you consider a whole-life policy?

At which stage of life do you think it makes most sense to take out a whole-life assurance policy? #Opinion

See Chapter 11 for personal financial life cycle

Jobs in the insurance industry

Insurance broker

A broker helps households and individuals to get the insurance that best fits their needs and their budget. Insurance brokers search the market to find the best policy and price for their client. Since most insurance brokers represent several insurance companies, they can offer their clients a wide range of policies. They are paid a commission by the insurance company for each policy sold.

Agent

An agent sells policies on behalf of only *one* insurance company.

Actuary

An actuary is employed by the insurance company to decide on the premium that should be charged based on the risk of a loss occurring and a claim being made. They use statistics and probability to assess risk. The greater the risk, the higher the premium will be.

KEY TERM

Risk means how likely a person is to make a claim and how costly any claim is likely to be.

Loss adjuster

A loss adjuster will investigate a claim for compensation on behalf of the insurance company and decide if the claim is covered by the insurance policy. They recommend the amount of compensation to be paid.

Taking out insurance

Before you can take out insurance, you must complete a **proposal form**. This is an application form that should be filled out by the person seeking insurance cover. It must be completed truthfully, disclosing all relevant information. This will enable the insurance company to make a realistic assessment of the risk involved and calculate the premium to charge.

An example of a completed proposal form is shown in Figure 9.2.

Car insurance proposal form	
Proposer	
Name	Callum Cunningham
Date of birth	01/04/1986
Type of licence	Full Irish licence
Email address	cjcunningham@xmail.ie
Postal address	22 St Joseph's Avenue Donegal Town, Co. Donegal
Occupation	Architect
Cover to commence from	22/06/2020
The Vehicle	
Make and exact model	Toyota Avensis
CC	1600cc
Fuel	Petrol
Registration number	201 DL 1595
Year of make	2020
Present value	€28,000
Where is the vehicle kept overnight? (tick as appropriate)	Garage ☐ Private property ☑ Public road ☐
Cover and Use	
Vehicle cover required (tick as appropriate)	Comprehensive ☑ Third party, fire and theft ☐ Third party only ☐
Estimated annual mileage	17,000 km
No-Claims Discount	
Do you hold insurance in your own name?	Yes ☑ No ☐
If yes, please specify start date	22/06/2014
Name of insurer	AXA Insurance
Expiry date	21/06/2020
Number of years No-Claims Discount	6
Driving History	
Have you had any accidents, losses or claims during the past five years?	No
Have you ever been convicted of any offence in connection with any motor vehicle?	No
Declaration	
I declare that the information given in this form is true.	
Signed Callum Cunningham	
Date 15/6/2020	

Figure 9.2 An example of a completed proposal form for car insurance

Details of the types of losses covered and the amount of compensation to be paid are set out in the insurance contract, which is called a **policy**. An insurance policy sets out:

- What is insured
- The insurable value of the item insured
- The types of loss covered
- The policy excess
- Exclusions
- The maximum amount of compensation that will be paid.

KEY TERM

The policy **excess** is the amount the insured person must pay for any loss or damage to the insured item. The insurance company pays the rest.

Policy excess example

Tracy is awarded €5,000 compensation for damage to her car following an accident. Tracy's policy carries an excess of €250, so the insurance company will actually pay €5,000 minus €250, or a total of €4,750 in compensation, as Tracy must pay for the first €250 of any claim.

KEY TERM

Exclusions are specific items or risks that are not insured.

By excluding certain high-risk activities, it may be possible for insurance companies to lower the average level of premiums. For example, an injury caused by skiing may be excluded from the terms of standard travel insurance policies. People who wish to insure themselves for these activities may need to pay an extra premium called a **loading** to reflect the higher level of risk.

How to calculate a house insurance premium

Example 1: Premiums

Margaret Finley's house insurance is due for renewal. Her insurance company has given her a quote of €12 per €10,000 value for the house and €20 per €5,000 value for the contents. She estimates that she should insure her house for €180,000 and her contents for €90,000. Calculate the insurance premium that Margaret will have to pay. #Calculate

Solution

House	$\frac{180{,}000}{10{,}000} \times €12 = 18 \times €12 = €216$	€216
Contents	$\frac{90{,}000}{5{,}000} \times €20 = 18 \times €20 = €360$	€360
Total premium		€576

BN

9.10 Shopping for home insurance

Reza is looking for new house insurance. He has some expensive sports equipment that will need to be insured separately because of its specialist nature. He calculates that he needs to make the following insurance provisions:

1. Buildings: €450,000
2. General contents: €110,000
3. Sports equipment: €3,000

He receives the following quotations:

- **Insure All Ltd** charges €1.50 per €1,000 for the buildings, €5 per €1,000 for the contents and €20 per €1,000 for the sports equipment.
- **Cover4U Ltd** charges €1.35 per €1,000 for the buildings, €4.50 per €1,000 for the contents and a flat rate of €120 for sports equipment up to a value of €5,000.

Calculate which insurance company offers the best value for money. Show your workings. #Calculate

Making a claim

In the event of an accident, loss or damage, the first step in making a claim is to talk to the insurance company. They will ask you to complete a **claim form**. This is a standard form from the insurance company that the insured must complete when seeking compensation for a loss. The claim form requires details of how the loss occurred and the amount being claimed. For items that have been stolen, you will usually need a reference number from a garda station, so you will have to report the theft.

Jones Insurance Ltd	
Name	Michael Martin
Address	Main Street, Enniscrone, Co. Sligo
Policy number	786543224F
Occupation	Teacher
Details of loss/damage	
Date	14 July 2020
Location	Enniscrone, Co. Sligo
Description of item lost/stolen	iPad
Value	€800
Date of purchase	12 November 2019
Was item lost/stolen reported to the gardaí? (tick yes or no)	☑ Yes ☐ No
If 'Yes' please state:	
Date reported	14 July 2020
Garda station	Enniscrone
Name of garda who took the details	Gavin Daly
Garda reference number	SL63532F
Signed	Michael Martin
Date	15 July 2020

Figure 9.3 An example of a completed claim form

KEY SKILLS

MIT BN

9.11 Proof of purchase

Jones Insurance Ltd will probably ask Michael for a receipt for the iPad. Why will they do this? #Opinion

9.12 Calculating the compensation

If Michael has a policy excess of €300, how much can he expect to get in compensation from his insurance company? #Calculate

9.13 Increasing the policy excess

Some insurance companies offer you the option to voluntarily increase the policy excess. How does this make a difference to:

(a) The *premium* when getting a quote for an insurance policy? #Identify #Explain

(b) The amount received as *compensation* when making a claim? #Identify #Explain

Average clause

The **average clause** applies in the case of underinsurance and partial loss, based on the principle of indemnity.

Underinsurance means that the insured item has not been insured for its full replacement value. This might be because the policy holder does not know the value or because they are trying to save money on their premium. As a result, the amount of compensation paid will not be enough to cover the loss. The insurance company will apply the average clause rule and will pay compensation in direct proportion to the value of the property actually insured.

Example 2: Average clause

A house was flooded and partially damaged. The actual value of the house is €250,000, but it is insured for only €200,000. The owners are claiming €20,000 compensation for the damage.

How much compensation will be paid out to the owners in this case? #Calculate

Solution

$$\text{Compensation} = \frac{\text{Insured value}}{\text{Actual value}} \times \text{Amount claimed}$$

$$= \frac{€200{,}000}{€250{,}000} \times €20{,}000 = €16{,}000$$

Since the homeowner has insured their property for only four-fifths of its replacement value, they are entitled only to four-fifths of any loss.

KEY SKILLS

BL

9.14 Name that term

What is the term we use when you do something to try to save money but it costs you money in the long run? #Research #Recall

PERSONAL FINANCE

Renewing an insurance policy

Insurers will send a **renewal notice** when your policy is due for renewal. At that time, it is always worth shopping around for a new deal, as you may be able to get the insurance more cheaply from another company.

IN THE NEWS

House insurance: Not a box-ticking exercise

House insurance may be more stable, but it is also a more complicated product than car insurance. There can be considerable differences between house insurance policies in terms of what they include and don't include. Which means it's not a box-ticking exercise. You've got to research what's out there and fit it to your needs and your budget.

Home insurance generally covers damage to the building, damage to contents, loss of or damage to valuables and injury to others in your home. You can actually get separate policies to cover these four risks, but in general, you'll get a reasonable mix of convenience and value with a single policy.

How much to insure for? The rule here is to insure your property for the cost of rebuilding it, not the market value. The Society of Chartered Surveyors has got a house rebuilding calculator on their website. It's important to get the amount just right. Underinsure and you may not have enough to repair or rebuild in the event of damage or destruction. Overinsure and you'll end up paying extra without incurring any additional benefit in the event of a claim.

Policies can differ substantially between insurers, so always check what's insured and what's not, particularly if your home is susceptible to risks like flooding or subsidence. In general, policies will tend to cover you against damage – from flood, fire, storm, vandalism, subsidence, burglary, impact and leakage of oil or water from a domestic appliance. Ordinary wear and tear is never covered.

Source: Irish Examiner, 6 June 2019

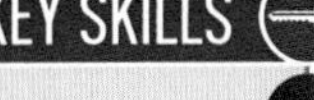

9.15 Insurance in your household

(a) Think about your own household. What types of insurance do you think you need? #Identify #Reflect

(b) Now ask what types of insurance cover your household has. Does your household have insurance you didn't think of? Which types of insurance does your family think are unnecessary or too expensive to have? #Research

KEY SKILLS

9.16 Accidentally on purpose

Peter and Angela decided to redecorate their living room. Once they had chosen the colours, they realised the carpet would no longer match. They didn't want to have the expense of buying a new carpet, so they decided they would 'accidentally' spill a bottle of bleach in the middle of it so they could claim for a new carpet.

What do you think about Peter and Angela's actions? Were they justified because, as they said, they 'pay enough insurance, so why not get something back'? Is this ethical or does it cause problems for other people with insurance? Do you hope they get away with it or do you hope the loss adjuster will see through their dishonesty? #Opinion

What are the benefits of insurance?

Insurance cannot prevent accidents happening, but it can help people to recover from the financial impact of a loss. Most people who take out insurance hope that they will never suffer an insurable loss.

- The compensation received allows policy holders to **replace or repair** items that have been **damaged or stolen**.
- While insurance has an obvious financial cost, many are willing to pay it because it protects them from the financial uncertainty of loss and buys them **peace of mind.**
- Salary protection and critical illness cover **can help to protect household income**.
- Life assurance gives families **financial security** in the event of sudden or unexpected death. As well as providing a cash payment, the policy may clear all outstanding mortgage debt.

Is insurance really necessary?

Costs and risks associated with insurance and non-insurance

If you drive a motor vehicle, you are required by law to have insurance, but most other types of insurance are optional and may not be necessary. It is up to each household to decide what types of insurance suit their needs and resources.

Insurance is just one aspect of household risk management. Before you decide whether to insure, you should follow these steps to manage your risk:

1. **Identify** the major sources of household or personal **risk**, e.g. the risk of fire damage to the home.
2. Take steps to **eliminate or reduce the risk**, e.g. install smoke alarms. These measures will also help to reduce premiums if insurance is required.
3. If necessary, **insure** against those risks that cannot be eliminated.

You need insurance with enough cover for potential losses. There are costs associated with having too little insurance cover, but also with having too much insurance cover.

KEY SKILLS

9.17 Too much or not enough?

Discuss and record what you think the costs and risks are for having:

(a) Too much cover

(b) Too little cover. #Discussion

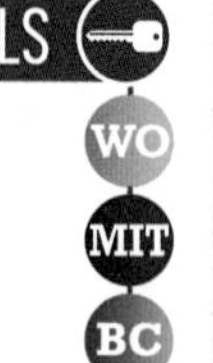

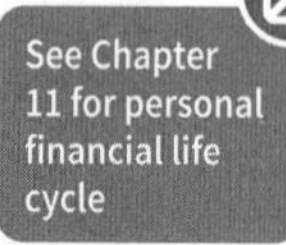
See Chapter 11 for personal financial life cycle

Decisions about insurance should be taken as part of your personal financial life cycle. Insurance needs should be reviewed and updated annually.

Whether or not a person takes out insurance is largely a personal decision, but if you have a mortgage, the lender will require that you have adequate insurance on your property and life assurance on the person(s) paying the mortgage to make sure the debt is paid in the event of their death.

Can all risks be insured?

The answer is no; some risks are **uninsurable**. In general, it is not possible to insure a risk where the insurer cannot work out the chances of a loss occurring. For example, you can't insure against failing an exam or making a business loss. Other types of uninsurable risk include losses that are certain to occur, such as a person who has a terminal illness who is trying to take out life insurance.

DID YOU KNOW...

Some celebrities insure parts of their body, such as their legs, their voice or their smile, if they rely on them to earn their living. Taylor Swift is rumoured to have her legs insured for $40 million in case she has an accident and is unable to dance on stage.

KEY SKILLS

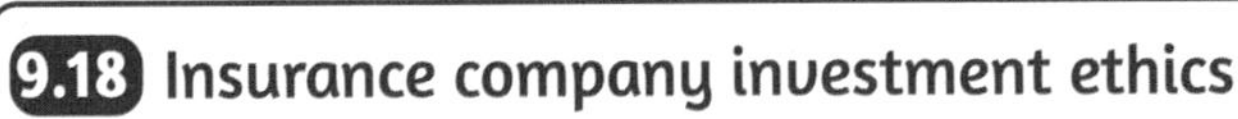

9.18 Insurance company investment ethics

When you buy insurance, the insurance company invests that money in order to make a profit. Is it important to you that those investments are ethical or should the insurance company go for the best monetary return? Write your views in your copy. #Discussion #Opinion

WO C MIT

IN THE NEWS

'Ghost brokers' leave thousands of motorists uninsured

A leading insurance company has claimed that more than 10,000 motor insurance policies have been taken out by so-called 'ghost brokers' who falsify information and sometimes use stolen credit cards to pay for policies on behalf of unsuspecting customers. The issue only arises when the insurance firm realises a stolen card was used, the policy is cancelled and unsuspecting consumers are driving around with no insurance. Aviva is dealing with up to 1,500 policies that have been taken out fraudulently.

Nataliya Nastechyk, who was duped by a ghost broker, paid more than €2,000 for her policy and several hundred euro as a brokerage fee, which was more than 50% less than what a legitimate company had quoted. She explained how the 'broker' spoke Russian, which was useful, as she was from Ukraine and had poor English at the time.

The group representing legitimate insurance brokers, Brokers Ireland, has said that 'ghost brokers' are not brokers and should instead be referred to as 'fraudsters'.

Source: RTÉ News, 21 November 2019

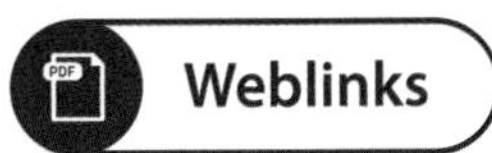

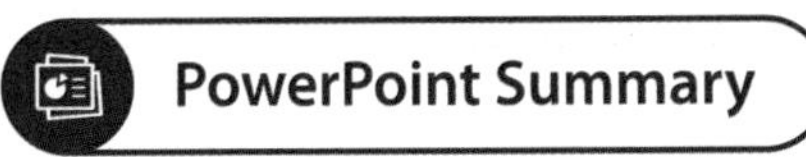

CHAPTER 10 PERSONAL TAXATION

LEARNING OUTCOMES IN FOCUS

1.4 Explain key personal taxes and charges and suggest the occasions when and why they might arise Links to 1.2, 1.5, 1.11, 3.2, 3.3, 3.4, 3.5, 3.10, 3.11

1.11 Interpret a wage slip and calculate personal tax liability arising from employment Links to 1.2, 1.4, 1.6, 2.3, 3.4, 3.5

LEARNING INTENTIONS FOR THIS CHAPTER

When you have completed this chapter you will be able to:

- Outline the role of taxation in a modern economy
- Discuss personal responsibilities in relation to taxation
- Describe the major household and personal taxes in Ireland
- Illustrate the impact of taxation on households and individuals
- Calculate the tax liability for a household or individual.

CHAPTER 10 KEY TERMS

Capital Acquisitions Tax (CAT)	Local Property Tax (LPT)	tax
Capital Gains Tax (CGT)	motor tax	tax audit
carbon tax	net pay	tax avoidance
customs duty	Office of the Revenue Commissioners	tax credit
deductions	Pay As You Earn (PAYE)	tax credits certificate
Deposit Interest Retention Tax (DIRT)	Personal Public Service Number (PPSN)	tax evasion
direct tax	progressive taxation	tax liability
emergency tax	regressive taxation	tax rate
excise duty	self-assessed income tax	taxation
gross pay	stamp duty	Universal Social Charge (USC)
income tax	standard rate cut-off point (SRCOP)	Value Added Tax (VAT)
indirect tax		Vehicle Registration Tax (VRT)

CHAPTER 10 KEY SKILLS

 Being Literate

 Being Numerate

 Communicating

 Managing Information and Thinking

 Managing Myself

 Working with Others

What are taxes?

Governments, just like households and businesses, need to generate income in order to pay their expenses. Most government revenue comes from **taxation**, which involves the government taking money from people and businesses in order to fund a range of public services. In Ireland, the state agency responsible for tax collection is the **Office of the Revenue Commissioners** (Revenue for short).

'In this world nothing can be said to be certain, except death and taxes.'
Benjamin Franklin, 1789

See Chapter 11 for personal financial life cycle

Tax is a compulsory payment to the government that is used to fund public services. Tax is charged on income or business profits or added to the cost of goods and services.

Taxation: Liability and responsibility

Your **tax liability** means the amount of tax you are required to pay. It is based on your income, wealth and spending habits. The more income and wealth you have, and the more money you spend on goods and services, the more tax you will be liable (or required) to pay.

Each person has a legal responsibility to pay the correct amount of tax – it's the law. There is also a social or ethical responsibility because everyone should pay their fair share. Without income from taxation, the government would not be able to fund public services. This would affect all citizens, but especially those on low incomes who can't afford to pay for these services privately.

You may think that tax is just for adults or people who are in employment, but people of all ages, including students, pay **Value Added Tax (VAT)** on many of the goods and services they buy. As you get older, your level of income and expenditure will rise and you will be liable for a greater range of taxes.

See Chapter 11 for financial planning for your future

Types of tax

Direct taxes

A **direct tax** is paid on income as it is *earned*. It is paid by the person on whom it is imposed (*levied*).

Examples include:

- Income earned under the PAYE income tax system.
- DIRT (Deposit Interest Retention Tax), which must be paid by deposit account holders who earn interest on savings.

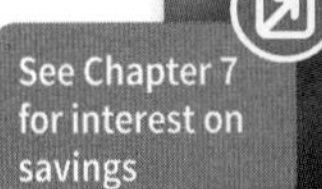

See Chapter 7 for interest on savings

Indirect taxes

Indirect taxes are paid on income as it is *spent*. Examples of indirect taxes are VAT, excise duty and customs duty. Indirect taxes are paid for by the end-consumer of goods and services.

One of the major criticisms of indirect taxes, such as VAT, is that the amount of tax is the same for all consumers. As a result, the burden of tax falls most heavily on those with low incomes because the amount paid in tax represents a far greater proportion of their income. Taxes that take a higher percentage of income from low-income earners are said to be **regressive**.

The burden of tax

A sofa costs €1,230, which includes €230 in VAT, levied at 23%. Billy and his friend Alex are each planning to buy the same sofa.

Billy earns €1,000 per week, so the €230 VAT payment represents 23% of his weekly income.

Alex earns €500 a week, so the €230 VAT payment will consume 46% of his weekly income.

A progressive system of taxation, such as income tax, where those earning higher incomes pay higher taxes, results in fairer or more equitable taxation. A **progressive tax** is one where the tax rate increases as income increases, so the more you earn, the more you pay.

KEY SKILLS

10.1 Is VAT a luxury tax?

Some people say taxation by VAT is better than a high rate of income tax because people can choose whether or not to spend money on items that carry a VAT levy. In the example above, Alex could choose to buy a cheaper sofa and so be taxed less. For this reason, VAT is sometimes called a luxury tax. Do you agree with this? Outline your reasons for agreeing or disagreeing. #Discussion

WO C BL MIT

Common household and personal taxes and charges

There are many different taxes. We'll look at the ones most likely to affect you and your family.

Pay As You Earn (PAYE) income tax

Workers pay tax on all types of earnings from employment, including wages, salaries, bonuses, overtime and benefits in kind.

Income tax is deducted at source. This means that the tax is calculated and submitted to Revenue by the employer rather than by the employee. From the worker's point of view, this system is very easy as the tax has already been deducted from their wages when they receive them.

Workers on very low incomes may not have to pay income tax.

KEY SKILLS

10.2 Income tax rates for the current year

What are the current rates of income tax? Record the rates and at what levels of income they are paid. #Research

MIT

Self-assessed income tax

Those who are self-employed or earn income that is not taxable under the PAYE system pay self-assessed income tax. Being self-employed means working for yourself rather than being an employee. Under **self-assessment**, the taxpayer calculates and makes the relevant tax payment themselves. These returns are subject to regular checks by Revenue, which are called **tax audits**.

Universal Social Charge (USC)

Incomes over a certain amount are subject to **USC in addition to income tax**. The amount of USC a taxpayer is liable for increases with income level.

KEY SKILLS

10.3 Calculating USC rates

MIT BN

Research the current rates of USC and the income levels they apply to. How much USC would someone earning €30,000 a year pay per month? #Research

Value Added Tax (VAT)

VAT is a tax on goods and services. Everyone who buys goods and services in Ireland pays VAT. VAT is included in the price of many everyday purchases, so you may not always be aware that you are paying it.

There are different VAT rates for goods and services in Ireland. Some essential goods, including certain foods, medicines and children's clothing, are free of VAT, while many goods and professional services currently carry a 23% VAT rate.

KEY SKILLS

10.4 VAT rates in Ireland

MIT BN

Research the current rates of VAT in Ireland. Find out the rate of VAT applicable on these items: #Research

(a) Milk
(b) Solicitors' fees
(c) DVDs
(d) Newspapers
(e) Crisps
(f) Books
(g) A meal in a restaurant
(h) A take-away meal
(i) Children's clothing
(j) Biscuits without chocolate
(k) Chocolate biscuits
(l) Bin collections
(m) Health supplements

Customs duties

Customs duty is a tax on goods imported into Ireland from outside the EU.

Excise duties

Excise duty is a tax levied (charged) on certain goods and materials, including:

- Motor fuel (petrol and diesel)
- Heating oil
- Natural gas
- Solid fuel (e.g. coal)
- Alcohol
- Tobacco.

KEY SKILLS 

WO C BL MIT

10.5 Does carbon tax tackle climate change?

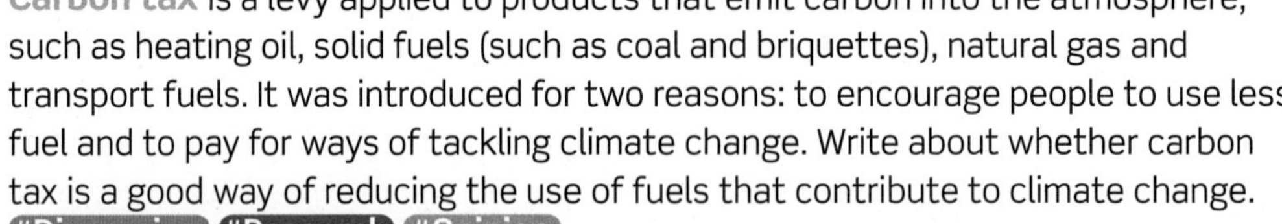

Carbon tax is a levy applied to products that emit carbon into the atmosphere, such as heating oil, solid fuels (such as coal and briquettes), natural gas and transport fuels. It was introduced for two reasons: to encourage people to use less fuel and to pay for ways of tackling climate change. Write about whether carbon tax is a good way of reducing the use of fuels that contribute to climate change.

#Discussion #Research #Opinion

Local Property Tax (LPT)

Owners of residential properties in Ireland are liable to pay this tax. The tax payable is based on the market value of a house/apartment and there are different levels of value (called bands).

KEY SKILLS

MIT BN

10.6 Local Property Tax bands

(a) What are the first five bands of LPT?

(b) What amount has to be paid in each band? #Research

Stamp duty

Stamp duty is charged on certain written documents. It is most commonly associated with the purchase of property, but it is also charged on cheques and financial cards (debit, credit and ATM cards).

KEY SKILLS 

MIT

10.7 Current stamp duty

What is the current stamp duty on:

(a) A debit card?

(b) A credit card? #Research

Proof of tax must be displayed on the vehicle at all times

Motor tax

This is a compulsory tax for all owners of motor vehicles. It is calculated on an annual basis and paid to the local authority (city or county council), which is responsible for the upkeep of local roads.

Ireland currently has two systems under which road tax is calculated for passenger cars. All cars made before 2008 have their road tax calculated based on the car's engine size. All cars made since 2008 have their road tax calculated based on the car's carbon dioxide emissions.

KEY SKILLS 

MIT MM

10.8 Using a reliable source for calculating motor tax

(a) Find a website that you could use for calculating motor tax in Ireland. How can you be sure this is a trusted website for this information? Record the name and website address. #Research

(b) Find a website address that you could use for calculating the VRT on a vehicle you are importing into Ireland and discuss why the website is reliable. #Research

Vehicle Registration Tax (VRT)

This is a separate once-off tax on buying and registering a new car or motorcycle in the state.

Deposit Interest Retention Tax (DIRT)

This is a tax on interest earned on savings. The tax is deducted at source by the financial institution.

See Chapter 7 for Deposit Interest Retention Tax

Capital Gains Tax (CGT)

Profits earned from the sale of assets such as property (other than a main residence) and investments are subject to CGT.

Profits (capital gains) arise when the value of an asset increases above its original purchase price. For example, an investor buys company shares for €5,000 and later sells them for €7,000. In this case, the capital gain of €2,000 would be liable for CGT.

KEY SKILLS

10.9 Current rate of CGT

What is the current rate of Capital Gains Tax? #Research

MIT MM

Capital Acquisitions Tax (CAT)

CAT is paid on gifts and inheritances. An inheritance is wealth (money, property, etc.) left to one person following the death of another. The gift or inheritance is liable for tax if its value is above a certain limit.

Impact of tax on households and individuals

The introduction of new taxes or an increase in existing tax rates has consequences for all taxpayers.

KEY SKILLS

10.10 The impact of more tax

WO MIT

Discuss the effect of introducing a new tax or a change in tax on each of the following for households/individuals. Following the discussion, make notes on the effects your class came up with.

Consequence of new taxes or an increase in existing taxes on:

(a) The cost of living

(b) Disposable income

(c) Savings

(d) Cash flow

Consequence of a decrease in taxes on:

(e) Public services

#Discussion

See Chapter 2 for income
See Chapter 3 for expenditure
See Chapter 4 for budgeting
See Chapter 7 for DIRT
See Chapter 35 for government expenditure

10.11 The effects of less tax

What would be the effect on households and individuals if taxes were abolished (done away with) or the tax rate is lowered? #Opinion

Tax avoidance and evasion

Understanding the taxation system, knowing your entitlements and being able to accurately calculate your tax liability are important steps in meeting your responsibilities and planning your financial future. You may be able to reduce your tax liability by knowing how to claim more tax reliefs or by spending your money in particular ways. Reducing the amount of tax you have to pay in this way is called **tax avoidance** and it is perfectly legal.

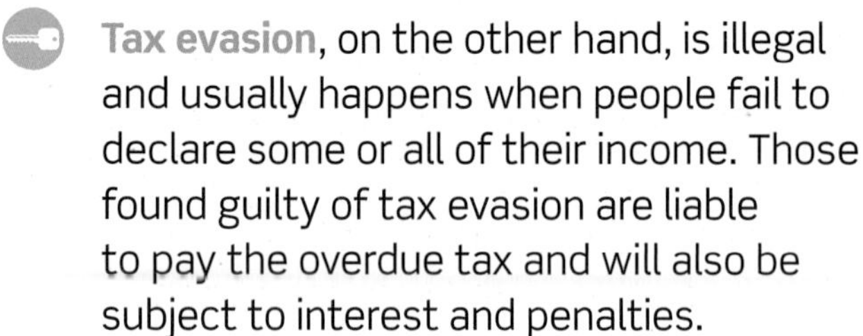

For example, Revenue allows eligible taxpayers to claim certain tax credits that will reduce the amount of tax they have to pay.

Tax evasion, on the other hand, is illegal and usually happens when people fail to declare some or all of their income. Those found guilty of tax evasion are liable to pay the overdue tax and will also be subject to interest and penalties.

Getting started with income tax

Danielle Whelan has just been offered her first job and will soon be earning some income of her own. Her new employer tells Danielle that she will have to pay income tax under the PAYE system.

The employer asks Danielle for her PPSN and sends it to Revenue to inform them that Danielle has started working.

> **KEY TERM**
>
> A **Personal Public Service Number (PPSN)** is an individual's unique reference number that is used in all dealings with public service agencies, including Revenue.

If you were born in Ireland, the Department of Employment Affairs and Social Protection would have allocated you a PPSN; if you weren't born in Ireland, you might have been given a number when you moved here or you might have to apply for one.

Once Danielle has a PPSN, she will need to register for tax. First-time employees should register online via myAccount on the Revenue website. Revenue will issue Danielle, through myAccount, details of her **tax credits certificate** and her standard rate cut-off point. This information will help her employer to calculate how much tax to deduct from her wages.

If Danielle fails to register for a tax credit certificate, her employer will have to apply **emergency tax** to her income.

> **KEY TERM**
>
> **Emergency tax** is a higher than normal rate of tax designed to encourage new employees to get their tax affairs in order as quickly as possible.

If you are on emergency tax, you will pay more tax than you need to for a while and will have very little take-home pay. Once the tax is sorted out, you will get back any tax you have overpaid.

The tax credits reflect Danielle's personal circumstances and include a PAYE tax credit and a single person's tax credit. This information is used to work out the deductions from her gross pay and what her net pay will be.

KEY TERM

The **tax rate** is the percentage of tax that is levied on a person's income. There are different rates: the standard rate (currently 20%) and the higher rate (currently 40%).

The **standard rate cut-off point (SRCOP)** is the amount of income that will be taxed at the standard rate of tax. Once a person's income goes above this level, the portion of income above the cut-off point will be taxed at the higher rate of tax.

Tax credit is an amount by which a person's annual tax bill may be reduced. This varies from person to person depending on their circumstances.

Gross pay is pay before all deductions. Gross pay = basic pay + overtime + bonuses + commission.

Deductions are all the payments that must be taken away from gross pay by the employer to calculate net pay. It includes tax, USC, pensions, trade union dues, and so on. This will vary from person to person.

Net pay is gross pay minus all deductions. It is also called take-home pay.

See Chapter 2 for payment received

Danielle Whelan

Tax credits

	Single person's tax credit	€1,650
+	Employee (PAYE) tax credit	€1,650
=	Total tax credits	€3,300 per year (€63.46 per week)
	Standard rate cut-off point	€33,800 per year (€650 per week)

KEY SKILLS

10.12 Danielle's tax rates BN

If Danielle earned €44,000 this year, how much of it would be taxed at 20% and how much at 40%? #Calculate

10.13 Danielle's monthly figures

If Danielle is paid monthly, what would her monthly figures be:

(a) For tax credits? (b) For SRCOP? #Calculate

10.14 Greg's monthly figures

Greg has been given annual tax credits of €2,960 and a standard rate cut-off point of €28,900. He is paid monthly, so what are his:

(a) Monthly tax credits? (b) Monthly SRCOP? #Calculate

Income tax calculation

Example 1: Single person weekly tax calculation

Assuming Danielle begins her job at the start of the tax year (1 January) and earns a gross wage of €800, here is her tax calculation for her first week of employment.

Taxable income €800

Step	Action	Tax	Explanation
1	Tax €650 @ 20%	€130.00	Apply standard rate 20% up to a maximum of the weekly standard rate cut-off point (€650.00) as per tax credit certificate
2	Tax €150 @ 40%	€60.00	Apply higher rate to pay in excess of the weekly standard rate cut-off point (€800 – €650 = €150)
3	Gross tax	€190.00	Add the standard rate tax figure to the higher rate tax figure
4	Less tax credit	€63.46	Tax credit as per tax credit certificate
5	Net tax	€126.54	Subtract tax credits from gross tax

Danielle also pays PRSI of 4% and USC of €30 on her gross wages.

6	PRSI €800 @ 4%	€32	4% PRSI paid on gross income
7	USC on €800	€30	USC calculation based on gross income

Danielle will have total statutory deductions of €188.54 (€126.54 + €32 + €30).

Her net (take home) pay for her first week of employment will be €611.46 (€800 – €188.54).

This example shows that tax calculation is another area of personal financial management that varies from person to person. Since personal circumstances and the rules governing taxation are likely to change over time, you should keep up to date with current tax policies. This helps to ensure that you and your household are paying the correct amount of tax and are benefiting from all tax credits to which you are entitled.

Up-to-date information on tax rates, credits and allowances is available on the Revenue website. Most changes to taxation are announced by the Minister for Finance when presenting the government's annual budget.

KEY SKILLS 

10.15 Today's PRSI rates

BN

Find out the current PRSI rates. #Research

KEY SKILLS

10.16 Grace's take-home pay

BN

Grace has a part-time job while she is at college. Her hourly rate is €11.15; standard rate cut-off point €33,800 per year; tax credits €3,300 per year; income tax rate is 20%, USC is 1% and PRSI is 4%. In her first week she worked 25 hours. How much will she take home? #Calculate

KEY SKILLS

10.17 Minimum wage in Ireland

BN

(a) What is the current national minimum wage? #Research

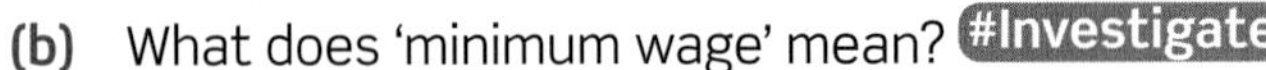

(b) What does 'minimum wage' mean? #Investigate

(c) Where did you find this information? What was it about this source that made you happy that the information is correct? #Evaluate

KEY SKILLS

10.18 Corporate tax avoidance

WO C

Some big companies have accountants who help the company to avoid tax. Tax avoidance, as we mentioned, is a legal way of not paying some tax. Although legal, do you think it is fair and ethical that some big companies can avoid tax in this way? How does corporate tax avoidance impact on other taxpayers? #Discussion

KEY SKILLS

10.19 Is the government like Robin Hood?

MIT BL

'When it comes to taxation, the government is a bit like Robin Hood because it takes from the rich and gives to the poor!' Write a short speech setting out your reasons for agreeing or disagreeing with this statement. #Presentation

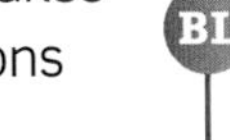

EXAM QUESTION

Junior Cycle 2019

Question 16 (c)

New Chapter, an award-winning traditional bookshop, has decided to diversify and start selling takeaway coffee, which is very much in demand by their customers and would also entice passers-by into the bookstore. They are concerned about a new proposal outlined below which appeared in a newspaper.

> **A proposed 'latte levy' could reduce disposable coffee cups by 250,000 a day.**
> The Government has proposed a new 15 cent levy on disposable coffee cups.
> *Irish Times*, March 2018

(i) Outline two benefits of the proposed 'latte levy'.

Question 17 (b)

(ii) Food2Go Ltd (a fast food retailer) pays VAT at the new rate of 13.5% following the increase in VAT rates announced in Budget 2019 for the hospitality sector. Answer the following questions.

- What does VAT stand for?
- What is VAT charged on?
- For whom is VAT a source of income?

 Weblinks

 PowerPoint Summary

CHAPTER 11

FINANCIAL PLANNING FOR YOUR FUTURE

LEARNING OUTCOMES IN FOCUS

1.3 Construct a personal financial life cycle to identify financial needs at different life stages

Links to 1.1, 1.2, 1.5, 2.3, 3.1, 3.2

LEARNING INTENTIONS FOR THIS CHAPTER

When you have completed this chapter you will be able to:

- Construct a personal financial life cycle to identify financial needs at different life stages
- Draft a personal financial life cycle to think about planning for your own financial needs
- Plan finances for different stages of your life.

CHAPTER 11 KEY TERMS

asset
estate
occupational pension
pension
personal financial life cycle
personal pension
will

CHAPTER 11 KEY SKILLS

- BL Being Literate
- BN Being Numerate
- C Communicating
- MIT Managing Information and Thinking
- MM Managing Myself
- SW Staying Well
- WO Working with Others

Financial resources

When you think about your financial resources, you may get frustrated about how little money you have as a teenager. You may begin to think about ways to increase your income. No doubt you already have an endless list of needs and wants to spend your money on!

The good news is that as you get older, your income levels are likely to increase greatly and become much more regular. The bad news is that the demands on your money are also likely to increase. You will have more money coming in, but also more money going out. Planning your finances for different stages of your life is important because it will allow you to deal with changes in your income and expenditure. It will also help you to meet different needs and wants that you will have as you grow older.

KEY SKILLS C MIT MM

11.1 Your future income

List possible sources of income you may have in the future. #List

11.2 Your future expenditure

List extra financial responsibilities you may have when you get older. Share both lists with your partner. #List

What is a personal financial life cycle?

A life cycle is a series of stages that a person goes through during his or her lifetime. A **personal financial life cycle** shows the changing financial needs a person will have at each stage of their life. A typical financial life cycle is shown in Figure 11.1.

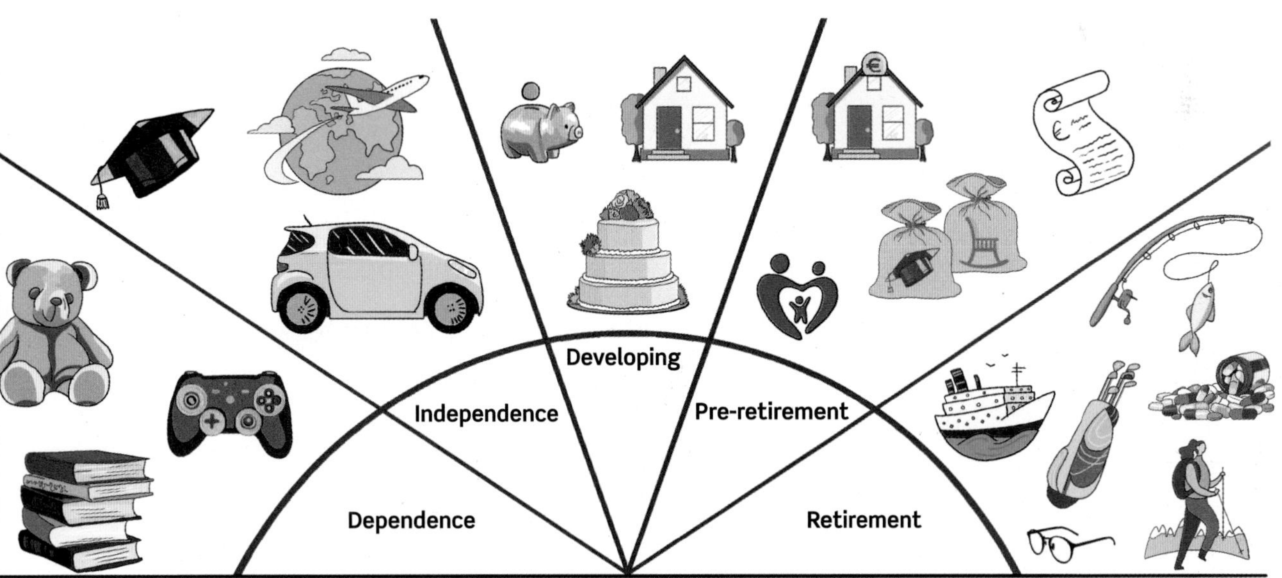

Figure 11.1 The personal financial life cycle

As you grow older, your financial needs and priorities will change. Understanding and **planning** for these ongoing changes is an important life skill.

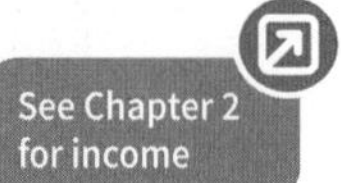

See Chapter 2 for income

For most of your childhood and teenage years, you are financially dependent on your parents or guardians. You have very few sources of income and most of your financial needs are met by your parents. Most of your personal income is disposable and most of your expenditure is discretionary.

KEY SKILLS

BL

11.3 Do you remember?

As a brief recap, explain the following in your own words:

(a) Disposable income

(b) Discretionary income. #Identify

When you leave school, you are likely to become more independent. As an adult, your financial needs will increase greatly. You may also reach a stage in your life when other people, such as children or other family members, become financially dependent on you. Later in life, you may be concerned with having enough money when you retire. You will also have to plan what happens to your estate when you die.

KEY TERM

Your **estate** is made up of everything you own. At the moment, it might be your bicycle, your books and your laptop or tablet. Later, it might include a car, a house and your savings.

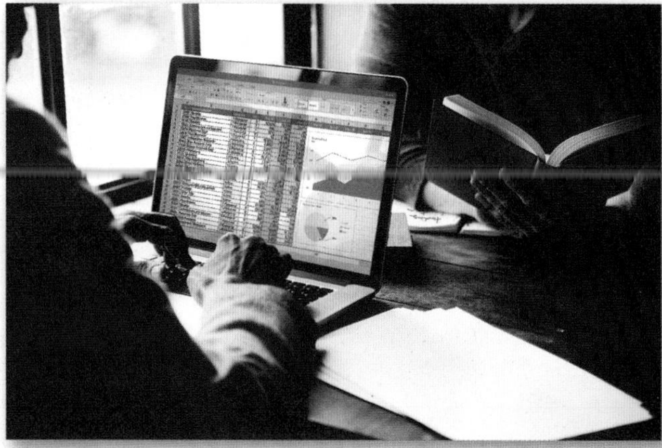

Financial planning

Financial planning is an ongoing process and plans need to be reviewed and revised from time to time. A plan is like a route map that sets out where you want to go and how you expect to get there. The benefit of planning is that people are prepared for each life stage well in advance. When you are ready for financial challenges before they happen, you will be in a better position to meet those challenges and enjoy the opportunities life offers.

Your financial needs will vary throughout your lifetime. Your financial goals and priorities will depend on your circumstances, values and life choices.

See Chapter 2 for planning and recording income

See Chapter 3 for planning and recording household expenditure

There is no perfect financial plan and it is not possible to adopt a 'one size fits all' approach. Every person is different, every life journey is different and every financial life cycle will be slightly different.

When you were younger, you probably didn't have much of your own money and planning was unlikely to be in your thoughts. We have looked at income and expenditure plans, so you have already started planning. This might be planning just one week at a time or it might involve longer-term planning to save for an expensive item you really want, such as a school tour, a games console or maybe even your first car. Starting when you are young will prepare you for planning your finances throughout your own personal financial life cycle.

Key financial planning during the personal financial life cycle

- Income and expenditure planning (budgeting) (see Chapters 2, 3 and 4)
- Risk management planning (insurance) (see Chapter 9)
- Taxation planning (see Chapter 10)
- Savings and investment planning (see Chapter 7)
- Retirement planning (pension)
- Estate planning. This is deciding what will happen to your assets after your death. An **asset** is something of value that you own. Making a will is part of this planning process. A **will** is a legal document containing instructions for what should be done with personal money and property after death.

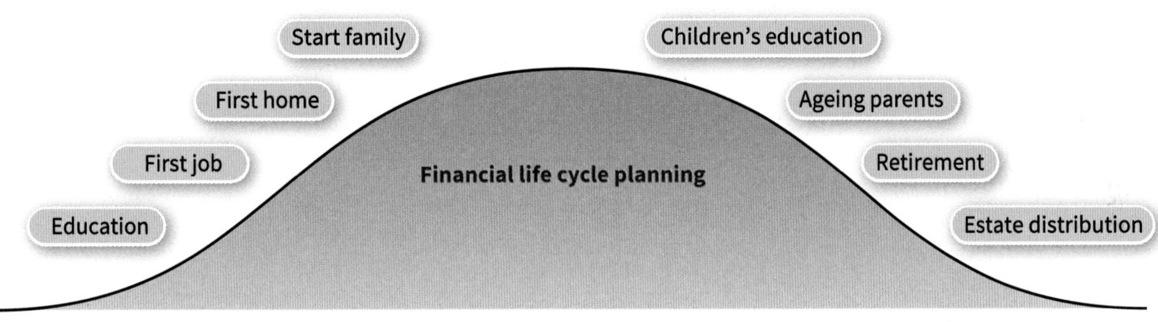

Figure 11.2 Financial life cycle planning

How your stage of life affects your personal financial life cycle

As you get older, your personal circumstances and lifestyle choices will impact your financial life cycle. For example, a 30-year-old single person with no children who rents an apartment will have different priorities than a married 30-year-old with two children and a mortgage.

Here are some of the main factors that may impact your financial planning:

- **Employment status:** Whether you are employed or unemployed.
- **Age:** Related to your earnings potential, your health, your family size and your spending priorities.
- **Number of dependents:** Children, partner, parents, etc.
- **Health status:** Medical treatment can be very expensive and developing a serious long-term illness has financial consequences. Medical insurance is also a financial consideration.
- **Economic outlook:** Unemployment levels, interest rates, taxation, etc.
- **Marital status:** Single, married, divorced, widowed, etc.

You should review your financial position and plans to reflect any changes in your circumstances. Some people revise their financial plan every year to check that it is still suitable for their circumstances; others revise it as their circumstances change.

Case study: How different decisions affect financial planning

Emily and Priyal are friends at school. Once they leave school, they take different life paths.

Emily

Emily completes her Leaving Certificate and decides to continue in full-time education. She gets a student loan and a part-time job so that she can pay college fees and day-to-day living expenses. She will continue to live at home during her first year in college, but hopes to move into rented accommodation in second or third year. Emily will rely on public transport, as she cannot afford to buy a car and is not in a position to take out a second loan. She is no longer covered by her parents' health insurance policy and feels she has no option but to go without private health insurance for a few years. She is hopeful that her college education will enable her to get a good job and she will then be in a position to repay her loan and save money to buy a car and a home of her own.

Priyal

Priyal completes her Leaving Certificate and seeks full-time employment. She finds a job in a neighbouring town but will continue to live at home in the short term. Priyal plans to move out of the family home in two or three years' time, but is prepared to wait until her job situation is more secure and she has some savings to support her. Priyal agrees to pay €100 a week to her parents. This is her contribution to household expenditure. She takes out a small credit union loan in order to buy a second-hand car, which she will use to travel to and from work and for socialising. Priyal will pay for her own motor and health insurance costs and is considering paying money into a pension fund.

11.4 Financial planning for Emily and Priyal

Having read Emily and Priyal's case studies, answer the following questions.

(a) List three major items of expenditure they will each have to plan for in the next five years. #List

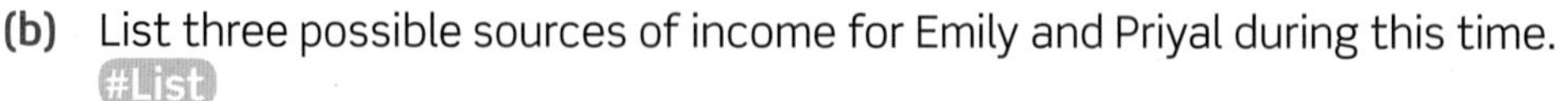

(b) List three possible sources of income for Emily and Priyal during this time. #List

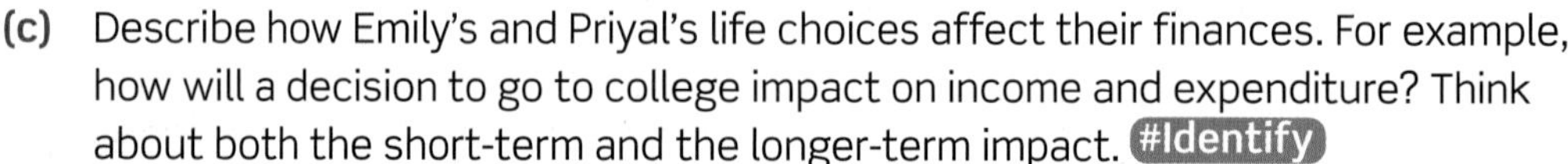

(c) Describe how Emily's and Priyal's life choices affect their finances. For example, how will a decision to go to college impact on income and expenditure? Think about both the short-term and the longer-term impact. #Identify

(d) Discuss with your partner possible events that might cause them to change their plans. #Discussion

PERSONAL FINANCE

When to plan and what to plan for

Dependence stage

In your early years, you probably didn't think about money, budgeting, saving or planning. You have been, and still are, very dependent on your parents or guardians for your financial needs.

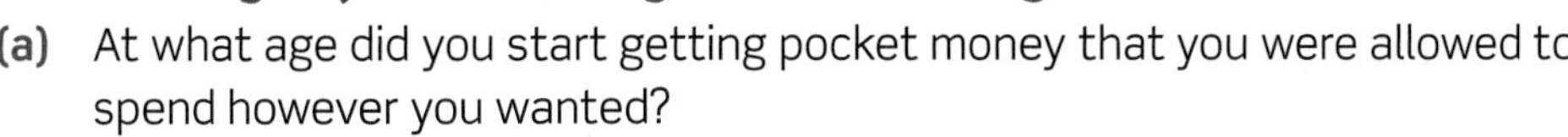

KEY SKILLS

MM C

11.5 When did you first receive your own money?

(a) At what age did you start getting pocket money that you were allowed to spend however you wanted?

(b) Do you have to work for your pocket money?

(c) Discuss whether you think it is a good idea to have to work to earn pocket money. Give reasons for your opinion. #Discussion #GroupWork

11.6 What's fair?

Some families have rules for children's income. For example, a certain amount of income must be saved. Discuss the benefits and drawbacks of this for the children and their parents. #Discussion

11.7 Should you budget when you're young?

Discuss the benefits of budgeting for teenagers. #Discussion

In your teens

In your younger teens, you are likely to be very dependent on your parents or guardians and gifts of money on special occasions. If you start working for money, you will have a greater appreciation of what money means. You may have started saving for more expensive items. When you are an older teenager, you will need to plan and prepare for your career and adult life. Your parents will be involved in this too, but you should take on some of the responsibility – after all, it's your life!

Key financial concerns will be:

- Full-time education and preparation for your career
- Income from part-time employment
- Considering future financial needs and resources.

KEY SKILLS

MIT MM SW

11.8 What else do you need?

List four other needs that a teenager may have. #List

11.9 Available income sources

List two possible sources of income available to a teenager, other than pocket money. #List

Independence stage

At this stage, people begin working and gain financial independence. If they are working, they will earn a wage or salary. If they are looking for a job, they may qualify for Jobseeker's Benefit. They will have greater personal income and more expenditure. People without families and mortgages may have relatively high levels of disposable income and enjoy lots of discretionary spending. This may be a good time to try to save some money to meet future needs and wants, such as saving for a deposit for a house.

At this stage, people will probably be thinking about:

- Finishing their education/apprenticeship/career preparation
- Starting work and building wealth
- Becoming financially independent
- Repaying student loans
- Beginning regular savings
- Buying/renting a home
- Household budgeting
- Insurance needs
- Starting a pension.

KEY TERM

A **pension** is a fund into which payments are made during a person's working life, and from which payments are later made to support them when they retire from work.

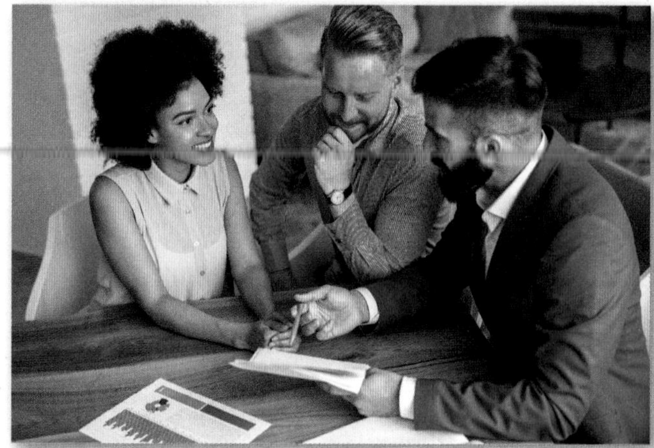

KEY SKILLS WO MIT

11.10 Changing the pension age

The government may consider changing the age at which the state pension is paid, perhaps delaying it for two years, until people reach the age of 68. Think of two reasons why the government would make this change. #Discussion

Pensions

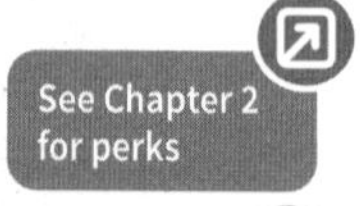

See Chapter 2 for perks

Anyone who has paid enough PRSI is eligible for the state pension. Some employers also have pension schemes and money is deducted from employees' wages to pay into it. The employer may make a contribution towards it as well. This is called an **occupational (work) pension** and is in addition to the state pension.

People who don't have an occupational (work) pension can pay into a **personal pension** that will give them extra income in addition to the state pension.

Professional advice is often the best way to plan your pension needs. Revisiting your plans every few years is a good idea to make sure you are still on the best path for the future.

KEY SKILLS

11.11 Saving for retirement

People who have just started work may feel that retirement is a long, long way off and they have lots to experience before then. Why is it advisable to start thinking about pensions as soon as you start work? Discuss your thoughts in pairs or small groups. #Discussion

WO MIT C BN SW

Developing stage

At this stage, people are likely to have more family and household commitments that will probably need extra household income. They may be earning a higher salary than when they started working and will qualify for payments like Child Benefit if they have children. Many people will get a mortgage at this stage of their lives. Householders should think about their insurance needs. People with families are likely to spend more of their income on current and future education needs for their children. If income levels allow, it may be possible to take investment opportunities. People at this stage will probably be thinking about:

- Increasing their income
- Paying mortgage/rent
- Personal savings/creating an emergency fund
- Children's education costs
- Household expenditure
- Life assurance
- Health insurance needs
- Pension
- Considering retirement goals
- Considering estate plans/making a will.

KEY SKILLS

11.12 Advantages of starting early

(a) If you started a pension plan in your twenties, what advantage would you have over people who started it later? #Opinion

(b) When do most people purchase life assurance? Suggest a reason for your answer. #Identify

MIT BN SW

Pre-retirement stage

People at this stage are likely to be near the top of the salary scale and may have been promoted in work. This will help to increase regular income.

A salary scale is like an income ladder that people can climb during their time in employment. When they start out they are near the bottom of the scale, but over time, as they grow in seniority and experience, they get paid more. After a certain number of years they reach the top of the scale.

Those who are parents will tend to have older children and education spending is likely to be for third level. Health insurance and pension planning become more important as a person gets older. There may also be a need to provide for increased levels of health and life insurance.

If they have not already done so, they should consider retirement goals and pension needs.

At this stage, people will probably be thinking about:

- Children's third-level education
- Savings
- Updating retirement plans
- Paying off a mortgage
- Life assurance
- Considering estate plans/making a will.

11.13 Changing wills at will

Why, do you think, do people alter their wills at different stages of their lives? #Opinion

MIT

Retirement stage

People at this stage have retired from work and will be living off their retirement income. They will have repaid their mortgage and may consider downsizing to top up their income (i.e. selling the family home and buying a smaller property that costs less).

People of retirement age will be thinking about:

- Children's education (third level)
- Pension entitlements
- Life assurance and health insurance
- Meeting the responsibilities of ageing parents
- Retirement planning
- Checking the contents of a will
- Inheritance planning.

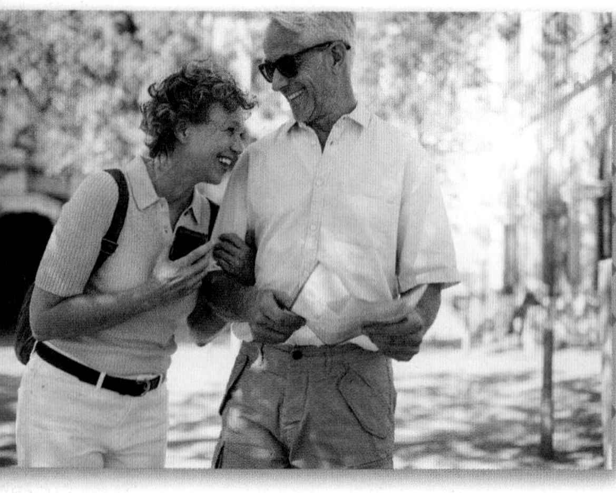

At retirement, people will be thinking about:

- Re-evaluating their living conditions – possibly buying a smaller home
- Spending based on retirement income
- Living off saved wealth
- Adjusting insurance for increased risk
- Considering what care needs they might have as they get older
- Finalising wills and estate plans.

KEY SKILLS

11.14 Income and expenditure over a lifetime

Complete question 5 in the Student Activity Book to identify your sources of income and the main items of expenditure throughout your life. You should include reasons for why you might need to save and suggest what debts you may have at each stage of your life. #Activity

Elder financial abuse: Demands from family members for money among issues – survey

Demands from family members for money are among the issues that arose in new research on elder financial abuse in a survey from Age Action and Ulster Bank. Forty-five per cent of the survey's respondents had dealt with suspected elder financial abuse cases.

There were more than 13,000 cases of elder abuse referred to the HSE up to the end of 2013. Financial abuse is the second most common form of elder abuse, accounting for more than one in five cases. Justin Moran, Head of Advocacy and Communications at Age Action, said: 'Every year, hundreds of older people are facing demands for money from family members, having their income withheld from them or finding their possessions taken. To make it worse, in the overwhelming majority of cases of elder abuse, the perpetrators are immediate family members.

Among the case studies detailed was the story of Sinéad, who has been diagnosed with dementia. During a period when she was experiencing reduced mental capacity, her son persuaded her to set up a joint bank account. Her son then used this account to obtain a credit card and made a number of purchases on the card for which Sinéad was charged. Afterwards, Sinéad realised what had happened. With the help of her daughter, she approached her bank, which recognised it as fraud and reimbursed her.

Source: Irish Independent, 15 June 2015

11.15 Reflecting on elder abuse

Discuss the following questions.

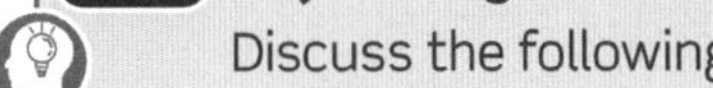

(a) Are you shocked by the number of cases of elder abuse involving money that the bank's staff have come across? Do you think it is a large number? #Reflect

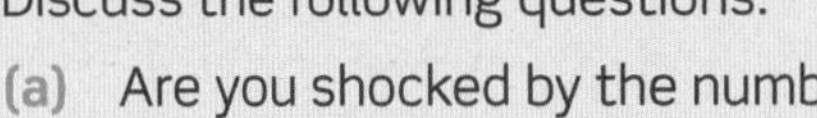
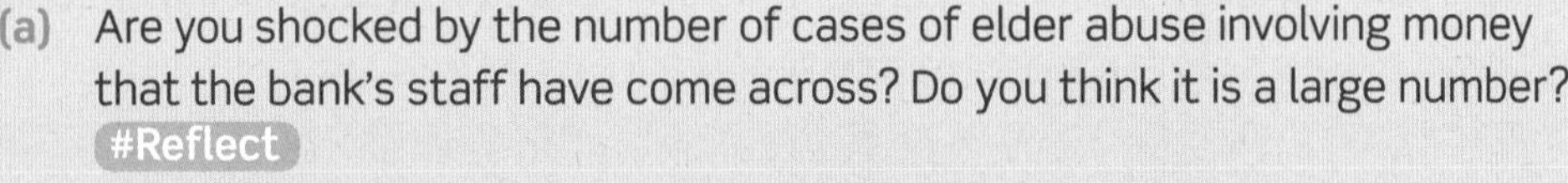

(b) Do you think more or fewer elderly people will suffer this kind of abuse in the future? Why do you think this? #Discussion

(c) How does reading this article make you feel? Can you imagine this happening to an elderly person you are fond of? Can you imagine it happening to you when you are elderly? How does that make you feel? #Reflect

(d) If you thought an elderly person you know was being abused in this way, would you report it? Give reasons for your answer. #Discussion

(e) What makes what Sinéad's son did to her a case of fraud? #Identify

Weblinks

PowerPoint Summary

PERSONAL FINANCE

CHAPTER 12

PROTECTING THE CONSUMER

LEARNING OUTCOMES IN FOCUS

1.7 Distinguish between and appreciate their rights and responsibilities as consumers (Links to 1.8, 1.9, 1.10, 3.1, 3.7, 3.8)

1.8 Compare the services provided by consumer agencies and financial institutions to assist and support customers (Links to 1.5, 1.7, 1.9, 1.10)

LEARNING INTENTIONS FOR THIS CHAPTER

When you have completed this chapter you will be able to:

- Explain what a consumer is
- Be a wise consumer
- Outline the responsibilities of a consumer
- Know and understand your rights as a consumer
- Describe the redress available if a good is faulty or a service is not up to standard
- Make a complaint orally or in writing, backed up by your knowledge of consumer laws
- Explain how relevant agencies can assist in resolving consumer complaints.

CHAPTER 12 KEY TERMS

- as described
- *caveat emptor*
- Commission for Communications Regulation (ComReg)
- Commission for Regulation of Utilities (CRU)
- Competition and Consumer Protection Commission (CCPC)
- consumer
- Consumers' Association of Ireland (CAI)
- credit note
- European Consumer Centre (ECC) Ireland
- extended warranty
- fit for purpose
- guarantee
- match the sample shown
- merchantable quality
- Office of the Ombudsman
- redress
- refund
- repair
- replacement
- retailer
- sample
- Small Claims Procedure
- unfair commercial practices

CHAPTER 12 KEY SKILLS

- BC Being Creative
- BL Being Literate
- BN Being Numerate
- 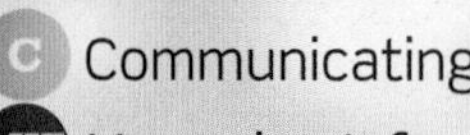 C Communicating
- MIT Managing Information and Thinking
-  MM Managing Myself
- SW Staying Well
- 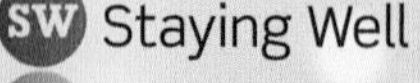 WO Working with Others

PERSONAL FINANCE

What is a consumer?

KEY TERM

A **consumer** is a person who buys goods or services for their own use.

Every time you buy a bar of chocolate, purchase a book or magazine, go to the hairdresser or barber to get a haircut or pay to download a song from the internet, you are a consumer.

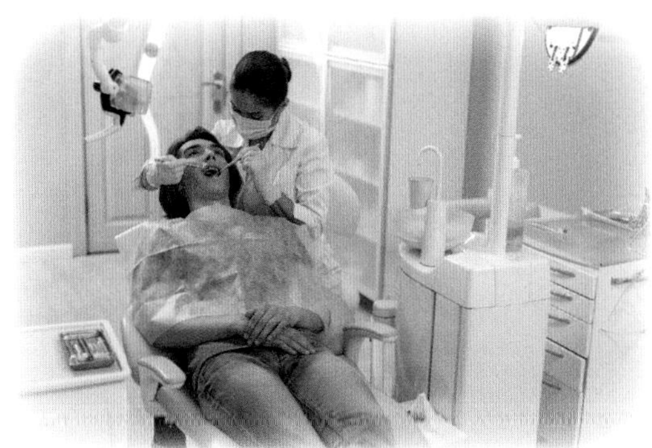

Consumers have different needs and wants. Most consumers' requirements when buying products are:

- Choosing products that will be useful and will best serve their needs
- Value for money
- High-quality products
- Finding out information about the product before they buy it
- Getting a good after-sales service if there is a fault or problem with the product.

See Chapter 1 for needs and wants

The wise consumer

See Chapter 1 for financial resources

As we discovered in Chapter 1, money is a scarce resource. When consumers want to buy something, they have to ask themselves some important questions, such as:

- Do I really need it or is it an impulse buy?
- Can I afford it?
- Is it a false economy?
- Will there be further costs once I have bought the item? Are there any hidden extra charges?
- Can I buy this product more cheaply elsewhere?
- Is it a safe product? Could it cause harm to me or to others when I use it?
- Is there an ethical cost in the way it was produced? Was it produced using slave labour? Did an animal suffer for this product? Has the environment been harmed because of it?
- Will I help to create jobs in Ireland by buying this product? (If the product is bought from abroad (imported), it will not help to create as many jobs in Ireland.)

KEY SKILLS: BL

12.1 Revisiting impulse buying and false economy

Can you recall the meaning of the terms 'impulse buying' and 'false economy'? Give an example of each. #Identify

KEY SKILLS: WO, C, BL, SW, MIT

12.2 Smart shopping for a smartphone

The latest smartphone has just arrived in the shops. You have been thinking of getting a new phone and you are trying to decide which model to go for. What questions would you ask yourself? In your group, list the questions, such as, 'Are there any hidden costs? If so, what are they?' Record your answers. #GroupWork

Information about products

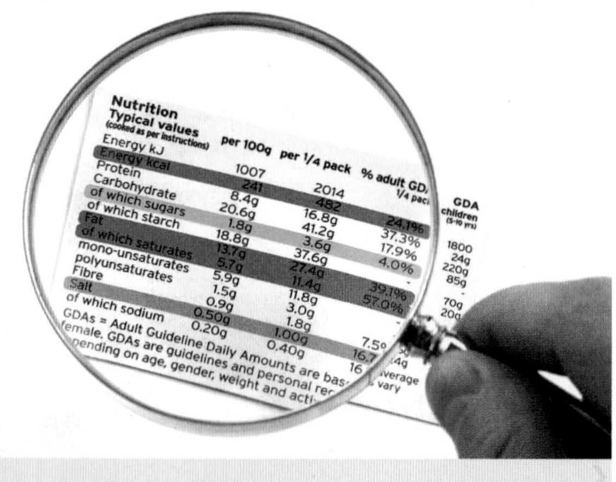

Example of a food label

Many products have labels listing the contents of the package, technology requirements or safety details. In particular, most packaged food products have a label. These labels give important information and shouldn't be ignored. The following information might be included on a food label:

- Name of product – the brand and the item
- Name and address of the producer/seller
- The weight of the product
- Price – the cost of the product
- Best before/sell by/use by date
- Ingredients – these are always listed in descending weight order, i.e. the heaviest items are listed first
- Country of origin
- Nutritional information

- Cooking/storage instructions
- Barcode – a series of lines and numbers that identify where the product was made, by which company and the cost of the product.

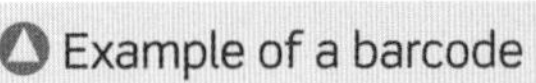
Example of a barcode

KEY SKILLS: MIT, BC, BL, BN, SW, MM

12.3 Product dates

(a) What does the 'best before' date mean? #Research

(b) What does the 'sell by' date mean? #Research

(c) What does the 'use by' date mean? #Research

(d) Is it legal for shops to have items on the shelf that have passed #Research
- The 'best before' date?
- The 'sell by' date?

(e) If the dates on the products are getting close, what might the shopkeeper do to make sure the items sell before they have to be taken off the shelf? #CreativeThinking

(f) Create a poster aimed at shoppers explaining 'best before', 'use by' and 'sell by' dates. Include information on how the consumer should make use of these dates. Make sure you include pictures in your poster. #Presentation

Value for money

Unit pricing

Question: Which is better value for money?

(a) 9-pack of Brand A multi-pack of cans of soft drink, which costs €5.00

(b) 16-pack of Brand B multi-pack of cans of soft drink, which costs €8.00

Answer:

(a) $\frac{\text{Price}}{\text{Quantity}} = \frac{5.00}{9}$ = 56c per can

(b) $\frac{\text{Price}}{\text{Quantity}} = \frac{8.00}{16}$ = 50c per can

In this case, Brand B is better value for money.

KEY SKILLS: BN, MIT

12.4 Calculating cost per unit

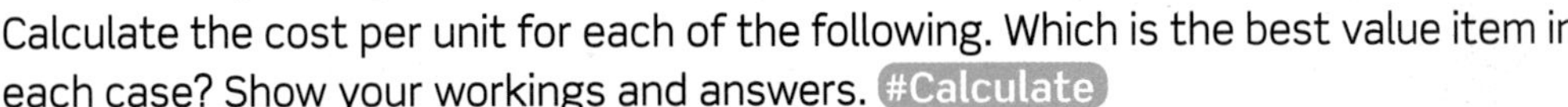

Calculate the cost per unit for each of the following. Which is the best value item in each case? Show your workings and answers. #Calculate

(a) (i) A 12-pack of Brand A pens at €9.12
 (ii) A 7-pack of Brand B pens at €5.25

(b) (i) A 500g box of Brand A breakfast cereal at €3.95
 (ii) A 650g box of Brand B breakfast cereal at €4.29
 (iii) A 700g box of Brand C breakfast cereal at €4.85

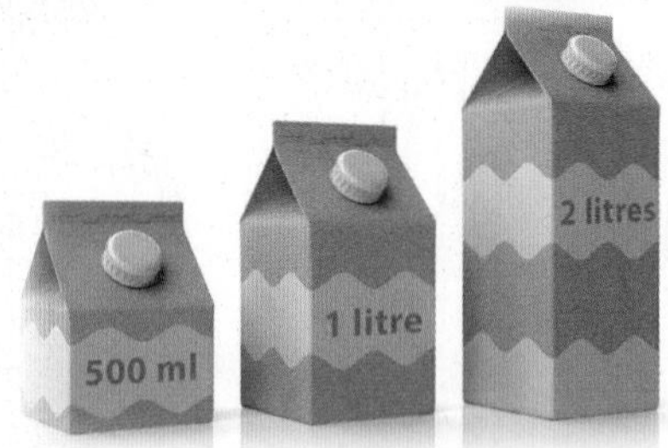

While a larger size is often better value for money, you might not use all of the product and it could therefore be a **false economy**. Before you buy a larger size of a product, even if it is better value for money, ask yourself if you need all of it or if you will use it before it goes out of date.

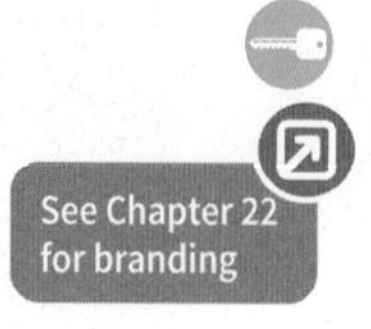
See Chapter 22 for branding

Own-label products carry the brand of the shop that sells them (the **retailer**). These products are usually cheaper than well-known brands and may represent better value for consumers. Most popular foods have an own-brand version in the bigger supermarkets.

Consumer responsibilities

If something seems too good to be true, it probably is! ***Caveat emptor*** is a Latin phrase that means 'let the buyer beware'. This means that consumers need to use common sense when buying goods and services.

Consumers have the following responsibilities:

- To behave wisely when buying goods and services.
- To avoid impulse buying and false economies.
- To shop around for the best value for money.
- To use products carefully and in accordance with the manufacturer's instructions to avoid damaging them.
- To dispose of packaging responsibly, recycling when possible.

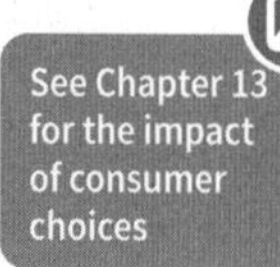
See Chapter 13 for the impact of consumer choices

- To consider the environmental and ethical impact of the products they consume. How will consumer choices impact on people and the planet?
- To keep receipts as proof of purchase. This is important if faulty goods need to be returned. In some cases the receipt may be used to show the start date for the product guarantee.
- To know their legal rights. Despite being protected by law when purchasing goods, consumers should always be careful when buying goods and services.

Although you can't insist on a refund if you change your mind about buying a product, many shops will give a refund or a credit note out of goodwill, meaning they trust their customers and want to help them.

12.5 Digital activity/research

Create a poster or infographic showing a wise consumer. Include suitable images and at least five key questions that a wise consumer should ask before purchasing a good or service. Create a display in your school to promote being a wise consumer where all class posters can be shown. #Create #Design

KEY SKILLS MIT BL C MM

12.6 Consumer ethics

Sarah has found a dress that she really wants to wear to a party, but it costs more than she can afford. Her friend Martina says, 'Buy it, wear it for the evening, then take it back to the shop the next day and get a refund.'

(a) Discuss what you think about this idea. Is it ethical? #Discussion #Ethics

(b) How does this behaviour impact on other consumers? #Identify

Legal rights of consumers

Consumers in Ireland are protected by two Irish laws:

- Sale of Goods and Supply of Services Act 1980
- Consumer Protection Act 2007.

They are also protected by EU laws, especially when buying online. Later in the chapter, we will look at some organisations that assist consumers who have been unfairly treated.

Sale of Goods and Supply of Services Act 1980

This law helps to protect consumers by providing them with a number of rights when they buy goods from a **trader**. Note that this law does not protect consumers if they buy goods from another consumer or private individual. You need to be very careful when buying goods privately, either from people you know or from resale sites such as DoneDeal and Gumtree. You should inspect the goods very carefully, as you have no right to return the goods once you have paid for them. While the goods may be a little cheaper in a private sale, the risks of being scammed may be higher and you won't have any guarantee from the seller.

Goods

According to the Sale of Goods and Supply of Services Act 1980, goods must:

- **Be of merchantable quality:** The good must be in fit condition to be sold. This means it must be safe, usable and of reasonable quality considering the price paid. For example, food must be edible up to the best before date. The standard of quality expected is linked to the price paid. For example, if you buy a brand new car, you will pay top price and expect the vehicle to be in perfect condition. If you buy a used car you will pay a lower price, but you cannot expect the same level of quality.
- **Be fit for the purpose intended:** The good must do what you expect it to do: a kettle must boil water, a phone must be able to make and receive calls, etc. If a consumer specifies a particular use, the goods sold to them must be capable of meeting that purpose. For example, a consumer may ask for a camera they can use underwater. If the retailer sells them a camera that is not waterproof, it is clearly not fit for its intended purpose.
- **Be as described:** The good must match the description given by the salesperson, packaging, brochure or advertisement, e.g. a jacket described as waterproof must not let rain in.

- **Match the sample shown:** For certain items bought from a showroom, just a sample will be available, such as tiles, wallpaper, sofas and carpets. When the item is purchased, it must be the same as the item shown to you in the shop and you must have an opportunity to check this.

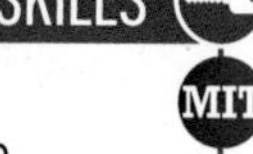

12.7 Jack's 'new' oven

Jack bought an oven from a man on an online advertising board. He went to the man's house to collect it. When he fitted it into his kitchen, he found that it did not work. Does he have any rights under the Sale of Goods and Supply of Services Act 1980? Record your answer and the reason. #Record

Services

The law states that services must be:

- **Provided by someone who has the necessary skills and qualifications:** We expect providers who charge for services, such as doctors, solicitors, electricians, mechanics and hairdressers, to be suitably qualified.
- **Provided with necessary care and attention:** Sometimes being qualified to provide a service is not enough. Service providers must also carry out the work with proper care and attention.
- **Carried out using goods or materials of merchantable quality:** For example, if you pay a mechanic for a car service that includes a new battery, the service provider must ensure that the parts and materials meet your requirements and reflect the price paid. If they simply replace your old battery with another second-hand battery, they are acting illegally and you would be well within your rights to seek redress.

Redress

If you buy a damaged or faulty item from a trader, you are legally entitled to some form of **redress** (remedy or compensation). There are three kinds of redress, known as the **3 Rs**:

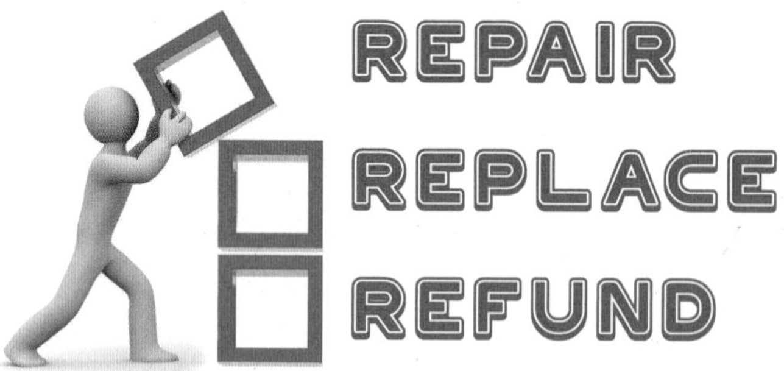

- **Repair:** The item may be fixed free of charge. The repair must be permanent.
- **Replacement:** You can have the same or an alternative product that is free from damage or faults.
- **Refund:** You can receive the cost of the item back, either in cash or as money paid back to your debit or credit card.

Consumers are *not* entitled to a refund, repair or replacement if they simply change their mind or if they caused the fault through careless use of the good.

A **credit note** allows a customer who has returned faulty goods to choose other goods of the same value from that shop. If the shop offers you a credit note, you have the right to refuse it and ask for a refund. This is because a credit note limits you to buying something else (of equal value) from the same shop, which may not suit you.

The longer you wait to make the complaint or the longer the fault occurs after you have bought the item, the less likely it is that you will receive a full refund; you may instead be offered a replacement, repair or partial refund.

WO C BL MIT SW MM

12.8 Returning an item

Have you or your family ever had a reason to take something back to a shop or return something by post? What were the circumstances and how was the situation resolved? Discuss the experience and share with your group.
#GroupWork #Discussion

12.9 Karen's new phone

Karen bought a new phone. She looked at the display model in the shop, but was given a new one in a sealed box to take home. When she got home, she showed her brother the box and he said, 'That's rubbish. You should have got the Xi57; it's way cooler.' Karen now didn't like the phone she had bought. She undid the seal, took out the phone and made a scratch over the screen. Then she went back to the shop, complained loudly that the phone was damaged, demanded her money back and went to a different shop to get the Xi57. Write the answers to the following questions:

(a) How could Karen have handled this situation better? #Identify

(b) Did Karen have any legal rights in this situation? If so, what rights did she have? #Identify

(c) How could this situation impact on: #Evaluate

- (i) Herself?
- (ii) The shop staff?
- (iii) The reputation of the shop and the manufacturer?
- (iv) The staff at the factory where the phone was made and packaged?

(d) How could Karen ensure she buys a phone with a good reputation in the future? #Plan

Responsibilities of sellers

The Sale of Goods and Supply of Services Act 1980 states that:

- Consumer complaints must be dealt with by the seller. You do not have to contact the manufacturer if an item is faulty. The retailer who sold you the item is responsible for dealing with your complaint, as your contract is with the shop.
- Retailers must respect consumers' rights when selling goods and services.
- Retailers cannot display signs that limit their responsibility, such as 'No refunds', 'No exchanges' or 'Credit notes only'.
- Guarantees and warranties are an addition to consumers' legal rights, but they do not replace them.

Guarantees and warranties

Some manufacturers offer a **guarantee**. This is a written statement promising to replace or repair an item that develops a fault within a certain time period, such as one year. Some shops offer consumers extended warranties at an extra cost to cover item repairs after the manufacturer's guarantee has run out. Consumers do not have to buy an extended warranty.

> KEY TERM
>
> A **guarantee** is a promise by the manufacturer or company that it will sort out any problems with a product or service within a specific, fixed period of time. It is usually free. It cannot take away any of your legal rights as a consumer.

> KEY TERM
>
> An **extended warranty** is like an insurance policy, for which you must pay a premium. For an extra fee the manufacturer or retailer will extend the guarantee for a longer time period.

Consumer Protection Act 2007

The **Consumer Protection Act 2007** tries to modernise and update consumer law in Ireland and it sets out what is expected of retailers. Unlike the Sale of Goods and Supply of Services Act, the Consumer Protection Act does not list any specific rights of consumers, but rather it provides protection for them in relation to misleading claims about goods, services and prices. It does this by making it illegal for retailers to act in particular ways.

Misleading claims

Businesses cannot make misleading claims about the business, their goods, services or prices. For example, a business cannot claim to be 'Ireland's oldest bakery' unless it really is Ireland's oldest bakery.

For **goods**, claims about the performance of a product, the ingredients it contains and the weight of the item must be truthful. Examples of misleading claims are:

- A claim that a product will remove acne when there is no scientific proof that it can
- A claim that a product is made in Ireland when in fact it is made elsewhere.

For **services**, claims about the time, place and effect of a service must be truthful. Examples of misleading claims are:

- A claim that a service is available throughout the country when it is available only in Cork and Galway
- A claim that a service will be provided within one hour (e.g. dry cleaning) if it will take longer
- A claim that mobile data is unlimited when there are extra charges if the consumer downloads more than 15GB of data.

For **prices**, the recommended retail price (RRP), previous prices and actual prices must be truthful. When a retailer advertises a previous price, the item must have been on sale at that price in the same location for 28 consecutive days within the previous three months.

Misleading practices

The Consumer Protection Act protects consumers against unfair practices whether they buy from a local shop or a business within the EU.

There are three main **unfair commercial practices**:

- **Misleading:** When false or untrue information is used to deceive the consumer, such as a butcher displaying a sign indicating it is an award-winning business when it has not in fact won any awards.
- **Aggressive:** When harassment, physical force or influence are used to force a consumer into buying a product, such as a mechanic carrying out more work on a car than was agreed in advance and refusing to return the car until the consumer pays for the work.
- **Prohibited:** The law lists 32 specific practices that are banned, for example:
  - Telling a consumer that they have won a prize and then demanding payment to claim the prize
  - Claiming a business is closing down when it is not.

IN THE NEWS

Major retailers fined over breaches of consumer legislation

The Competition and Consumer Protection Commission has released details of 40 enforcement actions taken against 33 traders in 2016. The commission, which is responsible for enforcing consumer protection legislation, uses its powers to stop practices that are misleading, unfair or harmful to consumers.

Twenty-seven fines of €300 were paid by 24 traders who failed to display the selling price of a product.

Seven compliance notices were issued to traders who charged more than the price displayed.

Creative Retail Solutions was issued with proceedings under the Sale of Goods Act in relation to its temporary store on Grafton Street in Dublin. The sign claimed it was the shop's policy not to provide refunds and that it would only exchange goods within 24 hours of purchase and with a receipt. 'This suggested to consumers that their statutory rights in relation to faulty goods were restricted,' the authority said.

Four enforcement actions were taken for failure to comply with or for providing misleading information about consumers' legal rights under the EU Consumer Rights Directive.

According to commission chair Isolde Goggin: 'Under consumer protection law, the selling price of every item offered for sale must be displayed clearly and accurately.'

Source: *Irish Times*, 6 March 2017

Distance selling and consumer rights

When you buy from a retailer located anywhere in the EU, you are protected by the EU **Consumer Rights Directive**. This Directive, which has been part of Irish law since 2014, protects consumers when buying online, over the phone or by mail order. It only applies to purchases from businesses located in the EU.

When you buy goods or services online, you have the right to:

- **Clear and accurate information before you buy:** Information such as the retailer's name and address; a description of the product or service; full details of price, including taxes, delivery and payment details; and details of your right to cancel and return goods should all be provided by the retailer in advance.
- **A refund if your goods are not delivered:** You should contact the seller to request a refund, which should be provided within 14 days. If you have paid by debit or credit card and the retailer fails to refund your money, you may be able to get your card provider to reverse the transaction. This is called **chargeback**.
- **Return faulty goods:** If you receive faulty goods, you have the same rights as if you had bought them in a shop. You should contact the retailer and return the goods in order to receive a refund. In this case, the retailer must cover the cost of returning the goods.

- **Return the item because you have changed your mind:** When you buy online, there's a 14-day **cooling-off period**. This means that within this period, you have the right to cancel an order for any reason, including a change of mind. If you choose to cancel the contract, you will usually have to pay the costs involved in returning the goods to the retailer. This must be done within 14 days of the cancellation date. The cooling-off period does not apply when goods have been made to order or have been personalised in some way, such as a hoodie with the customer's name on it. There is also no cooling-off period for perishable goods, such as fresh food; newspapers and magazines; CDs, DVDs and computer software that have been unsealed and used; gaming or lottery services; and services that have already commenced. For hygiene reasons, it is not possible to return swimwear or underwear.

- **Cancel a service:** The 14-day cooling-off period also applies to services, and retailers should inform you of your right to cancel. They should also make a copy of a standard cancellation form available to consumers.
- **Cancel digital purchases:** With digital purchases you must clearly agree to download or stream the content before you are liable for the costs. Retailers normally require you to do this on a website or via an app. If you have not already downloaded or streamed the content, you have a right to cancel a digital service. Consumers need

to be careful when setting up accounts to purchase digital content. In many cases you need to provide the retailer with your debit or credit card details and can sign up to buy extra content with a single click. This means that anyone who has access to your account can download or stream material and you will be charged.

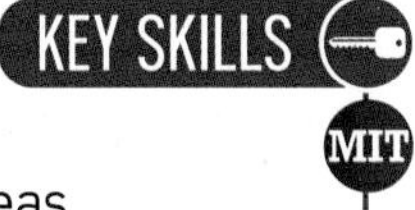

12.10 Cooling-off online?

MIT

Why, do you think, are online consumers entitled to this cooling-off period whereas consumers who buy goods in a shop are not? #Opinion

Beware!

If you buy goods and services from businesses located outside the EU, you may not have the same level of protection, so it's very important to do some research and make sure you are dealing with a reputable business and have read all the terms and conditions relating to the purchase. In particular, you should consider what rights you will have if goods are not delivered or need to be returned. Purchases from retailers outside the EU may also be liable for VAT and customs duty.

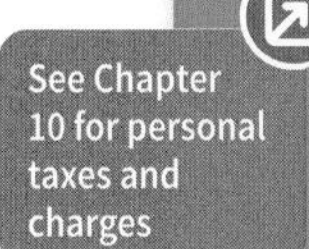

See Chapter 10 for personal taxes and charges

Making a complaint

If you discover a fault with a product you have purchased, you will need to make a complaint to the retailer. There are a few simple steps you should follow:

1. Stop using the item immediately.
2. Take the item back to the shop and ask to speak to the manager. If you still have the receipt or other proof of purchase, bring this with you. If the manager is unavailable, ask to speak to the person in charge.
3. Explain the problem clearly, including details of purchase and when you noticed a problem with the item. Be polite but firm. Know your rights under the Sale of Goods and Supply of Services Act 1980.

4. Decide which form of redress you would prefer: a refund, a replacement or a repair.
5. If the retailer does not offer a satisfactory result, you may need to send your complaint in writing (by letter or email), providing details of the problem. Keep a copy of all correspondence.
6. If the complaint is still not resolved, you may have to seek the advice of a third party, such as the Competition and Consumer Protection Commission or the Consumers' Association of Ireland (see pages 146–148).
7. If the complaint is still not resolved, make a claim through the Small Claims Procedure, if applicable (see page 148).
8. Go to court.

KEY SKILLS

12.11 Make a complaint guide

Either:

(a) Illustrate the steps outlined above for making a complaint by summarising them in a poster, an information leaflet or a presentation. Include suitable images.

Or:

(b) Create a podcast or video in which you advise people about what steps they should take to make a complaint. #Presentation

When is a consumer complaint not valid?

As a consumer, you do not have any rights:

- If you change your mind about the purchase
- If a fault arises due to your misuse of a product
- If you were told about the fault when you bought the good.

Writing a letter or email of complaint

Although it is best to complain politely and in person, sometimes you may have to make a complaint in writing. Letters usually follow a certain format, as shown in Figure 12.1.

You should include three separate paragraphs in the main body of the letter:

1. Describe the details of the purchase.
2. Give the details of the complaint and show how the situation breaches consumer law.
3. Explain what remedy (redress) you want.

Keep a copy of the letter to refer to in the future in case you need to take the matter to a consumer agency. This will provide proof that you have already tried to resolve the complaint yourself.

Example: A letter of complaint

Shannon Meehan bought a new Samsung phone in LMM Electrics that cost €199. After three days, she noticed that the battery wasn't charging properly and the phone kept switching itself off. By the end of the week, she noticed that the phone was not receiving any incoming calls, which were instead going straight to voicemail. Shannon rang LMM Electrics and asked for the name of the manager and the shop's address. She then wrote to the manager. Her letter is shown in Figure 12.1.

KEY SKILLS

12.12 Addressing the letter

Suggest a reason why Shannon rang the shop to get the name of the manager rather than addressing the letter to 'The Manager'. #Opinion

PERSONAL FINANCE

13 Harbour Road
Killybegs
Co. Donegal
18 October 2020

Ms Louise McMenamin
Manager
LMM Electrics
16 Main Street
Donegal Town
Co. Donegal

Re: Faulty phone

Dear Ms McMenamin,

On 10 October 2020 I purchased a Samsung phone costing €199 from LMM Electrics. I enclose a copy of my receipt.

The battery isn't charging properly and the phone switches itself off even when it hasn't been used. I have also discovered that all calls are going straight to voicemail and that there is no record of incoming calls to the phone. According to the Sale of Goods and Supply of Services Act 1980, goods should be of merchantable quality and fit for the purpose intended. This is clearly not the case with my new phone.

I would therefore like a replacement phone or a refund.

Yours sincerely,

Shannon Meehan

Shannon Meehan
Encl: 1

Address of consumer

Date

Address of retailer

Reference

Salutation

First paragraph: Details and date of purchase

Second paragraph: Details of complaint and reference to consumer legislation

Third paragraph: Request for remedy

Closing (note: use 'Yours sincerely' if you are using a name and 'Yours faithfully' if you are using Dear Sir/Madam)

Handwritten signature

Print name

Indicates that one extra item (the copy of the receipt) is enclosed with this letter

Figure 12.1 Sample letter of complaint

12.13 Write a letter of complaint

Write a letter of complaint about a waterproof jacket that leaked the first time you wore it in the rain. The shop you bought it from is Gleeson Ltd on the main street of your nearest town. You have phoned the shop to get the name of the manager, who is Desmond O'Rourke. #Activity

MIT

See questions 14–15 in your Student Activity Book for activities related to making a complaint.

It is also possible to contact a retailer via email in order to make a complaint. Shannon could have chosen to email her complaint to LMM Electrics. If so, her email would be as follows:

To: customerservice@LMM.ie

From: ShannonM@mail.ie

Subject: Faulty phone

On 10 October 2020 I purchased a Samsung phone costing €199 from LMM Electrics. I attach a copy of my receipt.

The battery isn't charging properly and the phone switches itself off even when it hasn't been used. I have also discovered that all calls are going straight to voicemail and that there is no record of incoming calls to the phone. According to the Sale of Goods and Supply of Services Act 1980, goods should be of merchantable quality and fit for the purpose intended. This is clearly not the case with my new phone.

I would therefore like a replacement phone or a refund.

Yours faithfully,
Shannon Meehan

Who can help you if you have a consumer complaint?

First, you should approach the shop or service company and give them an opportunity to fix the problem by providing you with a refund, replacement or repair. If there is no satisfactory resolution, you can take your complaint to a consumer agency.

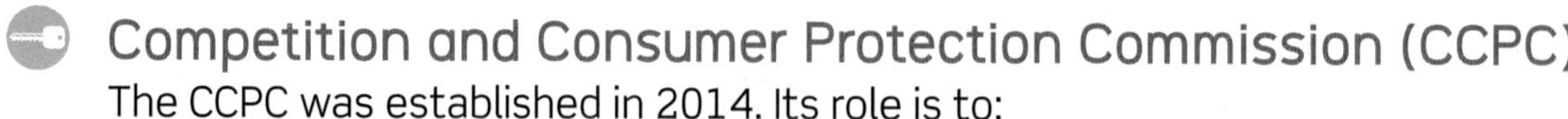

Competition and Consumer Protection Commission (CCPC)

The CCPC was established in 2014. Its role is to:

- Provide information and education to consumers about their personal finance and their consumer rights
- Conduct research into consumer matters
- Represent consumers' interests by advising government on possible changes to consumer law
- Enforce consumer protection law in Ireland.

The CCPC's website gives information about the organisation and your rights as a consumer.

Source: Competition and Consumer Protection Commission

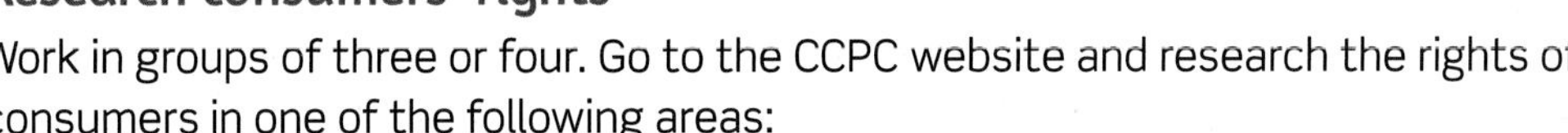

KEY SKILLS WO BC BL MIT

12.14 Research consumers' rights

134

Work in groups of three or four. Go to the CCPC website and research the rights of consumers in one of the following areas:

- Buying goods online
- Buying gift vouchers
- Paying a deposit when buying goods/services
- Mobile phone services and contracts
- Cancelled flights.

In your group, create a presentation/poster/infographic on the rights of consumers in the area you researched and then make a presentation about these rights to the rest of the class. Use the template in your Student Activity Book to complete a peer/self-assessment on this. #Presentation #GroupWork #Research

Consumers' Association of Ireland (CAI)

The **CAI** is an independent organisation, founded in 1966, that represents Irish consumers and seeks to protect their rights. Its website contains information on your rights as a consumer and answers to common consumer questions.

KEY SKILLS WO MIT BC C BL MM

12.15 Consumer rights in practice

Work in groups. The questions below need to be researched, so first decide how you will do this – will you all look up the same questions or will you divide the questions between you? Record your research findings. #Research #GroupWork

(a) Find answers to the following questions:

(i) What is a deposit?

(ii) Can you get your deposit back if you change your mind about buying the good?

(iii) Does a shopkeeper have to give you a receipt?

(iv) Why would you need a till receipt?

(v) What information will you find on a receipt?

(vi) If you lose your receipt and want to return a good to the shop, how might you prove you actually bought the item there?

(vii) If you buy something and then change your mind about wanting it, can you insist on a refund?

(viii) In what circumstances can you insist on a refund?

(ix) What is a credit note and when might you be given one?

(x) What are your consumer rights if you buy goods online from a business within the EU?

(xi) What are your rights if you buy goods online from an individual, e.g. on eBay?

(xii) What are your rights if you buy goods online from a business outside the EU?

(xiii) What taxes might you have to pay if you buy goods from a business outside the EU?

(b) What sources of information did you use? What made you confident that these were reliable sources? #Research #Evaluate

(c) When you have found answers to the questions, prepare a presentation or make a poster, infographic or booklet to give to the rest of the class to explain consumer concerns. You will need to decide between you how you are going to do this and make a plan for who for going to do what. #GroupWork #Presentation #Strategise

Office of the Ombudsman

The Office of the Ombudsman is responsible for investigating complaints from people who feel they have been unfairly treated by a public body, such as:

- Government departments
- Local authorities
- The Health Service Executive (HSE)
- Publicly funded third-level institutions
- Private and public nursing homes.

The ombudsman is independent, impartial and provides a free service. Before making a complaint to the ombudsman, you must first complain to the relevant public body. If your complaint is not resolved to your satisfaction, you can then complain to the ombudsman. The ombudsman website contains information on how to make a complaint, information videos and sample cases.

The word **ombudsman** is a Swedish word that means a representative or someone appointed to act for another person. The first ombudsman was appointed in Sweden in the early nineteenth century to investigate complaints about the king's ministers.

Ireland's first ombudsman was appointed in 1984.

Small Claims Procedure

The **Small Claims Procedure** is a quick, cheap and easy way to resolve a complaint about a faulty good or poor work by a service provider without having to hire a solicitor. If you have a complaint of this nature, you should first complain to the retailer or service provider yourself. If you cannot resolve the issue with them, you can go through the Small Claims Procedure. You can use the Small Claims Procedure if your claim is for €2,000 or less. The application fee is €25, which you send along with your application form.

You can complain online at the Courts Service website or by completing an application form and returning it to your local district court.

The Small Claims Registrar will inform the business about your claim. The business has 15 days to reply. If they do not reply, the claim will be undisputed, which means that the district court will direct the business to pay you the amount claimed.

European Consumer Centre (ECC) Ireland

The **ECC** in Ireland supports consumers who have a problem with a supplier of goods or services in another EU member state. ECC Ireland provides a free information advice service and assistance to consumers on their rights in the EU. Part of an EU-wide network of consumer centres, it can help to resolve consumer disputes that arise in other member states of the EU. It does this by trying to solve the dispute directly with the provider of goods or services and, if this fails, it will refer the case to another dispute resolution body that will try to solve the dispute.

ECC Ireland also researches issues of consumer interest to raise awareness of emerging trends among consumers.

Commission for Regulation of Utilities (CRU)

The CRU's mission is to protect the public interest in water, energy and energy safety. The CRU protects consumers by resolving complaints about energy companies that supply electricity, gas and water (including Airtricity, Bord Gáis, Energia, Electric Ireland and Flogas).

Common types of complaint include:

- Delays in getting connected
- Faulty meters
- Connection costs.

Consumers must first make the complaint to the relevant company themselves, either by phone or in writing. If the complaint is not resolved, the consumer can complain to CRU by email, letter or phone. The CRU website contains helpful information about the role of the CRU.

Commission for Communications Regulation (ComReg)

ComReg protects consumers of communications businesses such as:

- An Post
- Home phone providers
- Mobile phone providers
- Broadband providers.

Consumers must initially make a complaint to their provider. If this complaint fails, ComReg will contact the provider and seek an official response. Its website provides advice for consumers on how to make a complaint to their provider.

Consumer protection in the media

Newspapers and radio and TV programmes provide information and advice to consumers about their rights. Many newspapers and radio and TV shows have 'consumers affairs' features that offer up-to-date information on issues facing consumers.

KEY SKILLS

12.16 Consumer reporting

(a) In your group, research consumer protection in both local and national media (newspapers, radio and TV). Create a poster or presentation listing the different programmes/newspaper columns and the days when they are published/aired. #Research #GroupWork

(b) Summarise a particular case that you find interesting. Create a display in your classroom showcasing your research. #Create

KEY SKILLS

12.17 A valid complaint?

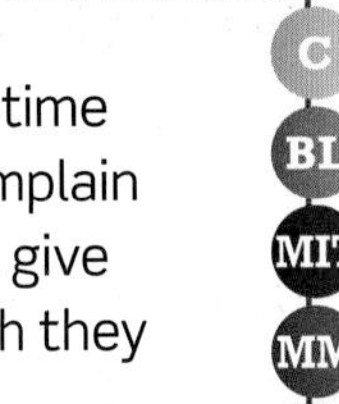

At the end of the exams, five friends went out for a meal. They had a great time and they all enjoyed the meal. After the first course, Graham said, 'If we complain about a couple of the meals not being cooked through properly, they might give us dessert for free.' Joshua was horrified, since everyone had said how much they enjoyed the food. #GroupWork

What would you say to Graham? Do you all agree with this reaction? Write down your conclusions, discussing the impact on:

- The whole dining group
- The waiting staff
- The kitchen staff
- Future visitors to the restaurant
- The restaurant business
- Other diners who may have overheard. #Discussion

Weblinks PowerPoint Summary

PERSONAL FINANCE

CHAPTER 13

THE IMPACT OF CONSUMER CHOICES

LEARNING OUTCOMES IN FOCUS

1.9 Debate the ethical and sustainability issues that arise from their consumption of goods and services and evaluate how they can contribute to sustainable development through consumer behaviour

Links to 1.1, 1.7, 1.8, 1.10, 2.5, 3.1, 3.5, 3.6, 3.7

LEARNING INTENTIONS FOR THIS CHAPTER

When you have completed this chapter you will be able to:

- Appreciate the role of the consumer in the marketplace and the wider economy
- Examine the impact of consumer behaviour on others – locally, nationally and globally
- Explore the ways in which consumer choices can influence the provision of goods and services, and how consumer power can change the lives of other people
- Explain what it means to be an ethical consumer
- Outline the concept of sustainability
- Debate the ethical and sustainability issues that arise from your consumption of goods and services
- Evaluate how you can contribute to sustainable development.

CHAPTER 13 KEY TERMS

boycott	ethical goods	renewable resources
carbon footprint	ethics	sustainability
consumerism	fair trade movement	sustainable consumption
corporate social responsibility (CSR)	green consumer	sustainable development
creative reuse	non-renewable resources	sweatshop
ethical consumer	quota	triple bottom line

CHAPTER 13 KEY SKILLS

- BC Being Creative
- BL Being Literate
- BN Being Numerate
- C Communicating
- MIT Managing Information and Thinking
- MM Managing Myself
- WO Working with Others

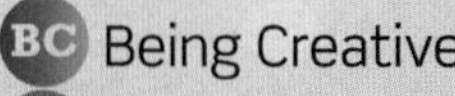

'Climate change is destroying our path to sustainability. Ours is a world of looming challenges and increasingly limited resources. Sustainable development offers the best chance to adjust our course.'

Ban Ki-moon, former Secretary-General of the United Nations

Some BIG questions!

Have you ever thought about the type of consumer you are?

- Are you an informed consumer, a responsible consumer, an ethical consumer or perhaps even a 'green' consumer? Do you understand what each of these involves?
- What factors influence your decision to buy a product? Is it the price, the quality, how well it works? Or do you simply choose products that are new or popular with your friends?
- Do you ever consider what goes into making the product? Do you know what materials and resources are used to produce it?
- Are you concerned about whether the materials or the finished product are recyclable?
- Do you ever consider where the product comes from or the many people who are involved in making and delivering that product to you? Do you think about how your consumer choices and actions can impact on their lives?
- What do you do with products when they no longer meet your needs? Do you make them available for reuse? Do you recycle them? Or do you simply throw them away and replace them with new ones?

These are all big questions, but many consumers give them very little thought. Our lives are busy, so when we go shopping we expect the shops to have the goods and services we need. We simply want to buy those items and just get on with enjoying them.

When we have finished with them, we want to be able to replace them with the latest version. We tend to focus on getting all the things we need and want, but we don't always consider the immediate and long-term impacts of our buying habits on our planet.

KEY SKILLS

MIT C

13.1 Consumer types

(a) What is your understanding of the different types of consumer mentioned in the first bullet point above? List some key characteristics or concerns of each type of consumer. #List

(b) Reflect on your answers to the 'Some BIG questions' section above. Would you change any aspects of your current consumer behaviour? Share your ideas with the person sitting next to you. #ThinkPairShare #Reflect

KEY TERM

Consumerism is a desire to buy increasing amounts of goods and services. It assumes that owning more goods is a sign of wealth and success.

People opposed to consumerism argue that ownership of goods is not a true measure of success and does not guarantee happiness. They're also concerned that our focus on consumption is having a negative impact on our planet. A lot of valuable and limited

resources are used to produce goods and often the end result is a lot of waste and pollution as consumers dump products in order to buy something new.

Throughout this chapter, we will discuss issues on both sides of this argument and you will be asked to consider your own consumer choices and the impact of these choices on the lives of others.

13.2 What sort of consumer are you?

MM MIT

Give an example from your own experience for each of the following and record your answers. #Record #Identify #Reflect

(a) Buying something with no thought to its social impact (e.g. buying an item because it was very cheap, even though it may have been made abroad by people in poor working conditions)

(b) Buying something having thought about its social impact, such as refusing to buy an item that is likely to have been made by people earning very little money

(c) Buying something with no thought to its environmental impact, such as a new phone when your old one was perfectly all right but you wanted a newer model

(d) Buying something with thought to its environmental impact, such as refusing to buy an item that has a lot of unnecessary packaging

In this chapter, you will think about the consumer choices you make so that as well as being an informed consumer, you will also be a more responsible, more ethical and more sustainable consumer.

In order for this to happen, you will need to consider the impact that your consumer choices can have at a local, national and even at an international level. You should also understand that consumers have the power to create demand for goods and services. They have the power to influence the types of goods and services supplied as well as the way in which they are produced.

Resources

All goods and services require the use of different types of resources. These may be:

- Natural resources – oil, gas, coal, water, agricultural land, etc.
- Human resources – workers.
- Capital resources – buildings, vehicles, machinery, equipment, etc.
- Financial resources – money.

In Strand 3 you will study economics, examining how these resources give rise to our four basic factors of production: land, labour, capital and enterprise. Many of these resources are limited, which often forces us to make choices about how we distribute and use them.

See Chapter 1 for resources

See Chapter 31 for scarcity and choice

The goods and services you consume will have an impact on the use of these resources and your spending habits can have consequences for a large number of people in many parts of the world.

In much the same way that a small stone thrown into a pond can create a ripple effect across the water, the individual buying decisions that you make can have a knock-on effect on the lives of others.

KEY SKILLS

13.3 Considering produce options

Think about buying a package of tomatoes in the local supermarket that were grown in the Netherlands rather than buying Irish tomatoes loose from the greengrocer. Discuss how this small decision might affect other people as well as the environment and record your conclusions. #Discussion

WO MIT C BL

Ireland ranked worst in EU for performance on climate action

IN THE NEWS

The Climate Change Performance Index (CCPI) 2019 concludes existing climate mitigation efforts in reducing carbon emissions 'will not enable Ireland to achieve either its EU 2020 or 2030 targets'. The report examines a total of 56 developed countries plus the EU average, and ranks them across a number of criteria. Reacting to the latest rankings, An Taisce's Climate Change Committee spokesman John Gibbons said it was 'another deeply embarrassing blow to Ireland's reputation as a good faith actor in terms of doing its fair share in tackling the global climate crisis'. Ireland is the top producer of plastic waste in Europe, generating an average of 61 kg per person every year – almost double what the UK produces. We produce the equivalent of nearly 2,000 water bottles, or 5,550 disposable coffee cups, per person annually.

Source: Irish Times, 10 December 2018

Non-renewable resources

Non-renewable resources are limited in supply or cannot be replaced. Examples include fossil fuels such as coal, oil and natural gas. Since we are using them up at a much faster rate than they can be replaced, they will eventually run out. While we cannot be certain about exact dates and quantities, many experts suggest that at current rates of usage, petroleum may only last a few more decades and coal is likely to be used up in less than 150 years.

13.4 What does the future hold?

According to the World Coal Association, there are an estimated 1.1 trillion tonnes of proven coal reserves worldwide. This means that at current rates of production, there is enough coal to last us around 150 years. Oil and gas reserves are equivalent to around 50 and 52 years, respectively, at current production levels.

These timelines are quite short. If the figures are correct, oil and gas are likely to be used up in your lifetime and coal in the lifetime of your children. How does this make you feel? Are you happy to hand this type of future to the next generation?

#Reflect #Consider

MIT

KEY SKILLS

13.5 Here today, gone tomorrow?

Do you think it's acceptable to use the world's resources as we want and then rely on scientists and inventors to find replacement fuels if they run out? Discuss this in your group. #GroupWork #Discussion

Renewable resources

Renewable resources are not limited in supply, won't run out and can be regrown, reused or recycled. Examples include wind, sunlight and trees.

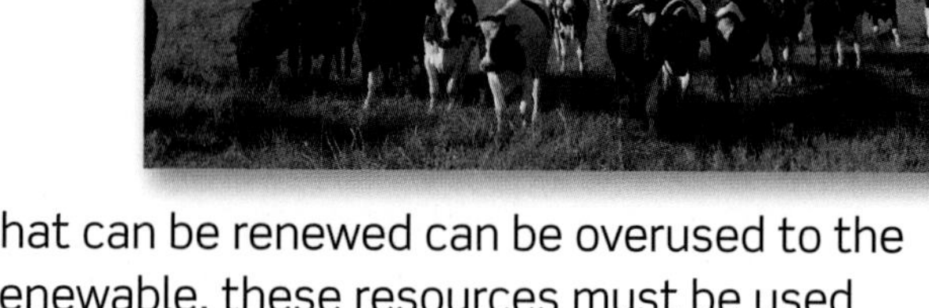

Sustainable consumption

There is a danger that even resources that can be renewed can be overused to the point of extinction. In order to be truly renewable, these resources must be used sustainably.

KEY TERM

Sustainability means using resources in a way that meets current needs but also preserves the resources for future generations.

KEY TERM

Sustainable development meets the needs of the present without undermining the ability of future generations to meet their needs.

IN THE NEWS

EU nations living far beyond the Earth's means – report

If everybody in the world lived like the average EU citizen, we would need 2.8 planets to meet our needs, according to a new report by the World Wide Fund for Nature (WWF) and the Global Footprint Network.

The report says the EU uses up almost 20% of the Earth's bio-capacity although it comprises only 7% of the world population.

It adds that none of the EU's member states has implemented sustainable consumption policies.

The WWF report says the EU's smallest and richest country, Luxembourg, was also the one that used up renewable resources the fastest. Just 46 days into the year, on 16 February, it had consumed its full share of the Earth's resources, it said.

The report says Ireland had used its annual share of nature's resources by 27 April.

'If everybody in the world had the same ecological footprint as an average EU resident – emitting as much carbon, consuming as much food, timber and fibres, and occupying as much built-up space – 10 May would be the date by which humanity would have used as much from nature than our planet can renew in a whole year,' the report said.

'For the rest of the year, humanity would have to live off depleting the natural capital of the Earth,' it said.

Source: RTÉ News, 9 May 2019

KEY SKILLS

13.6 How does this make you feel?

(a) What do you think about Ireland's use of global resources? #Opinion

(b) How do you feel about the need to cut back? #Reflect

(c) Can you suggest some practical steps that you and your family could take to cut back on your use of global resources? #Suggest #Plan

'We do not inherit the earth from our ancestors, we borrow it from our children.'

Native American proverb

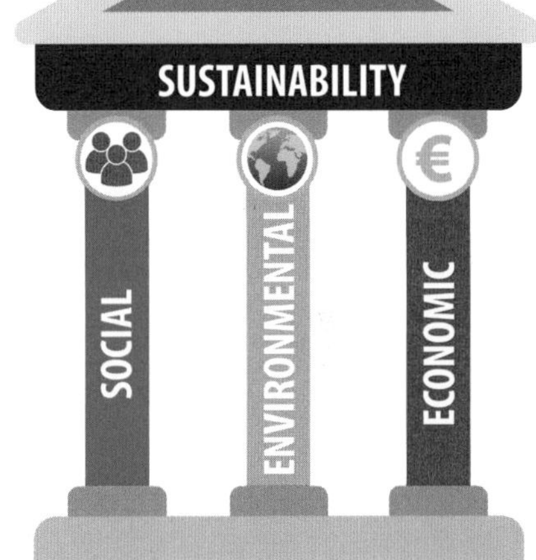

There are three core pillars of sustainability:

- Social – people
- Environmental – planet
- Economic – profit.

Sustainability involves carefully managing a resource in order to give it time to renew itself. For example, the fishing industry issues licences and also sets limits (called **quotas**) on the amount of fish that can be caught each year. These measures help to protect fish stocks and allow each species time to regenerate. While it would be possible to create more short-term wealth and employment by removing these restrictions, the long-term effect would be the extinction of many species of fish.

For that reason, unregulated fishing is not sustainable. This example also illustrates that there is often a conflict or trade-off between wealth creation (economic growth) and sustainability. Sustainable economic growth will be discussed further in Chapter 38.

See Chapter 38 for sustainable economic growth

KEY SKILLS

13.7 Regulated resources

(a) Can you think of other resources whose use is limited or controlled in order to preserve them and ensure we consume them sustainably? #Identify #List

(b) Are there other resources that you think might be added to this list in the future, especially as our population grows and demand for resources increases? #List

Since the choices we make as consumers can affect the lives of so many others, it is important for us to think about our buying habits and to make an effort to become sustainable consumers. **Sustainable consumption** means buying goods and services that do not harm society, the environment or the economy in the long term.

In order to better understand the impact of consumer behaviour on both the economy and the environment, let's look at the life cycle of a product.

KEY SKILLS

BC MIT WO MM BL C

13.8 Case study: Bananas

In groups, research one of the options below and prepare a presentation for the rest of the class. #Research #GroupWork #Presentation

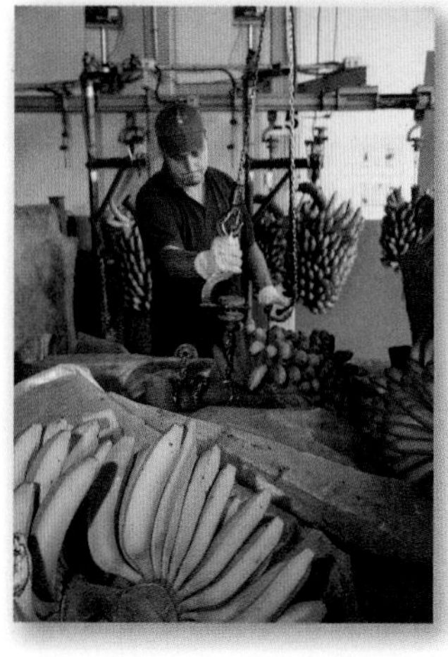

Group 1: Research how bananas get from large-scale plantations to Ireland's supermarket shelves. Make sure you provide information on how bananas are grown; how they are prepared for shipping; how they are transported to our supermarkets; and how they are stored before reaching the shelves.

Group 2: Research how fair trade bananas are grown, prepared for shipping and transported to our supermarkets. Make sure you note the benefits and drawbacks, if any, of fair trade bananas over conventionally grown bananas.

Group 3: Research how organic bananas are grown, prepared for shipping and transported to our supermarkets. Make sure you note the benefits of organically grown bananas over non-organically grown bananas.

KEY SKILLS

MIT C

13.9 Banana case study conclusions

When you have seen each group's presentation, discuss the following as a class and record your conclusions. #Discussion

(a) How do you feel about buying bananas now?

(b) Has this activity changed how you feel about wasting food?

(c) What are the reasons why people don't buy fair trade or organically grown bananas?

(d) Do you think the workers on large-scale plantations receive a fair wage for the work they do? How might wages differ depending on where the bananas are grown?

(e) How is eating an Irish-grown apple more beneficial for a sustainable economy than eating a banana grown thousands of kilometres away?

DID YOU KNOW...

The growth and development of fair trade

What is Fairtrade? © Fairtrade 2015

The **fair trade movement** began shortly after the Second World War and developed rapidly during the 1960s. Fair trade means that farmers and workers in developing countries are paid a fair price for their products, e.g. coffee, bananas or cocoa. It means they have decent working conditions and fair terms of trade. The idea continued to grow and resulted in the creation of Fairtrade International in 1997 and the creation of the international Fairtrade Mark in 2002. The umbrella organisation sets the Fairtrade Standards, supports producers and co-ordinates Fairtrade worldwide. In 2018 the number of Fairtrade producer countries reached 73, while more than 50,000 Fairtrade products were on sale in 158 countries across the world. In that same year global retail sales of Fairtrade products reached €9.8 billion.

The ethical consumer

KEY TERM

Ethical consumers only buy products that are produced in a fair and honest way. They avoid products that are known to harm or exploit other people or the natural environment.

Ethics and moral values refer to a person's ability to judge right from wrong. Ethical consumers choose goods and services that meet their needs and also reflect their sense of fairness, honesty and justice.

Ethical consumers are concerned about the following major issues:

- **Impacts on the environment:** Pollution, climate change, depletion of resources, habitat, generation and consumption of energy.
- **Impacts on people:** Exploitation of workers, child labour, human rights, unfair trading practices, irresponsible marketing.
- **Impacts on animals:** Animal testing, animal cruelty, factory farming.
- **Sustainability:** Meeting our current needs without undermining the ability of future generations to meet theirs. This is about making sure that resources are managed carefully and are not destroyed.

13.10 Ethical consumption in practice

Read the case study below and record your answers to the questions that follow. Discuss and debate the issues with your classmates. #Discussion

Case study

Your sister has asked that you buy her a particular branded item of clothing for Christmas. The brand is very stylish and popular at the moment, so you can understand why your sister has asked for it.

However, you are aware that the company that makes the clothing has recently been in the news because of its unethical trading practices. It has been accused of mistreating workers and employing child labour in some factories. In recent weeks, another division of the company has also been linked to the severe chemical pollution of a river in Asia and this has had a negative impact on local wildlife and citizens.

You have already made a personal decision that you would not buy or wear this brand of clothing yourself, and although you might be able to justify this purchase as a gift for your sister, you are not happy that your money would go to support this company.

(a) What do you see as the main ethical issues here?

(b) What would you do? Explain your choice. #Reflect #Ethics

The first step in becoming an ethical consumer is to become an **informed consumer**, as this will allow you to understand the issues involved and will help you to make choices that take into account your needs, your values and your financial circumstances.

Sometimes our financial resources may create a conflict between our ethical values and our need to get value for money. Lack of money may force us to make choices about our consumption. For example, a person with very little income may have to choose cheaper products in order to meet their needs. These products may be cheaper because they are replicas of branded goods or because the workers who made them have been underpaid. Likewise, many people who consume meat products may value and support the humane treatment of animals, but when it comes to buying goods, limited cash may mean that they are not willing or able to pay a little extra for free-range options.

This suggests that it is not always easy to act in an ethical way, but we should try to make the best choices possible with the resources and information available to us.

KEY SKILLS

WO MIT C

13.11 What are ethics worth to you?

In pairs, discuss whether you would be prepared to have fewer treats so that you could spend extra on something a little more expensive that you know has been ethically produced. For example, would you prefer to buy three cheap T-shirts from a shop known to source their clothes from countries with poor worker conditions, or one T-shirt from a shop that is certified as buying from companies that look after their workers? #Discussion #ThinkPairShare

Despite differences in values and purchasing power, there are a number of key elements that define ethical goods and ethical consumers.

Ethical goods are produced in a way that is kind to the environment and also to the people who produce them. This means the goods have been manufactured and distributed in a manner that minimises harm or damage to people and the environment.

Ethical consumers buy products and services that have been produced under ethical conditions.

- They make careful, considered and deliberate choices about the goods and services they buy.
- They take responsibility for their buying decisions.
- They avoid products and services that have a negative impact on society, on animals or on the environment.

Since many goods are produced by multinational companies that operate in several parts of the world, ethical consumers also try to ensure that workers are treated fairly and have safe working conditions regardless of where they work. It is only fair that all workers should be treated with dignity and respect and should receive a fair reward for their efforts.

In the past, campaigns against several well-known multinational companies, including Nike, Gap, Adidas, Primark and Marks & Spencer, have highlighted the exploitation of resources and workers used in producing goods. In some cases consumers were called upon to boycott these companies and their products.

'Consumers are increasingly interested in the world behind the product they buy. Life cycle thinking implies that everyone in the whole chain of a product's life cycle, from cradle to grave, has a responsibility and a role to play.'

Klaus Toepfer, former Executive Director, UNEP (United Nations Environment Programme)

Source: United Nations Division for Sustainable Development Goals

KEY TERM

A **boycott** is a voluntary act of protest in which consumers refuse to buy from or deal with a particular company.

DID YOU KNOW...

The word **boycott** entered the English language during the Land War in Ireland in the late nineteenth century (in about 1880). It comes from the name of a land agent, Charles Boycott, who worked for an absentee English landlord in Co. Mayo. Following a poor harvest, Boycott refused to lower rents for his tenants and even tried to evict some of them. In protest at his actions, local people shunned him. He was unable to buy or sell anything and even the postman refused to deliver his mail! He was unable to hire workers to harvest his crops. The 'boycott' was widely reported in the newspapers of the time and the word has been used ever since to describe this type of protest action.

KEY SKILLS

13.12 Boycott movements

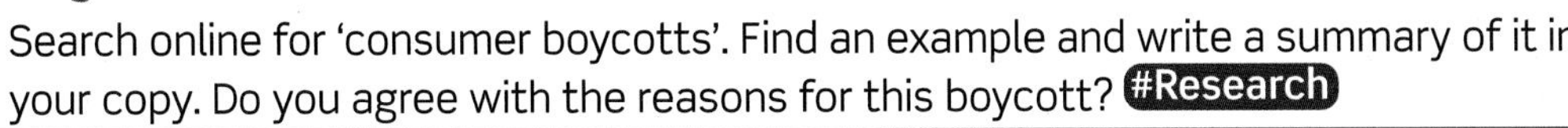

Search online for 'consumer boycotts'. Find an example and write a summary of it in your copy. Do you agree with the reasons for this boycott? #Research

IN THE NEWS

Fast fashion is hard to escape, but it is damaging our environment

Clothing is an example of an industry that does not always come up in conversations about sustainability, possibly because the vast majority of clothing purchased in Ireland is made elsewhere. This gives the clothing industry a feel that the products come from nowhere and only rarely, as in the case of the 2013 Rana Plaza factory building collapse in Bangladesh, which claimed 1,134 lives and left over 2,000 injured, is the real cost of fashion revealed to us.

The fast fashion industry is polluting, wasteful and growing yearly. The water footprint of cotton is enormous and has contributed to severe water shortages in many parts of the world. A single cotton shirt requires around the same amount of water as one person would drink in two and a half years. Polyester is a common synthetic material created from fossil fuels. In 2015, polyester production was responsible for carbon emissions equivalent to 185 coal-fired power plants running for a whole year, according to the World Resources Institute.

The people who make the clothes are often treated horrifically, possibly working in unsafe buildings, paid low wages and having virtually no workers' rights.

One might think that as each of us comes to own more clothing we end up buying less, but in fact, the amount of clothing purchased per person has increased by 60% in the last 20 years while the amount of times we wear an item has reduced by almost half, according to one study.

Source: TheJournal.ie, October 2019

The impact of ethical consumerism

The impact of ethical consumerism can be witnessed in all the following areas.

Increased emphasis on CSR

As a result of the growth of ethical consumerism, companies are more aware of the need to behave in a socially responsible manner. Many now invest a lot of resources, including money, in improving their **corporate social responsibility** (CSR).

See Chapter 38 for sustainable economic development

KEY TERM

Corporate social responsibility (CSR) is the duty of businesses to act in the best interests of all those who are affected by their activities (stakeholders), not just their owners (shareholders). Examples include paying employees a fair wage, preventing workplace bullying and operating in a way that is environmentally sustainable.

Businesses have come to realise the value of CSR to society and to the business itself, particularly in terms of consumer goodwill and positive public relations.

An organisation may develop a code of ethics in order to guide staff when making decisions or carrying out actions on behalf of the organisation. It tries to make sure that employees act in a way that is legal, decent, honest and fair. Examples of ethical responsibilities include:

- Making sure that employees are treated well and are paid a fair wage for their work
- Providing customers with high-quality products for a reasonable price
- Not engaging in false or misleading advertising
- Honouring contracts with suppliers and paying them on time
- Avoiding or minimising pollution of the natural environment.

Triple bottom line

Ethical and sustainable businesses look at the wider impact of their operations and decisions. They consider not only the profitability of their actions, but also the impact on society and the environment. This is known as the **triple bottom line**.

- A business that constantly loses money is unsustainable and will eventually close down, so they need a profit (the **financial** bottom line).
- Socially sustainable businesses must not destroy or undermine the communities that support them or that they seek to serve (the **social** bottom line).
- Business growth must not undermine or destroy the resources on which all life and development ultimately depend (the **environmental** bottom line).

This is very similar to the focus on profit, people and planet discussed on page 155.

Increased focus on 'green' consumerism

Green consumers force producers to take into account the impact of consumption on the environment, for example a reduction in the amount of harmful chemicals used in the manufacture of aerosols and fridges, the increased development and demand for 'green' energy and 'green' cars, etc.

Increased awareness of our carbon footprint

Your **carbon footprint** – also called an ecological footprint – is an approximate measure of all the greenhouse gases emitted either directly by you or on your behalf.

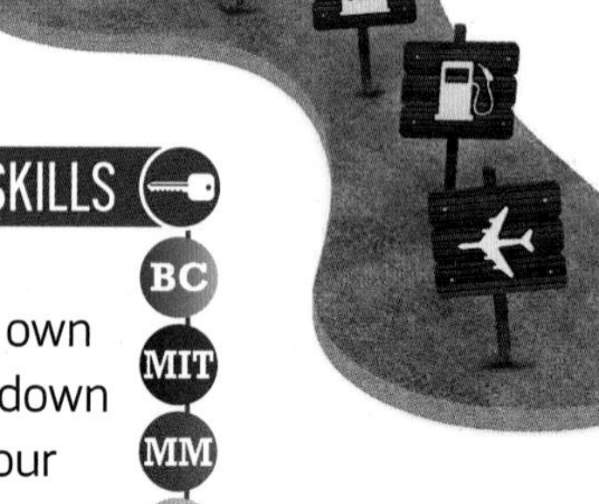

KEY SKILLS

13.13 Calculate your carbon footprint

BC MIT MM C BN

(a) Use an online carbon footprint calculator to calculate your own personal carbon footprint or that of your household. Write down your answers and create a poster showing the results of your research. #Research #Calculate

(b) Identify three changes you could make in your life in order to reduce your carbon footprint in a sustainable way. #Identify

Fair labour-certified garments

Brands that have this certification try to improve the pay and conditions of workers and tackle the global sweatshops where vulnerable employees are exploited.

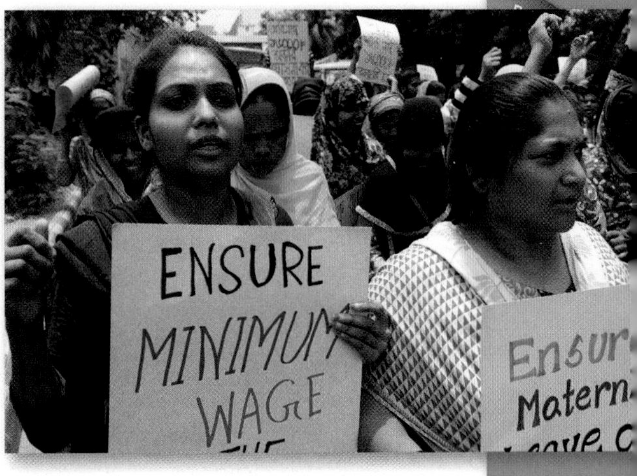

KEY TERM

A **sweatshop** is a factory or workplace where workers are employed at very low wages for long hours and under poor conditions. They are most often found in the clothing industry.

The promotion of animal welfare

Concerns in this area include how animals are used in scientific research, as a source of food or kept in zoos, farms and circuses, etc. Some businesses and brands, including The Body Shop, Faith in Nature and Weleda, were set up to make a clear commitment not to sell cosmetics that have been tested on animals.

Campaigners also highlight the ways in which human activities affect the welfare and survival of wild species. This includes the destruction of natural habitats.

Enterprise in action

The Body Shop

Anita Roddick started The Body Shop in March 1976. The mission statement of The Body Shop makes a commitment 'to dedicate the business to the pursuit of social and environmental change'. Its stores and products are used to help communicate human rights and environmental issues.

KEY SKILLS

13.14 Case study: Is The Body Shop living up to its founding vision?

Carry out some research into Anita Roddick and her vision for an ethical business. Research the current ownership and operation of The Body Shop and evaluate whether the business continues to live up to the values of its founder.

#Research #Evaluate

MIT BL

Sustainable resources and technologies

There is an increased demand for products made using sustainable resources and technologies. Examples include products made from recycled materials or replanted forests.

Reduce, reuse, recycle

The Reduce, Reuse, Recycle campaign has been very successful in reducing waste.

Enterprise in action

ReCreate

ReCreate is a social enterprise that collects clean, end-of-line materials from businesses and redistributes them to its members. The concept is known as **creative reuse**, which encourages the public to reuse materials that would normally be thrown away in all kinds of inventive ways.

Members pay an annual subscription fee and have unlimited access to the materials stored in ReCreate's Warehouse of Wonders. Businesses have their materials collected for free and have the opportunity to avail of a strong CSR programme. This encourages reuse on an industrial scale, which is ReCreate's main aim.

Additional income streams include art workshops, project funding, event management, a complementary shop and team-building programmes. ReCreate's vision is to continue to be an innovative, dynamic social enterprise inspiring curiosity, creativity and care for the environment.

ReCreate aims to:

- Provide accessible and affordable art materials and educational supplies to all
- Divert materials from landfill and raise environmental awareness around reuse (150 tonnes a year)
- Facilitate social inclusion, particularly in areas of disadvantage
- Provide quality work experience opportunities for those most distant from the labour market, including those with special needs.

ReCreate has learned that by just seeing materials on the shelves in its Warehouse of Wonders, members begin thinking about how they can reuse them. The items' original uses are being reinvented and creatively reused in every way possible, from children's art, school murals, sensory projects and festival installations all the way up to community gardens. The diverse range of materials and alternative/creative opportunities for reusing them really has no limits and ReCreate is making this possible for the whole community.

Source: ReCreate

United Nations Sustainable Development Goals

These are global objectives that target hunger, poverty, education and environmental sustainability.

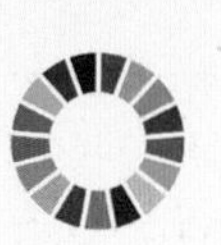

Source: United Nations Development Programme

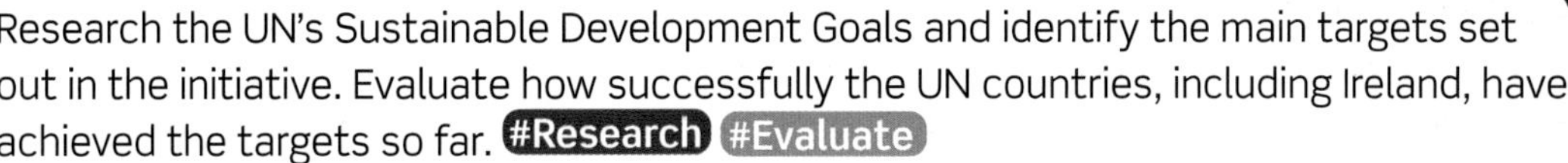

13.15 Which countries have hit the targets?

Research the UN's Sustainable Development Goals and identify the main targets set out in the initiative. Evaluate how successfully the UN countries, including Ireland, have achieved the targets so far. #Research #Evaluate

What can you do?

> 'Every time you spend money you're casting a vote for the kind of world you want to live in.'
> Anna Lappé, author and educator on sustainable food

❶ Engage in life cycle thinking

Consider the environmental and economic impacts of a product over its entire life cycle. This challenges us to be more mindful of the consumer choices we make. It requires us to take responsibility for the impact that our choices have on others. Issues we should think about include:

- Energy usage
- Working conditions
- Waste production
- Pollution effects
- Destruction of endangered ecosystems.

For example, if you realised that it takes 24 trees to create 50,000 sheets of office paper and 2.3 cubic metres of landfill space to dispose of it, you might choose paper made from recycled material or sourced from sustainably managed forests. Recycled paper creates 75% less air pollution and 35% less water pollution over its life cycle. Better still, only use paper when you really need to.

❷ Ask questions

Questions you might want to ask are:

- Where is the product made?
- What is it made of?
- How much energy does it consume?
- How are the workers who made it treated?

13.16 Evaluate ethical businesses

Research four organisations that certify ethical products (e.g. that do not use animal testing or that promote sustainable farming). Create a poster showing the logos and names of these organisations and what their purpose is. #Research

BC

❸ Support sustainable businesses

As demand for sustainable goods increases, producers will be more willing to supply them and prices are likely to fall. Consumers have the power to change things as businesses respond to consumer pressure.

❹ Reduce, reuse and recycle

Choose goods that are durable and will last a long time. It isn't always necessary to have the latest and most up-to-date products.

❺ Consider end-of-life disposal

Before disposing of products that no longer meet your needs, consider the environmental benefits of reuse and recycling. Where this is not possible, be sure to dispose of them in an environmentally responsible manner.

❻ Shop local where possible

Buying locally produced goods and services helps to reduce some of the environmental damage caused by **food miles** as goods are shipped from around the globe. It also helps to sustain Irish jobs and improves the local economy. The Foodmiles website can be used to calculate food miles on products you consume.

Enterprise in action

Shop local

Buying from locally owned businesses keeps money circulating closer to where you spend. Local shops use local services, accountants, insurance brokers and suppliers as well as employing local people, and they also carry a higher percentage of locally produced goods. Every €10 spent locally on Irish products generates €24 of benefit to the local community. Forty-five cents of every euro spent is reinvested locally in comparison to only 15 cents for the foreign multiples.

Source: Mark Fielding, Chief Executive of the Irish Small and Medium Enterprises Association (ISME)

KEY SKILLS

13.17 How does local spending benefit the local economy?

What are your thoughts on the claim that 'every €10 spent locally on Irish products generates €24 to benefit the local community'? How is this possible? Share your thoughts with the person next to you. #Discussion

Older Irish consumers 'care less about the ethics of businesses'

IN THE NEWS

New study suggests younger buyers are more likely to demand higher ethical standards

New research suggests that as Irish people age, they become less likely to want to do good through their shopping habits. Research published today suggests that older people are less likely to care about the ethics of the companies with whom they do business than those who reached adulthood in the 21st century.

The analysis, part of Accenture's 14th annual Global Consumer Pulse Research, which surveyed 30,000 people worldwide, including 420 in Ireland, suggests that most consumers here prefer to buy goods and services from companies that reflect their personal values and beliefs and are happy to ditch those that do not. It states that 59 per cent of Irish consumers want companies to take a stand on social, cultural, environmental and political issues, with younger consumers more likely to demand higher ethical standards.

Source: Irish Times, 17 December 2018

KEY SKILLS

13.18 Who should be leading the movement?

Read the newspaper article above. Do you think it is up to retailers or consumers to lead ethical consumerism? Record your thoughts in your copy. #Identify #Record

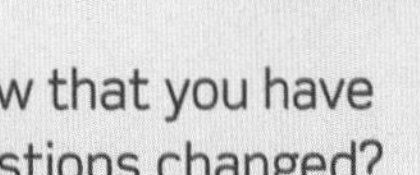

13.19 Rethinking the big questions

Reread the 'Some BIG questions' section on pages 151–152. Now that you have completed this chapter, have any of your answers to those questions changed? If so, how have they changed? Write down how your views have changed based on your new knowledge and understanding. Be specific about how your consumer behaviour will change as a result of your new knowledge and insight.

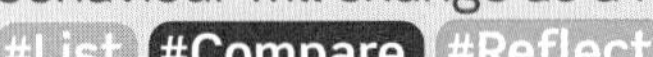

BL

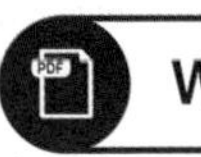

Weblinks

PowerPoint Summary

CHAPTER 14

THE BIGGER PICTURE: AN INTRODUCTION TO GLOBALISATION

LEARNING OUTCOMES IN FOCUS

1.10 Discuss and evaluate how globalisation and developments in technology impact on consumer choice and behaviour

Links to 1.2, 1.7, 1.8, 1.9, 2.6, 2.7, 3.1, 3.7, 3.8

LEARNING INTENTIONS FOR THIS CHAPTER

When you have completed this chapter you will be able to:

- Explain the term 'globalisation'
- Outline the reasons why companies engage in globalisation and foreign trade
- Explain what a transnational company is and the reasons why they locate in particular countries
- Explain the reasons why technology has increased globalisation
- Identify the impact of global companies and technology on consumer choice and behaviour.

CHAPTER 14 KEY TERMS

consumerism
delivery systems
economies of scale
electronic commerce (e-commerce)
foreign direct investment (FDI)
globalisation
inward investment
repatriation of profits
transnational company (TNC)

CHAPTER 14 KEY SKILLS

BC Being Creative
BL Being Literate
C Communicating
MIT Managing Information and Thinking
WO Working with Others

The world is becoming a smaller place

KEY SKILLS MIT

14.1 Is it a small world after all?

Some people say that the world is a smaller place than it used to be. What do you think they mean by this? Write down two reasons why you agree or disagree with this point of view. #List #Opinion #Reflect

What is globalisation?

KEY TERM

Globalisation is the process by which the world becomes interconnected as a result of increased trade and cultural exchange.

In effect the world becomes one big marketplace. Many big businesses have become transnational corporations (TNCs) with operations in many countries.

KEY TERM

A **transnational (or multinational) company** is one that carries out its business in many other countries as well as its own.

Globalisation has resulted in:

- Increased international trade.
- Greater dependence on the global economy. TNCs produce huge quantities of goods and rely on selling them to customers all over the world.
- Freer movement of capital, goods and services. Fewer barriers to trade means that goods, services and money can be moved around the globe more quickly and easily.
- Companies such as McDonald's and Starbucks trading throughout the world and treating it as a global market.

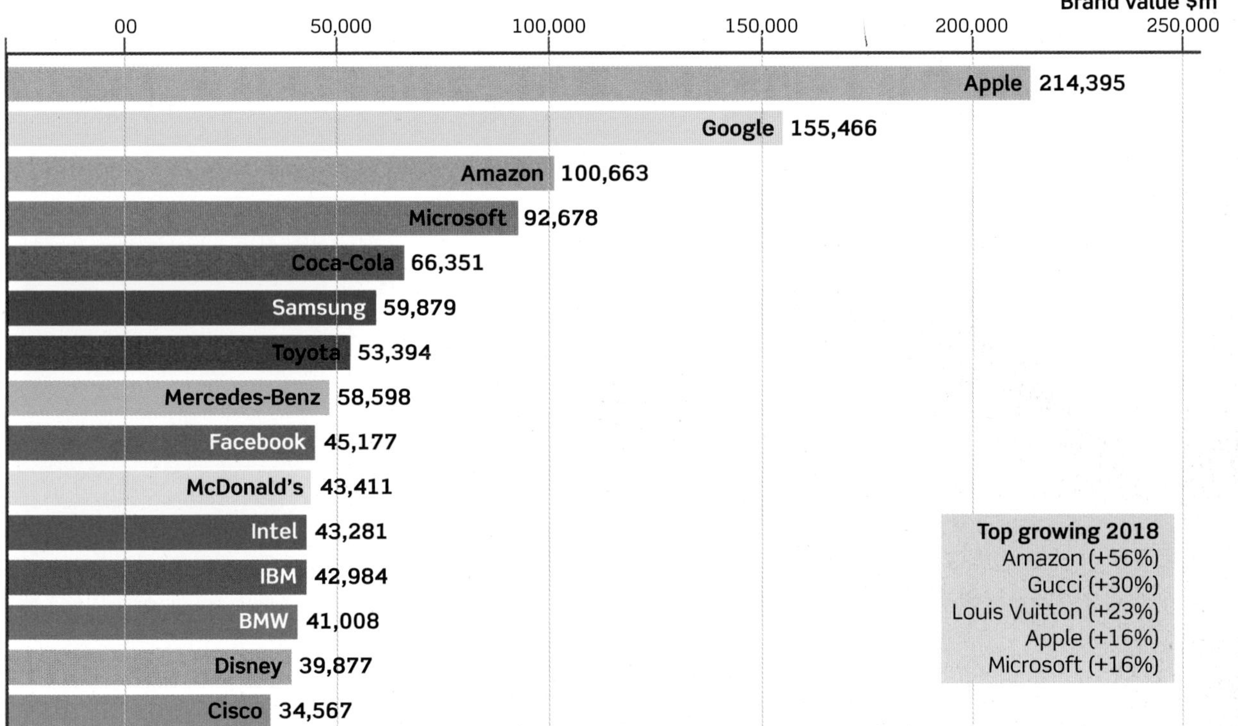

Figure 14.1 Top global brands in 2018 (*Source:* Interbrand)

Development of globalisation

Countries around the world have been trading internationally for hundreds of years. In the last 200 years this trade has expanded for a number of reasons:

- In the nineteenth century the Industrial Revolution made it possible to mass produce goods cheaply. Rapid population growth worldwide led to increased demand for these goods.
- The construction of the Suez and Panama canals made it quicker and easier to transport goods around the world by sea.
- The invention of the telephone made it easier and quicker for businesses to communicate internationally.
- The invention of aeroplanes allowed for faster transportation of goods and people internationally.
- Increased use of electricity meant that goods could be produced much faster.
- Barriers to international trade were reduced by international agreements that were made following the Second World War.
- Widespread use of television created global awareness of, and demand for, many products.
- The invention of modern technologies such as the computer, the internet and email have made it quicker and easier than ever before to communicate, advertise and sell globally.

KEY SKILLS

14.2 Globalisation factors

Which of the developments listed above had the greatest influence on globalisation, in your view? Give reasons for your answer and share these with your partner. Find out if another pair agrees with you. #ThinkPairShare #Collaborate

MIT BL C

A bigger percentage/proportion of national wealth is earned from overseas trade

More capital (money) is being moved between countries

Increased foreign direct investment

Increasing number of global brands, including from emerging countries

More global manufacturing, with (component) parts coming from many countries

Global supply chains and new trade routes, with raw materials coming from overseas

Increased levels of migrant workers, both within and between countries

Greater connectivity of people and businesses through mobile and Wi-Fi networks

Figure 14.2 A selection of key aspects of globalisation

Reasons for globalisation

The following factors have also helped the globalisation process.

- **Consumer demands:** A desire for more goods and services, known as consumerism, has been a major driving force behind the growth and development of globalisation. As income levels increase, consumers demand greater choice and are able to afford more goods and services from overseas markets.
- **Improvements in technology:** The internet and mobile technology have enabled greater communication between people in different countries and allowed businesses to trade internationally very easily. These changes in technology help consumers to satisfy their demand for more goods and services.
- **Economies of scale:** The cost per item reduces when operating on a large scale. The more widely you distribute the item, the more you are likely to sell; and the more you make, the cheaper the product becomes to produce. Global businesses produce on a vast scale and enjoy very low unit costs of production. This gives them a price advantage over smaller businesses.
- **Freedom of trade:** Organisations such as the World Trade Organization (WTO) and the EU encourage free trade between countries, which helps to remove restrictive barriers to trade between countries.
- **Labour availability and skills:** Countries such as India and China have lower labour costs and high skill levels among their workers. Manufacturing companies in particular will take advantage of this cheap supply of labour.
- **Transport improvements:** Goods and people can travel quickly between countries. The cost of transporting goods between countries has decreased, e.g. by using larger cargo ships or aircraft with longer ranges.

See Chapter 39 for international trade

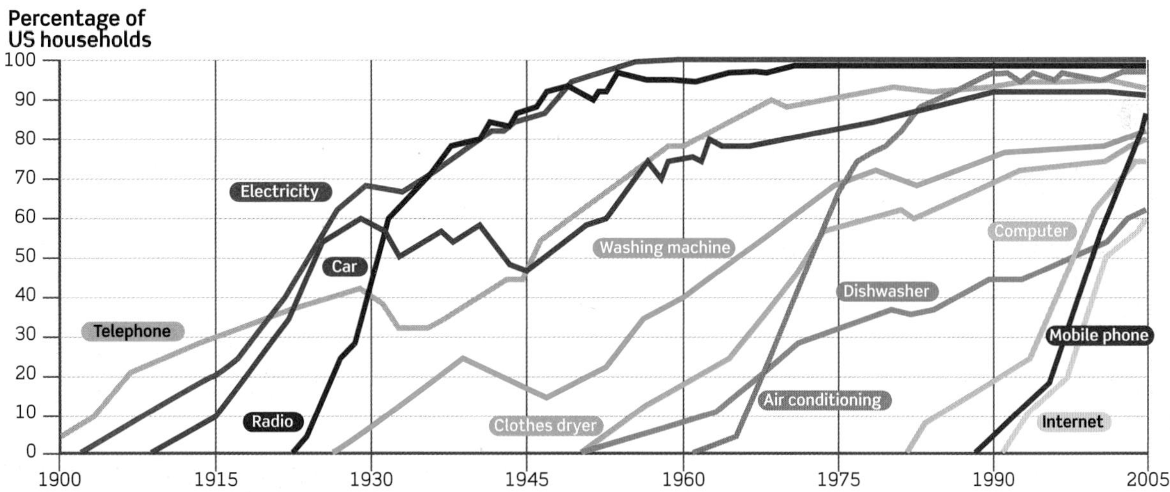

Figure 14.3 Speed of uptake of new household technologies in the USA

KEY SKILLS

14.3 Exploring the World Trade Organization

Research the following information about the World Trade Organization and record the answers:

(a) Where is the WTO based?

(b) When was the WTO established?

(c) How many member countries does the WTO have?

(d) When did Ireland become a member of the WTO?

(e) Who is Ireland's current ambassador to the WTO? #Research

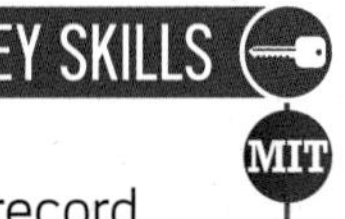

Let's Talk Future of Trade © World Trade Organization, 2019

Delivery systems

KEY TERM

Delivery systems are the ways in which products are transported from the manufacturer to the consumer.

Improvements in transportation and delivery systems have made it easier for businesses to sell globally. Commonly used delivery systems are road, rail, sea and air. The table below looks at the advantages and disadvantages of each.

Delivery system	Advantages	Disadvantages
Road	› Door-to-door deliveries are possible › Minimum handling of goods	› Roadworks/traffic congestion can cause delays › Environmentally damaging emissions › Not suitable for very bulky goods
Rail	› Suitable for bulky goods	› Fixed timetable/not flexible › Not every town has a railway station
Sea	› Suitable for transporting bulky goods worldwide › Cheaper than transporting by air	› Slow › Weather conditions can cause delays › Must link with another form of transport
Air	› Fast › Suitable for perishable goods	› Expensive › Must link with another form of transport

KEY SKILLS WO BC

14.4 Drones of the future

Drones are another method of delivery. Do you think drones will become a common way of delivering goods? In small groups, research delivery by drones and prepare a presentation, video or podcast to explain it to the rest of the class. #GroupWork

Transnational companies

Globalisation has resulted in many businesses setting up or buying operations in other countries. When a foreign company invests in a country, perhaps by building a factory or a shop, this is called **inward investment**, or **foreign direct investment (FDI)**. Ireland has been very successful at attracting FDI.

When companies have their head office in one country and operate in several different countries they are known as **transnational companies (TNCs)**. The US fast food chain McDonald's is a large TNC – it has over 36,000 restaurants in 120 countries.

Factors attracting TNCs to a particular country include:

- Cheap raw materials
- Good transport links
- Cheap and plentiful labour supply
- Attractive government policies, e.g. low corporation tax
- Access to markets where goods are sold – Ireland's membership of the EU provides access to European markets for all businesses located here.

See Chapter 40 for the European Union

KEY SKILLS

14.5 Ireland's business appeal

(a) Write out the economic attractiveness factors listed above. On a scale of 1 to 10, rate Ireland for each factor based on how attractive *you* consider this country to be to TNCs. #Rate

(b) When you have completed your rating, carry out some research into Ireland's attractiveness as a business location for inward investment. #Research

(c) In light of your research findings, reassess your original ratings and write a short note to explain why your opinion has changed or remains the same. If you have discovered any other factors that help to attract TNC investment to Ireland, add them to the list in your copy. #Compare

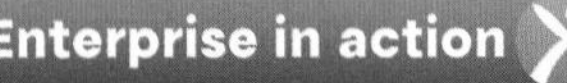

Microsoft, the world's biggest software company, established an Irish manufacturing facility in 1985 and employed 100 people. It now employs over 1,200 full-time staff and 700 contract staff in Sandyford, Dublin.

Microsoft Ireland is a subsidiary of the US software giant Microsoft, which sells, distributes and markets software globally from Dublin.

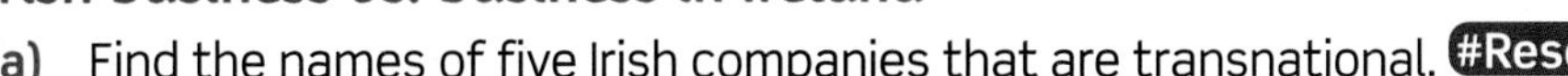

14.6 Irish business vs. business in Ireland

(a) Find the names of five Irish companies that are transnational. #Research

(b) Find the names of five foreign-owned companies that have their headquarters or are major employers in Ireland. #Research

Impacts of globalisation

Globalisation is having a huge effect, both good and bad, on the world economy and on people's lives.

Positive impacts

- **Employment:** TNCs help countries by providing new jobs and skills for local people.
- **Spin-off effects:** TNCs bring wealth and foreign currency to local economies when they buy local resources, products and services, and in doing so they support local businesses. This extra investment results in more tax being paid to the government, which can be spent on education, health and infrastructure.
- **Greater choice:** Consumers have access to a greater choice of goods and services than might be available in their local economy.
- **Lower prices:** TNCs benefit from lower production costs due to economies of scale. This might benefit consumers in the form of lower prices for goods and services.
- **New experiences:** Sharing ideas, experiences and lifestyles of different cultures. People can buy foods and other products that were not previously available.

Negative impacts

- **Benefits the rich more than the poor:** Globalisation operates mostly in the interests of the richest countries, which dominate world trade at the expense of poorer ones.
- **Local communities:** There is no guarantee that the wealth from inward investment will benefit local people where the company operates. Often profits are sent back to the home country of the TNC. This is called **repatriation of profits**.

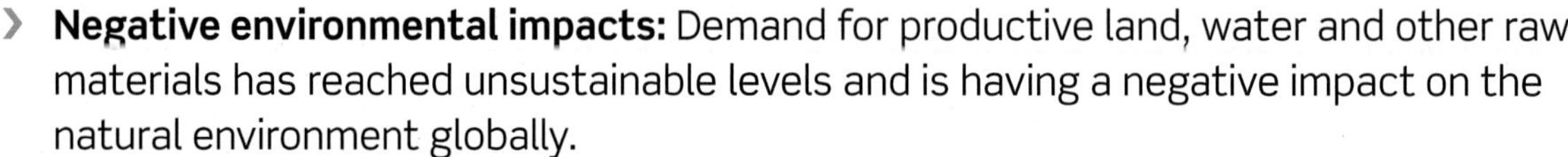

- **Negative environmental impacts:** Demand for productive land, water and other raw materials has reached unsustainable levels and is having a negative impact on the natural environment globally.
- **Crowding out:** Due to economies of scale, TNCs may drive small local companies out of business, resulting in higher unemployment and making the local economy heavily dependent on FDI.
- **Dominant global brands:** Globalisation might limit competition and global markets may be dominated by businesses with dominant brands and superior technologies.

KEY SKILLS

14.7 Ireland and overseas companies

Discuss whether you think it is good that Ireland attracts big companies from overseas to open branches here. Are there any negative consequences? Give reasons for your answers.

#Discussion #Opinion

BL MIT C WO

See Chapter 13 for the impact of consumer choices

Globalisation means that we can buy and sell goods abroad. This has advantages, but it can also mean that we are adding a lot of air miles to goods.

For example, if we buy tomatoes from abroad, a lot of transport costs are involved and the carbon footprint is larger than if we bought Irish tomatoes. It also means that we are not giving the Irish growers our business. If we export live animals abroad instead of their meat, they might be uncomfortable on trucks for many hours. If we create a demand for products made with palm oil, rainforests are possibly being destroyed to fulfil this demand.

KEY SKILLS WO

14.8 How much value do you place on yourself as a consumer?

How important is it to you that your ability to act as a global consumer does not conflict with your responsibilities as an ethical consumer? Do you think we give enough thought to this consequence of globalisation or do you think there is an 'out of sight, out of mind' mentality when it comes to buying goods? Record your thoughts. #Discussion #Reflect

The impact of developments in digital technologies

Improvements in digital technologies have increased globalisation by increasing trade and investment. Email, the internet, mobile phones and faster phone lines that quickly carry large amounts of information are now considered normal. The internet is a fast and convenient way for businesses all over the globe to communicate with each other, advertise and sell online.

This means that a company can have its headquarters in one country and branches in other countries. For example, Google's headquarters are in California, but it has more than 70 offices in over 40 countries, including Ireland.

Impact of technology on consumer choice and behaviour

Technology is a big part of our everyday lives. We use computers and mobile technology for school, work and social communication. Our behaviour as consumers is changing as a result of technology. For example, we can shop globally by using the internet to search for and buy goods from overseas retailers.

KEY SKILLS

14.9 Technology in your household

How do you and your family use technology to buy goods and services? List items you have purchased using technology. #List

Electronic commerce

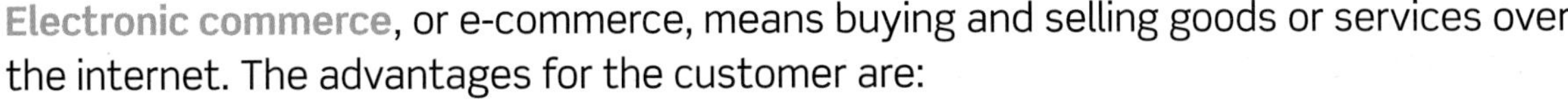

Electronic commerce, or e-commerce, means buying and selling goods or services over the internet. The advantages for the customer are:

- **Convenience:** Consumers can find what they are looking for without leaving their own home.
- **Choice:** Consumers are no longer limited to what shops they buy from and they can buy from abroad. Improvements in global transportation mean that goods can be shipped from anywhere in the world in a matter of days. Amazon is an example of a global business that has developed to meet this change in consumer shopping habits.

- **Product details:** There is likely to be greater information available online compared to what a member of staff might be able to provide in store. Consumers are becoming more informed as they can research products online before they buy and they can shop around for the best value for money.
- **Customer reviews:** There are many websites that customers can use to find out what other people think about a product or service and so make an informed decision when buying.

The disadvantages for the customer of buying online are:

- **No human interaction:** Some people prefer to deal with people when buying products or services.
- **Returning goods:** It can be inconvenient and expensive to return products that have been purchased online.
- **Fraud:** A website may take your money but have no intention of delivering the products.

See Chapter 12 for distance selling and consumer rights

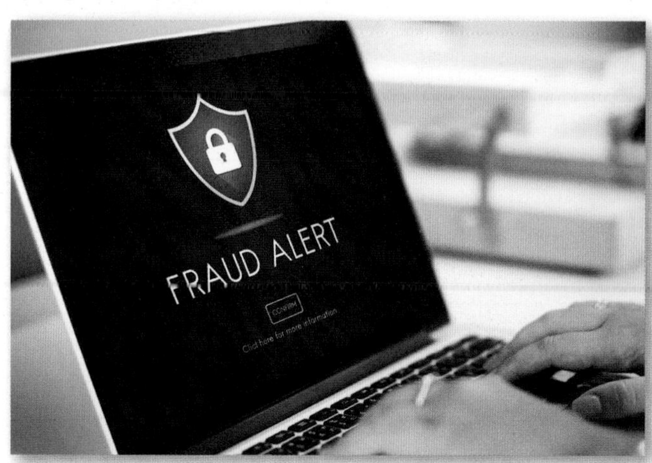

KEY SKILLS

MIT

14.10 When buying locally involves sacrifices

We are encouraged to 'shop local' and 'buy Irish', but sometimes shopping online and buying something from abroad is cheaper and more convenient. Do you think it is better to shop local, even if it costs a little more? Discuss this and write down the reasons for your answer. #Reflect #Opinion #Discussion

Weblinks

PowerPoint Summary

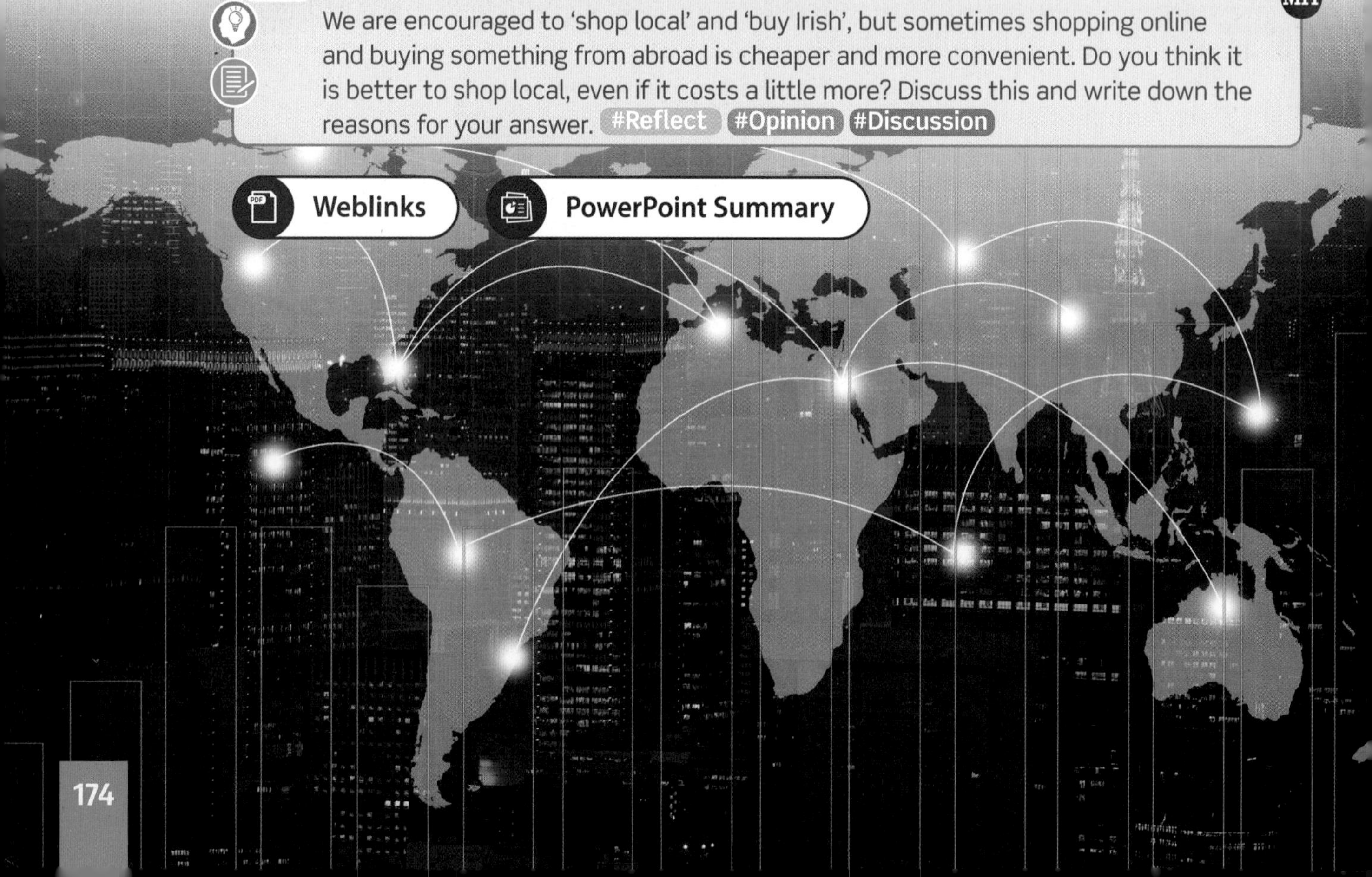

STRAND

ENTERPRISE

ENTERPRISE

THE SKILLS, CHARACTERISTICS AND ROLE OF THE ENTREPRENEUR

LEARNING OUTCOMES IN FOCUS

2.2 Describe the skills and characteristics of being enterprising and appreciate the role of an entrepreneur in an organisation, in society and to the economy

Links to 2.1, 2.3, 2.4, 2.9, 3.1, 3.2, 3.6

LEARNING INTENTIONS FOR THIS CHAPTER

When you have completed this chapter you will be able to:

- Define the term 'enterprise'
- Identify and illustrate enterprise in personal life, school, government and business
- Outline the characteristics and skills of entrepreneurs
- Profile an entrepreneur
- Appreciate the rewards and risks of being an entrepreneur
- Describe different categories of enterprise: financial, cultural and social
- Identify the reasons for starting a business
- Evaluate the role of an entrepreneur in an organisation
- Appreciate the role played by entrepreneurs in society and the economy
- Outline how entrepreneurs get ideas for businesses
- Identify and explain internal and external sources of new product or service ideas
- Explain the stages in the new product or service development process.

CHAPTER 15 KEY TERMS

brainstorming	intrapreneur
decisive	market research
enterprise	proactive
entrepreneur	prototype
feasibility study	realistic risk-taker
flexible	social entrepreneur
import substitution	test marketing
innovative	

CHAPTER 15 KEY SKILLS

- BC Being Creative
- BL Being Literate
- BN Being Numerate
- C Communicating
- MIT Managing Information and Thinking
- MM Managing Myself
- SW Staying Well
- WO Working with Others

What is enterprise?

KEY TERM

Enterprise is any attempt to start or do something new. Enterprise is about turning ideas into actions, using creativity and a willingness to try new things.

Enterprise is all around us!

Enterprise is not just about business. Enterprise can happen in many different areas of people's personal, working and social lives.

Enterprise in the home/personal life:

- Learning a new skill, such as playing a musical instrument or taking a part-time course to study computing or languages
- Carrying out some DIY to decorate or improve your house
- Starting to prepare household budgets to ensure you have enough money to pay your bills
- Selling unwanted household items, such as furniture, baby accessories and old games consoles, to make some extra cash.

Enterprise in school:

- Starting a student enterprise or mini company
- Students or teachers setting up a club/society
- Organising a school event or trip
- Introducing new subjects or a course like the Leaving Certificate Vocational Programme (LCVP) into the school.

Enterprise in the community:

- Local people setting up a sports club, youth club or scout troop
- A community establishing a Neighbourhood Watch scheme or Tidy Towns committee
- A group of people starting a Meals on Wheels service for the elderly.

Enterprise in the public service:

- In 2019 the government introduced the National Broadband Plan to supply broadband services to all parts of Ireland.
- Coillte was set up by the government to develop Irish forests.
- The Revenue Commissioners launched an online facility (ROS) to allow people to manage their tax affairs online.
- Local Enterprise Offices (LEOs) were set up to help Irish people set up their own businesses and create jobs in their local area. LEOs also run the Student Enterprise Programme to promote enterprise in Irish schools.

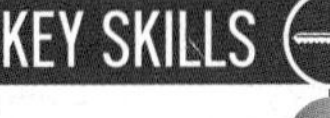

15.1 Being enterprising

In small groups, brainstorm ideas showing how you could be enterprising in your home, school and in your local community. To brainstorm, call out ideas as you think of them. Pick one person to write all the ideas down and they will hopefully spark new thoughts for the list. #GroupWork #Discussion

Enterprise in business

See Chapter 16 for types of enterprise

See Chapter 17 for impact of organisations

Business enterprise is a specific type of enterprise that provides a range of goods and services to consumers. Entrepreneurs start business enterprises.

KEY TERM

An **entrepreneur** is a person who takes the initiative as well as the personal and financial risk involved in setting up an organisation.

Business entrepreneurs will try to make a profit as a reward for their efforts. **Social entrepreneurs** use their enterprising skills to develop organisations that benefit the wider community. They are less concerned about making a profit than business entrepreneurs.

Mary Ann O'Brien is a business entrepreneur who set up Lily O'Brien's, one of Ireland's best-known chocolate brands.

Iseult Ward and Aoibheann O'Brien are the social entrepreneurs behind FoodCloud, an app that connects businesses with surplus food to local charities who need it. They have won several awards, including the Impact Award from Social Enterprise Ireland (2014), Newstalk's Women Mean Business Social Entrepreneurs of the Year (2016) and Businesswoman of the Year (2017).

Entrepreneurs are people who put a business idea into practice. They show initiative by making decisions and taking a chance to set up a business. Enterprise is about turning an idea into action.

Here are some examples of people who have identified business ideas and acted to turn them into a real business, making a profit in the process.

Enterprise in action

Smooth Remove

Smooth Remove, a product designed by a group of students from Boherbue Comprehensive School in Cork, won first prize at the 2019 national final of the Student Enterprise Programme. Primarily aimed at farmers, it helps people who find it painful or difficult to bend when removing footwear. It also helps to cut down on dirt from muddy boots.

Enterprise in action

Stripe

Have you ever bought anything online? Limerick brothers Patrick and John Collison, who started computer programming as teenagers, developed a web and mobile payments company called Stripe, which makes it easier for businesses to accept and manage payments. Now based in San Francisco, their business is valued at $20 billion and is fast becoming the main payments platform for online businesses. Stripe has a presence in 20 countries worldwide and has linked up with social media firms Twitter, Facebook and Pinterest to help create new 'buy now' buttons. Stripe also has an operation in Dublin with over 100 employees.

KEY SKILLS

15.2 Entrepreneurs

(a) Name three other entrepreneurs and the businesses they are associated with. You can choose local, national or international examples. #Research

(b) Look back at a few issues of your local county or city newspaper (probably most easily done online). Find an article about an entrepreneur and write about the person and the business they started. You might need to do a little more research online to get all the information you need about the person. #Research

(c) Local papers are a great way of finding out about entrepreneurs. Throughout this strand, keep a scrapbook or folder (physical or online) of articles about local entrepreneurs. In each case, summarise the article, highlighting the entrepreneurs' reasons for starting a business, the type of businesses they start and what support they receive. #Identify #Record

Characteristics and skills of entrepreneurs

While no two entrepreneurs are exactly alike, they often share many of the following characteristics and skills, which are commonly associated with entrepreneurial success.

Characteristics of entrepreneurs

A characteristic is a personality trait that you are born with. Entrepreneurs often possess many of the following enterprising characteristics that set them apart from other people.

Realistic risk-takers

Entrepreneurs are willing to risk their money (and time) to set up a business with no guarantee of success. Successful entrepreneurs are **realistic risk-takers**, which means they research carefully, weigh up the risks involved and take a chance only if they see a reasonable chance of success.

KEY SKILLS

15.3 Taking risks

What do you think are the main risks facing entrepreneurs? Suggest how some of these risks might be reduced. Write down your answers. #Record #Opinion #Reflect

Innovative

Being **innovative** means being able to do something in a new or different way. Entrepreneurs are good at coming up with new ideas or new ways of doing things. For example, Steve Jobs invented the iPhone, which was launched in 2007, the first smartphone of its kind.

KEY SKILLS

15.4 Innovation investigation

Carry out some research to find out what mobile phones were popular around 2007. Investigate why the iPhone was so innovative compared to other phones that were available at that time. #Research #Analyse

Proactive

Entrepreneurs are **proactive**, which means that they are prepared to make things happen, rather than waiting for someone else to act. Acting and taking a risk to turn ideas into reality is a key difference between entrepreneurs and inventors. Inventors are 'ideas' people, whereas entrepreneurs are 'action' people. Entrepreneurs take the lead in getting involved in new areas of business ahead of other people.

Flexible

Entrepreneurs accept change as natural. They learn from their mistakes and failures by adapting when things don't go according to plan.

Self-confident

Entrepreneurs believe in themselves and in their business idea. They believe they have what it takes to be successful and that they can cope with any setbacks.

Decisive

Entrepreneurs have the ability to make timely decisions and take responsibility for the decisions they make.

Determined/resilient

Entrepreneurs do not give up easily when faced with obstacles and failures. They are good at tackling problems, they stick with a task until it is completed and they can cope with setbacks.

DID YOU KNOW...

Thomas Edison, the inventor of the lightbulb, famously stated: 'I have not failed. I've just found 10,000 ways that won't work.'

James Dyson developed 5,127 prototype designs before he successfully produced the bagless vacuum cleaner!

James Dyson

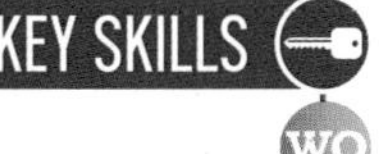

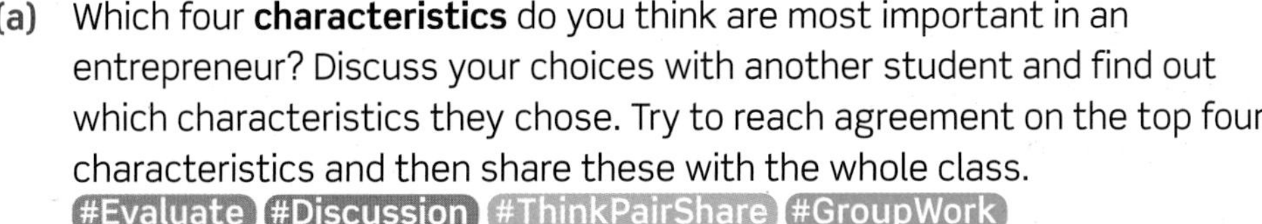

15.5 Characteristics of an entrepreneur

(a) Which four **characteristics** do you think are most important in an entrepreneur? Discuss your choices with another student and find out which characteristics they chose. Try to reach agreement on the top four characteristics and then share these with the whole class. #Evaluate #Discussion #ThinkPairShare #GroupWork

(b) Discuss whether an entrepreneur must have all the characteristics you have been looking at in class. #Discussion

Skills of entrepreneurs

A skill is an ability or expertise that people develop through practice, experience, learning or training. Entrepreneurs possess many of the following enterprising skills.

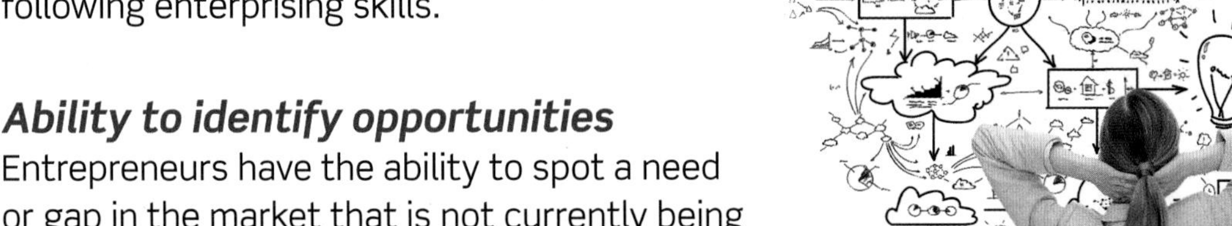

Ability to identify opportunities

Entrepreneurs have the ability to spot a need or gap in the market that is not currently being met and seize the opportunity by listening carefully to customers' needs and being aware of future business opportunities.

Planning and goal setting

Entrepreneurs learn to set strategic goals for themselves and their business using plans to achieve these goals. They also write a business plan when establishing their new/start-up business.

Time management

Entrepreneurs use their time carefully to achieve their goals. They make the best use of their time by prioritising daily tasks.

Ability to manage money

Entrepreneurs need to have good financial skills in order to prepare budgets and manage cash flow.

Human relations skills

Entrepreneurs use good communication and listening skills to get on with people, such as employees, suppliers, investors, customers and state agencies that provide support to entrepreneurs.

Ability to assess and manage risk

Entrepreneurs measure the risks involved in a potential course of action and take steps to minimise these risks. They are unlikely to engage in a new venture if they feel the risk of failure is too great.

KEY SKILLS

BC BL C

15.6 The nature of the entrepreneur

'Entrepreneurs are born and not made.' Write a short speech arguing for or against this statement. #Presentation #Debate

KEY SKILLS

WO BC MIT

15.7 Skills of an entrepreneur

(a) Which four **skills** do you think are most important in an entrepreneur? Write them down, giving reasons for your choices. Discuss your choices with another student and find out which skills they chose. Share your decisions with another pair of students or with the whole class. #Discussion #GroupWork #Evaluate #ThinkPairShare

(b) Discuss whether an entrepreneur must have all the skills you have been discussing in class. 

KEY SKILLS

BC

15.8 They've got what it takes!

Watch an episode of *The Apprentice* or *Dragons' Den* on TV or online. Assess which enterprising characteristics and skills the team leader/entrepreneur possesses using the template supplied in the Student Activity Book. #Research

Enterprise in action

From property to pastry: Roll It Hand Made All Butter Pastry

Mairéad Finnegan, owner of Roll It Hand Made All Butter Pastry

Mairéad Finnegan, a property surveyor, was looking for all-butter puff pastry and was surprised that she could find none made in Ireland, which has a worldwide reputation for producing quality butter. This was the **gap in the market** that Mairéad was looking for, and as work in the building sector was becoming scarce, she had the idea of establishing her own business producing hand-made all-butter pastry. Helped by a friend with a background in marketing and graphic design, she produced samples of her pastry and packaging and displayed them at a food festival near her home in Kells in 2012. She sold them all within hours. This gave her the confidence to approach her local SuperValu supermarket to ask them to stock her product, which they agreed to do. Mairéad took business courses with Leader and got mentoring and advice from local entrepreneurs through the Co. Meath Local Enterprise Office. She received grants towards equipment, marketing and new packaging. Mairéad found the advice from her mentor invaluable, especially for preparing business and financial planning. She now provides advice to new food start-ups in her local area and believes it's important to develop a strong local network of entrepreneurs.

Mairéad says that hard work, determination, the ability to cope with inevitable setbacks and confidence in herself and her product were crucial characteristics while establishing her business. Since starting Roll It Pastry, she has developed the skills of

time management, juggling production, finances, marketing and deliveries. Mairéad has entered and won a few prestigious food awards. Awards are important, as they help her to expand her network and keep her in touch with what other producers are doing. Running her own business gives Mairéad flexibility, as it allows her to work from home at times that suit her and her family. She gets a tremendous sense of satisfaction from knowing that she started the business from scratch and looks forward to expanding her product range and number of sales outlets.

15.9 Minding the gap

(a) What do think is meant by 'gap in the market'?

(b) What gap in the market did Mairéad take advantage of?

(c) How did Mairéad show initiative?

(d) How was Mairéad innovative?

(e) What characteristics did Mairéad say she needed to make her business work?

(f) What skills did Mairéad get help with **(i)** when she first started and **(ii)** as she grew her business?

(g) What demands on her time does Mairéad have?

(h) What goals has Mairéad set herself? #Identify #Opinion

Should entrepreneurial types become entrepreneurs?

Enterprise and employees

Not everyone with the characteristics and skills of an entrepreneur will want to actually become one. Entrepreneurs may be quite happy working for someone else, in which case their efforts can be used for the benefit of the business. Very often they develop a new product idea or find a better way to do something in order to save time and money for the business. The Sony PlayStation, Post-it notes and Gmail are all examples of products created by intrapreneurs.

An enterprising employee within an existing business is called an **intrapreneur**.

Google allows employees to spend 20% of their working week on a personal project, which has led to many of Google's best projects, including one many people use every day: Gmail, which was developed by Paul Buchheit.

DID YOU KNOW...

Swan Vesta matches saved thousands of pounds when a factory worker suggested putting sandpaper for striking the matches on only one side of each matchbox. The factory worker got his reward and retired a wealthy man!

Could you be an entrepreneur?

15.10 Could you be an entrepreneur?

155 Complete the self-assessment in the Student Activity Book to see how suited you are to being an entrepreneur. #Activity

KEY SKILLS MM

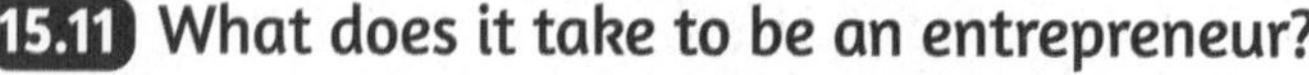

15.11 What does it take to be an entrepreneur?

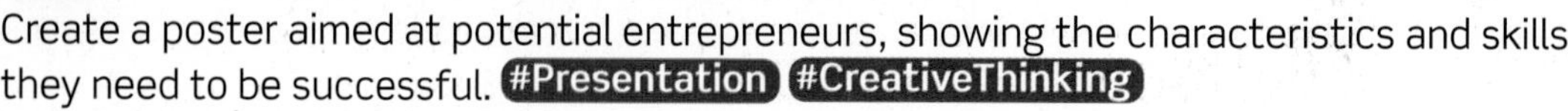

Create a poster aimed at potential entrepreneurs, showing the characteristics and skills they need to be successful. #Presentation #CreativeThinking

KEY SKILLS BC MM

Rewards and risks of self-employment

There are both rewards and risks for an entrepreneur in setting up their own business and becoming self-employed. There are many reasons why people might start up in business for themselves. For example:

- Entrepreneurs want to **be their own boss** and get to make all the key decisions in the business themselves.
- They want to **make the most of a gap in the market**. Many entrepreneurs start this way, such as Mairéad Finnegan.
- They want to **keep all the profits** of a business for themselves.
- Entrepreneurs want to **prove something to themselves** by showing they can start a business.

Entrepreneurs may currently be unemployed. By starting a business, they can **provide employment for themselves** (and possibly others if the business is a success).

They may want to **turn a hobby or interest in something into a business idea**. For example, an interest in rugby could lead someone to provide coaching to a local club or to set up a sports shop.

Rewards of being an entrepreneur

- You are your own boss and get to make all the decisions in the business.
- You can choose to keep all the profit the business makes.
- You can work flexible hours or have flexible opening hours to suit the needs of your customers.
- You have a great sense of satisfaction if the business is a success.

Risks of starting your own business

See Chapter 24 for unlimited liability

- You may lose the money you invested in the business if it fails. In some cases the entrepreneur may lose their own money or personal assets. This is a major risk of starting business as a sole trader.
- You will need to work long hours to get the business up and running and to oversee all aspects of the business.
- You may find it difficult to take time away from running the business.

- Sales may vary each week, so income is not guaranteed.
- You may not have all the necessary skills to set up and run a business.
- Your personal reputation and credit rating may suffer if the business fails.

We have already learned that entrepreneurs see opportunities and take action to generate rewards and value for themselves and others. The value created from their entrepreneurship can be financial, cultural or social.

The role of the entrepreneur in an organisation

An entrepreneur in an organisation:

- **Generates ideas:** Entrepreneurs use innovation and creativity to come up with new ideas or new uses for existing products.
- **Takes risks:** Entrepreneurs take a risk in order to put their ideas into practice and try to develop successful organisations.
- **Provides vision and motivation:** Entrepreneurs generate ideas and set out the organisation's future direction and goals. This vision is important for guiding and motivating all staff.
- **Provides leadership and management:** In start-up organisations, the entrepreneur is usually the manager (chief executive) and will provide leadership for others.
- **Creates long-term plans:** The entrepreneur turns their vision into business plans. These plans will be used to help raise finance for the new organisation and guide its future growth and development.
- **Raises finance:** If the entrepreneur does not have all the money, they need to finance the organisation and will need to attract investment and funding.

The role of the entrepreneur in society and the economy

Entrepreneurs have a big role to play in both community and economic development. Their work and its benefits can be felt at the local, national and sometimes even international level.

Role of entrepreneurs in the economy

- **Make use of resources:** Entrepreneurs use their creative ability to make the best use of resources available in a community or economy.
- **Provide goods and services:** Businesses started by entrepreneurs provide consumers with a range of goods and services.
- **Create jobs and wealth:** By starting new businesses, entrepreneurs help to create direct and indirect employment for themselves and for others.

See Chapter 13 for the impact of consumer choices

See Chapter 31 for scarcity and choice

KEY SKILLS

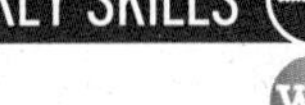

15.12 Direct and indirect employment

Working in pairs, discuss the difference between direct and indirect employment. Try to come up with some examples of each to share with your class.

#ThinkPairShare #GroupWork

- **Provide training and develop skills:** As a result of employment, workers become more skilled and are better able to contribute to their employer and to the wider community.
- **Raise standards of living:** Through their productive use of resources and an increased level of employment, entrepreneurs can help to improve the standard of living in a community or economy.
- **Taxation:** The entrepreneurs and their employees pay taxes to the government and this money can be reinvested into the local or national economy.
- **Foreign trade:** Irish entrepreneurs sell goods and services abroad (exports). In some cases, they also help reduce imports from other countries by producing goods and services in Ireland. All of this creates wealth for the Irish economy.

See Chapter 39 for foreign trade

Role of entrepreneurs in society

As well as the economic benefits outlined above, the work of entrepreneurs has the following positive benefits for society:

- **Provide services:** Organisations started by social entrepreneurs provide a range of services and supports that help many people in the community. Examples include clubs and charities.
- **Develop infrastructure and amenities:** The work of entrepreneurs helps a community to develop the range of facilities available to citizens. These may include improved transport, recreation or childcare facilities.
- **Increased standard of living:** By creating jobs and providing services, entrepreneurs help to improve the standard of living in their communities. In some rural areas, these jobs, services and clubs help to ensure that people can continue to live there.
- **Enterprise culture:** Entrepreneurs help to create a culture of enterprise and self-help in their communities. Their positive example can inspire other entrepreneurs.
- **Sponsorship:** Many entrepreneurs support and sponsor a variety of community-based organisations, including clubs and charities.

See Chapter 16 for social enterprise

Some entrepreneurs help to bring about social change. They use their enterprising skills and characteristics for the benefit of the community rather than for personal gain. We will examine their role and their impact on society in Chapter 16.

Sources of business ideas for entrepreneurs

To start in business, entrepreneurs obviously need a good idea. In some cases, people will first decide to set up a business before thinking about what sort of business they might run. The founders of Innocent Drinks, for example, were three friends who met at university and knew that they wanted to go into business together. They did some brainstorming until they came up with the idea of smoothies. **Brainstorming** is a way of working together as a group to generate ideas.

Other people might set up in business because they have an idea. James Dyson is an inventor who came up with the idea of a bagless vacuum cleaner. He took his idea to existing companies, who rejected it, so he set up his own company.

Entrepreneurs may also notice a **growing trend in the market** that helps them to come up with an opportunity for a new product or service. For example, in recent years the major move towards organically produced foods may create opportunities for selling seeds, growing organic food or producing ready meals from organic food. Other ideas can come from family and friends. For example, an idea could come from hearing a family member complain about not being able to buy a product or service that they need.

Entrepreneurs are very good at spotting a gap between what people want and what is currently available. They identify problems and come up with effective and creative solutions. If they can fill this gap, they have the potential for a successful business.

SW

15.13 Your business ideas

(a) In small groups, brainstorm different business ideas that could result from your hobbies and interests. Think about a business by yourself, and a business that could combine the interests of two or more of your group. Share your ideas with the rest of the class and note any interesting ideas that other groups had. #GroupWork #Discussion

(b) What do you think might be the drawbacks and the benefits of turning a hobby into a business? #Opinion

Pamela Laird: Moxi Loves

Founder of brand Moxi Loves, Pamela Laird is no stranger to the beauty industry. Her mother owned a beauty salon in Dublin and from a young age Pam loved all things beauty related. After school she spent evenings in the salon, staying until it closed. Watching her mum work long hours taught her the importance of hard work. After working in Brown Thomas aged 16 and setting up a nail bar in another department store when she left school, she established her own cosmetics brand, Moxi Loves. Rather than inventing something completely new, she decided to adapt existing products.

Pamela was inspired by trips away where she was unable to pack her normal beauty products due to the liquid restrictions in hand luggage. Her products – dry shampoo sheets, powder pods and cleanser-infused bare-faced pads (that activate when mixed with water) – are travel friendly, convenient and, most importantly, biodegradable.

Two previous products – Eye-catcher (individually wrapped cotton buds that contain eye make-up remover) and Tan Aid (wipes to correct self-tanning mishaps) – were discontinued due to EU laws that will ban single-use plastics and wipes. Although these laws haven't yet taken full effect, Pamela was proactive in moving towards more sustainable materials.

Pamela initially financed her business with a bank loan. She took part in *Dragons' Den* in 2017, but turned down three investors as she received a better offer from her distributor. In 2019 she appeared on *The Apprentice*, finishing in the final five.

Moxi Loves is currently stocked in Penneys, Arnotts and online via Cloud10 Beauty. Future plans include bringing 10 more products to market, expanding her stockists and selling in the UK and USA as well as in Ireland.

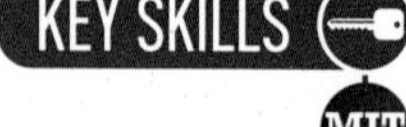

BL

15.14 Risky business

Having read the information about Pamela Laird, write down your answers to the following questions:

(a) Identify two risks that Pamela took when starting her business enterprise. #Identify #List

(b) Apart from risk-taking, describe two other enterprising skills or characteristics that Pamela displays. #Identify

Some entrepreneurs may spot something working well in another country and bring the idea back to their own country.

KEY SKILLS

WO

15.15 Gaps in the Irish market

Have you seen or read about something abroad that isn't yet available in Ireland and therefore could be a good business idea for someone here? #Reflect #GroupWork

Sources of new product ideas for existing businesses

Existing businesses also need new ideas to replace or improve their current products. Business ideas can come from inside the business (internal) or ideas may be generated from outside the business (external).

Internal sources

Sometimes new ideas come about by accident, but businesses usually have to make some effort to create a new product or service idea. These are some of the ways they might go about it:

- **Brainstorming sessions:** This involves people coming together and thinking of new ideas. Some of these ideas are rejected, while others are explored further.
- **Sales personnel:** Feedback from salespeople who are in touch with customers is a valuable source of information about customer needs and wants.
- **Ideas from employees in the business (intrapreneurship):** Employers may encourage employees to think of new ideas by rewarding good ideas with a bonus.

- **The research and development (R&D) department:** Dedicated research and development staff may discover a new product or improve an existing product or service. In 2018, Amazon.com spent $22.6 billion on R&D.

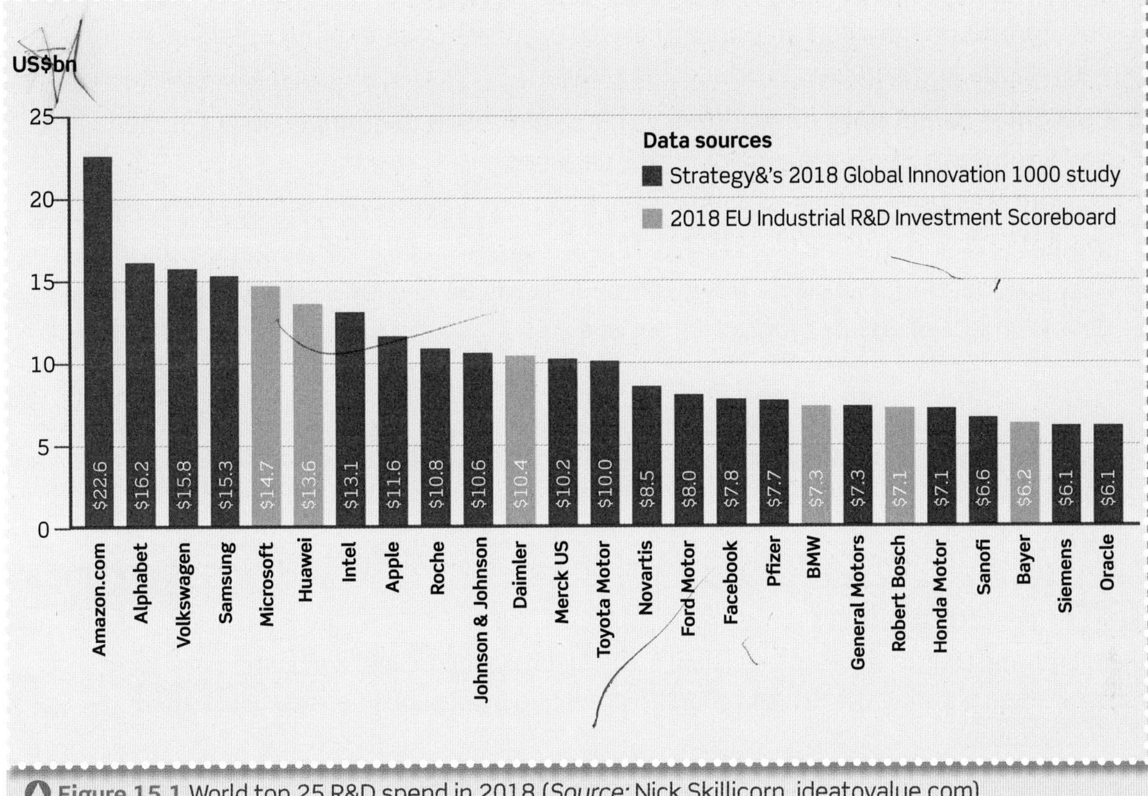

Figure 15.1 World top 25 R&D spend in 2018 (*Source:* Nick Skillicorn, ideatovalue.com)

KEY SKILLS

15.16 Innovation vs. success

(a) In groups of three or four, research what a global business is. For each business listed above, write down the type of business/industry they are involved in. #GroupWork #Research

(b) Indicate which companies in this top 25 list have operations such as headquarters, factory, administration centre or retail outlets in Ireland. #Research

(c) Does this bar chart suggest a link between innovation and success in global business? Explain the reason for your answer. #Discussion

BC

15.17 Accidental inventions

Search online using the query 'inventions made by mistake'. Pick five well-known inventions and create a poster with a short paragraph about each, alongside a photo of the product. Note the sources of your information. Put your posters around the classroom for everyone to look at. #Research

External sources

Ideas or motivation for new products and services are often driven by people and organisations outside the business.

- **Competitors:** This entails looking at competitors and using some of their product or service ideas, while being mindful of patent and copyright law (you cannot copy a business idea that is protected under copyright or patent). These are known as 'me too' products. For example, many electronics companies produce tablets that are similar to, but not exactly the same as, the iPad produced by Apple.

- **Import substitution:** Imports are goods and services bought from overseas. Some entrepreneurs may see an opportunity to create a business by replacing imports with goods and services produced in Ireland.
- **Customer complaints or feedback:** This could result in changes in or further developments to existing products or services.
- **Market research:** A business could use market research to identify gaps in the market and find market trends. The business can then fill these gaps with innovative new products and services. Market research will always be carried out in the development of a new product or service.

See Chapter 21 for market research

KEY TERM

Market research is gathering, recording and analysing information about consumer preferences for a good or service in order to make informed decisions about a potential market.

KEY SKILLS BC MIT

15.18 'Me too' products

Research 'me too' products in electronics and/or cosmetics. Create a poster or presentation showing the similar products produced by rival businesses. #Research #Presentation

KEY SKILLS MIT WO

15.19 Competition

If you were thinking about starting a car-washing or bakery business in your area, who would your competitors be? In pairs, make a list, noting where you found out the information, then share everyone's information through the teacher. #ThinkPairShare

Enterprise in action

Stira Folding Attic Stairs

Michael Burke founded Stira Folding Attic Stairs Ltd in 1982. The idea stemmed from a request to repair an imported attic stairs. Michael says, 'I looked at it and immediately saw the problem and an opportunity. The problem was obvious: inferior material was used on the arms. The opportunity was that the product was a great idea, it was just poorly made. As I had an engineering background it did not take long to build a **prototype** [a realistic working model] and test it out. I saw the problems with the design and began making improvements. It took six months to get the design sorted out, but when I was finished with it I had a strong, safe product to try out on the market.'

KEY SKILLS MIT

15.20 Innovation and entrepreneurship

Michael Burke did not invent the attic stairs, but he was innovative and entrepreneurial when it came to turning it into a successful business. How does the information above illustrate this? #Innovation

ENTERPRISE

The product development process

This process helps both entrepreneurs and businesses to develop ideas that have market potential and should ensure that the finished product has the best possible chance of success.

Product development is expensive and risky, so the business needs to take the following steps to be sure it is not making a mistake. At any point, the business may decide to halt the development process rather than launch a product that will generate losses.

Step	At this stage	Example
1 **Idea generation**	Think up as many new ideas as possible. No ideas should be ruled out at this point.	Following a brainstorming session, a group of students thinks it might be possible to set up a mini-company to produce one of the following: scented candles, cupcakes, T-shirts or wooden ornaments.
2 **Product screening**	The best ideas are considered further and any unworkable ones are rejected.	The students realise they don't have the resources or skills to make T-shirts, cupcakes or wooden ornaments. They think the scented candles offer the greatest potential for success.
3 **Concept development**	The chosen idea is developed into a product that will appeal to consumers. Identifying a unique selling point (USP) for the product allows you to make it different from other products on the market.	The students begin to consider the design of the candles and in particular the ingredients, shapes and scents that will make their candles different from those of their rivals. This will be their USP.
4 **Feasibility study**	A **feasibility study** is carried out to see if the idea is commercially viable: **(i)** Is it actually possible to make this product? **(ii)** Can it be produced and sold profitably in the current market?	The students research how to make candles and are confident they can make them with their own skills and resources. They also investigate the costs involved and speak to some potential customers about their willingness to buy the product. Based on their research, they decide that the scented candle idea is a realistic one and has potential to be profitable.
5 **Prototype development**	Develop a sample or model of the product so the developer can see exactly how it will be manufactured. The prototype can then be tested and, if necessary, altered to make it better.	The students begin to make prototype candles. It takes several attempts to get the correct mix of ingredients and to produce a candle that is good enough to be sold. Their fourth prototype is the most successful, so they agree that this should set the standard for all future production.
6 **Test marketing**	**Test marketing** means that the product is tested on a small sample of the market in order to identify possible faults and test customer reaction.	The students produce a batch of five candles, which they sell to neighbours and teachers. They receive very positive feedback on the quality of the candles and the scents. This gives them the confidence to produce a lot more candles.
7 **Product launch**	The product goes into full-scale production and is introduced to the market. The business will need to select a suitable marketing strategy to persuade consumers to buy the product.	The students invest in raw materials to produce 50 candles. They advertise in the school and get some free publicity in a local paper. They launch their product range by taking a stall at a local Christmas market.

See Chapter 22 for marketing mix

Table 15.1 The product development process

Weblinks PowerPoint Summary

ENTERPRISE

TYPES OF ENTERPRISE

LEARNING OUTCOMES IN FOCUS

2.1 Identify different types of financial, cultural and social enterprise and appreciate the role each plays in society

Links to 1.6, 2.2, 2.3, 2.5, 3.2, 3.4, 3.5, 3.6

LEARNING INTENTIONS FOR THIS CHAPTER

When you have completed this chapter you will be able to:

- Distinguish between financial, cultural and social enterprises
- Discuss the key features of each type of enterprise
- Appreciate the role played by different categories of enterprise in society.

CHAPTER 16 KEY TERMS

- commercial enterprise
- cultural enterprise
- economic growth
- enterprise
- financial enterprise
- not-for-profit
- shareholder
- social enterprise

CHAPTER 16 KEY SKILLS

- BC Being Creative
- C Communicating
- MIT Managing Information and Thinking
- WO Working with Others

Types of enterprise

In Chapter 15 we saw that entrepreneurs help to set up many different **enterprises** or organisations. In this chapter we will look more closely at the role that these enterprises play in our society.

Enterprises can be local, national or global.

- **Local organisations** operate in a specific local area, for example community groups, local newspapers and local shops.
- **National organisations** operate or have branches all over Ireland, for example the Football Association of Ireland (FAI) and Dunnes Stores.
- **Global organisations** are very large and have operations all over the world, for example McDonald's, Coca-Cola and the Red Cross.

Financial enterprises

A **financial (or commercial) enterprise** is set up to make a profit by selling a product or service. Most businesses, including banks, shops, airlines, etc., are financial enterprises. Some financial enterprises are set up and owned by one person (a sole trader), while others, like Apple and Google, are very large companies that operate all over the world and have thousands of owners (called **shareholders**) and millions of customers.

The role of financial enterprises in society

Financial enterprises have an important role to play in our society for the following reasons:

- **Goods and services:** Most financial enterprises provide goods and services for consumers, governments or other organisations.
- **Employment:** Financial enterprises provide direct and indirect employment.
- **Taxation:** Financial enterprises pay tax to the government. This money can be used to provide public services.
- **Finance:** Some financial enterprises, such as banks, building societies, credit unions and An Post, are directly involved in providing finance for others.
- **Economic growth:** By creating employment, paying taxes and supporting other enterprises, financial enterprises contribute to economic growth.

See Chapter 24 for forms of business ownership

See Chapter 36 for economic indicators

See Chapter 38 for economic growth

KEY TERM

Economic growth occurs when there is an increase in the amount of goods and services produced in an economy from one year to the next.

A non-commercial enterprise is one that has not been set up for the sole purpose of making a profit. These **not-for-profit** enterprises include many charities and voluntary organisations that provide a range of services and benefits to communities, for example the GAA and the Arts Council.

Support for financial enterprises

Local Enterprise Offices

Thirty-one Local Enterprise Offices (LEOs) across the country offer a range of supports and services to people interested in starting up a new business. These include:

- **Financial advice** to entrepreneurs and direct financial support for micro-businesses with fewer than 10 employees
- A **mentoring service** that enables entrepreneurs to seek advice from experienced business professionals
- A **business information, advisory and training service** that helps entrepreneurs to upskill in some areas of business management.

Enterprise Ireland

Enterprise Ireland is a government organisation that helps Irish start-up enterprises that have the potential to create employment by exporting their goods and services to overseas markets. Services provided by Enterprise Ireland include:

- **Financial support** for start-up and expanding enterprises
- Assistance with **research and development** (R&D) to help Irish enterprises become more innovative and competitive In international markets
- **Export assistance**, including introductions to overseas customers and information about selling in overseas markets.

Social enterprises

A **social enterprise** is one that puts people and community ahead of private and personal gain. The people who start such enterprises are known as social entrepreneurs. Social enterprises try to create jobs and tackle social, economic or environmental issues that affect the community. They are often owned by the community or by members. This makes them different from financial enterprises, which are owned by shareholders. Social enterprises can have both financial and social goals, but any profits they make are reinvested into the enterprise or the community or distributed to members.

The social enterprise sector in Ireland employs between 25,000 and 35,000 people in over 1,400 social enterprises. Examples of social enterprise include organisations involved in community radio, rural transport schemes, tourism, heritage products and local accommodation.

- **CoderDojo:** Established in 2011, CoderDojo started in Cork and has since expanded around the world. Volunteers provide young people with a free introduction to programming/coding, website development and game development.
- **Macra na Feirme:** This voluntary rural youth organisation provides a social outlet for members in sport, travel, public speaking, performing arts, community involvement and agriculture.
- **Camara Education:** Established in 2005, Camara provides technology at affordable prices to low-income communities as well as training and technical support to purchasers. It does this by taking unwanted computers from businesses and refurbishing them for reuse. As well as working in Ireland, Camara has provided IT equipment to disadvantaged students in Africa and the Caribbean.

- **Young Social Innovators (YSI):** This is Ireland's largest social awareness, active citizenship and education programme for 15- to 18-year-olds. Its main goal is to get young people involved in action that helps to improve the lives of others in their community.
- **Credit unions:** Credit unions perfectly illustrate an organisation with both financial and social goals. They exist to serve members' needs, not necessarily to make a profit. Surplus income generated is returned to members as a dividend or is used to improve or add services for members. Members' savings are used to fund loans to other members of the credit union. The money in a credit union stays in the local community.

Support for social enterprise

Social Entrepreneurs Ireland (SEI)

SEI is a not-for-profit organisation that helps social entrepreneurs by providing financial and practical support. Since it was set up in 2004, SEI funding of over €7 million has supported 264 social entrepreneurs. These projects have directly impacted 1.7 million people all over Ireland and created almost 1,500 jobs.

Clann Credo

This social investment fund was founded in Ireland in 1996. It provides loans to community organisations, charities and social enterprises.

KEY SKILLS

16.1 Clann Credo

Visit the Clann Credo website and discuss how this social organisation is different from most commercial lenders. #Research #Discussion

The role of social enterprises in society

- **Tackle social problems:** They raise awareness of and try to tackle social issues and problems such as unemployment and poverty.
- **Provide services:** They provide services and support for their communities by meeting community needs that are not served by the state or by commercial enterprises.
- **Employment:** While social enterprises often rely on the work of volunteers, some help to create employment in their local communities.
- **Finance:** Some social enterprises, such as SEI and Clann Credo, provide finance for other social enterprises.
- **Enterprise culture:** They help to create a culture of entrepreneurship and self-help, particularly in disadvantaged communities, which encourages and motivates others to follow their example.

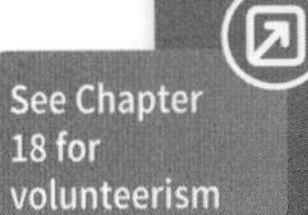

See Chapter 18 for volunteerism

Enterprise in action

Social enterprise: FoodCloud

According to the Environmental Protection Agency (EPA), approximately 1 million tonnes of food go to waste in Ireland each year. Much of this food is perfectly edible. Irish retailers have about 87,000 tonnes of surplus food a year, most of which is dumped at a cost of €8.5 million. The Statue of Liberty weighs 204 tonnes, so the amount of food wasted by businesses in Ireland each year is equivalent to over 426 Statues of Liberty.

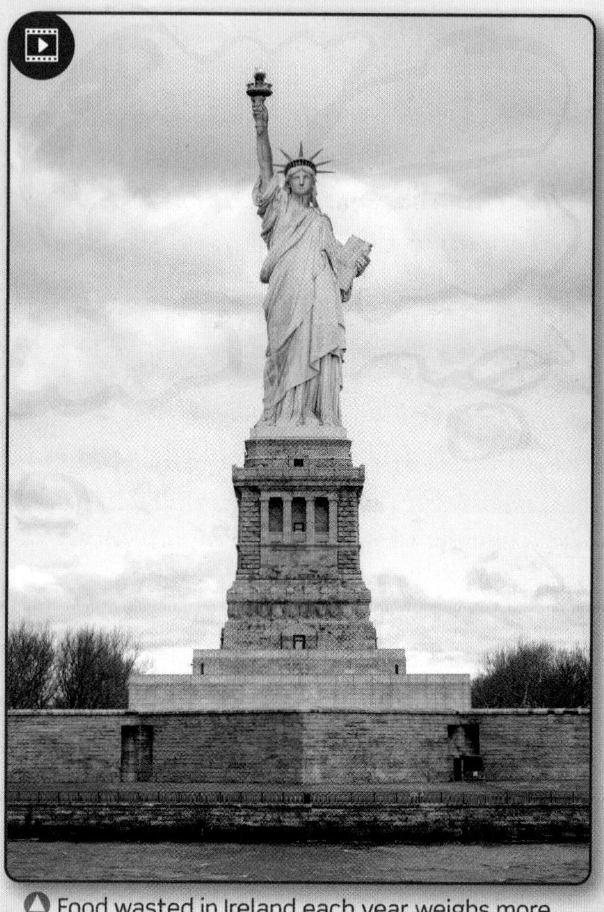

Food wasted in Ireland each year weighs more than 426 Statues of Liberty

To address this problem, social entrepreneurs Aoibheann O'Brien and Iseult Ward established FoodCloud, a social enterprise that connects businesses that have surplus food with charities that can use the food. In 2012, Aoibheann and Iseult researched ways of matching businesses and charities and quickly realised that technology was needed to do this efficiently and on a large scale throughout the country and the world.

They received support, funding and mentoring from Social Entrepreneurs Ireland, among others. They developed an app and website and launched FoodCloud in October 2013 with some cafés and one Tesco store. By July 2014, they had expanded to include all Tesco stores throughout Ireland, which now redistribute surplus food to a range of charities around the Republic of Ireland. FoodCloud also operates in the UK through a partnership with Fareshare and Tesco. Businesses use FoodCloud's app to upload details of surplus food and a collection time. This sends a text to a local charity, which replies to accept the offer and then collects the food.

There are now over 1,100 charities and 500 businesses on board.

Since its establishment, FoodCloud has redistributed 27,299 tonnes of food (the equivalent of 65 million meals) to 9,500 charitable groups around Ireland and the UK. Working with FoodCloud reduces the food bill for charities and allows them to redirect their funds into the other important services they provide.

For the businesses involved, it is a socially responsible and environmentally sensitive alternative to wasting good food.

KEY SKILLS

16.2 Social enterprise

(a) What enterprising characteristics and skills have Aoibheann and Iseult shown? #Identify

(b) What gap in the market did they seek to fill? #Identify

16.3 Social Entrepreneurs Ireland

Aoibheann and Iseult received mentoring, funding and support from Social Entrepreneurs Ireland. In small groups, research this organisation and find out what other social enterprises have received assistance from them. Present your findings to your classmates in a presentation or on a poster. #Research

Cultural enterprises

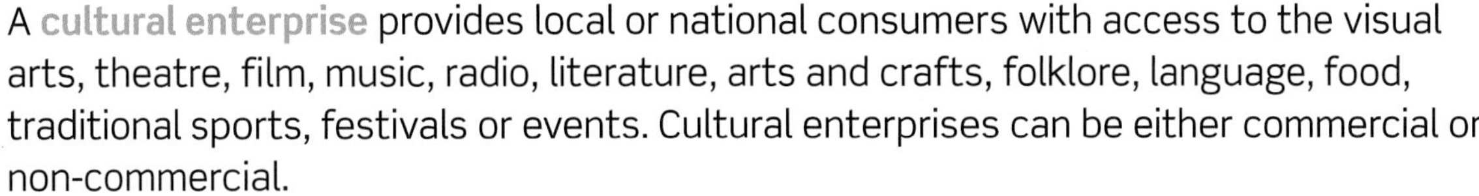

A **cultural enterprise** provides local or national consumers with access to the visual arts, theatre, film, music, radio, literature, arts and crafts, folklore, language, food, traditional sports, festivals or events. Cultural enterprises can be either commercial or non-commercial.

For example, your local community may have a library, theatre or arts centre, while GAA clubs and Comhaltas Ceoltóirí Éireann support Irish culture by promoting Irish sport, music, singing, dancing and language.

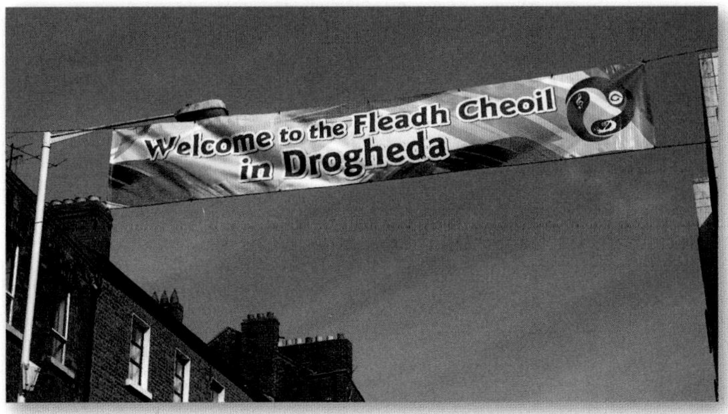

Other examples include:

- **Abbey Theatre:** Also known as Ireland's national theatre, the Abbey Theatre was established in 1904. It aims to promote Irish writers and artists and to produce a programme of interesting and exciting Irish and international theatre each year.

- **Fleadh Cheoil Na hÉireann:** Fleadh Cheoil means 'feast of music' and this traditional Irish music festival is an annual event run by Comhaltas Ceoltóirí Éireann. It also features the national finals for traditional music and singing competitions.

- **Electric Picnic:** This annual music and arts festival takes place in Stradbally, Co. Laois. It attracts over 50,000 people each year.
- **National Gallery of Ireland:** While the National Gallery of Ireland does not charge an entrance fee, its shop sells a range of goods, such as books, greetings cards, umbrellas and stationery, inspired by the gallery's collections.

- **Rose of Tralee International Festival:** The Rose of Tralee has been held annually in Tralee, Co. Kerry since 1959 and is one of Ireland's largest and longest-running festivals. While you may be familiar with the TV programme shown over two nights in August, the festival itself takes place over five days and includes live music, concerts, a fashion show, circus, funfair, fireworks and a Rose Parade. The event attracts over 50,000 people to Tralee each year.
- **Local cultural enterprise events:** Events take place throughout Ireland, usually festivals that promote the local economy. Examples include the Kilkenny Cat Laughs Comedy Festival, the Cork Jazz Festival and the Taste of Donegal Food Festival.

KEY SKILLS MIT

16.4 Cultural enterprises

Find out about the local cultural events or enterprises in your town or county. What benefits do these events bring to the local community? #Research

KEY SKILLS MIT

16.5 Social entrepreneurs

Research and profile a local, national or international social entrepreneur. Note the sources you used to find your answers. #Research #List

The role of cultural enterprises in society

- **Promote arts and culture:** Cultural organisations support and promote Irish culture, especially in areas such as music, sport and literature. They also help to ensure that people have easy access to cultural events and experiences.
- **Create employment:** Many cultural enterprises employ full-time staff to carry out and support their day-to-day operations.
- **Support the local economy:** Cultural enterprises can positively impact a local economy through direct employment and by promoting tourism and staging large events such as festivals.
- **Entertainment:** Cultural enterprises are not all about money and making a profit. Very often they exist simply to provide entertainment, which can have a positive impact on people's lives and wellbeing.

Support for cultural enterprise

Culture Ireland

Culture Ireland, a division of the Department of Culture, Heritage and the Gaeltacht, is responsible for promoting Irish arts worldwide. It creates and supports opportunities for Irish artists and companies to present their work at international showcases, festivals, venues and arts markets. It supports a range of artistic and cultural activities, including visual art, theatre, literature, music, dance, opera and film.

Arts Council of Ireland

The Arts Council of Ireland is a government organisation with responsibility for developing the arts. It works in partnership with artists, arts organisations and the government to promote and support the arts in Irish life.

Weblinks

PowerPoint Summary

ENTERPRISE

IMPACT OF ORGANISATIONS

LEARNING OUTCOMES IN FOCUS

2.5 Investigate the positive and negative impacts on a community of an organisation from an economic, social and environmental perspective

Links to 1.9, 2.1, 2.4, 2.6, 3.6, 3.7, 3.9, 3.10, 3.11

LEARNING INTENTIONS FOR THIS CHAPTER

When you have completed this chapter you will be able to:

- Recognise the difference between a social, an economic and an environmental perspective
- Outline the benefits that organisations bring to society, the economy and the environment
- Recognise the possible negative impacts of an organisation on a community.

CHAPTER 17 KEY TERMS

- clean technology
- community
- culture of enterprise
- economic growth
- economic perspective
- environmental perspective
- indirect employment
- infrastructure
- multiplier effect
- social perspective

CHAPTER 17 KEY SKILLS

- BC Being Creative
- BL Being Literate
- C Communicating
- MIT Managing Information and Thinking
- MM Managing Myself
- SW Staying Well
- WO Working with Others

Types of impact

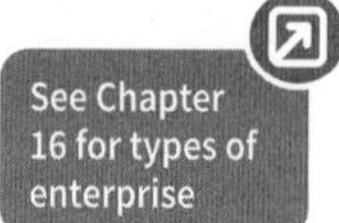
See Chapter 16 for types of enterprise

In this chapter we will look at some of the impacts that organisations can have on a community. The impact of a specific organisation may depend on whether it is a financial, social or cultural enterprise and also on the community in question.

> **KEY TERM**
>
> A **community** is a group of people who live in the same place or who have certain attitudes and interests in common.

An organisation's impact on a community can be:

- **Positive** – when it benefits a community
- **Negative** – when it involves costs or a loss to the community.

Communities can be very small, but they can also be global. As part of your study and to develop your understanding of the issues raised here, you should choose a number of organisations that you know of and investigate how they actually impact on a community.

We use different viewpoints or perspectives when looking at the impact of organisations on a community. A perspective is like a lens that helps us to focus attention on certain parts of an issue or problem. In this chapter we will use three different perspectives or points of view.

Economic perspective

See Chapter 1 for opportunity cost

See Chapter 32 for distribution of economic resources

How does an organisation impact on an economy? Consider money, wealth, employment and profits. We could also look at how to get the best value out of available resources and the choices that people have to make if their resources are limited. For example, available land may be scarce and an economic choice may have to be made about whether to use it for housing, shops or a new school. Each of these options will involve benefits and costs.

Social perspective

How does an organisation impact on people, communities and society? Consider how the actions of organisations impact on our relationships and interactions with others. For example, a new community centre can be a meeting place for local people and can provide an opportunity for new clubs to be started.

Environmental perspective

How does an organisation impact on our surroundings and natural resources? This includes how they impact on other living things. For example, a decision to clear an area of forest to build an industrial estate may have a negative impact on the local air quality and wildlife.

When making decisions about the overall impact of an organisation, we need to consider all three viewpoints and try to achieve the best, most sustainable outcome.

Economic
Economic growth
Profit
Employment
Resources
Standard of living

Social
Education
Community
Equal opportunities

Environmental
Natural resources
Pollution prevention
Environmental management

ENTERPRISE

Economic impacts of organisations

Positive economic impacts

From an economic perspective, the positive impact of an organisation refers to the financial or wealth benefits it brings to a community.

Area impacted	How organisations have a positive economic impact
Employment	Jobs are created in the organisation as well as spin-off jobs in related businesses such as transport, banking, suppliers and cleaning services.
Tax revenue	The organisation will contribute to local authority (city or county council) rates and taxes. This money is used to develop local **infrastructure** such as roads and parks.
Improved standard of living	The organisation's employees will have disposable income, which will enable them and their families to have more wealth, comfort, goods and services.
Economic growth	An increase in business activity in an economy will lead to an increase in the amount of goods produced and services provided from one year to the next. This is an indicator of economic growth. Economic growth benefits a community through increased employment and a higher standard of living.
Promotes an enterprise culture	Seeing local entrepreneurs establish businesses can lead to a culture of enterprise in an area, which can encourage more businesses to develop in the local community.
Multiplier effect	Money paid by an organisation to its employees and local suppliers leads to increased spending in the local community. This in turn supports other businesses, such as shops and restaurants. The impact of the initial payment is multiplied as it passes around the community. This is called the multiplier effect and illustrates the economic value of an organisation, especially a major employer, to a community. In the example below, you will see how a small increase in spending leads to a larger increase in economic output and wealth.

See Chapter 36 for effects of economic growth on households, businesses and the economy

See Chapters 36 and 38 for economic growth

KEY TERM

Infrastructure is the physical (e.g. buildings) and transport (e.g. roads, rail) structures and facilities (e.g. power supplies) needed for a society or enterprise to function.

The multiplier effect at work in a local economy

Eoin, a factory owner, has a good month and earns €1,000 extra income. In order to satisfy his needs and wants, he decides to employ Rashad, an electrician, to install new lighting in his house. Eoin pays Rashad €700 to carry out the electrical work. Rashad in turn will use some of this income to satisfy his own needs and wants, so he spends €500 in Sandra's shop. As a result of Rashad's spending, Sandra has now earned €500 in income.

In this example, the initial €1,000 of spending created an extra €1,200 (€700 + €500) in spending or economic output (a total of €2,200) for the local community. This is the multiplier effect and it shows how an organisation can provide a major economic benefit for a community.

Negative economic impacts

An increase in the number or size of organisations can negatively impact a community. It may take some time before the effects are felt by the community and they may not impact all members in the same way.

See Chapter 33 for demand and supply

Area impacted	How organisations have a negative economic impact
Pressure on resources	New organisations will increase the demand for available resources, which may increase both the scarcity and the price of these resources. For example, land prices may go up in a location that is popular with builders and developers. While new organisations may offer new services to a community, they may also increase pressure on existing public services and utilities (gas, electricity, water, telephone and broadband). If there is no increase in supply, many people are likely to suffer from reduced levels of service.
Housing	New organisations, especially those employing a large number of people, may create housing problems in a community. If employees want to live close to their place of work, demand for housing will increase. This will impact on land, property and rental costs, which are all likely to rise.
Crowding out	Large businesses may crowd out the local competition in a community. Because of their size and scale, it may be difficult for existing local businesses to compete on price and service levels. This could lead to business closure, which will cause unemployment.
Over-reliance	A community may become very dependent on one or two large organisations, especially for employment. If these organisations close down, there will be devastating impacts on the local community, including job losses, reduced incomes and lower levels of economic growth. The recent closure of the Bord na Móna boglands in the Midlands is an example of this.

17.1 Negative economic impacts

Investigate the negative economic impacts on a community following the closure of a major employer or organisation. If possible, find an example from your own area. In addition to researching online, it may be helpful to ask family members or teachers who may remember these organisations and events. #Research

BL MIT C

Google, Facebook, Twitter and several other large technology businesses have their EMEA (Europe, Middle East and Africa) headquarters in an area of Dublin known as the Silicon Docks. Many cafés, restaurants and bars have opened there to meet the needs of these employees, which has created more **indirect employment** in the area. However, rents in the area have risen sharply due to demand from employees who want to live locally. These employees earn large salaries and can afford to pay high rents, but this has resulted in other people being unable to afford to live there.

KEY SKILLS

17.2 Indirect employment (spin-off jobs)

(a) In pairs, list other types of business that exist to meet the needs of the workers in these large technology businesses. #List #ThinkPairShare

(b) Think of a business near where you live that has enabled other businesses to exist nearby. Name both the business and the dependent businesses. #Research

KEY SKILLS

17.3 Negative impacts

Can you think of any negative impacts that these large organisations may have had on the local community? #Suggest #Identify

Social impacts of organisations

Positive social impacts

From a social perspective, the positive impact of an organisation refers to how it improves the lives of people in the community.

Area impacted	How organisations have a positive social impact
More local services	There will be a growth in local services to meet the needs of local organisations (taxi/transport services, banks, credit unions, etc.). Local people can also use these services. Voluntary organisations also provide services for people in need (e.g. the Jack and Jill Foundation). Commercial enterprises often support and sponsor non-commercial organisations in their local community, which improves the level of services and increases community spirit.
Sustainable communities	Increased employment and services should make the community a more attractive place to live, especially for families and young people. This is likely to keep these people working, living and spending in the community and will help the community to survive and grow. If these people are forced to leave in order to find work, the community may not be sustainable, as schools, businesses and clubs close down.
Increased choice/ lower prices for consumers	New organisations should provide extra goods and services as well as greater competition in the marketplace. This generally leads to more choice and lower prices for consumers.
Improved quality of life	Successful social and cultural enterprises such as theatres, libraries, clubs and societies improve community spirit and increase social interaction. This leads to a better quality of life for local residents and makes the community a better place to live.

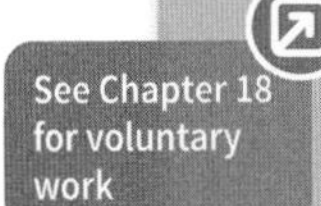

See Chapter 18 for voluntary work

Negative social impacts

Area impacted	How organisations have a negative social impact
Population	Large and sudden increases in the local population can transform a community. In some cases, local services such as schools, medical and leisure facilities may not be able to cope with the increase. Until new services are provided, access to them may be reduced.
Traffic	New organisations may generate extra traffic, and existing roads may not be able to deal with this increased volume. This may result in delays and the need for major upgrades to the road network.
Social tension	Sometimes local people feel that a new organisation is not a good fit for their community, either because of the disruption it causes or the type of organisation it is. This can cause a lot of bad feeling and resentment in the community. Examples include communities where a new prison or sewage treatment plant are to be located.

Environmental impacts of organisations

Positive environmental impacts

From an environmental perspective, an organisation can have a positive impact on the natural resources (land, air, water) or the physical environment of a community (see the table below).

Many modern organisations use **clean technology**. Clean technologies are designed to be more sustainable and to reduce negative environmental impacts. They are found in a range of industries, including manufacturing, energy, water and transportation. Examples include recycling and renewable energy as well as using information technology, electric vehicles and energy-efficient lighting.

Area impacted	How organisations have a positive environmental impact
Pollution controls	New developments, including factories, have to obey strict rules to limit pollution. Many high-tech industries use cutting-edge clean technology to minimise pollution and their environmental impact.
Recycling facilities	Organisations may develop recycling facilities that serve their own needs or the needs of the wider community to reduce waste going to landfill or incineration. Rehab and FoodCloud provide recycling services that have a positive impact on the natural environment. Some organisations use rainwater harvesting or recycling to reduce their consumption and environmental impact.
Energy efficiency	Industry is increasingly using renewable energy, which helps to keep pollution levels low. Building Energy Ratings (BER) have increased awareness and changed building practices.
Land usage	Organisations such as Tidy Towns use vacant land to develop community services and improve the local landscape. Local authorities provide parklands, while sporting organisations develop land to improve local facilities and the physical environment.

17.4 Environmental responsibility

What could your school do to be more environmentally responsible?
#ThinkPairShare #Reflect

17.5 Local businesses

Consider local businesses near you.

(a) How do they support the local community?

(b) How does their support benefit the local community? #Research

Negative environmental impacts

Area impacted	How organisations have a negative environmental impact
Pollution	Organisations may cause environmental pollution as a result of their operations and activities. This results from the generation of waste as well as noise and water pollution. Carbon emissions and global warming are currently huge areas of concern for the global community.
Unsustainable use of resources	As the number of organisations in a community increases, so does the demand for scarce resources. If they are not managed carefully, the resources may be damaged or lost for ever.
Habitat destruction	In order to provide development land for large organisations, some natural habitats may be cleared or destroyed. This has a negative impact on plants and wildlife and can also impact on the climate.

17.6 Unethical organisations

Being unethical means acting unfairly, unjustly or dishonestly. Use newspapers and/or news websites to find an organisation that has behaved unethically to customers, employees, suppliers, the government or the local community. Create a presentation, poster or infographic showing:

(a) How the business behaved unethically

(b) Who/what was affected

(c) What the consequences/effects were #Research #Presentation

Case study

Question:

A global hotel operator has announced plans to develop a major hotel and leisure facility on the south-east coast. The plan is to develop an indoor waterpark alongside a 75-bedroom hotel and conference centre. The facilities would be open all year round and would be targeted at local and overseas visitors.

Examine the impact of the proposal from economic, social and environmental perspectives.

Suggested solution:

Evaluation of the impact of a proposed new hotel and leisure facility

Positive impacts	Negative impacts
Economic impacts	
The development will create 400 short-term construction jobs and 250 long-term jobs when the hotel and leisure facilities are fully up and running. There is strong potential for spin-off jobs and services to meet the needs of staff and visitors.	The development may cause the closure of an existing local hotel, which would result in 20 jobs being lost.
The development will attract more tourists to the area and will boost the local economy. It is expected to generate €70–80m of extra spending in the region each year.	Local roads and transport infrastructure will need to be upgraded. This will cost roughly €200m and will be paid from tax revenues.
The local authority will receive additional revenue from taxation and commercial rates.	An increase in land prices and housing rental costs is likely.
Housing values are likely to increase as the area becomes a more desirable place to live.	
The facility will attract overseas visitors and will have a positive impact on the balance of payments.	
Social impacts	
When fully operational, the facility will provide the local community with a range of new leisure services.	There may be short-term pressure on some local services, as the development is likely to increase the local population.
The development and the economic benefits associated with it will improve the quality of life for many local people.	Some crowding out of smaller local businesses and tourist attractions may occur.
Environmental impacts	
The facility will use land that has been neglected and unsightly for several years. This will improve the appearance of the local environment. The development will also include some parkland development.	Some locals are concerned about the environmental impact of the construction process. The plan also requires a small section of local forest to be cut down.
The facility will use the most energy-efficient technology and will use solar energy to meet its needs.	There are some concerns about the amount of water the facility will require and fears that this will impact on supplies to the wider community.
Water harvesting will be a feature of the waterpark development.	The new development will generate more waste and wastewater. This will require existing facilities to be upgraded at a cost of €10m.

17.7 Impact analysis

Consider the arguments for and against the proposed new development set out on the previous page. Based on your analysis, decide whether you are in favour of it going ahead or are against the development. Write down at least three reasons for your decision. Compare your decision with others in your class and take a vote to see what the majority think. #Identify #Opinion #Compare #Reflect

Answer the following questions:

(a) Would you pay most attention to economic, social or environmental issues when assessing the impact of an organisation? Why would you make this choice? #Justify

(b) Why might other people have different views? #Opinion

(c) How do you think these differences of opinion should be resolved? #Opinion

Tayto Park owner confident screams from proposed new €15.5m rollercoaster won't impact residents

The screams by passengers on Tayto Park's planned new €15.5 million rollercoaster won't impact on nearby residents.That is according to Tayto Park owner Raymond Coyle, who said today that the new rollercoaster comes with a series of specific measures aimed at eliminating any noise impacts for nearby residents.

Last July, An Bord Pleanála turned down planning permission for Mr Coyle's previous rollercoaster plan due mainly to noise impacts from rollercoaster passengers' screams on nearby residents.

The new plan contains 14 separate noise reduction measures. Tayto Park is also constructing a 106-metre-long, six-metre-high sound barrier along the northern boundary of the Tayto Park site.

An Environmental Impact Statement (EIS) lodged with the plan states that the Coaster 2021 project has been specifically oriented away from residents' homes to ensure that patrons' screaming and shouting from the rollercoaster will be directed into Tayto Park and away from residents' homes.

Environmental consultants for the project, Malone O'Regan Environmental, state that 'there will be no increase in noise as a result of the proposed new rollercoaster'.

Planning documents lodged with the application state that if the plan is operational for 2021, visitor numbers will soar to 715,000. The numbers to attend Tayto Park in 2019 totalled 615,000. Mr Coyle said, 'Numbers have been flat the last two or three years and we need to do something about it.'

Twenty-five people will be employed during the construction phase and 40 if and when the new Coaster 2021 is operational.

Source: BreakingNews.ie, 3 March 2019

IN THE NEWS

Peat didn't just keep our homes warm, it fuelled local economy

Being sent to turn turf in the bog as a young lad in the Midlands was part of life but always felt like punishment. It was hard work that, at best, was rewarded with one or two pounds that you were only allowed to spend in instalments in the local shop.

Yet our micro-economy as children was largely replicated in the adult world. Fathers, brothers, uncles and neighbours worked in either Bord na Móna or ESB, two companies that propped up entire towns like where I grew up in Offaly. Peat wasn't just the fuel that kept our homes warm. It also fuelled almost every local enterprise, from the butchers to the collection basket at Mass. A sort of brown gold.

Yesterday, Climate Action Minister Richard Bruton visited my home parish of Ferbane to see what remains of a dying industry. It was announced last Friday that the ESB plans to close the nearby Shannonbridge power station as well as the Lough Ree plant in Co. Longford at the end of 2020.

Around 80 jobs in the area will be directly affected, but that's not even close to the full story. Another 1,000 Bord na Móna workers who have spent decades harvesting peat and servicing machinery also face into an uncertain future. Knowing that there were few alternatives for the workers, unions opposed the closures until it became inevitable.

In the 1980s and early 1990s, Ferbane was known as a GAA stronghold. But as the bogs depleted and the opportunities to get a job with 'the Board' decreased, so did the number of young people willing or able to stay. At the time there was a realisation that the bogs couldn't be exploited forever, but the phrase 'climate action' wasn't part of the conversation. And the community was largely left to fend for itself, which it did.

Over the years, shops and pubs closed. An empty coffin was carried symbolically up the main street when Ulster Bank threatened to pull out in 2004. It left anyway.

But it hasn't been all bad. ESB gave money towards the development of a small business park and as nearby towns like Athlone and Tullamore grew on the back of foreign direct investment, so did the potential for employment.

As he drove through the town in his hybrid car yesterday, Mr Bruton would have passed the old power station site, which has been fenced off since that February. It is now finally a building site, courtesy of a South Korean energy company and an Offaly firm that is developing new power facilities based on battery storage technology. The project won't bring many jobs, though.

The minister went to Lough Boora Discovery Park, a sanctuary for wildlife and a haven for locals. For years it has been a much-valued local amenity. Now that the secret is out, around 100,000 people a year take the potholed road to what was once a flooded wasteland. There are walking trails, a coffee shop, art installations and the park guarantees to exhaust even the most active of kids.

A big part of the government's plan seems to be to create more places like Lough Boora – but while the bog restoration takes some work, in the long run it only sustains a handful of jobs. Mr Bruton talked about the €6m 'Just Transition' fund for the Midlands, which is to be topped up with another €5m from ESB. He promised to 'try to develop an alternative future for these people'. But the experience suggests there are no quick fixes for the problems facing the Midlands.

Source: *Irish Independent*, 12 November 2019

KEY SKILLS MIT MM

17.8 Community impacts

Using the template in question 9 in your Student Activity Book, list and evaluate the ways in which Tayto Park, Bord na Móna or one of the other listed organisations impacts a community from an economic, a social and an environmental perspective. Clearly define your chosen community (local, national or global). #List #Evaluate

WORK, EMPLOYMENT AND VOLUNTEERISM

LEARNING OUTCOMES IN FOCUS

2.3 Differentiate between employment, work and volunteerism, identifying and describing features, benefits, rewards and careers within each

Links to 1.11, 2.1, 2.2, 2.4, 3.1, 3.10, 3.11

LEARNING INTENTIONS FOR THIS CHAPTER

When you have completed this chapter you will be able to:

- Differentiate between work, employment and volunteering
- Explain the benefits and rewards of work and employment
- Discuss different types of employment
- Explain the term 'unemployment'
- Outline the reasons why people volunteer
- Identify the benefits and rewards of volunteering to individuals, organisations and society
- Identify careers relevant to your interests and subjects.

CHAPTER 18 KEY TERMS

casual employee	job sharing
contract of employment	labour force
employee	part-time employees
employer	self-employed
employment	teleworking
fixed-term employees	unemployment
flexitime	volunteering
full-time employees	work

CHAPTER 18 KEY SKILLS

- BC Being Creative
- BL Being Literate
- C Communicating
- MIT Managing Information and Thinking
- MM Managing Myself
- SW Staying Well
- WO Working with Others

What is work?

You may or may not be paid for work. Examples of unpaid work include doing housework, doing your homework, practising a musical instrument and voluntary work.

KEY TERM

Work is any productive activity that requires effort.

- If you are paid for the work you do, it is called employment.
- If you agree to carry out unpaid work, it is called volunteerism.

KEY TERM

Employment is work for which a person receives a payment (a wage or salary).

Work	Employment
May or may not be paid	Payment is received
No contract	Contract of employment
No legal rights	Legal rights

KEY TERM

Employees are people who work for employers in return for a payment.

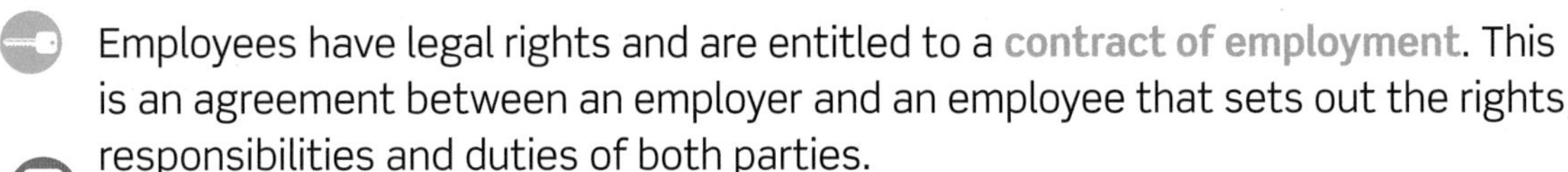

Employees have legal rights and are entitled to a **contract of employment**. This is an agreement between an employer and an employee that sets out the rights, responsibilities and duties of both parties.

See Chapter 19 for contract of employment, and rights and responsiblities of employers and employees

KEY TERM

An **employer** is someone who pays another person to work for them.

Most people work to earn an income. This gives a person a secure standard of living, which allows them to buy goods and services to satisfy their needs and wants.

See Chapter 1 for needs and wants

KEY SKILLS

18.1 Minimum wage

What is the current minimum wage in Ireland for a person aged:

(a) Over 18?

(b) Under 18? #Research

ENTERPRISE

Types of employment

Full-time employment	**Full-time employees** usually work 35 hours or more per week. They receive a salary or a full week's wage when working full time. The times might be regular, e.g. 9 a.m. to 5 p.m., or change from week to week.
Part-time employment	A **part-time employee** could work up to 30 hours a week. They are paid for the hours they work.
Fixed-term employment	Many people are employed on a **fixed-term** basis, e.g. for a 10-month contract. Their temporary employment finishes when the contract term ends.
Casual employment	**Casual employees** are on standby to do work as required without fixed hours. They are employed only when work is available. Sometimes they work seasonally. For example, some hotel staff are only required to work during peak holiday times and may not work during the off-season. However, these workers are treated as employees for employment rights purposes.
Self-employment	People who are **self-employed** work for themselves. They may receive a wage and take their income from the profits they make in the business.
Job sharing	In **job sharing**, two employees together make up one working week in a particular role. They share the hours, workload and pay associated with the job.
Flexitime	**Flexitime** means that an employee can start and finish work at a time that suits them each day as long as they do the hours stated in their contract.
Teleworking	In **teleworking**, the employee works from home and carries out their duties as if they were working on the business premises. The employee needs to have a phone and an internet connection to respond to email and communicate easily with co-workers, customers, etc.

See Chapter 15 for entrepreneurs

KEY SKILLS

18.2 Review and recall

MIT BL

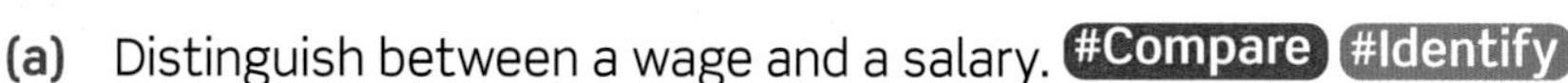

(a) Distinguish between a wage and a salary. #Compare #Identify

(b) Explain each of the following payment methods used to reward employees:
- Time rate
- Piece rate
- Commission
- Bonus. #Explain

See Chapter 2 for income

KEY SKILLS

18.3 Employment contracts

MIT MM

(a) Think of two examples of jobs that might have a fixed-term contract. #Identify

(b) What benefits might there be for an employee who is offered a temporary or short-term contract? #Opinion

KEY SKILLS MIT

18.4 Seasonal employment

Some casual employees are known as seasonal workers. List five examples of employment that might be seasonal. #List

KEY SKILLS MIT

18.5 Self-employment

List five different examples of work carried out by self-employed people. #List

KEY SKILLS MIT

18.6 Job sharing

Why do you think employers offer job sharing rather than creating two part-time jobs? #Opinion

KEY SKILLS MIT

18.7 Flexitime

Why do you think that schools do not operate on flexitime? #Opinion

KEY SKILLS MIT SW

18.8 Teleworking

(a) What are the advantages of teleworking: #Identify
- To the employer?
- To the employee?

(b) What disadvantages of teleworking could you foresee: #Identify
- For the employer?
- For the employee?

KEY SKILLS WO BL

18.9 Working for yourself

In groups, discuss the advantages and disadvantages of self-employment. Write down your conclusions. #GroupWork #Discussion

Rewards and benefits of work and employment

- Both work and employment help to achieve goals.
- Both help to develop talents and skills, which may help us to get a new job or a promotion in the future.
- Both work and employment provide a sense of satisfaction and personal achievement as a result of doing something worthwhile.
- Work and employment are important for developing self-esteem. This is especially true of employment. Getting praise or being rewarded for our work has a positive effect on our self-esteem.
- Both work and employment help us to meet new people and develop our social skills.
- Some types of employment provide an opportunity to travel, either within Ireland or internationally.
- Employment provides income in the form of wages and salaries. Employees may also receive benefits in kind, such as company cars or free products.

Unemployment

Members of the labour force who cannot find paid work are classified as unemployed.

KEY TERM

The **labour force** refers to all those people of working age (16–65) who are willing and able to work for payment.

The labour force does not include retired people, full-time students or those who have an illness or disability that prevents them from working for payment.

A healthy and growing economy tends to have low levels of unemployment. Those who are unemployed usually receive some form of financial payment from the Department of Employment Affairs and Social Protection, such as Jobseeker's Benefit or Jobseeker's Allowance. This money is designed to help them meet their daily needs and to provide short-term financial support until they find a job.

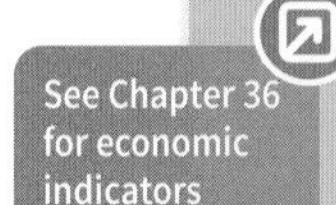
See Chapter 36 for economic indicators

Voluntary work

KEY TERM

Volunteering is when people carry out some work or activity without payment for their time and effort.

A voluntary organisation is a group of people who come together and carry out unpaid work that aims to help others or the environment. Voluntary organisations can be local, national or international. Many of these voluntary groups are social organisations. They rely on unpaid volunteers, but some also have paid employees.

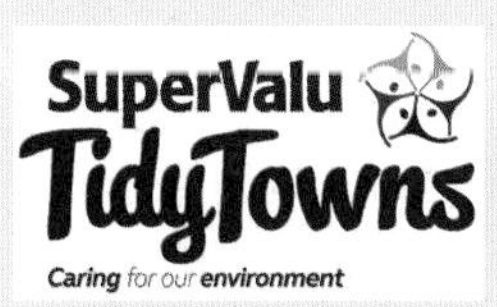

Local, national and international voluntary groups and organisations in Ireland

18.10 Voluntary organisations

(a) Working in pairs, sort the voluntary organisations whose logos are shown above under the following headings:

- Local voluntary groups
- National voluntary organisations
- International voluntary organisations. #ThinkPairShare #Classify

(b) In small groups, investigate what local and national voluntary organisations exist in your locality. Create a poster or presentation about five different organisations, showing the name, logo and purpose of each organisation. #Research #Presentation #GroupWork

Why do people volunteer?

- They are passionate about a cause, such as preventing animal abuse, keeping their neighbourhood tidy or preserving a natural habitat.
- They have personal experience of a cause, for example an illness, so they want to help others who are going through the same thing.
- They have received help themselves and now want to 'give back' and help others who are in a similar situation.
- They have time available and want to help their community.
- They have a skill that is needed and they want to put it to good use.
- They enjoy the work and get satisfaction from doing it.

KEY SKILLS BL BC C MM

18.11 Voluntary work

(a) If you do voluntary work, prepare a presentation for your class explaining what the voluntary organisation is, what it does and the work you do. Let people know why you find this work valuable. Include some relevant images. #Presentation

Or:

(b) If you don't currently do voluntary work, think about what you would like to do and why. Research organisations you could volunteer to help and prepare a presentation on what the voluntary body is, what it does and why you would like to work with them. #Justify #Research #Presentation

Working for a voluntary organisation

Most people who work voluntarily do so part time in order to fit it in with their other commitments, such as earning a living or looking after a family. Some people might give their time for one event; others might do one hour a week; while others, such as Transition Year students or retired people, might devote weeks or months at a time to voluntary work. In some cases this may involve voluntary work overseas. Voluntary groups will always be grateful for any time and help you can offer them.

18.12 Volunteering

Do you think it is important that people work as volunteers? Discuss your feelings on giving your time for free.

SW

Benefits and rewards of volunteerism

Benefits and rewards to the individual volunteer

- Volunteering is a chance to learn new skills and an opportunity to use existing skills.
- It can lead to paid employment in the future and provides an opportunity to get work experience and may lead to paid employment in the future.
- It shows initiative and personal enterprise and it also highlights a person's willingness to work with and for others, which is all likely to impress future employers.
- It offers a chance to make new friends and improve social and interpersonal skills.
- It enhances personal satisfaction and wellbeing – it makes you feel good and helps to improve self-esteem.

Benefits and rewards to the organisation

- Volunteers bring a range of new skills, expertise and ideas to the organisation.
- Volunteers are often passionate about the issue or the cause. Every organisation benefits from having passionate and highly motivated people involved.
- If volunteers are unpaid, more funds can be directed towards the organisation's main aims and activities. For example, a homeless charity can use all the money it receives to help reduce homelessness.
- Volunteers may act as ambassadors for the organisation in the wider community. This creates positive publicity and helps to spread the values and good name of the organisation.

Benefits and rewards to society/the economy

- The ideals of giving and helping others in order to improve our community lie at the very heart of volunteerism. Communities tend to improve when members work together.
- Many voluntary organisations play an important role in reducing social isolation. Examples include sports clubs, men's sheds and charities that assist homeless people or the elderly. Reducing isolation also helps to limit the potential for antisocial behaviour.
- The work of unpaid volunteers reduces the financial burden on the local and national government, which allows money to be spent on other goods and services.
- Volunteering gets things done! Society benefits from a greater range of community services and activities, ranging from coaching local teams to providing medical services overseas.

What job will suit you?

'Find a job you love and you'll never work a day in your life.' This saying means that our working lives will be more interesting and rewarding if we work in jobs that suit our interests and qualities. It may be possible to do unpaid work or volunteer in order to develop your skills, especially if it's in an area that interests you. Alternatively, you could take an online quiz and see what jobs it recommends for you. It's never too early to start planning your future career!

KEY SKILLS

18.13 Finding your career path BC

Look at the example in Figure 18.1 of suitable careers for someone who is interested in languages. In your copy, write down your hobbies and your favourite subject and consider the careers that might suit you. #List #Identify

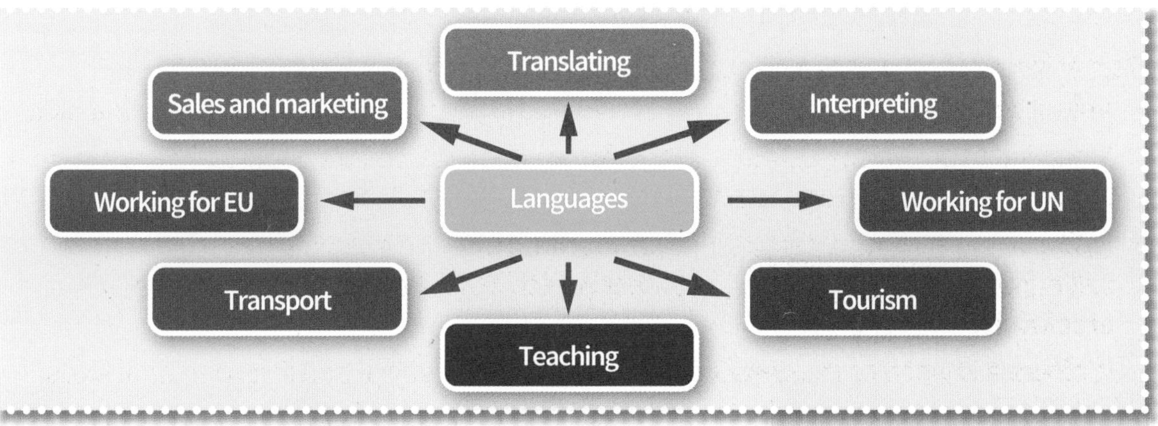

Figure 18.1 Suitable careers for a language expert

Weblinks

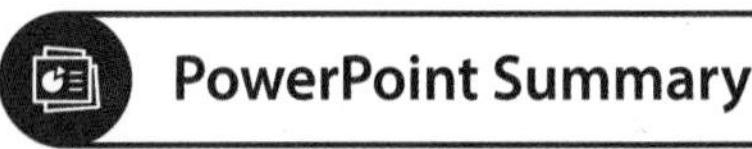
PowerPoint Summary

ENTERPRISE

RIGHTS AND RESPONSIBILITIES OF EMPLOYERS AND EMPLOYEES

LEARNING OUTCOMES IN FOCUS

2.4 Distinguish between the rights and responsibilities of employer and employee from a legal, social, environmental and ethical perspective

Links to 1.9, 2.2, 2.3, 2.5, 3.4, 3.6, 3.11

LEARNING INTENTIONS FOR THIS CHAPTER

When you have completed this chapter you will be able to:

- Appreciate that rights also bring responsibilities
- Outline the rights and responsibilities of employees
- Outline the rights and responsibilities of employers
- List and briefly explain the laws that protect employees
- Explain the term 'industrial relations'
- Outline the role of trade unions
- Explain why employees might join a trade union
- Outline different types of industrial action.

CHAPTER 19 KEY TERMS

absenteeism
arbitration
conciliation
contract of employment
curriculum vitae (CV)
employee
employer
go-slow
industrial action
industrial relations
Labour Court
national minimum wage
official strike
overtime ban
probationary period
redress
responsibility
right
shop steward
staff turnover
token stoppage
trade union
work to rule
Workplace Relations Commission (WRC)

CHAPTER 19 KEY SKILLS

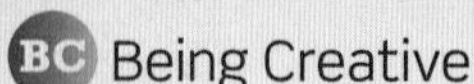

BC Being Creative
BL Being Literate
BN Being Numerate
C Communicating
MIT Managing Information and Thinking
WO Working with Others

ENTERPRISE

Rights and responsibilities

In Chapter 18 you learned about employment. In this chapter you will learn about the rights and responsibilities of employees and employers.

An **employer** is a person or business that pays employees for their work.

Employees are people who work for employers in return for a payment.

A **right** is something you are entitled to receive, for example to be treated fairly or to receive at least the minimum wage.

A **responsibility** is a duty or something you should do, such as treat others with respect.

With rights come responsibilities. Rights and responsibilities can be classified as follows:

- **Legal/statutory:** These are rights and responsibilities set out in law, such as the right to be treated equally regardless of age, gender, marital status, etc.
- **Social:** A responsibility to respect the rights of others and to act in the best interests of society as a whole.
- **Environmental:** Ensuring that the actions of individuals and organisations do not damage the environment. This is the basis for sustainable development.
- **Ethical:** Doing what we believe to be right, such as treating employees fairly. Employers should not exploit or mistreat employees. While this might potentially be profitable, it is certainly not ethical.

See Chapters 13 and 38 for sustainability

In practice, many rights and responsibilities are a combination of some or all of the above. For example, discrimination in the workplace is illegal as well as being both socially and ethically wrong.

Legislation protecting employees

Some of the main laws that protect employees in Ireland are:

- Protection of Young Persons (Employment) Act 1996
- Employment Equality Acts 1998–2015
- Unfair Dismissals Acts 1977–2015

Protection of Young Persons (Employment) Act 1996

This law protects young workers under the age of 18 and prevents young workers doing late-night work. Children aged 14 may do light work outside of school term. Children aged 15–16 may also do light work and this may be during school term. There are limits on the number of hours that may be worked and when the work may be done, with a complete ban on work between 8 p.m. and 8 a.m.

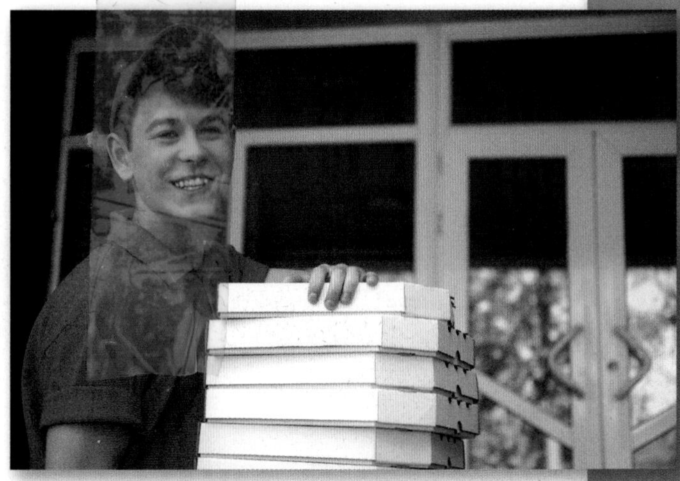

The law describes light work as work that is non-industrial and is not likely to be harmful to the safety, health or development of children, and is not harmful to their attendance at school or their participation in vocational guidance or training programmes.

Young people between 16 and 18 years of age may become employees, but there are restrictions on the maximum number of hours that can be worked and generally they cannot work between 10 p.m. and 6 a.m.

An employer of a child or young person must:

- See a copy of the employee's birth certificate
- Get a letter of consent from the child's parent/guardian if the employee is under 16
- Keep records of the employee's details, such as date of birth and the hours worked.

KEY SKILLS

19.1 Protection of Young Persons (Employment) Act 1996

BC RL MIT

Create a poster or infographic that could be given to young people from the age of 14 explaining the Protection of Young Persons (Employment) Act 1996. Set out the main points of the Act so that a young worker could refer to it to check that their conditions of employment are legal. **#Research**

Employment Equality Acts 1998–2015

These laws define discrimination as 'the treatment of one person in a less favourable way than another person is, has been or would be treated'. These laws outlaw discrimination on nine grounds:

- Age
- Gender
- Race
- Sexual orientation
- Religion
- Family status
- Marital status
- Disability
- Membership of the Travelling community.

All aspects of employment are covered, including:

- Hiring and training employees
- Equal pay
- Opportunity for promotion
- Dismissal (being sacked)
- Conditions of work
- Advertising for employees.

ENTERPRISE

Unfair Dismissals Acts 1977–2015

This Act states that employees cannot be dismissed for the following reasons:

- Age
- Becoming pregnant
- Religious beliefs
- Political beliefs
- Race
- Sexual orientation
- Being a member of the Travelling community
- Being a member of a trade union (see page 225)
- Taking part in an official strike
- Taking legal action against an employer.

Redress: Employees who have been unfairly dismissed may get their job back or receive financial compensation.

Valid reasons for dismissal include:

- **Incompetence:** Not carrying out the work to the required standard.
- **Misconduct:** The employee has broken the rules of their employment.
- **Redundancy:** An employee loses their job because the role is no longer required.
- **Unqualified:** The employee does not have the necessary qualifications needed to do the job.
- **Incapability:** Unable to do the job due to lateness or constant absences.

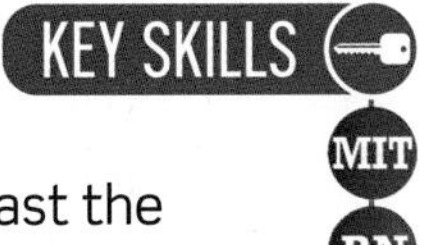

19.2 Unfair dismissal and discrimination

179 Using the Venn diagram in the Student Activity Book, compare and contrast the reasons for unfair dismissal under the Unfair Dismissals Acts and the reasons for which discrimination is outlawed under the Employment Equality Acts. #Compare

MIT BN

Rights of employees

Legal rights

> Employees have a legal rights to tips
> law coming soon for right to request working at home

Employees are protected by a number of employment laws. They have the right to:

- Receive at least the legal minimum wage – employees should always receive a fair day's pay for a fair day's work
- Receive a written contract of employment
- Receive the correct amount of paid holidays
- Work in a workplace that is safe and healthy
- Receive proper rest breaks during work
- Be provided with all information about them that is held by their employer.

Minimum wage

KEY TERM

The **national minimum wage** is the lowest average hourly rate that can be paid by an employer to an employee.

Some workers, including those under 18 and workers in certain industries, can be paid less than the national minimum rate. A national minimum wage does not prevent an employer paying a higher wage.

Contract of employment

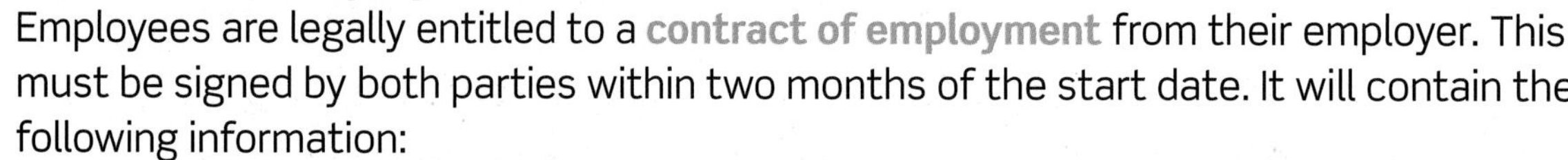

Employees are legally entitled to a **contract of employment** from their employer. This must be signed by both parties within two months of the start date. It will contain the following information:

1. Employer's name and address.
2. Employee's name and address.
3. Job title.
4. Job description.
5. Code of conduct.
6. Date of commencement and duration of contract: When the contract begins and how long it lasts for and whether it is a temporary or permanent contract.
7. What the employer reasonably expects the normal length of the employee's working day and week to be, in a standard week.
8. Payment: The salary or wages that you receive, when you receive them (weekly, monthly, etc.), how you receive them, overtime rate, etc.
9. Holiday entitlements: Employees have a legal entitlement to 20 days' paid annual leave, although some jobs may give more. There may also be rules about when you can take holidays and details of other types of statutory leave, e.g. parental, maternity, etc.
10. Duration/length of contract/probationary period, if any.
11. Any other conditions of the job (hours of work/location).
12. Pension arrangements.
13. Sick leave entitlements: How many days before a doctor's certificate is needed, details of payment while you are ill.
14. Signatures of the employer and the employee.

KEY TERM

A **probationary period** is a specified trial period at the start of the employment to see if the employee is suitable for the position.

KEY SKILLS

19.3 Contract of employment

182

Complete the blank contract of employment template in your Student Activity Book. #Activity

BL MIT

ENTERPRISE

Social rights

- To work in a safe and respectful atmosphere, free from danger, bullying or discrimination
- To join a trade union if they choose to do so.

KEY TERM

A **trade union** is an organisation that represents workers, protects their rights and negotiates with employers on pay and conditions of work.

Environmental rights

- To have a safe and healthy working environment
- To be provided with necessary safety equipment and protective clothing
- Not to be asked to carry out work that breaches environmental regulations.

Ethical rights

- To receive a fair day's pay for a fair day's work
- To have their religious and cultural beliefs respected
- Not to be asked to do anything unethical or illegal.

KEY SKILLS

19.4 Working conditions around the world

C BL MIT

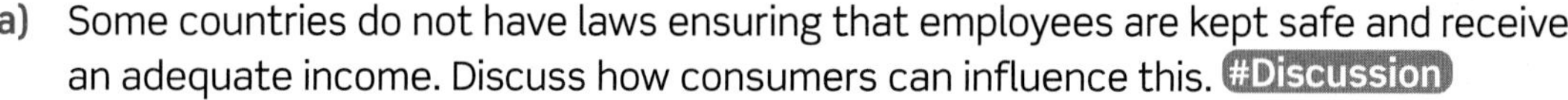

(a) Some countries do not have laws ensuring that employees are kept safe and receive an adequate income. Discuss how consumers can influence this. #Discussion

(b) Compare the rights of people working in Ireland and people working in better or worse conditions in other countries. #Research #Compare

Responsibilities of employees

Legal responsibilities

Employees should:

- Carry out their duties as stated in their contract of employment
- Follow workplace rules and safety instructions
- Respect their employer's property
- Wear protective clothing and equipment provided by their employer
- Attend all training provided by the business
- Not discriminate against or bully other employees.

Social responsibilities

Employees have the responsibility to:

- Treat customers, co-workers and the employer with respect
- Work with and support fellow workers in order to achieve the aims of the business
- Be loyal to their employer and not disclose confidential business information.

Environmental responsibilities

Employees should carry out work in an environmentally responsible way and follow all environmental regulations and procedures; for example, they should not dump waste illegally.

Ethical responsibilities

Employees should:

- Do a fair day's work for a fair day's pay
- Be on time for work
- Not be absent from work without a valid reason, for example illness or a family emergency
- Be honest and truthful in all aspects of their work.

KEY TERM

The practice of regularly staying away from work without good reason is called **absenteeism**. High levels of absenteeism can lead to staffing and operational problems for employers.

Rights of employers

Legal rights

- To decide the aims and objectives of the business
- To hire suitable staff for their business
- To dismiss dishonest or unsuitable staff.

Social rights

Employers have the right to expect a reasonable effort from all employees.

Environmental rights

Employers have the right to expect employees to carry out their work in an environmentally responsible way and to follow all environmental regulations and procedures.

Ethical rights

Employers have the right to expect:

- Loyalty and honesty from their staff
- That staff will respect their property and good name
- A fair day's work from their staff for a fair day's pay
- That staff will act in an ethical way when carrying out their work or making decisions.

Responsibilities of employers

Legal responsibilities

Employers should:

- Comply with all employment and privacy laws.
- Give employees a written contract of employment.

- Pay agreed wages. They must pay at least the minimum wage to their employees and give equal pay to men and women.
- Ensure that all employees are treated equally in the business and that there is no bullying or harassment.
- Not discriminate when advertising, recruiting or promoting staff (see Employment Equality Acts, page 218).
- Ensure that the workplace is safe and that employees have healthy working conditions. For example, workers on building sites should wear hard hats and protective footwear.
- Provide employees with the holidays and leave that they are legally entitled to, such as maternity/paternity/parental leave.
- Deduct and submit tax – Pay As You Earn (PAYE), Pay Related Social Insurance (PRSI) and Universal Social Charge (USC) – from their employees' pay and keep employment records, including Revenue payments, for each employee.
- Provide employees with all information requested by them. Under data protection laws, workers can ask to see all the information their employer holds about them.
- Use fair procedures when dealing with staff redundancy. Employers should operate a fair selection process for redundancy, usually on the basis of last in, first out.

KEY SKILLS

19.5 Voluntary redundancy

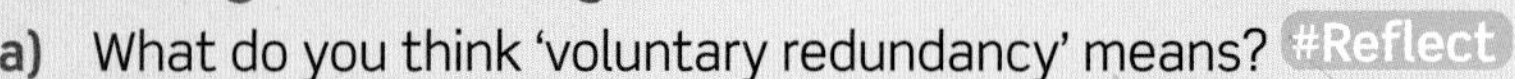

(a) What do you think 'voluntary redundancy' means? #Reflect

(b) Why do you think employees might agree to it? #Opinion

Social responsibilities

Employers should:

- Respect employees' right to join a trade union.
- Consult with employees on issues that will impact on staff. If employees feel they have been included in decision-making, they are more likely to accept decisions and work hard to achieve them.
- Respect employees' privacy and their personal and cultural beliefs.
- Act in the best interests of the wider group of stakeholders, not just shareholders, when operating the business.

Environmental responsibilities

Employers' responsibilities are to:

- Create a positive and healthy working environment that looks after the needs of employees
- Operate their business in a sustainable and environmentally responsible manner. This may include waste reduction, increased recycling and responsible sourcing of raw materials.

Ethical responsibilities

Employers should:

- Be open, honest and truthful in all dealings with employees
- Pay employees a fair wage for the work they do
- Not exploit or take advantage of workers in any way.

KEY SKILLS

19.6 Employers' responsibilities

In groups, create a poster or infographic showing the responsibilities of employers. #GroupWork

Employee records

Employers are required to keep records on all their employees. Employee records help an employer to make decisions about pay rises, promotions and dismissals. The details they keep are usually:

- Personal details, such as the employee's full name, address, date of birth, PPS number and contact names and telephone numbers in case of an emergency
- The completed job application form or CV
- The employee's behaviour record, including attendance, punctuality and work performance
- Timesheets
- A copy of the employee's employment contract
- Records of PAYE, PRSI and USC paid.

KEY TERM

A **curriculum vitae (CV)** is often used by someone who is applying for a job. It is a written summary of the job applicant's personal details, work experience, qualifications and achievements.

Industrial relations

KEY TERM

Industrial relations refers to the relationship that exists between employers and their employees in the workplace.

If there are good industrial relations in a workplace, staff will be motivated, hard-working and happy. There are likely to be very few disputes or strikes, which means that the business, the employees and the customers will not lose out on income or services due to **industrial action**.

In contrast, poor industrial relations can lead to disputes in the workplace, high absenteeism, high staff turnover, strikes, loss of income and customers, and bad publicity for the business.

KEY TERM

Staff turnover refers to the number of employees who leave an organisation and have to be replaced by new staff.

KEY SKILLS

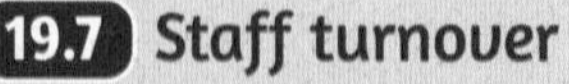

19.7 Staff turnover

(a) Why is a high rate of staff turnover bad for an organisation? #Opinion #Reflect

(b) What could an organisation do to reduce its level of staff turnover? #Suggest

Trade unions

All employees have the right to join a trade union. Workers join trade unions and pay subscriptions to them because their trade union:

- Negotiates with employers for better pay and working conditions for its members
- Represents workers who have disputes with their employers
- Represents employees at discussions about national pay agreements. These are agreements on issues like pay and conditions that are made between employers, trade unions and the government.

Examples of trade unions include SIPTU (Services, Industrial, Professional and Technical Union) and Mandate, which represents retail and bar workers.

The trade union representative in the workplace is known as a **shop steward**. This is an employee elected by the workers to represent them in dealings with the employer.

KEY SKILLS MIT WO BC

19.8 Trade unions

In small groups, research one of the following trade unions (or another union of your choice) and create a poster or infographic on it, including its full name, the type of employees it represents and an outline of how it protects the rights of its members. #GroupWork #Research

- Connect
- CPSU
- CWU
- FSU
- INMO
- INTO
- Mandate
- SIPTU

KEY SKILLS MIT C

19.9 Industrial relations

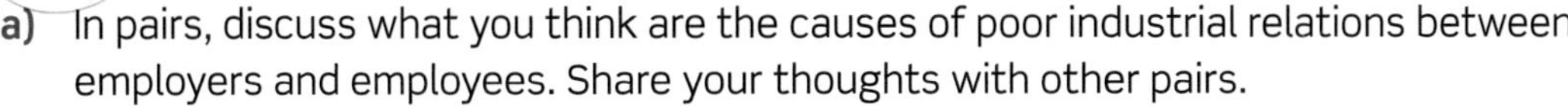

(a) In pairs, discuss what you think are the causes of poor industrial relations between employers and employees. Share your thoughts with other pairs.

(b) Discuss how many industrial disputes are the result of employees being denied their rights. #Opinion #Discussion #ThinkPairShare

Types of industrial action

Industrial disputes can result in a range of actions, such as:

- **Official strike:** Employees refuse to work for the employer. The trade union must hold a secret ballot and give the employer one week's notice of the strike action.
- **Work to rule:** Workers do only what is in their job description and nothing else. For example, doctors in a hospital may refuse to do any administrative work, for example answering phones, and will only deal directly with the treatment of patients.
- **Go-slow:** Workers do their work, but at a slower pace. This means they are less productive.
- **Overtime ban:** Workers refuse to do overtime.
- **Token stoppage:** Workers stop working for a short period of time, for example for three hours. This can disrupt the flow of work on the day it happens.

KEY SKILLS 

MIT BL

19.10 Industrial relations disputes

Research recent industrial relations disputes using newspapers or the internet. Find answers to these questions:

(a) In which sector (for example retail, medicine) did the dispute take place?

(b) Which trade union and which employer were involved?

(c) What was the dispute about?

(d) If the dispute has been resolved, how was this achieved? **Or:** If it has not yet been resolved, how would you suggest this could be achieved? #Research

Industrial Relations Act 1990

This Act states that employees engaging in **industrial action** (strikes, etc.) cannot be stopped or sued by the employer for losses suffered as a result of industrial action, provided the employees held a secret ballot and gave the employer one week's notice of the industrial action.

KEY SKILLS

MIT BL

19.11 Young people, work and employment

Write down your own personal views about young people, work and employment. Consider the following:

(a) Do you think young people should be allowed to be employed outside the home? Explain your reasons. If you think they should be allowed to work outside the home, what age and working hours do you think are appropriate? #Reflect

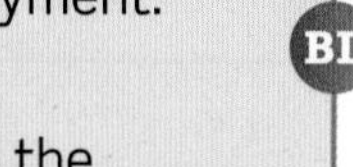

(b) Do you think young people should be taxed on any income they earn from employment? Explain why/why not. #Justify

(c) What other legal protection should the law provide to young workers? #List #Opinion

Workplace Relations Commission (WRC)

The Workplace Relations 2015 Act set up the **Workplace Relations Commission (WRC)**, which is an independent statutory body. Its role is to improve workplace relations between employers and employees. It ensures that employers obey all employment laws and helps to resolve disputes by assisting in talks between employers and employees. This process is known as **conciliation**. For example, the WRC might invite an employer and trade union who are in dispute to sit down and talk about a possible agreement. The WRC will not put forward a solution, but will act as an independent mediator (third party) to try to get both sides to discuss their differences and find a compromise or solution.

Labour Court (LC)

The **Labour Court (LC)** can help to resolve disputes that were not resolved by the Workplace Relations Commission. It investigates disputes and recommends a solution in a process known as **arbitration**. It is the court of last resort in industrial relations matters.

KEY SKILLS

MIT

19.12 WRC and LC

Research the functions of the Workplace Relations Commission and the Labour Court. #Research

Weblinks

PowerPoint Summary

ENTERPRISE

IMPACT OF DIGITAL TECHNOLOGIES

LEARNING OUTCOMES IN FOCUS

2.6 Discuss the impact of digital technologies on an organisation, debating the associated rewards and costs

Links to 1.10, 2.5, 2.7, 2.8, 3.7

LEARNING INTENTIONS FOR THIS CHAPTER

When you have completed this chapter you will be able to:

- Explain the term 'digital technologies'
- Identify a range of technologies used by enterprises
- Describe the benefits of using digital technologies
- Outline the cost of using digital technologies
- Explain the opportunities for enterprises when using digital technologies
- Appreciate the impact of digital technology on consumers.

CHAPTER 20 KEY TERMS

- applications (apps)
- blog
- broadband
- cloud computing
- capital expenditure
- customer relationship management (CRM)
- database
- digital technologies
- e-commerce
- hacking
- hardware
- impact
- information and communications technology (ICT)
- internet of things (IoT)
- m-commerce
- social media
- software
- tablet
- video conferencing
- vlog
- Wi-Fi

CHAPTER 20 KEY SKILLS

- BL Being Literate
- C Communicating
- MIT Managing Information and Thinking
- MM Managing Myself
- SW Staying Well
- WO Working with Others

Digital technologies in organisations

KEY TERM

Digital technologies are a set of technological tools and resources used to communicate and create, distribute, store and manage information, for example mobile phones, apps, tablets and computers.

'I've come up with a set of rules that describe our reactions to technologies:

1 Anything in the world when you're born is normal and ordinary and is just part of the way the world works.
2 Anything that's invented between when you're 15 and 35 is new and exciting and revolutionary and you can probably get a career in it.
3 Anything invented after you're 35 is against the natural order of things.'

– Douglas Adams, *The Salmon of Doubt*

In this chapter we will learn about the impact of digital technology on organisations.

An **impact** is an effect or influence on something. The impact of digital technologies on an organisation can be:

- **Positive** – when it benefits the organisation
- **Negative** – when it involves costs or a loss to the organisation.

As consumers, we use our phones, tablets and computers in a variety of ways.

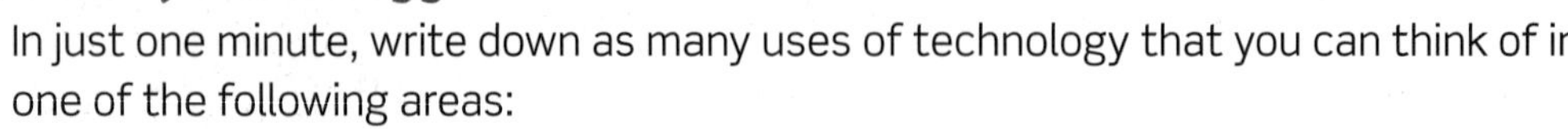

KEY SKILLS

20.1 Uses of technology

In just one minute, write down as many uses of technology that you can think of in one of the following areas:

(a) Your home
(b) Your school
(c) A local business you are familiar with. #List

Consider the quote above and remember that it's okay to include technologies that aren't necessarily new. If they've been around for a while, you may just take them for granted! Swap your list with your partner and see how many uses you had in common. Share your combined list with the whole class. #Record #ThinkPairShare

Organisations also use technology in a variety of ways:

- To design and produce products
- To conduct market research
- To prepare financial budgets and accounts
- To communicate with suppliers, customers and employees
- To promote and sell their products and services online.

In order to compete with rivals, organisations need to invest in and make effective use of technology. The technology an organisation uses can affect how the business operates, how orders are processed, how stock shortages are identified, how sales are analysed, etc. If the technology is out of date, business opportunities may be missed and competitors may gain an advantage.

> **KEY TERM**
>
> **Information and communications technology (ICT)** refers to the use of technology to send, receive, gather, store, analyse, distribute and communicate information.
>
> **Hardware** is the physical parts of a computer, such as the monitor, scanner and printer.
>
> **Software** refers to the programs that provide instructions to a computer, for example spreadsheets and word processing.

Digital technologies used by organisations

There are many technologies that a business can use to save time and money. Some will be familiar to home users too. The following examples of common current technologies is not a complete list and it will be constantly changing as old technologies become outdated and new technologies replace them.

- **Word processing** for writing reports, letters, business plans, etc.
- **Spreadsheets** for recording employees' wages/salaries, recording cash flow, preparing accounts, creating charts, etc.
- **Databases** for recording employee, customer and supplier details, stock items and other relevant data. Databases allow users to store and search for large amounts of information quickly. They can also be used to create reports that show, for example, best-selling products. They can speed up decision-making by making it easy to find information quickly.

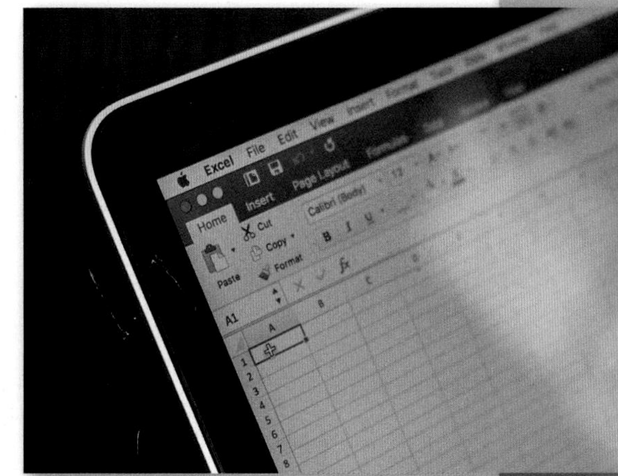

> **KEY TERM**
>
> A **database** is a computer program that files and stores information in a very structured way so that it can be searched for specific details.

- **Desktop publishing** for creating brochures, leaflets, flyers, catalogues, etc.
- **Presentation packages** (e.g. PowerPoint) for creating slideshows for meetings, etc.

- **Electronic point of sale (EPOS)** for scanning barcodes, printing till receipts, taking payments by debit cards, credit cards and digital wallets, updating stock records and providing sales reports.
- **Email** for communicating both internally and externally with suppliers, customers, banks and other stakeholders.
- The **internet** is a global network connecting computers, tablets and smartphones and enabling them to exchange information. Most enterprises have their own website to promote and/or sell their product or service and communicate with existing and potential customers. Advertising and selling products through websites has allowed global e-commerce to flourish. Many people use their smartphones to buy products – this is called mobile commerce, or m-commerce.
- Cloud computing for saving, storing and accessing information remotely on the internet (the cloud). Enterprises can save money by storing information online, as this reduces the need for lots of hardware as well as the number of ICT staff needed to maintain equipment. However, cloud computing requires excellent broadband and Wi-Fi connections.
- Wi-Fi allows computers, tablets, smartphones and other devices to connect to the internet wirelessly. It operates within a certain area range, for example a building. Most businesses have broadband, which allows information to be transferred between computers at a high speed. Many consumers expect businesses such as libraries, transport services, shops, cafés, restaurants and hotels to provide free Wi-Fi; businesses that do not may lose customers to competing businesses.
- Video conferencing allows people in different locations to communicate using audio and video. Video conferencing reduces the need to travel to meetings, which saves time and money. Skype and Facetime are examples of this type of technology.
- Businesses use social media to keep in touch with customers and to promote products and services to a potential global market. Social media is a powerful marketing and advertising platform for many businesses. Social media platforms such as Facebook, Instagram and Twitter have millions of daily users and consumers are often influenced by what they see or read on social media.

KEY SKILLS

20.2 Social media platforms

(a) Name four social media platforms other than Facebook. #List

(b) Which social media platforms would you recommend to:

(i) A magazine aimed at teenagers?

(ii) A business selling holidays to 18–30-year-olds?

(iii) A hotel selling short breaks to the over-60 age group?

Provide reasons for your answers. #Identify #Research

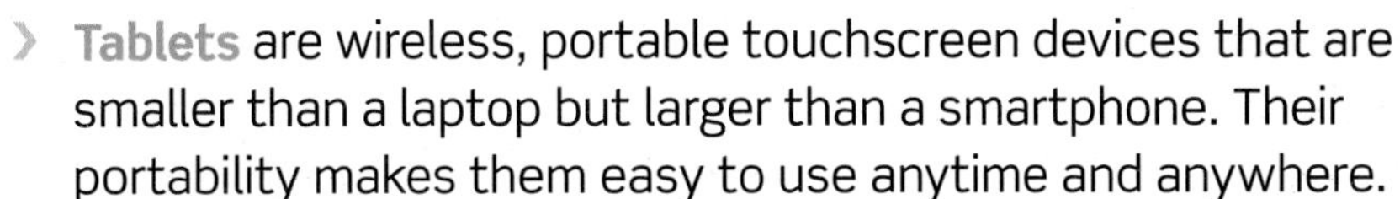

- **Tablets** are wireless, portable touchscreen devices that are smaller than a laptop but larger than a smartphone. Their portability makes them easy to use anytime and anywhere.

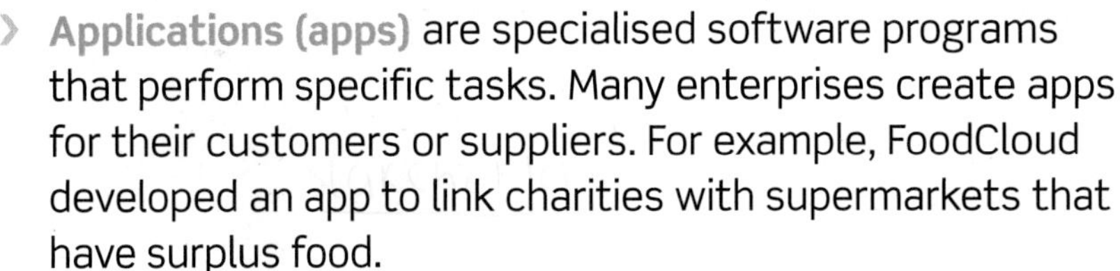

- **Applications (apps)** are specialised software programs that perform specific tasks. Many enterprises create apps for their customers or suppliers. For example, FoodCloud developed an app to link charities with supermarkets that have surplus food.

See Chapter 16 for social enterprise: FoodCloud

KEY SKILLS

20.3 Choosing digital technologies

MIT C

Chris and Claire have decided to open a new restaurant.

(a) What digital technologies would you advise them to invest in? #Opinion

(b) In each case, briefly explain why they would need it and what it will be used for. #Justify

(c) Share your thoughts with a classmate and identify any technologies that you didn't consider. #ThinkPairShare

(d) Share your combined list with the whole class. #ThinkPairShare

Benefits and rewards of using digital technology

Digital technologies have many benefits for a business, which can be categorised as follows:

- Recruiting and managing staff
- Market research and marketing
- Production
- Finance
- Administration.

Recruiting and managing staff

- **Job vacancies and interviews:** Job vacancies can be advertised online, which will increase the number of applicants. Video conferencing can be used to interview shortlisted candidates to reduce travel costs.
- **Online shared calendars:** Employees can use online shared calendars to view staff meetings and appointments.
- **Emails and texts:** Email and text messaging can be used to communicate with staff.
- **Online training:** Staff can avail of online training, which they can complete at their own pace.
- **Teleworking:** Staff might be able to work from home (teleworking) through the use of broadband, email, telephone and video conferencing.

Market research and marketing

- **Loyalty cards:** Information on consumers' spending habits can be gathered through store loyalty cards, which are swiped or scanned when purchasing goods. This allows businesses to target special offers at consumers. The loyalty card benefits the consumer in the form of discounts, but it also helps the retailer by providing information about the consumer's spending habits.

IN THE NEWS

McDonald's Corp has announced that it is buying Israel's Dynamic Yield. The latter company's technology helps marketers personalise customer interactions.

McDonald's will pay more than $300 million for Dynamic Yield. McDonald's said it would use Dynamic Yield's technology to change its digital drive-through menu displays to show food based on the time of day, weather, current restaurant traffic and trending menu items.

Source: Hospitality Ireland, 1 April 2019

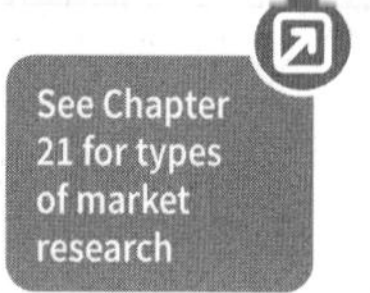
See Chapter 21 for types of market research

- **Online surveys:** Market research can be gathered and analysed quickly and easily by using online surveys.
- **Direct marketing:** Customer information stored on databases can be used for direct marketing purposes. This involves information about products or special offers being sent directly to specific customers who are likely to be interested. Customers can be contacted by email, phone or through social media. However, organisations must be aware of their responsibilities under the General Data Protection Regulation (GDPR), which became law in 2018. This regulation is designed to protect personal information and data and limits how organisations can collect, use and share it.
- **Websites and social media:** Products and services can be promoted and sold globally using a company website and social media can be used to target customers.
- **Emails and texts:** Text messages and emails can be used to communicate directly with customers who have opted in to the service to encourage them to buy products, inform them of sales or special offers, remind them of appointments, etc.

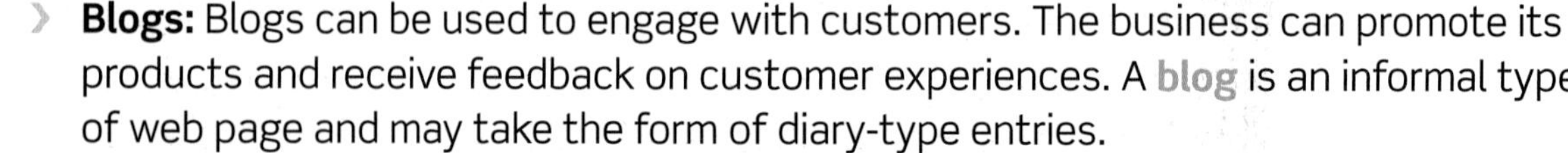

- **Blogs:** Blogs can be used to engage with customers. The business can promote its products and receive feedback on customer experiences. A **blog** is an informal type of web page and may take the form of diary-type entries.

Production

- **Research:** Suppliers can be researched online to find the cheapest source of raw materials.
- **Stock control:** The information gathered from the EPOS can be used to automatically reorder stock when it runs low.

- **CAD, CAM and CIM:** CAD (computer-aided design), CAM (computer-aided manufacture) and CIM (computer-integrated manufacturing, which is similar to robotics) can be used to speed up the product development process and produce high-quality products. All of these processes use technology to design and manufacture products.

Finance

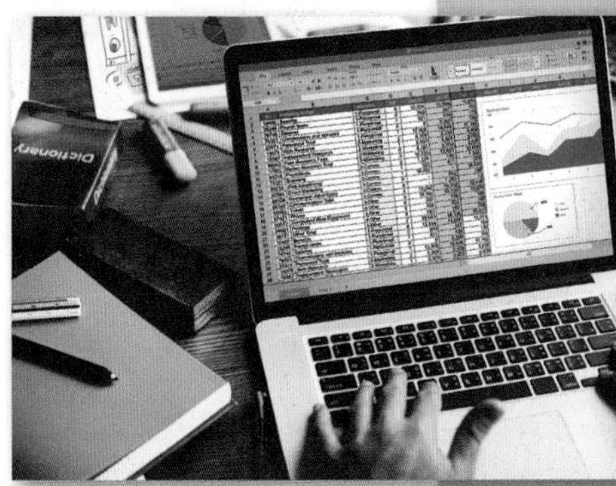

- **Spreadsheets:** Spreadsheets can be used to prepare accurate cash flow forecasts and accounts.
- **Formulas:** Formulas can be copied to speed up the calculation of accounts.
- **Graphs and charts:** Graphs and charts can be created to analyse and interpret financial information.
- **Presentations:** Presentation software can be used to make financial information more engaging when looking for investment.
- **Loans:** It is possible to research loan comparisons and apply for loans online.

Administration

- **Decision-making:** Decision-making is much faster because information is easier to access.
- **Writing:** Writing personalised letters and reports is more efficient with word processing and email.
- **Tax returns:** A business can file tax returns online through Revenue Online Service (ROS).

Digital technology and business costs

Investing in technology can be a major cost for businesses. However, using technology can also lead to many cost savings.

Cost increases

- **Capital costs:** There will be capital costs when installing new technology. Capital expenditure refers to once-off or long-term spending needed to upgrade technology, for example the cost of buying new computers or phones or installing a server or Wi-Fi network.
- **Recruitment and training:** Cost of recruiting and training specialist staff along with the loss of working time while staff are being trained.
- **Information loss:** Risk of information loss through staff error or computer hacking. Hacking is when someone gains unauthorised access to computer data. In 2018, Facebook reported that the accounts of up to 50 million of its users were hacked due to a security flaw in their system.
- **Back-up:** Risk of loss of information if storage is not backed up.
- **Website:** Cost of designing, maintaining and hosting a website.
- **Anti-virus software:** Cost of anti-virus software for business laptops, computers and tablets.

- **Health and safety:** Health and safety issues for staff through repetitive strain injury, eye strain, backache, etc. Employees who work on computers/laptops for long periods should take frequent breaks from using the screen to avoid eye strain.
- **Cost of technology failure or breakdown:** In 2012, Ulster Bank paid compensation to customers and a €3.5 million fine when computer failure prevented customers from accessing their accounts.
- **Redundancy costs:** The use of technology may displace human workers, which means that businesses may have to make redundancy payments to staff.

Cost reductions

- **Website:** A company's website can be used to advertise its business and as an online store. The site can be updated on a regular basis, which eliminates the need to produce printed catalogues.
- **Number of workers:** Using certain new technologies can reduce the number of workers required. For example, ATMs and online banking reduce the need for bank staff, while many supermarkets now use self-scanning checkouts.
- **Teleworking:** Teleworking cuts down on costs by reducing the need for large premises for staff to work in.
- **Email:** Emails can be sent to many people much more quickly and cheaply than sending letters.

Opportunities associated with using digital technology

- **Production:** The increased use of technology in production allows for standardisation and mass production, resulting in increased output and reduced costs.
- **Sales and marketing:** Using digital technology in sales and marketing allows businesses to see what consumers are buying and to pick which sector of the market to focus on.
- **Customer relationship management (CRM):** CRM describes the use of a variety of strategies and technologies to manage interactions with customers. For example, information gathered from websites, blogs and social media can offer useful insights into a customer's purchase history and preferences.
- **Salespeople:** Salespeople can use smartphones and laptops to access updated information at any time.
- **Travel and meetings:** A business can use email and video conferencing to reduce the costs of travel and meetings.
- **Employees:** Technology can reduce the number of people employed in the business or improve the efficiency of those employed.

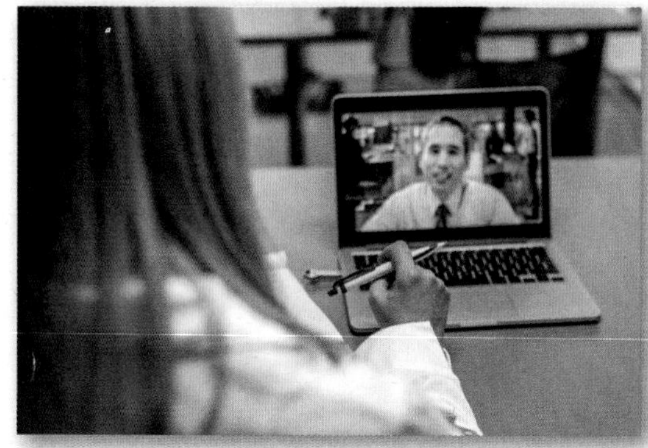

- **Automation:** Routine tasks can be automated, which means employees' time is available for more creative tasks.

KEY SKILLS MIT C

20.4 Going low-tech?

Do you think any business can survive these days without technology? Discuss, thinking about a window-cleaning business, a bank and a farm (or another business of your choice). #Discussion

Case study: A cost–benefit analysis of digital technology in retailing

A clothing retailer with several branches throughout Ireland has decided to rebrand its business in order to appeal to a younger target market. A target market is a group of people to whom a business is aiming to sell its products or services. As part of the rebranding, it is also considering a large investment in digital technology. The main elements of the plan are as follows:

- Make maximum use of point-of-sale technology for marketing and payment purposes.
- Upgrade the company website to include a new online catalogue and sales facility. The current website is very outdated, as it was designed to appeal to an older target market who make limited use of online technology.
- Blog in an effort to communicate with the target market. Many blogs are written by social media 'influencers'. These are people who can influence consumers by promoting or recommending goods and services on social media. Some influencers use video to support their blogs – these are called **vlogs**.

- Invest in iBeacon technology to target individual customers with products. This technology requires customers to download an app to their phone. Once they enter the retail store, they receive details of special offers and specific products that they have browsed or 'liked' online.

- Introduce in-store hubs and virtual displays to provide customers with images and information on product lines. In-store hubs use touchscreen technology and allow customers to view product details, including prices, sizes and availability. Customers can also use the technology to order goods that are currently out of stock. The virtual displays are large screens that show products to customers as they move around the store.

DID YOU KNOW...

The **internet of things (IoT)** is a computing concept that describes how everyday objects and devices (cars, smartwatches, fridges, traffic signals) can be connected to the internet and are able to interact and share information with other devices. The information they share can be useful for the way we make products or manage transport and healthcare systems.

Cost-benefit analysis of the proposed investment in digital technology

This looks at what costs are involved in getting the new technology and compares them with the benefits the organisation will get from using the technology. By weighing up both sides to see if the benefits outweigh the costs, the organisation hopes to make the best decision.

Technology	Costs	Benefits
Point-of-sale technology	› Requires a minor upgrade of existing technology	› Essential for payments in a cashless society › Increases sales of specific products at point of purchase
Website upgrade	› Major investment required › Will need to employ specialist staff or hire a professional web designer	› The business will have a greater online presence › Increased interaction with target market › Increased online sales
Blogs	› Developing a blog will be time-consuming and offers no guarantee of success › Hiring an existing fashion blogger may have a lower cost and a greater appeal	› Increased interaction with target market › Ability to use social media as a marketing tool › Ability to get feedback from customers helps with market research
iBeacon	› Costs of developing app and acquiring technology › Risk of annoying some customers with constant push notifications about products	› More targeted advertising and an ability to cater for individual customer needs and preferences › Useful for market research purposes
In-store hubs	› Expensive to programme and install the technology › May be time-consuming to maintain and update › May be a costly duplication of technology if iBeacon is also in use	› Less intrusive than iBeacon technology › Can encourage customers to order out-of-stock items
Virtual displays	› Cost of purchase, programming and installation	› Once installed, they are cheap to update and maintain › Reduce the need to create large in-store displays › Increase availability of revenue-generating floor space

Evaluation and conclusion	Bearing in mind the costs and benefits set out above, management decided: › To upgrade the point-of-sale technology › To update the website and outsource the blog in order to promote the business online › To invest in iBeacon technology and in-store virtual displays › That the benefits of in-store hubs did not justify the costs involved, so no investment would be made in this technology.

ENTERPRISE

Impact of digital technology on consumers

Digital technology is now a big part of our everyday lives and the growth of the internet and mobile phone technologies have played a major role in this development. Businesses use our obsession with technology to sell us more goods and services. The use of social media influencers, notifications and personalised content are all examples of ways in which businesses try to influence our buying decisions.

Social media influencers are often paid to promote products to their followers. The Advertising Standards Authority for Ireland (ASAI) states that such posts must be clearly marked as marketing communications using *#ad, #sp* (sponsored post) or similar.

See Chapter 22 for celebrity endorsement/ influencers

KEY SKILLS

20.5 Digital technology and consumers

Debate the impact of these technologies on your buying habits. Do you believe that they are a powerful influence? Outline your views to the class. #Debate #Discussion

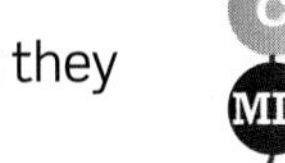

KEY SKILLS

20.6 Your use of social media

The phrase 'if you're not paying for it, you're the product' is often used in relation to social media, blogs and websites. What do you think this means? How does this make you feel about your use of social media? #Opinion #Reflect

IN THE NEWS

'A tweet from Kendall Jenner can be worth more than a €500k marketing budget'

Shane O'Sullivan, owner of Easilocks, explains how social media has helped his business to grow.

After I took over my dad's salon, I looked at different services that would offer more of a profit. We started providing hair extensions, which in 2005 were only starting to become a popular service.

We introduced that service into the salon on top of the hairdressing and it quickly became the most popular and profitable part of the salon.

We started getting the attention of celebrity models who would come exclusively to our salon to have their hair extensions done and became the go-to salon for the service in Dublin. People were travelling from all over the country and across from the UK just to come to us.

Three years ago we had a celebrity client in the salon that I had done hair extensions for and she had tweeted about Easilocks.

Twitter had just started to become popular and it was a more innocent time of social media when people weren't getting paid to post about a product. She tweeted how happy she was and the next day we had over 100 emails from people enquiring where they could get their hair done like this celebrity they follow.

Twitter, Facebook and Instagram create such massive awareness instantly, which is a tool smaller businesses, like my own, didn't have at our disposal 10 years ago. Even if you had a marketing budget of €500,000, it would still be hard to replicate some of the success you can get from a celebrity endorsement on social media, like model Kendall Jenner.

Source: The Journal.ie, 2 October 2016

KEY SKILLS 

20.7 Online influencers

(a) Make a list of any online influencers or vloggers you follow or have heard of. #List

(b) Why do you think these people are so popular and influential? #Opinion

(c) Did you know that they have to clearly state if they are paid to promote a product? Suggest a reason why you think this is required. #DoYouKnow

(d) Do you think you would ever be influenced to buy products or services as a result of this type of promotion or endorsement? Why/why not? #Justify #WhatDoYouThink

KEY SKILLS

20.8 Online selling

(a) Explain two advantages of online selling/e-commerce for consumers. #Explain

(b) Outline one risk of online selling/e-commerce for consumers. #Outline

KEY SKILLS

20.9 Technology terms

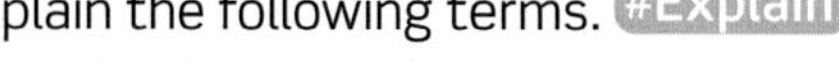

(a) Explain the following terms. #Explain

(i) Cloud computing

(ii) Video conferencing

(iii) Electronic point of sale

(iv) Push notification

(b) The following abbreviations are used in information and communications technology (ICT). In your copy, write down what each abbreviation stands for. #Identify

(i) CAD

(ii) CIM

(iii) CAM

(iv) EPOS

EXAM QUESTION

Junior Cycle 2019

Question 16(a)

New Chapters is an award-winning traditional bookshop located in Tinahely, Co. Wicklow.

(v) Investing in information and communications technology (ICT) can bring many benefits to a local business like New Chapters. Illustrate how the business could use technology to its advantage.

(vi) Outline two possible costs for New Chapters associated with investing in ICT.

 Weblinks

 PowerPoint Summary

MARKET RESEARCH

LEARNING OUTCOMES IN FOCUS

2.7 Conduct market research in order to investigate an entrepreneurial opportunity and analyse, interpret and communicate the research findings using relevant terminology and representations

Links to 1.10, 2.6, 2.8, 2.9, 3.3

LEARNING INTENTIONS FOR THIS CHAPTER

When you have completed this chapter you will be able to:

- Define the term 'market research'
- Outline the benefits of carrying out market research
- Distinguish between field research and desk research
- Explore the advantages and disadvantages of field research and desk research
- Conduct market research and analyse the results of that research
- Interpret and communicate your research findings.

CHAPTER 21 KEY TERMS

bar chart	personal interview
desk research	pie chart
field research	postal survey
focus group	primary research
market research	sampling
marketplace	secondary research
observation	survey
online survey	telephone survey

CHAPTER 21 KEY SKILLS

- BC Being Creative
- BL Being Literate
- BN Being Numerate
- C Communicating
- MIT Managing Information and Thinking
- WO Working with Others

As you learned in Chapter 16, new products and services are constantly being developed to meet consumer needs. Existing products or services may also be redesigned or updated. During the new product development process, entrepreneurs have to screen ideas and drop unworkable products. One method of screening is to conduct market research.

What is market research?

KEY TERM

Market research is gathering, recording and analysing information about consumer preferences for a good or service in order to make informed decisions about a potential market.

Businesses conduct market research to help ensure that they provide the goods and services that customers need and want and to help them stay ahead of their competitors.

Benefits of carrying out market research

Market research helps a business to reduce the risk of failure by finding out:

- Information about **customers' needs and wants**
- **Consumers' reactions to changes** to an existing product or service
- Information about their **competition**
- The **best price to charge** their customers
- Consumers' reactions to **how the product is promoted**, for example whether or not an advertising campaign is effective
- The likely **level of demand/sales** for a new product or service.

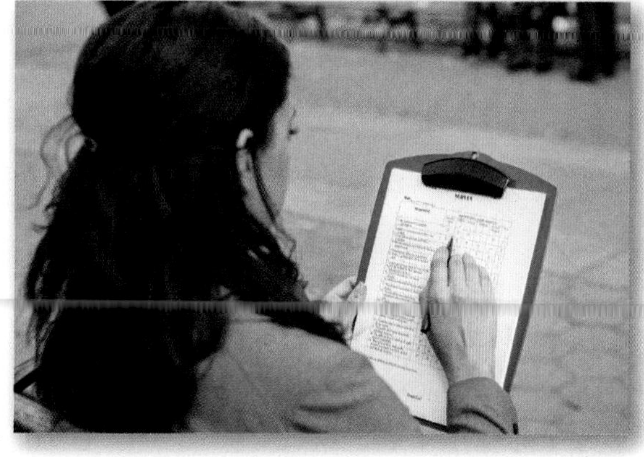

Market research should help businesses to make informed decisions about new products and services or changes to existing products and services.

Uses of market research

Enterprises use market research for the following reasons:

- **To identify what is happening in a market.** For example, Apple may want to identify trends in sales of iPads or smartphones.
- **To identify what is likely to happen in the future.** For example, Sunway Travel may research the kinds of holidays people are interested in taking in the next three years so that they can provide suitable trips.
- **To explain the causes of changes in the market.** For example, Nissan might research why sales of the Qashqai in Europe have declined slightly since 2011, as shown by their sales reports.
- **To investigate new market possibilities.** For example, SuperValu could test a new product in stores in Galway to test consumer reaction before launching nationwide.
- **To identify gaps in the market** that are not already being served by competitors and provide a product or service that fills that gap. For example, Kellogg's might identify a demand for a new type of breakfast cereal that nobody is currently producing.

Types of market research

There are two main types of market research: field research and desk research.

KEY TERM

Field research involves gathering information directly from the marketplace.

Desk research involves analysing information that has already been collected.

Field research

Field research involves going to the **marketplace** (the people who might buy your product or service) to gather information first-hand for a specific purpose. It is also known as **primary research** and is carried out by making direct contact with existing customers or potential customers.

Methods of field research include:

1. **Surveys:** Face-to-face or written questionnaires.
2. **Focus groups:** Meeting with a group of customers to discuss their opinions about a product.
3. **Observation:** Looking at customers' buying habits.

1 *Surveys*

A **survey** involves asking consumers questions about products and services. The responses will be analysed by market researchers. Questions should be clear and they should not be leading (suggesting certain answers). Question types include:

- Closed – requiring a 'yes' or 'no' answer.
- Multiple choice – allows several possible responses.
- Open-ended – allows consumers to say what they like rather than be confined to a specific answer. These are useful for gathering reactions or opinions. For example, you might ask 'Did you like the chocolate bar?' The consumer might just say 'No', which isn't very helpful. However, if you ask 'What did you like and dislike about the chocolate bar?', they might say, 'I liked the taste but the texture was unpleasant, so I wouldn't buy it.' This provides the business with more detailed information.

'Robin Hoodies' Student Enterprise Market Research Survey

Please indicate your answer by ticking the appropriate boxes below.

1. *Gender*

   Male ☐ Female ☐

2. *What year are you in?*

   First ☐ Second ☐ Third ☐
   TY ☐ Fifth ☐ Sixth ☐

3. *Are you interested in buying a school hoodie?*

   Yes ☐ No ☐

4. *If you answered 'Yes' to Q3, how much would you be prepared to pay for the hoodie?*

   Up to €15 ☐ Up to €20 ☐ Up to €25 ☐

5. *If you answered 'Yes' to Q3, what size would you buy?*

   Small ☐ Medium ☐ Large ☐

6. *If you answered 'Yes' to Q3, what would you like to be on the hoodie?*

   School name ☐
   School crest ☐
   Class signatures ☐

   Other (please specify) ______________________

7. *What is your favourite colour?* ______________________

Figure 21.1 An example of a survey

The questioning can be done by personal interview, by post, by phone or online. Each method has its advantages and disadvantages (see Table 21.1). It would be impossible to survey all consumers, so market researchers usually select a small number of people to represent all consumers. This is called **sampling**.

Method	Advantages	Disadvantages
Personal interview Face-to-face interview between the market researcher and consumer using a questionnaire (the interviewer usually fills out the responses on behalf of the consumer)	› Allows for detailed responses › The question or answer can be clarified	› Time-consuming › Expensive › Consumers may feel uncomfortable answering some questions face to face and may be dishonest in their responses
Postal survey Questionnaires are sent and returned through the post	› Cheaper than a personal interview, as there is no interviewer involved › People can answer in their own time	› Very low response rate › Responses may take a long time to be returned

Method	Advantages	Disadvantages
Telephone survey A series of questions are asked over the telephone	› Cheaper than a personal interview › People can be chosen from a wide geographical area › The question or answer can be clarified	› Difficult to get people to respond, particularly if you contact them at busy times › People may provide quick responses to get the survey over quickly
Online survey Survey is published on a website or sent via email	› Cheapest method (no printing, postage, phone calls or interviewer costs) › People worldwide can take part › People can answer in their own time › Responses can be analysed automatically	› Many people ignore on-screen pop-ups or ignore the option to complete a survey › The opinions of consumers who are not online are ignored

Table 21.1 Advantages and disadvantages of survey methods

KEY SKILLS

21.1 Survey questions

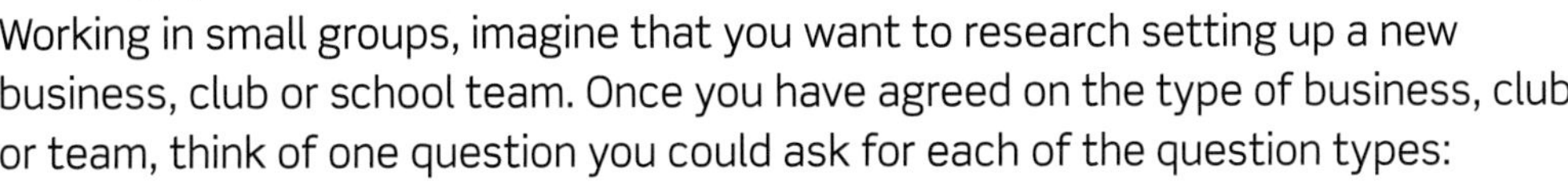

Working in small groups, imagine that you want to research setting up a new business, club or school team. Once you have agreed on the type of business, club or team, think of one question you could ask for each of the question types:

- Closed
- Multiple choice
- Open-ended

One person from each group reads out the questions when asked to do so. You should write down any questions that other groups had that your group did not. #GroupWork

WO C BL MIT

KEY SKILLS

21.2 Survey methods

Following on from activity 21.1, which survey method would you choose? Discuss your reasons in small groups. Conduct a survey among the class to identify the most popular choice. #Survey #Evaluate #ThinkPairShare

WO C BL MIT

2 Focus groups

A **focus group** is a group of consumers brought together to discuss a particular product or service.

- **Advantage:** It is an efficient way to gather reactions and opinions from a group of people at the same time.
- **Disadvantage:** Some members of the group may dominate the responses and influence the views of other group members.

❸ *Observation*

Observation involves watching or viewing consumers in action, for example:

- The number of customers selecting a specific product during a particular period in a store
- The time it takes to select a particular product
- How much attention is given to an in-store display.

This method is often used in retail stores such as supermarkets.

- **Advantages:** Large numbers of people can be observed in one location. It is a relatively cheap method of market research, as there is no need to employ staff to interview consumers.
- **Disadvantages:** It is time-consuming and provides only limited information. For example, it shows what products are purchased, but it might also be useful to know *why* those products were chosen.

KEY SKILLS

MIT BL BN

21.3 Observing students' habits

Conduct an observation on one of the following over the next week:

(a) The type of lunches that students buy or bring to school
(b) The snacks bought at break-time in your school
(c) How students travel to school, e.g. walk, cycle, car, bus
(d) The breakdown of customers in your local supermarket who use a trolley or a basket

Record your observations and share your results with your class.
#Investigate #Record

Analysing field research findings

After you gather your market research, you need to analyse the findings. Closed questions (those that require a yes/no or multiple-choice answer) are easier to analyse than open-ended questions (for example, Q7 in the sample survey in Figure 21.1).

For example, if 75 people answered a survey and 50 of those were female and 25 were male, the findings would be as follows:

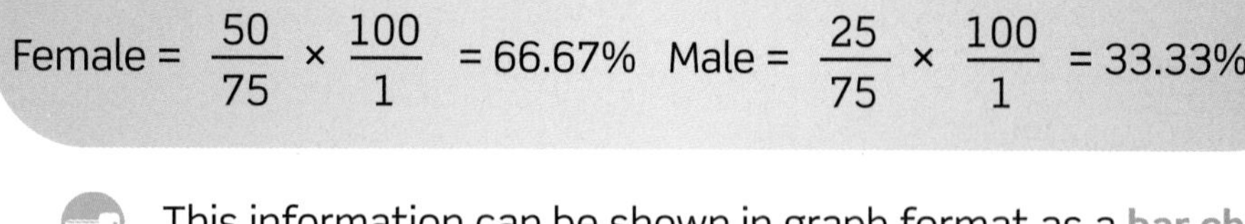

N = 75 (number of respondents) Female = 50, Male = 25

$$\text{Female} = \frac{50}{75} \times \frac{100}{1} = 66.67\% \quad \text{Male} = \frac{25}{75} \times \frac{100}{1} = 33.33\%$$

This information can be shown in graph format as a **bar chart** or **pie chart**, such as the one in Figure 21.2.

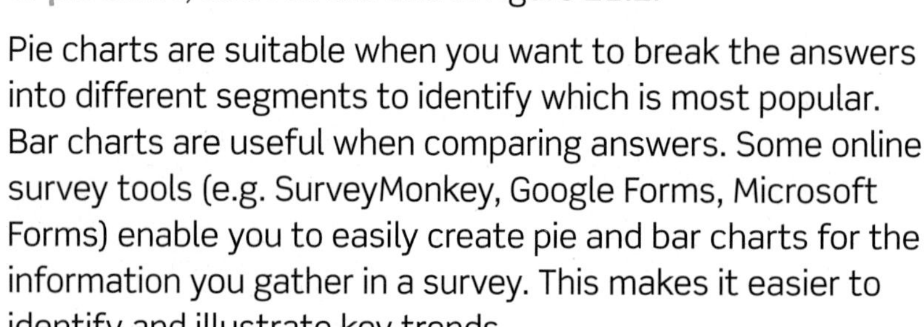

Pie charts are suitable when you want to break the answers into different segments to identify which is most popular. Bar charts are useful when comparing answers. Some online survey tools (e.g. SurveyMonkey, Google Forms, Microsoft Forms) enable you to easily create pie and bar charts for the information you gather in a survey. This makes it easier to identify and illustrate key trends.

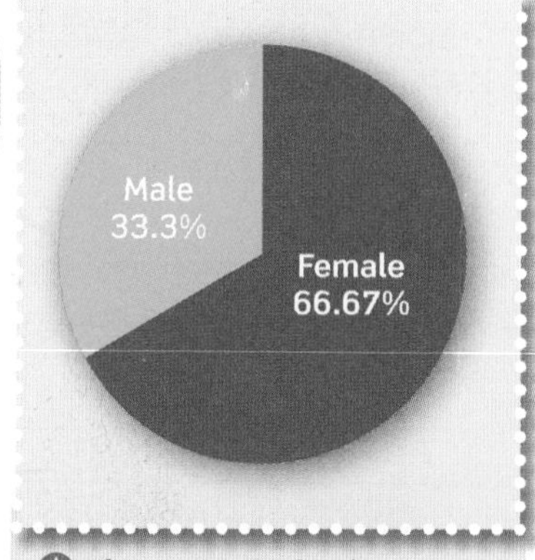

Figure 21.2 Pie chart showing the gender of respondents

Example

Sally's Organic Smoothies wanted to find out customers' views of their new Tropical Popical Pomegranate and Pineapple smoothies. They carried out a survey of 1,000 of their existing customers in March 2022 and the results were as follows:

Q1 *How many times have you purchased Tropical Popical smoothies?*

Never	645
Once	290
Twice	40
Three times	20
Four or more times	5

Q2 *If you answered 'Once', are you planning to buy it again?*

Yes	30
No	260

Q3 *What are your reasons for buying smoothies (any flavour) from Sally's Organic Smoothies?*

	Number of respondents	%
Advertising	150	$\frac{150}{1,000} = 15\%$
Taste	500	$\frac{500}{1,000} = 50\%$
Price	100	$\frac{100}{1,000} = 10\%$
Organic ingredients	250	$\frac{250}{1,000} = 25\%$

The results show that 35.5% (355 out of 1,000) of the sample group surveyed have tried Tropical Popical Pomegranate and Pineapple smoothies. This shows that the advertising for the new product is successfully attracting customers. However, very few customers make repeat purchases, which suggests that there is a problem with the product. Sally's Organic Smoothies needs to consider changing the recipe of the smoothie or dropping it altogether.

Two years ago, in March 2020, Sally's Organic Smoothies had asked 500 existing customers a similar question to Q3 about why they bought smoothies. The results at that time were as follows:

	Number of respondents	%
Advertising	50	$\frac{50}{500} = 10\%$
Taste	225	$\frac{225}{500} = 45\%$
Price	200	$\frac{200}{500} = 40\%$
Organic ingredients	25	$\frac{25}{500} = 5\%$

The pie charts below compare the results of the Sally's Organic Smoothies research in 2020 and 2022.

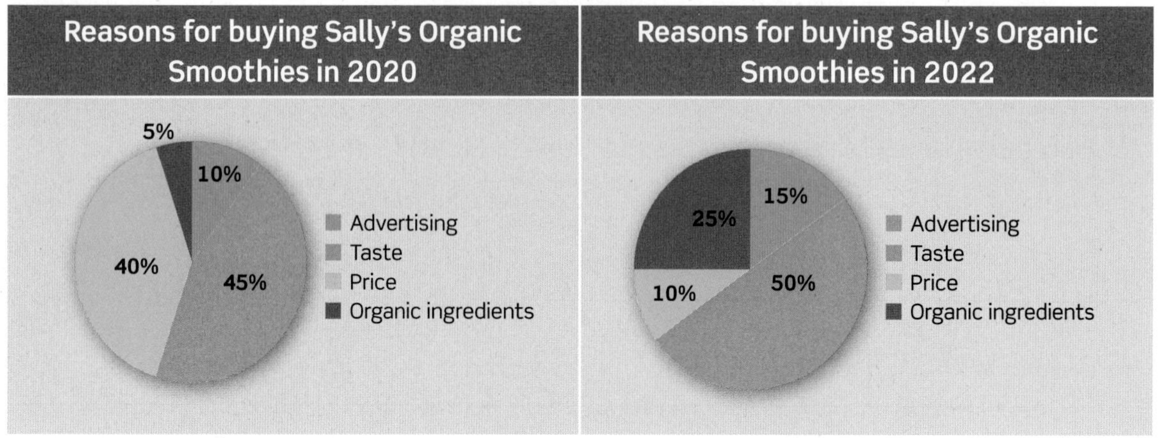

Calculations (2020 survey):

Reason for buying	Angle for pie chart (Note: a circle = 360°)
Advertising	360° × 10% = 36°
Taste	360° × 40% = 144°
Price	360° × 45% = 162°
Organic ingredients	360° × 5% = 18°

An analysis of these pie charts could look like this:

- Taste was the most important factor in purchasing smoothies in both years.
- The use of organic ingredients increased as a reason for purchasing Sally's Organic Smoothies from 5% in 2020 to 25% in 2022, which is a five-fold increase.
- Price decreased in importance from 2020 to 2022.

Recommendations:

Sally's Organic Smoothies should promote the taste and organic ingredients in future advertising and promotions. It may be possible to increase the price of the smoothies without affecting sales.

Market research results are often displayed at meetings using slides (PowerPoint, Prezi, Google Slides) or communicated in a report.

DID YOU KNOW...

See Chapter 20 for digital technologies used by organisations

Businesses use technology to conduct market research. Some retailers gather information about consumers' purchasing habits using their loyalty cards, which are scanned at the electronic point of sale (EPOS).

Many retailers also use social networking sites such as Facebook, Twitter or Instagram to test customer reactions to products or services.

KEY SKILLS MIT

21.4 Market research and social networking

What disadvantages might there be to using information gathered through social networking sites? Write your answers down. #Evaluate

KEY SKILLS WO MIT BL BC C

21.5 Market research survey: A piece of cake!

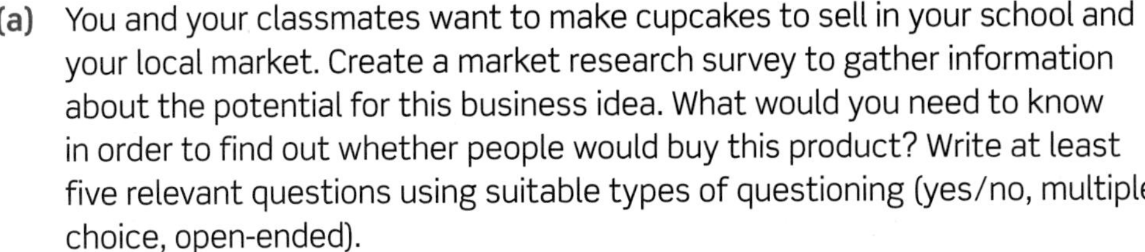

(a) You and your classmates want to make cupcakes to sell in your school and your local market. Create a market research survey to gather information about the potential for this business idea. What would you need to know in order to find out whether people would buy this product? Write at least five relevant questions using suitable types of questioning (yes/no, multiple choice, open-ended).

(b) Pick at least 20 people as your sample to answer your survey. How will you choose these people to answer your survey? How might the sample size impact the reliability of your results?

(c) Present the results of your survey graphically where possible (pie charts, bar charts, etc.).

(d) Create an online version of the survey using one of the free tools available on the internet, such as SurveyMonkey, Microsoft Forms or Google Forms.

(e) Email the survey to 20 people, such as friends, family or classmates. Explain that the survey is a school assignment. Analyse the results (graphically if possible). #GroupWork #Research #Investigate

Advantages and disadvantages of field research

Advantages	Disadvantages
› Up-to-date information is gathered › Relevant information is gathered for the specific needs of the business	› Time-consuming › Expensive › Requires skill to conduct

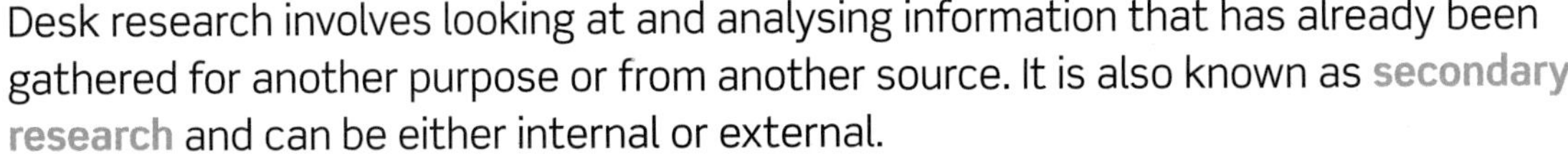

Desk research

Desk research involves looking at and analysing information that has already been gathered for another purpose or from another source. It is also known as **secondary research** and can be either internal or external.

Examples of desk research

Example of desk research	How it might be used
Business sales reports	Past sales records and business reports will help to identify the most and least successful products that the business has sold in the past.
Newspapers and magazines	Newspaper and magazine articles may contain information about competitors or consumers, such as market size, products or international trends.
Internet	Check competitors' products and prices online and find information about market size and trends.
Central Statistics Office (CSO)	The CSO provides information on the population of towns and cities throughout Ireland as well as information on age, gender, marital status, etc. The Household Budget Survey gives information on the spending patterns of households on different types of goods.

Advantages and disadvantages of desk research

Advantages	Disadvantages
› Easy to obtain, as it uses information that is already available › Quick to gather › Cheaper than field research, as it does not require trained interviewers	› As the information gathered is not for the specific needs of the business, it may not be as useful or relevant as primary research › Information may be outdated › The researcher may have to read a lot of information to find what they need

21.6 Desk research

Which type of desk research do you think would be the best way to find information about the following?

(a) A company's competitors

(b) Potential customers

(c) Market size #Evaluate

21.7 Using your desk research

(a) Using the CSO website, find the 10 most popular girls' and boys' names for babies born last year. #Research

(b) Make a list of the types of business that would find this information useful. #List

(c) Find another piece of research on the CSO website and explain how a business might turn it into a business opportunity. #Investigate

(d) Find an article in a local or national newspaper that contains information that might be of use to a local business. Copy or cut out the article and insert it in your copybook. Highlight the most useful information and write down why it is useful. #Research

Brexit blamed for drop in new car sales

Sales of new cars in January were down almost 13% compared with the same month last year.

There were 32,374 191 car registrations last month, down from 37,023 in January 2018 – a 12.6% reduction – according to figures released by the Society of the Irish Motor Industry (SIMI) today.

There were monthly declines in new car registration figures last year, something SIMI puts down to 'the substantial impact of Brexit'.

Used car imports in 2018 reached the highest level on record – 100,755 – accounting for 44.5% of the total car market in 2018. Used car imports for January 2019 (9,006) saw a very slight decrease of 0.6% on January 2018 (9,061).

Electric vehicle registrations increased significantly, with 811 registrations in January 2019, which is more than for the whole of 2017 and over 60% of the total for the whole of last year.

While electric vehicle numbers are still relatively low, they are showing strong growth – increasing from less than 1% of the market last year to a 2.6% market share in January this year.

Diesel continues to be the market leader in 2019 with a 49% share, despite an 8% decline on January 2018. Petrol has grown to 40% and hybrids currently account for 7% of the new car market.

Source: The Journal.ie, 1 February 2019

21.8 The Brexit effect

(a) What is Brexit? #Explain

(b) In your opinion, why has Brexit impacted on car sales in Ireland? #Justify

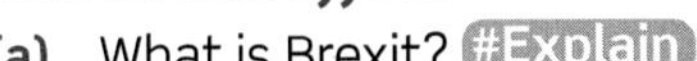

(c) Which two pieces of information in the survey might a car dealer find most useful in identifying future trends for their business? #Analyse

(d) Is the information in this article an example of desk or field research for **(i)** SIMI and **(ii)** a car dealer? #Research #Analysis #Evaluate

21.9 Market research skills and importance

Find out more about the job of a market researcher.

(a) What skills does a market researcher need?

(b) Evaluate the importance of a market researcher in an organisation. #Research

Weblinks

PowerPoint Summary

ENTERPRISE

CHAPTER 22

MARKETING MIX

LEARNING OUTCOMES IN FOCUS

2.8 Devise and apply a marketing mix in order to promote a new or existing product or service

Links to 2.6, 2.7, 2.9, 3.3

LEARNING INTENTIONS FOR THIS CHAPTER

When you have completed this chapter you will be able to:

- Define the term 'marketing'
- Explain the concept of target markets
- Illustrate your understanding of a marketing mix
- Create a marketing mix for a product of your choice
- Draw and label a product life cycle
- Outline a range of factors that impact on the selling price of goods and services
- Outline the various elements of the promotion mix
- Identify different types of advertising and advertising media
- Appreciate the powerful influence that marketing has on consumers.

CHAPTER 22 KEY TERMS

4Ps	marketing	product life cycle
advertising	marketing mix	promotion
Advertising Standards Authority for Ireland (ASAI)	media	promotion mix
brand	niche market	psychological pricing
channels of distribution	peak load pricing	public relations
competitive advertising	penetration pricing	reminder advertising
competitive pricing	persuasive advertising	social media
cost-plus pricing	place	sponsorship
generic advertising	premium pricing	target market
informative advertising	price	unique selling point (USP)
	product	

CHAPTER 22 KEY SKILLS

- BC Being Creative
- BL Being Literate
- C Communicating
- MIT Managing Information and Thinking
- MM Managing Myself

- SW Staying Well
- WO Working with Others

ENTERPRISE

What is marketing?

KEY TERM

Marketing is the process of identifying and satisfying customer needs and wants while making a profit.

Market research can be used to gather information about customers' needs and wants.

See Chapter 21 for uses of market research

Most goods and services are aimed at a specific group of consumers called a **target market**.

A **target market** is the group of people to whom a business aims to sell its products or services.

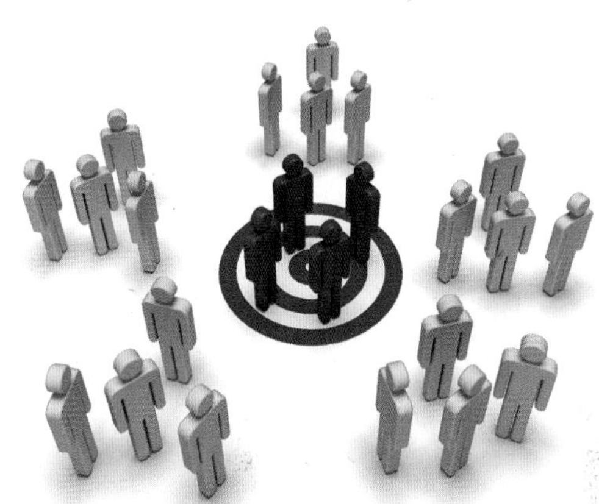

Target markets may be based on a range of criteria, including age, gender, location, income level, product usage, lifestyle, etc. For example, the main target market for Lego is children and their parents. The main target market for this textbook is Junior Cycle Business Studies students and their teachers.

KEY SKILLS

MIT

22.1 Identifying target markets

Identify the target market for the following:

- Kellogg's Coco Pops
- Kellogg's Special K
- Nissan Micra
- Tesla cars
- Starbucks
- *Business Post* newspaper #Identify

Some products or services are targeted at very small gaps in a larger market. These are known as **niche markets**. Bridal shoes are an example of a niche product within the shoe market.

A **niche market** is a small, specialised segment of a larger market for a particular product or service. For example, folding bicycles are a niche market: many people want bicycles, but only a small part of that market (e.g. commuters) want to use a folding bike.

22.2 Target markets of ads: Who's the customer?

(a) While watching television, listening to the radio or reading a magazine, take note of five adverts. For each one, name the advert and identify:
- What target market the advert is aimed at
- What the advert includes to appeal to that target market. #Research

(b) Do you think any of the adverts were aimed at people like you? #Opinion

(c) Did you find these adverts appealing? Explain your answer. #Identify #Opinion #Justify

22.3 Radio stations

There are many national Irish radio stations. Discuss the following questions with your classmates and record your answers. #ThinkPairShare

(a) Why, do you think, are there several different stations rather than just one? #WhatDoYouThink

(b) Find out the names of all the different national radio stations, then find out a little about each one and identify the target market for each. #Research #Identify

(c) For each radio station, list three examples of the type of products or services that would be advertised on that station. #List

Marketing mix

KEY TERM

The **marketing mix** is a combination of four elements that can help a business to market its products to its target market and maximise profits.

The four elements of the marketing mix (also known as the **4Ps**) are:

- Product
- Price
- Place
- Promotion.

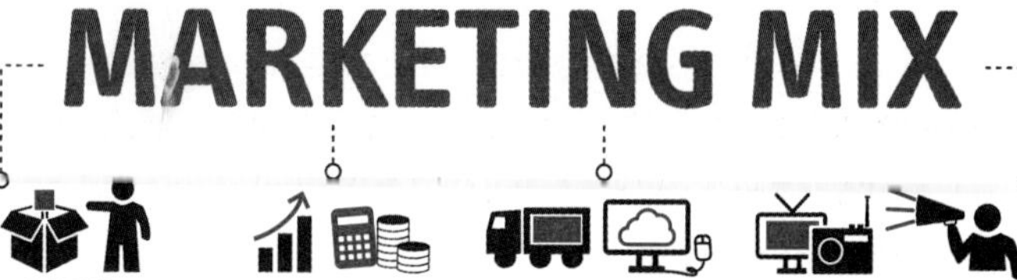

The goal is to combine these elements in a way that increases customer satisfaction and product sales. Think of the marketing mix as being like a recipe: it is important to get the right mix of ingredients or it will not be totally successful.

A marketing mix can be developed for both new and existing products. Marketers need to make sure that the marketing mix for any product is kept up to date. It may need to be changed from time to time for reasons such as the introduction of rival products, changing demand, product life cycle stage, etc.

Product

In the marketing mix, the product element includes:

- Design
- Product life cycle
- Branding
- Unique selling point (USP).

KEY TERM

A **product** is an actual item (either a physical good or a service) provided to meet consumers' needs.

Design

Design is the first stage in making a product. Well-designed products are useful, attractive, easy to use and long-lasting. With greater focus now being placed on sustainability, product design is becoming more important. Designers should think about the impact of their product at every stage of its life cycle, including the materials used, the manufacturing process, the environmental impact of using the product as well as the end-of-life issues such as disposal, reuse and recycling.

DID YOU KNOW...

Swedish studio Form Us With Love designed the Kungsbacka kitchen units for IKEA. Twenty-five plastic bottles are used in each kitchen unit, which also uses reclaimed industrial wood.

'A plastic bottle is not waste; it is a resource,' said Jonas Pettersson, Form Us With Love CEO. 'We have to challenge the excuses for not using waste as a resource by showing how to best put these materials back into production, making affordable, democratic products that will last.'

Source: Dezeen magazine website

See Chapter 1 for making the most of your resources

See Chapter 13 for sustainable consumption

Product life cycle

KEY TERM

The **product life cycle** is the different stages that a product goes through from the time it is launched until it is taken off the market. It is usually illustrated on a five-stage diagram that shows the changes in product sales over time.

Most products have a limited lifespan due to changes in fashion, consumer taste and new inventions. While products last for different lengths of time, they all move through a product life cycle that contains five stages:

1. **Introduction:** The new product is launched. Sales will be slow until consumers become familiar with it.
2. **Growth:** Sales increase rapidly as more consumers learn about the product.
3. **Maturity:** Sales growth increases at a slower pace and may start to level off, often due to competitors entering the market.
4. **Saturation:** Sales reach their peak because there are many competitors in the market and because most consumers in the target market already have the product. This makes it difficult to increase sales, as there are fewer new customers available.
5. **Decline:** Sales fall due to changes in taste/fashion or the introduction of a new or better product. Eventually the product will be withdrawn from the market.

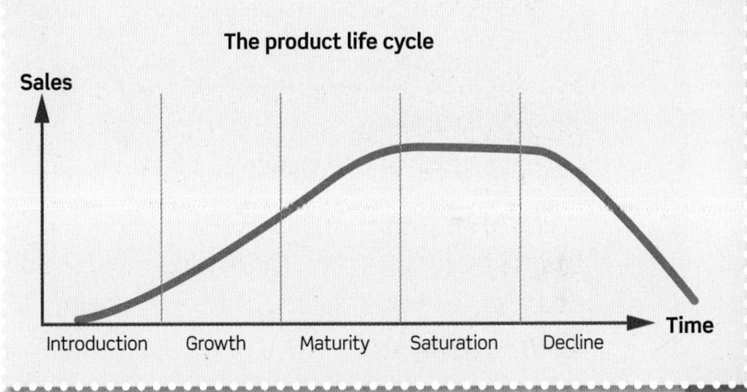

KEY SKILLS

22.4 Product life cycle

206

(a) Draw a product life cycle diagram in the space provided in the Student Activity Book. Don't forget to label both axes and give your diagram a title. #Activity

(b) Identify which stage of their product life cycle you think each of the following products are at. Suggest a reason for your decision.

- Kellogg's Corn Flakes
- CDs
- Electric cars
- Levi jeans
- A brand new range of Adidas running shoes

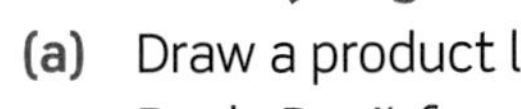

#Research #Identify

Branding

KEY TERM

A **brand** is a name, symbol, design or other feature that makes a product easy to recognise and distinguishes it from competing products.

Most brands are developed by the producer, but some are created by retailers. Branding has the following advantages:

- It helps a business to increase sales because consumers know and trust the brand.
- It makes products easy to recognise, which means that it is easier to introduce new products with a brand name. For example, the Apple Watch is successful because Apple already has a good reputation for making other products.

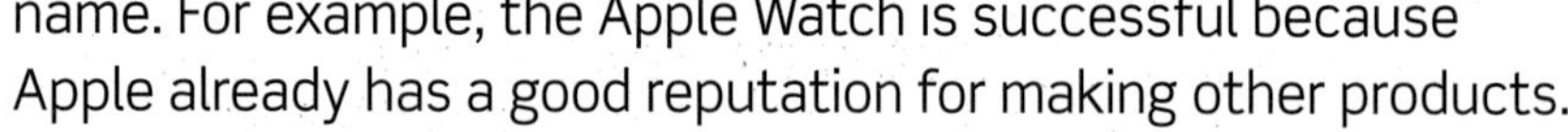

- It encourages customers to buy upgrades or new products from the same brand (known as brand loyalty).
- Higher prices can be charged for branded products, as consumers often associate them with better quality and are willing to pay extra for this.

KEY SKILLS

22.5 Brands

In pairs, think of five examples of brands. Discuss what identifies them as a brand and helps to distinguish them from similar products. #ThinkPairShare

Own branding

Some large shops have their own brand products, such as Tesco Finest or Dunnes Stores' Simply Better. Own-label brands are generally developed by a retailer rather than by a producer.

KEY SKILLS

22.6 Choosing a brand

Think of the last time you bought runners or a mobile phone. Discuss the following questions with your partner and write down your responses.

(a) Did the brand influence your choice of product?

(b) Can you identify other competing brands or products?

(c) Why did you choose the brand you did? #ThinkPairShare #Opinion

Unique selling point

A business will try to create a **unique selling point (USP)** for its product or service. This is what makes the product different from its competitors. For example, Volvo's USP is safety, while Toyota's is reliability.

ENTERPRISE

Price

KEY TERM

The **price** is the amount of money a seller charges a customer for a product or service.

The price of a product often depends on demand and supply. If lots of people want to buy a product (high demand) but only a small amount of the product is available (low supply), the price of the product will generally increase. Why do you think this is the case?

See Chapter 33 for demand and supply

Other factors that a business may consider when setting the price include:

- The cost of making the product
- The target market for the product – their income level and ability to pay
- The amount of profit the business wants to make
- Where the product is in its life cycle
- The price charged for competing products.

Pricing strategies

Based on the factors above, businesses use different pricing strategies to decide how to price their products or services. Some of the more common pricing strategies are:

- **Cost-plus pricing:** The business calculates how much it costs to produce a product, then adds a percentage mark-up to make a profit. For example, if a product costs €4 to produce and the manufacturer wants a 50% mark-up, they will sell the product for €4 + 50% (€2) = €6.
- **Competitive pricing:** The business sets a price that is similar to rival products. For example, Coca-Cola and Pepsi have similar prices. Ryanair and Aer Lingus also compete on price, so when Ryanair has a sale, Aer Lingus often has a sale too.
- **Premium pricing:** The business charges a permanently high price to convey an image of exclusivity or quality, for example BMW cars, designer clothing, perfume.
- **Penetration pricing:** The business charges a low price when a product is new to the market to get consumers interested in it. Once the product becomes known, the business may increase its price.
- **Peak load pricing:** A business charges a higher price during periods of high demand and lowers the selling price when demand falls. For example, the price of airline flights increases during summer months and school holidays, but in winter, when demand is lower, prices will usually be cheaper.
- **Psychological pricing:** A business may set a price slightly below a round number in the belief that consumers will see it as cheaper, for example €599 rather than €600. The fact that one starts with a 'five hundred' and the other with a 'six hundred' may help to disguise the fact that there is only a €1 difference in price. It is called psychological pricing because the potential saving is really only in the mind of the consumer.

22.7 Pricing strategy

Think of a recent purchase you made. Identify what type of pricing strategy you think was used. Justify your answer with a reason. #Identify #Strategise

Place

KEY TERM

Place refers to where customers will buy the product and the channel of distribution used to get the product to this location.

Channels of distribution refers to the way in which the product gets from the manufacturer to the consumer.

A product or service must be distributed in a way that is convenient for the consumer. There are four main ways the product can get from the manufacturer to the consumer:

1. The **manufacturer** sells in bulk to **wholesalers**, who sell in smaller quantities to **retailers**, who then sell to the consumer. Many goods, including sweets and soft drinks, are sold in this way.
2. The **manufacturer** sells to large **retailers** (such as Dunnes and Tesco) that can buy in bulk and sell to consumers. Bread and tinned goods are examples.
3. The **manufacturer** sells to the **wholesaler**, who then sells directly to the **consumer**, for example buying a book from Amazon.
4. The **manufacturer** sells directly to the **consumer**, for example farm shops, mail order, online shopping.

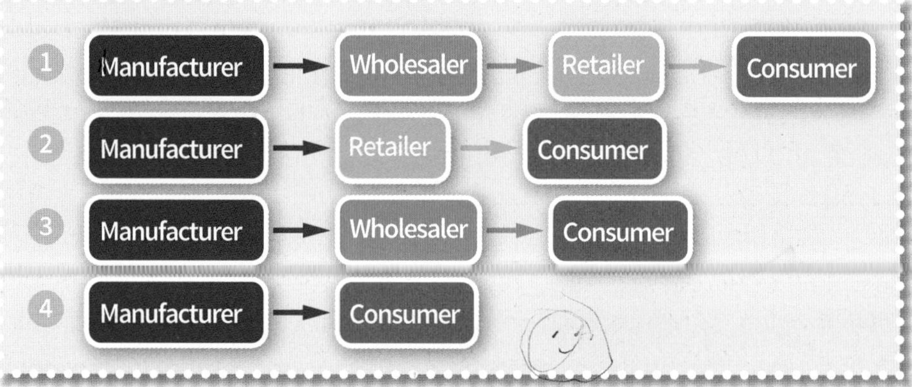

The channel used depends on:

- **The product itself:** Some products, such as fresh fruit, have a short shelf life, so they need to be delivered to retailers or consumers quickly.
- **Legal requirements:** Some products must be sold through a certain channel, for example certain medicines can be sold only by a pharmacist.
- **The image of the product:** Some products have a high-quality image, which means they will be sold only in exclusive retailers, such as Brown Thomas.

Different types of retailer

Department stores sell a wide range of products in different departments, such as women's clothing, menswear, children's wear, accessories, cosmetics, household goods, etc. Examples include Debenhams, Arnotts and Brown Thomas.

Chain stores usually specialise in a type of product and have many different branches throughout the country. Examples include River Island, Oasis, Easons and Boots.

Supermarkets sell a wide range of products, including food, drink, cleaning products, toiletries, etc. Examples include SuperValu, Dunnes and Tesco.

Discount retailers sell products at a reduced price. Examples include Dealz and EuroGiant.

Franchises operate using a licence from a franchisor. Examples include McDonald's and Subway. See page 287 for a detailed explanation of the franchise operating model.

See Chapter 24 for franchises

Independent retailers are small businesses that are usually owned by a sole trader. Examples include local boutiques, small newsagents and a village shop.

Online stores are shops set up on the internet. Sometimes they exist solely on the internet and sometimes physical shops also sell online. Examples include Amazon and Tesco.

KEY SKILLS MIT

22.8 Types of retailer

(a) Think of one of the main streets in your nearest town or city. List the shops and note what kind of retailers they are. #List #Classify

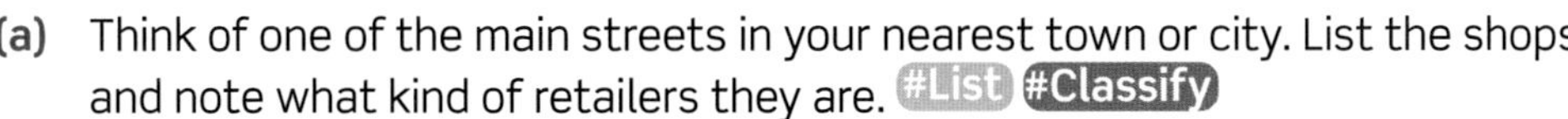

(b) On your list, mark the shops that also sell online. #Classify

(c) Think of five items that you or your family bought recently. Which type(s) of retailer did you purchase them from? #List #Identify

KEY SKILLS MIT

22.9 Online selling

Many businesses use technology to sell directly to consumers, either through a website or through an app. Some businesses sell exclusively online, such as ASOS and Ryanair. With the person sitting next to you, discuss two advantages and two disadvantages of online selling for:

- The business
- The consumer.

Write down your conclusions. #ThinkPairShare

Promotion

KEY TERM

Promotion means making customers aware of the product or brand in order to increase sales and create brand loyalty.

Businesses use promotion to:

- Launch a new product
- Increase sales of existing products
- Improve the image of the business.

KEY TERM

The **promotion mix** is the combination of promotional activities that a business uses to communicate with existing and potential customers.

Businesses can promote their goods and services in many ways, including:

- Advertising
- Sales promotion
- Public relations
- Sponsorship
- Personal selling
- Social media
- Merchandising
- Celebrity endorsement/influencers
- Product placement.

Advertising

Advertising involves communicating with the public to let them know about a product and get them interested in buying it. Advertising is the promotion method that we are probably most familiar with. It is paid for by businesses and is directed at a large target audience rather than individual consumers. Advertisements follow the AIDA model:

- **A** – attract **attention**.
- **I** – capture the **interest** of the consumer.
- **D** – stimulate **desire** for the product.
- **A** – lead to **action** (purchasing the product).

Adverts can reach a large number of potential consumers across a range of target markets.

There are five different categories of advertising:

1. **Informative advertising** provides information about a product or service to the general public.
2. **Persuasive advertising** convinces/persuades people that they need a particular product or service.
3. **Competitive advertising** is used by businesses to convince people that their product is better than their competitors' products.
4. **Reminder advertising** is used to remind customers that a product is still available and continues to be good value for money.
5. **Generic advertising** is when firms in an industry work together to produce an advertisement to persuade people to buy that particular type of product rather than a specific brand. For example, all milk is advertised by the National Dairy Council.

22.10 Types of advertising

Look through magazines and newspapers to find at least one example of each of the five different categories of advertising. Copy these or (if it belongs to you) cut out the advertisement and stick it in your copybook. Write notes by the side of the advert to explain its main message. #Research #Evaluate

Advertising media

The medium used for advertising will depend on:

- The target market for the product
- The advertising budget available.

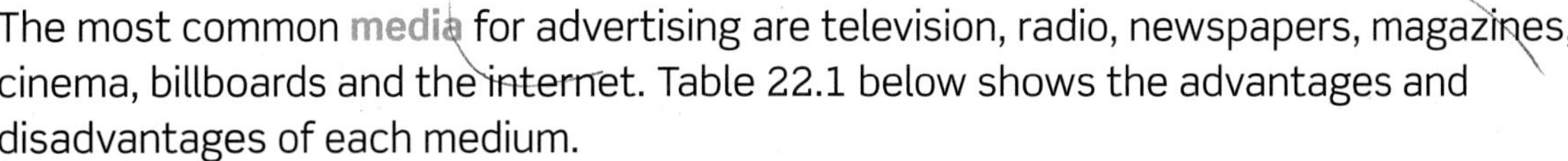

The most common **media** for advertising are television, radio, newspapers, magazines, cinema, billboards and the internet. Table 22.1 below shows the advantages and disadvantages of each medium.

Medium	Advantages	Disadvantages
Television	› Can reach a national or global audience › Can demonstrate the product › Can target specific audiences during particular TV shows	› Expensive to produce and put on TV, especially during popular programmes › Some people skip the adverts, while others channel hop to avoid adverts › Many people watch Netflix, etc. and cannot be targeted by adverts
Radio	› Cheaper than TV advertising › Can target specific audiences based on the radio programme and/or station › Local radio adverts are suitable for local businesses › More captive audience than TV, as people are less likely to switch stations › Jingles can make adverts memorable	› There's no option to rewind or listen again on radio › People can't see the product › Lack of images makes it impossible to demonstrate the product
Newspapers	› Full-page adverts are attention-grabbing › Can provide lots of information that can be re-read › Can target specific markets depending on the newspaper chosen › Local newspapers are suitable for local businesses	› National full-page adverts are expensive › Newspapers contain lots of adverts, so it can be difficult to stand out › No sound or video content to demonstrate the product › A short shelf life means that adverts may not be visible for very long
Magazines	› High visual impact, as they are usually printed in colour › Can target specific markets › Are kept by readers for a longer time than newspapers, so may be viewed repeatedly	› No sound or video content to demonstrate the product › Competitors may advertise in the same publications
Cinema	› Shown to a more captive audience than TV adverts › Can demonstrate the product › Can target specific audiences during particular movies, for example toys advertised during Disney movies	› Limited to cinema-going audience › Expensive to produce

cont'd

Medium	Advantages	Disadvantages
Billboards	› Strong visual impact › Can be displayed in busy locations › Useful for short messages	› Are ignored by many people › Can only convey a limited amount of information
Internet/ websites	› Relatively cheap to create and share › Sound and video can be used › Some online adverts go viral and can reach a global audience › The number of times an advert is viewed online can be monitored › Detailed information can be placed on a business website and can be read at a time that is convenient to the consumer	› Internet users increasingly shut down pop-up ads or skip adverts at the start of videos

Table 22.1 Advertising media

MIT C BC BL

22.11 Code-breaker

(a) What is the image in Figure 22.1 called?

(b) Which of the advertising media in Table 22.1 would you find these on?

(c) Why are they included on adverts?

(d) Where else, other than adverts, could you find them?

(e) Explain what this is and why it is used. Provide instructions for using the code. (If you don't know, ask someone in your class to demonstrate it to you.) #Investigate #Evaluate

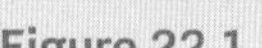
Figure 22.1

DID YOU KNOW...

The cost to air a 30-second TV advert during the Super Bowl, the most high-profile TV event in the United States, was $5.25 million in 2019. That doesn't even include the cost of making the advert, which can also run into millions of dollars. The reason businesses are prepared to pay so much is because the adverts will be viewed by at least 114 million people in the United States alone and many more worldwide. Super Bowl adverts are also often posted online, providing further exposure for the business.

KEY SKILLS

BC MIT BL

22.12 TV advertising

From your own experience or by talking to other people, find out what kinds of adverts are shown during different programmes at various times and on various days. What does this tell you about the target market? Compare your results with your classmates. From your research, write a short report on targeted advertising on TV. #Research #Report

Advertising ethics

Advertisements should not mislead or offend customers or make false claims about products or services.

The **Advertising Standards Authority for Ireland (ASAI)** is a body set up and financed by the advertising industry that ensures that all marketing communications are legal, decent, honest and truthful. The ASAI investigates complaints made by the public. Its website contains a list of recent complaints.

KEY SKILLS

22.13 Children and advertising

Class debate: Do you think adverts for toys and sweets should be shown during children's television programmes? Justify your opinion with arguments for or against.
#Discussion #Ethics #Opinion #Justify

Sales promotion

Sales promotions are incentives offered to customers to get them to buy products. These incentives often include short-term tactics to improve sales, such as:

- Free samples
- Buy one, get one free (BOGOF)
- Gifts with purchase
- Bonus packs, e.g. 50% extra free
- Loyalty card schemes
- Money-off vouchers/coupons/discount codes
- Competitions
- In-store merchandising/point-of-sale materials, e.g. posters, displays.

KEY SKILLS

22.14 Sales promotions

(a) What are the benefits of sales promotions to the consumer?

(b) What are the disadvantages of sales promotions to the consumer?
#Evaluate #Identify

Public relations/publicity

The role of **public relations** is to help create a positive image of the business. This may be achieved by organising charitable events, giving back to the local community or by minimising any negative story about the business. Businesses often create press releases to inform the media of new products or provide free samples of their products to magazine editors so that they might be featured in an article.

KEY SKILLS

22.15 Publicity

(a) How is publicity different from advertising?

(b) Although publicity is not paid for directly in the same way as advertising, in what ways will it cost the business money? #Investigate

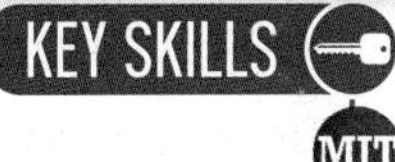

Sponsorship

Businesses sometimes sponsor events, sports competitions, teams or venues, such as the 3 Arena and Aviva Stadium. They do this by providing financial support in return for promoting the business and/or its products. Businesses can benefit from the success of those they sponsor and can become popular with customers who support or visit the sponsored event, team, competition or venue. Businesses and other financial enterprises try to partner with social or cultural enterprises that are a good match for their brand or share the same values. For example, SuperValu, a business made up of locally owned shops, sponsors both the GAA and Tidy Towns, both of which have strong local and community links.

See Chapter 17 for social impacts of organisations

KEY SKILLS MIT

22.16 Sponsorship

List five examples of sponsorship. Include local, national and international examples. #List

Personal selling

Personal selling involves salespeople selling directly to new or existing customers. This form of promotion uses the salespeople's specialist knowledge to inform and encourage the customer to buy the product.

The message used can be personalised to the individual customer. Personal selling is often used to sell high-priced products, for example cars, electrical goods, jewellery, cosmetics in large department stores, specialist machinery and financial services such as insurance and pension products.

Social media

Social media provides businesses and organisations with a quick, cheap and easy way to promote products and services to a potentially global audience. Most businesses now have at least one social media account (Snapchat, Facebook, YouTube, Twitter, Instagram) where they share photos or videos of new products with existing and potential customers.

Social media can also promote interactive communication with customers and businesses can gather feedback on potential new products.

Facebook founder Mark Zuckerberg

Merchandising

This can involve using in-store displays and promotions designed to generate consumer interest in a specific product. It can include in-store product sampling, such as free tasters in supermarkets.

Merchandising also refers to spin-off products used to promote a core product or brand. For example, Disney uses merchandising to promote its brand and movies. This often involves the creation of branded clothing, toys and other items linked to characters from Disney movies, for example *Toy Story* pencil cases.

Celebrity endorsement/influencers

Many companies provide free products to influencers who will tell their followers about the products on Instagram, Snapchat or Facebook. If a celebrity is seen with a product, it can quickly and effectively increase the appeal of that product.

Enterprise in action

Marissa Carter, the entrepreneur behind Cocoa Brown, paid Joyce Bonelli, make-up artist to the Kardashians, to be her brand ambassador. The product then reached the radar of some of the biggest beauty influencers in the world without Marissa having to pay the individual celebrities a cent.

Kylie Jenner
@KylieJenner

Time for #TanningThursday with @CocoaBrownTan by @CarterMarissa #FlawlessFauxGlow #BestTan #1HourTan

Marissa says, 'We were only in 28 stores in New York when Kylie put up a photo of herself wearing the tan, but we sold out within 24 hours. There was a knock-on effect because overnight, it turned us into an internationally recognised brand.'

Source: RTÉ Lifestyle, 18 August 2017

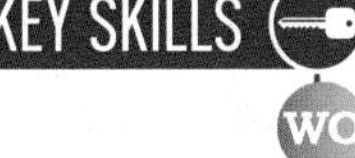

22.17 Celebrity endorsements

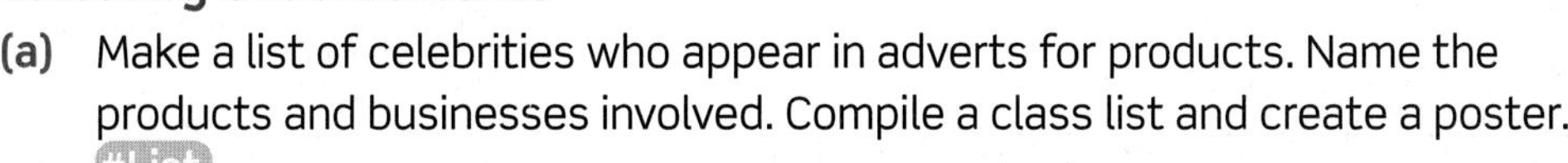

(a) Make a list of celebrities who appear in adverts for products. Name the products and businesses involved. Compile a class list and create a poster. #List

(b) Would you buy a product because it had a celebrity endorsement? Why would their involvement encourage you to buy the product? #Discussion

WO MIT SW BC

Product placement

Businesses often pay a lot of money for their latest products to appear in TV programmes or movies – for example, Audi cars featured in the *Iron Man* trilogy. The product's presence can be enough to persuade people to buy it because they like the show or the actor or just because continually seeing it makes them recognise it.

KEY SKILLS

MIT

22.18 Product placement

Look out for product placement when you watch a movie or a TV programme. What product was used? If you can't spot any products, search online for articles about product placement to find out what programmes or movies have featured products. Make a list. #Identify #List

Marketing mix for Fujifilm Instax

Product:

- Brightly coloured, small square-shaped camera
- Provides users with instant prints
- Competing products from Polaroid, including Instant Film Camera.

Price:

- Ranges from €62 to €90 depending on where the customer buys it
- Product is competitively priced compared to rivals.

Place:

- Online, e.g. Fujifilm website, Amazon, Littlewoods Ireland
- In stores, e.g. Harvey Norman, DID Electrical, Boots, camera shops.

Promotion:

- TV adverts
- Sponsorship of TV programmes on the E! TV channel
- Celebrity endorsement by Taylor Swift.

KEY SKILLS MIT BC

22.19 Marketing mix

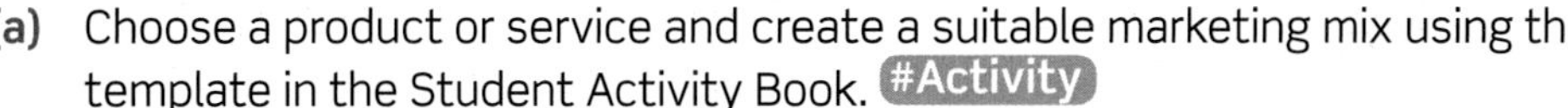

210 (a) Choose a product or service and create a suitable marketing mix using the template in the Student Activity Book. #Activity

211 (b) Think of a new product or service that you or your classmates could produce or offer. Identify the target market for this product or service and create a marketing mix for it using the template in the Student Activity Book. #Innovation

KEY SKILLS MIT MM

22.20 The power of marketing

Read the quotes below. Write a short reflection to outline your thoughts on the power of marketing to influence consumers. #Reflect #Opinion

> 'We all need to become more customer-focused and recognise the power of marketing to sell more diamonds.'
> Nicky Oppenheimer, former chairman of De Beers

> 'Advertising is legalised lying.'
> H.G. Wells, author of *War of the Worlds*

> 'If people believe they share values with a company, they will stay loyal to the brand.'
> Howard Schultz, former chairman of Starbucks

> 'Never underestimate the power of social media to build brand trust and recognition.'
> Socially Tailored Marketing

Weblinks

PowerPoint Summary

ENTERPRISE

CHAPTER 23 FINANCIAL PLANNING FOR ORGANISATIONS

LEARNING OUTCOMES IN FOCUS

2.11 Assess the importance of planning an organisation's cash flow, propose suitable sources of finance to manage expenditure and prepare a budget

Links to 1.2, 1.5, 1.12, 2.9, 2.10, 2.12, 2.13, 3.2, 3.4

LEARNING INTENTIONS FOR THIS CHAPTER

When you have completed this chapter you will be able to:

- Explain the importance of cash flow to an organisation
- Outline the need for organisations to plan their future cash flow
- Outline the consequences of poor cash flow for an organisation
- Explain the concept of working capital
- Explain the importance of effective working capital management
- Prepare and analyse a cash flow forecast for an organisation
- Distinguish between short-, medium- and long-term sources of finance for an organisation
- Assess the major short-, medium- and long-term financial needs of an organisation
- Describe and evaluate the major sources of finance for an organisation
- Outline the factors that will influence an organisation when choosing a source of finance.

CHAPTER 23 KEY TERMS

accrued expenses	crowdfunding	fixed assets	receipts
balanced forecast	current expenditure	grant	sale and leaseback
capital expenditure	debenture	hire purchase	surplus
cash flow	debtors	leasing	venture capital
cash flow forecast	deficit	liquidity	working capital
credit	expenditure	matching principle	
creditors	factoring	net cash	

CHAPTER 23 KEY SKILLS

BC Being Creative

BN Being Numerate

C Communicating

MIT Managing Information and Thinking

WO Working with Others

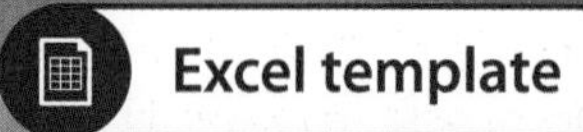

Step-by-step accounts

Excel template

ENTERPRISE

Cash flow

Managing the flow of money is an important task for all types of organisation.

KEY SKILLS

23.1 Review and recall MIT

In Chapter 16 we discussed different types of enterprise. Can you list two examples each of financial, social and cultural enterprises that you have studied? #List

KEY TERM

Cash flow (or **liquidity**) is the movement of money into and out of an organisation. It measures the ability of an organisation to pay its day-to-day expenses and debts.

If an organisation does not manage its cash flow carefully it may have problems paying its bills, which can negatively impact its ability to carry out its day-to-day operations.

Some organisations are seasonal and may receive a lot of their income over a short period of time, such as in the summer or at Christmas. They need to manage this cash to ensure that they can pay ongoing expenses that may have to be paid all year round. For example, it is not uncommon for producers of chocolate to make 40% of their total annual sales in the Christmas period. Other seasonal businesses include farming and tourism-related organisations.

Consequences of cash flow problems

- **Unable to pay bills:** Cash shortages make it hard to pay bills on time. This can lead to losing important suppliers or services. If wages are not paid, this will also cause industrial relations problems.
- **Loss of discounts:** Some suppliers offer discounts if bills are settled quickly. If an organisation is short of cash, it will struggle to make these payments and will lose out on cash discounts.
- **Penalties for late payment:** An organisation may be charged extra if they are late paying their debts.
- **Poor reputation and credit rating:** An organisation that makes a habit of late or missed payments will get a bad name and its credit rating may suffer. This will make it harder and more expensive to borrow money in the future.

See Chapter 8 for credit rating or creditworthiness

- **Lost opportunities:** If an organisation is short of money, it may miss out on a chance to invest, expand or buy more assets. An asset is an item of value owned by an organisation.

See Chapter 29 for assets

- **Increased borrowing costs:** Cash shortages may need to be solved by extra borrowing. This will increase debt levels in the organisation and it will also have to repay the borrowings with interest. As a result, there will be more pressure on future cash flow.
- **Business failure:** Poor liquidity (cash flow) is the single biggest reason for business failure, so keeping a balance between total income and total expenditure should be a key priority for business managers.

Many businesses get into financial difficulty because they try to grow too quickly. For example, entrepreneurs often try to increase their profit by selling more goods, usually on **credit**. 'On credit' means that the goods will be sold now, but payment won't be received for up to 30 days. This can create a cash flow problem as the business may need to pay for raw materials, operating costs, staff wages, etc. before it receives payment for the goods sold. If it cannot pay these bills, the business may close even though it seems to be profitable and increasing its sales.

The business operating cycle

Since there is often a time delay between payment of expenses (cash outflows) and receipts (cash inflows), organisations need to find a way to continue operating despite this temporary shortage of cash. They need to manage their working capital very carefully, which requires them to manage cash, debtors and stock.

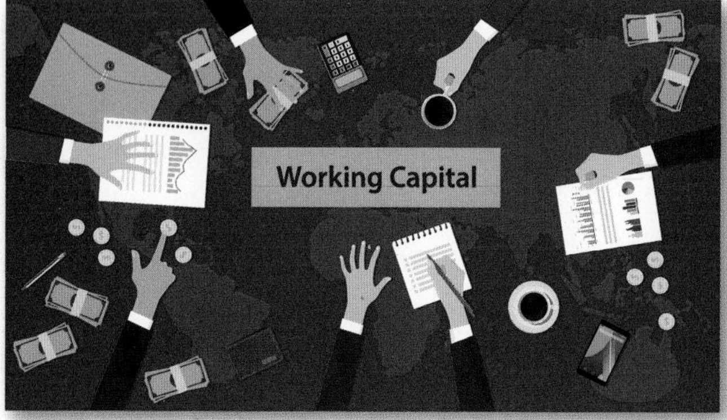

Working capital is the money available to fund the organisation on a day-to-day basis.

Working capital = Current assets – Current liabilities

Examples of current assets include cash, debtors and stock, etc.

Examples of current liabilities include bank overdraft, creditors, expenditure due, etc. Current liabilities are also known as 'creditors falling due within one year'.

Managing debtors

Debtors are people who owe money to an organisation, usually because they have been sold goods or services on credit. This means that there is a delay between the sale of goods or services and the receipt of payment for them. Thirty days is a common period of credit, but in some cases it may be longer. Since the organisation must continue to pay its operating expenses in the meantime (raw materials, wages, transport, light and heat, etc.), it must make sure that cash is being received from debtors on a regular basis (see also page 295).

KEY SKILLS

23.2 Credit

(a) Write down two types of business that do not provide credit to customers. #Research

(b) Do you think that businesses that do not offer credit have cash flow problems? Give reasons for your answer. #Opinion

Managing stock

Organisations should always aim to keep the ideal amount of stock. This means not having too much or too little stock, but having just the right amount to meet the demands of the market. An organisation that has too little stock will be unable to meet customer demands and is likely to lose potential sales (see also page 297).

See Chapter 25 for stock

KEY SKILLS

23.3 Overstocking

MIT

What are the costs to an organisation of having more stock than it needs? #Investigate

Managing cash flow

KEY TERM

A **cash flow forecast** is very similar to a household budget except that it is prepared by an organisation. It is a financial plan that shows expected monthly income and planned expenditure. Cash flow forecasts also help to identify future surpluses and deficits.

Once it has been identified, managers can make plans to deal with excess income or expenditure. For example, the organisation may need to arrange for a short-term loan to cover cash shortfalls or may invest cash surpluses to earn deposit interest.

See Chapter 4 for household budgets

Cash flow forecasts

Why prepare a cash flow forecast?

The benefits of preparing a cash flow forecast include the following:

- **To help organisations to live within their means:** If an organisation can predict its expected monthly receipts, it can plan its monthly spending to match it.
- **To encourage organisations to think about their spending:** Managers will need to consider the timing and amount of all payments.
- **To predict future cash flow problems:** They allow organisations to identify months when there will be a lot of expenses. Managers can then take steps to spread these payments out over several months or borrow the money needed.
- **To allow managers to plan for large items of future expenditure:** For example, this might be the purchase of fixed assets. A cash flow forecast also helps the organisation to set aside money for these items.
- **To show how much cash the organisation expects to have left over at the end of each time period:** This is called their **net cash** and is the difference between planned income and planned expenditure.

A **balanced forecast** refers to a situation where planned income exactly equals planned expenditure.

A **surplus** occurs when planned income is greater than planned expenditure.

A **deficit** occurs when planned expenditure is greater than planned income.

Cash flow forecasts focus on two specific areas:

- Receipts (income)
- Payments (expenditure).

Receipts (income received by organisations)	Payments (expenditure made by organisations)
Sales receipts (or operating income)	Purchase of raw materials
Investment income/deposit interest	Purchase/rental of fixed assets
Receipts from debtors	Dividends to shareholders
Income from grants	Taxation (VAT, import duty, etc.)
Borrowings	Payments to creditors
Share capital (money invested by owners)	Overheads/operating expenses (including wages)
VAT refunds	Loan repayments

KEY TERM

Fixed assets are items owned by the business and intended for long-term use, such as premises, equipment and vehicles.

Creditors are people to whom an organisation owes money, usually because they have supplied the organisation with goods or services on credit.

Preparing a cash flow forecast

On the next page is a cash flow forecast for ABC Ltd. It outlines the receipts and payments of this company.

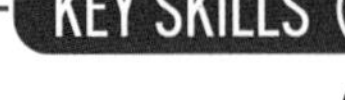

23.4 Review and recall

MIT

Before you begin to analyse the cash flow forecast for ABC Ltd on the next page, write an explanation of each of the following key terms associated with budgets and cash flow forecasts. Where appropriate, outline how each one is calculated. #Record

- Total receipts/income
- Total payments/expenditure
- Net cash
- Opening cash
- Closing cash
- Surplus
- Deficit

See Chapter 4 for household budgets

Cash flow forecast for ABC Ltd					
	May €	June €	July €	August €	Total (May–Aug) €
RECEIPTS					
Cash sales	70,000	70,000	90,000	100,000	330,000
Grant	45,000				45,000
Receipts from debtors	12,000	15,000	15,000	20,000	62,000
Total receipts (A)	**127,000**	**85,000**	**105,000**	**120,000**	**437,000**
PAYMENTS					
Cash purchases	35,000	35,000	48,000	35,000	153,000
Wages	16,000	16,000	16,000	16,000	64,000
Light & heat		4,600		7,400	12,000
Payments to creditors	5,000	10,000	9,000	7,000	31,000
ICT equipment		35,000			35,000
Delivery costs	6,000	6,000	6,000	6,000	24,000
Rent	5,500	5,500	5,500	5,500	22,000
Machinery			85,000		85,000
Insurance	800	800	4,800	800	7,200
Total payments (B)	**68,300**	**112,900**	**174,300**	**77,700**	**433,200**
Net cash (A – B)	58,700	(27,900)	(69,300)	42,300	3,800
Opening cash	12,000	70,700	42,800	(26,500)	12,000
Closing cash	70,700	42,800	(26,500)	15,800	15,800

Interpreting cash flow forecasts

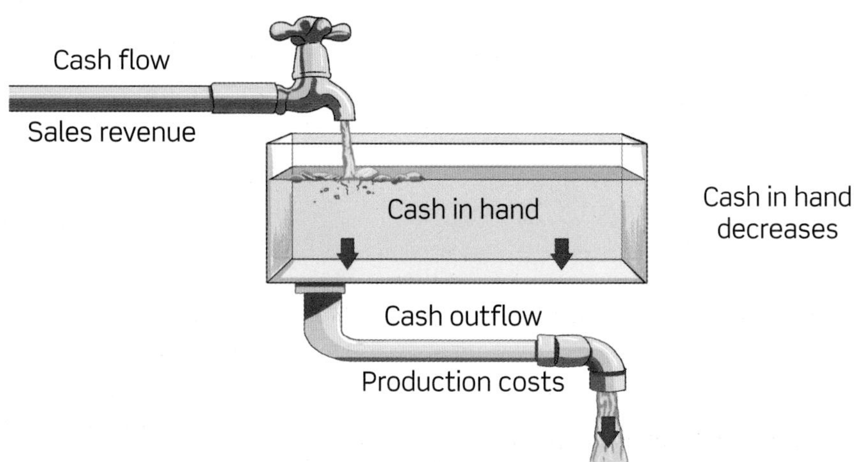

- Cash flow forecasts will highlight 'problem' months for the organisation. A figure in brackets is a minus amount and represents a deficit for that month. This is never an ideal situation for any organisation, but it may be acceptable in the short term if the deficit can be made up from available cash reserves (opening cash). For example, in June, ABC Ltd expects to have a net cash deficit of (€27,900). However, they can afford this because they will have €70,700 left over from May, which can be used to cover this planned overspend in June.

- ABC Ltd's cash flow forecast shows that the business expects to receive more income in May and August than they plan to spend. This will leave them with net cash surpluses of €58,700 in May and €42,300 in August. This is a healthy cash flow situation.
- Looking at the four-month period, we can also see that ABC's total expected receipts are greater than their total planned payments, which will give them a small overall net cash surplus of €3,800. They will have a positive cash flow over the four-month period, but there are big differences between expected receipts and planned payments in some months. These monthly differences are likely to create cash flow problems and illustrate the importance of planning.
- In June and July, ABC expects to have a net cash deficit. In June, the planned overspend of €27,900 can be met out of opening cash reserves, but in July the deficit of €69,300 is greater than the available opening cash. This means that ABC Ltd will face an overall (closing cash) shortfall of €26,500 at the end of July.
- A closing cash deficit is always a serious problem for an organisation, since this money will need to be made up from borrowing. An organisation that has an ongoing cash flow problem of this type will have trouble paying bills and may have to rely on short-term borrowings.
- Fortunately for ABC Ltd, their liquidity problems are for a short time only – the cash flow forecast indicates that they will have overcome the deficit by the end of August. The bank will want to see this cash flow forecast if ABC Ltd decides to apply for a bank overdraft.

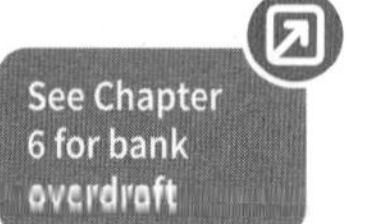
See Chapter 6 for bank overdraft

Dealing with a cash flow deficit

ABC Ltd could use one or more of these solutions to deal with its cash flow problems:

1. **Increase income:** This can be difficult to do, especially in the short term. The organisation might have a sale to increase sales revenue or they could try to collect money due to them from debtors.
2. **Reduce expenditure:** The organisation could cut costs in order to limit its spending, being careful to reduce non-essential spending first. For example, it may be possible to buy cheaper raw materials or reduce operating hours and costs. It may also be possible to spread large payments out over a longer time period, which helps to avoid dealing with a very large item of expenditure in just one month.
3. **Borrow:** The organisation might choose to take out a loan and borrow the money needed to make up the shortfall. In this case, ABC Ltd could organise a bank overdraft, which will enable them to pay their bills in July. They would need to get permission from their bank to do this.

The solution will often involve a combination of two or more of these strategies, for example increase sales revenue and also cut expenditure.

Dealing with a cash flow surplus

When an organisation predicts that it will have a large surplus, it may consider how to make the best use of that money. For example:

1. **Save or invest it until it is needed:** This is relevant for organisations whose income is seasonal.
2. **Repay an existing loan:** This will improve future cash flow by reducing future interest and loan repayments.
3. **Fund some extra expenditure:** For example, use it to buy assets or increase staff pay.

The importance of cash flow planning

- An organisation can calculate its expected **receipts (income)** each month and can identify patterns and differences across a time period. This is especially useful for organisations whose revenue may be seasonal.
- It allows an organisation to plan its monthly **expenditure (payments)**. This planned spending should ideally be in line with expected revenue, but the organisation needs to identify months when this will not be possible.
- It helps an organisation to identify months where it is likely to have a cash surplus or deficit so that they can plan for this situation in advance. In the case of a cash **deficit** (or **shortfall**), it can take action to minimise its negative impact on the organisation.
- The organisation can use the cash flow forecast to support a **loan application**. It will help to illustrate the need for finance to a potential lender and the organisation's ability to repay any borrowings.

BN MIT

23.5 Cash flow forecast

Look at the cash flow forecast for Active Ltd and answer the questions that follow.

Cash flow forecast for Active Ltd					
	August €	Sept €	Oct €	Nov €	Total (Aug–Nov) €
RECEIPTS					
Cash sales	90,000	90,000	110,000	140,000	430,000
Receipts from debtors	15,000	22,000	28,000	35,000	100,000
Total receipts (A)	**105,000**	**112,000**	**138,000**	**175,000**	**530,000**
PAYMENTS					
Cash purchases	38,000	38,000	47,000	68,000	191,000
Wages	19,000	19,000	21,000	24,000	83,000
Light & heat	5,600		6,400		12,000
Vehicles		55,000			55,000
Delivery costs	6,000	6,000	8,000	10,000	30,000
Rent	5,200	5,200	5,200	5,200	20,800
Machinery			95,000		95,000
Insurance	1,100	1,100	5,100	1,100	8,400
Total payments (B)	**74,900**	**124,300**	**187,700**	**108,300**	**495,200**
Net cash (A – B)	30,100	(12,300)	(49,700)	66,700	34,800
Opening cash	22,000	52,100	39,800	(9,900)	22,000
Closing cash	52,100	39,800	(9,900)	56,800	56,800

(a) What are the reasons why Active Ltd would prepare a cash flow forecast? #List #Investigate

(b) Identify two examples of capital expenditure in the above cash flow forecast. #Identify

(c) In which month(s) will Active Ltd experience cash flow problems? #Identify

(d) Suggest two possible solutions to these liquidity problems. #ProblemSolving

(e) Create a single bar chart or trend graph to show and compare total receipts and total payments for August–November for Active Ltd. #Presentation #Analyse

Financial needs of organisations

Managing cash flow is just one aspect of financial planning for organisations. Managers need to ensure that the organisation has enough money to meet its long- and short-term needs.

Organisations need finance for a variety of reasons:

- **Short-term needs** involve items of expenditure that must be paid within the current financial year, such as raw materials, wages, light and heat, telephone, advertising, insurance and transport costs. Since these are day-to-day costs that must be paid regularly and repeatedly, they are also known as **current expenditure**.
- **Medium-term needs** involve spending on items that are likely to last beyond the current financial year, such as the purchase of vehicles and digital technology equipment. These are examples of **capital expenditure**, as the items will be owned and used by the business for one to five years.
- **Long-term needs** include the purchase of items that will provide benefits to the business over an extended period of time (usually more than five years), such as premises and machinery. These are also examples of capital expenditure.

KEY SKILLS

MIT

WO

23.6 Short-, medium- and long-term needs

With your partner, discuss whether each of these is a short-, medium- or long-term need.
#Discussion #ThinkPairShare

(a) An office telephone bill

(b) A delivery van

(c) A packaging machine for a factory

(d) A fridge for a restaurant

(e) Furniture for the reception area of a voluntary organisation

(f) Marketing leaflets for a hotel

(g) A stable for a horse-riding school

Sources of finance

The **matching principle** ensures that organisations use a source of finance that is most suited to their specific needs – in other words, that short-, medium- and long-term needs are financed (or matched) with short-, medium- and long-term sources of finance.

See Chapter 8 for matching principle

- Short-term finance will be repaid within one year. It is used to pay day-to-day expenses, such as buying raw materials, paying wages and creditors, etc.
- Medium-term finance will be repaid between one and five years. It will be used to pay for vehicles and equipment, etc.
- Long-term finance will be repaid over a period longer than five years. It is used to purchase premises and large items of machinery and equipment that the organisation will use for a long time.

Factors that influence the source of finance

Organisations must consider the following when choosing a suitable source of finance.

- **The purpose of the finance:** Is it for day-to-day purposes (working capital) or is it to fund long-term goals or the purchase of fixed assets?
- **The amount of finance required:** Large amounts are usually spread out over a longer time period. This will reduce monthly repayments, which will help with monthly cash flow (liquidity).

- **Cost of finance:** Borrowers should compare the annual percentage rate (APR) of each possible source.
- **Control:** How will the source of finance impact on ownership and control of the organisation? For example, issuing new shares will allow new shareholders to have a say in how an organisation is run.
- **Security required:** What collateral will be needed to protect the lender in case of non-payment? Some sources of finance, including mortgages, may require assets to be set aside in the event of default. If the borrower fails to repay the loan, the lender can claim the assets and sell them to recover the money owed to them.

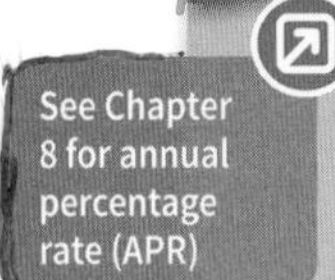

See Chapter 8 for annual percentage rate (APR)

See Chapter 8 for collateral

Table 23.1 gives a summary of common needs for and suitable sources of finance for organisations.

Short-term needs	Short-term sources of finance (repaid within 1 year)
Stock Raw materials Wages Transport Light and heat Insurance Advertising	Bank overdraft Accrued expenses Credit card Trade creditors Factoring debt Invoice discounting
Medium-term needs	**Medium-term sources of finance (repaid in 1–5 years)**
Vehicles Computers and ICT equipment	Leasing Hire purchase Medium-term loan
Long-term needs	**Long-term sources of finance (repaid in 5+ years)**
Premises Land Machinery Expansion Fixtures and fittings	Share capital (equity) Venture capital Retained profit Grants Sale and leaseback Debentures/long-term loan Mortgage Crowdfunding

Table 23.1 Common organisational needs and suitable sources of finance

Borrowing in any form can be costly and risky. For each potential source of finance, managers will need to consider the costs, benefits and potential risks.

Short-term sources of finance

Source	Explanation	Cost/risk
Bank overdraft	The organisation can withdraw more money from their current account than they have in it. The overdraft must be arranged in advance. The bank will limit the amount that can be withdrawn.	Interest will be paid on the amount overdrawn. The financial institution can cancel the overdraft at short notice.
Trade creditor	A creditor is a person or business we owe money to, usually because we have bought goods or services on credit from them.	Cash discounts for prompt payments will be lost. Interest may be charged on overdue amounts.
Accrued expenses	**Accrued expenses** means that the organisation can use certain services (expenses) for up to two months before it needs to pay for them, such as electricity, phone and broadband. Businesses also pay VAT collected from their sales every two months. This money is paid to the Revenue Commissioners, but a business can use this money in the short term before the VAT bill has to be paid.	If the bill is not paid on time, the service could be disconnected. Failure to pay bills could damage the organisation's credit rating.
Credit card	Credit allows the card holder to buy now and pay later. They are not suitable for all business purchases but may be used to pay for some staff expenses, such as travel costs, fuel, accommodation, meals, etc.	Interest is charged on the balance outstanding.
Factoring debt	When a business sells goods on credit, it will be owed money by its debtors. It may not receive the cash in time to meet its ongoing payments. **Factoring** allows the debt to be sold for less than its value, but the cash will be received quickly. (See example on the next page.)	Very expensive, as debts are often sold at a big discount.
Invoice discounting	A form of factoring that allows an organisation to borrow money owed to it by customers (debtors). A debtor is someone who owes us money. Unlike factoring, the organisation is responsible for collecting payments from its debtors and will forward payment to the bank.	Interest is charged on the amount borrowed.

See Chapter 10 for Value Added Tax

Table 23.2 Short-term sources of finance

An example of factoring

Elite Ltd is owed €100,000 by Thrifty Ltd for goods sold on credit. Thrifty Ltd is slow in paying the debt, so Elite Ltd approaches a factoring company, which agrees to take over the total debt of €100,000 but at a discounted price of €80,000. Elite Ltd no longer has an outstanding debt and has improved its cash position with an immediate payment of €80,000.

The factoring company will receive €100,000 when it collects the debt and will earn a €20,000 profit on the deal. Most commercial banks offer factoring services to their business customers.

KEY SKILLS MIT

23.7 Overdraft

Megan and Julie run a seaside restaurant. They have an overdraft facility on their bank account, but don't use it all the time.

(a) Why do you think they have the facility when they seem not to need it? #WhatDoYouThink #Investigate

(b) Are there times of year when they might need it more than others? #Investigate

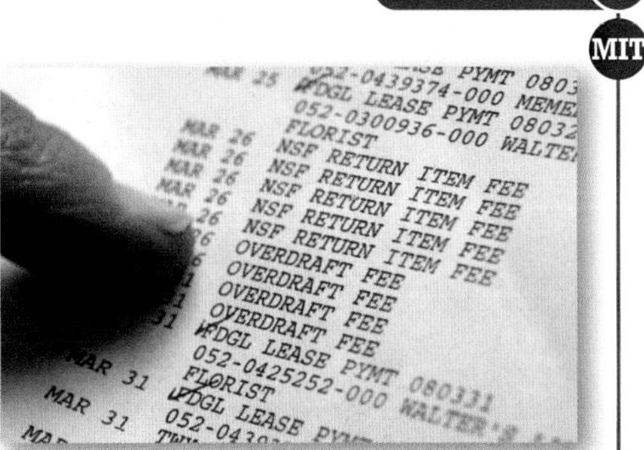

KEY SKILLS MIT

23.8 Business credit card

Galvin's sells veterinary products to veterinary practices around the country. Each of its 10 salespeople has a business credit card to use when they are on the road.

(a) What do you think the salespeople use their credit cards for? #WhatDoYouThink #Investigate

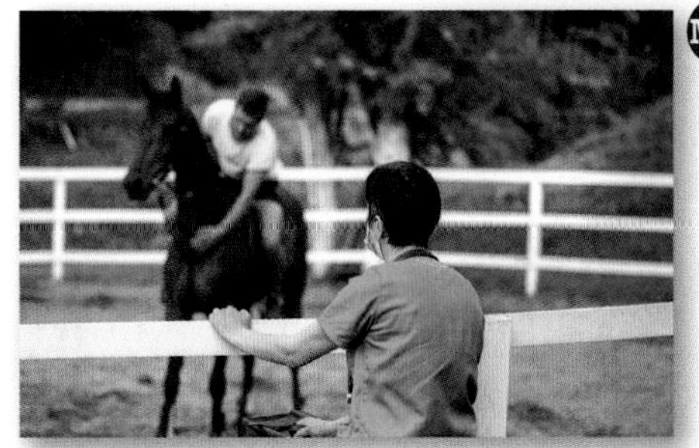

(b) What are the benefits of using business credit cards to:

(i) The salespeople?

(ii) The business? #Investigate

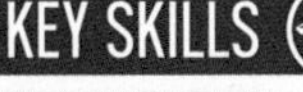
KEY SKILLS MIT

23.9 Credit terms

Some large businesses require long credit terms from small suppliers and may not pay the supplier for two or three months. What problems could this cause for the smaller businesses? #CreativeThinking

KEY SKILLS

MIT

23.10 Factoring

In the case of factoring, who does the factoring company have to credit-check? #Investigate

Medium-term sources of finance

Source	Explanation	Cost/risk	Security required
Leasing	Leasing means renting an asset over a number of years. The lease agreement allows a business to have possession and use of the asset provided they make fixed regular payments to the leasing company.	Expensive. Over a long period of time, the cost will be greater than the purchase price of the asset. Ownership is never transferred and the asset remains the property of the leasing company.	None, as ownership remains with the leasing company.
Hire purchase (HP)	In hire purchase, the purchaser pays an initial deposit and a finance company pays the balance to the seller. The purchasing business then pays back the finance company with an agreed number of fixed regular payments.	Expensive. The APR may be over 20%. Failure to meet the repayment schedule will result in the assets being repossessed (taken back).	None, as ownership is not transferred until the final payment is made.
Medium-term loan	Available from banks and credit unions. Borrowers make fixed payments (which cover repayment of the loan plus interest) over an agreed time period, usually between one and five years.	The APR is usually cheaper than a bank overdraft. Failure to repay the loan can result in legal action and a poor credit rating.	Collateral may be required.

Table 23.3 Medium-term sources of finance

KEY SKILLS MIT WO C

23.11 Hire purchase

Why is hire purchase often used as a last resort by businesses? #ThinkPairShare

HP

Hire Purchase

ENTERPRISE

Long-term sources of finance

Note: In the table below, 'Impact on control' looks at how new investors or lenders may have a say in the future running of the organisation.

Source	Explanation	Cost/risk	Impact on control	Security required
Share capital/ equity	Capital is money invested into a business by its owners. The owners are called shareholders. In return for their investment, a profitable business may pay them a dividend (a portion of profits paid to shareholders).	There are no fixed interest payments involved in selling shares.	Issuing new shares will reduce the existing shareholders' control. Each share provides a shareholder with a vote in running the business.	None
Venture capital	**Venture capital** is money invested in new or high-risk businesses. Venture capitalists usually invest capital in return for shares in the business. The 'dragons' on *Dragons' Den* are venture capitalists. Some banks offer venture capital finance to business start-ups.	Venture capitalists look for a good return on investment, e.g. a shareholding in the business and dividend payments.	If the venture capitalist takes shares, they will have some control over the business.	None
Retained profit	A portion of the annual profits is put back into the organisation. Reinvesting the profits can be used to purchase fixed assets or to fund expansion. This is only suitable for existing businesses, as a start-up business will not have any retained profits to use.	Very little cost and risk involved, as the money already belongs to the organisation and there is no increase in external debt.	None	None, as the organisation's own money is being used
Grants	A **grant** is money provided by the government, local authority or EU. It may be used to pay for staff training, buy machinery or create employment. Start-up businesses may also receive grants to fund market research.	Grants are free from interest charges and usually do not have to be repaid as long as they are used for their intended purpose.	None, but the agency providing the grant may attach strict conditions on the use of the grant.	None

cont'd

Source	Explanation	Cost/risk	Impact on control	Security required
Sale and leaseback	A business may decide to use **sale and leaseback** to 'cash in' on the value of its premises by selling it to an investor while at the same time signing a long-term lease with the new owner. This allows the business to keep using the premises.	Annual rent charge. Loss of future increases in the value of the premises.	The organisation will lose control over the asset once it is sold. This will reduce the value of the fixed assets of the business.	None
Debenture	A **debenture** is a long-term loan with a fixed interest rate and a specific repayment date.	Fixed interest payments must be paid each year, so the organisation must generate enough income to pay these. The amount borrowed must be repaid in full by the due date; failure to do so may lead to loss of assets.	None	Collateral will be required in the form of fixed assets, such as title deeds of property.
Mortgage	Specifically used to purchase property. Typically repaid over 20–30 years.	If the borrower cannot repay the debt, the lender can sell the property and recover the money owed.	While the lender will not have control over the organisation, they have a legal claim to the property. This may limit the organisation's ability to sell or dispose of this asset.	The lender will secure a legal claim on the property and may repossess it in the event of non-payment by the borrower.
Crowdfunding	**Crowdfunding** means seeking small amounts of funding from a large number of people. The investors will receive a reward for investing in the organisation depending on how much they invest, such as early access to products or shares in the business. GoFundMe is a well-known crowdfunding website that can be used to raise donation- or equity-based funding.	Need to find a large number of investors in order to reach the target.	In some cases the investors may own shares in the organisation, which will give them a say in its operation and a share of profits.	None

Table 23.4 Long-term sources of finance

KEY SKILLS

23.12 Selling shares

Why might a company find it difficult to sell more shares? #ThinkPairShare #Investigate

Businesses here raise €165m in venture capital funding

Irish businesses raised more than $185m (€165.6m) in venture capital (VC) funding in the three months to 30 September, according to the latest Venture Pulse from global consulting and accountancy group KPMG.

Financial technology company Fenergo closed the largest deal, valued at $74.5m (€66.7m). It was followed by Dublin-founded student loan specialist Future Finance, which raised $26m (€23m).

'Ireland continues to attract a significant amount of attention from VC investors and fintech remains a very hot sector,' said Anna Scally, partner at KPMG.

Elsewhere, global VC investment dropped to $55.7bn in the third quarter of this year, from $65bn in quarter two. The volume of deals also fell to 4,154 from 5,138. In Europe, VC fundraising topped $9.8bn.

So far this year, Europe has seen $28.76bn in VC investment – well above the record $26.98bn reported in 2018.

Source: Irish Independent, 4 November 2019

MIT

23.13 Venture capitalists

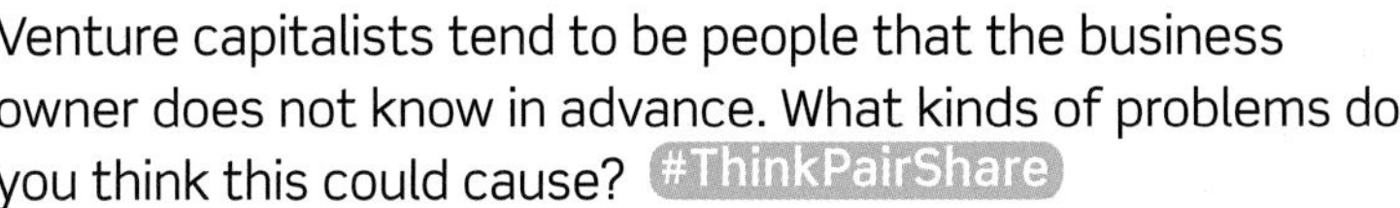

Venture capitalists tend to be people that the business owner does not know in advance. What kinds of problems do you think this could cause? #ThinkPairShare

23.14 Reinvesting profits

Why is it a good idea for any business to put some of its profits back into the company to make cash available for purchases? #ThinkPairShare #Investigate

KEY SKILLS

23.15 Grants supporting businesses

(a) Research what organisations in your local area offer grants to start-up businesses.

(b) What types of grants do they provide? How much grant aid is available to organisations?

(c) Apart from grants, what other types of support do these organisations provide to start-up businesses?

(d) Research organisations that offer grants to existing businesses. Find out how much grant aid is available to these businesses. #Research

IN THE NEWS

Easons launches Munster sale and leaseback deals worth over €4m

Stationery and book seller Easons has launched sale and leaseback deals for three stores that it owns in Limerick City, Tralee, Co. Kerry and Clonmel, Co. Tipperary.

These sales are part of Easons's plan to sell 13 properties in the Republic, which could generate €60m, of which about €20m would be invested in its retail business. The rest of the proceeds will be divided among its 220 shareholders.

It has already sold a retail outlet in Carlow town that it had let to another retailer and in January Easons agreed a deal to sell its 184,886 sq. ft warehouse on 8.4 acres at St Margaret's in north Dublin to Irish property fund Iput for €19m.

Sale and leaseback deals are also among the options being considered for its flagship store on O'Connell Street in Dublin as well as its store on Patrick Street in Cork city centre, but the future timing and details of those have not yet been decided.

Source: Irish Independent, 27 August 2019

KEY SKILLS MIT

23.16 Sale and leaseback

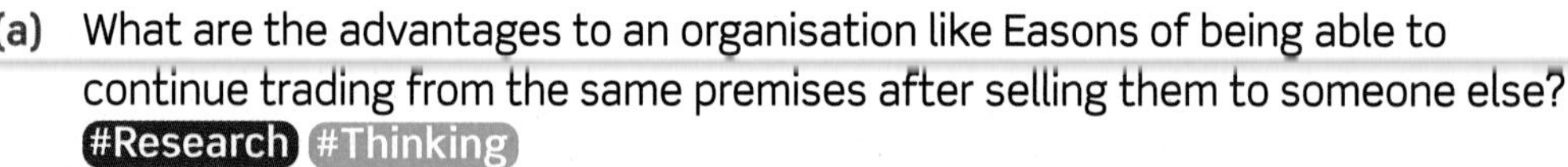

(a) What are the advantages to an organisation like Easons of being able to continue trading from the same premises after selling them to someone else? #Research #Thinking

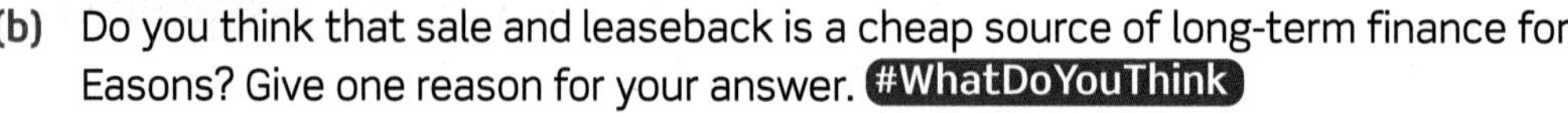

(b) Do you think that sale and leaseback is a cheap source of long-term finance for Easons? Give one reason for your answer. #WhatDoYouThink

(c) What are the possible drawbacks for Easons of using sale and leaseback as a source of long-term finance? #Research #Opinion

KEY SKILLS MIT BC C

23.17 Crowdfunding

Research crowdfunding websites and find an organisation that has raised money this way. Prepare a presentation for the rest of the class. Include:

(a) Details about the organisation

(b) Why it needed the capital

(c) What rewards are available for investors

(d) Whether or not the campaign was successful

(e) What happened after the funding was received #Research #Presentation

Weblinks

PowerPoint Summary

WRITING A BUSINESS PLAN

LEARNING OUTCOMES IN FOCUS

2.9 Develop a simple business plan for a new or existing product or service

Links to 2.2, 2.7, 2.8, 2.11, 2.12, 2.13, 3.3

LEARNING INTENTIONS FOR THIS CHAPTER

- Carry out a SWOT analysis
- Outline the purpose of a business plan
- Identify the main headings in a business plan
- Complete a business plan for a new or existing product or service.

CHAPTER 24 KEY TERMS

- business plan
- franchise
- franchisee
- franchisor
- limited liability
- partnership
- private limited company
- SMART goals
- sole trader
- SWOT analysis
- unlimited liability

CHAPTER 24 KEY SKILLS

- BC Being Creative
- BL Being Literate
- MIT Managing Information and Thinking
- WO Working with Others

The business plan

KEY TERM

A **business plan** is a written description of a business's aims, strategies, target markets and financial forecasts. It explains what the business plans to do and how it plans to do it.

A business plan is also useful to help the entrepreneur(s) identify the resources and finance that are needed to start the business as well as the marketing and production needed to ensure the business is a success.

When an entrepreneur starts a new business or requests a loan from a financial institution, either for a start-up business or to fund expansion for an existing business, they will need to prepare a business plan in order to provide information about:

- The background and history of the business
- The team of people involved in setting up and managing the business
- The product or service being offered
- How the business will produce the goods or service
- Details about the market for the product or service: size of market, target market, marketing mix, etc.
- How the business will be financed and its ability to repay loans
- The structure of the business.

Anyone who is starting a business should write a business plan, even if they are not seeking external finance, as it is a good way of looking at where the business is now, where it is heading and how it will get there.

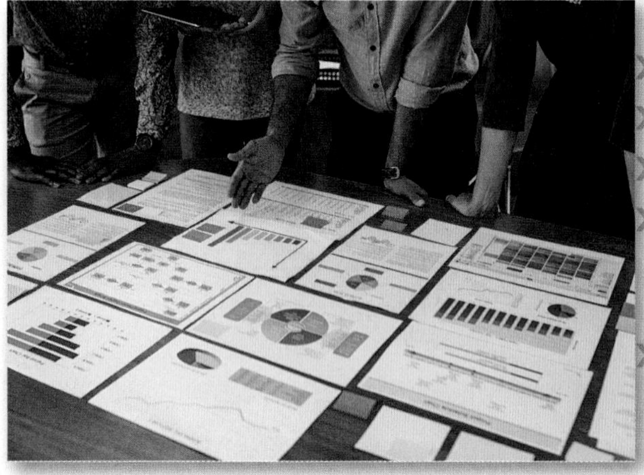

The purpose of a business plan is to:

- Establish whether the business is likely to succeed
- Help the business raise the finance it needs
- Set targets to be achieved
- Help the entrepreneur to focus on the future goals of the business to benchmark future profits and/or growth targets
- Support a proposed expansion or the development of a new product or service by an existing business.

A business plan will contain the following headings.

Section 1: Background of the business

- The aims and objectives of the business, i.e. what it is set up to do
- What products/services it will provide
- The name and address of the business.

Section 2: The business team

- The people involved in the business, including their educational details and past experience.

Section 3: Market and marketing

- A brief description of the market
- The current and potential size of the market
- The number of competitors already in the market
- The marketing mix strategy, including product, price, place and promotion.

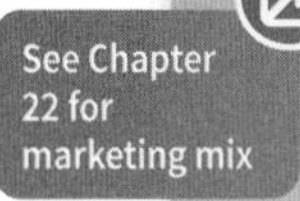
See Chapter 22 for marketing mix

Section 4: Production

- An outline of all premises and equipment available to the business
- The production process to be used, for example job production (single/one-off products), batch production (group of similar products) or mass production (products produced in very large quantities).

Section 5: Costings and finance

- How much it costs to produce the item (cost price) and what mark-up/profit margin will be added on to get the price it will be sold at (selling price)
- Details about any existing loans that the business has
- The amount of finance required and the purpose for which it is needed
- How the finance is to be repaid
- Detailed cash flow forecasts and projected profits for two or three years.

Section 6: Structure of the business

- The legal structure of the business (sole trader, partnership, private limited company or franchise – see page 287).

Planning

Planning involves setting goals for the business and deciding on ways to achieve these goals. When setting goals, always remember that they should be **SMART**:

S	**Specific**	Define a specific, clear goal.
M	**Measurable**	It must be possible to measure whether or not the goal has been achieved.
A	**Agreed**	Goals are much more likely to be reached if they are agreed and accepted by all those involved in achieving them.
R	**Realistic**	It must be possible to achieve the goal using the resources (including time) available. If the goal is not realistic, people will not be motivated by it.
T	**Timed**	This gives the goal a target date to be achieved by.

For example, an entrepreneur might set her goal as 'making my business more successful in the future'. This goal is hard to plan for because it is unclear what 'success' means or how it will be measured. 'The future' is also vague. A SMART goal might be 'to increase market share in Ireland by 8% in the next five years'. This is more clearly defined and easier to measure. It should also make it easier to plan for.

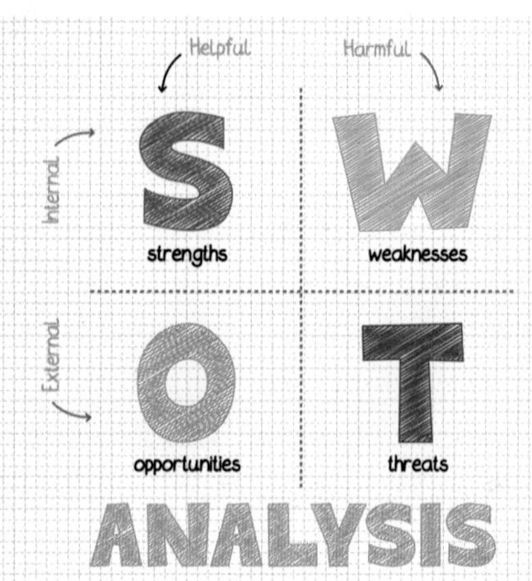

SWOT analysis

Before writing a business plan, it may be useful to carry out a SWOT analysis. A SWOT analysis is not an actual plan, but it helps to identify positive and negative aspects of the business that can be promoted or improved by future plans.

KEY TERM

A **SWOT analysis** identifies the current strengths and weaknesses of a business as well as the opportunities and threats facing it.

Strengths and opportunities are positive factors, while weaknesses and threats are negative factors. Strengths and weaknesses are internal factors (elements inside the organisation), which the business has control over. Opportunities and threats are external factors (elements outside the organisation), which the business has no control over. Completing a SWOT analysis forces a business to consider its current position and the situations it might face in the future.

Businesses may consider asking employees, managers, customers and suppliers to identify factors for each element of the SWOT analysis.

Let's look at an example of a SWOT analysis for McDonald's.

Strengths	Weaknesses
› Strong brand name › Global recognition	› High staff turnover, which means spending money on hiring and training new staff › Over reliance on fast food, which does not have a reputation for being healthy
Opportunities	**Threats**
› Offer healthier food options › Open new branches	› Competition from other fast food businesses › Sugar tax on soft drinks › Tax increase on fast food items

Table 24.1 SWOT analysis for McDonald's

KEY SKILLS

24.1 SWOT analysis

MIT WO BC

(a) Why might business owners ask for input from other people (stakeholders) into the SWOT analysis? #Investigate

230

(b) Working in pairs, identify a business that you are familiar with (local, national or international). Using the template in the Student Activity Book, complete a SWOT analysis for this business. Give at least two examples for each element. #ThinkPairShare #GroupWork #Collaborate

See Chapter 11 for personal financial life cycle

(c) Individuals and other types of organisations, not just businesses, may also carry out a SWOT analysis. At what points of life might an individual carry out a SWOT analysis on themselves? #CreativeThinking

Forms of business ownership

When establishing a business, an entrepreneur will need to decide on the legal structure of that business. Ownership structures in Ireland include:

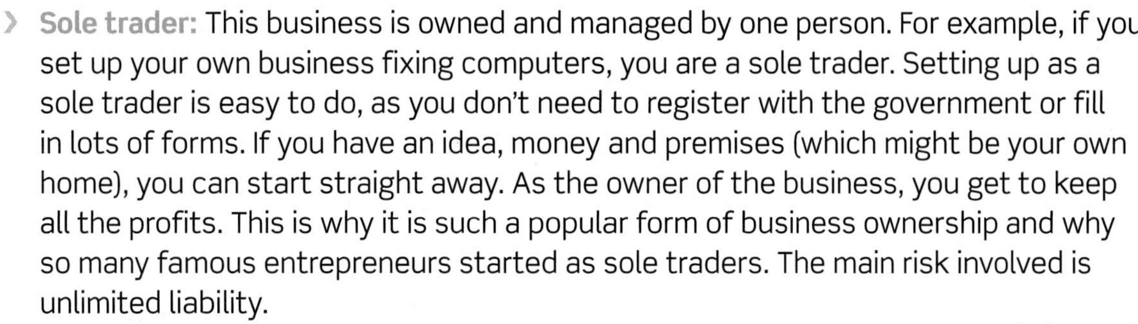

- **Sole trader:** This business is owned and managed by one person. For example, if you set up your own business fixing computers, you are a sole trader. Setting up as a sole trader is easy to do, as you don't need to register with the government or fill in lots of forms. If you have an idea, money and premises (which might be your own home), you can start straight away. As the owner of the business, you get to keep all the profits. This is why it is such a popular form of business ownership and why so many famous entrepreneurs started as sole traders. The main risk involved is unlimited liability.

KEY TERM

Unlimited liability means that the sole trader is personally responsible for the debts of the business.

- **Partnership:** A partnership is created when 2–20 people set up in business. Partnerships are common with solicitors, doctors, accountants, auctioneers and estate agents, although any business can have partners, such as a shop or a sandwich-making business. Partners share the workload, the risks and the profits.
- **Private limited company:** A private limited company is a business set up by between one and 149 people, called shareholders. The business has Limited or Ltd in its name because the liability of the owners is limited to what they originally invested in the business (**limited liability**). This means that unlike a sole trader, individual shareholders are not personally liable for company debts. It cannot advertise its shares to the general public – if shares are sold, this will be done privately.

Franchises

Some entrepreneurs choose to become part of an existing business by buying a franchise.

KEY TERM

A **franchise** is when one firm (the **franchisor**) sells the right to use its products and its brand name to another business (the **franchisee**) in return for a fee and a share of the profits.

An example of a franchise business is Supermac's. In return for an initial fee and a percentage of the revenue earned, franchisees can use the Supermac's name and sell Supermac's products. Although the franchisee owns the business, they use Supermac's methods and products and must follow strict rules set down by the company. Other popular franchises in Ireland are McDonald's, Subway, Chopped and Domino's Pizza.

KEY SKILLS

MIT BL BC

24.2 Your new franchise

Search online for franchises that are for sale in Ireland. Choose one that appeals to you and write a short report on:

- What the business is
- Why you like the idea
- Where you could locate your business and why you have chosen this location
- What skills you could bring to the business. #Research #CreativeThinking

Advantages of franchises

- The idea already exists, so the entrepreneur can look at the track record of the existing business and see if the product/service works. This reduces the risk for the franchisee.
- The brand name may be well established. If people have heard of the business already, this may make it easier to get customers.
- The franchisor provides support and training, so the franchisee benefits from the franchisor's guidance, training, products and equipment.
- Costs such as marketing can be shared between the franchisees. Promotion of the brand benefits each franchisee, as it spreads the cost and allows the business to advertise on national TV and in the national press.

Disadvantages of franchises

- A negative response to one franchisee might affect them all. If there is a problem with one franchise, for example in relation to quality or service, this will reflect badly on all the other franchises.
- Franchisees must follow strict rules when operating the business, so there is a loss of control. There may be disputes between the franchisee and the franchisor. The person selling the franchise might want to keep a high level of control over how things are done, but the person buying it might want more freedom to make their own decisions.

Example of a business plan

Luxury Furniture Ltd

Luxury Furniture Ltd has been operating for 10 years in Co. Carlow. It manufactures luxury tables and chairs for the Irish market. Recent market research it carried out has shown a demand for a luxury bedroom furniture range. A bank loan is needed for expansion. The business owners have prepared a business plan to support their application.

Business Plan – Luxury Furniture Limited (Ltd)

Section 1: Background of the business

The business, Luxury Furniture Ltd, has its headquarters in Market Street, Tullow, Co. Carlow.

The objective of Luxury Furniture Ltd is to make and sell high-quality tables and chairs for the Irish market.

Section 2: The business team

The shareholders of the company are Michael O'Neill and Gráinne O'Neill.

Michael is responsible for production and design. He holds an engineering degree from UCD and has been working in furniture manufacturing for over 20 years. He has invested €30,000 in the business.

Gráinne qualified in business management and administration in IT Carlow in 2009 and has several years' managerial experience in the manufacturing sector. She is the managing director and finance manager. She has also invested €30,000 in the business.

Section 3: Market and marketing
It is estimated that the Irish market for luxury furniture is growing and is worth around €10 million per annum. There are currently seven competitors based throughout the country. The product is a luxury brand, therefore the price charged is a premium price.

The main form of promotion is advertising on local and national radio stations, online and in magazines. The products are sold through a national network of furniture retailers.

Section 4: Production
The fixed assets of the business are the premises in Market Street, Tullow (which consists of production, office, showroom and display areas), industrial saws, equipment and two delivery vans. The company produces the tables and chairs in batch production.

Section 5: Costings and finance
The cost price per chair is €100. With a mark-up of €50, each has a selling price of €150. The cost price per table is €700. With a mark-up of €300, each has a selling price of €1,000.

The company has no existing borrowings (loans) and wishes to borrow €100,000 in order to finance expansion. This money will be used to:

- Build an extension to the premises
- Purchase another delivery van
- Develop a bedroom furniture range
- Update the company website to enable increased sales, both within Ireland and internationally.

The loan is required for 10 years and will be paid for out of estimated future income.

Section 6: Structure of the business
Luxury Furniture Ltd is a private limited company.

Signed:

Michael O'Neill   Gráinne O'Neill

Date: 30/12/2020

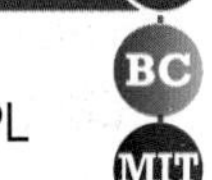

24.3 Business plan

231 233

(a) Using the templates in the Student Activity Book, write a business plan for PL Ltd and Lightbody's Bakery Ltd using the details supplied. #Activity

(b) Choose a local, national or global business that you are familiar with and prepare a simple business plan for the organisation. Use the headings provided in the example above and carry out whatever research is necessary. #Research

ENTERPRISE

CHAPTER 25

BUSINESS DOCUMENTS

LEARNING OUTCOMES IN FOCUS

2.10 Complete and interpret key business documents that an organisation uses to manage its transactions for accountability purposes

Links to 1.2, 2.9, 2.11, 2.12, 2.13, 3.2, 3.4

LEARNING INTENTIONS FOR THIS CHAPTER

When you have completed this chapter you will be able to:

- Appreciate the importance of record-keeping in business
- Identify and complete the documents used by businesses when buying and selling goods
- Outline the procedures for dealing with incoming and outgoing business documents
- Analyse the information in business documents
- Explain the key terms associated with business documents.

CHAPTER 25 KEY TERMS

B2B	debit note	quotation
bad debt	delivery note	receipt
bank reference	E&OE (errors and omissions excepted)	statement of account
carriage paid	estimate	stock control
cash discount	invoice	terms of sale
COD (cash on delivery)	letter of enquiry	trade discount
credit note	payment terms	trade reference
CWO (cash with order)		VAT

CHAPTER 25 KEY SKILLS

- BC Being Creative
- BL Being Literate
- BN Being Numerate
- C Communicating
- MIT Managing Information and Thinking
- WO Working with Others

The importance of business documents

Nearly everything that happens in a business relies on some sort of written record. When you receive wages, you get a payslip; when all the staff need to know something, they are sent a memo; when a client needs to be contacted, they are sent an email or a letter. Having a record is important because it helps people in the organisation to remember what took place or was agreed.

Sometimes the document is electronic, but it is still considered a document. In this chapter we will look at the business documents that are involved in buying and selling goods.

25.1 Business documents

Why do businesses use documents when buying and selling goods? List all the reasons you can think of. #List #Think

Table 25.1 is a summary of all the documents that firms may use for selling goods.

	Document	Sender		Receiver
1	Letter of enquiry	Buyer	→	Seller
2	Quotation	Seller	→	Buyer
3	Order	Buyer	→	Seller
4	Delivery note	Seller	→	Buyer
5	Invoice	Seller	→	Buyer
6	Credit note	Seller	→	Buyer
7	Debit note	Seller	→	Buyer
8	Statement of account	Seller	→	Buyer
9	Payment	Buyer	→	Seller
10	Receipt	Seller	→	Buyer

Table 25.1 Summary of transaction documents

1 Letter of enquiry

When a business wants to buy from another business (known as business-to-business, or **B2B**), they will often write a letter or email of enquiry, particularly if they have not dealt with the business before. A letter or email will help a business to keep a record of the enquiry.

The buyer might contact several different businesses to ask about availability of goods, prices and the terms of sale.

KEY TERM

The **terms of sale** are the conditions attached to a sale, such as who pays for delivery, what discount is available and when the invoice (bill) has to be paid.

25.2 Letter of enquiry

Why should a buyer write a letter or email of enquiry to at least three businesses that offer the same goods for sale? #Investigate #Opinion

Figure 25.1 shows a typical letter of enquiry.

O'Brien Electrical Ltd
12 Main Street
Trim
Co. Meath
Tel: (046) 123 4566/Fax: (046) 987 6544
Email: office@obrienelectrical.ie
www.obrienelectrical.ie

02/11/2022

Downtown Wholesalers Ltd
Water Street
Clonakilty
Co. Cork

Re: Quotation request

Dear Sir/Madam,

Please quote your best price and terms of sale for the following goods:
10 Windspool dishwashers
15 Windspool washing machines
50 Meteor electric blankets

Yours faithfully,

James O'Brien

James O'Brien
Purchasing Manager

Figure 25.1 Example of a letter of enquiry

Dealing with the letter of enquiry

Seller (incoming)	Buyer (outgoing)
On receipt of a letter of enquiry: › Check stock and prices. › Prepare a quotation. › File the original for reference.	Before sending a letter of enquiry: › Check the name and address of the seller. › Check the quantities required. › File a copy for reference.

KEY SKILLS

25.3 Choose a supplier for your new business

You have just set up a business selling sports kit and equipment. Decide on your business name and address. Research three sportswear suppliers and write a letter or email of enquiry to one of them, using the contact details that you have found online, requesting 10 each of your county GAA kits in sizes small, medium and large, and 40 footballs. (*Note:* You are not required to actually send the letter.) #Research

C BC BL

2 Quotation

When the enquiry is received, the seller will check the current prices and prepare a quotation.

KEY TERM

A **quotation** is a written document that a seller sends to a potential buyer that shows the price of the goods and any terms of sale.

Terms of sale

The terms of sale are the conditions attached to a quotation and any future sale. They might include:

- **Delivery:** If the quotation says **carriage paid**, the seller of the goods will cover the cost of delivering the goods to the buyer. Otherwise, they will quote a cost for postage or delivery by courier.
- **E&OE:** This stands for 'errors and omissions excepted'. This means that the seller will not be held responsible if an error has been made and it can correct the price if it has made a mistake.
- **Trade discount:** A reduction of the selling price given to business customers. It is subtracted before the VAT is added on.
- **Cash discount:** An extra discount may be given if the goods are paid for promptly, for example a 5% cash discount for payment within 14 days. Sellers offer this extra incentive to encourage quick payment.
- **VAT:** A tax on goods and services. It must be charged on each transaction in the channel of distribution.
- **CWO (cash with order):** Payment must be made when the order is placed for the goods.
- **COD (cash on delivery):** Payment must be made when the goods are delivered.
- **Payment terms:** Details of the credit and payment terms. For example, a buyer may have up to 30 days to pay for the goods.

When the buyer has received all the quotations that they asked for, they will compare them and make a decision about who to purchase from.

25.4 Terms of sale

Businesses offer different terms of sale. For example, one business may require CWO, while another may offer customers 30 days' credit. Likewise, businesses may offer different levels of trade discount. With a partner, discuss why you think this happens. Share your thoughts with another pair. Write down your conclusions. #Discussion

WO MIT C

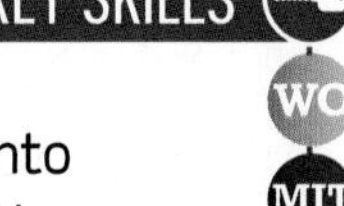

C

25.5 To buy or not to buy?

With your partner, discuss what factors (other than price) buyers will take into account when deciding which supplier to buy from. Share your thoughts with another pair and record your answers. #Discussion #GroupWork

Figure 25.2 shows a typical quotation.

Quotation **No. 0076**

Downtown Wholesalers Ltd

Water Street
Clonakilty
Co. Cork
Tel: (091) 654 3276/Fax: (091) 789 6543
Email: office@downtownwholesalers.ie
www.downtownwholesalers.ie

06/11/2022

To: O'Brien Electrical Ltd
12 Main Street
Trim
Co. Meath

Quantity	Description	Model no.	Unit price €
10	Windspool dishwashers	DW500	200.00
15	Windspool washing machines	WM350	150.00
50	Meteor electric blankets	EB776	50.00

These prices are valid for orders within 21 days
All goods include a trade discount: 10%
Carriage paid
VAT rate: 20%
Payment terms: Payment in full within 30 days.

Signed: Robert Walsh
Sales Manager
E&OE

Figure 25.2 Example of a quotation

KEY SKILLS BL C

25.6 Who's who?

Who is the buyer and who is the seller in this quotation?
#Identify

KEY SKILLS BL C

25.7 COD and credit

Downtown Wholesalers requires new customers to pay COD for their first order. They will consider offering credit terms to customers for future orders if they provide a trade or bank reference. Why is payment of cash on delivery (COD) required for the first order, but the buyer may be given credit for future orders? #Investigate #Opinion

Dealing with the quotation

Buyer (incoming)	Seller (outgoing)
On receipt of a quotation: › Check the quotation against the letter of enquiry. › Check prices and availability of goods. › Compare with other quotations. › File the original for reference.	Before sending out a quotation: › Check the details against the letter of enquiry. › Check all prices and terms of sale. › File a copy for reference.

Selling goods on credit

Many suppliers sell goods to their business customers on credit. This means that the goods are delivered to the buyer, but no payment is made at that time. The buyer is usually given up to 30 days to pay for the goods. This allows the buyer time to sell the goods before they have to pay for them.

The risk for the supplier is that the buyer will take the goods and not be able to pay for them later. If the goods have been sold but the buyer goes out of business, the supplier may not be able to recover either the goods or the money owed to them. This is called a bad debt and it will not be repaid.

KEY TERM

A **bad debt** is a debt that cannot be recovered.

Because of the risk of bad debts, businesses should carry out credit checks on all new customers. A credit check will show if the customer has other unpaid debts or has had previous financial problems. It would be unwise to sell goods on credit to a customer who is not creditworthy.

See Chapter 8 for credit rating or creditworthiness

New customers could also be asked to provide a bank reference or a trade reference. A **trade reference** comes from another supplier that they have previously bought goods on credit from. It should support their application for credit by confirming that they have reliably paid their bills in the past. A **bank reference** is a letter from a bank confirming that the business is creditworthy.

Organisations should always try to collect money owed to them as quickly as possible by sending out invoices (bills) and reminders promptly to customers. Suppliers may also offer cash discounts to those who pay quickly and charge interest on overdue amounts. This is all part of having an effective credit control policy aimed at reducing cash flow problems and the risk of bad debts.

See Chapter 23 for cash flow forecast

25.8 Estimates

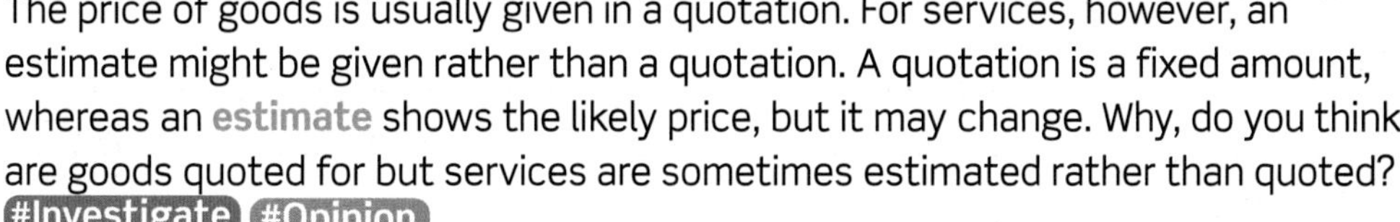

The price of goods is usually given in a quotation. For services, however, an estimate might be given rather than a quotation. A quotation is a fixed amount, whereas an **estimate** shows the likely price, but it may change. Why, do you think, are goods quoted for but services are sometimes estimated rather than quoted? #Investigate #Opinion

3 Order

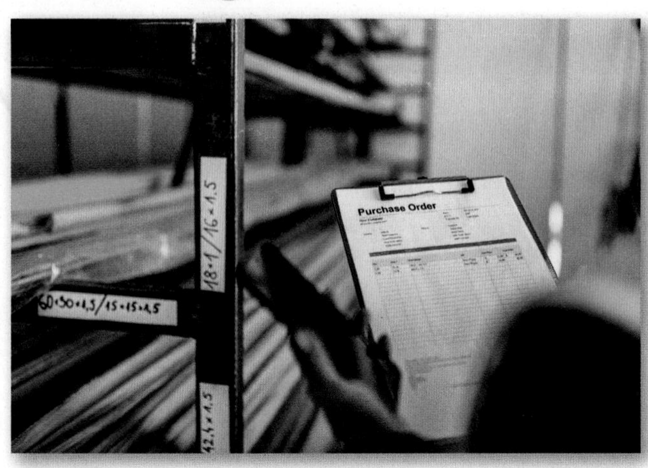

Once the buyer has decided which business offers the best prices and terms, they will place an order for the goods. They may order all the items on the quotation or just some of them.

An order is a written document sent by a buyer to a seller requesting the supply of a quantity of goods listed. The order might be made by telephone, email, on an order form or by letter. A record of the order should be kept.

An order might look similar to the one shown in Figure 25.3.

Order **Order No. 554**

O'Brien Electrical Ltd
12 Main Street
Trim
Co. Meath
Tel: (046) 123 4566/Fax: (046) 987 6544
Email: office@obrienelectrical.ie
www.obrienelectrical.ie

10/11/2022

To: Downtown Wholesalers Ltd
Water Street
Clonakilty
Co. Cork

Please supply the following goods as per your Quotation No. 76.

Quantity	Description	Model no.	Unit price €
10	Windspool dishwashers	DW500	200.00
15	Windspool washing machines	WM350	150.00
50	Meteor electric blankets	EB776	50.00

Signed: James O'Brien

James O'Brien, Purchasing Manager

Figure 25.3 Example of an order

Dealing with the order

Seller (incoming)	Buyer (outgoing)
On receipt of an order: › Deal with the order quickly to avoid losing business. › Check that all goods are in stock. › Check details of prices and terms against the quotation. › File the original for reference.	Before sending out an order: › Check quantities and product details. › Check the quotation to ensure the seller has the ordered goods in stock. › File a copy for reference.

Effective purchasing

Effective purchasing is about buying the right quantity of the right goods at the right time and at the right price. The goods should also be of the right quality.

Stock control

An efficient business must engage in **stock control**. It will try to ensure the ideal stock level at any given time. This simply means not having too much or too little stock.

When deciding on the right level of stock to keep, a business should consider the following factors:

- **Storage:** Does the business have enough space to hold the required level of stock?
- **Costs:** Carrying greater levels of stock will mean that insurance costs will increase.
- **Level of customer demand:** A business may have to stock up on extra products, such as before Christmas.
- **Lead time:** How long does it take for an order to be delivered from the supplier? The longer the delivery time, the more stock a business will have to hold.
- **Type of stock:** Some goods, such as vegetables and milk, are perishable and will go off quickly. Businesses will usually only carry a limited stock of perishable goods. The major cost associated with having too little stock (known as a stockout) is potential loss of sales.

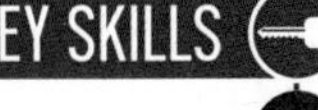

25.9 Stock control

(a) Why, do you think, is one person (usually the purchasing manager) employed to co-ordinate all the ordering for the business? #Think

(b) What are the potential costs involved for a business that orders too much stock? #Investigate

4 Delivery note

Once the sale has been agreed, the seller will start to complete the order and prepare a delivery note and invoice.

KEY TERM

The **delivery note** is a document sent by the seller to the buyer that lists the items being delivered.

When the goods are delivered to the buyer's address, the person making the delivery will ask the buyer to sign the delivery note. This is proof that the goods were delivered. Figure 25.4 shows an example of a delivery note.

Delivery Note **No. 0124**

Downtown Wholesalers Ltd

Water Street
Clonakilty
Co. Cork
Tel: (091) 654 3276/Fax: (091) 789 6543
Email: office@downtownwholesalers.ie
www.downtownwholesalers.ie

15/11/2022

To. O'Brien Electrical Ltd
12 Main Street
Trim
Co. Meath

Re: Order No. 554

Quantity	Description	Model no.	Unit price €
10	Windspool dishwashers	DW500	200.00
15	Windspool washing machines	WM350	150.00
50	Meteor electric blankets	EB776	50.00

Comment: Goods received and counted but individual items not checked

Signed: James O'Brien

James O'Brien, Purchasing Manager

Figure 25.4 An example of a delivery note

In the example on the previous page, James O'Brien took delivery of the goods from Downtown Wholesalers, but because of the size of the order and the fact that each item was packed individually, he did not examine each item. He noted this before signing the delivery note.

Dealing with the delivery note

Buyer (incoming)	Seller (outgoing)
On receipt of a delivery note: › Compare the delivery note with the order to ensure the correct goods were delivered. › Check that the quantities actually delivered match the delivery note. › Check that the goods are in perfect condition. › Sign the delivery note and return it to the delivery driver. › File the copy for reference.	Before sending out a delivery note: › Check that the goods being delivered match the order. › Check that all the goods are in perfect condition. › Check the delivery address. › File the original for reference.

25.10 Review and recall

MIT BL

(a) Explain why a delivery note is important to (i) the seller and (ii) the buyer of the goods. #Investigate

(b) Do you think the buyer should check the goods before they sign the delivery note? Explain the reason for your answer. #Opinion #WhatDoYouThink #Reflect

5 Invoice

An **invoice** is a document that gives details of the quantity and price of the goods being sent. It also includes terms of sale and details about carriage.

An invoice will be sent either with a delivery or by post.

The invoice acts as the final bill for the goods delivered. It must contain the following information:

- The name and address of the supplier
- The name and address of the buyer
- A unique invoice reference
- The date the invoice was issued
- A complete list of the products or services provided
- The net amount owed for the goods (not including VAT)
- The total amount of the invoice (including VAT)
- The payment terms of the invoice, including details of cash discounts.

Figure 25.5 shows an example of an invoice.

Invoice **No. 10524**

Downtown Wholesalers Ltd

Water Street
Clonakilty
Co. Cork
Tel: (091) 654 3276/Fax: (091) 789 6543
Email: office@downtownwholesalers.ie
www.downtownwholesalers.ie
VAT registration no. IE494037J

Date: 15/11/2022

To: O'Brien Electrical Ltd
12 Main Street
Trim
Co. Meath

Your order number: 554

Quantity	Description	Model no.	Unit price (€)	Total (€)
10	Windspool dishwashers	DW500	200.00	2,000.00
15	Windspool washing machines	WM350	150.00	2,250.00
50	Meteor electric blankets	EB776	50.00	2,500.00
	Total (excluding VAT)			6,750.00
	Discount at 10%			675.00
	Subtotal (excluding VAT)			6,075.00
	VAT at 20%			1,215.00
	Total (including VAT)			7,290.00

E&OE

Payment terms: Full payment required by cheque or credit transfer within 30 days.

Cash discount: 5% for full payment within 7 days.

Downtown Wholesalers Ltd, registered no. 494037J, registered at Water Street, Clonakilty, Co. Cork

Figure 25.5 An example of an invoice

Some businesses send a copy of the invoice via email instead of printing and posting it. Based on this invoice, O'Brien Electrical owes €7,290 to Downtown Wholesalers for the goods listed on the invoice. They must pay within 30 days, but if they pay within a week they can reduce the amount owed by 5% (€364.50).

ENTERPRISE

Dealing with the invoice

Buyer (incoming)	Seller (outgoing)
On receiving an invoice: › Check the invoice against the delivery note. › Check that the prices are the same as on the quotation. › Check all calculations. › Record details in the purchases accounts (an account is used to keep a record of all business transactions). › File the original for reference.	Before sending out an invoice: › Match the goods listed against the order. › Check that the prices match the quotation. › Check the discounts and terms of sale. › Check the customer's name and address. › Check all calculations. › Record details in the sales accounts. › File a copy for reference.

See Chapter 5 for analysed cash book

See Chapter 26 for ledger accounts

Note: The information contained on the invoice is used to write up the accounts of the seller. The invoice acts as a source document for the financial records.

KEY SKILLS

25.11 Invoice

MIT

What are the advantages to the seller of sending an invoice by email?
#Investigate

6 Credit note

KEY TERM

A **credit note** is a document sent by the seller to the buyer to explain a reduction in the amount owed. It is issued when goods that have been purchased on credit are returned to the seller and it would not be appropriate to provide a cash refund.

The credit note is sent if any of the following situations occur:

- The customer was overcharged
- The wrong goods were delivered
- Faulty or damaged goods were returned.

The day after the goods were delivered, James O'Brien unpacked and checked each item. He discovered that three of the dishwashers were damaged and returned them to Downtown Wholesalers. The supplier issued a credit note to O'Brien Electrical for the damaged goods.

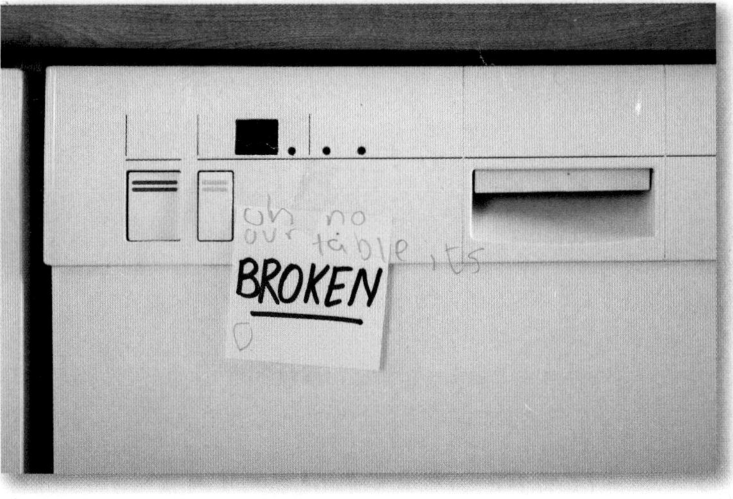

Figure 25.6 shows a credit note.

Credit Note **No. 886**

Downtown Wholesalers Ltd

Water Street
Clonakilty
Co. Cork
Tel: (091) 654 3276/Fax: (091) 789 6543
Email: office@downtownwholesalers.ie
www.downtownwholesalers.ie
VAT registration no. IE494037J

19/11/2022

To: O'Brien Electrical Ltd
12 Main Street
Trim
Co. Meath

Ref. Invoice number 10524

Quantity	Description	Model no.	Unit price (€)	Total (€)
3	Windspool dishwashers (damaged)	DW500	200.00	600.00
	Total (excluding VAT)			600.00
	Trade discount 10%			60.00
	Subtotal			540.00
	VAT 20%			108.00
E&OE	Total (including VAT)			648.00

Downtown Wholesalers Ltd, registered no. 494037J, registered at Water Street, Clonakilty, Co. Cork

Figure 25.6 An example of a credit note

The credit note shows that O'Brien Electrical now owes €648 less to Downtown Wholesalers Ltd.

Dealing with the credit note

Buyer (incoming)	Seller (outgoing)
On receiving a credit note: › Check that the details match the returned goods. › Check all calculations. › Record the reduction in the amount owed to creditors in the accounts. › File the original for reference.	Before sending out a credit note: › Check that the details match the returned goods. › Check all calculations. › Record the reduction in the amount owed by the debtor in the accounts. › File a copy for reference.

KEY SKILLS

25.12 Review and recall

MIT BL

'Credit note' is a business term that can have slightly different meanings depending on the situation or context it is used in. How does the definition of 'credit note' used in this chapter differ from the one used in Chapter 12: Protecting the Consumer? Comment on any similarities you notice between the two uses of the term. #Compare #Reflect

KEY SKILLS

25.13 Why no cash refund?

MIT

Why did Downtown Wholesalers issue a credit note rather than a cash refund to O'Brien Electrical when the faulty goods were returned? #Think #Explain

7 Debit note

A debit note is issued if either of the following situations occur:

- The buyer has been undercharged
- The buyer received goods but was not charged for them on the invoice.

KEY TERM

A **debit note** is sent by the seller to the buyer. It will increase the amount owed. It is used when there has been an undercharge on an account.

In terms of layout a debit note looks almost identical to a credit note, but it will have the effect of increasing the amount owed by the buyer rather than reducing it.

In our example, all goods ordered by O'Brien Electrical Ltd were invoiced correctly, so there was no need for Downtown Wholesalers to issue a debit note.

Dealing with the debit note

Buyer (incoming)	Seller (outgoing)
On receiving a debit note: › Check all calculations. › Record the increase in the amount owed to creditors in the accounts. › File the original for reference.	Before sending a debit note: › Check all calculations. › Record the increase in the amount owed by debtors in the accounts. › File a copy for reference.

On 22 November O'Brien Electrical paid €5,000 to Downtown Wholesalers in part payment for the goods invoiced on 15 November. They do not qualify for an early payment discount as they did not pay for the goods in full. The money was paid directly into the supplier's account by credit transfer.

8 Statement of account

The method used in the statement of account is known as the **continuous balancing method**. This is the same approach as is used on a bank statement.

See Chapter 6 for bank statements

The statement works on the following rules/assumptions:

- The balance shown at the start of the month/period is the amount owed by the buyer to the seller at that date.
- Any entry in the debit column will increase the amount owed and is added to the previous balance in order to get the new balance.
- Any entry in the credit column will reduce the amount owed and is subtracted from the previous balance in order to get the new balance.
- The last balance shows the amount owed as on that date.

Statement of Account **No. 229**

Downtown Wholesalers Ltd

Water Street
Clonakilty
Co. Cork
Tel: (091) 654 3276/Fax: (091) 789 6543
Email: office@downtownwholesalers.ie
www.downtownwholesalers.ie
VAT registration no. IE494037J

30/11/2022

To: O'Brien Electrical Ltd
12 Main Street
Trim
Co. Meath

Date	Details	Debit €	Credit €	Balance €
1/11/22	Balance			3,200.00
15/11/22	Invoice No. 10524	7,290.00		10,490.00
19/11/22	Credit Note No. 886		648.00	9,842.00
22/11/22	Payment (credit transfer)		5,000.00	4,842.00

E&OE

Terms: 4% 14 days

Downtown Wholesalers Ltd, registered no. 494037J, registered at Water Street, Clonakilty, Co. Cork

Figure 25.7 An example of a statement of account

An example of a statement of account is shown above in Figure 25.7. It shows that on 1 November O'Brien Electrical owed €3,200 to Downtown Wholesalers. This is based on previous business and orders that are yet to be paid for.

The invoice also illustrates the purchase of more goods on credit during November, the return of damaged goods and a part-payment for one order. Finally, the statement of account shows the balance outstanding at the end of the month. This is the closing balance and represents the amount of money owed by O'Brien Electrical on 30 November.

KEY TERM

A **statement of account** is sent by the seller to the buyer. It is a summary of all the transactions between the two firms over a particular period of time. It shows the full amount owed and will act as a demand for whatever payment is still owed.

The phrase '4% 14 days' means that the buyer will get a 4% discount if they pay in full within 14 days of the statement being issued. *Note:* If a debit note had been issued during this month, it would appear in the debit column of the statement and would increase the balance owed.

Dealing with the statement of account

Buyer (incoming)	Seller (outgoing)
On receiving a statement: › Check the opening balance. › Check the statement against the invoices, credit notes and/or debit notes received. › Check that all payments have been recorded. › Check all calculations and the closing balance. › Pay the amount due by the due date. › File the original for reference.	Before sending out a statement: › Check the opening balance. › Check invoice amounts. › Check debit and credit note amounts. › Check that payments have been recorded. › Check all calculations and the closing balance. › File a copy for reference.

KEY SKILLS BN MIT

25.14 Statement of account

If O'Brien Electrical Ltd pays the outstanding amount from their November statement on 12 December, will they be entitled to the cash discount? Explain your answer. #WhatDoYouThink #ProblemSolving

9 Payment

When goods are sold for cash, payment may be made when the order is made (CWO) or when the goods are delivered (COD). The payment may be made in cash or, more likely, through other forms of payment, such as a cheque or bank credit transfer. If immediate CWO or COD is not required, payment should be made within the credit terms given, such as 30 days.

10 Receipt

Receipts should be filed away safely, as they may be required as proof of payment in the future.

KEY TERM

A **receipt** is a written document stating that goods have been paid for. It is signed by the seller and given to the buyer.

An example of a receipt is shown in Figure 25.8. It is proof of the €5,000 payment made by O'Brien Electrical on 22 November.

Receipt **No. 375**

Downtown Wholesalers Ltd

Water Street
Clonakilty
Co. Cork
Tel: (091) 654 3276/Fax: (091) 789 6543
Email: office@downtownwholesalers.ie
www.downtownwholesalers.ie
VAT registration no. IE494037J

Date: 22/11/2022

Received from: O'Brien Electrical Ltd

The sum of: Five thousand euro (€5,000) in part payment of invoice number 10524.

With thanks:

Steven Monahan

Accounts Manager

Figure 25.8 An example of a receipt

Dealing with the receipt

Buyer (incoming)	Seller (outgoing)
On receiving a receipt: › Check that the figure matches the payment. › Record the payment in the creditors account. › File the original for reference.	Before sending out a receipt: › Check that the figure matches the payment. › Record the payment in the debtors account. › File a copy for reference.

KEY SKILLS

25.15 Business documents

(a) In pairs, create an infographic or poster showing the documents that might be created as part of the buying/selling process between two businesses. Use Table 25.1 as a guide. #ThinkPairShare #GroupWork #Collaborate

(b) What documents might be used if a service is being purchased rather than goods, such as an accountant hired to do work for a business? Make a list. #List

EXAM QUESTION

Junior Cycle 2019

Question 5

Using the information given on the invoice extract below, copy these figures into your copy and complete the blank boxes.

	€
Total (excluding VAT)	25,000
Trade discount (12%)	
Subtotal	
VAT (23%)	
Total (including VAT)	

 **Weblinks**

 **PowerPoint Summary**

CHAPTER 26

DOUBLE ENTRY BOOKKEEPING

LEARNING OUTCOMES IN FOCUS

2.12 Prepare a cash account to monitor income received and payments made by an organisation, evaluate its financial position and recommend a course of action; post figures to relevant ledgers and extract a trial balance

Links to 1.2, 1.13, 2.9, 2.10, 2.11, 2.13, 3.2

LEARNING INTENTIONS FOR THIS CHAPTER

When you have completed this chapter you will be able to:

- Explain the term 'double entry bookkeeping'
- Prepare an analysed cash book, post to the ledger and extract a trial balance
- Account for VAT on sales and purchases
- Appreciate the value of bookkeeping in recording and evaluating an organisation's financial performance.

CHAPTER 26 KEY TERMS

account
analysed cash book (ACB)
double entry bookkeeping
folio
general ledger (GL)
ledger
opening balance
purchases
sales
share capital
trial balance

CHAPTER 26 KEY SKILLS

MIT Managing Information and Thinking

Step-by-step account

Excel template

Note: You may or may not be using Business Studies Record Books in your class. For those who are, we have included references to them throughout Chapters 26 to 30. If you are not using them, you can ignore all references to Record Books and continue using whatever template, spreadsheet or copybook your teacher has instructed you to use.

Why keep accounts?

A business must keep an accurate and up-to-date record of all its financial transactions. Together, they support the day-to-day operations of the business and help to tell its financial story.

Business accounts can help with the following areas of business operation:

- **Identifying and recording sources and pattern of income:** Business documents and analysed cash book are used for these purposes.
- **Identifying and recording expenditure patterns and amounts:** Business documents and analysed cash book are used for these purposes.
- **Keeping track of cash flow:** Cash flow forecasts help to plan income and expenditure and also identify future surpluses and deficits.
- **Calculating profitability:** Final accounts help to calculate the level of profitability at the end of each year.
- **Calculating tax returns:** Final accounts indicate profit that tax must be paid on and illustrate expenses, which are tax deductible. Ledger accounts are also used to record VAT.
- **Valuation of the business:** Final accounts illustrate the financial make-up of the business and include information on assets, liabilities and capital.

See Chapters 5, 25 and 27 for analysed cash book, business documents and income statement

See Chapter 23 for cash flow forecast

See Chapters 27 and 28 for income statement (trading and P&L account)

See Chapter 25 for business documents

See Chapter 29 for the statement of financial position (balance sheet)

In this chapter we will briefly revise the rules for recording transactions in the analysed cash book (Record Book 1). We will also look at general ledger accounts (prepared in Record Book 3) before illustrating how both record books combine to create a system of double entry bookkeeping. The abbreviation A/C is used for account.

The information contained in the analysed cash book and ledgers comes from the business documents. For example, invoices received from suppliers contain information used to write up the purchases and VAT amounts in the general ledger.

DID YOU KNOW...

International Accountants' Day is on 10 November every year. That date was chosen because on 10 November 1494, Italian mathematician Luca Bartolomeo de Pacioli published *Summa de Arithmetica, Geometria, Proportioni et Proportionalita (Everything About Arithmetic, Geometry and Proportion)*, which included the first ever work on double entry bookkeeping. Although double entry bookkeeping had already been used for centuries, Luca Pacioli became known as the father of modern accounting and he proposed the use of the trial balance. He also said that a person should not go to sleep at night until the debits equalled the credits!

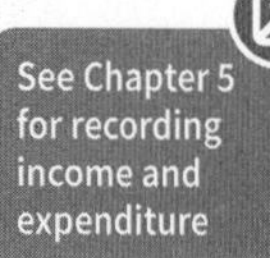

See Chapter 5 for recording income and expenditure

The analysed cash book

Cash transactions are a specific type of financial transaction where money is used to settle a transaction on the same date that it takes place. In bookkeeping, we use an **analysed cash book (ACB)** to record receipts of money coming into the business and payments of money going out of a business. The rule that is used when entering transactions in the analysed cash book is as follows:

Cash book rule

Debit (**Dr**) money received by the business	**Credit** (**Cr**) money paid out by the business

Dr **Analysed cash book** Cr

Dr: MONEY IN	Cr: MONEY OUT

Opening cash and bank balances

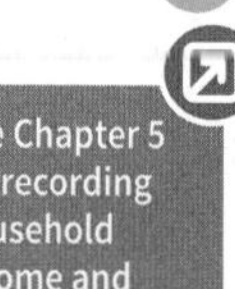

See Chapter 5 for recording household income and expenditure

The **opening balance** refers to the cash or bank balance at the beginning of an accounting period. In some months, a business may have cash left over from a previous month. This is shown as a Balance b/d on the debit side of the analysed cash book.

Example 1: Opening balance

This is a Bank account that has an opening balance of €2,500 on 1 January 2022.

Dr **Bank A/C** Cr

Date	Details	F	Total	Date	Details	F	Total
1 Jan 2022	Balance b/d		€2,500				

If the business has overdrawn its account and has a bank overdraft, it owes money to the bank. This is recorded as a Balance b/d on the credit side of the analysed cash book.

Note regarding Folio (F): This is a reference column. We will explain and use it later in this chapter as part of our double entry approach to bookkeeping.

Example 2: Opening balance for bank overdraft

Here is a Bank A/C that has an opening bank overdraft of €3,000 on 1 January 2022. Note that the opening balance appears on the credit side.

Dr **Bank A/C** Cr

Date	Details	F	Total	Date	Details	F	Total
				1 Jan 2022	Balance b/d		€3,000

Ledgers

Ledgers are the books that all individual **accounts** are recorded in.

These accounts are used to bring together:

- All transactions involving a particular business or person **OR**
- All transactions involving a particular type of income or expense.

Therefore, we could have accounts called Michael O'Neill A/C, Electricity A/C, Wages A/C, etc.

Having a separate account for each makes it much easier to keep track of all the money and transactions associated with each person, business, expense or source of income. We simply have to look at that account in the ledger to see a record of all transactions, receipts and payments.

We will be using the **general ledger (GL)**. This is used to record all the expenses that are involved in running a business, such as rent and electricity. As part of a double entry system of bookkeeping, the information in the analysed cash book must also be recorded in the ledgers. In bookkeeping this is referred to as 'posting to the ledgers'.

Double entry bookkeeping

As its name suggests, **double entry bookkeeping** requires that every transaction be entered twice in the accounts. This is because there is both a 'giving' element and a 'receiving' element involved – one account gives something, while another account receives something.

T-account

Debit the receiver	Credit the giver

When dealing with cash transactions, this will require:

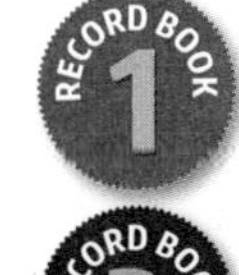

- One entry in the analysed cash book (Record Book 1)
- One corresponding entry in the appropriate general ledger account (Record Book 3).

Example 3: Double entry for expenses

O'Connor Ltd paid a €400 bill for light and heat by direct debit from its bank account on 6 April 2022.

The €400 payment from the bank account is recorded on the credit side of the analysed cash book (the Bank account is the 'giver').

The transaction is also entered on the debit side of the Light & Heat A/C in the general ledger (the Light & Heat account is the receiver).

The entry in the Bank A/C shows:

- The date of the transaction (6 April 2022).
- Where the money went/the name of the other account involved (Light & Heat).
- A reference or **folio** to indicate where the corresponding double entry is (GL). In this example, it is in the Light & Heat account in the general ledger (GL). Having this folio will make it easier to locate the other entry and check the information later on.
- The amount of the transaction (€400).

There is a corresponding (matching) entry in the Light & Heat A/C. The two accounts are shown below.

Dr				Bank A/C (ACB)			Cr
Date	**Details**	**F**	**Total**	**Date**	**Details**	**F**	**Total**
				6 April 2022	Light & Heat	GL	€400

Dr				Light & Heat A/C (in GL)			Cr
Date	**Details**	**F**	**Total**	**Date**	**Details**	**F**	**Total**
6 April 2022	Bank	ACB	€400				

The entry in the Light & Heat account shows:

- The date of the transaction (6 April 2022)
- Where the money came from/the name of the other account involved (Bank A/C)
- A reference or folio to indicate where the corresponding double entry is (ACB)
- The amount of the transaction (€400).

As we post from the analysed cash book to the general ledger, we follow the rule:

Double entry rule

A **debit entry in the ACB** will be posted to the **credit** side in the ledger.

A **credit entry in the ACB** will be posted to the **debit** side in the ledger.

This is because for every debit, there is a corresponding credit.

Note: When working with these types of transaction, deal with the analysed cash book entry first, remembering to debit money in and to credit money out. Once you have correctly worked out this entry, put the general ledger entry on the opposite side.

If we stick to this double entry rule, the total value of debit entries in the accounts will match the total value of credit entries. Later on, we will use a trial balance to test if this is the case.

Accounting for share capital

KEY TERM

Share capital is the money invested into a business by its owners. This money is often invested at the time the business is being set up, but extra share capital can be invested at a later date.

Example 4: Double entry for investment of share capital

On 1 April 2022, Michael O'Connor started a business and invested €40,000 of his own money into the business bank account. The double entry needed to record this transaction is as follows.

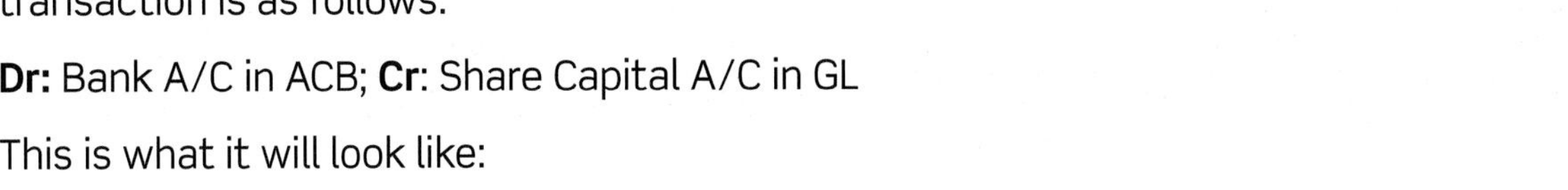

Dr: Bank A/C in ACB; **Cr**: Share Capital A/C in GL

This is what it will look like:

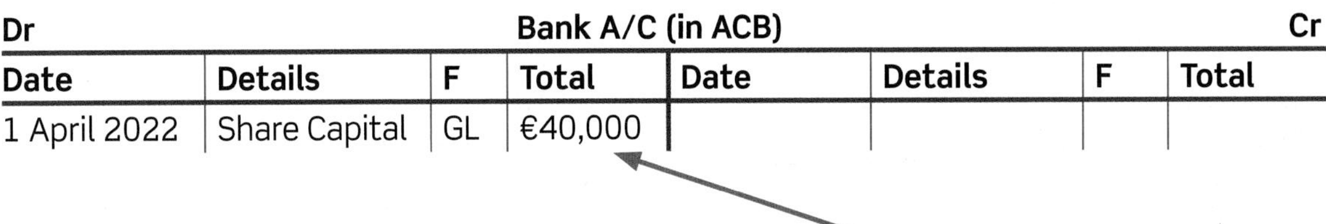

Dr **Bank A/C (in ACB)** **Cr**

Date	Details	F	Total	Date	Details	F	Total
1 April 2022	Share Capital	GL	€40,000				

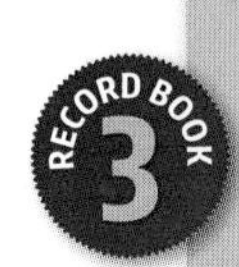

Dr **Share Capital A/C (in GL)** **Cr**

Date	Details	F	Total	Date	Details	F	Total
				1 April 2022	Bank	ACB	€40,000

Accounting for sales, purchases and VAT

When dealing with business accounts, the terms 'sales' and 'purchases' have specific meanings and are slightly different from our everyday use of the words, which simply mean to sell or buy something.

In accounting terms, **sales** refers specifically to money received when a business sells goods that are part of its normal day-to-day business activity. For example, any revenue a greengrocer earns from selling fruit and vegetables would be classified as sales and entered in the Sales A/C in the general ledger. However, money generated from the sale of an old delivery van would not be regarded as sales revenue since the greengrocer is not in the business of selling vehicles.

Similarly, the term **purchases** refers specifically to goods that a business buys and intends to resell as part of its normal day-to-day business activity. For example, if a greengrocer buys a box of apples, this would be entered into the Purchases A/C in the general ledger.

KEY SKILLS

26.1 Where to park the van?

If the greengrocer buys a replacement delivery van, would this be entered in the Purchases A/C? Explain your answer. #Opinion #Investigate

VAT

The VAT for all sales and purchases will be recorded in a single VAT account by each business. The VAT element of both sales and purchases transactions should not be included as part of sales or purchases figures in the respective ledger accounts.

Example 5: Double entry for cash purchases with VAT

On 2 June 2022, O'Connor Ltd bought goods for resale and paid by cheque. The cost of the goods was €300 plus €60 VAT. The entries needed to record this transaction are as follows:

1. Dr: €300 to the Purchases A/C in the GL
2. Dr: €60 to the VAT A/C in the GL
3. Cr: €360 to the Bank A/C in the ACB

The total of the two debit entries (purchases + VAT) is €360, which is equal to the amount credited to the Bank A/C. This is in keeping with the rule that **every debit entry must be matched by an equal and corresponding credit entry**.

This is what it will look like:

Analysed cash book (Bank account and credit side only)

Date	Details	Folio	Bank	Purchases	VAT
2 June 2022	Purchases	GL	€360	€300	€60

Purchases A/C (in GL)

Dr							Cr
Date	**Details**	**F**	**Total**	**Date**	**Details**	**F**	**Total**
2 June 2022	Bank	ACB	€300				

VAT A/C (in GL)

Dr							Cr
Date	**Details**	**F**	**Total**	**Date**	**Details**	**F**	**Total**
2 June 2022	Bank	ACB	€60				

Example 6: Double entry for cash sales with VAT

On 5 June 2022, O'Connor Ltd sold goods for cash and the money was lodged to the company's bank account. The goods were sold for €500 plus €105 VAT. The entries needed to record this transaction are as follows:

1. Dr: €605 to the Bank A/C in the analysed cash book (see explanation below)
2. Cr: €500 to the Sales A/C in the GL
3. Cr: €105 to the VAT A/C in the GL

Total debits equals total credits

The total of the two credit entries (sales + VAT) is €605, which is equal to the amount debited to the Bank A/C. This is in keeping with the rule that **every debit entry must be matched by an equal and corresponding credit entry**.

This is what it will look like:

Analysed cash book (Bank account and debit side only)

Date	Details	Folio	Bank	Purchases	VAT
5 June 2022	Sales	GL	€605	€500	€105

Sales A/C (in GL)

Dr							Cr
Date	**Details**	**Folio**	**Total**	**Date**	**Details**	**Folio**	**Total**
				5 June 2022	Bank	ACB	€500

VAT A/C (in GL)

Dr							Cr
Date	**Details**	**Folio**	**Total**	**Date**	**Details**	**Folio**	**Total**
				5 June 2022	Bank	ACB	€105

Accounts commonly found in the general ledger include:

- Sales A/C
- Purchases A/C
- VAT A/C
- Wages A/C
- Light and Heat A/C
- Rent A/C
- Advertising A/C
- Share Capital A/C: Records investment into the business by owners/shareholders
- Carriage In A/C: Records the cost of having purchases delivered to the business
- Carriage Out A/C: Records the cost of delivering goods sold to customers
- Vehicles A/C: Records the purchase or sale of vehicles by the business
- Machinery A/C: Records the purchase or sale of machinery by the business
- Bad Debts A/C: Records the cost of debts that the business cannot recover (this usually happens when goods are sold to customers on credit and they do not pay the money owed).

The trial balance

A business will have many accounts to prepare and mistakes can sometimes be made. Therefore, it is important to check that all accounts have been prepared correctly. In bookkeeping, we use the trial balance to carry out this check.

A **trial balance** is simply a list of account balances. In the trial balance (Record Book 2), we list all the balances b/d from the ledger accounts and the cash/bank balance from the analysed cash book. In doing this, we use the following rule:

A **debit balance in the ledger or ACB** will appear as a **debit in the trial balance**.

A **credit balance in the ledger or ACB** will appear as a **credit in the trial balance**. This is because the double entry has already occurred and the balances from each account are simply being listed.

If the rules for double entry bookkeeping have been followed correctly, the trial balance should balance. This means that the total of the debit balances matches the total of the credit balances.

If the trial balance totals do not match, a mistake has been made somewhere in the accounts and will have to be corrected. Once the trial balance has been completed correctly, the information can be used to prepare the company's final accounts.

Example 7: Analysed cash book, ledger and trial balance

Byrne Ltd had the following bank transactions. You are required to enter these in the analysed cash book, post to the (general) ledger and extract a trial balance as on 31/1/22. Use the following analysis columns in the analysed cash book:

Dr: Sales, VAT, Capital

Cr: Purchases, VAT, Wages, Insurance

Bank transactions:

3 January 2022	Cash sales lodged, receipt no. 1, €20,000 plus VAT €4,600
7 January 2022	Cash purchases, cheque no. 1, €7,500 plus VAT €500
8 January 2022	Paid wages, cheque no. 2, €2,000
12 January 2022	Shareholders invested €50,000 and this was lodged
18 January 2022	Paid insurance, cheque no. 3, €3,500

Suggested solution:

Analysed cash book of Byrne Ltd

(Dr) **(Cr)**

Date	Details	Rcpt	F	Bank	Sales	VAT	Capital	Date	Details	Chq	F	Bank	Purchases	VAT	Wages	Insurance
2022				€	€	€	€	2022				€	€	€	€	€
03/01	Sales	1	GL	24,600	20,000	4,600		07/01	Purchases	1	GL	8,000	7,500	500		
12/01	Capital		GL	50,000			50,000	08/01	Wages	2	GL	2,000			2,000	
								18/01	Insurance	3	GL	3,500				3,500
								31/01	Balance c/d			61,100				
				74,600	20,000	4,600	50,000					74,600	7,500	500	2,000	3,500
01/02	Balance b/d			61,100												

General ledger

Dr **Sales A/C** Cr

Date	Details	F	Total	Date	Details	F	Total
2022			€	2022			€
				03/01	Bank	ACB	20,000

Dr **VAT A/C** Cr

Date	Details	F	Total	Date	Details	F	Total
2022			€	2022			€
07/01	Cash purchases	ACB	500	03/01	Cash sales	ACB	4,600
07/01	Balance c/d		4,100				
			4,600				4,600
				08/01	Balance b/d		4,100

Dr **Purchases A/C** Cr

Date	Details	F	Total	Date	Details	F	Total
2022			€	2022			€
07/01	Bank	ACB	7,500				

Dr **Wages A/C** Cr

Date	Details	F	Total	Date	Details	F	Total
2022			€	2022			€
08/01	Bank	ACB	2,000				

Dr **Capital A/C** Cr

Date	Details	F	Total	Date	Details	F	Total
2022			€	2022			€
				12/01	Bank	ACB	50,000

Dr **Insurance A/C** Cr

Date	Details	F	Total	Date	Details	F	Total
2022			€	2022			€
18/01	Bank	ACB	3,500				

Trial balance of Byrne Ltd as on 31 January 2022

Details	F	Dr	Cr
		€	€
Capital	GL		50,000
Sales	GL		20,000
Purchases	GL	7,500	
Wages	GL	2,000	
Insurance	GL	3,500	
VAT	GL		4,100
Bank	ACB	61,100	
		74,100	74,100

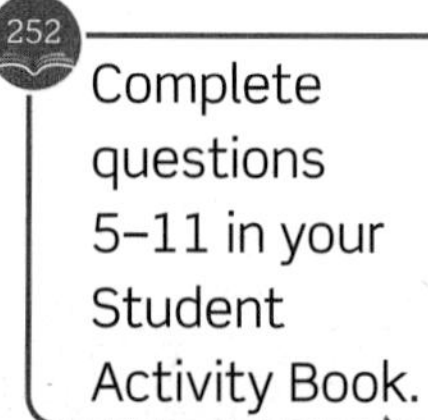

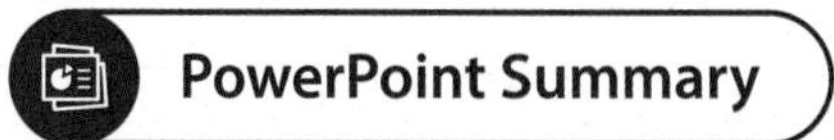

INCOME STATEMENTS 1: THE TRADING ACCOUNT

LEARNING OUTCOMES IN FOCUS

2.13 Prepare final accounts to assess the financial performance of an organisation at the end of a trading period, analyse and evaluate its financial position and recommend a course of action

Links to 1.13, 2.9, 2.10, 2.11, 2.12, 3.2

LEARNING INTENTIONS FOR THIS CHAPTER

When you have completed this chapter you will be able to:

- Explain the term 'final accounts'
- Outline the reasons why businesses prepare final accounts
- Outline the purpose of the income statement (trading account)
- List and explain the key elements of an income statement
- Prepare an income statement (trading account) in order to calculate gross profit.

CHAPTER 27 KEY TERMS

carriage inwards
closing stock
cost of goods sold
cost of sales
customs duty
final accounts
gross profit
import duty
income statement
opening stock
profit and loss account
purchases
sales
trading account

CHAPTER 27 KEY SKILLS

BC Being Creative
BL Being Literate
BN Being Numerate
MIT Managing Information and Thinking

Step-by-step account

Excel template

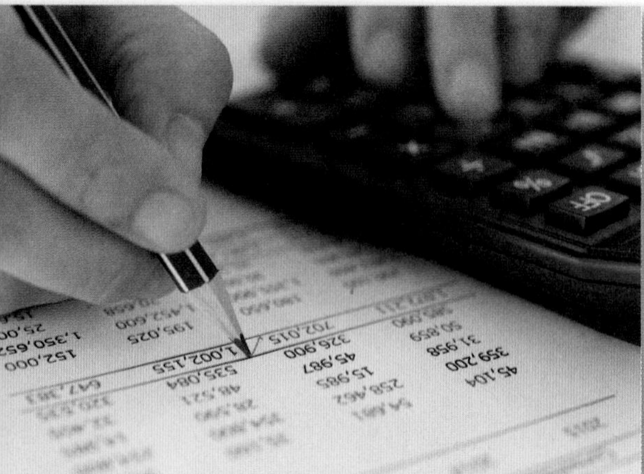

Introduction to final accounts

Every year, an organisation needs to answer two important questions:

1. How much profit (or loss) did it make this year?
2. How much is the organisation worth?

To find the answers to these questions, a company will prepare a set of accounts.

The answer to the profit or loss question can be found by preparing an income statement (trading, profit and loss account).

The question about company value can be answered by preparing a statement of financial position (balance sheet).

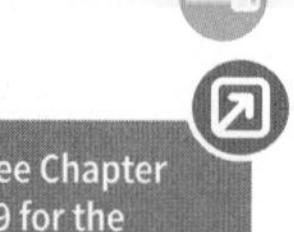

See Chapter 29 for the statement of financial position

Collectively, these are referred to as **final accounts**. Companies are required by law to prepare a set of final accounts at the end of each financial year, also known as the trading period. This is a 12-month period for which the final accounts have been prepared. It may begin on any date, as the company's year may or may not have begun on 1 January.

The income statement

See Chapter 28 for income statement (profit and loss account)

KEY TERM

An **income statement** is made up of a trading account and a profit and loss account.

The **trading account** section calculates the gross profit (or loss) that the business has made from selling its products or services.

The **profit and loss account** calculates the net profit (or loss) after deducting expenses from the gross profit figure.

If the company is profitable it will also need to show how the profit will be distributed and calculate the financial reserves that the company has at year end. This is the amount of money that belongs to the company and can be reinvested back into the business. It is a bit like savings for a household.

The trading account section of an income statement is used by a business to calculate gross profit or gross loss on its core activities. This is the **gross profit** (or loss) generated by a business as a result of making and selling its products. It does not include expenses, such as electricity or wages.

Gross profit = Sales – Cost of sales

Cost of sales may also be known as cost of goods sold.

Consider the following simple example:

- Imagine that you went to a supermarket and bought some baking ingredients. The total cost of your purchases was €40.

- You then used these ingredients to make cupcakes, which you sold to family, friends and neighbours for €90.
- Your gross profit in this situation would be €50, as this is the difference between your sales revenue and the cost of your purchases (€90 – €40 = €50 gross profit).

278 Complete question 7 in your Student Activity Book.

This simple example illustrates the concept of gross profit. However, it makes certain assumptions that may not be realistic. For example, it assumes:

- You had no ingredients to begin with (opening stock) and that since you sold all the goods you purchased, you had no goods left over at the end (closing stock).
- There were no other costs associated with purchasing, making or selling the goods.

Since all of these are real possibilities for a business, it will be necessary to consider how each one will impact on our calculation of gross profit. First, we will define the key terms that you will come across in the income statement (trading account).

KEY TERM

Sales is the value of the goods sold by the business.

Opening stock is the cost of goods held in stock at the beginning of the financial year. This may be stock of finished goods and/or raw materials.

Purchases is the cost of goods bought during the year. These goods are bought with the specific intention of reselling them.

Carriage inwards is the cost of having purchases delivered to the business.

Customs duty is a tax paid on purchases from countries outside the EU. This item may also appear as **import duty**.

Closing stock is the value of goods held in stock at the end of the financial year. This may be stock of raw materials and/or finished goods.

Cost of sales/cost of goods sold is the cost to the business of selling the goods that were actually sold during the trading period.

You will need to *learn* the items that appear in an income statement (trading account) and also the order in which they appear. You will also need to *practise* preparing trading accounts, as this is the only way to make sure you can correctly calculate gross profit or loss.

The most basic income statement (trading account) will have just four items and they will appear in the following order:

1. Sales
2. Opening stock
3. Purchases
4. Closing stock

Example 1: Basic income statement (trading account)

Prepare an income statement (trading account) for Zing Ltd for the year ended 31/12/2022 from the following information:

- Sales €450,000
- Purchases €280,000
- Opening stock €5,000
- Closing stock €11,000

Income statement (trading account) for Zing Ltd for year ended 31/12/2022

	€	€
Sales		450,000
Less cost of sales:		
Opening stock	5,000	
+ Purchases	280,000	
Cost of goods available for sale	285,000	
– Closing stock	11,000	
Cost of sales		274,000
Gross profit		**176,000**

Subtract 'Cost of sales' from 'Sales'

Points to note:

- The cost of sales takes account of the opening stock held by the business at the start of the year plus the additional goods purchased during the year.
- It is also necessary to subtract the value of the closing stock that remains unsold at the end of the year. Since these goods will not be sold until the next financial year, we need to subtract them from this year's accounts. The closing stock for this financial year will become the opening stock for next year.

279 Complete questions 8–9 in your Student Activity Book.

KEY SKILLS BN BL MIT

27.1 Practice: Income statements (trading accounts)

Prepare income statements (trading accounts) from the information supplied for the year ended 31/12/2022. (If you are using Business Studies Record Books, use Record Book 2 for each of the following questions.) #Calculate

(a)

Sales	€550,000
Purchases	€290,000
Opening stock	€15,000
Closing stock	€17,000

(b)

Sales	€930,000
Purchases	€680,000
Opening stock	€8,000
Closing stock	€12,000

(c)

Sales	€850,000
Purchases	€480,000
Opening stock	€15,000
Closing stock	€16,000

(d)

Sales	€435,000
Purchases	€265,000
Opening stock	€15,000
Closing stock	€16,000

Example 2: Income statement (trading account) with carriage inwards and customs duty

Prepare an income statement (trading account) for Zing Ltd for the year ended 31/12/2022 from the following information:

- Sales €450,000
- Purchases €280,000
- Carriage inwards €4,000
- Customs duty €2,000
- Opening stock €5,000
- Closing stock €11,000

RECORD BOOK 2

Income statement (trading account) of Zing Ltd for year ended 31/12/2022

	€	€
Sales		450,000
Less cost of sales:		
Opening stock (1/1/2022)	5,000	
+ Purchases	280,000	
+ Customs duty	2,000	
+ Carriage inwards	4,000	
Cost of goods available for sale	291,000	
– Closing stock (31/12/2022)	11,000	
Cost of sales		280,000
Gross profit		**170,000**

Subtract

Point to note:

- In this example, the cost of sales is increased due to the payment of transport (carriage in) and importation costs (customs duty). Since both of these items increase the cost of purchasing goods, they are added to purchases.

Complete questions 10–12 in your Student Activity Book.

KEY SKILLS

27.2 More practice: Income statements (trading accounts)

MIT BN

Prepare income statements (trading accounts) from the information supplied for the year ended 31/12/2022. (If you are using Business Studies Record Books, use Record Book 2 for each of the following questions.) #Calculate

(a)

Sales	€355,000
Purchases	€280,000
Carriage inwards	€14,000
Customs duty	€12,000
Opening stock	€5,000
Closing stock	€11,000

(b)

Sales	€685,000
Purchases	€483,000
Carriage inwards	€1,650
Customs duty	€8,000
Opening stock	€15,000
Closing stock	€19,700

(c)	Sales	€480,000	(f)	Sales	€502,000
	Purchases	€380,000		Purchases	€348,000
	Carriage inwards	€5,000		Carriage inwards	€5,500
	Customs duty	€8,000		Customs duty	€6,370
	Opening stock	€4,000		Opening stock	€9,570
	Closing stock	€10,000		Closing stock	€13,920
(d)	Sales	€630,000	(g)	Sales	€700,000
	Purchases	€570,000		Purchases	€474,000
	Carriage inwards	€26,200		Carriage inwards	€8,500
	Customs duty	€18,800		Customs duty	€7,800
	Opening stock	€5,000		Opening stock	€15,000
	Closing stock	€16,000		Closing stock	€19,000
(e)	Sales	€922,000	(h)	Sales	€644,000
	Purchases	€670,000		Purchases	€304,000
	Carriage inwards	€6,500		Carriage inwards	€16,500
	Customs duty	€8,900		Customs duty	€12,400
	Opening stock	€11,000		Opening stock	€19,000
	Closing stock	€14,000		Closing stock	€13,200

Remember!

If you are having trouble remembering the contents of the trading account (section of the income statement) and the order in which they appear, remember that 'some old people can drive cars in space!'

Sales	Some
Opening stock	Old
Purchases	People
Customs **D**uty	Can Drive
Carriage **I**n	Cars In
Closing **S**tock	Space!

KEY SKILLS

BC BL

27.3 Make it your own

Think up your own saying to remember the contents and order in which they appear in the trading account section of the income statement. #CreativeThinking

Weblinks

PowerPoint Summary

INCOME STATEMENTS 2: THE PROFIT AND LOSS ACCOUNT

LEARNING OUTCOMES IN FOCUS

2.13 Prepare final accounts to assess the financial performance of an organisation at the end of a trading period, analyse and evaluate its financial position and recommend a course of action

Links to 1.13, 2.9, 2.10, 2.11, 2.12, 3.2

LEARNING INTENTIONS FOR THIS CHAPTER

When you have completed this chapter you will be able to:

- Differentiate between gross profit and net profit
- Illustrate the difference between current and capital expenditure
- Prepare an income statement (profit and loss account) in order to calculate net profit
- Explain how business profits may be distributed
- Prepare a profit and loss appropriation account to calculate the closing reserves for a company at the end of its financial year.

CHAPTER 28 KEY TERMS

- audit fees
- bad debt
- capital expenditure
- carriage inwards
- carriage outwards
- current expenditure
- depreciation
- expenses
- fixed assets
- overheads
- profit and loss account
- profit and loss appropriation account
- reserves (retained profit)
- revenue expenditure

CHAPTER 28 KEY SKILLS

- BL Being Literate
- BN Being Numerate
- MIT Managing Information and Thinking

Step-by-step account

Excel template

See Chapter 27 for income statements (trading accounts)

Income statement

Remember, an income statement is made up of a trading account and a profit and loss account.

Accounting for expenses

In addition to the costs of sales outlined in the previous chapter, a business will have other expenses that will reduce their overall level of profit. These expenses, also called **overheads**, include a range of additional costs involved in operating a business. Examples include rent, wages, insurance, advertising and delivery costs.

These items will be included in the company's **profit and loss account**. This section of the income statement is used to calculate the net profit (or net loss) for the financial year. It lists all administration, financial, sales and distribution expenses for the year.

All expenses are subtracted from gross profit. For example:

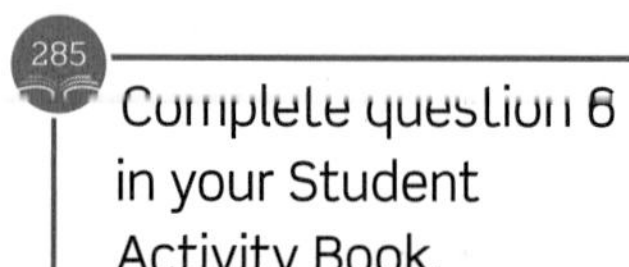
285 Complete question 6 in your Student Activity Book.

	€
Gross profit	50,000
– Expenses	20,000
Net profit	30,000

If the expenses are greater than the gross profit, this will result in a net loss for the trading period.

KEY SKILLS BN MIT

28.1 Net profit/loss

What net profit/net loss do the following result in? Show your workings. #Calculate

(a) Gross profit €125,000; Expenses €47,500

(b) Gross profit €250,000; Expenses €53,000

(c) Gross profit €75,000; Expenses €91,300

Capital expenditure vs. current expenditure

Capital expenditure is not recorded in the income statement – it is recorded in the statement of financial position (balance sheet).

See Chapter 29 for the statement of financial position (balance sheet)

KEY TERM

Capital expenditure refers to money spent on the purchase of items that will last for several years. These items are called **fixed assets**, for example buildings, vehicles, machinery and equipment.

KEY TERM

Current expenditure (also called **revenue expenditure**) refers to expenses involved in the day-to-day running of the business. Examples include advertising and fuel costs for vehicles.

Items of current expenditure are included in the income statement (profit and loss account). Note that the day-to-day operating and maintenance costs associated with fixed assets are regarded as current expenditure and are therefore included in the profit and loss account. For example, the purchase of a vehicle is not recorded in the income statement (profit and loss account), whereas the running costs of the vehicle are recorded in the expenses section of the income statement (profit and loss account).

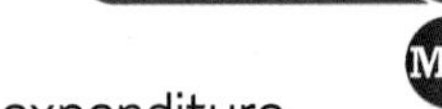

KEY SKILLS

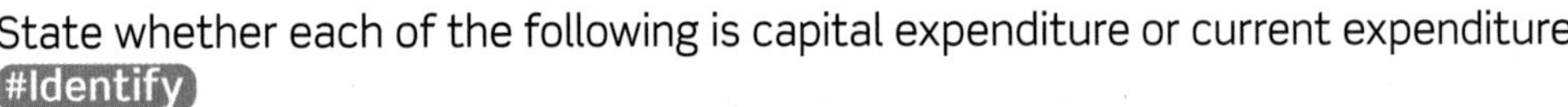

28.2 Capital and current expenditure

MIT

State whether each of the following is capital expenditure or current expenditure. #Identify

(a) A telephone bill
(b) A new telephone cabling system for the whole factory
(c) Servicing the company's fleet of cars
(d) A new car for the sales representative
(e) An oil tank for the heating oil
(f) Filling the tank with oil

Expenses

The following are some of the most common business **expenses** that appear in the income statement (profit and loss account).

- Wages and salaries
- Insurance
- Light and heat
- Telephone
- Rent and rates
- Postage and stationery
- Repairs
- General expenses
- Office expenses
- Cleaning expenses
- Travel expenses
- Advertising
- Selling expenses
- Vehicle operating expenses
- Marketing expenses
- Interest on loans
- Bank overdraft interest
- Audit fees[1]
- Carriage outwards[2]
- Bad debts[3]
- Depreciation of fixed assets[4]

Points to note:

1 **Audit fees:** An auditor's role is to examine company accounts in order to ensure that they have been properly prepared and that the accounts present a true and fair picture of the financial position of the business.

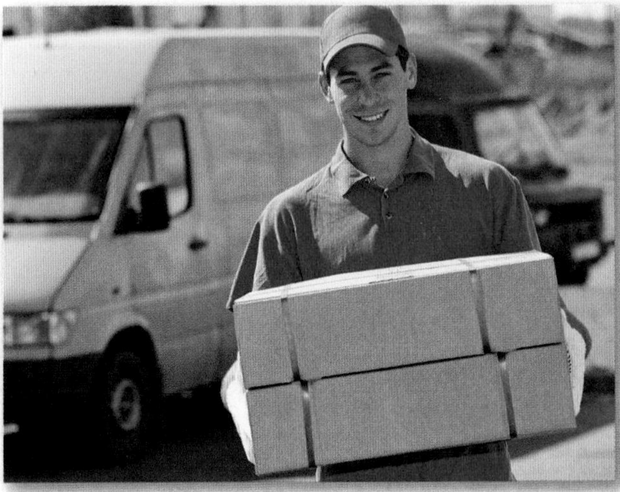

2 **Carriage outwards:** The transport and delivery costs associated with selling goods to customers. This expense is different from **carriage inwards** (the cost of having purchases from suppliers delivered), which is entered in the trading account.

3 **Bad debts:** When a debtor is unable to repay the debt, the money is written off as a non-recoverable loss. It is treated as an expense in the income statement (profit and loss account).

4 **Depreciation:** A reduction in the value of a fixed asset due to age, usage, and wear and tear. Businesses generally 'write off' a portion of the asset's value each year. For example, a new vehicle that is expected to have a working life of five years would be depreciated by 20% each year.

Example 1: Basic income statement (profit and loss account) with expenses

Use the following information provided by Intra Ltd to prepare a profit and loss account for the year ended 31/12/2022.

- Gross profit €180,000
- Wages €56,000
- Rent €12,000
- Light and heat €4,700
- Carriage outwards €3,000
- Advertising €8,300
- Office expenses €2,000

Income statement (profit and loss account) for Intra Ltd for year ended 31/12/2022

	€	€	€	Notes
Gross profit			180,000	P&L section of the income statement begins with gross profit
Less expenses:				
Wages		56,000		
Rent		12,000		
Light and heat		4,700		
Office expenses		2,000		
Carriage outwards		3,000		
Advertising		8,300	86,000	Subtract total expenses
Net profit			94,000	Net profit = Gross profit – Expenses

The profit and loss account begins with gross profit (or loss) and ends with the calculation of net profit (or loss). In practice, it is really just an extension of the trading account. Remember that these two accounts together make up the income statement.

286 Complete questions 7–11 in your Student Activity Book on preparing profit and loss accounts.

KEY SKILLS BN BL MIT

28.3 Profit and loss accounts

Use the information provided to prepare a profit and loss account for Benny & Hughes for the year ended 31/12/2022. #Calculate

Gross profit	€230,000	Carriage outwards	€3,000
Wages	€66,000	Advertising	€6,300
Rent	€16,100	Office expenses	€2,500
Light and heat	€9,700		

ENTERPRISE

RECORD BOOK 2

From trial balance to net profit

At the end of the financial year, the ledger accounts and analysed cash book will be balanced and totalled and a trial balance will be drawn up. This is simply a list of ledger and cash book balances at the end of the accounting period. These figures will be used to prepare the final accounts for the business.

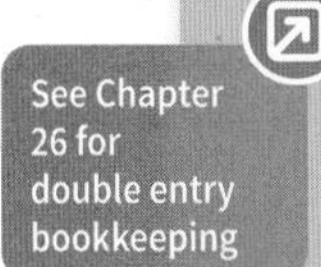

See Chapter 26 for double entry bookkeeping

Stages in the record-keeping process

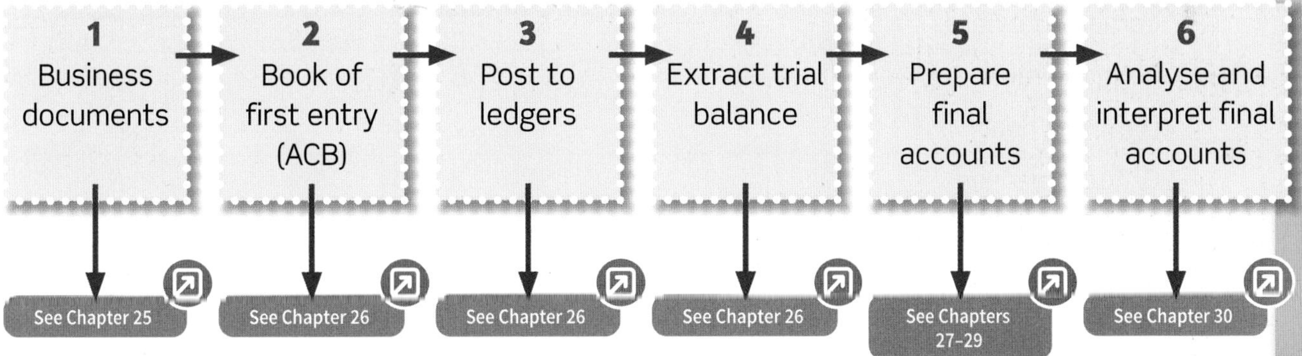

Points to note:

- The information from the business documents (invoices, credit notes, etc.) is posted to the book of first entry (analysed cash book).
- Double entry bookkeeping requires that figures from the analysed cash book are also posted to the ledger accounts.
- Accounts are balanced and totalled and a trial balance is extracted (drawn up).
- Figures from the trial balance are used to prepare the final accounts.
- The accounts must be analysed to get a better understanding of the current financial position of the business.

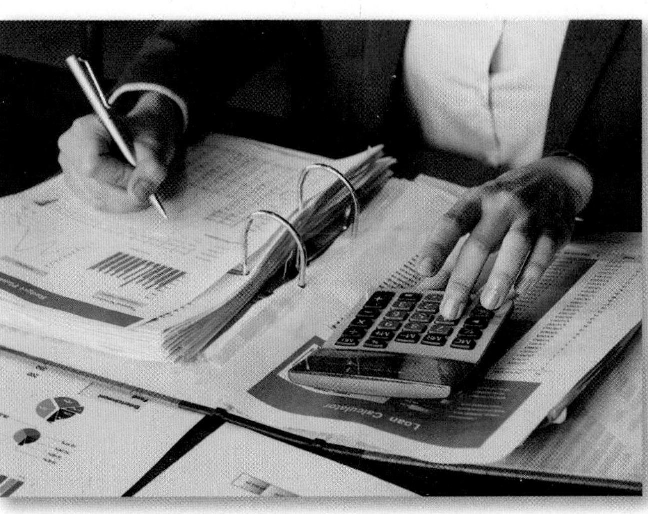

Example 2: Income statement with combined trading, profit and loss account

Use the following information to prepare an income statement (trading, profit and loss account) for Fresh Ltd for the year ended 31/12/2022.

In this example, the following abbreviations are used:

- T = Trading account item
- Exp = An expense in the profit and loss account.

Trial balance of Fresh Ltd on 31/12/2022

	DR €	CR €	Notes
Sales		234,500	T
Purchases	155,000		T
Opening stock	16,000		T
Customs duty	2,500		T
Carriage inwards	4,000		T
Salaries	25,000		Exp
Carriage outwards	8,000		Exp
Rent and rates	6,700		Exp
Light and heat	12,000		Exp
Office expenses	3,300		Exp
Depreciation on equipment	2,000		Exp
	234,500	234,500	
Closing stock (as on 31/12/2022) €11,500			T

Points to note:

- Closing stock is not included in the trial balance, but is listed as an extra item below the trial balance. It needs to be included in the trading account section of the income statement.
- Before preparing the income statement (trading, profit and loss account), it is helpful to identify each item in the trial balance and make a note of where it will appear in the final accounts.

Here is the completed income statement (trading, profit and loss account).

Income statement (trading, profit and loss account) for Fresh Ltd for year ended 31/12/2022

	€	€	€
Sales			234,500
Less cost of sales:			
Opening stock (1/1/22)		16,000	
Purchases		155,000	
Customs duty		2,500	
Carriage inwards		4,000	
Cost of goods available for sale		177,500	
– Closing stock (31/12/22)		11,500	
Cost of sales			166,000
Gross profit			68,500
Less expenses:			
Salaries		25,000	
Rent and rates		6,700	
Light and heat		12,000	
Office expenses		3,300	
Carriage outwards		8,000	
Depreciation: equipment		2,000	57,000
Net profit			11,500

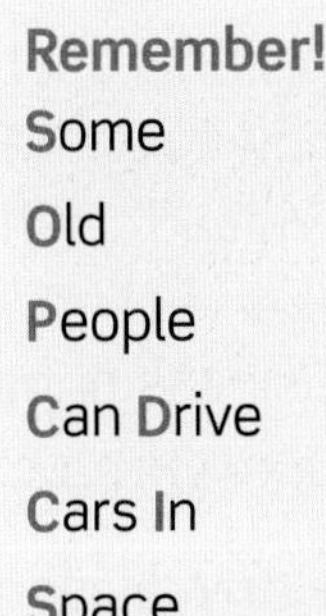

KEY SKILLS

28.4 Preparing an income statement (trading, profit and loss account)

BN MIT

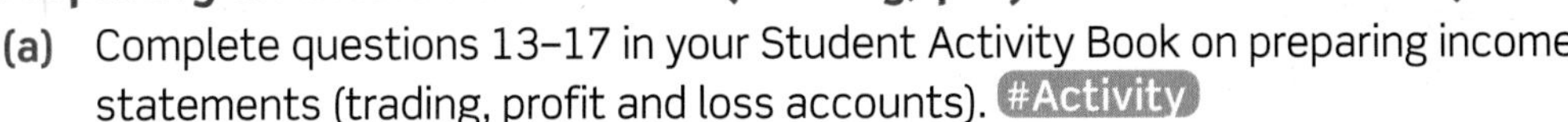

289 (a) Complete questions 13–17 in your Student Activity Book on preparing income statements (trading, profit and loss accounts). #Activity

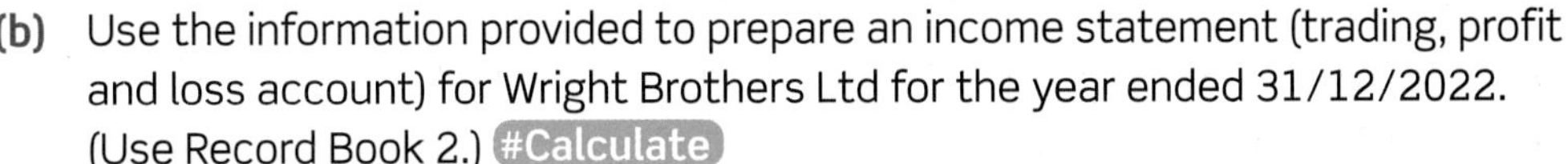

(b) Use the information provided to prepare an income statement (trading, profit and loss account) for Wright Brothers Ltd for the year ended 31/12/2022. (Use Record Book 2.) #Calculate

- Sales €820,000
- Purchases €440,000
- Opening stock €8,000
- Closing stock €6,000
- Carriage inwards €3,000
- Customs duty €9,000
- Wages and salaries €55,000
- Carriage outwards €6,600
- Rent and rates €8,400
- Light and heat €3,750
- Office expenses €4,500
- Repairs €7,100

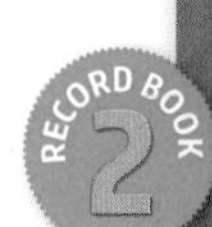

Monitoring expenses

An organisation should monitor business expenses/overheads to ensure that it is not paying more than it needs to and to maximise net profits. It can do this by:

- Cutting down on usage (if possible) if bills are higher than normal, e.g. turning down heating, switching off lights when not in use
- Shopping around for the best deal and switching to a different provider if necessary.

The profit and loss appropriation account

This final section of the income statement (trading, profit and loss account) is used to show how the annual profit is distributed. Some of the profit might be used to pay a dividend to shareholders, with the rest held as retained profits (also known as revenue **reserves**) and used for future investment in the business, for example to expand the business or purchase new assets.

The P&L appropriation account contains the following entries:

- Any dividends paid by the business during the current financial year. These are subtracted from the net profit or loss.
- Any reserves or retained profits carried forward by the business from previous years. These are added to the net profit or loss.

Net profit − Dividends paid + Opening reserves = Reserves (retained profits) at year end

Example 3: Profit and loss appropriation account

The layout of a profit and loss appropriation account is as follows.

Profit and loss appropriation account of Fresh Ltd for year ended 31/12/2022

	€	€	Notes
Net profit		11,500	
– Dividends paid		10,000	Portion of profit paid to shareholders
		1,500	
+ Opening reserves (1/1/2022)		30,000	Retained profit from previous years
Reserves (retained profit) 31/12/2022		31,500	Retained profit at the end of this financial year

Points to note:

- If dividends have already been paid to shareholders, they will be listed in the trial balance as dividends paid.
- The opening reserve (if one exists) will be listed in the trial balance.
- The closing reserve represents the retained profit or reserves at the end of the current financial year.

KEY SKILLS BN MIT

28.5 Profit and loss appropriation account

291

(a) Complete questions 20–23 in your Student Activity Book on preparing profit and loss appropriation accounts. #Activity

(b) Use the information provided to prepare a profit and loss appropriation account for Jackson and Perkins Ltd for the year ended 31/12/2022. #Activity #Calculate

Net profit	€325,000
Dividends paid	€16,000
Opening reserve (1/1/2022)	€42,000

(c) Use the information provided to prepare a profit and loss appropriation account for Christopoulos Pharmaceuticals Ltd for the year ended 31/12/2022. #Activity #Calculate

Net profit	€714,000
Dividends paid	€35,000
Opening reserve (1/1/2022)	€57,000

Example 4: Complete income statement (trading, profit and loss and appropriation account)

From the following information, prepare an income statement (trading, profit and loss and appropriation account) for Sunny Ltd for the year ended 31/12/2022.

Cash sales	€420,000	(T)
Cash purchases	€225,000	(T)
Opening stock	€23,000	(T)
Customs duty	€2,000	(T)
Closing stock	€13,750	(T)
Carriage inwards	€6,000	(T)
Rent	€12,800	(P&L Exp)
Light and heat	€3,250	(P&L Exp)
Wages	€65,000	(P&L Exp)
Carriage outwards	€4,000	(P&L Exp)
Telephone	€5,150	(P&L Exp)
Depreciation on vehicles	€10,000	(P&L Exp)
Opening reserves (1/1/2022)	€50,000	(App)
Dividends paid	€6,000	(App)

Income statement (trading, profit and loss and appropriation account) of Sunny Ltd for year ended 31/12/2022

	€	€	€
Sales			420,000
Less cost of sales:			
Opening stock (1/1/22)		23,000	
Purchases		225,000	
Customs duty		2,000	
Carriage inwards		6,000	
Cost of goods available for sale		256,000	
– Closing stock (31/12/22)		13,750	
Cost of sales			242,250
Gross profit			177,750
Less expenses:			
Wages		65,000	
Rent		12,800	
Light and heat		3,250	
Telephone		5,150	
Carriage outwards		4,000	
Depreciation on vehicles		10,000	100,200
Net profit			77,550
Less dividends			6,000
			71,550
Add opening reserves (1/1/2022)			50,000
Reserves (retained profit)			121,550

Remember!
Some
Old
People
Can Drive
Cars In
Space

KEY SKILLS

28.6 Income statement (trading, profit and loss account)

BN MIT

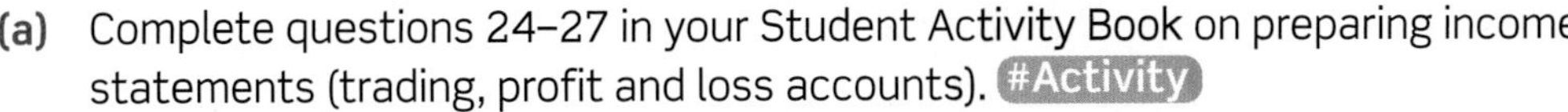

293 (a) Complete questions 24–27 in your Student Activity Book on preparing income statements (trading, profit and loss accounts). #Activity

(b) Use the information provided to prepare an income statement (trading, profit and loss account) for Grace Fashions Ltd for the year ended 31/12/2022. #Activity #Calculate

› Cash sales	€385,000
› Cash purchases	€175,000
› Opening stock	€13,500
› Closing stock	€13,750
› Carriage inwards	€3,200
› Rent	€16,000
› Depreciation on machinery	€8,000
› Light and heat	€5,250
› Wages	€32,000
› Carriage outwards	€7,000
› Telephone	€7,950
› Opening reserves (1/1/2022)	€41,000
› Dividends paid	€17,000

(c) Use the information provided to prepare an income statement (trading, profit and loss account) for Film & Vinyl Ltd for the year ended 31/12/2022. #Activity #Calculate

› Cash sales	€970,000
› Cash purchases	€645,000
› Opening stock	€43,000
› Closing stock	€23,450
› Carriage inwards	€7,600
› Customs duty	€900
› Rent	€16,000
› Depreciation on vehicles	€7,000
› Light and heat	€5,250
› Repairs	€6,000
› Wages	€72,000
› Carriage outwards	€1,200
› Telephone	€1,150
› Opening reserves (1/1/2022)	€82,000
› Dividends paid	€25,000

Weblinks

PowerPoint Summary

THE STATEMENT OF FINANCIAL POSITION (BALANCE SHEET)

LEARNING OUTCOMES IN FOCUS

2.13 Prepare final accounts to assess the financial performance of an organisation at the end of a trading period, analyse and evaluate its financial position and recommend a course of action

Links to 1.13, 2.9, 2.10, 2.11, 2.12, 3.2

LEARNING INTENTIONS FOR THIS CHAPTER

When you have completed this chapter you will be able to:

- Outline the purpose of a statement of financial position (balance sheet) and list its main elements
- Distinguish between fixed assets, current assets and creditors falling due within one year
- Explain the term 'working capital' and understand its significance
- Distinguish between authorised share capital and issued share capital
- Prepare a statement of financial position (balance sheet)
- Illustrate the impact of adjustments to final accounts
- Prepare a complete set of final accounts
- Prepare a set of final accounts for a not-for-profit organisation.

CHAPTER 29 KEY TERMS

assets
authorised share capital
capital
capital employed
closing stock
creditor
creditors falling due after more than one year
creditors falling due within one year
current assets
debt capital
debtor
depreciation
equity capital
fixed assets
issued share capital
liabilities
liquidity
net assets/net worth
statement of financial position
working capital

CHAPTER 29 KEY SKILLS

 Being Numerate

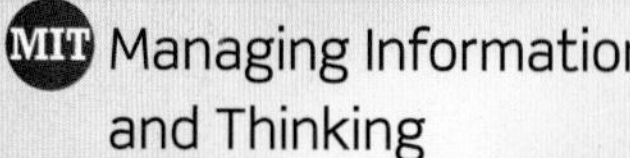 Managing Information and Thinking

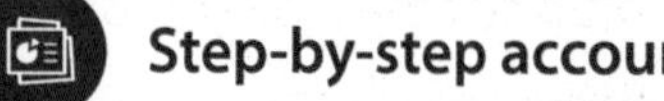 Step-by-step account

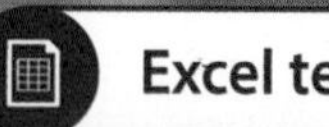 Excel template

The statement of financial position (balance sheet)

The **statement of financial position** (balance sheet) illustrates the year-end value of a business's assets and liabilities (creditors) and outlines details of where it gets its money from (its capital structure).

> KEY TERM
>
> **Assets** are items of value owned by the organisation.
>
> **Liabilities** refers to money owed by the organisation.
>
> **Capital** is all the money invested in the organisation and used to generate income. It comes from shareholder investments, long-term borrowings and retained profits (reserves).

The income statement (trading, profit and loss account) illustrates yearly totals for the trading period, so the title always includes 'for year ended', while the statement of financial position (balance sheet) reflects the financial status of a business on a given day. It's a bit like the difference between a video and a photograph: one covers a *period* of time, whereas the other is a *snapshot* at a specific time.

What is in the statement of financial position (balance sheet)?

The following will be in the statement of financial position (balance sheet):

1. Fixed assets
2. Current assets
3. Creditors falling due within one year (current liabilities)
4. Working capital
5. Total net assets
6. Capital employed.

1 Fixed assets

These are items owned by a business and intended for long-term use, such as premises, equipment, vehicles, etc. They may depreciate over time and their valuations in the statement of financial position (balance sheet) will need to be reduced in order to show this and give a more realistic value of the assets.

2 Current assets

This is cash or any asset that can be converted to cash in the short term (within one year).

Examples in this category include:

- Cash
- Bank deposits
- Money owed to the business by debtors
- Stock of goods.

The term '**debtor**' refers to someone who owes money to another person or business, usually because they have been sold goods or services on credit. This means that they have been supplied with the goods but they will not pay for them until an agreed future date, usually within 30 days.

See Chapter 23 for managing debtors

3 Creditors falling due within one year (current liabilities)

These are short-term debts owed by the business.

A **creditor** is someone that an organisation owes money to, usually because they have sold goods or services to the organisation on credit.

Examples include:

- Bank overdraft
- Accrued expenses (unpaid bills)
- Money owed to trade creditors (suppliers).

4 Working capital

Working capital = Current assets – Creditors falling due within one year (Current liabilities)

Working capital provides a good indication of a business's short-term liquidity.

See Chapter 23 for cash flow and liquidity

KEY TERM

Liquidity refers to cash flow and shows whether the business can generate enough short-term income to pay its short-term debts.

See Chapter 30 for analysing and assessing financial accounts

For example, if a business has current assets valued at €100,000 and creditors falling due within one year (current liabilities) of €30,000, it will have a positive working capital of €70,000. This suggests that there is not a problem with liquidity in the short term and that the business will be able to pay all its bills.

We will look at the significance of these issues in more detail in the next chapter.

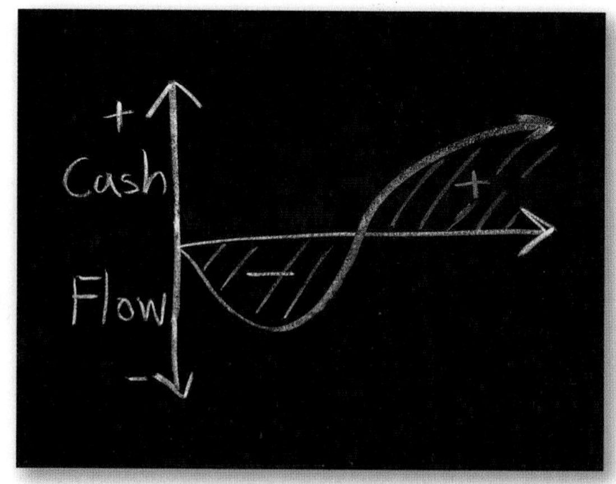

5 Total net assets

This is also called **net worth**. It shows what the business would be worth if it were to sell its assets and pay its short-term debts.

Total net assets = Fixed assets + Working capital

6 Capital employed

Capital employed is the total of the 'financed by' section of the statement of financial position (balance sheet). It sets out the capital structure of a business.

This section of the statement of financial position (balance sheet) contains:

- Details of the business's share capital.
- Long-term loans taken out by the business. These are **creditors falling due after more than one year** and will not be repaid during the current financial year.
- Retained profits or reserves held by the business for future reinvestment.

Capital comes from two main sources: investments by shareholders (**equity capital**) or borrowings (**debt capital**).

Authorised vs. issued share capital

When a company is being set up, its owners must set an upper limit for the amount of share capital that it can issue. This maximum limit is called the **authorised share capital**.

For example, Flash Ltd may have an authorised share capital of €500,000, made up of 500,000 individual shares with a value of €1 each.

The **issued share capital** of a company indicates the number of shares it has actually issued (sold) to date. For example, Flash Ltd may have an issued share capital of €300,000, comprising 300,000 €1 shares.

BN

29.1 How much extra capital?

From the information provided above, calculate how many extra shares Flash Ltd may choose to issue in the future if it needs to raise extra capital. #Calculate

When the statement of financial position (balance sheet) is completed, the total net assets figure should equal the capital employed figure. When this happens, the statement of financial position (balance sheet) has balanced.

Example 1: Preparing a statement of finacial position (balance sheet)

Use the following information to prepare a statement of financial position (balance sheet) for Kahouna Ltd as at 31/12/2022. The company has an authorised share capital of €700,000.

Premises	€320,000
Machinery	€170,000
Bank (deposits)	€23,000
Closing stock	€14,000
Debtors	€18,000
Bank overdraft	€7,500
Creditors	€9,500
Issued share capital	€440,000
Long-term loans	€78,000
Reserves	€10,000

Statement of financial position (balance sheet) of Kahouna Ltd as at 31/12/2022

	€	€	€	
Fixed assets	**Cost**	**Depreciation**	**Net book value**	← These headings apply to the fixed assets section only
Premises	320,000	–	320,000	← Assets have not depreciated in value
Machinery	170,000	–	170,000	←
Total fixed assets	490,000	–	490,000	← Book value of fixed assets
Current assets				
Bank	23,000			
Closing stock	14,000			
Debtors	18,000	55,000		← Total current assets
Less creditors falling due within 1 year (current liabilities)				
Bank overdraft	7,500			
Creditors	9,500	17,000		← Total creditors falling due within one year
Working capital			38,000	← CA – CFD*
Total net assets			**528,000**	← Total fixed assets + Working capital
Financed by:				
Creditors falling due after more than 1 year (long-term loan)			78,000	
Capital and reserves	*Authorised*	*Issued*		
Ordinary share capital	700,000	440,000		← Must show both authorised and issued share capital
+ Reserves		10,000	450,000	
Capital employed			**528,000**	← This matches the total net assets

*CA = current assets; CFD = creditors falling due within one year

Points to note:

As with the income statement (trading, profit and loss account), it is important to use the standard layout for a statement of financial position (balance sheet).

KEY SKILLS

MIT

29.2 Statement of financial position (balance sheet)

(a) In which part of the statement of financial position (balance sheet) – fixed assets, current assets, creditors falling due within one year (current liabilities) or financed by – will you find the following? #Identify

(i) Premises
(ii) Creditors
(iii) Closing stock
(iv) Long-term loans
(v) Debtors
(vi) Machinery
(vii) Bank (deposits)
(viii) Issued share capital
(ix) Bank overdraft

300

(b) Complete questions 10–14 in your Student Activity Book for more practice on this topic. #Activity

Adjustments to final accounts

The figures used to prepare a business's final accounts are contained in the trial balance. Sometimes, however, extra information may be available that is not contained in the trial balance but it needs to be included in the final accounts. These items are usually listed below the trial balance and are treated as adjustments to final accounts.

There are two specific adjustments to final accounts that you need to consider:

- **Closing stock:** The value of goods held in stock at the end of the financial year. This may be stock of raw materials or finished goods.
- **Depreciation:** A reduction in the value of a fixed asset due to age, usage, and wear and tear. Businesses generally 'write off' a portion of the asset's value each year. For example, a new vehicle that is expected to have a working life of five years would be depreciated by 20% each year.

Each of these adjustment items needs to be **entered twice in the final accounts**: once in the income statement (trading, profit and loss account) and again in the statement of financial position (balance sheet).

Closing stock appears:

- In the income statement (trading account section)
- As a current asset in the statement of financial position (balance sheet).

Depreciation appears:

- As an expense in the income statement (trading, profit and loss account)
- In the fixed assets section of the statement of financial position (balance sheet). Depreciation will be subtracted from the asset's cost price in order to calculate its net book value (the current value of the asset).

Example 2: Accounting for depreciation

Machinery that cost €50,000 is to be depreciated by 20%. Depreciation is calculated as follows: €50,000 × 20% = €10,000.

This €10,000 will first be included in the list of expenses contained in the income statement (trading, profit and loss account). It will also appear in the statement of financial position (balance sheet) as follows:

Statement of financial position (balance sheet) extract (as at 31/12/2022)

	€	€	€	Notes
Fixed asset	**Cost**	**Depreciation**	**Net book value**	
Machinery	50,000	10,000	40,000	NBV = Cost price – Depreciation

Points to note:

The net book value (NBV) represents the current value of the fixed asset and reflects the impact of age and wear and tear. If no account is taken of depreciation and assets are included at their original cost price, it will over-state the actual value of the assets and would give a false impression of the financial strength of the business.

Example 3: Preparing final accounts, including adjustments

Here is a fully worked example of final accounts, including adjustments.

Use the information below to prepare an income statement (trading, profit and loss account) for Speed Ltd for the year ended 31/12/2022. Also prepare a statement of financial position (balance sheet) on that date.

Speed Ltd has an authorised share capital of 400,000 €1 ordinary shares.

The following abbreviations are used in this example to indicate where each item appears in the final accounts.

T	Trading account section of the income statement (trading, profit and loss account)
P&L Exp	An expense in the P&L section of the income statement (trading, profit and loss account)
App	Appropriation account section of the income statement (trading, profit and loss account)
SFP (FA)	Statement of financial position (balance sheet) (fixed assets section)
SFP (CA)	Statement of financial position (balance sheet) (current assets section)
SFP (CFD)	Statement of financial position (balance sheet) (a creditor falling due within one year)
SFP (Fin)	Statement of financial position (balance sheet) (financed by section)

Trial balance of Speed Ltd as at 31/12/2022

	€ Dr	€ Cr	Notes
Sales		380,000	T
Purchases	200,000		T
Carriage inwards	1,100		T
Rent	13,200		Exp
Opening stock	4,000		T
Wages	48,000		Exp
Customs duty	1,200		T
Telephone	4,000		Exp
Dividends paid	14,000		App
Light and heat	11,500		Exp
Carriage outwards	3,000		Exp
Premises	160,000		SFP (FA)
Vehicles	40,000		SFP (FA)
Office expenses	1,800		Exp
Cash in hand	4,000		SFP (CA)
Machinery	90,000		SFP (FA)
Creditors		12,000	SFP (CFD)
Debtors	11,000		SFP (CA)
Bank overdraft		8,000	SFP (CFD)
Advertising	4,200		Exp
Issued share capital		150,000	SFP (Fin by)
Reserves (P&L balance)		37,000	App
5-year loan		24,000	SFP (Fin by)
	611,000	**611,000**	

The following additional information is provided on 31/12/2022:

- Closing stock (31/12/2022) €10,000 – T and SFP (CA)
- Vehicles are to be depreciated by 20% – Exp and SFP (FA).

Income statement of Speed Ltd for year ended 31/12/2022

	€	€	€	Notes
Sales			380,000	**Some**
Less cost of sales:				
Opening stock		4,000		**Old**
+ Purchases		200,000		**People**
+ Customs duty		1,200		**Can Drive**
+ Carriage inwards		1,100		**Cars In**
Cost of goods available for sale		206,300		
– Closing stock		10,000		**Space**
Cost of sales			196,300	
Gross profit			183,700	
Less expenses:				
Wages		48,000		
Telephone		4,000		
Light and heat		11,500		
Office expenses		1,800		
Rent		13,200		
Advertising		4,200		
Carriage outwards		3,000		
Depreciation on vehicles		8,000	93,700	Depreciation =
Net profit			90,000	20% of €40,000
– Dividends paid			14,000	
			76,000	
+ Opening reserves			37,000	
Closing reserves			113,000	

Statement of financial position for Speed Ltd as at 31/12/2022

	€	€	€	Notes
Fixed assets	**Cost**	**Depreciation**	**Net book value**	
Premises	160,000	–	160,000	
Vehicles	40,000	8,000	32,000	Cost – Depreciation = NBV
Machinery	90,000	–	90,000	
	290,000	8,000	282,000	
Current assets				
Cash in hand	4,000			
Debtors	11,000			
Closing stock	10,000	25,000		
Creditors falling due within 1 year (current liabilities)				
Bank overdraft	8,000			
Creditors	12,000	20,000		
Working capital			5,000	
Total net assets			**287,000**	
Financed by:				
Creditors falling due after more than 1 year (5-year loan)			24,000	
	Authorised	*Issued*		Must show both authorised and issued share capital
Share capital	400,000	150,000		
+ P&L reserves		113,000	263,000	This figure is taken from the income statement
Capital employed			**287,000**	Total net assets = Capital employed

29.3 Review and reflect

(a) Illustrate your understanding of the term 'depreciation'. #Illustrate

(b) How does depreciation impact on the value of assets? #Evaluate

(c) Why do you think it is necessary to list assets at their net book value (Cost price – Depreciation) rather than their cost price? #Opinion

(d) Complete questions 15–16 in your Student Activity Book for more practice on this topic. #Activity

KEY SKILLS BN MIT

29.4 Final accounts

Use the information in the trial balance to prepare the final accounts of Bravo Ltd for the year ended 31/12/2022. Bravo Ltd has an authorised share capital of €300,000. (Use Record Book 2.) #Calculate

Trial balance of Bravo Ltd on 31/12/2022

	Dr €	Cr €
Cash sales		37,000
Cash purchases	12,900	
Opening stock (1/1/2022)	2,600	
Insurance	1,600	
Advertising	1,800	
Wages	10,000	
Vehicles	25,000	
Machinery	29,760	
Debtors	4,500	
Creditors		3,500
Cash at bank	2,340	
Issued share capital		50,000
	90,500	**90,500**

Note: Stock on 31/12/2022 was €6,000.

KEY SKILLS BN MIT

29.5 Browne Ltd's final accounts

Prepare Browne Ltd's final accounts from their trial balance. Browne Ltd has an authorised share capital of €350,000. (Use Record Book 2.) #Calculate

Trial balance of Browne Ltd on 31/12/2022

	Dr €	Cr €
Cash sales		250,000
Cash purchases	120,000	
Opening stock (1/1/2022)	1,500	
Carriage inwards	5,000	
Insurance	6,000	
Rent	6,000	
Office expenses	3,000	
Advertising	4,500	
Dividends paid	15,000	
Premises	210,000	
Machinery	39,000	
Debtors	7,500	
Creditors		11,000
Bank overdraft		9,000
Cash	2,500	
Issued share capital		150,000
	€420,000	**€420,000**

Note: Stock on 31/12/2022 was €15,000.

305 There are a number of other trial balances in the Student Activity Book for you to practise preparing the final accounts (questions 17–22). Do as many as you need to until you feel confident with your work.

Final accounts of not-for-profit organisations

Not-for-profit organisations such as clubs, charities and community groups also need to prepare final accounts. These accounts are used to support applications for loans and grants and to show members how money was received and spent during the year.

Since these accounts are not required to show profitability, they will look a little different from those prepared by companies and other commercial enterprises. (Remember, commercial enterprises are those whose main aim is to make a profit.)

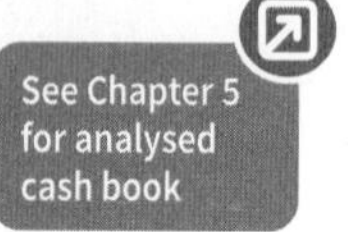
See Chapter 5 for analysed cash book

Not-for-profit organisations will record all money received or paid out in an analysed cash book and these figures will eventually be used to prepare a set of final accounts.

Commercial enterprises	Not-for-profit organisations
Main goal is to make a profit. Profits belong to shareholders, who may receive a dividend.	**Making a profit is *not* the main goal.** Surplus income is reinvested to help achieve organisational goals or to benefit members.
Accounts are prepared by **accountants** and double-checked by **auditors.**	Accounts are prepared by the **finance officer** or **treasurer** and may be checked by an auditor.
Income > Expenditure = **Profit** Expenditure > Income = **Loss** These are recorded in the income statement.	Income > Expenditure = **Surplus** (excess income) Expenditure > Income = **Deficit** (excess expenditure
Sales are the main source of income or revenue.	**Subscriptions, donations and/or grants** are major sources of income or revenue.
Issued share capital is recorded in a statement of financial position (balance sheet).	**Accumulated fund** is recorded in the statement of financial position (balance sheet).

Table 29.1 Final accounts prepared by commercial enterprises and not-for-profit organisations

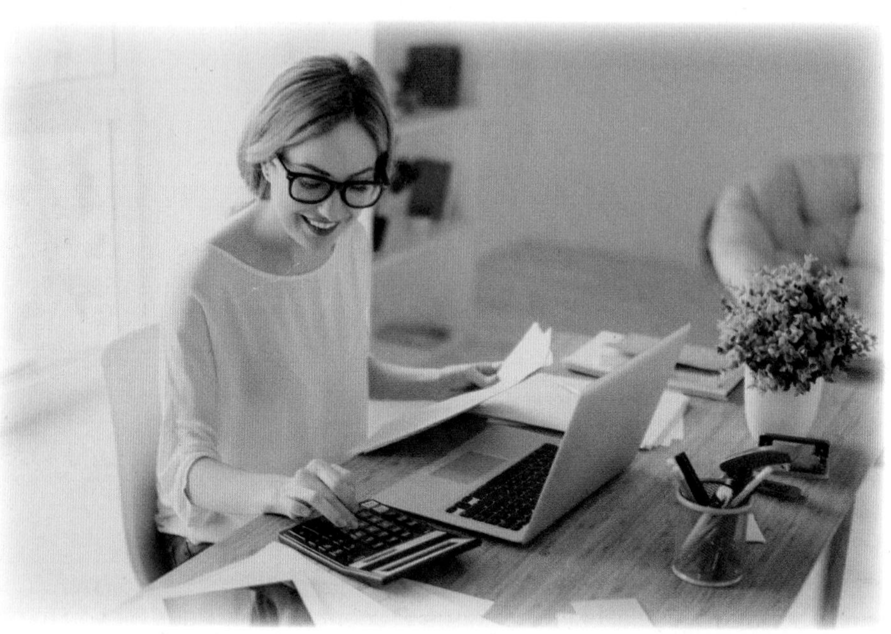

Example 4: Final accounts of a not-for-profit organisation

Barrtown Community Development Association prepared the following final accounts for the year ended 31/12/2022.

Income statement of Barrtown Community Development Association for year ended 31/12/2022

	€	€
Revenue:		
Donations	18,000	
Grants	27,000	
Fundraising income	6,800	51,800
Less expenditure:		
Programme expenses	29,000	
Rent	3,100	
Insurance	4,300	
Light and heat	8,400	
General expenses	2,700	
Depreciation on equipment	2,000	49,500
Surplus income		**2,300**

Statement of financial position (balance sheet) of Barrtown Community Development Association as at 31/12/2022

Fixed assets	Cost €	Depreciation €	Net book value €
Equipment	20,000	2,000	18,000
Current assets			
Cash	900		
Debtors	3,100	4,000	
Creditors falling due within 1 year (current liabilities)			
Bank overdraft	1,300		
Creditors	1,700	3,000	
Working capital			**1,000**
Total net assets			**19,000**
Financed by:			
Accumulated fund		16,700	
Surplus income (reserves)		2,300	
Capital employed			**19,000**

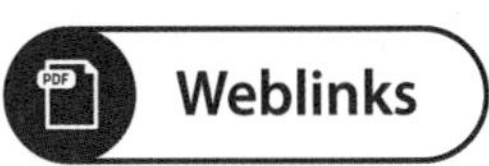

ENTERPRISE

CHAPTER 30

ANALYSING AND ASSESSING FINANCIAL ACCOUNTS

LEARNING OUTCOMES IN FOCUS

2.13 Prepare final accounts to assess the financial performance of an organisation at the end of a trading period, analyse and evaluate its financial position and recommend a course of action

Links to 1.13, 2.9, 2.10, 2.11, 2.12, 3.2

LEARNING INTENTIONS FOR THIS CHAPTER

When you have completed this chapter you will be able to:

- List the stakeholders who use the financial information provided by organisations
- Outline the key financial concerns of each of these stakeholders
- Analyse and evaluate the financial position of an organisation
- Prepare a report to communicate financial information to stakeholders
- Use your analysis to recommend a course of action.

CHAPTER 30 KEY TERMS

acid test ratio	liquidity
current ratio	low gearing
debt capital	net margin
dividend	net profit percentage
equity capital	profitability
gearing	quick ratio
gross margin	ratio analysis
gross profit percentage	stakeholder
high gearing	working capital ratio

CHAPTER 30 KEY SKILLS

- BL Being Literate
- BN Being Numerate
- C Communicating
- MIT Managing Information and Thinking

Analysing an organisation's financial position

In the previous chapters we learned how to prepare final accounts for an organisation. In this chapter we will take a closer look at those final accounts in order to better understand the financial story being told.

When we analyse the financial position of an organisation, we look at the evidence available in order to understand how well the organisation is meeting its financial goals. This requires us to examine cash flow forecasts and final accounts to identify patterns and trends. These patterns and trends should help us to make a judgement about the financial management of the organisation. Once this evaluation has been completed, it should be possible to offer advice about how to improve the organisation's financial performance.

Ratio analysis

One possible approach that can be used to help with this investigation is **ratio analysis**.

Ratios are helpful because they focus on financial performance in percentage terms rather than money terms. This makes it easier to compare organisations of different sizes.

Ratios are most useful when they are used to compare performance over a long period of time or against other businesses in the same industry. This makes it easier to compare different companies and different years.

There are three main categories of financial ratio:

1. **Profitability** ratios analyse the profit made during the financial year.
2. **Liquidity** ratios look at cash flow in the organisation and measure its ability to pay short-term debts on time. Poor liquidity is a major cause of organisational failure.
3. **Gearing** ratios look at how the organisation is financed and consider how much of its capital comes from external sources. This is long-term debt and must be repaid with interest, so having a lot of it can create financial problems.

Users of financial information

Stakeholders is a collective term used to describe everyone who is involved in or affected by the activities of an organisation.

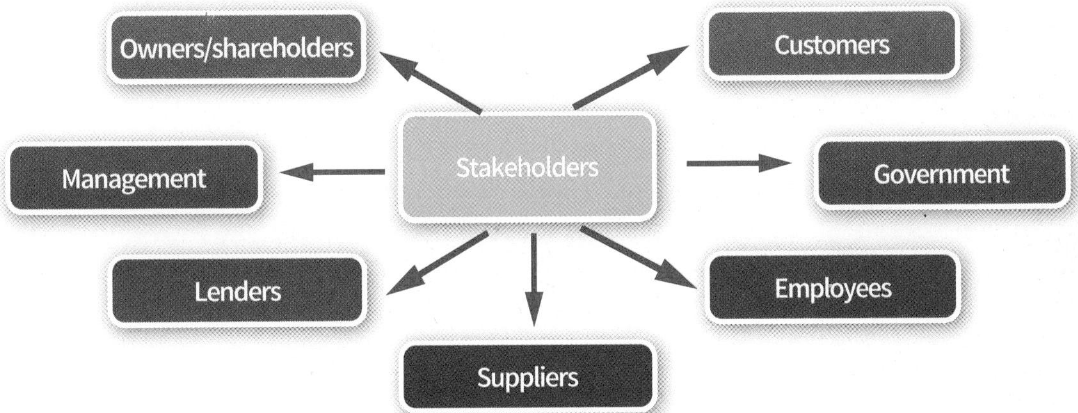

Although their reasons for doing so may be different, the following stakeholders will have an interest in analysing financial information.

1 Employees and managers

Both employees and managers may be interested in all financial aspects of the organisation because their long-term job security may depend on the organisation remaining profitable.

Employees may be rewarded for high levels of profitability, either through wage increases or performance-related bonuses.

2 Shareholders

As the owners of a business, shareholders will mainly be concerned with profitability and the payment of dividends.

> **KEY TERM**
>
> A **dividend** is the share of profits paid to shareholders. It is a reward for their investment in the organisation.

Potential shareholders will also be interested in return on investment.

3 Lenders

All existing and potential lenders will be concerned with liquidity, as this measures the organisation's ability to pay its debts.

Lenders will also be concerned with the organisation's ability to repay debts and with gearing (see page 359). High levels of external debt increase the pressure on an organisation to make repayments and also increase the chances of non-payment or default.

4 Suppliers

Liquidity will be the main concern for suppliers, especially those who supply goods on credit. An organisation that is having cash flow problems may struggle to pay its bills on time, which increases the likelihood of bad debts for suppliers. (A bad debt is one that cannot be repaid.)

5 Government

The government collects tax on company profits (corporation tax) and will therefore be interested in profitability levels.

Organisations also submit a range of other taxes and charges, including VAT, PAYE and PRSI.

Calculating ratios

In the examples that follow, all information will be taken from the accounts of Euro Ltd, whose final accounts for the year ended 31/12/2022 are set out on the next page. For comparison purposes, the company has also provided a copy of its key figures for the previous four years' trading. Where relevant, the industry average is also provided. The industry average allows us to compare the performance of Euro Ltd to other businesses in the same industry. It shows us whether or not their financial performance is above or below average for that type of business.

ENTERPRISE

Summarised income statement (trading, profit and loss account) of Euro Ltd for year ended 31/12/2022

	€
Sales	350,000
Less cost of sales	178,000
Gross profit	172,000
Less expenses	82,000
Net profit	90,000
– Dividend paid	14,000
	76,000
+ Opening reserves (1/1/2022)	37,000
Closing reserves (31/12/2022)	113,000

Statement of financial position of Euro Ltd as at 31/12/2022

	€	€	€
Fixed assets	**Cost**	**Depreciation**	**Net book value**
Premises	160,000	–	160,000
Vehicles	40,000	8,000	32,000
Machinery	90,000	–	90,000
	290,000	8,000	282,000
Current assets			
Cash in hand	4,000		
Debtors	11,000		
Closing stock	10,000	25,000	
Creditors falling due within 1 year (current liabilities)			
Bank overdraft	8,000		
Creditors	12,000	20,000	
Working capital			5,000
Total net assets			**287,000**
Financed by:			
Creditors falling due after more than 1 year (5-year loan)			24,000
Capital and reserves	*Authorised*	*Issued*	
Ordinary share capital	350,000	150,000	
Reserves		113,000	263,000
Capital employed			**287,000**

Profitability

We will now look at some of the ways that profitability can be measured.

Gross profit percentage

Profitability can be measured by the **gross profit percentage**, which is also known as the **gross margin**.

$$\textbf{Gross profit percentage} = \frac{\text{Gross profit}}{\text{Sales}} \times \frac{100}{1}$$

The 2022 gross profit percentage for Euro Ltd is therefore:

$$\frac{172{,}000}{350{,}000} \times \frac{100}{1} = 49.1\%$$

This means that Euro Ltd makes 49c gross profit from every €1 of sales revenue it receives from customers.

Total sales revenue

KEY SKILLS

30.1 Where does the money go?

Why are profits lower than money received by the business? What happens to the rest of the money it receives from customers? #WhatDoYouThink #Reflect

This figure can be measured against the gross profit percentage for previous years and against the industry average for this year:

Euro Ltd gross profit percentage (previous four years)

2018	2019	2020	2021
35%	30%	35%	40%
2022 INDUSTRY AVERAGE		42%	

The trend graph for the five-year period 2018–2022 is shown in Figure 30.1.

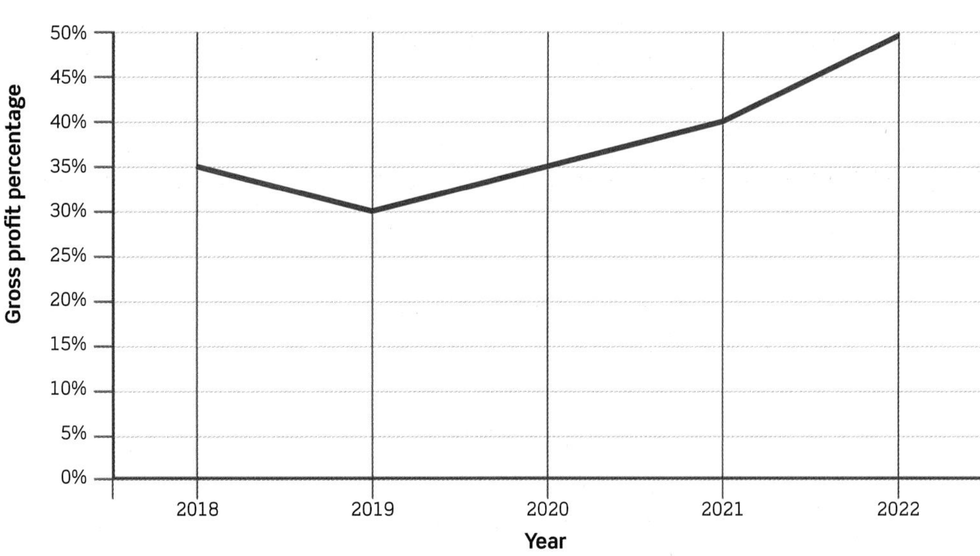

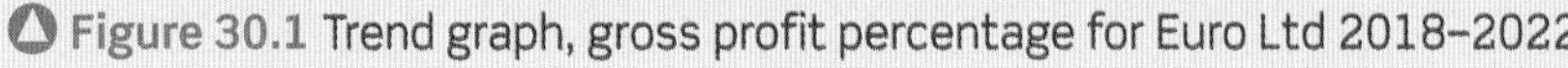
Figure 30.1 Trend graph, gross profit percentage for Euro Ltd 2018–2022

Commentary and evaluation

With the exception of a drop in profitability in 2019, Euro Ltd has seen an improvement in its gross profit margin over the five-year period. The 49.1% figure in 2022 is the best in the five-year period and suggests that sales have improved and that the cost of sales is under control. The result is also well above the industry average for 2022 and is very positive.

KEY SKILLS

30.2 Gross margin BN C MIT

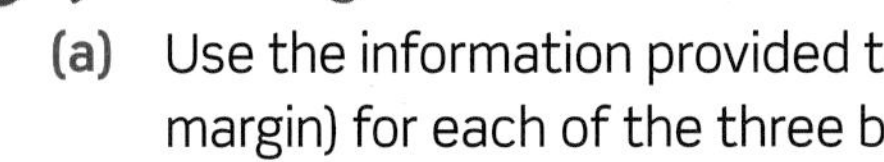
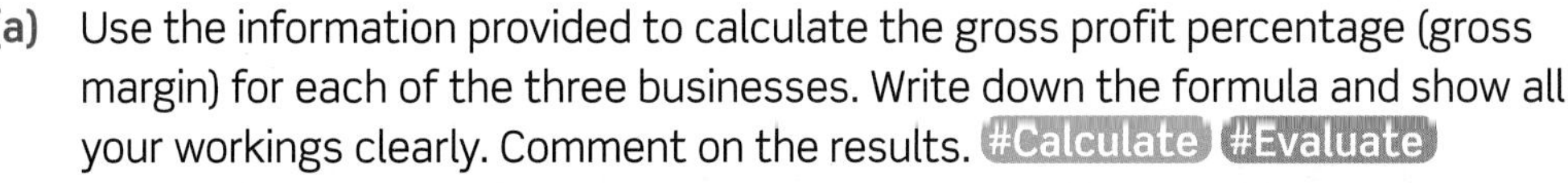

(a) Use the information provided to calculate the gross profit percentage (gross margin) for each of the three businesses. Write down the formula and show all your workings clearly. Comment on the results. #Calculate #Evaluate

Alpha Ltd		Beta Ltd		Gamma Ltd	
Gross profit	€360,000	Gross profit	€275,000	Gross profit	€360,000
Sales	€800,000	Sales	€500,000	Sales	€1,200,000

317 (b) Complete question 5 in your Student Activity Book for more practice on this topic. #Activity

Net margin

Profitability can be measured by the **net profit percentage**, which is also known as the **net margin**.

$$\text{Net profit percentage} = \frac{\text{Net profit}}{\text{Sales}} \times \frac{100}{1}$$

The 2022 net profit percentage for Euro Ltd is therefore:

$$\frac{90{,}000}{350{,}000} \times \frac{100}{1} = 25.7\%$$

This means that Euro Ltd makes 25.7c net profit from every €1 of sales revenue that it received from customers.

The figure for net profit percentage can be measured against the net margin for previous years and against the industry average for this year:

Euro Ltd net profit percentage (previous four years)

2018	2019	2020	2021
11%	10%	14%	17%
2022 INDUSTRY AVERAGE		20%	

KEY SKILLS BN C

30.3 Euro Ltd net profit percentage

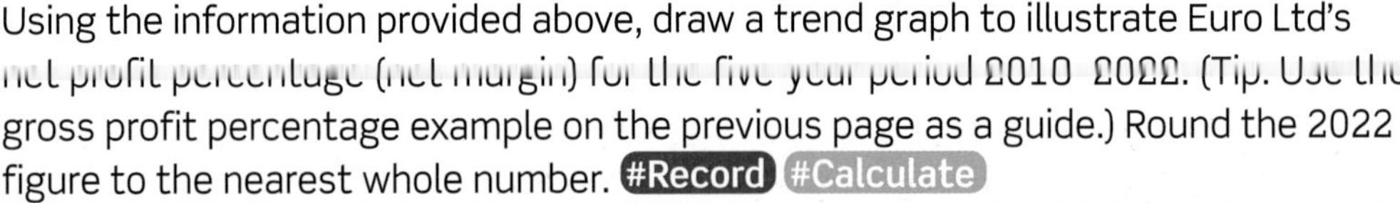

Using the information provided above, draw a trend graph to illustrate Euro Ltd's net profit percentage (net margin) for the five-year period 2018–2022. (Tip: Use the gross profit percentage example on the previous page as a guide.) Round the 2022 figure to the nearest whole number. #Record #Calculate

Commentary and evaluation

Euro Ltd has seen a year-on-year improvement in net profit percentage between 2021 and 2022, with figures rising from 17% to 25.7%. This continues a positive trend since 2019, which has seen a steady increase over the period. The result is also above the industry average for 2022.

KEY SKILLS BN MIT

30.4 Alpha, Beta and Gamma net profit percentages

(a) Use the information provided to calculate the net profit percentage (net margin) for each of the three businesses. Write down the formula and show all workings clearly. Comment on the results. #Calculate #Evaluate

Alpha Ltd		Beta Ltd		Gamma Ltd	
Net profit	€200,000	Net profit	€175,000	Gross profit	€360,000
Sales	€800,000	Sales	€500,000	Expenses	€180,000
				Sales	€1,200,000

(b) Complete question 6 in your Student Activity Book for more practice on this topic.

Return on capital employed

Profitability can be measured by the return on capital employed (ROCE), which is also known as the return on investment (ROI). This is an important measurement for shareholders and potential investors.

$$\text{Return on capital employed} = \frac{\text{Net profit}}{\text{Capital employed}} \times \frac{100}{1}$$

The 2022 return on capital employed for Euro Ltd is:

$$\frac{90{,}000}{287{,}000} \times \frac{100}{1} = 31.36\%$$

Return on capital employed is useful when comparing different companies' profitability because it indicates how well the business is using its capital to generate income. By comparing the return on capital employed available on different investment options, potential investors can choose the best possible option. It is also useful to compare the return on capital employed from an investment in company shares with the return on a (risk-free) investment in a financial institution.

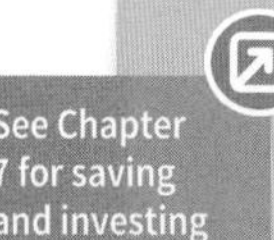

See Chapter 7 for saving and investing money

See Chapter 11 for financial planning for your future

For example, if money can be invested in a bank for a guaranteed 3% return with no risk, an investor might avoid the higher risk involved in a business investment:

- Where the return is estimated (but not guaranteed) to be 5% **AND**
- Where their money (capital) is not guaranteed to be returned.

Only the potential for a very high return on capital employed will convince an investor to risk money on buying shares in a business. Therefore, a business will try to keep its ROCE as high as possible, as it makes it easier to attract investment.

Euro Ltd return on capital employed (previous four years)

2018	2019	2020	2021
20%	20%	28%	26%
2022 INDUSTRY AVERAGE		22%	

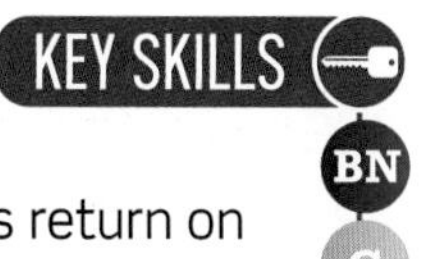

KEY SKILLS

30.5 Euro Ltd's ROCE

Using the information provided, draw a trend graph to illustrate Euro Ltd's return on capital employed for the five-year period 2018–2022. Round the 2022 figure to the nearest whole number. #Record

BN C MIT

Commentary and evaluation

Euro Ltd has seen a year-on-year improvement in its return on capital employed, from 26% in 2021 to 31.36% in 2022. This figure is well above the 'risk-free' rate of return currently available from financial institutions. It is also well above the industry average for the year and is therefore a positive result, which will be very pleasing to managers and investors.

KEY SKILLS BN MIT

30.6 Investment rates

Research the best available rate on offer from Ireland's major financial institutions for an investor with €100,000 and a willingness to leave the money on deposit for up to:

- One year
- Three years
- Five years

Record your findings and the source of your information. Can you be sure that your research findings are reliable? Explain one reason for your answer. #Research

KEY SKILLS BN MIT

30.7 Alpha, Beta and Gamma ROCE

(a) Use the information provided to calculate the return on capital employed for each of the three businesses. Write down the formula and show all workings clearly. Comment on the results. #Calculate #Evaluate

Alpha Ltd		Beta Ltd		Gamma Ltd	
Net profit	€200,000	Net profit	€175,000	Gross profit	€360,000
Capital employed	€1,000,000	Capital employed	€900,000	Expenses	€180,000
				Capital employed	€600,000

318 (b) Complete question 7 in your Student Activity Book for more practice on this topic. #Activity

Liquidity

See Chapter 23 for the importance of cash flow planning

There are several ways that liquidity can be measured. You may recall from previous chapters that liquidity is about cash flow and an organisation's ability to pay its debts as they fall due.

Working capital ratio (current ratio)

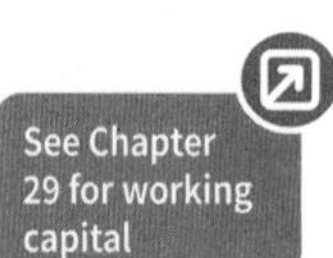

See Chapter 29 for working capital

This ratio is really asking the following question: Does the business have enough short-term assets to generate the cash it needs to pay short-term debts?

Working capital ratio = Current assets : Creditors falling due within one year (Current liabilities)

The 2022 working capital ratio for Euro Ltd is therefore:

25,000 : 20,000 = 1.25 : 1

We get the answer by dividing both sides by the number on the right-hand side.
So:
25,000/20,000 = 1.25 and
20,000/20,000 = 1
The answer expressed as a ratio is 1.25 : 1.

This indicates that Euro Ltd should be able to generate enough cash in the coming year to pay its short-term debts. However, the result is below the ideal level of 2 : 1.

Euro Ltd current ratio (previous four years)

2018	2019	2020	2021
1.8 : 1	1.2 : 1	2.5 : 1	3 : 1
2022 INDUSTRY AVERAGE		2.3 : 1	

Commentary and evaluation

When we consider the five-year trend, it is clear that Euro Ltd has generally improved its cash flow position between 2018 and 2022. The 2022 figure of just 1.25 : 1 is below the recommended minimum of 2 : 1 and also represents a major disimprovement since 2021. It is also below the industry average, which suggests that the liquidity problem is unique to Euro Ltd and is not a reflection of overall market conditions.

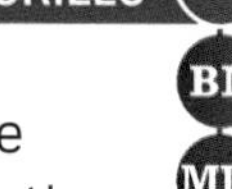

KEY SKILLS BN MIT

30.8 Alpha, Beta and Gamma current ratio

Use the information provided to calculate the current ratio for each of the three businesses. Write down the formula and show all workings clearly. Comment on the results. #Calculate #Evaluate

Alpha Ltd		Beta Ltd		Gamma Ltd	
Current assets	€400,000	Current assets	€700,000	Current assets	€360,000
Creditors falling due within 1 year	€200,000	Creditors falling due within 1 year	€400,000	Creditors falling due within 1 year	€900,000

Acid test ratio (or quick ratio)

This ratio is a stricter test of liquidity than the working capital ratio. It accounts for the fact that some current assets, especially stock, can take time to convert to cash.

The most common current assets in order of liquidity (how easily they can be converted to cash) are:

- **Cash:** It is already cash!
- **Bank deposits:** These are 'near cash' and can usually be withdrawn on demand or at short notice.
- **Debtors:** Will typically be given 30 days to pay, but may pay sooner if required or if offered discounts. There is also the option to avail of factoring if cash is urgently required.
- **Closing stock:** It may take quite a long time to sell large amounts of stock, which may require huge discounting of prices. For this reason, the acid test ratio excludes

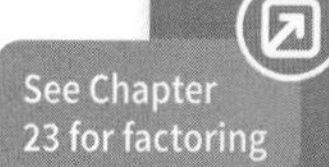

See Chapter 23 for factoring

the closing stock figure from the current assets and asks the question: If we have a lot of money tied up in stock, does the business still have enough short-term assets available to repay short-term debts?

Acid test = Current assets – Closing stock : Creditors falling due within one year (Current liabilities)

The 2022 acid test for Euro Ltd is therefore:

(€25,000 – €10,000) : €20,000
= 15,000 : 20,000
= 0.75 : 1

We get the answer by dividing both sides by the number on the right-hand side. So:
15,000/20,000 = 0.75 and
20,000/20,000 = 1
The answer expressed as a ratio is 0.75 : 1.

Euro Ltd acid test ratio (previous four years)

2018	2019	2020	2021
1.4 : 1	1 : 1	1.9 : 1	2.5 : 1
2022 INDUSTRY AVERAGE		2.3 : 1	

Commentary and evaluation

The ideal or benchmark figure for the acid test ratio is 1 : 1. Euro Ltd has achieved this target in each of the previous four years, but its 2022 figure of just 0.75 : 1 is below both the required level and the industry average. This result suggests that for every €1 it owes, Euro Ltd may only be able to raise 75c in the coming year. This sharp decline in liquidity is a worrying sign and shows that the business may have a large portion of its available cash tied up in stock. This can create liquidity problems if it needs to generate cash quickly.

KEY SKILLS BN MIT

30.9 Alpha, Beta and Gamma acid test ratio

(a) Use the information provided to calculate the acid test for each of the three businesses. Write down the formula and show all workings clearly. Comment on the results. #Calculate #Evaluate

Alpha Ltd		Beta Ltd		Gamma Ltd	
Current assets	€400,000	Current assets	€700,000	Current assets	€360,000
Closing stock	€150,000	Closing stock	€100,000	Closing stock	€200,000
Creditors falling due within 1 year	€200,000	Creditors falling due within 1 year	€400,000	Creditors falling due within 1 year	€900,000

(b) Complete question 10 in your Student Activity Book for more practice on this topic. #Activity

Gearing

Gearing focuses on the capital structure of the organisation. It compares the proportion of finance provided by debt capital to the proportion of finance provided by equity capital (or shareholders).

It asks the question: How much of the organisation's capital comes from borrowing and how much comes from shareholders?

Debt capital : Equity capital

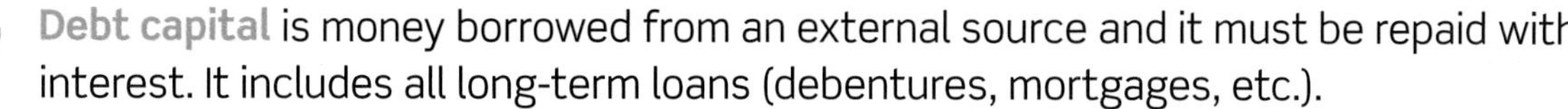

Debt capital is money borrowed from an external source and it must be repaid with interest. It includes all long-term loans (debentures, mortgages, etc.).

Equity capital is money received by selling shares. Equity capital is a cheap source of finance and does not have to be repaid. However, shareholders have a say in how the business is run and will expect to receive a share of the annual profits in the form of a dividend. Equity capital includes issued share capital and reserves.

If debt capital > equity, the organisation is highly geared.
If equity capital > debt capital, the organisation is lowly geared.

Low gearing is less risky since the organisation has less borrowing and is under less pressure to repay interest and debts.

High gearing has a greater level of risk because the organisation has more debt, which must be repaid with interest. During periods of slow growth, it may struggle to earn the levels of income required to meet these repayments.

Organisations that are highly geared may also find it more difficult to raise extra funding, since potential lenders and investors may be unwilling to loan money to a business that already has high levels of debt.

Euro Ltd's 2022 gearing position is as follows:

Debt capital		:	**Equity capital**	
Long-term loan	€24,000	:	Issued share capital	€150,000
			+ Reserves	€113,000
	= €24,000	:	€263,000	
	= 0.09	:	1	

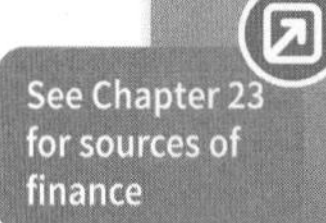

See Chapter 23 for sources of finance

We get the answer by dividing both sides by the number on the right-hand side. So:
24,000/263,000 = 0.09
263,000/263,000 = 1
The answer expressed as a ratio is 0.09 : 1.

Commentary and evaluation

In 2022, Euro Ltd is very lowly geared and most of its capital comes from equity. This means that the business has very little external debt and will not be under pressure to generate high levels of income to repay debt.

KEY SKILLS BN MIT

30.10 Alpha, Beta and Gamma gearing

Use the information provided to calculate the gearing for each of the three businesses. Write down the formula and show all workings clearly. Comment on the results. #Calculate #Evaluate

Alpha Ltd		Beta Ltd		Gamma Ltd	
Equity capital	€650,000	Equity capital	€400,000	Equity capital	€550,000
Debt capital	€350,000	Debt capital	€500,000	Debt capital	€250,000

KEY SKILLS BN MIT

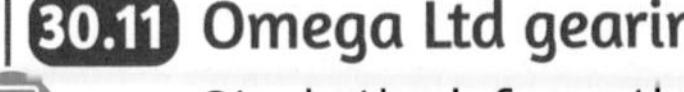

30.11 Omega Ltd gearing

Study the information extracted from the final accounts for Omega Ltd and answer the questions that follow.

Final accounts	2020	2021
Income statement (summary)	**€**	**€**
Sales	220,000	340,000
Gross profit	100,000	120,000
Net profit	75,000	105,000
Statement of financial position (summary)	**€**	**€**
Current assets (including closing stock)	380,000	570,000
Creditors falling due within 1 year (current liabilities)	190,000	400,000
Closing stock	60,000	85,000
Reserves	85,000	95,000
Issued share capital	320,000	340,000

(a) Calculate the gross profit percentage and the net profit percentage for 2020 and 2021. Show your workings. Comment on the trend.

(b) Calculate the acid test ratio for 2020 and 2021. Comment on the trend. #Calculate #Evaluate

Report writing

A **report** is a written document used to communicate information from which conclusions and recommendations can be drawn. Reports are quite structured and contain many common elements. They must be accurate, brief and clear, especially since they will be used as a basis for decision-making.

Having used ratio analysis to assess the financial performance of a business, it may be helpful to prepare a report to provide stakeholders with relevant information. Using this report template will ensure that you include all the information needed.

Report template

1. **Title:** A report on ...
2. **To:** For whom is the report written?
3. **From:** By whom is the report written?
4. **Date:** When was the report written/published?
5. **Terms of reference:** What is the report about? What was the writer asked to investigate?
6. **Introduction:** Introduces the topic and explains how the investigation was carried out.
7. **Main body of report:** Detailed analysis of the topic under investigation.
8. **Conclusions/recommendations:** What are the main findings and what action should now be taken?
9. **Signature of author:** The person who wrote the report should sign it.

CBA tip: You could use this type of report structure when presenting CBA material in written format. This would depend on your chosen topic and the type of material involved, but a report is one suitable written format.

Example: Report writing

Orla Power is a financial consultant. The directors of Euro Ltd have asked her to analyse and assess the financial performance of their company for the year 2022. They have specifically requested feedback on profitability and liquidity and have also asked Orla to present her findings in a written report.

Orla examined the final accounts of Euro Ltd (as shown throughout this chapter) and carried out a detailed ratio analysis of the figures. She has prepared the report shown in Figure 30.2 for the company directors, based on the template above.

1 **A Report on the Financial Performance of Euro Ltd in 2022**

2 **To:** The Directors of Euro Ltd

3 **From:** Orla Power, Financial Consultant

4 **Date:** 4 March 2023

5 **Terms of reference:** To analyse the final accounts of Euro Ltd and present a detailed assessment of its financial performance for the year ended 31/12/2022.

6 I have examined the final accounts of the company for 2022 and carried out a detailed ratio analysis. I have presented my main findings below under the following headings:

- Profitability
- Liquidity

7 **Profitability for 2022:**

- The gross profit percentage for the year is 49.1%.
- The net profit percentage for the year is 25.7%.
- The return on capital employed is 31.36%.

Comment: All these figures are very positive and represent an improvement in profitability levels since 2021. They are also above the industry average figures for profitability.

Liquidity for 2022:

- The working capital ratio for the year is: 1.25 : 1.
- The acid test ratio for the year is: 0.75 : 1.

Comment: There has been a worrying decline in liquidity since 2020. The liquidity figures are below the recommended minimum.

8 **Conclusions/recommendations**

The overall profitability position of the business is very strong. It continues to grow and is well ahead of rivals in the industry. Management should try to ensure that this positive trend is maintained, although they need to be careful about trying to grow the business too quickly, especially where they are buying and selling goods on credit. The worsening liquidity position highlighted by my analysis may suggest that current profitability levels are not sustainable.

I suggest that the business attempts to increase its level of cash sales, reduce its overall stock levels and make sure that it collects cash on time from debtors. All of these actions should help to improve liquidity in the year ahead.

9 **Signed:** Orla Power

Orla Power, Financial Consultant

Figure 30.2 Sample report on accounts

KEY SKILLS MIT BL

30.12 Liquidity

(a) What three things does Orla Power suggest that Euro Ltd should do to improve liquidity (cash flow)? #Identify

(b) How will each of these three things help to improve liquidity? #Evaluate

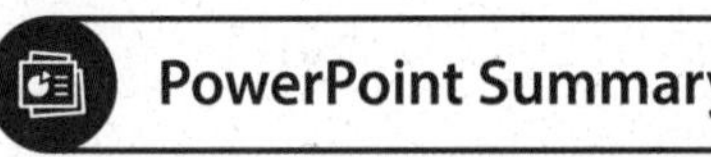

Weblinks

STRAND THREE
OUR ECONOMY

SCARCITY AND CHOICE

LEARNING OUTCOMES IN FOCUS

3.1 Explain how scarcity of economic resources results in individuals having to make choices; predict possible consequences of these choices

Links to 1.1, 1.2, 1.3, 1.6, 1.7, 1.9, 1.10, 2.2, 2.3, 3.2, 3.3, 3.6, 3.10, 3.11

LEARNING INTENTIONS FOR THIS CHAPTER

When you have completed this chapter you will be able to:

- Explain what economic resources are
- Identify and explain each of the factors of production
- Describe how individuals and organisations use each of the factors of production to create goods, services and wealth
- List the rewards associated with each factor of production
- Explain how scarcity, choice and opportunity cost impact on the production of goods and services.

CHAPTER 31 KEY TERMS

capital	needs
economic resources	opportunity cost
economics	rational choice
enterprise	scarcity
factors of production	supply
financial cost	utility
labour	wants
land	

CHAPTER 31 KEY SKILLS

- BC Being Creative
- BN Being Numerate
- C Communicating
- MIT Managing Information and Thinking

What is economics?

KEY TERM

Economics is a social science that studies how people with limited resources make choices in order to satisfy their needs and wants. These people include individuals, organisations and governments.

Economic resources are the factors or inputs used to produce and distribute goods, services and wealth.

There are two important points here:

1. Resources are **scarce** (limited in supply).
2. Scarce **resources must be used efficiently** in order to satisfy needs and wants.

When making choices about limited resources, we must distinguish between needs and wants.

Needs, wants and choices

All individuals have both needs and wants.

See Chapter 1 for resources, needs and wants

KEY TERM

A **need** is something we simply can't do without. It is essential for our survival or plays a very important part in our daily lives, for example food and clothing.

A **want** is something that we would really like to have. It may improve our quality of life but it is not essential, for example a mobile phone or a holiday.

Most people in Ireland have similar needs and wants for goods such as clothes, food, housing, furniture and electrical equipment and for services/service providers such as electricians, satellite TV and broadband. As consumers, we depend on different sectors of the economy to supply us with these goods and services.

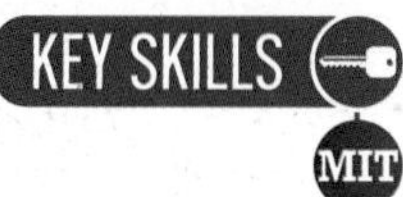
KEY SKILLS

31.1 Review and recall

(a) Distinguish between a good and a service. #Distinguish

(b) Suggest one example of a need and one example of a want for both a good and a service. #Suggest

KEY SKILLS

31.2 To each their own

(a) List one need and one want for each of the following.
- (i) A teenager in Ireland
- (ii) Your school
- (iii) Your local area
- (iv) A charity that helps homeless people
- (v) A start-up business #Identify #List

(b) What are the needs and wants of people living in the following?
- (i) A drought-stricken country
- (ii) A war-ravaged country #Identify #List

We all have a limited income (scarce financial resources) and don't have enough money to buy all the things we want, so we have to make choices. There are two costs involved when we buy goods and services: a financial cost and an opportunity cost.

The **financial cost** is the price of the item we choose to buy.

The **opportunity cost** is all the other things we could have spent our money on but can't buy now due to lack of money. When we decide to use our money for one particular purpose, we lose the chance (opportunity) to do something else with that money. For example, if you have €10 and choose to spend it on a T-shirt, you will not be able to use that money to buy phone credit. In this example, the financial cost of the T-shirt is €10 and the opportunity cost is the phone credit that you now cannot buy.

See Chapter 1 for financial and opportunity costs

Understanding this idea of opportunity cost is important for getting the best value out of our money.

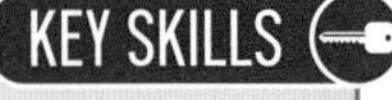

31.3 You can't always get what you want ...

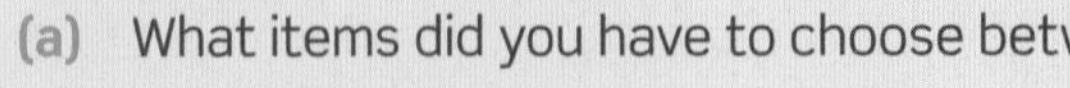

Think of a recent time when you didn't have enough money to buy everything you wanted and had to make a choice. #Reflect

(a) What items did you have to choose between?

(b) What was the opportunity cost?

(c) What was the financial cost?

(d) What influenced your final decision about which item to choose?

Businesses and governments have scarce resources too. This forces them to make choices between alternatives and also gives rise to opportunity costs. For example:

- A business wants to expand and has €100,000 retained profit. It must decide whether to hire more employees or invest in research and development.
- The Minister for Public Expenditure and Reform must decide whether to spend money on building a new national children's hospital in Dublin or a range of smaller healthcare projects and facilities across the country.

IN THE NEWS

Rising cost of national children's hospital a scandal in the making

When all the bills are paid four or five years from now, the price of the state's biggest construction project will probably come close to €2 billion. Throughout this period, there will be little money to build anything else in the health sector, unless the purse-strings are loosened further.

Source: Irish Times, 22 December 2018

IN THE NEWS

Individuals may be held accountable over cost of children's hospital

The knock-on effect of the overspending on the €1.43 billion project is causing concern among backbench TDs, who fear long-promised capital projects in their areas may be considerably delayed as a result.

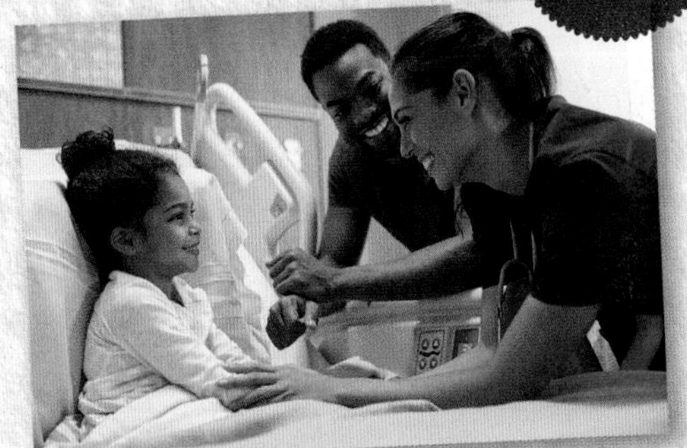

Government sources confirm they have not considered a list of projects to be delayed in order to divert resources to the children's hospital. The Cabinet is not expected to consider the issue until next week, but there is sure to be strong opposition to projects in other departments being delayed, Ministers say privately.

Source: Irish Times, 4 February 2019

Individuals, businesses and governments make rational choices when faced with scarce resources. A **rational choice** is one where the expected gains outweigh the expected losses.

When choosing between two or more alternatives, we will choose the one that will provide us with the greatest benefit or satisfaction from our limited resources. The economic term for this is **utility**. For example, you may decide that it is more useful to spend your money on a new phone rather than a new laptop. You have decided that the phone offers a higher level of utility than the laptop or any other alternative use for your money.

This is linked to the idea that consumers make rational choices. A rational decision is one that is based on reason or logic. For example, if you are shopping for a new phone, you will make the rational choice to buy from the shop that is selling the phone you want at the cheapest price. By making rational choices based on our understanding of usefulness (utility), we hope to gain the maximum value and benefit from our scarce resources.

See Chapter 12 for the wise consumer

The problems, of course, are that it is not always easy to work out which alternative offers the best utility and that people don't always make the most rational choices. For example, buying something on impulse may not involve any thoughts about usefulness or long-term benefit. This spur-of-the-moment decision may be an irrational choice and can have negative consequences in the long run, especially if you run short of money to pay essential bills.

See Chapter 3 for impulse buying

KEY SKILLS

MIT C BN

31.4 Government expenditure and where it goes

(a) Go to the Where Your Money Goes website and research how the government spent money in the most recent budget. Do you agree with the choices made? #Research

(b) Decide how you would allocate the money to make the best use of limited resources. Create a bar chart comparing your choices with the choices made by the government. Explain your decisions in a paragraph. #Justify #Presentation

(c) In a class discussion, debate the choices you have made. Would other classmates have made different choices? Why? #Discussion #Debate

Factors of production

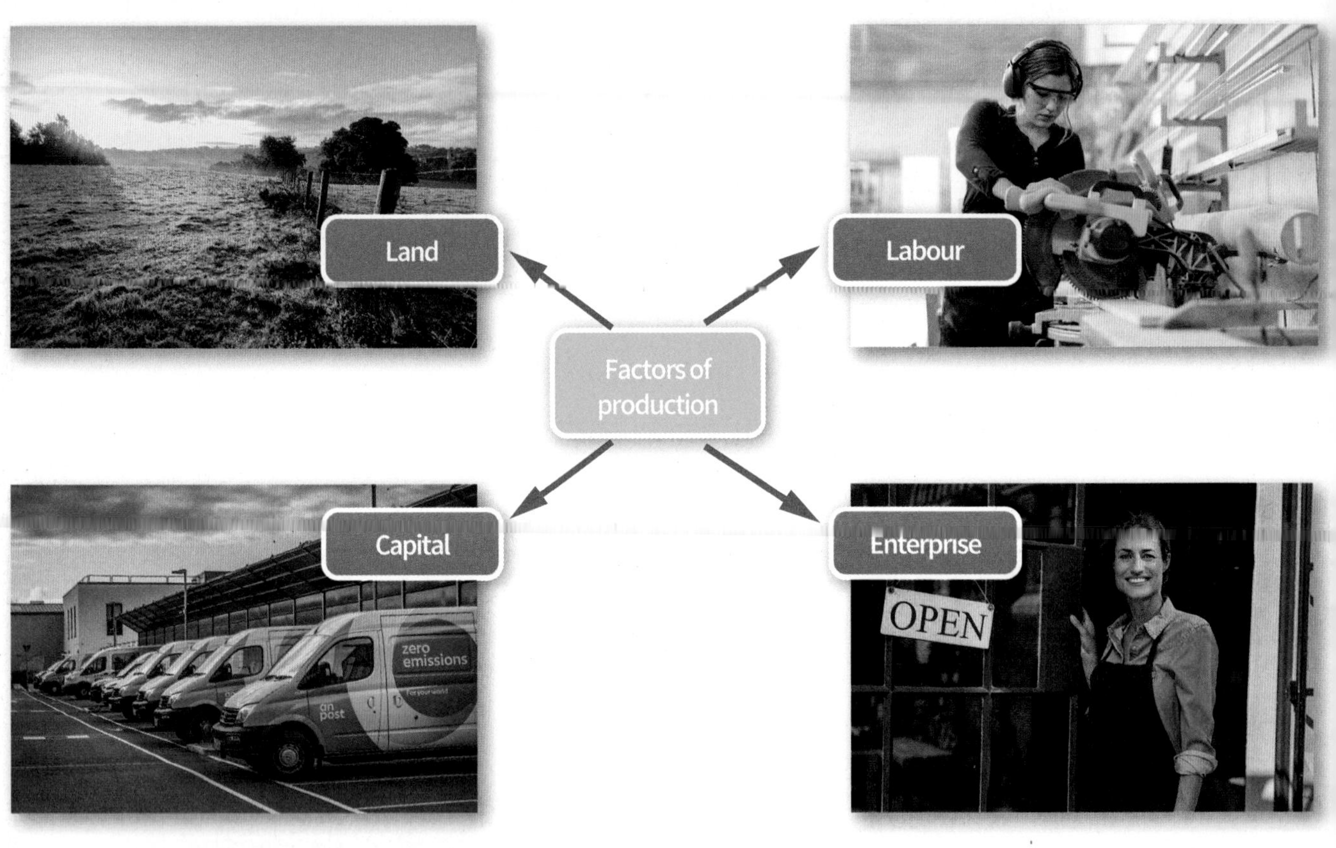

Figure 31.1 Factors of production

KEY TERM

The **factors of production** are the economic resources needed to produce goods and services.

These are the resources available to us. All goods and services are produced from a combination of these factors.

Factor	Description	Example	Reward
Land	Anything provided by nature and used to produce goods and services.	› Seas, rivers, fields, mines, forests, climate › Non-renewable resources are limited, e.g. oil, coal › Renewable resources include solar power, wind energy, water	Rent
Labour	The people involved in producing a good or service.	› Carpenters, farmers, factory workers, game developers, teachers, electricians	Wages
Capital	Physical items made by people and used in the production of goods or services.	› Buildings, machinery, vehicles, computers	Interest
Enterprise	Any attempt to start or do something new. Enterprise brings together land, labour and capital to produce a product or a service.	› Developing new and original products and services	Profit

Table 31.1 Factors of production

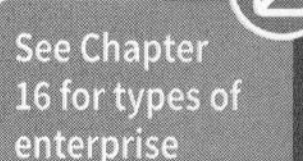

See Chapter 16 for types of enterprise

Every business needs to bring these four factors of production together to produce goods and services. For example, the factors of production for Ben & Jerry's ice cream will be:

Land	Cows that produce the milk used to make the ice cream graze on the land. Sugar beet and fruit are grown to make flavourings for the ice cream.
Labour	Ben & Jerry's employs people (production, marketing, etc.) to produce and sell ice cream.
Capital	Machinery and equipment are required to make the ice cream. Delivery vans are needed to deliver it to shops.
Enterprise	Ben Cohen and Jerry Greenfield founded the business by investing $12,000 and opening a shop in a former petrol station in Vermont, USA, in 1978 after they completed a course in ice cream making.

See Chapter 15 for enterprise

KEY SKILLS

MIT BC

31.5 How businesses use the factors of production

334

Choose an entrepreneur or business that you are familiar with. It may be local, national or international. Using the template in the Student Activity Book, show how the entrepreneur or business has used each factor of production to produce a good or service. Using the template, create a poster, infographic, presentation, podcast or video to present your results to your classmates.

#Research #Presentation

Scarcity

Economic resources have three things in common:

- They have value.
- They have alternative uses.
- They are scarce or limited in supply.

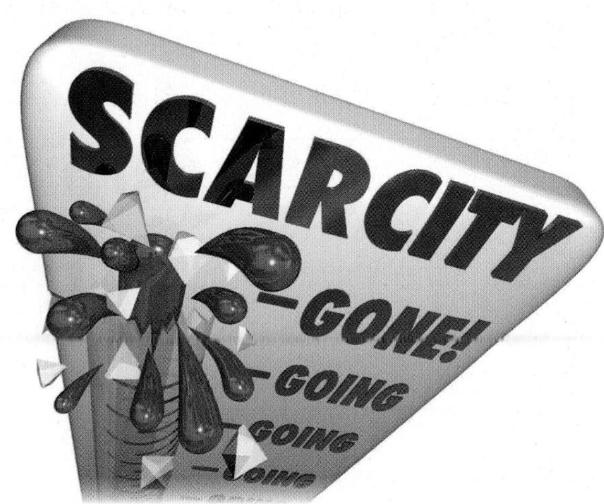

See Chapter 33 for supply

KEY TERM

Supply is the quantity of a resource that is available at a given time or price.

We do not have endless supplies of land, labour, capital or enterprise to meet the wants, or indeed the needs, of all people. As resources are scarce, choices must be made about:

- **What** will be produced
- **How** it will be produced
- **Where** it will be produced
- **Who** will receive the goods and services.

EXAM QUESTION

Junior Cycle 2019

Question 10

Copy the table into your copy and write in the missing terms.

Factors of Production	
1. ______	**2.** ______
3. ______	**4.** Enterprise

Weblinks PowerPoint Summary

DISTRIBUTION OF ECONOMIC RESOURCES

LEARNING OUTCOMES IN FOCUS

3.2 Explain how individuals, organisations (profit and not-for-profit) and the government work together to distribute economic resources used to produce goods and services

Links to 1.1, 1.2, 1.3, 1.4, 1.5, 2.1, 2.2, 2.10, 2.11, 2.12, 2.13, 3.1, 3.4, 3.5, 3.6, 3.9, 3.10

LEARNING INTENTIONS FOR THIS CHAPTER

When you have completed this chapter you will be able to:

- Distinguish between different economic systems
- Identify the benefits and problems associated with each of these economic systems
- Distinguish between the public sector, private sector and third sector
- Outline the role played by each of these sectors in the allocation and distribution of economic resources.

CHAPTER 32 KEY TERMS

- capitalism
- centrally planned economy
- circular flow of income
- economic resources
- economic system
- economy
- free market economy
- mixed economy
- private sector
- public sector
- public–private partnerships (PPP)
- third sector
- voluntary sector

CHAPTER 32 KEY SKILLS

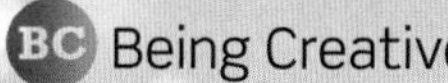

- BC Being Creative
- BL Being Literate
- C Communicating
- MIT Managing Information and Thinking
- WO Working with Others

What is an economy?

An **economy** refers to the way in which goods and services are made, sold and used in a country. The goal of an economy is to make the most effective use of available resources. This involves making choices about how best to maximise output and benefits while minimising costs.

Economic resources

In this chapter we will focus on the way in which individuals, organisations and the government work together to spread economic resources throughout the country in order to maximise outputs and minimise costs.

> **KEY TERM**
>
> **Economic resources** are the inputs that are used to create goods or provide services – in other words, land, labour, capital and enterprise (the factors of production).

Economic systems

Countries have to make the best use of their scarce resources. Choices have to be made about:

- ***What* will be produced:** This may depend on the supply of raw materials and demand for products. For example, concerns about the impact of fossil fuels and increased consumer demand have led many car manufacturers to increase their production of electric vehicles.
- ***How* it will be produced:** In the past most goods were produced by people, but goods are increasingly produced by machinery. For example, many car production lines use robotics and automation to carry out work previously done by humans.
- ***Where* it will be produced:** This is influenced by the availability of the factors of production, including raw materials and labour. For example, a mobile phone manufacturer may choose to make all its products in Asia because it is located close to important raw materials and because of the plentiful supply of cheap labour.
- ***Who* will receive the goods and services:** For example, will the goods or services be freely available to people or will they be sold to those who can afford to pay for them?

See Chapter 32 for distribution of economic resources

The amount of choice that individuals have depends on the economic system in the country.

> **KEY TERM**
>
> An **economic system** is the method that countries use to distribute economic resources and trade goods and services.

An economic system deals with the:

- Use of scarce resources
- Production of goods and services (economic outputs)
- Distribution of goods and services across the economy
- Role of the government and non-government sectors of the economy.

When we examine the different approaches to the distribution of economic resources, we will see that some countries rely heavily on the government (public sector), whereas others have less state involvement, so more goods and services are produced by the private sector.

> **KEY TERM**
>
> The **public sector** is the part of the economy that is owned and controlled by the government. It provides services to the public that may or may not be provided by the private sector. It consists of local and national government and state-owned organisations.

> **KEY TERM**
>
> The **private sector** refers to businesses owned by private individuals that produce and sell goods and services with the aim of making a profit.

There are a number of different economic systems. Each country must choose the one that is most suited to its economic needs, values and preferences.

The three main economic systems are:

- A centrally planned economy
- A free market economy
- A mixed economy.

Centrally planned economy

A **centrally planned (or command) economy** is one where the government has a lot of control over economic resources and decision-making.

Communism is the most extreme example of a centrally planned economy. Under this economic model, the state controls all the factors of production and makes all the decisions about what goods and services will be produced. This can lead to a lack of competition and choice when it comes to goods and services. For these reasons, this model is sometimes seen as inefficient. Some people also dislike the amount of control that the government has over people's lives, including access to healthcare, education, employment, media and the internet.

Havana, Cuba: a centrally planned economy

All organisations are owned by the government and private citizens have no involvement in business ownership. North Korea and Cuba are examples of centrally planned economies.

Washington, DC, USA: a free market economy

Free market economy

A **free market** (or **capitalist**) economy is one where private individuals control resources, own businesses and make all the decisions about what goods and services will be produced. Prices are decided by the level of demand from consumers and the willingness of businesses to supply goods and services. The USA is an example of a free market economy.

See Chapter 33 for demand and supply

Mixed economy

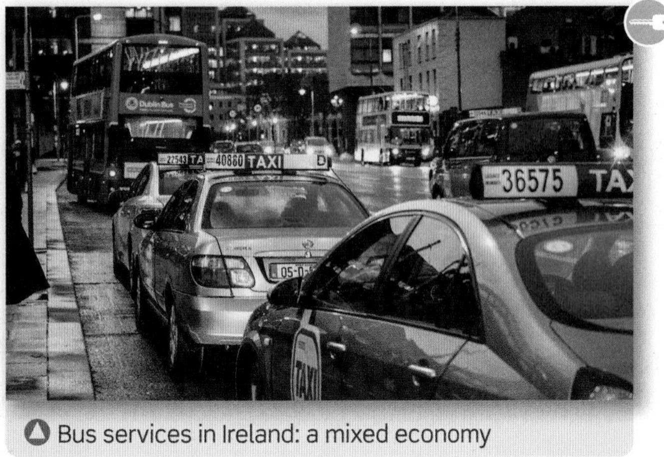

Bus services in Ireland: a mixed economy

A **mixed economy** is one that combines elements of the free market and centrally planned systems. It involves sharing the production of goods and services between government and private individuals. Ireland is an example of a mixed economy.

While most goods and services are produced by private businesses, there is still a lot of government involvement in services such as security, health, transport and education. For example, if a consumer wants to travel in Dublin, they can take a Dublin Bus (public sector) or a taxi (private sector).

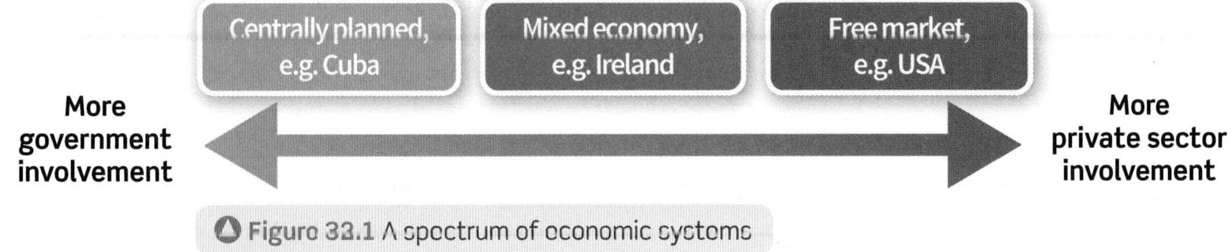

Figure 33.1 A spectrum of economic systems

Centrally planned and free market systems are at opposite ends of the economic spectrum. A mixed economy, which has elements of both of these systems, lies somewhere in the middle.

In reality, there are no examples of purely free market or centrally planned economies in the world today – every country lies somewhere between these two extremes.

Countries that have 'big government' involvement are socialist in nature. This means there is a belief that the production, distribution and exchange of goods, services and resources should be owned or controlled by the community as a whole. Examples include China, Denmark and Sweden. These economies typically have:

- High personal taxation
- A high level of state services
- A more equal distribution of wealth and resources.

As we move towards the free market end of the spectrum, the level of government involvement decreases. Examples of countries that operate this type of economic system include the USA, Hong Kong and Singapore. These economies typically have:

- Lower levels of taxation
- Lower levels of public services
- A less equal distribution of wealth and economic resources
- A huge income gap between the rich and the poor in society.

See Chapter 31 for scarcity and choice

As discussed in Chapter 31, the choices that people make about how best to manage and distribute scarce economic resources are based on their preferences and their estimation of utility. Some economies choose to rely heavily on the public sector, whereas others choose to rely on the private sector. There is no 'right' or 'wrong' way, but each has its own advantages, disadvantages and consequences.

KEY SKILLS

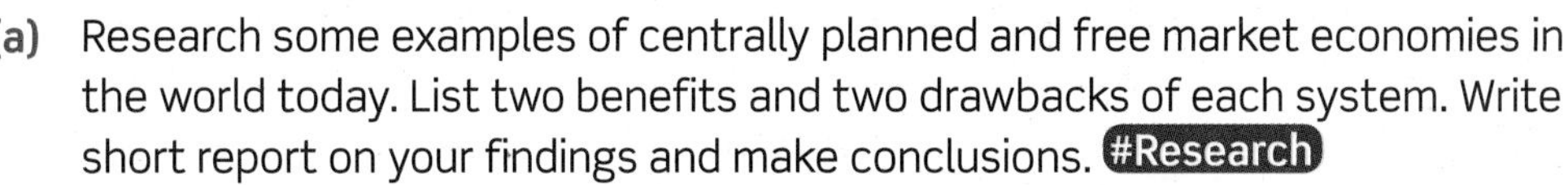

32.1 Economic systems around the world: Pros and cons

(a) Research some examples of centrally planned and free market economies in the world today. List two benefits and two drawbacks of each system. Write a short report on your findings and make conclusions. #Research

(b) With a partner, discuss which economic system you think is best. Justify your answer with examples. #Discussion #Debate

Sectors of the economy

In Ireland, goods and services are produced and distributed through three sectors:

- **Public sector:** The part of the economy that is owned and controlled by the government.
- **Private sector:** Businesses owned by individuals that produce and sell goods and services with the aim of making a profit.
- **Third sector/voluntary sector:** Social enterprises and not-for-profit organisations such as charities and voluntary organisations.

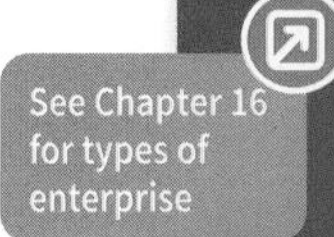

See Chapter 16 for types of enterprise

Public sector

The public sector is made up of local and national government and state-owned organisations.

Local government

Ireland has 31 local authorities (city and county councils), which provide a range of public services locally. Local authorities promote the interests of the local community and help to distribute economic resources through the services they provide. These include:

- Housing
- Planning services
- Road maintenance
- Fire services
- Pollution control
- Local environment protection
- Facilities and services to support the arts, culture, sports, leisure, libraries and recreation.

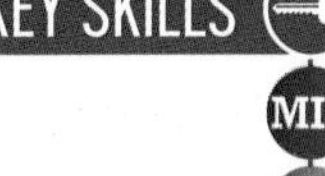

KEY SKILLS

32.2 Local authorities

(a) What is the name of your local authority? #Research

(b) Create a poster with the title 'Know Your Local Authority' to explain how it serves the community. #Create #Explain

National government

Government departments help to distribute economic resources by providing a range of services. Table 32.1 lists some examples.

Government department	Services provided
Department of Health	Hospitals, treatment, surgeries, healthcare
Department of Education and Skills	Education and training, schools, state examinations
Department of Agriculture, Food and the Marine	Support services to agriculture, fisheries, food and forestry
Department of Culture, Heritage and the Gaeltacht	Responsible for the protection and presentation of Ireland's heritage and cultural assets, advancing the use of the Irish language and supporting the development of the islands
Department of Communications, Climate Action and Environment	Responsible for the telecommunications and broadcasting sectors and regulates, protects and develops Ireland's natural resources

Table 32.1 Government departments and what they do

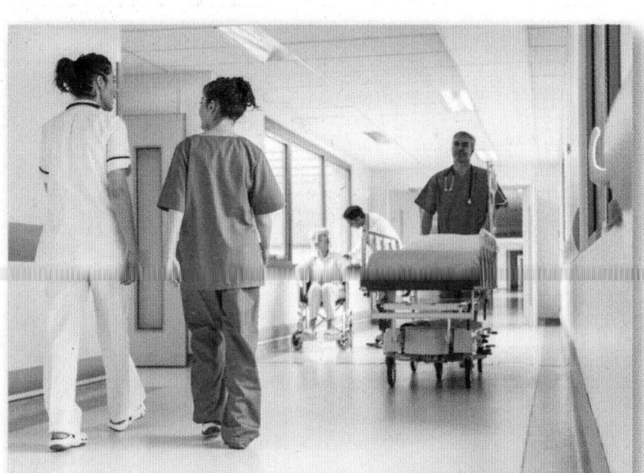

KEY SKILLS

32.3 Government departments and the services they provide

Go to the government's website (www.gov.ie) and research the services provided by the other government departments. Search for 'List of Government Departments'. Create a poster showing all the government departments and the services they provide, using Table 32.1 as a template. #Research

BC BL C MIT

State-owned organisations

State-owned organisations are set up by the government. There are two categories:

- **Commercial:** These charge for their product or service.
- **Non-commercial:** These provide services free of charge that are seen as necessary to develop the country.

Table 32.2 lists some examples of commercial and non-commercial state-owned organisations.

Commercial state-owned organisations		
Transport	Bus Éireann Irish Rail	Dublin Bus Dublin Airport Authority
Entertainment	RTÉ	
Communications	An Post	
Energy	Electric Ireland Ervia	
Natural resources	Coillte Bord na Móna	
Non-commercial state-owned organisations		
Regulation	Environmental Protection Agency Health and Safety Authority	
Marketing	Fáilte Ireland Bord Iascaigh Mhara Bord Bia	
Business development	Enterprise Ireland Local Enterprise Offices IDA Ireland	

Table 32.2 Some commercial and non-commercial state-owned organisations

Private sector

The private sector includes businesses owned by individuals that produce and sell goods and services with the aim of making a profit.

Business	Sector
Musgrave	Retail
Supermac's	Fast food
River Island	Retail
Aviva	Insurance
CRH	Building materials
Allergan Inc.	Pharmaceuticals
Penneys	Retail
Applegreen	Energy
Glanbia	Food

Table 32.3 Examples of private sector businesses

KEY SKILLS

BC

32.4 Private sector businesses

Create a poster showing the names and logos of 10 private sector businesses. Make sure you include local and national examples. #Illustrate #Create

Public-private partnerships

Sometimes the government (public sector) works with private sector enterprises to provide important services or infrastructure. This co-operative approach to resource distribution is called a **public-private partnership (PPP)**. Examples include private sector enterprises designing, building and operating infrastructural projects including motorways, schools and water treatment plants.

Third sector/voluntary sector

See Chapter 16 for types of enterprise

The third sector consists of social enterprises and not-for-profit organisations such as charities and voluntary organisations. Examples include Foróige, the Rehab Group and Pavee Point. These not-for-profit, citizen-based groups that operate independently of government are often referred to as non-governmental organisations (NGOs).

Not-for-profit organisations

See Chapter 18 for volunteerism

Charities are set up to benefit others by raising money, for example through collections, events or charity shops. They depend largely on volunteers.

The aims of charities depend on the cause for which they were established, but they include relieving poverty, helping vulnerable people and providing funding for animal welfare and medical research. Table 32.4 lists some examples of national charities.

Charity	Aim
Oxfam Ireland	To reduce poverty
ISPCA (Irish Society for the Prevention of Cruelty to Animals)	To prevent cruelty to animals, promote animal welfare and proactively relieve animal suffering
Focus Ireland	To support people across Ireland who are homeless or at risk of losing their homes
Irish Cancer Society	Provides free nationwide services for cancer patients and their families; funds innovative cancer research to find better ways of diagnosing and treating cancer; and advocates for cancer patients at a public policy level

Table 32.4 Examples of national charities

KEY SKILLS

32.5 Your local charities

In pairs or small groups, research a charity local to you and identify:

- Who they support
- What services they provide
- How they raise money.

Present your findings as a poster or presentation and display it for the rest of the class.

#Research #Presentation

MIT C BC WO BL

Voluntary organisations

Voluntary organisations provide services for their members. They raise finance by charging a membership fee and sometimes by organising fundraisers. They are managed and run by an elected committee, with help from volunteers. Examples include golf clubs, GAA clubs and tennis clubs.

KEY SKILLS

32.6 Clubs in your area

(a) In small groups, research local clubs.

(b) Create a map of your local area and indicate where each club is located.

(c) Create a poster with a brief outline of local clubs that can be used to inform people who move to your area.

#Research #Create

MIT C BC WO BL

Social enterprises

Social enterprises, unlike private sector businesses, have a social or environmental aim. While they are run in a businesslike way, they aim to make a profit to benefit a specific cause rather than the owners.

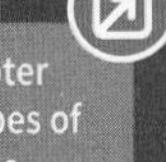
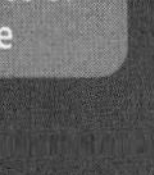

See Chapter 16 for types of enterprise

KEY SKILLS

32.7 Third sector organisations

The following are examples of third sector organisations:

- DSPCA
- Irish Cancer Society
- ISPCC
- Jack and Jill Foundation
- GAA.

Select one of these organisations or a local example that you know of. Write a short report on your chosen organisation under the following headings:

- History of the organisation
- Aims and objectives
- Sources of finance
- Services provided. #Research

MIT BL C

The circular flow of income

The **circular flow of income** shows how economic resources and wealth move through an economy. It shows how individuals, organisations and the government work together to distribute the economic resources used to produce goods and services.

In a simple economy, households provide businesses with the factors of production (land, labour, capital and enterprise). In return for these resources, businesses pay households a reward. This flow of resources and rewards between households and businesses is illustrated in Figure 32.2.

Businesses use these factors to produce goods and services, which they sell to households.

Households in turn spend money on the goods and services produced by firms. This money is then used by firms to pay households for their work.

This process repeats itself and creates a circular flow of income in the economy.

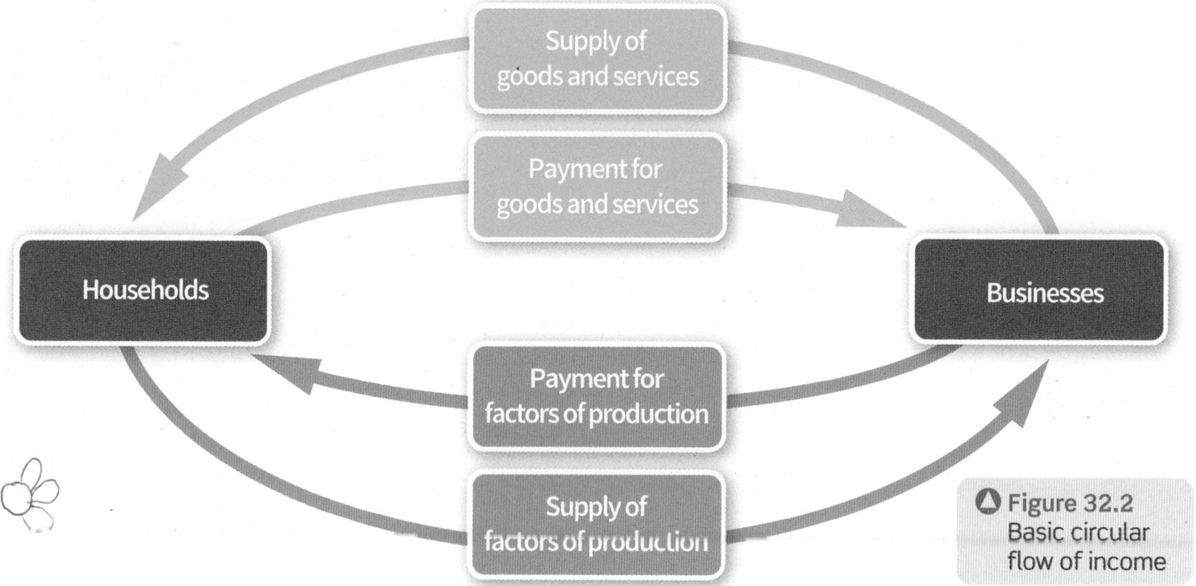

Figure 32.2 Basic circular flow of income

In reality, not all economic resources and income flow directly between households and businesses. Where households do not spend all their income, savings create a leak from the circular flow. Banks can lend this money, which is then injected back into the economy. Similarly, some income leaks from the circular flow as households and businesses pay taxes to government. In most economies, this money is returned to the circular flow through government spending. We will take a more detailed look at the role played by the government in income redistribution in Chapter 35.

See Chapter 35 for government revenue and expenditure

In an open economy like Ireland, which is heavily involved in international trade, imports and exports also impact on the circular flow of income. Money spent on imports is a leakage from the circular flow, while revenue generated by exports injects money back into the economy. We will take a more detailed look at the role and impact of international trade in Chapter 39.

See Chapter 39 for international trade

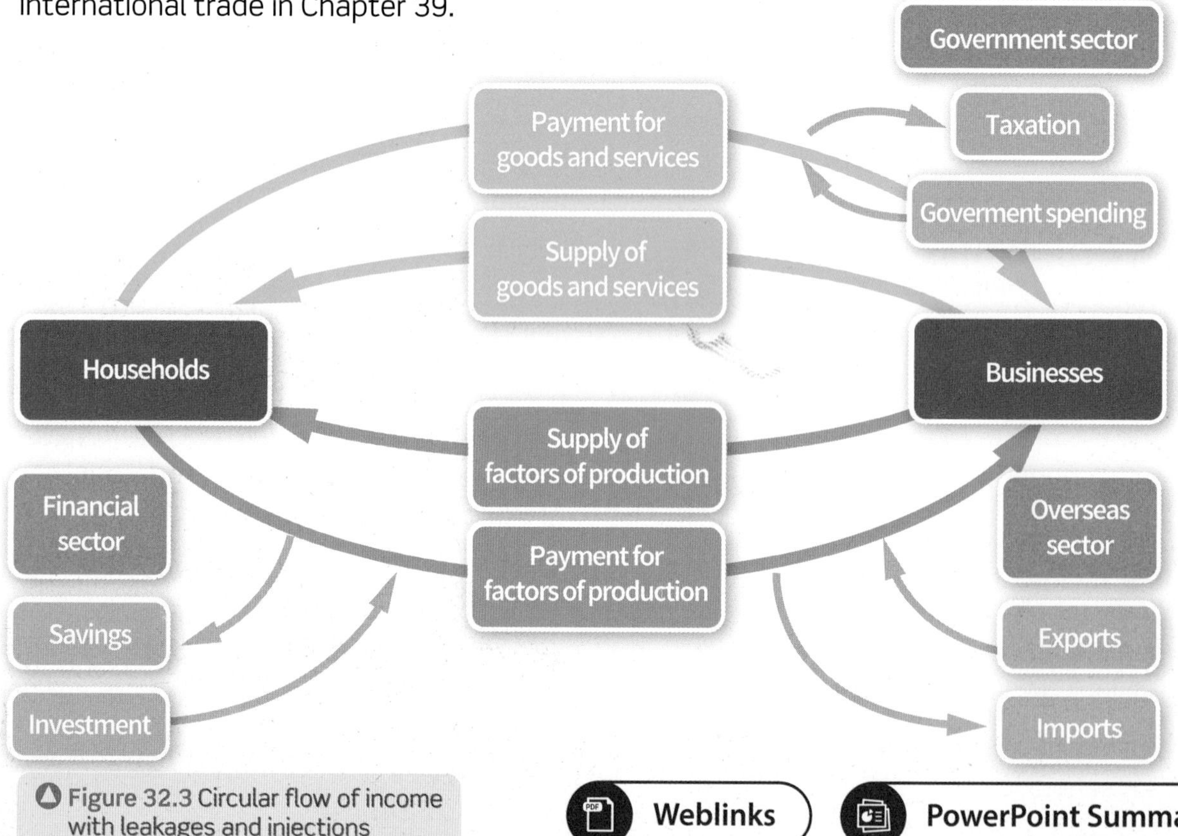

Figure 32.3 Circular flow of income with leakages and injections

Weblinks

PowerPoint Summary

DEMAND AND SUPPLY

LEARNING OUTCOMES IN FOCUS

3.3 Evaluate how changes in the supply and demand of goods and services in different markets can affect prices

Links to 1.4, 1.9, 2.7, 2.8, 2.9, 3.1, 3.5, 3.6, 3.7, 3.8, 3.10, 3.11

LEARNING INTENTIONS FOR THIS CHAPTER

When you have completed this chapter you will be able to:

- Explain what a market is and illustrate examples of markets commonly found in Ireland
- Explain what is meant by 'demand'
- Outline the relationship between the level of demand for a good or service and its price
- List factors, other than price, that impact on the demand for goods and services
- Distinguish between normal and inferior goods
- Explain what is meant by 'supply'
- Outline the relationship between the level of supply of a good or service and its price
- List factors, other than price, that impact on the supply of goods and services
- Understand and illustrate the concept of market equilibrium
- Evaluate how changes in the supply and demand of goods and services in different markets can affect prices.

CHAPTER 33 KEY TERMS

complementary goods	market equilibrium
demand	normal goods
demand curve	price
demand schedule	quota
effective demand	substitute goods
equilibrium	supply
inferior goods	supply curve
market	

CHAPTER 33 KEY SKILLS

- BL Being Literate
- BN Being Numerate
- C Communicating
- MIT Managing Information and Thinking
- WO Working with Others

What is a market?

KEY TERM

A **market** is a place where buyers and sellers connect with each other in order to trade or exchange goods and services.

Most markets are actual locations where buyers and sellers meet face to face and exchange goods and services (for example, supermarkets and farmers markets). These are **final markets**, where finished goods and services are bought and sold.

Other markets include:

- **Factor markets:** Where the factors of production are bought and sold. This includes the property market (land), labour market (labour), money market (capital) and stock market (where company shares are bought and sold).
- **Commodities markets:** Where raw materials used in the production of goods and services are bought and sold, for example agricultural products (wheat, barley, etc.), energies (oil, gas, etc.) and metals (gold, silver, copper, etc.).

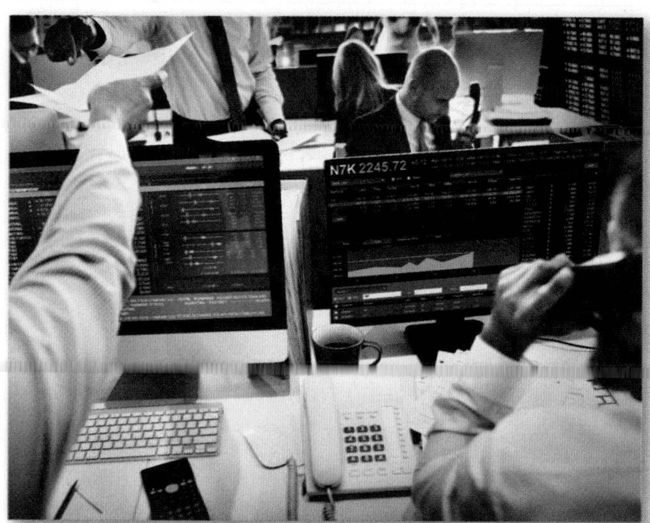

Some of these markets, for example the property and labour markets, are not located in an actual place, but the existence of buyers and sellers creates the conditions for a market to exist.

Buyers, as consumers, create demand for goods and services. Sellers try to meet this consumer demand by supplying the goods and services required.

In this chapter we will analyse how the interaction between buyers and sellers impacts on market prices.

Demand

KEY TERM

Demand refers to the quantity of a product that buyers are willing to purchase at a given price.

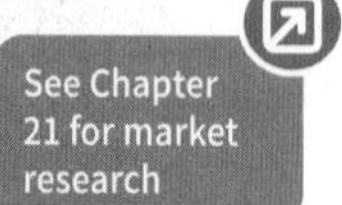
See Chapter 21 for market research

We have seen how businesses carry out market research to gather information about the market for their goods and services. As part of that research, they try to find out how much of a particular product customers are willing to buy. They also try to discover how much customers are willing to pay for the product. This type of research helps a business to establish the level of demand for their goods and services.

Effective demand is a willingness to buy, backed up by an ability to pay. Effective demand is real or actual demand. For example, you might say that you would be willing to buy the latest iPhone, but if you don't have the money to buy it, you don't have effective demand for that product.

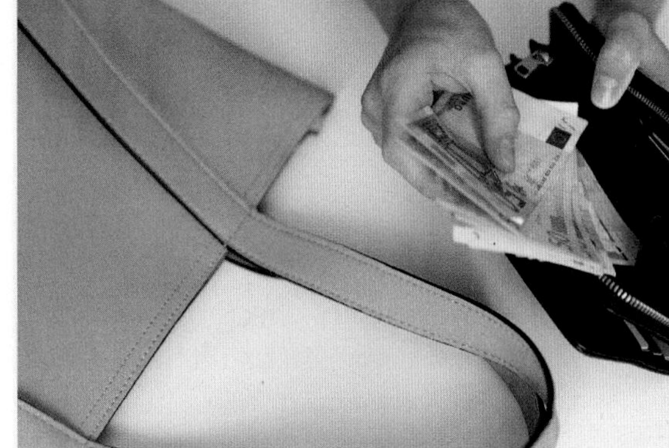

Consumer behaviour

When looking at consumer demand, economists make the following assumptions about consumer behaviour.

See Chapter 12 for consumers

Assumption	Example
Consumers are **rational**, which means that they will choose the cheaper option if offered two similar goods at different prices.	If the same mobile phone is available at different prices in two shops, you will choose to buy it from the shop with the lower price. This is the rational (sensible) thing to do.
Consumers have to make **choices** to get the best use out of their limited resources.	If you don't have enough money to meet all your needs and wants, you will have to choose between them.
Consumers will try to get as much benefit or satisfaction (known as **utility** in economics) as possible from their limited resources.	When choosing between alternatives, you will try to work out which one is most useful to you at this point in time. You may decide that it is more useful for you to spend your money on a new laptop rather than a new mobile phone.
The benefit or satisfaction (utility) that a consumer receives from consuming a good or service decreases over time. This is known as the **law of diminishing marginal utility**.	You will enjoy one bar of chocolate and perhaps two, but the more chocolate you consume, the less you will enjoy each extra bar. This means that you may be willing to spend your money on two or three bars of chocolate, but after that point you may decide that there is more benefit (utility) to be had from spending your money on something else.

See Chapter 31 for needs, wants and choices

Demand for a product is rarely fixed and will tend to change over time.

33.1 Law of diminishing marginal utility

Retailers often offer price discounts to consumers who are willing to buy multiples of the same product, for example buy one, get a second one half price; or three for the price of two. Explain how the law of diminishing marginal utility might influence this decision by retailers. #Explain #Decide #Reflect

KEY SKILLS MIT C

33.2 Demand and trends

Think of products that were strongly in demand a few years ago, but for which there is very little demand nowadays. What do you think caused the level of demand for these products to change? #Consider #Recall #Think

KEY SKILLS MIT BL C

33.3 Seasonal trends

Identify products or services for which the level of demand is seasonal (demand varies depending on the time of year). Does the price of these goods vary at different times of the year? Explain your answer with relevant examples. #Illustrate #Explain

Relationship between demand and price

Many factors influence the level of demand for a product, but its price is the most important factor.

Price refers to the amount of money expected or paid for a product or service. For most normal goods and services:

- When price is reduced, demand will increase.
- When price increases, demand will fall.

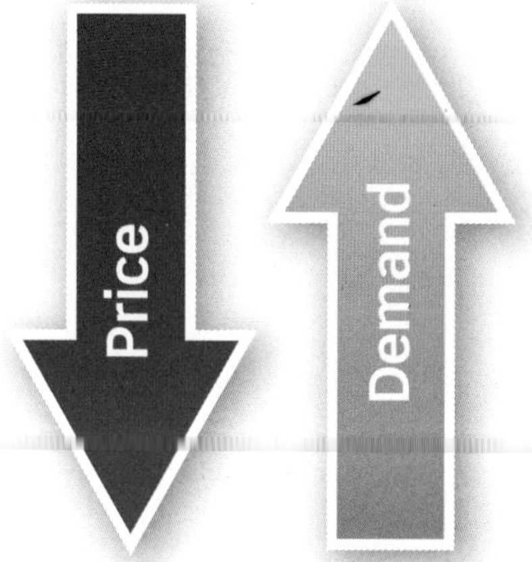

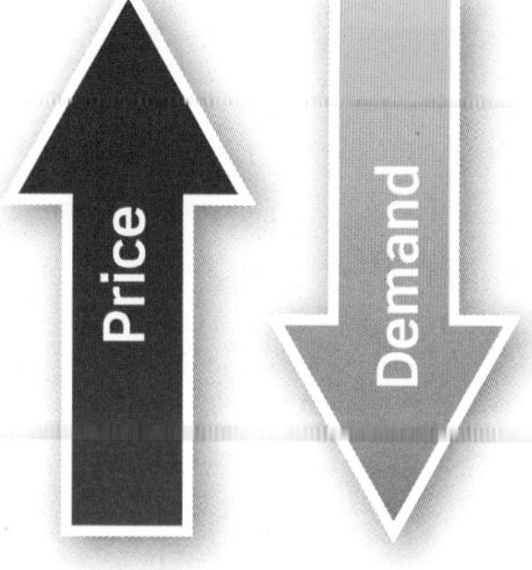

Figure 33.1 The relationship between demand and price

In general, lower prices will increase demand for a product. This is because a lower price makes the product more attractive and affordable for buyers. For example, if a customer goes to a shop to buy some oranges, the lower the price is, the more they will tend to buy – maybe two kilograms instead of one.

The opposite is also true: higher prices tend to reduce demand for a product. When the price increases, buyers may choose to stop buying a product entirely or they may switch to buying an alternative product instead. If the price of oranges increases, consumers may decide they are poor value for money and may decide to spend their money on apples or grapes instead.

There are many real-world examples that illustrate this relationship between demand and price:

- Elite professional sports stars are in great demand and command the highest prices (transfer fees) and wage levels.

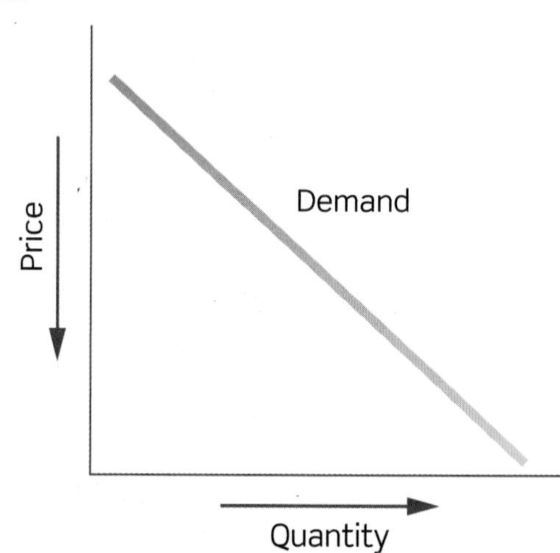

Figure 33.2 The law of demand: the lower the price, the higher the quantity demanded

- In the housing market, increased demand for family homes in some areas has caused house prices to rise.
- Ticket prices for very popular sporting and music events will be higher than less popular ones, which reflects the expected level of demand.

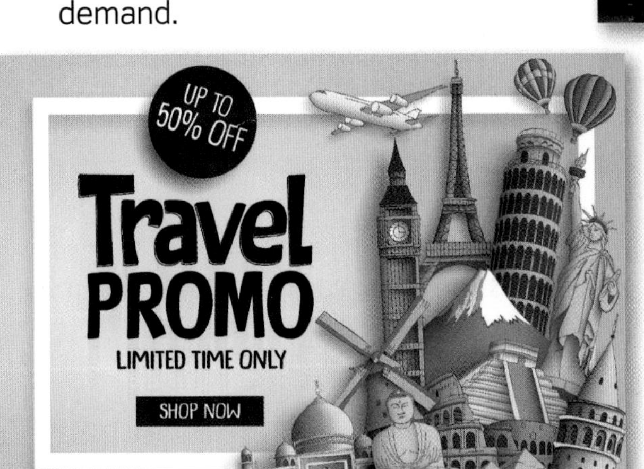

- Hotel and flight prices generally increase during school holidays, as this is a peak season for family holidays or travel. In the winter, many hotels offer reduced-price 'special offers' to create extra demand during the off season.

These examples illustrate that an increase in demand causes prices to rise in the market, while a decrease in demand causes prices to fall.

Demand schedule

A **demand schedule** shows the number of goods demanded by customers at different price levels.

Table 33.1 shows a demand schedule for a mobile phone, the Sonix424. It shows the number of phones that customers would buy per week at various prices.

Price	Quantity demanded
€50	200
€100	160
€150	120
€200	80

Table 33.1 Demand schedule for the Sonix424

The demand schedule indicates that a price increase from €50 to €100 will see a fall in the number of mobile phones demanded per week (from 200 units to 160 units). If the price is set at €200 per phone, there will only be market demand for 80 phones.

When prices rise, demand will fall because some consumers may no longer be able to afford the phone or may think it is no longer good value for money. If this happens, consumers may decide to buy another brand of phone. This is known as a **substitute good**.

If the price of the phone is reduced, demand will rise because more consumers can afford the item or consider it to be better value for money at the new lower price.

Demand curve

We can use the information from the demand schedule to plot a demand curve for the Sonix424 mobile phone (see Figure 33.3).

> **KEY TERM**
>
> A **demand curve** is a graph that illustrates the expected demand for a product at various price levels.

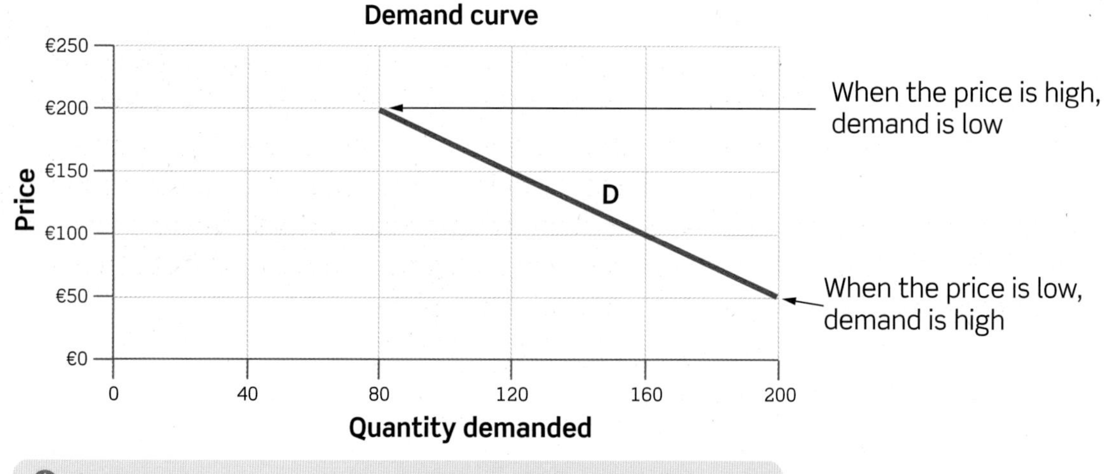

Figure 33.3 Demand curve for a Sonix424 mobile phone

When drawing a demand curve, the horizontal (x) axis shows the number of products demanded at a given price, while the vertical (y) axis shows the various prices that may be charged.

Figure 33.3 shows that the demand curve slopes downwards and that a smaller quantity is demanded at higher prices, whereas demand increases when the price is reduced.

Figure 33.4 shows that price changes cause movements along a demand curve. Movement along a demand curve means that a change in price will cause the quantity demanded to move from one point on the demand curve to another.

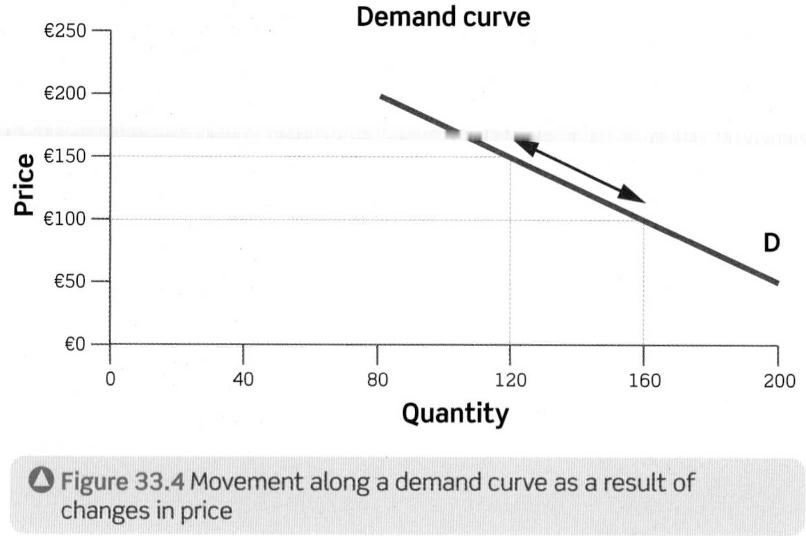

Figure 33.4 Movement along a demand curve as a result of changes in price

Under normal market conditions, a business cannot control both price and demand. For example, if the price of the Sonix424 mobile is set at €150, the level of demand is decided by consumers. As we have seen, they will reduce their demand for the product at higher prices.

KEY SKILLS

MIT BN

33.4 Making smart pricing choices

Will a retailer of Sonix424 mobile phones have a higher level of sales revenue with a selling price of €50 or €100? Explain your answer. #Calculate #Explain

Note: Sales revenue is calculated by: Number of phones sold × Selling price per phone.

Other factors affecting demand

Demand for a product can be affected by other factors apart from price. A change in these factors will cause the demand curve to shift (move) left or right. This means we will need to draw a new demand curve, either to the right or left of the original one (see Figure 33.5). An improvement in demand conditions will cause the demand curve to shift to the right (D2).This is because at every price, consumers will demand more. A negative change in demand conditions will cause the demand curve to shift to the left (D1), which shows that less will be demanded at every price.

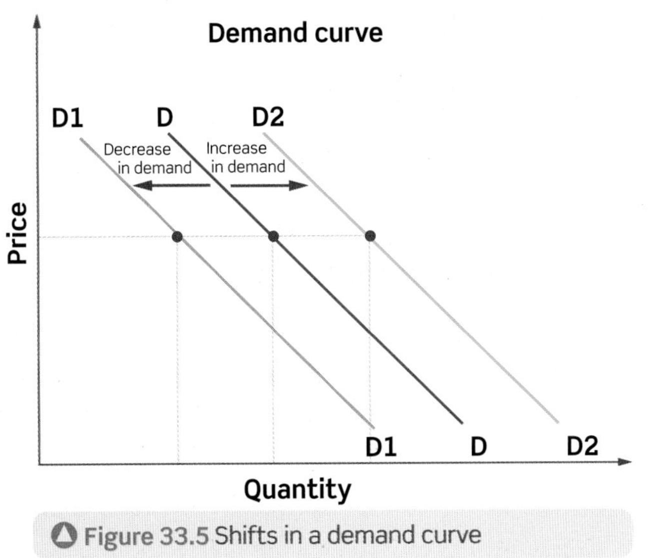

Figure 33.5 Shifts in a demand curve

The following factors will cause a shift in the demand curve for a product.

❶ *Price of substitute products*

A substitute good is one that can be used instead of another good. Different brands of the same type of product, such as mobile phones, can be substituted for each other. In some cases consumers may also replace one product with another similar product even though it may not be exactly the same, for example replacing tea with coffee or one brand of cola with another.

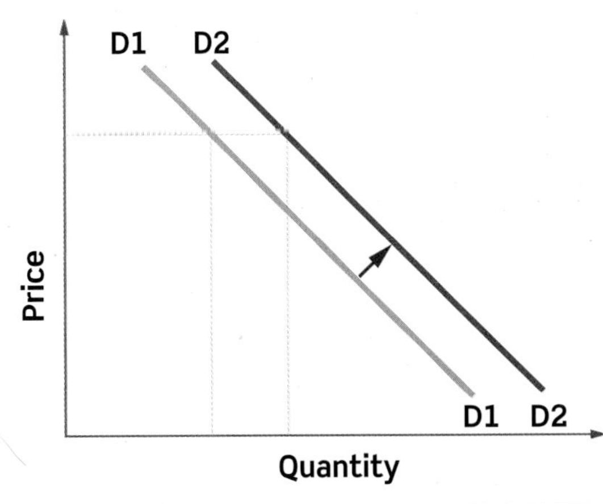

Figure 33.6 There is a shift in demand for one product (Coca-Cola) when the price of a substitute product (Pepsi) increases

If the price of substitute products is reduced, consumers will demand more of the substitute, which may reduce demand for other products.

A price reduction for the substitute product (coffee) may cause demand for tea to fall as people switch to the cheaper alternative. Likewise, a price increase for Pepsi is likely to lead to an increase in demand for a substitute product such as Coke.

❷ *Price of complementary goods*

A **complementary good** is a product that is used with another product. In some cases consumers need to buy both products, for example printers and ink cartridges. A change in demand for one will impact on demand for the other. For example, if the price of printers increases, demand for printers will fall (the law of demand). This will in turn lead to a reduced level of demand for printer ink.

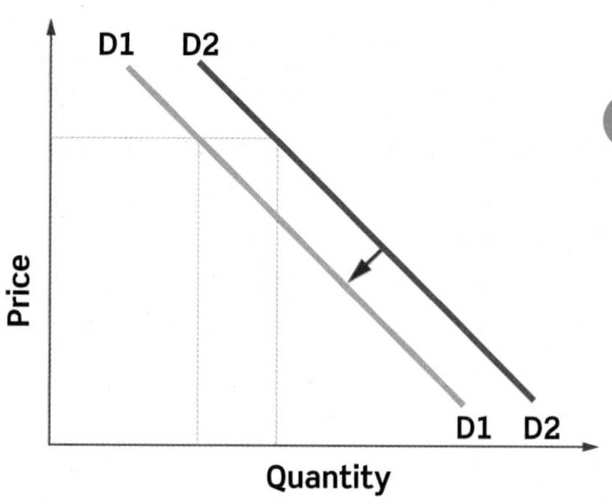

Figure 33.7 There is a shift in demand for printer ink when the price of printers increases

KEY SKILLS

MIT

33.5 Examples of substitute and complementary products

Outline your understanding of the terms 'substitute goods' and 'complementary goods' by giving one example of a substitute product and one example of a complementary product for each of the following goods and services:

- A Zanussi dishwasher
- Nescafé coffee
- Potatoes
- A train ticket to Galway
- A Sony PlayStation

#Outline #Illustrate #Connect

❸ *Fads and fashions*

As consumer tastes change, demand for products will also change. Fashionable goods or brands will see a sharp increase in demand, while those that are unfashionable will experience reduced levels of demand. For example, demand for music downloads and online movie streaming has increased, while demand for CDs and DVDs has declined.

❹ *Advertising*

Products that are heavily advertised may see an increase in demand, especially in the short to medium term, as consumers want to try the product. Examples include new magazines, games and toys.

❺ *Changes in population or market size*

An increase in the birth rate will lead to increased demand for baby products. Similarly, population trends can also impact on demand for housing and public services. For example, the demand for school places in your local area may have increased or decreased recently in line with population changes.

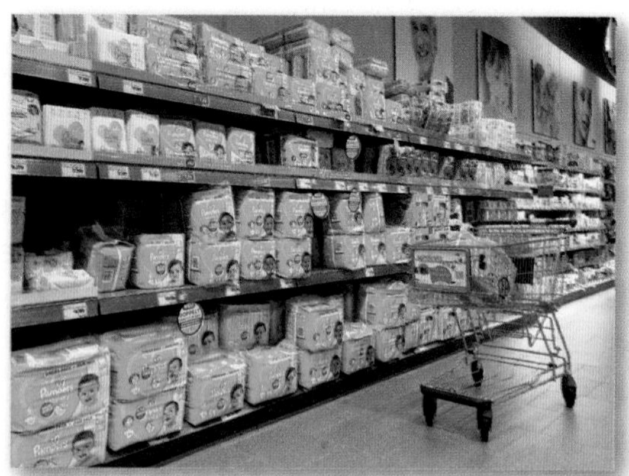

❻ *Seasonal factors*

Demand for some products changes depending on the time of year. Obvious examples include chocolate products at Christmas and Easter, ski clothing in winter and ice cream in summer.

7 Price expectations of buyers

If buyers expect prices to increase in the future, they may increase current demand to try to beat the price rise. On the other hand, if buyers expect prices to fall in the future, they may delay their purchase in order to avail of lower prices. This will reduce current demand. This often happens in the property market.

8 Income levels

Most goods are normal goods because if a person's income increases, they will be able to buy more expensive goods and services. For example, they may choose to buy more expensive cuts of meat, more premium-brand clothing or a more expensive car.

KEY TERM

A **normal good** is one that will be in greater demand when the buyer's income rises.

An **inferior good** is one for which there will be less demand when the buyer's income rises.

With inferior goods, demand falls when income rises. Cheaper cuts of meat and own-brand products are examples of inferior goods, as consumers tend to demand less of them when their income increases. For many consumers, buying generic or own-brand goods is a sensible choice when income levels decline and is in keeping with the guidelines for effective household budgeting.

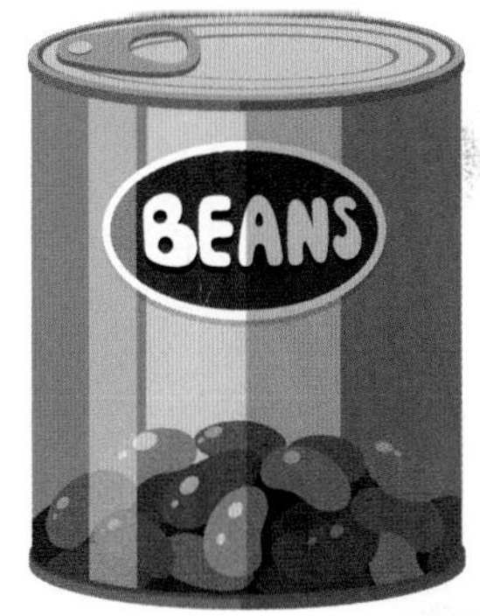

The term 'inferior' does not refer to the quality of the goods, but rather reflects the affordability of the goods. It is an economic term that indicates that these goods will experience a drop in demand when income increases.

See Chapter 4 for household budgets

33.6 Normal or inferior goods?

In pairs, discuss the following list of goods and services. Decide which are examples of normal goods and which are examples of inferior goods. #Decide #Justify

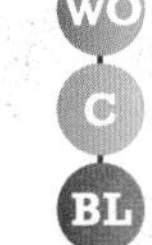

- Instant noodles
- Diamonds
- Gym memberships
- Smart TVs
- Potatoes
- Generic (unbranded) headphones
- BMW cars
- Public transport
- Own-brand bacon
- Foreign holidays
- Organic fruit and vegetables
- Second-hand cars
- Own-brand breakfast cereal

Supply

KEY TERM

Supply refers to the quantity of a product that producers are willing to sell at a given price.

Producers are willing to supply more of a good when its price increases. This is because there is potential to sell more goods and make more profit.

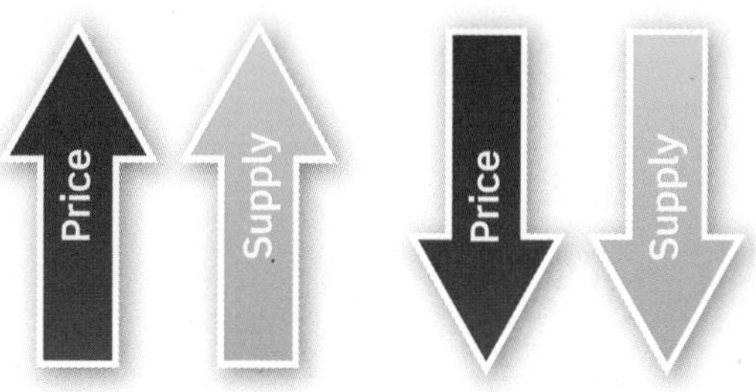

Figure 33.8 The relationship between supply and price

For most goods and services:

- Supply will increase when the selling price increases.
- Supply will decrease when the selling price drops.

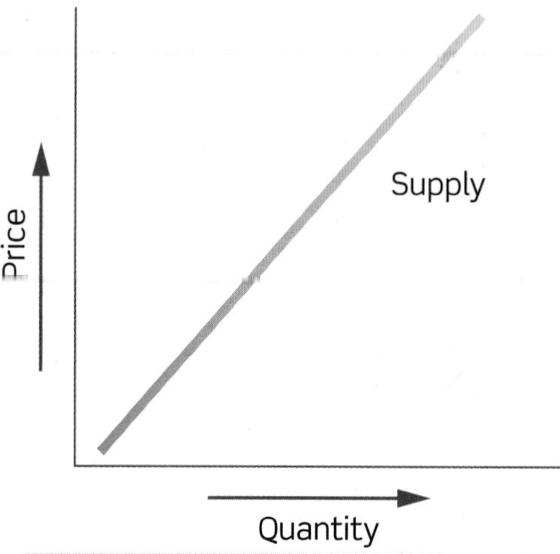

Figure 33.9 Law of supply: the higher the price, the more is supplied

Relationship between supply and price

There are many real-world examples that illustrate this relationship between supply and price:

- Global oil and gas prices fell when countries with these commodities produced more oil. The increase in supply resulted in lower gas and oil prices for households and businesses.

- A very warm summer may lead to a bumper crop of strawberries. To get rid of the excess supply, farmers will need to lower the price of strawberries. This lower price should encourage consumers to buy more strawberries.
- Following a spell of bad weather there may be a shortage of wheat, so the price of wheat will increase sharply.
- If a large number of new workers arrive in a city, the supply of labour may be greater than the number of jobs available. This excess supply of labour is likely to drive wages down, especially if the new arrivals are willing to work for lower wages.

Supply schedule

A supply schedule shows how much a firm is willing to supply at particular prices. The supply schedule shown in Table 33.2 shows the quantity of mobile phones (model Sonix424) that the producer is willing to supply (per week) at various prices.

Price	Quantity supplied
€50	80
€100	100
€150	120
€200	140

Table 33.2 Supply schedule for the Sonix424

Supply curve

We can use the information from the supply schedule to plot a supply curve for the Sonix424 mobile phone (see Figure 33.10).

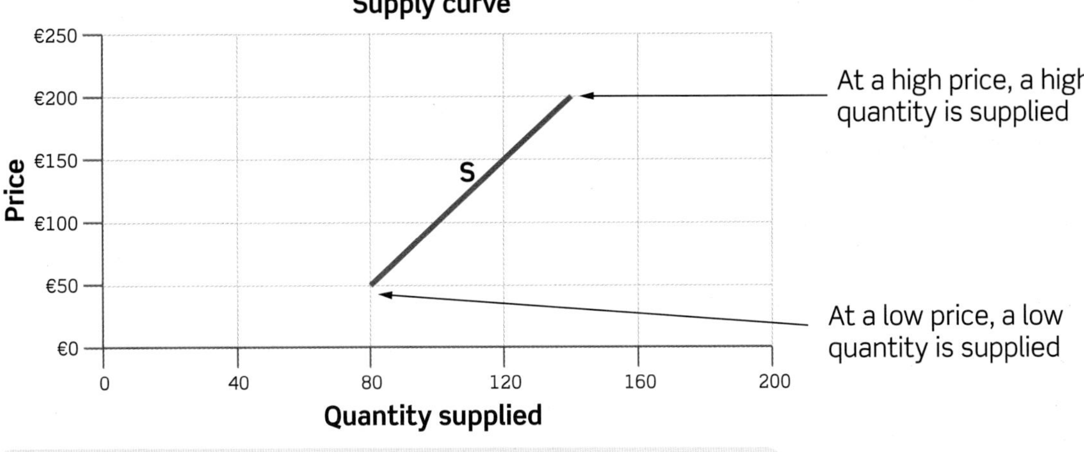

Figure 33.10 Supply curve for a Sonix424 mobile phone

KEY TERM

A **supply curve** is a graph that illustrates the quantity of a product that a seller is willing and able to supply at a series of price points.

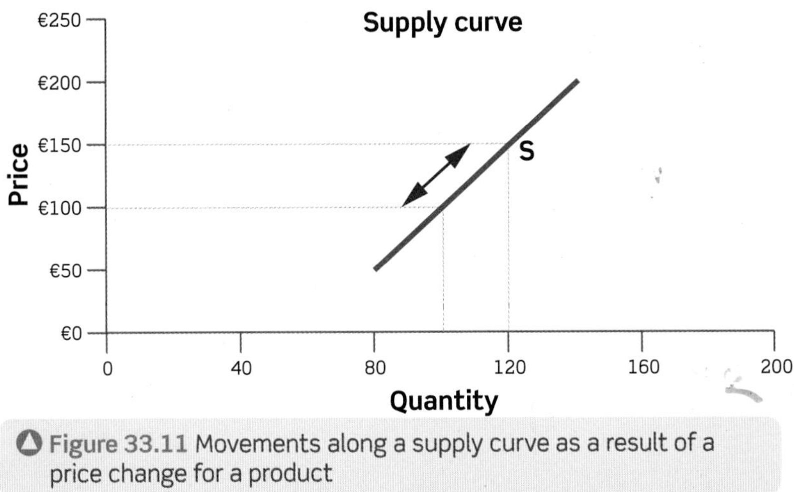

Figure 33.11 Movements along a supply curve as a result of a price change for a product

Figure 33.11 shows that changes in price will cause movements along the supply curve. Movements along a supply curve mean that a change in price will cause the quantity supplied to move from one point on the supply curve to another.

Other factors affecting supply

Other factors apart from price can impact on the quantity of goods supplied. These factors will cause the supply curve to shift right or left at a given price. An improvement in supply conditions will cause the supply curve to shift to the right. A negative change in supply conditions will cause the supply curve to shift to the left.

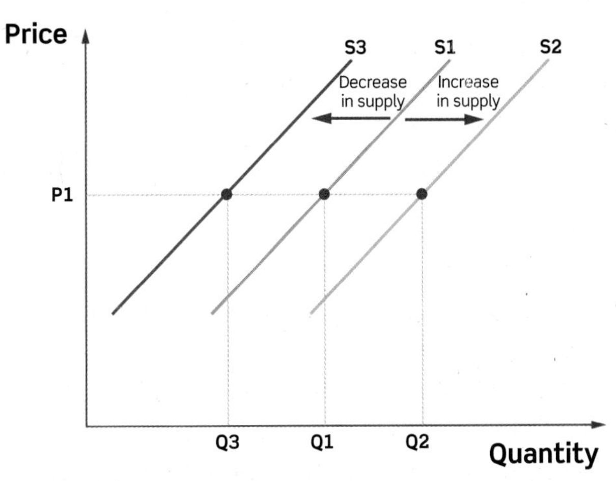

Figure 33.12 Shifts in a supply curve

The following factors can all affect supply.

❶ *Environmental conditions*

Weather can impact the supply of crops available. For example, a very wet summer may reduce the wheat harvest and will cause the supply curve to shift to the left. This indicates a reduced level of supply at each price point.

❷ *Production and development costs*

See Chapter 15 for product development

Producers of goods and services incur costs. These costs include product development, manufacturing costs, wages, raw materials and transport costs. When costs are low, more goods will be supplied at all different price levels, causing the supply curve to shift to the right.

❸ *Technology*

See Chapter 20 for the impact of technology

Technology helps businesses to be more efficient and productive. As a result of the increased use of technology (for example, robotics), production costs may be reduced and this will lead to an increased level of supply.

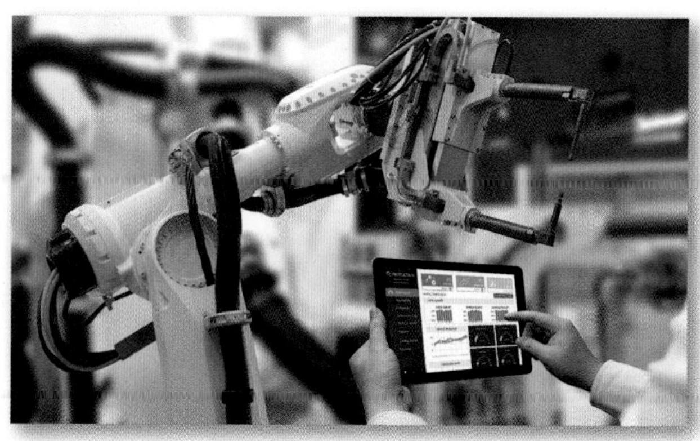

❹ *The number of suppliers*

If new suppliers enter a market, supply will increase and prices will fall. The Irish retail sector experienced this with the arrival of overseas supermarket chains such as Aldi and Lidl. Ryanair's entry into the marketplace in the 1980s and 1990s also saw increased capacity (supply) and lower prices on flights between Ireland and Europe.

❺ *Expectations of sellers*

If sellers expect prices to increase, they may store current supplies in the hope of selling them at a higher price in the future. For example, during a property crash, property owners may delay selling their property as they will not be able to make much money due to low market prices. They are likely to wait until the market improves and prices begin to rise again. The opposite will happen if suppliers think that prices will fall.

❻ *Government intervention*

Taxes and government regulations can all impact on quantities supplied. Higher taxes (VAT) and extra regulations will increase costs and reduce supply. Supply will also be reduced where quotas are applied.

KEY TERM

A **quota** is a limit on the number of goods made available for sale. For example, the fishing industry has a quota on the number of fish they are allowed to catch. This means that the supply available has a legal limit.

Finding a balance between demand and supply

In the marketplace, supply and demand interact until a balanced or **equilibrium** position is reached. At this price point, the quantity supplied will equal the quantity demanded. This should mean that sellers can sell all that they produce and buyers can buy all that they want at that price. If we plot our demand and supply curves (from Figures 33.3 and 33.10) on the same axis, we can see the **market equilibrium** price level for the Sonix424 mobile phone, as shown in Figure 33.13.

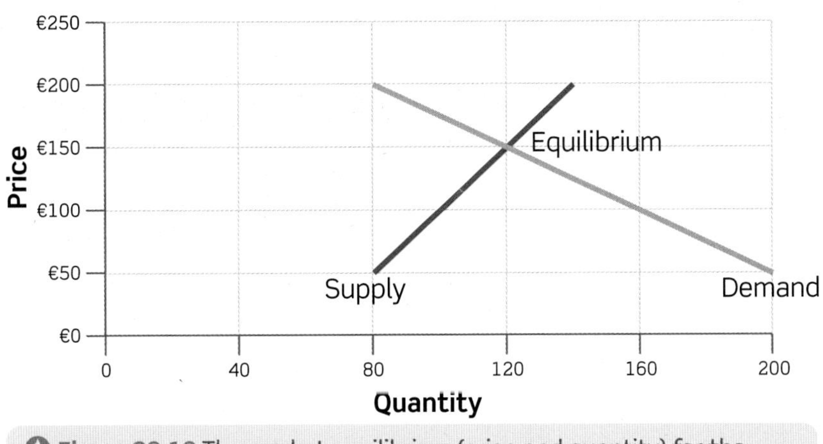

Figure 33.13 The market equilibrium (price and quantity) for the Sonix424 mobile phone

The diagram clearly shows that supply will equal demand at a market price of €150. At this market equilibrium price, weekly demand is 120 units and this is also the quantity that sellers are willing to make available for sale.

The laws of supply and demand explain how the interaction of supply and demand affects the price of goods and services.

We have already seen that high levels of demand for a good will cause the price of that good to rise. Equally, if there is a large supply of a good but not enough demand (excess supply), the price of that good will fall.

Let's now examine how the law of supply and demand operates in the property market and how the interaction of supply and demand will set an equilibrium price for property.

Case study: Demand and supply in action

Interaction of supply and demand in the property market

Each housing transaction involves a buyer and a seller. When there is high demand for property in a particular area and good-quality housing is scarce, house prices will tend to rise.

During a property boom in Ireland from 2000 to 2006 and again recently, an increase in demand led to big price increases. This extra demand was caused by several factors, including:

- **Income levels:** Wage and employment levels became high. Low interest rates made borrowing cheaper, so buyers generally had more money to spend.
- **Price of alternatives:** Increases in rent encouraged many people to consider buying their own property.
- **Fads and fashions:** Homes in some locations became extremely desirable. It was also quite common for people to own investment properties (properties they rented out for the rental income), which further fuelled demand.
- **Changes in population and market size:** There was a large increase in the number of new buyers entering the property market.
- **Price expectations of buyers:** As market prices continued to rise, consumers began to see this as an inevitable trend. Many looked to get on the 'property ladder' because they expected future price rises to make property unaffordable for them.
- **Advertising:** Property was heavily advertised and mentioned in the media. This helped to heighten the significance or fashionability of home ownership.

On the supply side, there was a shortage of good-quality family homes and also a shortage of available land on which to build them. Over time, the land shortage became less of a problem as more land was rezoned for housing.

In this climate of strong demand, limited supply and rising prices, it was a sellers' market and many houses were sold for prices well above the original asking price. Many sellers held auctions to ensure they achieved the best possible price for their property.

Prices in the Irish property boom peaked in 2006. By 2007, property prices levelled out and the market reached an equilibrium position. Rising prices and a weak economy reduced demand, while supply increased as more property developers entered the market. From 2007 to 2013, demand for Irish property fell enormously and there was a large oversupply of property in some areas. Mortgage approvals also declined by nearly 75%.

In keeping with the law of supply and demand, Irish property prices decreased. In some areas of the country, house prices fell by over 50% between 2007 and 2010. Prices of apartments fell by even greater amounts.

House prices began to increase again from 2013 as demand increased. In some urban areas prices rose very quickly as demand greatly exceeded supply. It also takes a lot of time and money to increase the housing supply and many property developers were unable or unwilling to build new houses immediately. This led to further price rises and buyers had to pay more to secure houses that were in short supply. As supply gradually increased, the level of price increases slowed down.

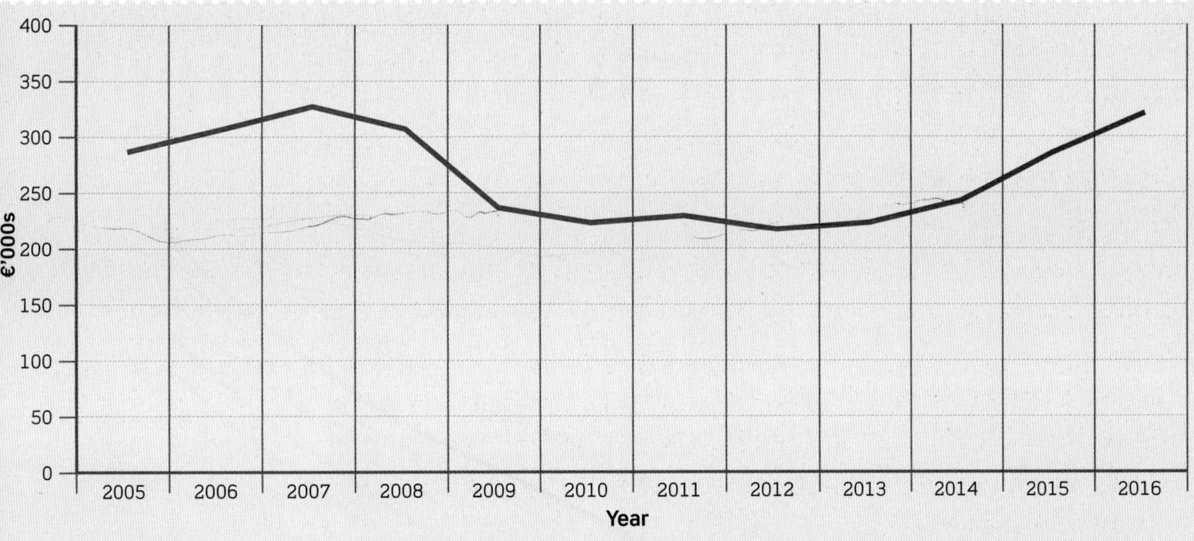

Figure 33.14 Average house prices in Ireland, 2005–2016 (*Source:* Department of Housing, Planning and Local Government)

This case study illustrates how the constant interaction of supply and demand impacts on market prices. It also clearly shows that demand, supply and price are all market variables and are likely to change over time.

KEY SKILLS

33.7 Property values and the Irish housing market

(a) Why do you think the prices of apartments fall more quickly than the prices of houses? #Opinion

(b) Research the major trends in the Irish housing market from 2013 to the present day. Focus in particular on the current situation and state whether it is caused by too much demand or an over-supply of property. #Research

(c) Investigate what measures have been taken, mainly by government, to try to stabilise the Irish property market since 2013. Prepare a short presentation using a format of your choice. #Investigate #Presentation

KEY SKILLS

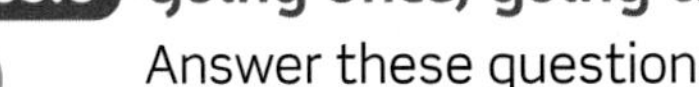

33.8 Going once, going twice

Answer these questions based on the 'Demand and supply in action' case study.

(a) Discuss the interaction of supply and demand at an auction. #Discussion

(b) Suggest a reason why sellers of property or rare antiques often use auctions to sell their goods. #Consider #Opinion

 Weblinks

 PowerPoint Summary

OUR ECONOMY

THE PURPOSE OF TAXATION

LEARNING OUTCOMES IN FOCUS

3.5 Examine the purpose of taxation from a financial, social, legal and ethical perspective

Links to 1.4, 1.5, 1.9, 1.11, 2.1, 3.2, 3.3, 3.4, 3.9, 3.10, 3.11

LEARNING INTENTIONS FOR THIS CHAPTER

When you have completed this chapter you will be able to:

- Explain the term 'taxation'
- Outline the principles of a fair tax system
- Examine the purpose of tax from a financial, social, legal and ethical point of view.

CHAPTER 34 KEY TERMS

- certainty
- convenience
- debt servicing
- economy
- equality
- fairness
- inflation
- Office of the Revenue Commissioners
- redistribution of wealth
- social objective
- taxation

CHAPTER 34 KEY SKILLS

- BL Being Literate
- BN Being Numerate
- C Communicating
- MIT Managing Information and Thinking
- WO Working with Others

OUR ECONOMY

What is taxation?

KEY TERM

Taxation is the way the government collects money to pay for public services.

The **Office of the Revenue Commissioners** ('Revenue' for short) is the state body responsible for collecting all taxes in the Republic of Ireland.

See Chapter 10 for personal taxation

See Chapter 35 for government revenue

Individuals and businesses must pay a range of different taxes. For example:

Revenue
Cáin agus Custaim na hÉireann
Irish Tax and Customs

- Tax on the income of employed people is deducted from their pay, collected by the employer through the PAYE system and paid to Revenue.
- Corporation tax on business profits is paid directly to Revenue.
- VAT on goods and services is included in the price of most products and services. It is collected by the supplier and paid to Revenue.
- Excise duty is charged on tobacco products, alcohol products, petrol, diesel, cars and bets.

The money collected is used to provide services to people living in Ireland, for example to build schools, hospitals and roads and to pay the wages of teachers, nurses and gardaí. The government also uses it to achieve a number of other social and economic goals, which we will discuss later in this chapter.

Principles of a fair (ethical) tax system

While few people want to pay taxes, most realise that they are necessary and provide benefits.

Adam Smith, 1723–1790

Taxes must be fairly imposed on all people living in a country. Adam Smith, an economist who lived in the eighteenth century, described principles of taxation (which he called the canons of taxation) in his book *The Wealth of Nations*. Although this was published in 1776, these principles are still used by governments today when imposing taxes.

A fair tax system should have the following principles:

Equality	The amount of tax that a person has to pay should be related to their ability to pay – in other words, those who earn more should pay more.
Certainty	The amount of tax that a person must pay should be clear and predictable. (Most taxes are a fixed amount or percentage, which makes them easier to predict and calculate.)
Economy	The cost of collecting a tax should be less than the amount that will be collected.
Convenience	It should be easy for each person to pay their taxes when they fall due. For example, it is easy for an individual to pay VAT since the tax is included in the price we pay for a good or service.

Along with Smith's canons of taxation, **tax should not act as a disincentive**. If taxes are too high, people may decide that it is not worthwhile working, as Revenue may take most of their income. Likewise, if corporation taxes are too high, it may discourage people from being entrepreneurial and prevent existing businesses from expanding.

Very high taxes can lead to a shadow or black economy, where people evade tax. For example, a service provider may insist on being paid in cash so that there is no bank record of the transaction. This would make it easier to hide that income from Revenue and allow the service provider to make more profit. However, this means that the state loses out on tax revenue and has less money to spend on public services.

See Chapter 10 for personal taxation and tax evasion

Also, because they are evading tax (which is illegal and unethical), they may be able to offer cheaper prices than other service providers who are obeying the law and paying their fair share of tax. This may result in some businesses closing down because they cannot compete with those who are operating in the shadow economy. This in turn impacts on all their staff, who will lose their jobs.

The government uses tax to redistribute income. A fair tax system should be used to collect money from those who earn higher incomes in order to look after those in our society who need help, for example to provide Jobseeker's Benefit to those who do not have a job and are currently looking for work.

KEY SKILLS

MIT C WO

34.1 Identifying taxes

In small groups, research the answers to the following. #Research

(a) Identify three taxes that the government collects from individuals.

(b) Identify three taxes that the government collects from businesses.

(c) List three different services provided by money raised through taxes in Ireland.

(d) Identify two new taxes that have been introduced in Ireland in recent years.

34.2 Taxing principles

In groups of three or four, discuss whether each of the following taxes follows the principles of **(i)** equality **(ii)** certainty **(iii)** economy and **(iv)** convenience. #GroupWork #Discussion

(a) Income tax (PAYE)

(b) VAT

The purpose of taxation

Taxes are imposed for a variety of reasons, which can be classified under four main headings:

- **Financial reasons:** Using taxation as a source of income to fund government spending.
- **Social reasons:** Using taxation to try to improve society and people's lives.
- **Legal reasons:** Complying with the law of the land.
- **Ethical reasons:** Using tax in ways that are just and fair to all.

Financial reasons

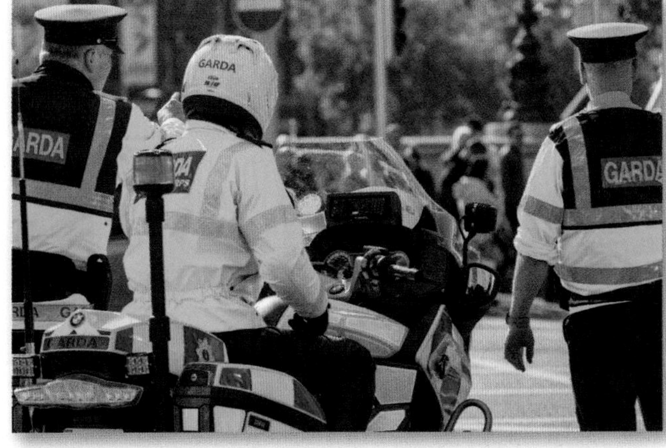

- **Financing the work of government:** The government uses the money to pay for the services it provides to people living in Ireland, for example education, health, policing and social welfare payments.
- **Meeting economic objectives:** Taxes may be used to control inflation. For example, if the prices of goods and services are increasing too quickly, the rate of income tax may be increased so that take-home pay is reduced and people have less disposable income to spend. Less consumer spending leads to lower demand and lower prices for goods and services.

KEY TERM

Inflation is a sustained increase in the general level of prices from one year to the next.

- **Assisting enterprise:** Money collected from taxes is used to encourage and help entrepreneurs. State bodies such as Enterprise Ireland and Local Enterprise Offices provide grants or services to entrepreneurs or businesses.
- **Repaying the national debt:** Interest and repayments have to be paid on money that the government borrows.

DID YOU KNOW...

At the end of 2019, Ireland's national debt was over €205 billion. Can you imagine how much money is required simply to pay the interest?

KEY TERM

Debt servicing means paying the interest on our national debt.

KEY SKILLS

34.3 Irish national debt and its costs

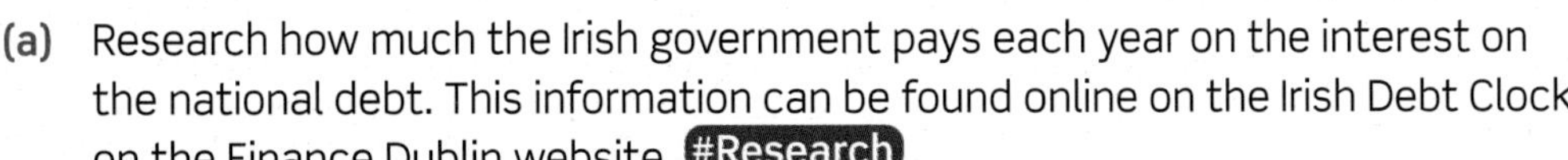

(a) Research how much the Irish government pays each year on the interest on the national debt. This information can be found online on the Irish Debt Clock on the Finance Dublin website. #Research

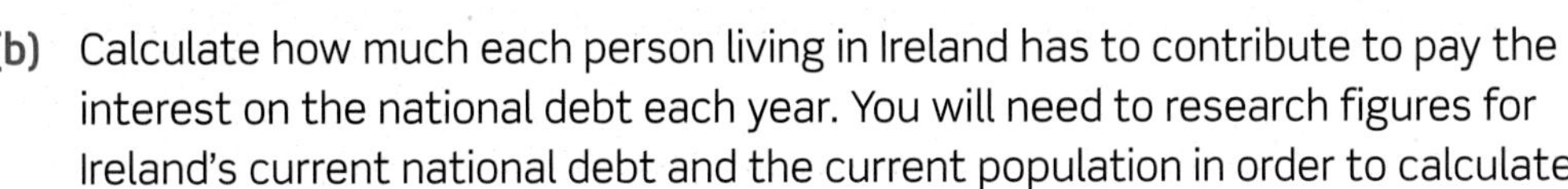

(b) Calculate how much each person living in Ireland has to contribute to pay the interest on the national debt each year. You will need to research figures for Ireland's current national debt and the current population in order to calculate this. #Calculate

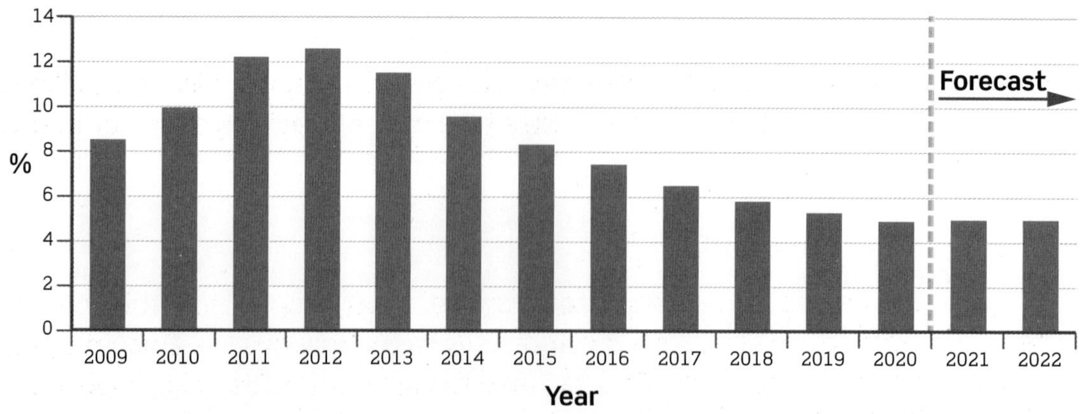

Figure 34.1 Interest payments as a percentage of government revenue (*Source:* Department of Finance, Central Statistics Office)

KEY SKILLS

MIT

BL

34.4 Paying the debt

Figure 34.1 shows the percentage of government revenue (income) that goes towards servicing Ireland's national debt.

(a) What does the trend suggest about Ireland's debt levels between 2010 and 2013? #Analyse

(b) Apart from a reduction in borrowing and interest payments, suggest one other reason for the trend between 2013 and 2017. #Suggest

(c) What does the forecast section of the graph suggest about the government's expectations for future borrowing? Explain your answer. #Explain

Social reasons

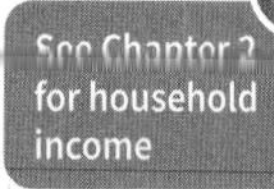

See Chapter 2 for household income

- **Redistributing wealth and income for the common good:** A major purpose of taxation is to transfer money from those on high incomes to those on lower or zero incomes. This allows the government to provide for those in our society who need help to bridge the gap between their actual income and what their income needs to be in order for them to have a reasonable standard of living.
- **Meeting social objectives:** Taxes are used to promote behaviour that may have a positive impact on society and discourage behaviour that may have a negative impact on society. For example, excise duty is placed on tobacco and alcohol products, as their consumption can seriously harm a person's health. The government also introduced a plastic bag levy on single use plastic bags from retailers in order to reduce litter and the impact of plastic waste on the environment. The government may lower the Vehicle Registration Tax (VRT) on electric vehicles in order to encourage people to buy them, which would reduce carbon emissions into the atmosphere.

DID YOU KNOW...

A carbon tax was introduced in 2010. Since then, all carbon dioxide emission sources have been taxed. The tax is used to encourage manufacturers and suppliers to provide low-carbon services and products to households. Low-carbon products use natural gas, as this has the lowest carbon content of any of the fossil fuels and therefore it is seen as being the cleanest.

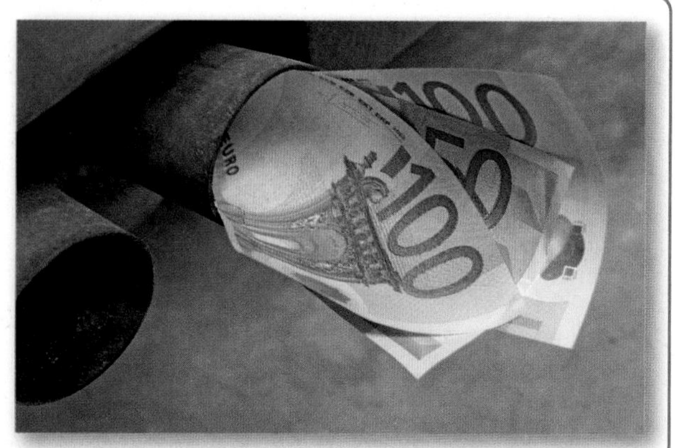

Legal reasons

- **Fulfilling a legal requirement:** Paying taxes is compulsory under Irish law. Individuals and businesses that do not pay their taxes face high interest payments and severe penalties.

Ethical reasons

- **Fairness:** Tax must be fair and apply to everyone, depending on their ability to pay. The income lost to the state as a result of tax evasion reduces the amount available to spend on essential services. This can lead to higher tax rates being imposed in order to collect more revenue. If some people avoid their responsibility and do not pay their fair share of tax, others will have to pay more to make up the difference, which is unfair.

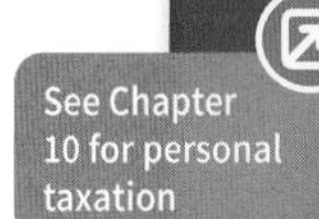
See Chapter 10 for personal taxation

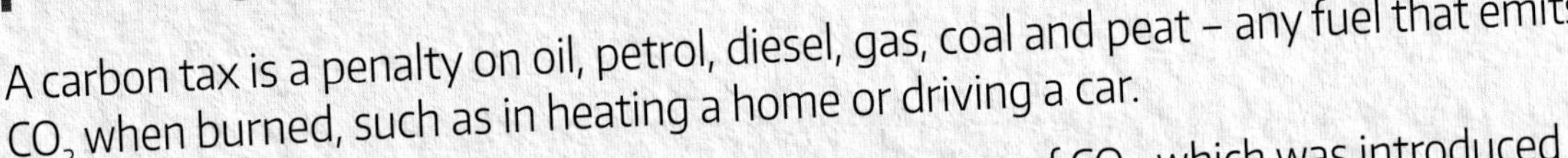

Can carbon tax be used to change behaviour while also protecting the less well-off?

IN THE NEWS

A carbon tax is a penalty on oil, petrol, diesel, gas, coal and peat – any fuel that emits CO_2 when burned, such as in heating a home or driving a car.

We already have a carbon tax levied at €20 per tonne of CO_2, which was introduced in 2010. It raises €400 million a year, but this goes straight into the Exchequer rather than funding green alternatives. It adds about €2.10 to the cost of a 40kg bag of coal, 45 cents to a bale of briquettes and 5.3 cents to a litre of diesel.

The tax is set to increase to €30 per tonne, but the emphasis will be on 'carbon pricing' and putting in place a penalty for damaging the environment.

There will be a clear signal to increase the tax steadily to €80 per tonne by 2030, when it will no longer be possible to buy briquettes, but all other fossil fuels will be much more expensive.

Supporters of the tax say it's critical to shifting human behaviour to the extent necessary to decarbonise Ireland. This means shifting to using renewable energy and making it cheaper to use less polluting options, such as using an electric vehicle or a heat pump in the home rather than an oil burner.

Is a carbon tax unfair on people who are dependent on fossil fuels?

Carbon taxes, if incorrectly or unfairly applied, hit people who are dependent on fossil fuels or those who live in 'fuel poverty'. This is particularly true for people living in rural areas, who may not have an alternative to a diesel or petrol car. Many people cannot afford to switch to an electric vehicle, for example.

But it's possible to protect the less well-off. One way is to give the revenue back to consumers or householders by way of a dividend and to increase fuel allowances for those on social welfare.

Carbon taxes work and if well designed, with supports for the less well-off, can significantly reduce emissions. When combined with other measures, such as improved public transport or congestion charges, it can yield substantial reductions.

If you spend less than the average person on polluting things, you end up with a cash bonus. If you spend more on polluting things, you end up out of pocket. This can shift behaviours in big numbers towards using less polluting fuels.

A clear pathway of increases gives consumers, households and businesses time to adjust and change their behaviour/lifestyle.

What happens next?

A policy of increasing carbon taxes will be endorsed in a government report on tackling climate disruption.

A consultation process will then consider how those who are most dependent on fossil fuels can be protected and how the revenue raised will be used to support the transition. Options include funding or subsidising the adoption of renewable technology or the retrofitting of homes to make them fuel efficient and zero-carbon.

Source: Irish Times, 27 May 2019 and updated 6 June 2019

MIT BL

34.5 Carbon tax

After reading the article above, answer the following questions.

(a) Explain each of the underlined terms. Research them if necessary. #Research

(b) What is your understanding of the 'polluter pays' principle as it relates to taxation? #Explain

(c) Is the proposed carbon tax an example of a direct or indirect tax? Explain your answer. You may need to return to Chapter 10 to revise these terms. #Explain

(d) How well do you think the proposed carbon tax meets the principles of taxation set out on page 397? #Opinion #Evaluate

34.6 Legal – but ethical?

In Chapter 10 you learned about the difference between tax avoidance, which is legal, and tax evasion, which is not legal. Do you think that tax avoidance by individuals or businesses is ethical? Explain your reasons to your partner, then debate this with the rest of the class. #Discussion #Ethics #Opinion

Weblinks PowerPoint Summary

CHAPTER 35

GOVERNMENT REVENUE AND EXPENDITURE

LEARNING OUTCOMES IN FOCUS

3.4 Differentiate between different sources of government revenue and government expenditure

Links to 1.1, 1.2, 1.4, 1.11, 1.12, 2.1, 2.4, 2.10, 2.11, 3.2, 3.5, 3.8, 3.9, 3.10, 3.11

3.10 Use their knowledge, and information from a range of media sources, to discuss current economic issues and present an informed view

LEARNING INTENTIONS FOR THIS CHAPTER

When you have completed this chapter you will be able to:

- Define the term 'national budget'
- Explain the need for a national budget
- Identify sources of government revenue and items of government expenditure
- Distinguish between balanced, surplus and deficit budgets
- Outline the impact of budget decisions on Irish society.

CHAPTER 35 KEY TERMS

- balanced budget
- budget deficit
- budget surplus
- capital expenditure
- capital revenue
- current expenditure
- current revenue
- Department of Finance
- Department of Public Expenditure and Reform
- government expenditure
- government revenue
- infrastructure
- national budget
- neutral budget
- privatisation

CHAPTER 35 KEY SKILLS

- BC Being Creative
- BN Being Numerate
- C Communicating
- MIT Managing Information and Thinking

 **Step-by-step accounts**

 **Excel template**

The national budget

The role of the government is to run the country. Providing public services is an important part of this task. Ireland has a **mixed economy**, which means that some goods and services are provided by the private sector, while the government (or public sector) provides many others.

See Chapter 32 for distribution of economic resources

In previous chapters we discussed how the government has to use available **resources** to provide the best possible level of public services. Since the government does not have enough resources to meet all demands for public services, it needs to prioritise some services over others. This means that the government has to make choices that will have both financial and opportunity costs.

For example, if the government chooses to spend €200 million on a new hospital, this money will not be available for spending on schools, roads or museums. Those schools, roads and museums that cannot now be built are the opportunity cost of building the hospital.

Preparing a national budget

The **national budget** is the government's financial plan for the year ahead. It shows expected revenue and planned expenditure.

An Roinn Caiteachais Phoiblí agus Athchóirithe
Department of Public Expenditure and Reform

The Department of Finance and the Department of Public Expenditure and Reform work together to ensure that the government has enough money to run the country. They estimate how much money each government department will need in order to provide its services. They must also decide how to raise the revenue required to pay for these services.

- The **Department of Public Expenditure and Reform** assesses each department's request for money and must approve government spending before it can take place.
- The **Department of Finance** is responsible for all decisions about taxes and government borrowing.

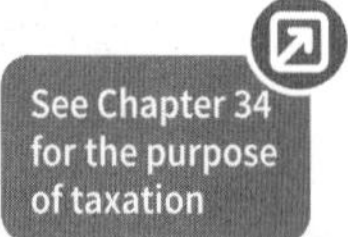
See Chapter 34 for the purpose of taxation

Each year, the Minister for Finance outlines the government's financial plan for the coming year when the national budget is announced in the Dáil. Before making this financial plan, the government needs to consider the revenue (or income) available to it.

Government revenue

Government revenue refers to all money received by the government.

Government revenue can be divided into two distinct categories:

- **Current revenue:** Money received by the government on a regular, ongoing or day-to-day basis. The vast majority of this revenue comes from taxation.
- **Capital revenue:** Money received on an irregular or once-off basis. This is normally non-tax revenue.

The government's current revenue comes from a number of sources, as outlined in Table 35.1.

Source	Description
Income tax	Tax on wages and salaries.
Universal Social Charge (USC)	Another tax on income.
Pay Related Social Insurance (PRSI)	Insurance paid by employers and employees that is used to fund social welfare payments, such as Illness Benefit and Maternity Benefit.
Value Added Tax (VAT)	Tax on the value added to goods at each stage of their production. This tax is paid by the consumers who buy the finished goods.
Corporation tax	Tax on company profits.
Excise duty	Tax charged on goods such as alcohol, tobacco and fuel products.
Customs duties	A tax on goods coming into Ireland from countries outside the EU.
Local Property Tax (LPT)	Tax on residential properties.
Capital Gains Tax (CGT)	Tax on the profits earned from investments. These profits usually arise from an increase in the value of shares or investment properties.
Capital Acquisitions Tax (CAT)	Tax on gifts and inheritances.
Dividends from state companies	As the sole or major shareholder, the state is entitled to receive a share of any profits earned by state companies such as the ESB and An Post.
Stamp duty	A tax for registering legal documents, especially when buying property.

Table 35.1 Major sources of government current revenue

The government's capital revenue comes from a number of sources, as outlined in Table 35.2.

Source	Description
Sale of state-owned companies	The sale of state-owned companies into private ownership is called **privatisation**. For example, in 2015 the government sold its 25% stake in Aer Lingus to the IAG Group for €335 million. Some bus routes previously operated by Bus Éireann and Dublin Bus have also been privatised in recent years.
Borrowings	Our government borrows money from other governments or from financial institutions in order to fund its spending plans.
European Union (EU) grants	The Irish government receives billions of euros from a variety of EU funding schemes. For example, in 2018 the government received €82 million from the European Regional Development Fund, which is used to support important economic and social projects.

Table 35.2 Major sources of government capital (non-tax) revenue

35.1 Where do governments get their money?

The table below lists a government's estimated income for next year.

Revenue source	Amount of revenue (€m)
Income taxes (including USC)	22,905
Value Added Tax (VAT)	15,140
PRSI	12,755
Corporation tax	9,480
Excise duties	5,940
Stamp duties	1,675
Capital Gains Tax (CGT)	1,000
Local Property Tax (LPT)	486
Capital Acquisitions Tax (CAT)	495
Customs duties	365
Dividends from state companies	285
Other sources	1,770
Total planned revenue	**72,296**

(a) Calculate the percentage of overall revenue that each of the following sources in the table represents. #Calculate

(i) Income tax

(ii) VAT

(iii) Corporation tax

(b) Do any of these figures surprise you? Comment on the figures. #Opinion

(c) Create a bar chart to illustrate the top five sources of government revenue. Round figures to the nearest €100 million. #Presentation #Graph #Illustrate

Government expenditure

KEY TERM

Government expenditure refers to all money spent by the government.

Government expenditure can be divided into two categories:

- **Current expenditure:** Money spent by the government on a regular or ongoing basis. The majority of government current expenditure involves day-to-day spending on essential public services, including health, education, security, etc. Operating costs and wages for public sector workers account for a large portion of government current expenditure.
- **Capital expenditure:** Spending on 'once-off' projects or on infrastructure that will have long-term benefits for the country.

KEY TERM

Infrastructure is the basic facilities, structures and services needed for a country to function. It includes water, power lines, transport and communications systems, schools and hospitals.

Spending	Purpose
Current expenditure	
Social protection	Payments and income supports such as pensions, Child Benefit and Jobseekers' Benefit
Healthcare	Day-to-day running costs of hospitals and healthcare facilities, e.g. nurses and doctors, wages, buying medicine, and light and heat
Education	To enable schools and colleges to be run efficiently, e.g. paying teachers' salaries, light and heat, and maintenance of school buildings
Justice	Our legal and judicial systems, e.g. judges' wages, garda wages and operating costs of prisons
Agriculture	To help farmers and ensure that this important sector is maintained, e.g. income supports to farmers, grants and other funding for a wide variety of rural development schemes
Defence	Maintaining the defence of our country, e.g. wages to members of the defence forces and civilians working for the sector, maintenance of facilities, training costs, etc.
Transport and tourism	Maintaining our existing transport systems and providing funding for tourism promotion agencies such as Fáilte Ireland
Capital expenditure	
Public transport	Building new rail networks, buying new trains and buses
Health	Building new hospitals, buying new equipment and ambulances
Education	Building or extending schools, buying furniture and ICT equipment for schools

Table 35.3 Examples of government current and capital expenditure

KEY SKILLS BN MIT BC C

35.2 How do governments spend their money?

The table below lists a government's planned expenditure for next year.

Government department	Planned expenditure (€m)
Employment Affairs and Social Protection	20,630
Health	17,110
Education and Skills	10,770
Debt servicing and EU payments	9,600
Housing, Planning and Local Government	4,040
Justice and Equality	2,770
Transport and Tourism	2,300
Agriculture, Food and the Marine	1,600
Children and Youth Affairs	1,501
Public Expenditure and Reform	1,250
Defence	1,010
Other expenditure	3,456
Total planned expenditure	**76,037**

(a) Calculate the percentage of overall expenditure that the government plans to spend on the following areas: #Calculate
- (i) Social Protection
- (ii) Health
- (iii) Education and Skills
- (iv) Debt servicing and EU payments

(b) Do any of these figures surprise you? Comment on the figures. #Opinion

(c) Create a bar chart to illustrate the top five items of government expenditure. Round figures to the nearest €100 million. #Illustrate #Graph

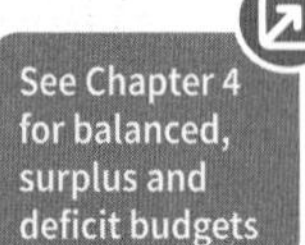
See Chapter 4 for balanced, surplus and deficit budgets

The government will combine its income and expenditure plans in order to create a budget. This is just like a household budget or a businesses cash budget, but on a much bigger scale. Depending on the relative amounts of revenue and expenditure, the government may have a balanced budget, a budget surplus or a budget deficit.

A budget deficit

If we combine the figures from the tables in Activities 35.1 and 35.2, we can see the following situation:

Total expected revenue (A)	€72,296 million
Total planned expenditure (B)	€76,037 million
Difference (A – B)	(€3,741 million) Deficit

This is a **budget deficit** since planned expenditure is greater than expected revenue. This suggests that the government is living beyond its means and will have to increase revenue, cut spending and/or borrow money to finance its plans.

A budget deficit is generally seen as a negative outcome and often arises because the government has failed to meet its revenue targets or because public expenditure is out of control.

As a member of the EU, Ireland must also follow strict financial rules that aim to control budget deficits. For these reasons, the government will try to keep its budget deficits to a minimum.

See Chapter 40 for the EU

In some circumstances, having a budget deficit, especially a small one, may be a deliberate and positive economic policy choice by the government. A deficit means that the government is injecting more money into the economy (through spending) than it is taking out (through taxation). The government may use this approach if it wishes to boost the level of economic growth.

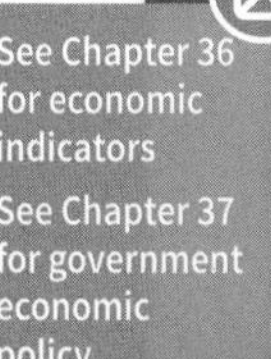
See Chapter 36 for economic indicators
See Chapter 37 for government economic policy

Solutions to a budget deficit

There are three possible ways of reducing or eliminating a budget deficit. Governments tend to use a combination of all three:

- **Increase planned revenue** by raising taxation levels or selling state assets.
- **Reduce planned expenditure** by cutting the level of public services.
- **Borrow money** to bridge the gap between revenue and expenditure. This is a short term solution since paying interest and repaying borrowings will impact on future budgets.

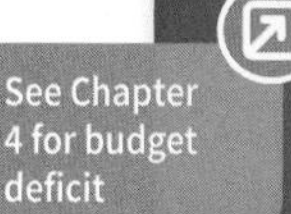
See Chapter 4 for budget deficit

KEY SKILLS C MIT

35.3 Solving a budget deficit

Discuss why a government would use a combination of all three strategies to resolve a budget deficit. #Discussion #Opinion

A balanced budget

If the government expects that planned revenue will be equal to planned expenditure, it will be a **balanced budget**.

The following figures illustrate a balanced budget situation:

Planned revenue (A)	€72,000 million
Planned expenditure (B)	€72,000 million
Balance (A – B)	€0

In this situation, the government is taking money out of the economy through taxation, but is returning the same amount of money to the economy via spending on public services. For this reason, a balanced budget is also called a **neutral budget**.

A budget surplus

If planned revenue is expected to be greater than planned expenditure, the government will have a **budget surplus**.

Just as with household budgeting, a budget surplus shows that the government is living within its means. It could decide to use some of the surplus money to cut taxes or increase the level of services it plans to provide.

The following figures illustrate a budget surplus:

Planned revenue (A)	€72,000 million
Planned expenditure (B)	€68,000 million
Budget surplus (A – B)	€4,000 million

In a surplus situation, the government is taking more money out of the economy (through taxation) than it is putting back in (through spending). This will reduce the overall amount of money and spending in the economy.

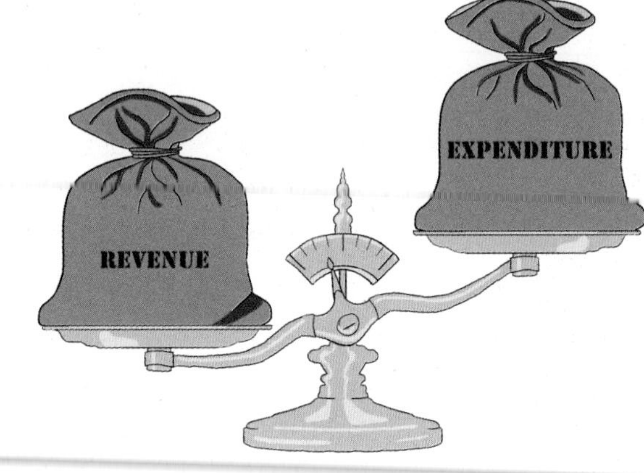

Irish budget trends

Figure 35.1 illustrates the pattern of budget surpluses and deficits in Ireland during the 12-year period from 2006 to 2018.

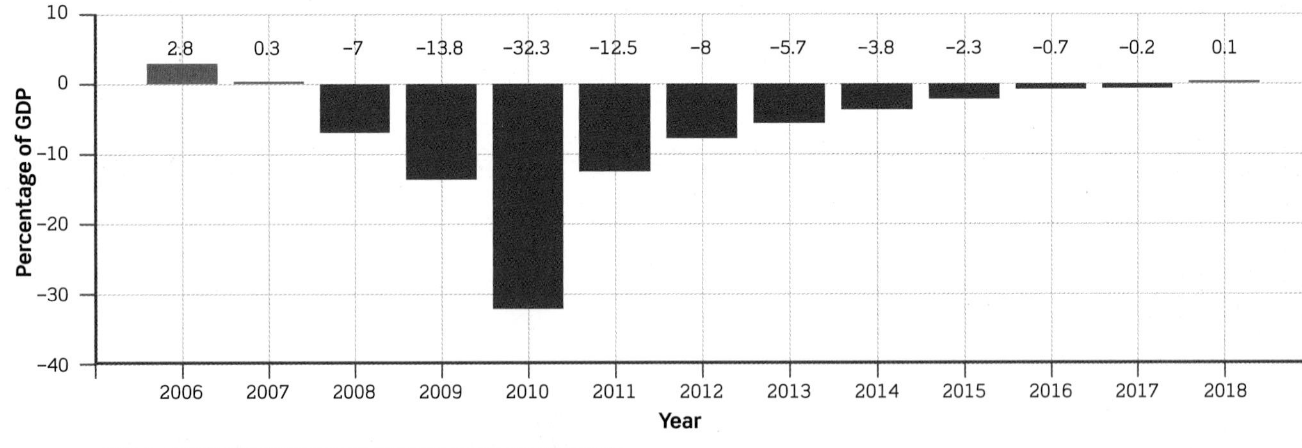

Figure 35.1 Ireland's budgets, 2006–2018

KEY SKILLS

35.4 Irish budget trends

(a) Research the national budget position in Ireland for all the years since 2018. #Research

(b) Comment on the trends and suggest possible reasons for them. #Opinion

Weblinks

PowerPoint Summary

ECONOMIC INDICATORS

LEARNING OUTCOMES IN FOCUS

3.9 Explain the relevance of economic indicators such as inflation, employment rates, interest rates, economic growth, national income and national debt for individuals and the economy

Links to 2.5, 3.2, 3.4, 3.5, 3.6, 3.8, 3.10, 3.11

3.10 Use their knowledge, and information from a range of media sources, to discuss current economic issues and present an informed view

LEARNING INTENTIONS FOR THIS CHAPTER

When you have completed this chapter you will be able to:

- Identify and explain each of the major economic indicators
- Describe the effects of the economic indicators on Ireland's households, businesses and the economy
- Calculate the rate of inflation
- Calculate the rate of economic growth
- Identify and explain the economic cycle.

CHAPTER 36 KEY TERMS

- balance of trade
- Consumer Price Index (CPI)
- cost-push inflation
- debt servicing
- deflation
- demand-pull inflation
- economic boom
- economic cycle
- economic depression
- economic growth
- employment
- exporting
- full employment
- gross domestic product (GDP)
- gross national product (GNP)
- imported inflation
- importing
- inflation
- interest rates
- multiplier effect
- national debt
- national income
- National Treasury Management Agency (NTMA)
- recession
- unemployment

CHAPTER 36 KEY SKILLS

- BL Being Literate
- BN Being Numerate
- C Communicating
- MIT Managing Information and Thinking

Economic indicators

Economic indicators show the direction that an economy is going or is likely to go in the future. These indicators are pieces of **economic information that highlight the condition of the economy** and allow economists to assess its overall health.

Depending on how well the economy is performing, the government may decide to continue with existing policies or adopt new ones to improve the situation.

In this chapter we will consider six economic indicators and discuss their impact on households, businesses and the economy. They are:

1 Inflation
2 Employment levels
3 Interest rates
4 National debt
6 National income
6 Economic growth.

1 Inflation

KEY TERM

Inflation is a sustained increase in the general level of prices of goods and services from one year to the next.

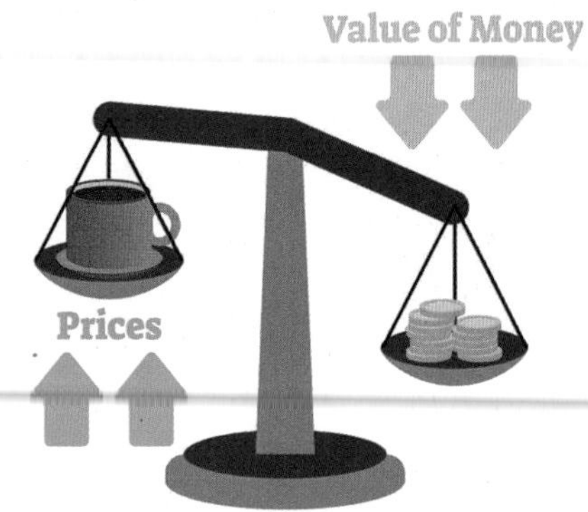

The official rate of inflation is measured by the **Consumer Price Index (CPI)**. In Ireland, the Central Statistics Office (CSO) collects approximately 53,000 prices every month and compares these to the corresponding prices from the previous month to find out the CPI.

Calculating the rate of inflation

The formula is:

$$\frac{\text{Difference in cost of living between Year 1 and Year 2}}{\text{Cost of living in Year 1}} \times 100$$

Example

The cost of living for a household in 2019 was €8,500 and the cost of living in 2020 was €8,755. Calculate the rate of inflation.

Solution:

$$\frac{\text{Difference in cost of living between Year 1 and Year 2}}{\text{Cost of living in Year 1}} \times 100$$

$$\frac{€8{,}755 - €8{,}500}{€8{,}500} \times 100$$

$$\frac{€255}{€8{,}500} \times 100$$

$$= 3\%$$

KEY SKILLS BN MIT C BL

36.1 Inflation in Ireland

The following are the inflation rates in Ireland for the years 2011 to 2019.

Year	2011	2012	2013	2014	2015	2016	2017	2018	2019
Inflation rate	2.6%	1.72%	0.48%	0.2%	−0.3%	0%	0.4%	0.5%	1.2%

(a) Draw a trend graph to illustrate Ireland's inflation rate for the years 2011 to 2019.

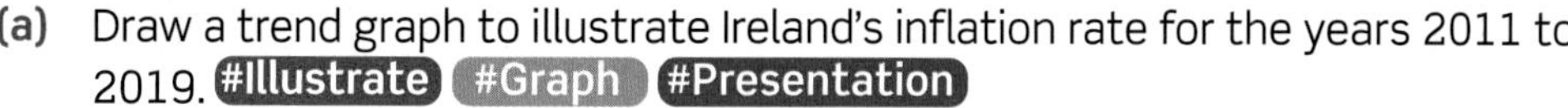

(b) Research Irish inflation rates since 2019. Comment on the trend and the possible reasons for that trend. #Research

The 2015 inflation rate was a negative figure, indicating that average prices fell during that year. This is called **deflation**. It tends to happen when the economy is weak.

KEY SKILLS MIT

36.2 Deflation in Ireland

(a) Do you think that deflation would be a positive situation for you and your household? Explain your answer.

(b) Do you think deflation is a positive situation for the Irish economy as a whole? Explain your answer. #WhatDoYouThink

What causes inflation?

Inflation is caused by any of the following.

- When the cost of producing goods increases, for example because the cost of wages or raw materials rises, the cost increase is likely to be passed on to the consumer. This is called **cost-push inflation** since the extra costs push up the price of goods.
- If the cost of imported raw materials increases, the price of the finished goods using these raw materials will rise. This is called **imported inflation**. For example, if the cost of imported flour increases, it may lead to higher prices for bread and other products that use this imported ingredient.

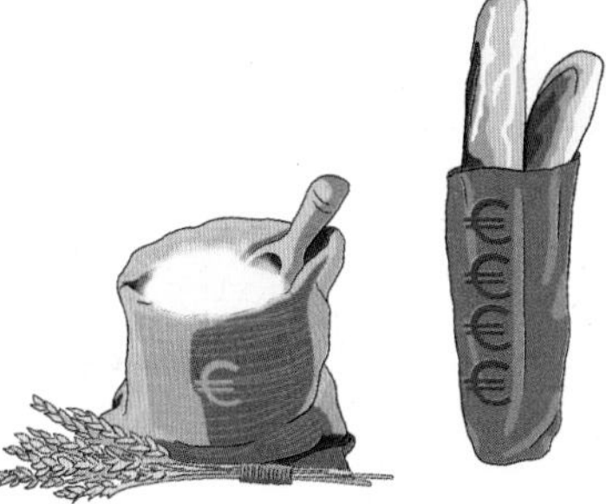

KEY TERM

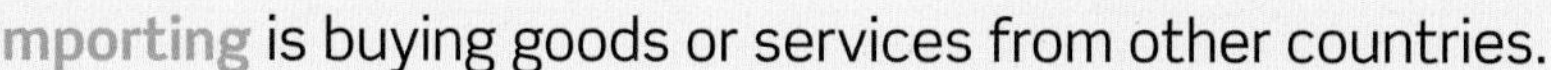

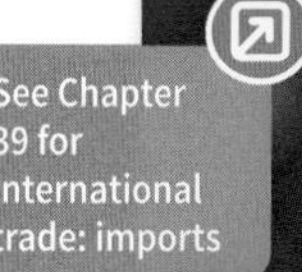

- An increase in indirect taxes, such as VAT or excise duties, will automatically increase the price of a product. For example, if the Minister for Finance announces a 5 cent increase in excise duties on fuel in the budget, fuel prices will increase immediately as service stations pass on the increase to motorists. This makes the annual cost of running a car more expensive.

- If the demand for goods or services is greater than the supply, the price will rise. Consumers will have to compete with each other for the items that are scarce, which will drive up the price. This is known as **demand-pull inflation** since the excess demand pulls the price upwards. For example, house prices often rise sharply when the demand for homes is greater than the available supply. Buyers who can afford to pay more will do so in order to get the house they want. This strong demand pulls the average price of property upwards.

KEY SKILLS

36.3 Make a choice about inflation

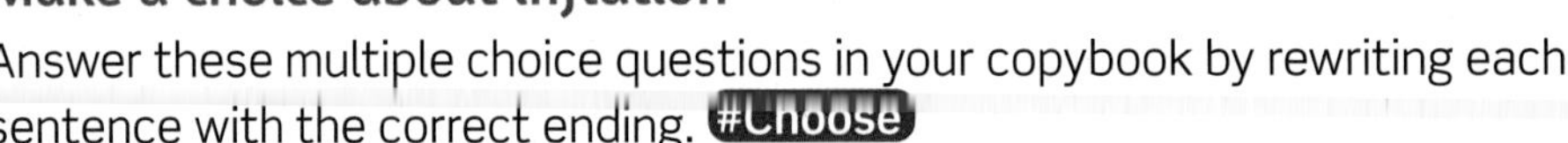

Answer these multiple choice questions in your copybook by rewriting each sentence with the correct ending. #Choose

(a) Inflation could be caused by the VAT rate:
- (i) Being reduced
- (ii) Being increased
- (iii) No longer being applied to electrical goods

(b) Cost-push inflation could be caused by:
- (i) The minimum wage being raised by €1.50
- (ii) The price of electricity going down
- (iii) Tax on profits being reduced by 2%

(c) Imported inflation could be caused by:
- (i) Increased ferry charges between the UK and Ireland
- (ii) A poor wheat harvest in the USA, increasing the price of this product
- (iii) The price of oil remaining steady

(d) Demand-pull inflation could be caused by:
- (i) An increase in wages for construction workers
- (ii) An increase in building costs
- (iii) An increase in the number of people who want to buy a home

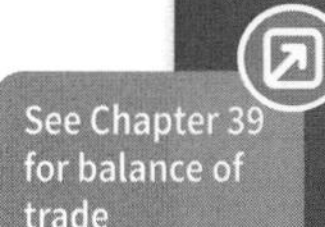

The impact of high inflation on households, businesses and the economy

Individuals	Businesses	Economy
› Inflation reduces the purchasing (buying) power of money. Higher prices means that consumers will not be able to buy as many goods and services, which will result in a lower standard of living. › Inflation may stop people saving money if the rate of interest they earn on savings is less than the rate of inflation. This is because the interest received will not match the price increase of goods and services, so people would actually be better off spending their money than saving it (see example below).	› Workers may demand wage increases so that they can afford the same amount of goods and services as they did before inflation. This is called a cost of living increase. This will increase business costs and will result in lower profits or higher prices. If the wage increase is not paid, workers may go on strike. › Rising business costs will discourage expansion and investment.	› Irish-made goods and services will be more expensive and it will become more difficult to sell them abroad. This may result in job losses and rising unemployment. › The higher cost of Irish-made goods will result in relatively cheaper imported goods and services. This has a negative impact on our balance of trade and may also cause job losses (see below). › Government spending may increase due to rising costs and increased social protection payments to match the rate of inflation.

See Chapter 39 for balance of trade

KEY TERM

The **balance of trade** measures the difference between the value of imported and exported goods.

Exporting is selling goods or services to other countries.

Consider this example.

Last year Declan had €100. He could have used this money to buy a new pair of football boots that cost €100, but he decided to postpone the purchase and put his money in a savings account that paid 2% APR. When he withdrew his money at the end of the year, he had €102.

However, if the rate of inflation in the economy is 5%, the price of the football boots will have risen to €105 and Declan will no longer have enough money to buy the boots.

In money terms, Declan is better off as he now has €102 rather than €100, but the purchasing power of his money has been reduced and it will allow him to buy fewer goods than it did a year ago. In real terms (which accounts for the effects of inflation on money), Declan is now worse off than he was last year. This may discourage Declan from saving future income.

KEY SKILLS 

36.4 Inflation in Ireland and the EU

(a) Find out the current rate of inflation in Ireland.

(b) How does it compare to the average rate of inflation across the European Union (EU)? #Research

2 Employment levels

The **labour force** is all the people of working age (16 to 65) who are willing and able to work. This definition does not include retired people, full-time students or those who have an illness or disability that prevents them from working.

36.5 Population and the labour force

Use the CSO website to find out the current size of Ireland's population and labour force. Calculate the labour force figure as a percentage of the total population. #Research

Formula: $\frac{\text{Labour force}}{\text{Total population}} \times \frac{100}{1}$

Members of the labour force who are able to find work are said to be **employed**. Those who cannot find work are classified as **unemployed**. The levels of employment and unemployment in an economy are important indicators of its economic wellbeing. A healthy and growing economy will tend to have low levels of unemployment.

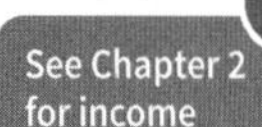

See Chapter 2 for income

People who are unemployed usually receive some form of financial payment from the Department of Employment Affairs and Social Protection, such as Jobseeker's Benefit or Jobseeker's Allowance. This money is meant to help them meet their daily needs and to provide short-term financial support until they find a job.

Calculation of unemployment level

In 2023, the labour force of a country was 3 million and 300,000 people were unemployed. Calculate the unemployment level.

$$\frac{\text{Number of unemployed people}}{\text{Total number in labour force}} \times \frac{100}{1}$$

Example

$$\frac{300{,}000}{3{,}000{,}000} \times 100$$

= 10% unemployment

All governments aim to have as many people in employment as possible. This will increase government revenue (due to higher tax revenue – PAYE, VAT, etc.) and reduce government expenditure (fewer social welfare payments).

Full employment refers to a situation where almost all members of the labour force are employed. In Ireland, an unemployment rate of around 4% is regarded as full employment. This is because there will always be some people who are between jobs or who have recently qualified and are looking for a job. Some members of the labour force may also have a disability that prevents them from finding suitable employment, while others may be full-time carers. For all these reasons we will never see a figure of 0% unemployment, but governments aim to get as close to it as possible.

KEY SKILLS

MIT BN BL

36.6 Unemployment in Ireland

The following table shows the unemployment levels in Ireland for the years 2011 to 2019.

Year	2011	2012	2013	2014	2015	2016	2017	2018	2019
Unemployment rate	14.5%	14.7%	12.5%	10.0%	9.5%	8.2%	6.7%	5.8%	4.8%

(a) Draw a trend graph to illustrate the unemployment rate in Ireland for the years 2011 to 2019. #Presentation #Illustrate #Graph

(b) Research the unemployment rate for each year since 2019. Continue your trend graph with this information. #Research

(c) What can you say about the unemployment rate from 2011 to the present? What do you think has caused this trend? #Think #Opinion #Analyse #Interpret

The effect of high unemployment for households, businesses and the economy

Households	Businesses	Economy
› There will be a decrease in consumer demand for goods and services as people lose their jobs and their income levels fall. › Many households will have a lower standard of living. Those facing long-term unemployment (12 months or more) may suffer from poverty and may find it difficult to maintain their skills and find new employment. › Some workers may have to emigrate to find employment.	› It may be harder to attract extra finance as investors will be less willing to invest at a time of falling demand. › There may be a reduction in sales and profits as consumers have less disposable income. › The emigration of highly qualified or skilled workers makes Ireland a less attractive location for foreign direct investment (FDI). This loss of important, talented workers is often called brain drain.	› There will be reduced economic activity due to a reduction in disposable income. › The shadow/black economy may grow and social problems may increase.

The effect of low unemployment for households, businesses and the economy

Households	Businesses	Economy
› There will be increased consumer demand for goods and services as people find jobs and their income levels increase. › Many households will have a higher standard of living and more disposable income. › Some workers who left Ireland to find employment may return. › Some people who chose not to seek employment in the past (e.g. stay-at-home parents) may decide to look for work outside the home.	› Employers may need to pay higher wages in order to recruit and keep skilled staff. › There may be an increase in sales and profits as consumers have more disposable income. › It may be easier to attract extra finance as investors will be more willing to invest at a time of increasing demand.	› There will be increased economic activity due to an increase in disposable income. › Some sectors of the economy may suffer from staff shortages. Workers from other countries may come to Ireland to take up available employment. For example, in January 2020 there was an estimated shortfall of 30,000 construction workers in Ireland to meet housing demands.

KEY SKILLS

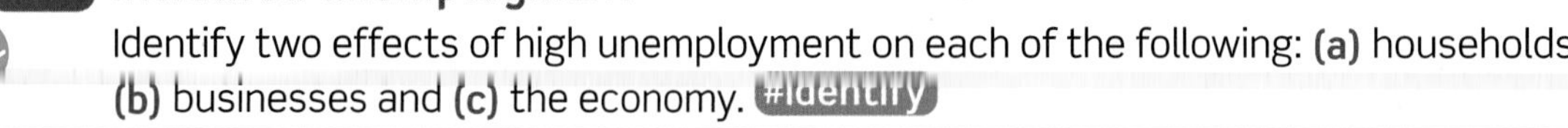

36.7 Increased unemployment

Identify two effects of high unemployment on each of the following: **(a)** households **(b)** businesses and **(c)** the economy. #Identify

3 Interest rates

KEY TERM

Interest rates are the cost of borrowing money expressed as a percentage of the amount borrowed or they are the reward for money saved.

Low interest rates encourage individuals and businesses to borrow more and they reduce the cost of existing borrowings. This is likely to increase the level of spending and investment in the economy. On the other hand, people are less inclined to save when interest rates are low.

Because Ireland is a member of the euro area, interest rates in Ireland are controlled by the European Central Bank (ECB).

See Chapter 40 for the EU

OUR ECONOMY

The effect of low interest rates for households, businesses and the economy

Households	Businesses	Economy
› Access to cheaper finance will result in more borrowing and more spending. › People with existing loans will have more disposable income, as repayment costs are reduced. A reduction in the cost of mortgages will be a huge benefit to households. › Extra borrowing will increase the level of household debt. › People are less likely to save money when interest rates are low.	› Expansion and new product development will be easier because of cheaper loans. This will lead to increased profitability and employment. › Repayments on any existing loans will fall, leading to lower business costs. The business may become more competitive and therefore sales, exports and profits should increase.	› Increased borrowing and spending will lead to an increase in revenue (VAT) for the government. › Increased investment will help to reduce unemployment and the level of social protection payments. › The cost of servicing the national debt will be reduced. › Very low interest rates may discourage householders from saving their money. The extra consumer spending will lead to increased business profits.

The effect of high interest rates for households, businesses and the economy

Households	Businesses	Economy
› Higher interest rates will make borrowing more expensive, which will result in less borrowing. › People with existing loans will have less disposable income as repayment costs are increased. An increase in the cost of mortgages will be a huge burden for many households. › Less borrowing will reduce the level of household debt in the longer term. › People will be more likely to save when interest rates are higher.	› Expansion and new product development will be more difficult because of higher borrowing costs. This will lead to lower levels of profitability and employment. › Repayments on any existing loans will rise, leading to higher business costs. The business may become less competitive and therefore sales, exports and profits will decrease.	› Less borrowing and spending will lead to a decrease in revenue (VAT) for the government. › Lower levels of investment will increase unemployment and the level of social protection payments. › The cost of servicing the national debt will be increased. › Higher interest rates may encourage households to save their money. This will reduce consumer spending and may lead to business closures.

375

Complete questions 21–27 in your Student Activity Book on the effects of interest rates. #Activity

4 National debt

KEY TERM

The **national debt** is the total amount of money that a country's government has borrowed.

Ireland's national debt rose from €65 billion in 2008 to €205 billion in 2019 due to the government's need to fund large budget deficits and to provide financial support to the banks.

IN THE NEWS

Public indebtedness was stable over the 1995–2007 period, averaging around €43 billion per annum. The financial crisis had a major adverse impact on public indebtedness in Ireland, with a massive accumulation of debt over the 2008–2013 period. At the end of 2013, public sector obligations peaked at €215 billion, a fivefold increase from the level immediately preceding the crisis. The level of public debt has been broadly stable at just over €200 billion since then. This represents the equivalent of €42,000 for every person resident in the state. On a per capita basis, public debt in Ireland is the third highest among the world's advanced economies, surpassed only by Japan and the US.

Source: Department of Finance *Annual Report on Public Debt in Ireland*, September 2018

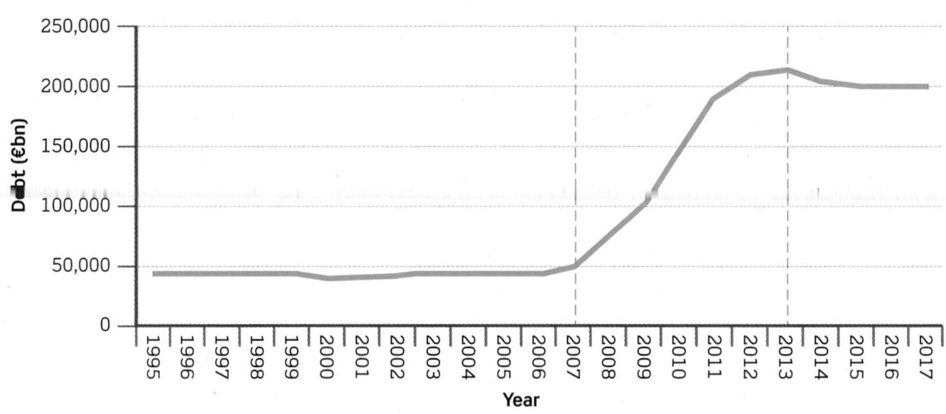

Figure 36.1 Gross public debt (€m) (*Source:* CSO and European Commission)

KEY SKILLS

36.8 Investigate national debt

MIT BL BN

(a) Investigate what happened to the Irish economy during the financial crisis that began in 2007. #Research #Investigate

(b) From your research, suggest one reason why Ireland's debt level increased so quickly. #Evaluate

(c) Considering our high level of national debt, do you think it is better for the government to plan for budget surpluses or budget deficits in the years ahead? Explain your answer. #Consider #Explain #Opinion

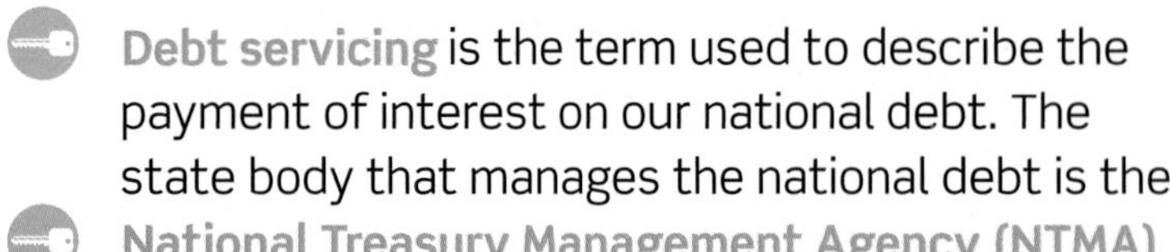

Debt servicing is the term used to describe the payment of interest on our national debt. The state body that manages the national debt is the **National Treasury Management Agency (NTMA)**.

eland still paying €14m a day in interest on national debt

;O figures show government debt stood at €206 billion st year, up from €201 billion previously.

ıe Republic paid out €14 million a day, or €5.2 billion in 018, in interest to service the national debt, new figures ıow.

he CSO's *Government Finance Statistics* report shows overnment debt rose to €206 billion last year, up from 201 billion in 2017, and remains one of the highest per-apita debt burdens in Europe.

Source: Irish Times, 15 April 2019

BN

36.9 National debt

(a) What is the current amount of Ireland's national debt? You can visit the Irish Debt Clock on the Finance Dublin website to find out.

(b) Which country in Europe has the highest national debt?

(c) Which country in the world has the highest national debt? #Research

The impact of national debt on households, businesses and the economy

Households	Businesses	Economy
› Taxes may increase to help fund repayment of the government's loans. › Government spending may be reduced, which will negatively impact the level of public services being provided.	› Consumers with less disposable income will buy fewer goods and services. › Reduced consumer demand may lead to job losses. › A negative economic climate will reduce business investment.	› Borrowing money to pay for essential public services (teachers, gardaí, nurses, etc.) is not sustainable. As a result, these services are likely to be cut back. › Debt has a significant opportunity cost. Money spent on debt servicing is not available for other important needs, including infrastructure and public services.

5 National income

KEY TERM

National income is the total value of all new goods and services produced within a country in a year.

National income is normally expressed as either gross domestic product or gross national product. **Gross domestic product (GDP)** and **gross national product (GNP)** measure the total value of the goods and services produced in a country in one year. GDP or GNP allow us to compare changes in national income from one year to the next. This year-on-year change is used to measure the level of growth in an economy.

6 Economic growth

KEY TERM

Economic growth occurs when there is an increase in the quantity of goods and services produced in an economy from one year to the next. It is measured by year-on-year changes in GNP (or GDP).

Calculation of rate of economic growth

$$\frac{\text{Difference between Year 1 and Year 2}}{\text{Production in Year 1}} \times 100$$

Example

The total value of goods produced in 2019 was €80,000 and in 2020 it was €85,000. Calculate the rate of economic growth.

Solution

$$\frac{\text{Difference between Year 1 and Year 2}}{\text{Production in Year 1}}$$

$$\frac{€85{,}000 - €80{,}000}{€80{,}000} \times 100$$

$$\frac{€5{,}000}{€80{,}000} \times 100$$

Rate of economic growth = 6.25%

The economic cycle

KEY TERM

The **economic cycle** is the way in which the level of economic activity changes over time.

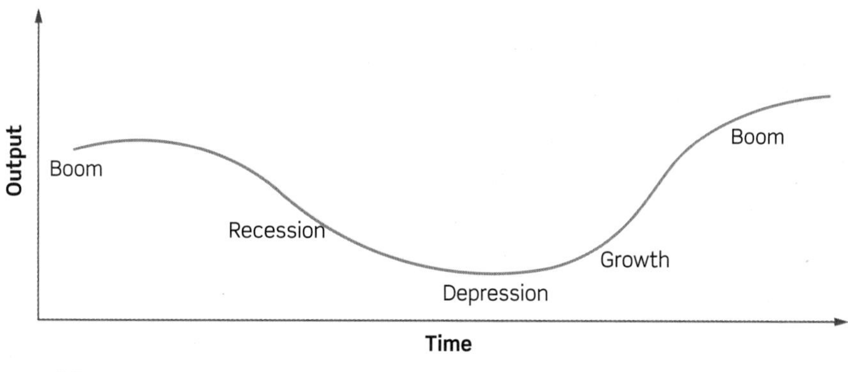

Figure 36.2 The economic cycle

- **Economic growth** occurs when the quantity of goods and services produced in the economy increases from one year to the next. Economic growth is likely to increase when taxation and interest rates are low and investment and employment levels are high. Ireland experienced a period of economic growth from 2014 to 2020.
- **Economic boom** describes a continuous period of rapid economic growth. Ireland experienced an economic boom during the 'Celtic Tiger' years (1994 to 2006).
- A **recession** is a general slowdown in the level of economic activity. Officially, an economy that experiences negative economic growth in two consecutive quarters (six months in a row) is said to be in recession. During a recession, GDP, demand for goods and services, investment, household incomes, business profits and inflation all fall. Ireland experienced a severe recession between 2007 and 2010.
- An **economic depression** occurs when a recession is severe and continues for a long period of time. The Great Depression of the 1930s affected many economies worldwide.

KEY SKILLS

36.10 The economic cycle

Research Ireland's current economic growth rate. Based on your research findings, explain which part of the economic cycle Ireland is in at this time. #Research

MIT BL BN

Economic growth in Ireland

The economic cycle can be seen if we examine the 12-year period from 2006 to 2018 in Ireland. Figure 36.3 shows that during this time, Ireland's economic growth:

- Declined sharply as the recession began in 2007 and remained negative until 2010
- Increased at a slow pace until 2013
- Was much stronger in 2015
- Economic growth increased (at a slower rate) between 2016 and 2018.

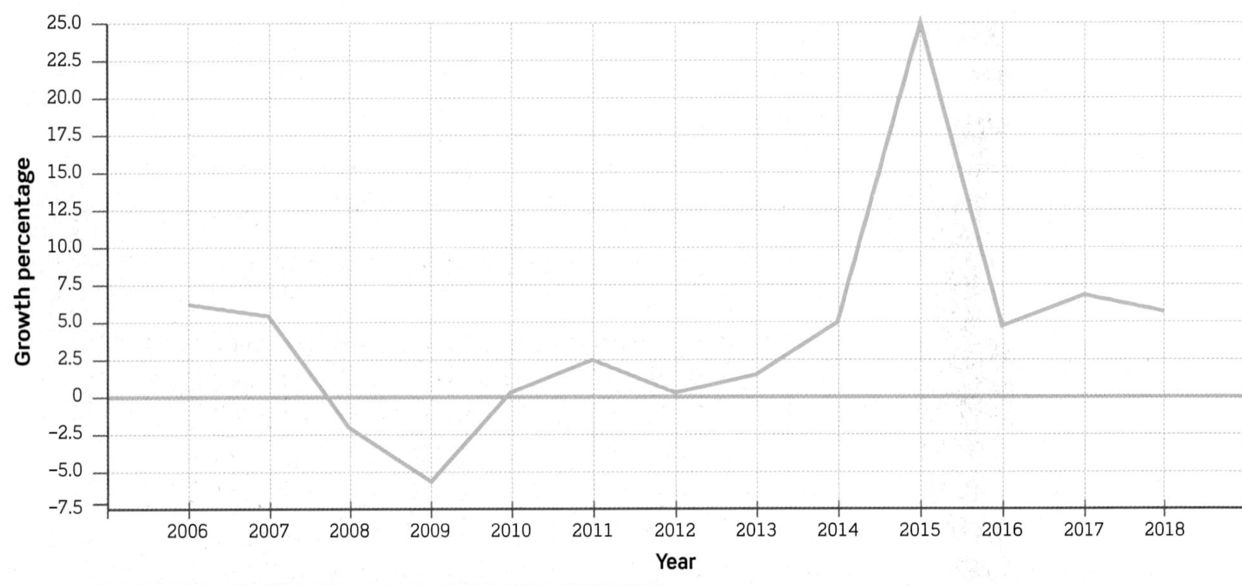

Figure 36.3 Economic growth in Ireland, 2006–2018

KEY SKILLS BN MIT BL

36.11 Economic growth

The table shows the figures for economic growth in Ireland and for the world from 2006 to 2018.

(a) Draw a line graph plotting these two series of figures. #Presentation #Illustrate #Graph

(b) Comment on economic growth, comparing Ireland with the rest of the world (average). #Compare #Comment #Analyse

(c) Research the rate of economic growth in Ireland for each year since 2018. #Research

(d) Research why the 2015 growth rate in Ireland was so high. #Research #Analyse

	Economic growth	
Year	**Ireland (%)**	**World (%)**
2006	6.3	4.1
2007	5.5	3.9
2008	–2.2	1.5
2009	–5.6	–2.1
2010	0.4	4.1
2011	2.6	2.8
2012	0.2	2.3
2013	1.4	2.4
2014	5.2	2.5
2015	25.1	2.9
2016	5.0	3.4
2017	7.22	3.8
2018	6.65	3.0

KEY SKILLS MIT BN 

36.12 GDP growth rate

The following figures show the year-on-year GDP growth rate in an economy for 2015 to 2019.

Year	2015	2016	2017	2018	2019
GDP growth rate (%)	5.2	5.6	5.1	7.8	3.8

Draw a trend graph to illustrate the growth rate of GDP in this economy for the years 2015 to 2019. #Graph #Presentation 

The effects of economic growth on households, businesses and the economy

Households	Businesses	Economy
› There will be increased employment and a decrease in social protection payments. › There will be an increase in living standards. › More goods and services will be available for consumption.	› There will be an increase in new businesses start-ups and a decrease in the number of business failures. › **Multiplier effect:** As more money is spent in the economy, demand increases, which will encourage production. This will lead to increased employment, which will lead to increased demand.	› The government will have more revenue from taxation, especially income tax from extra employees and VAT on increased consumption. › The extra tax revenue will enable the government to provide better public services. › There will be a decrease in the national debt, as the government will have to borrow less money. It may also be able to use extra tax income to repay existing debt. › There will be less emigration and more immigration because there will be greater demand for labour as the economy grows. › There may be strong economic growth and inflation. When the economy grows rapidly, some resources become scarce, which causes prices to rise. › Continuous economic growth, even at low rates, requires extra factors of production, which may put pressure on scarce resources. It can also lead to a lot of environmental damage as land is cleared for agriculture and the development of industry.

See Chapter 38 for sustainable development

Everything you need to know about Ireland's economy

Ireland's economy is outperforming most other eurozone countries, with almost full employment and rising real wages. So why are Irish consumers among the most pessimistic in Europe?

Although it was among the nations hardest hit by the 2007/8 economic crisis, Ireland's economy has bounced back. The European Commission forecast in February 2019 that the Irish economy would grow by 4.1% that year, the second highest growth rate in Europe.

The EU forecast was slightly down on its previous prediction, but unemployment is heading down towards 5% and real wages rose by 3.2% last year, while prices increased by only 0.7%.

Income inequality has fallen by 8% in recent years thanks to a big increase in the national minimum wage two years ago. Ireland has also been doing well in promoting gender equality, coming ninth in the World Economic Forum Gender Gap Index, ahead of France, Denmark, Germany and the UK.

Ireland was ranked 24th out of 137 nations in the World Economic Forum Global Competitiveness Index last year. However, the report highlighted the need to improve infrastructure and cut bureaucratic burdens on business. An OECD report last year highlighted the need to boost productivity too.

Source: World Economic Forum, 19 March 2019

36.13 Good news?

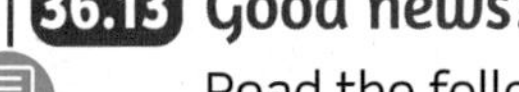

Read the following statement and answer the questions below: 'The news item above paints a positive picture of Ireland's recent economic performance.'

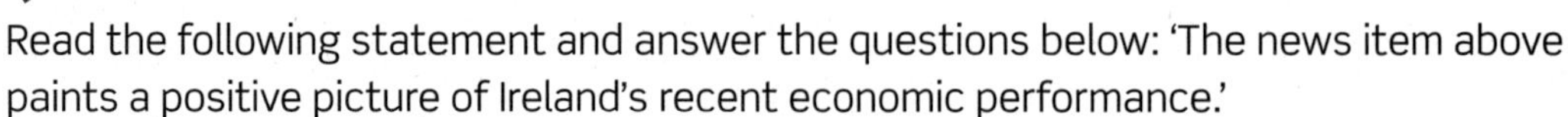

(a) Explain, giving three reasons, why you agree or disagree with this statement. Use the evidence presented in the news article to support your point of view. #Evaluate #Justify

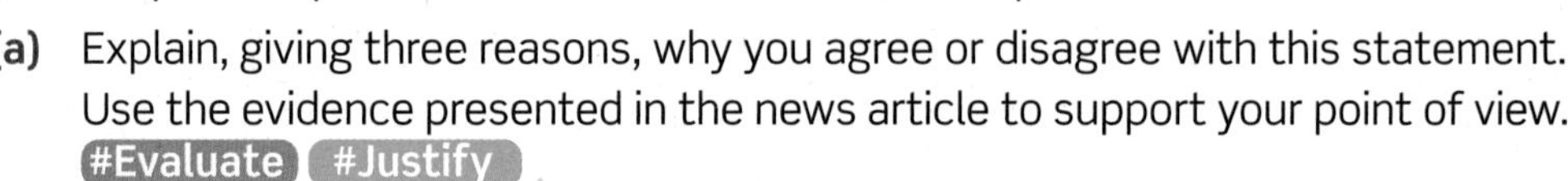

(b) Based on the evidence in the article, state one reason why somebody might have a different view from your own. #WhatDoYouThink #Analyse

EXAM QUESTION

SEC Sample Paper
Question 10

'The Irish economy is growing three times faster than any other European country.'
– Adapted from the *Irish Times*, February 2018

State two ways in which economic growth can have a positive impact on a small town in rural Ireland.

 **Weblinks**  **PowerPoint Summary**

GOVERNMENT ECONOMIC POLICY

LEARNING OUTCOMES IN FOCUS

3.11 Evaluate the benefits and costs of a government economic policy and assess who enjoys the benefits and who bears the costs

3.10 Use their knowledge, and information from a range of media sources, to discuss current economic issues and present an informed view

LEARNING INTENTIONS FOR THIS CHAPTER

When you have completed this chapter you will be able to:

- Understand the main aims of government economic policy
- Describe some of the different types of government economic policy
- Evaluate the costs and benefits of a government policy
- Analyse and discuss current economic issues.

CHAPTER 37 KEY TERMS

economic policy
fiscal policy
foreign direct investment (FDI)
indigenous firms
industrial policy
monetary policy
policy
primary sector
secondary sector
tertiary sector

CHAPTER 37 KEY SKILLS

- BC Being Creative
- BL Being Literate
- C Communicating
- MIT Managing Information and Thinking
- MM Managing Myself
- WO Working with Others

What is government economic policy?

KEY TERM

Government **economic policy** refers to all the ways in which the government tries to have an impact on the economy.

A **policy** sets out proposed actions and guidelines for an organisation to follow. All organisations write their own policies. Some are required by law (for example, a health and safety policy) and some are created by choice (for example, an internet usage policy). Your school will have a number of policies that set out how your school complies with laws or wants its students and staff to behave.

KEY SKILLS 

37.1 School policies

Your school has many policies. Investigate any two of them and explain how they benefit the school community as a whole.

#GroupWork

WO MIT C BL

Governments also have a number of policies, including ones that are designed to deal with the country's economy. Current examples in Ireland include Project Ireland 2040 and the National Development Plan 2018–2027. These long-term plans aim to improve Ireland's economic, social and environmental progress.

The main aim of government economic policy is to create a stable economic climate that promotes:

- Full employment
- Low inflation
- Sustainable economic growth
- Industrial and regional development
- Social and income equality
- Development of infrastructure
- International trade.

While many government policies have an economic impact, we will confine our discussion to the following major policies:

- Fiscal policy
- Monetary policy
- Industrial policy
- Direct intervention policy.

Fiscal policy

Fiscal policy (also called budgetary policy) is how the government sets the levels of taxation and spending in the economy in order to achieve its economic goals. We saw in Chapter 35 (Government Revenue and Expenditure) that this means creating national budgets. Fiscal policy also deals with the redistribution of wealth and resources.

For example, the government may decide to increase income tax rates for higher earners and use some of this money to increase public services for the less well-off. In recent years, the government has also started to use carbon taxes and grants to try to promote more sustainable energy usage by households and industry. Examples include grants for improving the energy efficiency of houses and to help with the purchase of electric vehicles.

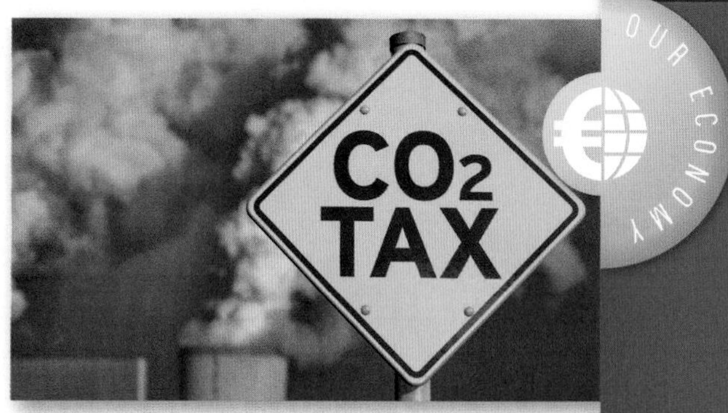

Monetary policy

Monetary policy is used to control the supply of money available in an economy at a particular time. It is also used to set interest rates and to help control inflation.

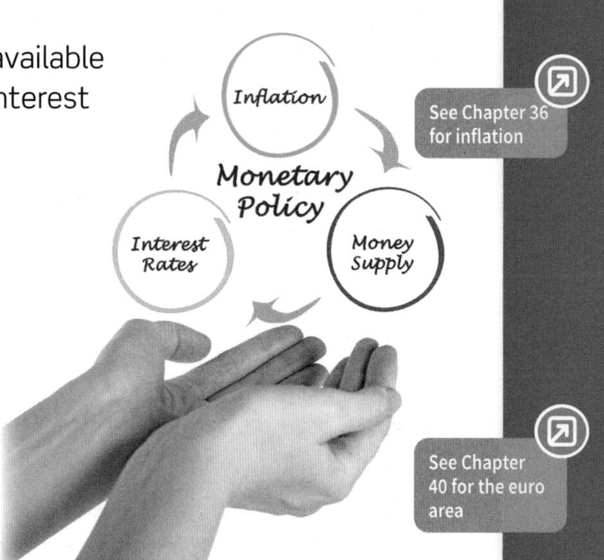

See Chapter 36 for inflation

For example, higher interest rates and a smaller supply of money will tend to reduce borrowing and spending. This will help to keep prices under control.

The European Central Bank (ECB) sets the interest rates and controls the supply of money in all euro area countries, including Ireland. This means that the Irish government has little or no control over monetary policy. Countries outside the euro area have a greater ability to control their supply of money and their interest rates.

See Chapter 40 for the euro area

Industrial policy

The government's **industrial policy** encourages the development and growth of the three sectors of the economy (primary, secondary and tertiary).

Sector	Description	Examples
Primary	Extractive industries that use natural resources to produce goods.	Farming, fisheries, mining, forestry, etc.
Secondary	Manufacturing and construction industries, which use raw materials from the primary sector to make other goods.	Computer manufacturers, furniture makers, builders, etc.
Tertiary	Service industries that are not directly involved in making any goods, but provide a huge range of services for households and businesses. This is currently the largest sector in the Irish economy, accounting for over 75% of total employment.	Banks, education services, hairdressers, medical services, transport companies, etc.

The government encourages both indigenous (local) businesses and foreign direct investment (FDI), as they create employment in the economy.

> **KEY TERM**
>
> **Indigenous firms** are business that are established and owned by local people.

See Chapter 14 for globalisation

> **KEY TERM**
>
> **Foreign direct investment (FDI)** occurs when a foreign company invests in our country, perhaps by building a factory or a shop to produce and sell its goods or services.

See Chapter 32 for state-owned organisations

Direct intervention policy

The government's direct intervention policy deals with setting up semi-state enterprises to provide goods and services that are not produced or supplied by the private sector. These enterprises provide jobs in the public sector, which are paid for by the taxpayer. Many are operated on a commercial basis, with profits going to the state or reinvested back into the organisation. Examples include An Post, Horse Racing Ireland and RTÉ.

> **KEY SKILLS** MIT BL
>
>  **37.2 State-owned enterprises in Ireland**
>
>  List three other examples of semi-state enterprises in Ireland. 

Evaluating government economic policy

Government economic policies impact the success of the economy as a whole, the taxes paid by households and the public services available to citizens. For this reason, all citizens should keep up to date with important economic developments and debates.

>  MIT MM BL
>
> **37.3 Stay informed**
>
>  Create a scrapbook (actual or digital) to which you can add news articles about topical economic issues and policies. This useful resource will enable you to keep up to date with ongoing developments and will help with future evaluation of government policy. You may be able to use some of the information you have gathered as inspiration or research material for your classroom-based assessment (CBA). #Research #Presentation

Researching economic issues

Use the questions in Table 37.1 to help you evaluate economic issues. The answers to these questions will inform your opinions and may even help to influence the actions of the organisation you work or volunteer for in the future.

Question	Reason
What is the economic issue?	You need to understand the issue and the impact it might have.
What caused the economic issue?	Understanding the cause may highlight the solution or help to avoid future problems.
What is the government doing about it?	How the government is dealing with the issue will impact you. You need to know whether there is already an economic policy in place or whether there is going to be one. If there is a policy, when was it introduced and has it started having an effect yet?

Question	Reason
Do other countries have a similar economic policy?	If so, how similar is it to the Irish policy and how successful has it been? Your answer to this question will help you to decide how effective our government's policy might be.
What are the benefits of the economic policy? What problem(s) will this policy help to solve?	How will the policy have a positive impact on our society and economy? What are the benefits? Who will/does it benefit and how will they benefit? Will it benefit everybody or just some people?
Are there any costs associated with the policy? Will there be financial or opportunity costs associated with the policy?	Who will bear the cost? Who in society will suffer the negative impacts of this policy? Will they suffer financial or opportunity costs?
Do you agree with the economic policy that is in place?	Why/why not? If not, how would you deal with the issue?
Can you see the benefits of the policy for Ireland, for its citizens, for you personally and for your organisation?	If it benefits one section of society but has costs for another, is this acceptable for the overall good of the country?

Table 37.1 Questions to consider when researching and evaluating economic policies

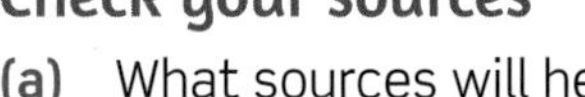

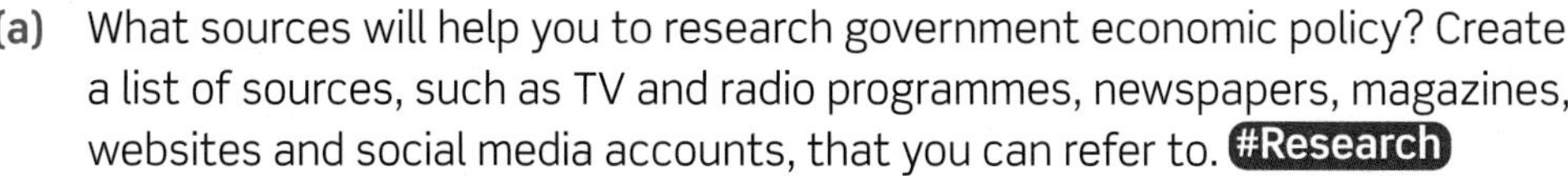

Assessing government economic policies

Any policy needs to be assessed from time to time to see if it is achieving its goals. If it is not working, it may be necessary to change or abandon it.

A cost–benefit analysis

The first stage in assessing any economic policy is to carry out a cost–benefit analysis. This weighs up all the costs associated with the policy and balances them against the potential benefits. The benefits should outweigh the costs.

What are the costs and who bears them?

Every policy decision will involve both a financial cost and an opportunity cost. For example, the decision to spend €2 billion (financial cost) on the national children's hospital means that this money is not available for spending on schools or social housing (opportunity costs).

Before introducing a new policy, the government must consider the costs involved as well as the impact that these costs will have on the country and its citizens.

Taxpayers usually bear the costs of government policy, either through increased taxation or cutbacks in public services. Even if the money is borrowed, future tax revenue will be used to service the debt and make loan repayments.

In terms of cost, some policy decisions impact more heavily on specific groups of citizens. For example:

- Introducing a residential property tax impacts home owners.
- Imposing the Universal Social Charge impacts all those in employment.
- Raising the national minimum wage increases wage costs for all employers.

KEY SKILLS

MIT

37.5 Who is affected?

Who bears the greatest cost for the following decisions? #Think

(a) Cutting the rate of Child Benefit

(b) Increasing the pupil–teacher ratio

What are the benefits and who receives them?

Some citizens may benefit directly from government economic policy. Others may benefit indirectly. Some examples that illustrate the benefits of government economic government policy include the following:

- Providing grants for FDI will directly benefit those who get jobs with these overseas employers. Extra corporation tax collected from FDI companies will have indirect benefits for many citizens, as the government may be able to reduce income tax or increase spending on public services.
- Cutting income tax rates will directly benefit all employees. Businesses may receive indirect benefits when these workers choose to spend their additional disposable income.

IN THE NEWS

OUR ECONOMY

'Sugar tax' on fizzy drinks raises €32m, but none of it goes on tackling obesity

The nation's craving for sweet, fizzy drinks generated €31.72m in the first year of the sugar tax – but not a cent has been directly spent on tackling the obesity crisis. The tax on sugar-sweetened drinks came into force in May 2018 in a bid to wean children in particular off high-calorie soft drinks. But all of the proceeds have gone into the Exchequer pool, unlike the UK, which is specifically targeting its sugar tax to fund sports and breakfast clubs.

The tax is, however, having the positive effect of forcing more drinks manufacturers to reformulate their recipes for popular products and reduce their sugar content to avoid the levy.

Professor Donal O'Shea, the HSE's lead on obesity, is to make a renewed bid to get the government in the upcoming budget to pump a substantial slice of the takings from the tax into improving lifestyle habits and also the treatment of people who are severely overweight. 'It is a missed opportunity not to use some of the revenue raised in prevention and treatment of obesity,' he said. 'There is a government policy and action on obesity, but it needs resources.'

The annual budget for the Healthy Ireland fund has remained around €5m, which is not going far enough, as stark figures show at least one in five children is overweight or obese. One in four adults is classed as obese.

Asked if it intended to direct some of the sugar tax take to fighting obesity, a spokesperson for the Department of Finance said that dedicating the revenue from a specific tax for a particular expenditure purpose was not a feature of the Irish tax system in general. This would reduce the flexibility of the government to prioritise and allocate funds as necessary at a particular time.

'An annual budget is allocated to the Department of Health as part of the estimates process, and that is assigned according to the needs within that department, including in relation to measures to tackle the problem of obesity.'

'The reality is that we are at increased financial risk by not treating obesity properly,' Professor O'Shea said.

He welcomed the fact that the tax is leading to a cut in the sugar content of a growing number of fizzy drinks.

The tax allows a levy of 16c per litre for drinks with 5–8g of sugar per 100ml. It rises to 24c a litre for varieties with more than 8g. When VAT is included, this works out at 20c per litre for drinks with 5–8g of sugar per 100ml and 30c per litre for drinks with more than 8g of sugar per 100ml.

Some products, such as Lucozade, Fanta, Sprite and Vimto, changed their recipes so that they contain less than 5g of sugar and avoid the tax. Others, including Coca-Cola and Pepsi, still produce classic varieties with the traditional sugar-sweetened recipe.

A 330ml can of cola contains 139 calories and 35g of sugar, equivalent to more than eight teaspoons.

Source: Irish Independent, 8 July 2019

A cost–benefit analysis of the sugar tax

What is the economic issue?

- The negative impact of obesity on our society and the increasing costs associated with poor diet and ill health.
- This is a socio-economic issue, which means that it impacts on the wellbeing of both our society and our economy.

What caused the economic issue?

- An increase in the marketing, availability and consumption of food and drink products that have a high sugar content. This has led to greater levels of ill health. A large number of people suffer from obesity, heart disease, type 2 diabetes and other diet-related problems.
- This obesity epidemic has resulted in huge economic costs. A 2012 study* into the economic cost of obesity in the Republic of Ireland estimated the annual cost to be €1.13 billion. This figure includes direct treatment and healthcare costs as well as indirect economic costs, such as absence from work and premature death.

**Source:* Safefood

See Chapter 34 for social reasons for taxation

What is the government doing about it? Is there an economic policy in place?

- The government introduced a sugar tax on 1 May 2018 that increased the price of high-sugar drinks. It was hoped that this would reduce their consumption.
- Drinks with more than 8g of added sugar per 100ml are taxed at 24 cents per litre (30 cents including VAT). Pure fruit juices are exempt from the tax as are dairy products on the basis of their nutritional value.
- The additional government revenue raised from the tax could be used to fund education programmes designed to promote healthy eating.

Do other countries have a similar economic policy? If so, how successful has it been?

Several other countries have introduced sugar taxes, with mixed results:

- Mexico successfully introduced a sugar tax, which resulted in a 6% reduction in purchases of sugary drinks. Norway, Finland and France have also successfully introduced sugar taxes.
- Denmark introduced a tax on fatty foods in 2011 and had plans for a sugar tax. However, it scrapped both taxes after a year because many consumers engaged in cross-border shopping in Germany in order to avoid the levy.

What are the benefits of the economic policy?

- Estimated savings on direct healthcare costs, including doctors' fees and medicines, of €398 million per year.*
- Estimated indirect economic benefits, due to higher productivity and lower mortality, of €728 million per year.*
- Total financial benefit to the economy of €1.13 billion per annum.*
- Tax revenue of €32 million and an expected reduction in obesity levels by around 1.25% (or 10,000 people).

**Source: Irish Times*, 23 December 2015

Are there any costs?

- **Cost of collection:** Revenue has expressed concerns that it may cost more to introduce and collect the tax than it will generate in tax revenue.
- **Possible loss of FDI:** The introduction of the sugar tax may make Ireland a less attractive location for multinational soft drinks companies to locate, which may cost jobs.

Do you agree with the economic policy? If not, how would you deal with the economic issue?

- The cost–benefit analysis above indicates that the economic cost of obesity is very high and needs to be reduced. Previous attempts using education alone have not worked, so it seems reasonable that another approach should be taken.
- Despite concerns over collection costs and the regressive nature of a flat tax, which is likely to fall more heavily on low-income families, the analysis suggests that the introduction of the sugar tax has increased tax revenues and has the potential to reduce government spending on healthcare.
- Because the tax has only been in place for a short time, it is probably too soon to be sure of the long-term benefits and a review of the policy should be carried out in a few years' time.

KEY SKILLS

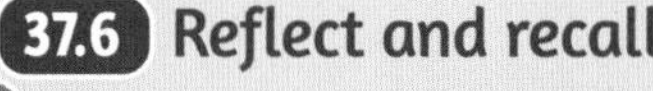

37.6 Reflect and recall

BC

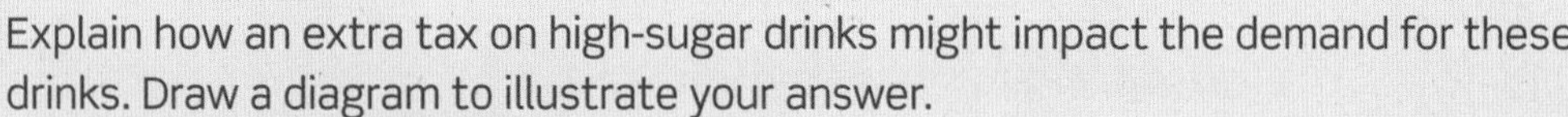

Explain how an extra tax on high-sugar drinks might impact the demand for these drinks. Draw a diagram to illustrate your answer.

#Evaluate #Presentation #Reflect

BL

37.7 A cost–benefit analysis

388

Consider the costs and benefits associated with one of the following government economic policy proposals and complete the cost–benefit analysis template in your Student Activity Book, following the example we have given for the sugar tax above. Consider the costs and benefits **(i)** from the government's point of view and **(ii)** from your own and your family's point of view. #Research

(a) Decentralisation (a proposal to move some government services and departments away from major cities like Cork and Dublin and relocate them in large rural towns)

(b) A decision to scrap the Universal Social Charge

(c) A decision to build enough social housing to eliminate social housing lists

(d) A proposal to provide free state-funded childcare for all pre-school children

(e) A proposal to introduce a 'wealth tax' for all those with incomes over €100,000 per annum

(f) A decision to privatise a major public sector business such as An Post or Córas Iompair Éireann (CIÉ)

(g) A proposal to reintroduce college fees for all students

(h) A decision to provide free GP care and prescription medication for everyone

(i) A proposal to increase the level of carbon tax on fuel

(j) Any other economic policy decision of your choice – it may be something that has a direct impact on you or your family or it may be something that is topical or in the news at the moment

PowerPoint Summary

OUR ECONOMY

SUSTAINABLE ECONOMIC DEVELOPMENT

LEARNING OUTCOMES IN FOCUS

3.6 Explain how economic growth can impact positively and negatively on society and the environment and justify the promotion of sustainable development

Links to 1.1, 1.9, 2.1, 2.2, 2.4, 2.5, 3.1, 3.2, 3.3, 3.7, 3.8, 3.9, 3.10, 3.11

3.10 Use their knowledge, and information from a range of media sources, to discuss current economic issues and present an informed view

LEARNING INTENTIONS FOR THIS CHAPTER

When you have completed this chapter you will be able to:

- Explain the term 'economic growth'
- Outline the key features of economic growth
- Identify the positive and negative effects of economic growth on society and the environment
- Appreciate the need for sustainable development
- Explain the term 'business ethics'
- Suggest ways the government can influence the impact of business on society and the environment.

CHAPTER 38 KEY TERMS

business ethics
corporate social responsibility (CSR)
economic growth
Environmental Protection Agency (EPA)
social costs
sustainable development
Sustainable Energy Authority of Ireland (SEAI)

CHAPTER 38 KEY SKILLS

- BC Being Creative
- BL Being Literate
- C Communicating
- MIT Managing Information and Thinking
- MM Managing Myself
- SW Staying Well
- WO Working with Others

Economic growth and its effects on society and the environment

KEY TERM

Economic growth occurs when there is an increase in the quantity of goods and services produced in an economy from one year to the next. It is measured by year-on-year changes in GNP (or GDP).

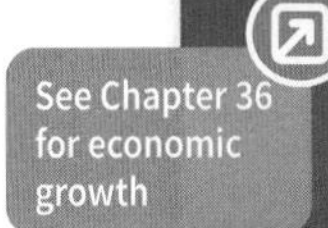

See Chapter 36 for economic growth

Economic growth is likely to increase when taxation and interest rates are low and investment and employment levels are high.

Positive effects of economic growth

- There will be an increase in employment and a decrease in social protection payments.
- An increase in economic growth will lead to an improvement in the standard of living for employees.
- The government will have more revenue from the collection of extra taxation.
- The government will be able to provide better public services.
- More goods and services will be available for consumption.
- There will be a decrease in the national debt, as the government will have to borrow less money.
- There will be a decrease in the number of business failures and an increase in new business start-ups.
- There will be less emigration and/or more immigration.
- The extra money available through increased employment will be spent on goods and services, which will lead to further economic growth.
- Economic growth leads to an increase in demand for higher education, as people have more money to spend on education. Interestingly, there is also a positive relationship between higher education standards and economic growth, as businesses tend to locate near a supply of well-educated workers.
- Countries with high economic growth spend more money on infrastructure, such as transport, telecommunications, supply of water, electricity and gas. This in turn leads to further increases in economic growth, as better infrastructure makes it easier for businesses to trade.
- An increase in living standards has a positive effect on life expectancy.

DID YOU KNOW...

In Ireland in 1915, the average life expectancy was just over 49 years for both men and women, while currently it is just over 78 for Irish men and just under 83 for Irish women.

KEY SKILLS

38.1 How to live longer

In pairs, discuss why an increase in living standards (more income, better healthcare and housing, etc.) has a positive impact on life expectancy. Share your reasons with the whole class and listen to your classmates' reasons.

Negative effects of economic growth

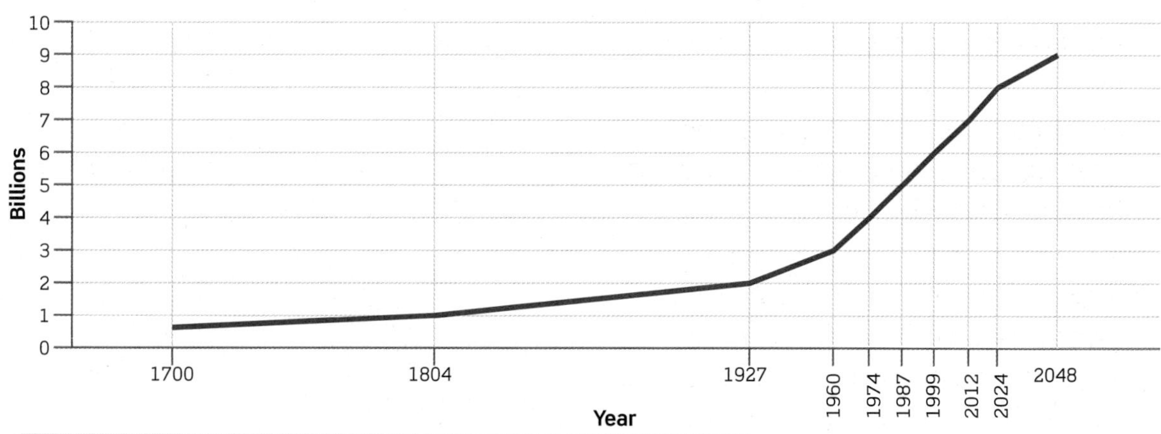

Figure 38.1 World population since 1700 and projected to 2048

See Chapter 31 for scarcity and choice

See Chapter 33 for demand and supply

- Better living standards have led to people living longer. There are now more people alive than at any point in history and the number is growing. As economic resources are scarce, food production and supply may not be able to keep up with demand from a growing population.
- An increase in living standards and an increase in the number of people in full-time employment with less time at home can lead to people spending money on convenience foods, which cause obesity when consumed to excess.
- The economy may become over-reliant on a particular industry. For example, during the Celtic Tiger economic boom (1994–2006), the Irish economy was over-reliant on the construction sector, so when the economic crash occurred there was very high unemployment in this sector.

DID YOU KNOW...

Over two-thirds of Irish people are overweight or obese. The annual cost of obesity in Ireland is over €1 billion. Almost 40% of this is in direct healthcare costs, while the remainder is indirect costs, such as lost productivity and absenteeism.

- Economic growth may lead to the destruction of natural habitats to build factories.
- Economic growth may cause increased pollution, for example air pollution caused by the fossil fuels required by planes and cargo ships that are used to export goods around the world.
- Increased traffic congestion may be caused by delivering more goods, which in turn increases exhaust emissions, adding to pollution and greenhouse gases.
- More landfill sites will be required for large amounts of consumer waste.
- Since the Industrial Revolution in the late eighteenth century, business activity has contributed to climate change due to the increased use of fossil fuels (coal, oil, gas), which release carbon dioxide into the atmosphere. This has increased greenhouse gases, causing the surface temperature of Earth to rise. China and India are two of the most densely populated countries in the world, with over 36% of the world's population between them. As these economies develop, they will use increasing amounts of already limited fossil fuels.

DID YOU KNOW...

The number of wild animals living on Earth is set to fall by two-thirds by 2020, part of a mass extinction that is destroying the natural world on which humanity depends. Animal populations plummeted by 58% between 1970 and 2012, with losses on track to reach 67% by 2020. The destruction of wild habitats, hunting and pollution were to blame.

(*Source: The Guardian*, 27 October 2016)

- Economic growth may cause income inequality – the gap between the rich and poor has increased significantly in recent decades.
- Economic growth may lead to the destruction of landmarks and sites of historical importance.

The social and environmental impact of economic growth should not be underestimated, especially when we consider the demands it places on scarce resources (factors of production). For example, a 3% increase in economic growth each year requires a doubling of inputs and resources over a 34-year period.

See Chapter 31 for factors of production

DID YOU KNOW...

The USA has 5% of the world's population but consumes 30% of the world's resources and generates 30% of the world's waste. If all countries consumed at US rates, we would need three to five planets!

Existing resources are already being consumed at enormous rates, so it seems unlikely that we could consider doubling that rate of consumption in the future. If we do it will have implications for our planet and for future generations, but if we don't it may impact on our ability to achieve economic growth. Does this suggest that we need to rethink our priorities and goals at a global level? Are we willing to take a longer-term view of the impact of our consumer choices? How will all of this impact on our current lives and the lives of future generations?

See Chapters 31 and 32 for economic resources

DID YOU KNOW...

The Kyoto Protocol of 1997 is an international treaty that established legally binding commitments to reduce greenhouse gases. There are financial penalties for countries that fail to achieve their targets. Ireland signed this protocol and must abide by it.

KEY SKILLS MIT BL MM C

38.2 Your opinion

'I don't care about being popular. I care about climate justice and the living planet. Our civilisation is being sacrificed for the opportunity of a very small number of people to continue making enormous amounts of money.' Greta Thunberg

Write a short personal response outlining how you feel about the Greta Thunberg quotation. Do you think she makes a good point? Do you agree with her? What difference, if any, do you think her words and actions will have? Explain your thinking clearly. #WhatDoYouThink #Reflect #Opinion

DID YOU KNOW...

In 2013, a Mayan pyramid in Belize was destroyed. The pyramid, called the Noh Mul temple, which was approximately 2,300 years old, was destroyed by a construction company for use as gravel for road filler. Only a small part of the pyramid was left standing.

KEY SKILLS

38.3 Share your thoughts

Discuss how it makes you feel when you read or hear stories like the one about the Mayan temple being bulldozed. Should profit ever come before heritage and environment? Should the people responsible for this destruction be penalised lightly or heavily? #Opinion #Discussion

Sustainable development

KEY TERM

Sustainable development is development that meets the needs of the present without limiting the ability of future generations to meet their own needs.

DID YOU KNOW...

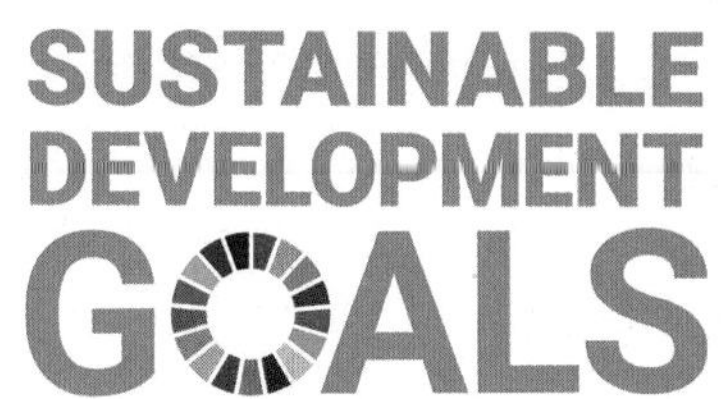

The United Nations has 17 Sustainable Development Goals to transform the world, including one on economic growth. Some of the targets include:

- An increase of 7% in GDP in the least developed countries
- Stopping forced labour, human trafficking and child labour
- Protecting workers' rights
- Promoting safe and secure working environments for all workers
- Achieving full and productive employment for all men and women, including people with disabilities, by 2030
- Reducing the proportion of young people not in employment, education or training by 2030.

Sustainable economic growth requires countries to create conditions where the economy is stimulated without harming the environment. Job opportunities and decent working conditions are also required for the entire working-age population.

In recent years, consumers and businesses have become more aware of the need to be socially responsible and take the environment into account when producing goods and services. Examples of this include:

- Using sustainable raw materials
- Replanting raw materials, such as trees
- Recycling waste products
- Increasing the use of environmentally friendly products
- Decreasing pollution
- Using renewable energies such as solar panels and wind power.

DID YOU KNOW...

Velvet, the toilet tissue brand, replaces three trees for every one they use to make their toilet tissue. To date they have planted over 7 million trees around the world.

KEY SKILLS  MIT BL

38.4 Your sustainable goal

(a) Visit the United Nations Sustainable Development Goals website. Choose one goal that interests you and read the information provided to find out about the targets linked to that goal. #Research

(b) Suggest three specific actions that the Irish government could take to help reach those targets and achieve your chosen goal. #Suggest

(c) When you have completed this task, visit Ireland's Sustainable Development Goals (SDGs) data hub website to investigate the progress that Ireland has made in terms of achieving that goal. #Evaluate

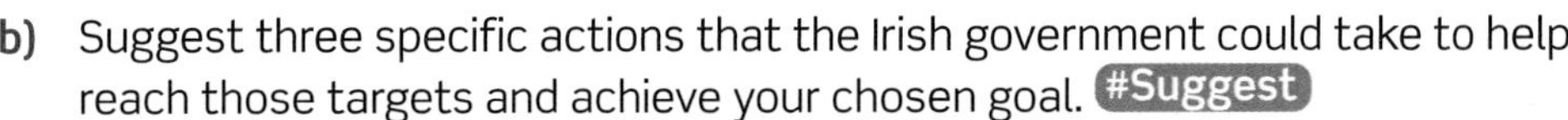

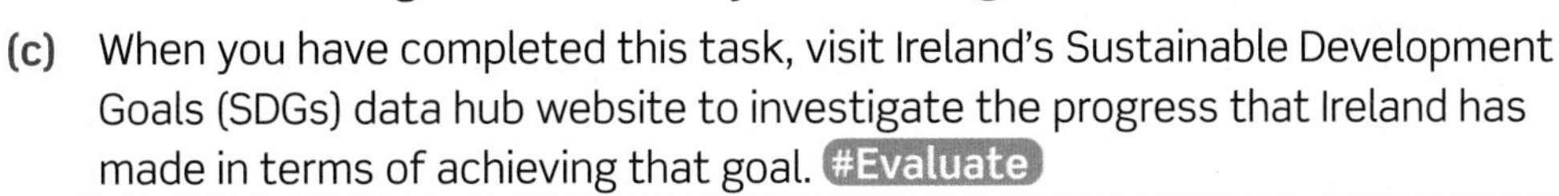

Irish Sustainable Development Goal 'champions' to be recognised

IN THE NEWS

UN SDGs set ambitious environmental targets to be achieved by 2030

Achieving all 17 UN Sustainable Development Goals will be a challenge 'but it is possible if everyone across society gets involved', according to Minister for the Environment Richard Bruton.

Irish organisations and individuals who are leading by example in achieving the UN Sustainable Development Goals (SDGs) are to be recognised by the government as an inspiration for others to follow.

The 17 SDGs are an ambitious set of targets to be achieved by 2030, covering the social, economic and environmental requirements for a sustainable future. They cover policy areas such as poverty eradication, economic development, protection of the environment, addressing climate change, access to health and education services, gender equality, peaceful societies and human rights.

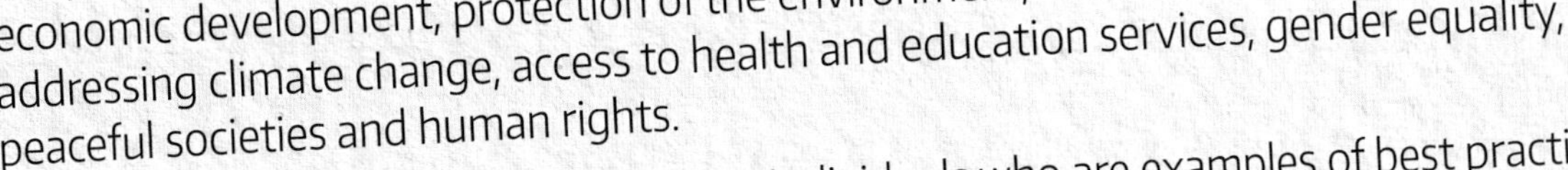

'SDG Champions' will be organisations or individuals who are examples of best practice and who 'will inspire others to contribute in whatever way they can to Ireland's attainment of the goals', according to Mr Bruton.

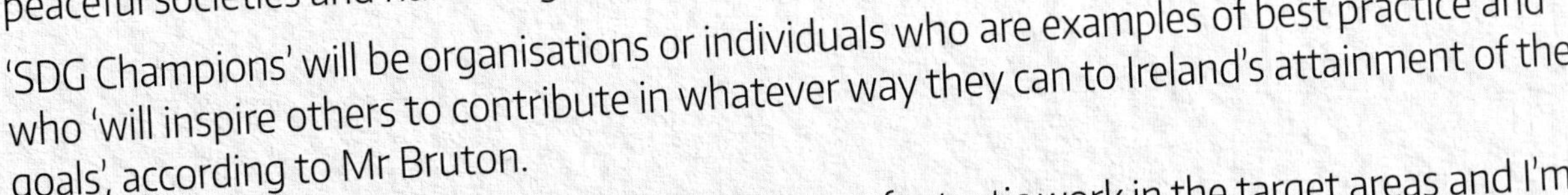

'Many organisations across Ireland are doing some fantastic work in the target areas and I'm keen to harness this good work to inspire others to contribute in whatever way they can,' he told the third meeting of the National SDG Stakeholder Forum in Dublin Castle.

The government has committed to fully implementing the goals, Mr Bruton said. An implementation plan has been put in place and a senior officials group established, led by the Department of the Taoiseach, to ensure this commitment is met.

Source: Irish Times, 31 January 2019

KEY SKILLS  MIT BC

38.5 Sustainable energy zone

Research how Dundalk, Co. Louth became Ireland's first sustainable energy zone in 2007. Create an infographic to show:

- What a sustainable energy zone is
- How Dundalk is managing this
- What its aims are. #Research #Presentation

KEY SKILLS

38.6 Your zone

What steps (if any) has your local village/town/city taken to be more sustainable? What other steps could it take?

#Research

MIT BL SW

Producing sustainable products

As natural resources continue to be consumed and depleted, businesses are under increasing pressure from governments, consumers and retailers to produce sustainable products. Many have begun to adopt a 'total life cycle' approach and examine the environmental cost of the product across all stages of its production and disposal.

The cradle-to-grave approach to sustainability

The total life cycle approach looks at the sustainability of a product 'from cradle to grave'. This requires businesses to consider all of the following.

Production and sourcing of raw materials

The questions that need to be asked are:

- Are raw materials sourced in an ethical way and from sustainable sources?
- What is the impact on the workers, communities and economies involved in the production of raw materials?

Product manufacturing processes

Many businesses have changed how they produce their goods in order to reduce the social and environmental costs of their activities. **Social costs** are the costs to society of business activity. Cutting down rainforests and environmental pollution are examples of social costs because everyone in society suffers the consequences of these actions.

The impact of product distribution

Production facilities should be located close to the source of raw materials and/or consumers in order to minimise transportation and its environmental impact. Modes of transport that rely on fossil fuels should be eliminated or reduced.

The impact of product usage by consumers

This used to be seen as being beyond the control of a business, but attitudes have changed and more businesses are designing and marketing their products to reduce the social and environmental costs associated with their use.

The makers of all electrical goods are required to display an energy rating for each of their products. This helps consumers to make an informed choice when buying products, as they can see which product provides the greatest energy efficiency.

KEY SKILLS

MIT C WO MM

38.7 Energy ratings

(a) Discuss whether you think an energy rating score is a good or bad thing for producers and consumers.

(b) Would you like to see rating scales applied to other goods? Explain your answer.

#Discussion #WhatDoYouThink

See Chapter 1 for resources

See Chapter 13 for the impact of consumer choices

The impact of product disposal

Producers may try to influence consumer attitudes and behaviour by using recyclable materials and packaging. They may also support efforts or policies designed to promote the sustainable disposal of product waste. Examples include using refillable containers for many products and the promotion of the 'reduce, reuse, recycle' campaign.

In some industries the government may take action to make producers accountable for product disposal. For example, WEEE Ireland helps members to meet their producer responsibility through the collection, recovery and recycling of waste electrical and electronic equipment and batteries.

KEY SKILLS

MIT

BC

BL

38.8 Making a difference

(a) What does WEEE stand for?

(b) Who does WEEE work for?

(c) How does WEEE work with schools? #Research

(d) Create a poster that could go on the wall in schools to encourage them to work with WEEE. Display the posters in your classroom or school. #Presentation

The benefits of the life cycle approach

The life cycle approach to sustainability offers the following benefits.

Take a longer-term view

Decisions made at individual or industry level should aim to promote long-term sustainability. Quotas in the fishing industry are a good example of this type of long-term thinking. The industry realises that there is little point in increasing short-term production and job creation if the long-term consequences would lead to the extinction of some species and the eventual demise of the industry.

Japan resumes commercial whaling

IN THE NEWS

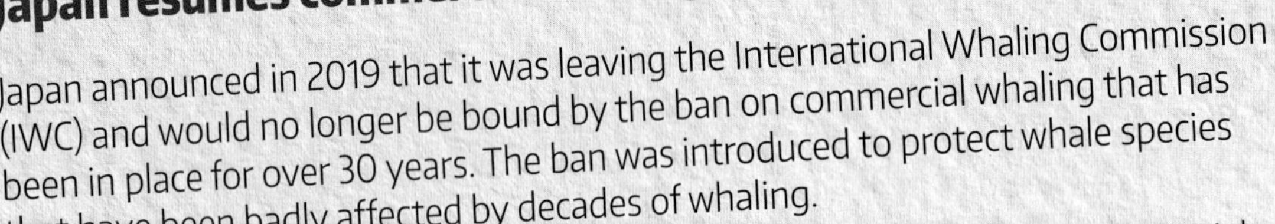

Japan announced in 2019 that it was leaving the International Whaling Commission (IWC) and would no longer be bound by the ban on commercial whaling that has been in place for over 30 years. The ban was introduced to protect whale species that have been badly affected by decades of whaling.

Japan began whaling for scientific research a year after a 1986 ban on commercial whaling, aiming to gather what it called crucial population data. Critics said the programme was simply commercial whaling in disguise after the meat of animals taken in scientific whaling ended up on store shelves and in restaurants.

The annual quota for commercial whaling, including minkes, sei whales and Bryde's whales, is 227. The quota, to be set annually, is less than the 330 whales Japan harvested in the Antarctic until recently.

There has been widespread criticism from across the globe at Japan's decision to return to commercial whaling.

Source: RTÉ News, 1 July 2019

Focus on the bigger picture

See Chapter 13 for the impact of consumer choices

Our decisions have consequences – the actions that we take can impact on others at different stages of the life cycle. This wider focus should also prevent stakeholders at one stage of the life cycle from taking actions that simply push the problem or the negative consequences to another stage. This also emphasises interdependence and shared responsibility.

Promote positive action and sustainable behaviour

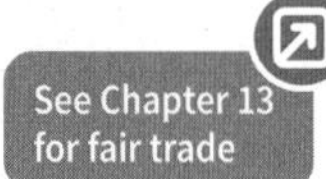

See Chapter 13 for fair trade

Since we are aware of the negative consequences, we are in a better position to take steps to reduce or eliminate them. The fair trade campaign is a good example – it began when retailers and consumers supported the calls for a fairer share of wealth and better working conditions, especially for producers and suppliers of raw materials.

Corporate social responsibility (CSR)

Many businesses now have a **corporate social responsibility (CSR)** policy. CSR sets out how the organisation will act to benefit society and/or the environment. A CSR policy has the following benefits for the business:

- The reputation of the business will improve as it reduces its negative impact on the environment and society.

- Customers who care about the environment are likely to buy from the business.
- The business can attract top-quality staff who share their aims.

Dell is an American computer manufacturer that produces and sells PCs and laptops directly to the consumer through its company website. Each order can be customised to the consumer's specific requirements. Dell employs over 100,000 people worldwide and has a comprehensive CSR policy.

Dell minimises negative impacts on the environment by reducing waste and preventing pollution in its factories. All boxing materials are made from recycled materials. Its products are designed to reduce air pollution and consumers can recycle used computers, monitors and printers for free when they purchase a new Dell product.

KEY SKILLS

MIT

38.9 CSR in action

(a) Use Dell's website to research its corporate responsibility policy and identify what steps it takes to reduce its impact on the environment and local communities. #Research

(b) Croke Park became the first stadium in Ireland and the UK to be certified for sustainability and environmental protection. Research the steps Croke Park takes to minimise its impact on the environment and identify whether your local GAA grounds could adopt similar steps. #Research

(c) Consider a manufacturer located near you. Find out whether it has a CSR policy and, if so, what it prioritises. #Investigate

Business ethics

Business ethics are moral principles that influence the way a business behaves to consumers, suppliers, employees, shareholders, the government and society. Business ethics tells businesspeople what is the right and wrong thing to do in any situation.

By behaving ethically, a business can attract consumers and staff who agree with its aims. The business may also receive awards for being ethical.

An ethical business will behave responsibly towards all stakeholders and the environment.

Ethical responsibilities of an organisation to its stakeholders	
Consumers	› Provide high-quality goods and services at a fair price.
Suppliers	› Pay suppliers on time. › Source supplies from sustainable sources, e.g. Fairtrade suppliers.
Employees	› Fair pay. › Equal pay for all employees. › Adopt health and safety procedures.
Shareholders	› Run the business in the best interests of the shareholders. › Provide a fair return on investment.
Government	› Pay all taxes on time. › Obey the law.
Society	› Ensure the business does not negatively affect the local environment.

DID YOU KNOW...

In November 2015, Nestlé (which produces a range of products, such as Cheerios breakfast cereal, Nescafé coffee, Rowntree sweets and pet foods) commissioned an investigation of their supply chain and found that slave labour was being used to produce pet food in Thailand. Nestlé has since taken steps to protect workers.

KEY SKILLS

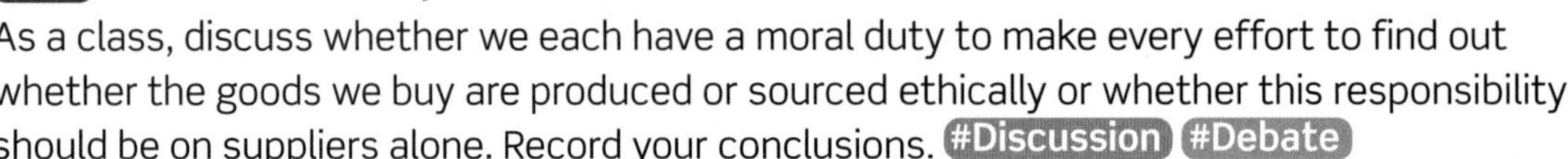

38.10 Consumers' responsibilities

As a class, discuss whether we each have a moral duty to make every effort to find out whether the goods we buy are produced or sourced ethically or whether this responsibility should be on suppliers alone. Record your conclusions. #Discussion #Debate

WO C MIT

Role of government in reducing negative impacts of business on society

Central and local government have a clear role to play in reducing the negative impact of business and economic growth on society and the environment. They can do this by:

- Passing laws such as the Safety, Health and Welfare at Work Act 2005 and the Consumer Protection Act 2007 to ensure that workers and consumers are protected from unsafe business practices
- Refusing planning permission to a business that, for example, wants to build a factory that would harm the environment or the health of local people or would cause traffic congestion in an area
- Introducing a charge to limit damage caused by pollutants and waste, for example the levy on plastic shopping bags that was introduced in 2002 to reduce the consumption of disposable plastic bags.

DID YOU KNOW...

The plastic bag levy introduced in 2002 had an immediate effect on consumer behaviour. Usage dropped from an estimated 328 bags to 21 bags per person per year.

38.11 Planning in your local area

Research the website of your local authority to see if any planning applications have been made that could have a negative impact in your local area. #Research

Government organisations that protect the environment

Environmental Protection Agency (EPA)

The **Environmental Protection Agency (EPA)** is a public body that was established in 1992. It helps to protect Ireland's environment by providing advice to businesses through publishing reports and guidance on air quality, biodiversity, climate change, green business, waste, drinking water, noise and genetically modified organisms (GMOs). It also enforces environmental law; monitors, analyses and reports on the environment; and conducts environmental research.

Sustainable Energy Authority of Ireland (SEAI)

Established in 2002, the **Sustainable Energy Authority of Ireland (SEAI)** is Ireland's national energy agency. It aims to promote sustainable energy by:

- Developing renewable sources of energy
- Improving energy efficiency
- Reducing the impact of energy use on the environment
- Providing advice to consumers
- Managing grants for home improvement to reduce energy consumption.

Something to think about

Could doughnuts really be the answer to sustainable economic development? Kate Raworth, an Oxford economist, has challenged the traditional economic models that are based on endless economic growth. She says that this type of model is unsustainable because it does not meet the needs of millions of people and overuses many of the Earth's valuable and limited resources. She says that the traditional circular flow of income is not realistic because it ignores the following:

- Our economy is totally connected to the environment. We rely on natural resources to meet many of our needs and wants, but these resources are not endless.
- The unpaid work of parents and volunteers and the economic trade of the barter economy add value to our lives and our economies, but these are not counted in the circular flow. Bartering involves swapping goods and services – for example, you cut your elderly neighbour's grass and they look after your pet while you are away on holiday.
- Current models based on endless growth have failed to meet the needs of millions and have resulted in the unequal use of resources and distribution of wealth.

As an alternative, Kate Raworth thinks we need to look at a doughnut-shaped economic model, which helps to identify a balance between meeting the basic needs of all people without overusing the Earth's resources.

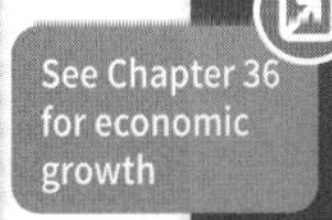
See Chapter 36 for economic growth

See Chapter 32 for circular flow of income

The centre ring of the doughnut lists basic human needs. People who are living in this space do not have enough of these. They are falling short of their minimum human needs for a range of things that will improve their lives and wellbeing. Economists' aim should be to ensure that everyone at least reaches the line labelled 'social foundation' (or floor), as this is the minimum requirement for these basic human needs.

climate change
ocean acidification
chemical pollution
nitrogen and phosphorous loading
freshwater withdrawals
land conversion
biodiversity loss
air pollution
ozone layer depletion
ECOLOGICAL CEILING
THE SAFE AND JUST SPACE FOR HUMANITY
SOCIAL FOUNDATION
REGENERATIVE AND DISTRIBUTIVE ECONOMY
OVERSHOOT
SHORTFALL
water
food
health
education
income and work
peace and justice
political voice
social equality
gender equality
housing
networks
energy

At the same time, we need to ensure that we do not overshoot the limits of the planet's resources, especially in relation to each of the nine areas listed on the outer ring. This is seen as the ecological (or environmental) ceiling and links back to the need for sustainable development that has been explored in this chapter. There is already evidence that we have problems with at least four of these environmental issues:

- Climate change
- Biodiversity loss
- Air pollution
- Ozone layer depletion.

The doughnut model suggests that the global economy needs to operate in the space between the social foundation and the ecological ceiling. Think of this as the dough in the doughnut! This area allows us to meet the needs of our population and also protect the natural environment that current and future generations depend on.

In her book *Doughnut Economics*, Kate Raworth outlines the need for a circular economy that is based on the regeneration and reuse of resources. She argues that there are plenty of profitable ideas that will improve human wellbeing and be environmentally responsible. Enterprises need to look at their activities through the lens of doughnut economics.

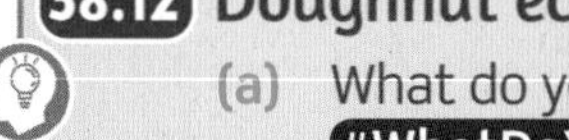

38.12 Doughnut economics

(a) What do you think of Kate Raworth's ideas? Do you think they are realistic? #WhatDoYouThink

(b) Do you think we need to rethink our approach to economic development? Why/why not? #WhatDoYouThink

(c) What questions would you like to ask her about her ideas and suggestions? What more do you need to know? #Reflect #Investigate

You could research this topic further by listening to Kate Raworth. To do this, search for a video of Kate Raworth speaking at the TEDx Conference in Athens in 2014.

PowerPoint Summary

INTERNATIONAL TRADE AND GLOBALISATION

LEARNING OUTCOMES IN FOCUS

3.7 Debate the implications of globalisation of trade, including the benefits and challenges of international trade

Links to 1.7, 1.9, 1.10, 2.5, 2.6, 3.3, 3.6, 3.8, 3.10, 3.11

LEARNING INTENTIONS FOR THIS CHAPTER

When you have completed this chapter you will be able to:

- Explain the term 'international trade'
- Illustrate the difference between importing and exporting
- Explain the difference between visible and invisible trade
- Outline the reasons why Ireland trades with other countries
- Outline the benefits and challenges for Irish business when it trades with other countries
- Differentiate between the balance of trade and the balance of payments
- Explain the term 'globalisation'
- Debate the implications of the globalisation of trade
- Appreciate how interconnected the world is and how the actions of some impact on many others.

CHAPTER 39 KEY TERMS

balance of payments	importing
balance of trade	international trade
deregulation	invisible exports
economies of scale	invisible imports
embargo	invisible trade
Enterprise Ireland	quota
exporting	subsidy
free trade	tariff
global business	trade barriers
global marketing (4Ps)	visible exports
	visible imports
globalisation	visible trade

CHAPTER 39 KEY SKILLS

- BC Being Creative
- BL Being Literate
- BN Being Numerate
- C Communicating
- MIT Managing Information and Thinking

What is international trade?

KEY TERM

International trade is the buying (**importing**) and selling (**exporting**) of goods and services between different countries.

Ireland is one of the most open economies in the world. This means that Ireland is an economy that engages very strongly in international trade. Ireland exports nearly 80% of what it produces.

International trade is divided into visible and invisible trade:

- **Visible trade** involves physical goods that can be seen going out of and coming into Ireland, for example food and cars.
- **Invisible trade** involves services. No physical goods can be seen going out of or coming into Ireland as a result of the sale or purchase of services, for example insurance, banking and tourism.

What is importing?

KEY TERM

Importing is buying goods or services from other countries. When this happens, money leaves the country.

Imports are divided into visible and invisible imports:

- **Visible imports** are the physical goods that Ireland buys from other countries, for example cars, oil, coal and fruit.
- **Invisible imports** are services that Ireland buys from other countries, for example Irish people going on holiday abroad, foreign bands performing in Ireland, Irish students going abroad on school tours, giving a foreign firm the contract to build our roads and Irish people buying services such as insurance and transport from foreign businesses.

KEY SKILLS

39.1 Ireland's imports

MIT

(a) Write down 10 goods or services that you think Ireland imports. #List

(b) Research Ireland's major imports, then compare your list from part (a) to the list you found from your research. Was there anything that surprised you about the actual list? Share your lists with your partner, then with the class. #Research #ThinkPairShare

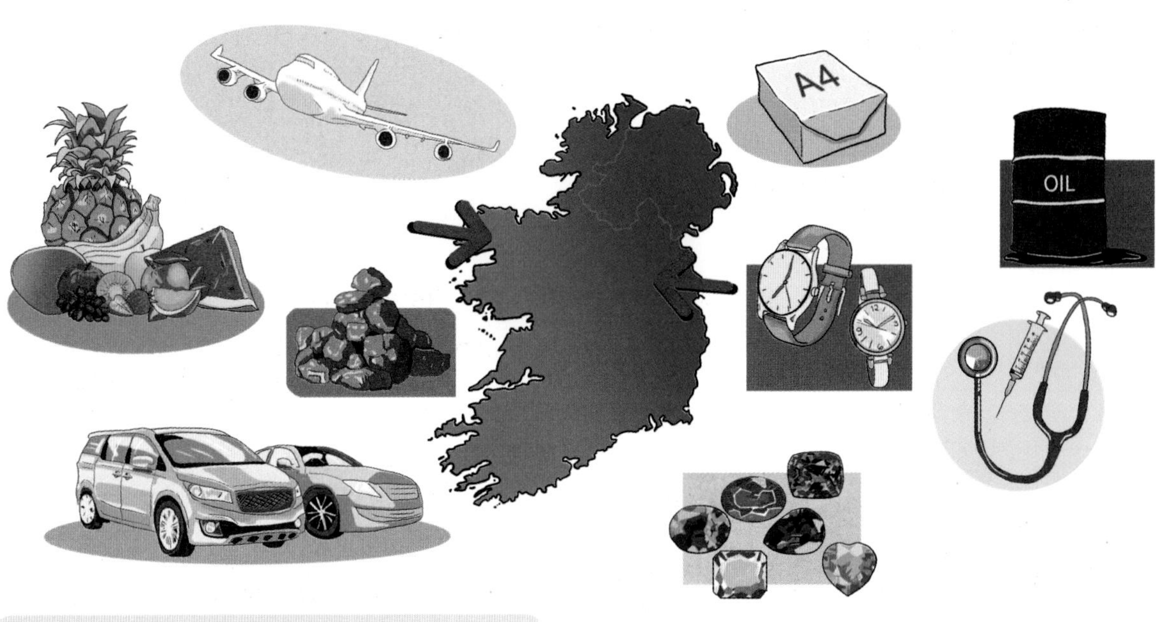

Figure 39.1 Some of Ireland's visible imports

Why does Ireland import goods and services?

Ireland is not able to provide all the goods and services we need for the following reasons:

- **Climate:** Ireland does not have the climate to grow certain products, such as oranges, bananas and coffee.
- **Raw materials:** Ireland lacks the essential raw materials or natural resources that would enable us to produce certain goods, such as oil, coal and steel.
- **Choice for consumers:** Irish consumers want to have a variety of goods and services to choose from, such as fruit, clothing, electrical goods, etc.
- **Skills:** Certain countries have people with the skills to make certain products, for example Swiss watches. There is a lack of skills and tradition in producing some goods or services, which is a limiting factor in production.
- **Cost:** Foreign goods may be cheaper than comparable Irish goods.
- **Small domestic market:** The Irish market is small, so certain products cannot be produced economically and must be imported, for example cars.

What is exporting?

KEY TERM

Exporting is selling goods or services to other countries. In the case of all exports, money comes into the country.

Exporting is divided into visible and invisible exports:

- **Visible exports** are the physical products or goods that Ireland sells to other countries, for example meat, dairy products, live animals, ICT equipment, pharmaceuticals.
- **Invisible exports** are services that Ireland sells to other countries, for example Spanish students coming to Ireland to learn English and an Irish band performing in another country.

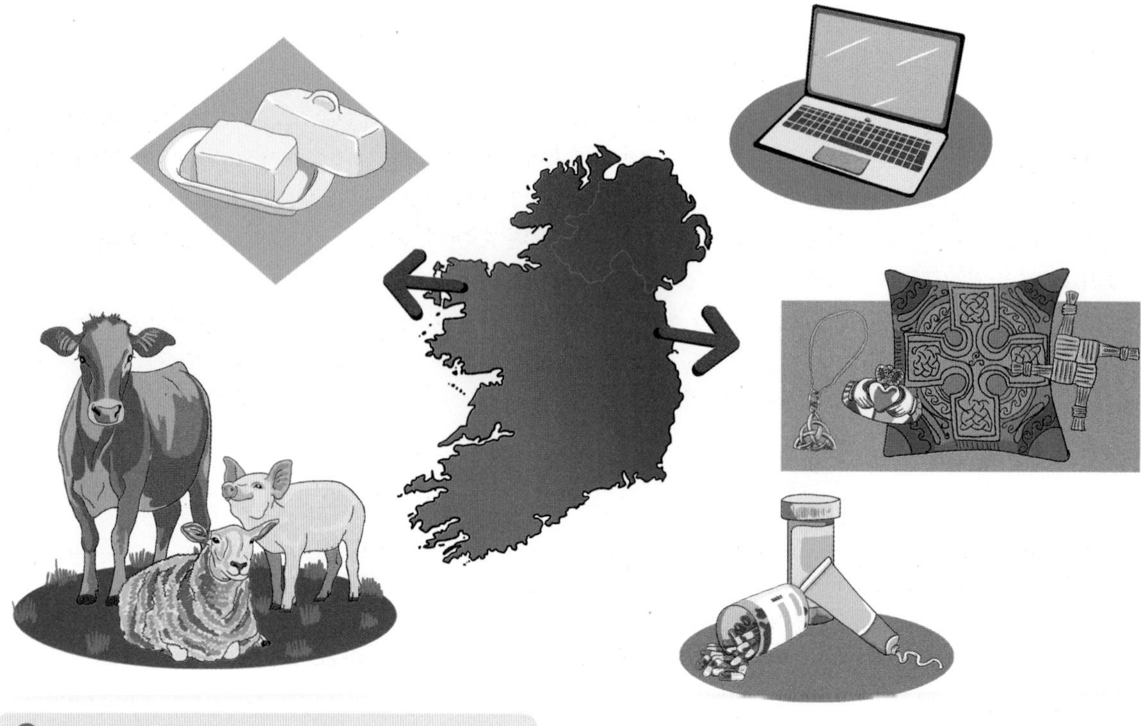

Figure 39.2 Some of Ireland's visible exports

Why does Ireland export goods and services?

- **Increased sales/profits:** Irish firms can increase their sales and profits by exporting their excess output to a foreign market. This also helps them to overcome the problem of having a small domestic market.
- **Employment creation:** Exporting helps to support jobs in Ireland. The more we sell, the more people we need to make the goods.
- **Demand:** There is demand from consumers abroad for Irish products, such as for our high-quality food products like beef and butter.
- **Earn foreign currencies:** The receipt of foreign currencies can boost our country's reserves and provides the finance to help pay for imports.

KEY SKILLS

MIT

39.2 Playing both sides

Some items might appear on both export and import lists, such as clothes and ICT equipment.

(a) Why might Ireland both import and export ICT equipment?

(b) What other items might be both imported and exported? #Compare

Ireland's main trading partners

Ireland is a small open economy, which means that we rely heavily on trading (importing and exporting) with other countries, but our level of trade is not large enough to impact on the global economy. Some of our trading partners have much greater economic power, and changes in their economies can impact on the entire global economy. Examples include the USA, UK and China.

	Exports	Imports
Trading partners	› United States › United Kingdom › Belgium › Germany › Switzerland › France › The Netherlands › Spain	› United Kingdom › United States › Germany › China › The Netherlands › France › Japan › Switzerland
Goods and services	› Machinery and equipment › Computers › Chemicals › Medical devices › Pharmaceuticals › Food › Animal products	› Petroleum and petroleum products › Cars › Machinery › Textiles and clothing › Aircraft and transport equipment
Value (2018)	€141 billion	€92 billion

Table 39.1 Ireland's exports and imports

39.3 Partners in trade

(a) Research the most recent figures for the value of goods imported from Ireland's main trading partners. #Research

(b) Carry out the same exercise for the exports. #Research

(c) Compare the two sets of figures graphically using a trend graph, pie chart or bar chart. #Compare #Presentation #Illustrate #Graph

(d) What do these figures tell you? #Evaluate

(e) Create a presentation, poster or infographic to show your results. #Presentation

How is international trade measured?

KEY TERM

The **balance of trade** is the difference between visible exports and visible imports over a period of time, usually one year. It accounts for trade in **goods** only.

Balance of trade = Visible exports − Visible imports

Visible exports > Visible imports = Balance of trade surplus

Visible exports < Visible imports = Balance of trade deficit

A surplus means that there is a net inflow of money coming into an economy from sales to overseas customers.

KEY TERM

The balance of payments is the difference between total exports and total imports over a period of time, usually one year. It accounts for trade in both **goods and services**.

The balance of payments shows the flow of money coming into and going out of a country.

Balance of payments = Total exports – Total imports

Total exports > Total imports = Balance of payments surplus

Total imports < Total exports = Balance of payments deficit

How to calculate the balance of trade and balance of payments

Question

The following data relates to the international trade of a country for 2022:

	€
Visible imports	1,150 million
Invisible imports	1,300 million
Visible exports	1,250 million
Invisible exports	1,380 million

From the above data, calculate **(i)** the balance of trade and **(ii)** the balance of payments.

In each case, state whether it is a surplus or a deficit balance.

Solution

(i) *Balance of trade*

	€ (m)
Visible exports	€1,250
– Visible imports	– €1,150
Surplus	€100

(ii) *Balance of payments*

Total exports	€2,630	(€1,380 + €1,250)
– Total imports	– €2,450	(€1,150 + €1,300)
Surplus	€180	

KEY SKILLS

BN

39.4 International trade

The following data relates to the international trade of a country for 2022:

	€
Visible imports	1,570 million
Invisible exports	1,620 million
Visible exports	2,050 million
Invisible imports	1,950 million

From the above data, calculate **(a)** the balance of trade and **(b)** the balance of payments.

In each case, state whether it is a surplus or a deficit balance. #Calculate

Benefits of international trade for Irish businesses

- **Increased sales:** With fewer than 5 million consumers, the Irish market is quite small. By exporting, Irish businesses can increase sales and access much larger markets. This is very important for industries that rely heavily on exports. For example, Ireland exports over 80% of the beef we produce.
- **Lower costs:** Irish businesses have to increase production to satisfy demand from abroad. The more products that are made, the cheaper it becomes to make each one. This is known as economies of scale.
- **Spreads risk:** A business can spread risk by not relying on its local market alone.
- **Raw materials:** Irish businesses need to import some raw materials as we do not produce them in Ireland, for example oil.

Challenges of international trade for Irish businesses

- **High costs:** Ireland is an island, so transportation is more difficult and more expensive for Irish exporters, as goods can only be transported abroad by plane or ship.
- **Languages:** Irish exporters may need to make their websites available in many languages for customers in different countries, for example Ryanair. They may also have problems when trying to communicate with overseas customers via phone and email, etc.
- **Exchange rates:** If the euro increases in value, the price of Irish products in countries that do not use the euro will become more expensive. This is because overseas customers have to pay more of their own currency to buy the euros needed for the Irish products. This may lead to a reduction in demand for Irish exports. However, if the euro decreases in value, it will be more expensive for Irish importers to buy raw materials from countries that are not in the euro area.
- **Getting paid:** Trying to collect payments from businesses in other countries can be difficult.
- **Competition from low-cost economies:** Irish wages are quite high by international standards. This means that it is much cheaper to produce goods in other countries, particularly in Asia and Africa. It is difficult for Irish manufacturers to compete on cost against goods manufactured in low-wage economies.

EU/Mercosur trade deal

In 2019, the EU agreed the Mercosur trade deal with four South American countries: Brazil, Argentina, Paraguay and Uruguay. The agreement includes detailed rules and regulations covering a wide range of areas and is designed to increase trade between the EU and the Mercosur countries.

The European Union is Mercosur's largest trade and investment partner and its second biggest trade in goods partner. A total of 20.1% of Mercosur exports in 2018 went to the EU.

In 2018, the EU exported €45 billion worth of goods to the four South American countries.

The Irish Farmers' Association (IFA) expressed concern about the importation of South American beef to EU markets and suggested that the potential impact on Irish farmers could be a loss of between €500 and €750 million.

Source: RTÉ News, 29 June 2019

KEY SKILLS MIT

39.5 Opportunities and challenges

How does this news item about the Mercosur trade deal illustrate both the opportunities and the challenges for Irish businesses that arise from international trade? #Reflect #Analyse #Illustrate

Free trade

KEY TERM

Free trade occurs when countries can buy and sell without any trade barriers or restrictions, such as customs duties on goods.

See Chapter 40 for the European single market

The member countries of the European Union (EU) enjoy free trade when trading with each other.

DID YOU KNOW...

The World Trade Organization (WTO) had 164 members as of May 2019. The WTO helps governments to sort out trade problems and encourages the removal of barriers to trade.

Barriers to trade

Governments impose **trade barriers** to limit or restrict international trade. Examples include the following:

- **Tariff:** This is a tax, for example customs duties and import duties, that a country adds to imports to make them more expensive and therefore less attractive for customers to buy. It encourages consumers to buy home-produced products.
- **Quota:** Countries limit the amount of a good that can be imported into their country. This should increase demand for home-produced goods and services. For example, a government may limit the number of cars that can be imported in one year.
- **Embargo:** A country can put a complete ban on goods being imported from a certain country. Consumers will have no choice but to buy the home-produced goods. This may be for health or political reasons. For example, British beef was temporarily banned from most EU countries during an outbreak of BSE (mad cow disease) in the 1990s.
- **Subsidy:** This is a direct payment to a domestic producer. It will reduce the cost of production and make exports cheaper. It boosts employment and improves the balance of trade, for example Irish farmers receiving direct farm payments from the EU.

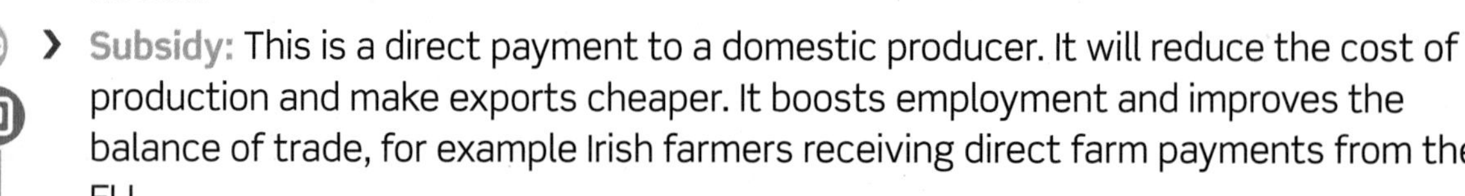

See Chapter 40 for the European Union

Why do countries impose barriers to free trade?

- **To protect their domestic industries:** Industries may have difficulty competing with industries in other countries, so the government may choose to protect them by limiting these imports.

- **To protect domestic employment:** Competition from foreign producers can lead to job losses in the domestic economy, especially if consumers switch from home-produced goods to cheaper imports. Limiting imports may help to protect jobs in some industries.
- **To protect against 'cheap labour' economies:** Domestic firms may not be able to compete with countries where workers are paid low wages, so a government might restrict imports from these countries.
- **National security:** Free trade can result in the spread of animal diseases. For example, if there is an outbreak of foot and mouth disease abroad, the government will ban the importation of cattle to protect this vital industry.

Enterprise Ireland

Enterprise Ireland is the state agency that helps Irish businesses that want to sell their products or services to other countries.

- It provides market research information on foreign markets to Irish businesses.
- It organises trade fairs and exhibitions for Irish businesses to show their products to foreign buyers.
- It provides advice on everything to do with foreign trade, including all documentation, how to get paid, labelling of goods, etc.

Globalisation

Globalisation is the process by which the world becomes interconnected as a result of increased trade and cultural exchange. In effect, the world becomes one big marketplace.

KEY TERM

A **global business** sees the world as one market and production location. It provides the same product worldwide.

KEY TERM

A global business uses a **global marketing** strategy, which involves the same marketing mix of product, price, place and promotion (the **4Ps**) throughout the world to build a global brand. Coca-Cola and McDonald's are examples of global businesses.

The growth in globalisation and global businesses, with their quality produce at cheap prices, is a challenge for Irish exporters. Irish exporters will have to become more efficient and provide products with a unique selling point (USP) to survive the competitive threat from global firms.

KEY SKILLS

39.6 Around the globe

(a) List three other examples of global businesses.

(b) List two examples of Irish global businesses. #Research

Reasons for the development of global businesses

- **Increased sales:** To increase sales and to make higher profits, especially if the business's home market is saturated (it cannot increase its sales any more in its home market).
- **Mass production:** This allows the business to have economies of scale – the more they produce, the lower the cost per unit. For example, when larger quantities are produced, the producer may get bulk buying discounts for raw materials, while some fixed costs, such as rent, advertising, etc., are spread across a larger number of goods. All these factors increase the total cost of production, but help to reduce the production cost per item. In this way, large-scale production leads to economies or savings.
- **Reduction in barriers to trade:** More economies are open to international trade, while advances in digital technologies and transportation make it quicker and cheaper to operate across the globe.

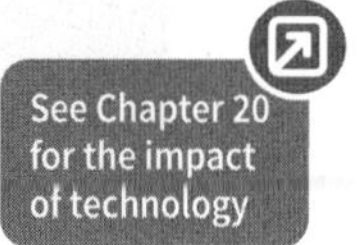
See Chapter 20 for the impact of technology

- **Developments in digital technology:** Communication is faster and easier with the use of video conferencing, email, etc. This has made it easier to manage global businesses.

DID YOU KNOW...

16 hours. 960 minutes. 57,600 seconds.

This is the amount of time it took to send the first transatlantic cable from Valentia Island to Newfoundland in 1858. This might be unthinkable in today's world, where a tweet is posted all over the world in less than one second, but at the time it was ground-breaking. Before that, it took weeks to get a message across the Atlantic.

The Valentia Transatlantic Cable was one of the first steps in a global communications revolution that has led us to be able to transmit messages instantaneously today.

The transatlantic cable was one of the first steps in making Ireland an open, globalised economy. Suddenly, Valentia, London, Newfoundland and New York were connected. What were once distant lands were brought together.

The work didn't stop when the first message was transmitted in 1858. Those 16 hours to send a message were reduced to minutes with the laying of the next cable in 1866 with improvements in technology.

From a speech by Minister Paschal Donohoe to the Valentia Transatlantic Cable Foundation

Global marketing

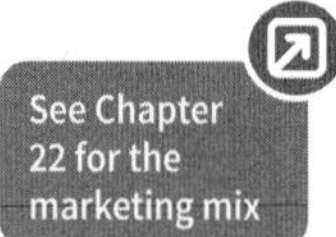
See Chapter 22 for the marketing mix

A global business will sell the same product in the same way all over the world using the global marketing mix (the 4Ps). The global business will concentrate on similarities across world markets. They will make as few changes as possible to their marketing mix to keep production costs down.

Global product

The company will try to use the same brand name and have the same product design all over the world. The product may need to be adjusted to reflect technical, legal and language differences, for example a left-hand-drive car or packaging may need to be changed to cater for the needs of the local market. McDonald's adjusts its menu to fit local tastes. India is the only country where McDonald's doesn't serve beef products, as Hindus believe the cow is sacred and don't eat its meat.

DID YOU KNOW...

'The joy of pizza is that bread, sauce and cheese works fundamentally everywhere, except maybe China, where dairy wasn't a big part of their diet until lately,' explains Domino's CEO, J. Patrick Doyle. 'And it's easy to just change toppings market to market. In Asia, it's seafood and fish. It's curry in India. But half the toppings are standard offerings around the world.'

Global price

Global firms try to charge the same price in each market, but the price may vary in different countries due to the following factors:

- A higher standard of living in some countries may lead to the company charging a higher price, as customers have more disposable income.
- More expensive transport costs to get the product into a country may lead to a higher price.
- More competition may lead to lower prices.
- Exchange rate fluctuations may cause the price to change.

Despite these issues, goods and services are priced relative to their main competitors.

Global place

This is how the global company gets their product to the market. The company could sell directly to customers or use a distribution agent. Many global businesses rely on local agents and distributors to deliver their products. For example, Coca-Cola distributes its product through 250 bottling partners worldwide, while McDonald's uses a franchise model.

See Chapter 24 for franchises

Global promotion

The company will try to use the same advertising all around the world, but this may not always be possible because of differences in language and culture.

Global companies often try to use marketing to localise their global products and make them more appealing to different cultures. For example, in 2014 Coca-Cola launched the 'Share a Coke' campaign and included names on the bottles. In Ireland they

used names such as Aoife and Oisín, whereas in China, where it is disrespectful to call people by their first name, they replaced the names with terms like 'close friend' or 'classmate'. This illustrates how the company used a global marketing strategy to appeal to customers in different markets.

KEY SKILLS

39.7 Global success?

Research other examples of global marketing campaigns that have been very successful or complete failures. Prepare a short presentation or infographic to illustrate the strategy and outline the reasons for its success or failure. #Research #Presentation

Implications of globalisation

For businesses

- **More competition:** Businesses will face greater competition as barriers to international trade are removed (a process called **deregulation**).
- **More export opportunities:** Bigger markets will lead to more export opportunities. This is important for Ireland because our home market is quite small and exporting is necessary for growth.
- **Economies of scale:** Mass production (the manufacture of huge numbers of identical products) is a feature of globalisation. It also reduces unit costs for production, distribution and marketing. Small businesses will find it hard to compete with global businesses on cost and price.
- **Need for quality and innovation:** Scale is important to serve global markets, but this is not possible for smaller producers. Irish business may need to rely on high quality or innovation as alternative ways of competing in global markets.
- **Takeovers:** Successful businesses may be taken over by larger global companies.

For consumers

- **Lower prices:** Consumers may benefit from lower prices as global producers use economies of scale to cut production costs. Some goods that were previously too expensive for many people, for example mobile phones and televisions, have become more affordable and are now owned by huge numbers of people worldwide.
- **Increased choice:** Consumers benefit from a greater choice of products and brands. Sometimes, however, there is less real competition in the market, as global producers own many of the 'competing' brands. Nestlé, Procter & Gamble and Unilever are examples of global businesses that own several brands in the same product sector.

Procter & Gamble products

KEY SKILLS

39.8 Reflect and recall

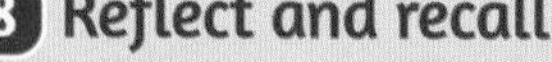

From a marketing point of view, can you think of any reason why a global company would own several different brands in the same product sector? #Reflect

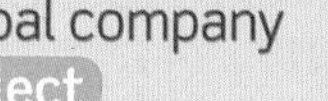

For the economy and society

- **More trade:** Globalisation has led to a huge increase in the volume of international trade.
- **Employment:** Globalisation has led to increased levels of employment, but there have been changes in the types of employment. In some cases this has led to concerns about low pay and job losses in some industries.
- **Increased use of resources:** The economic growth and production demands caused by globalisation have put a greater strain on scarce resources. This has led to a lot of environmental damage and concerns about climate change.
- **Transport and communications:** Globalisation has helped to bring about advances in transport and communications networks, but it has also led to concerns about 'air miles' as products are transported around the world to meet consumer demands.
- **Foreign direct investment (FDI):** Globalisation has increased the level of FDI in many regions. Countries compete against each other to attract this type of inward investment in the hope that it will lead to greater employment and economic growth. In Ireland, most of this inward investment and job creation has been in the Dublin region, which has led to a big urban/rural divide in terms of investment and employment opportunities. Many rural communities have seen a fall in population as people move away to seek employment in large cities.
- **Distribution of wealth:** While globalisation has increased the income level and wealth of many people worldwide, the wealth is not being shared equally and the wealth gap between rich and poor has increased.
- **Cultural issues:** Globalisation relies on selling the same products to all consumers, which has led to concerns about cultural uniformity, where everyone wants to be the same or to copy Western or European lifestyles. This can have a negative impact on other cultures and creates a misleading impression that consumerism is a desirable thing and a measure of wealth or success.

KEY SKILLS

39.9 International trade

MIT BL

(a) Distinguish between the balance of trade and balance of payments. #Distinguish

(b) Outline three benefits of international trade for Irish businesses. #Outline

(c) Outline three challenges of international trade for Irish businesses. #Outline

EXAM QUESTION

Junior Cycle 2019
Question 2

Answer true or false to each of the following statements about globalisation.

(i) Companies have access to bigger markets.
(ii) Consumers have less choice.
(iii) Increased trade leads to increased pollution.

Weblinks

PowerPoint Summary

OUR ECONOMY

CHAPTER 40

THE EUROPEAN UNION

LEARNING OUTCOMES IN FOCUS

3.8 Discuss the economic and social benefits and challenges of Ireland's membership of the EU

Links to 1.7, 1.10, 3.3, 3.4, 3.6, 3.7, 3.9, 3.10, 3.11

3.10 Use their knowledge, and information from a range of media sources, to discuss current economic issues and present an informed view

LEARNING INTENTIONS FOR THIS CHAPTER

When you have completed this chapter you will be able to:

- Explain the term 'European Union'
- Outline the main aims of the European Union
- Explain the term 'trading bloc'
- List the main decision-making and administrative institutions of the EU
- Outline the role of MEPs in representing EU citizens
- Explain the term 'single European market'
- Discuss the major economic and social benefits of Ireland's membership of the EU
- Discuss the major challenges associated with Ireland's membership of the EU.

CHAPTER 40 KEY TERMS

- Brexit
- Common Agricultural Policy (CAP)
- Council of the EU
- Court of Auditors
- Court of Justice of the EU
- euro area
- European Central Bank (ECB)
- European Commission
- European Council
- European Parliament
- European Social Fund (ESF)
- eurozone
- foreign direct investment (FDI)
- Member of the European Parliament (MEP)
- shared sovereignty
- single European market (SEM)

CHAPTER 40 KEY SKILLS

- BC Being Creative
- BL Being Literate
- BN Being Numerate
- C Communicating
- MIT Managing Information and Thinking
- WO Working with Others

Origin and aims of the European Union

The European Union (EU) was established shortly after the Second World War in an attempt to prevent future conflict between former enemies. Originally it was known as the European Economic Community (EEC) and had just six members. Many other countries have since joined, including Ireland in 1973.

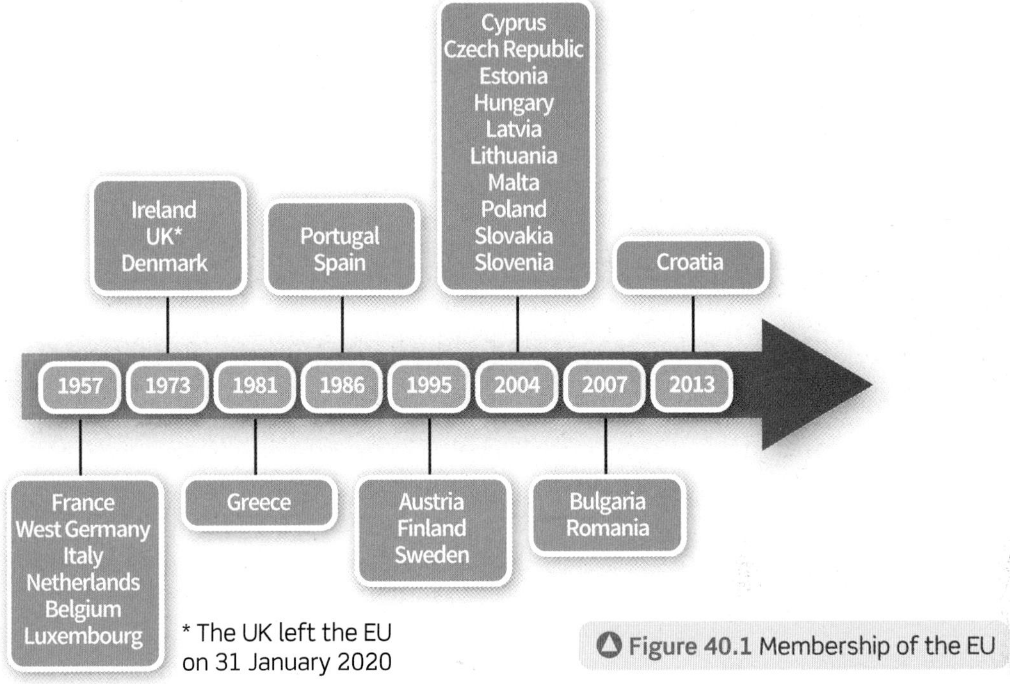

* The UK left the EU on 31 January 2020

Figure 40.1 Membership of the EU

KEY SKILLS

40.1 Join the club

405 How many countries are currently members of the EU? List them in your Student Activity Book. **#Research**

MIT

The EU is a kind of 'club' for European countries. Its members agree to join and to follow the club rules. Each member must pay a fee and in return they receive certain benefits, including the support and co-operation of fellow members.

Club members share ideas and resources and work together to achieve common goals. Member countries also work collectively to promote and improve the position of the EU globally.

The European Union has three main aims:

- To establish European citizenship – this means protecting human rights and freedoms
- To ensure freedom, security and justice for EU citizens
- To promote economic and social progress – this involves the single market, the euro, environmental protection and social and regional development.

As it currently exists, the EU is based on the idea of **shared sovereignty**. This means that each country is willing to give up control over some parts of its government in order to work with others to achieve common goals, standards and laws.

In June 2016, the majority of citizens in the United Kingdom voted to leave the EU. The term **Brexit** was coined to describe Britain's exit from the EU. The impact of Brexit on Ireland will be discussed later in this chapter (see page 471).

The single market
© European Union, 2019

The four freedoms

The EU operates as a single market and has created a free trade area for members, without any barriers to trade across the whole of the EU. A key part of this single European market (SEM) is the 'four freedoms': the free movement of goods, services, capital (money) and people across the EU.

40.2 Freedom of movement

MIT BL

(a) If you have ever travelled abroad, what evidence have you seen of your ability to travel freely within the EU?

(b) How do you think this is different from travelling to non-EU countries such as the USA or Australia?

(c) What are the benefits to you of the EU freedom of movement for all citizens of member states? #Reflect #Consider

European Union institutions

While each member country still has the power to make most of its own laws, a number of EU institutions enact and enforce EU law. These EU rules apply to all member countries and may take priority over domestic laws.

European Council

European Council meetings are summit meetings held regularly by EU heads of state (prime ministers, presidents, our taoiseach, etc.). These meetings are used to set out priorities and the general strategy for the development of the EU. They usually discuss major issues facing the EU, for example debt problems, migration and security concerns.

Once the overall agenda has been set by the European Council, responsibility for day-to-day decision-making in the EU lies with its three main institutions:

- The European Commission
- The European Parliament
- The Council of the European Union.

Together, these are known as the EU's institutional triangle.

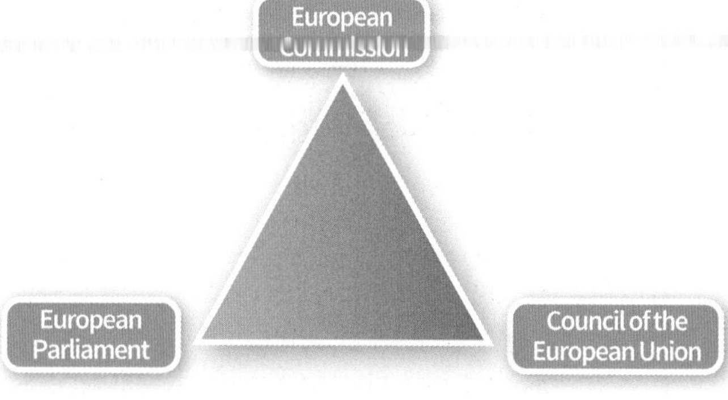

Figure 40.2 The EU's institutional triangle

European Commission

Commissioners are responsible for the day-to-day management of the EU. Each member state has a commissioner who has responsibility for a particular area of EU policy, such as agriculture or transport. A commissioner's job is similar to that of a government minister in Ireland.

The main functions of the European Commission are to:

- Propose new laws. The Commission works very closely with the Parliament and the Council of the EU to achieve this aim.

The European Commission building in Brussels

- Enforce EU law.
- Manage the EU's budget.
- Represent the EU internationally. For example, the EU trade commissioner attends World Trade Organization (WTO) talks, while the environment commissioner attends international conferences on climate change.

KEY SKILLS MIT

40.3 Ireland's representative

Find out the name of the current European Commissioner from Ireland. Identify the portfolio that he or she is responsible for. #Research

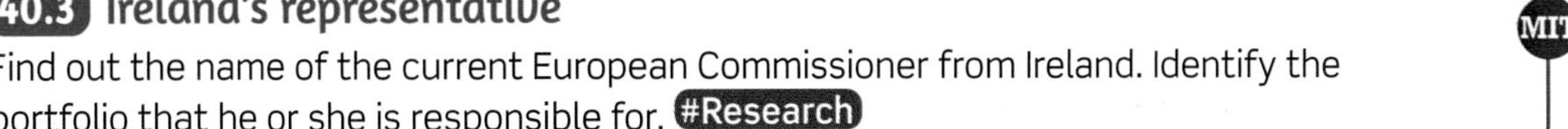

European Parliament

Members of the European Parliament (MEPs) are directly elected by EU citizens. Each member state has a set number of MEPs based on its population. Elections take place every five years.

KEY SKILLS MIT BN

40.4 Ireland's MEPs

(a) How many MEPs does the Republic of Ireland have? #Research

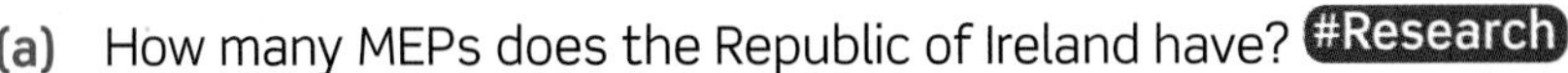

(b) How many members does the European Parliament have? #Compare

(c) What proportion of the Parliament are Ireland's MEPs? #Calculate

(d) Do you think we have enough MEPs to represent us? Explain your answer. #WhatDoYouThink

(e) Where is the European Parliament located? #Investigate

The role of the European Parliament

The main functions of the European Parliament are to:

- Represent EU citizens
- Help introduce legislation
- Approve the EU budget.

KEY SKILLS MIT

40.5 Ireland's European constituencies

For European Parliament elections, Ireland is divided into electoral regions called constituencies.

(a) What are the names of these constituencies?

(b) How many MEPs does each of these constituencies have?

(c) What are the names of the MEPs who are currently elected to represent your area of the country? #Research

The European Parliament

Council of the European Union

Council members are government ministers from EU member states. The membership of the Council depends on the topic being discussed – for example, finance ministers discuss budget issues, whereas agriculture ministers debate agricultural policy.

The main functions of the EU Council are to:

- Set goals and co-ordinate policy
- Pass laws
- Approve the EU budget
- Sign international agreements.

Court of Auditors

The Court of Auditors monitors EU spending to ensure that taxpayers' money is not being wasted. It checks that money given to member states is used for the purpose intended and it presents the European Parliament and the Council with an annual report each year.

The European Court of Justice

Court of Justice of the EU

Each EU member state appoints a judge to the Court of Justice, which makes sure that EU laws are applied fairly and consistently in all member states. The Court has the power to force governments and businesses to comply with EU laws.

European Central Bank (ECB)

The ECB:

- Sets the monetary policy of the EU. It controls interest rates and the supply of the euro.
- Keeps the level of inflation in the **euro area** under control.
- Ensures that the euro is a safe and secure currency.
- Issues euro notes and coins.

The European Central Bank

KEY TERM

The **euro area** (also known as the **eurozone**) is the collective name for the EU member states that share a common currency, the euro.

KEY SKILLS

40.6 The euro area

Which EU member states are members of the single currency or euro area? List them in your Student Activity Book. #Research

Benefits of EU membership for Ireland

The benefits to Ireland of EU membership can be divided into economic benefits and social benefits.

OUR ECONOMY

Economic benefits of EU membership

- The single European market (SEM) allows for free movement of goods, services, capital and citizens.
- The removal of customs barriers has **reduced costs for importers and exporters**.
- The EU provides a **larger market for exports**, which allows Irish businesses to reach 450 million consumers compared with a domestic population of under 5 million.
- Ireland is **less dependent on the UK** than it once was as a market for exports, as you can see from Table 40.1.

See Chapter 39 for exports

	1973	2015
UK	55%	16%
Other EU countries	21%	44%
USA	10%	23%
Rest of the world	14%	17%

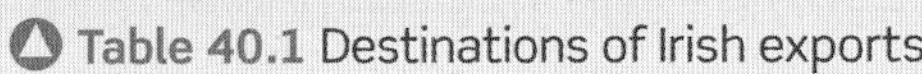
Table 40.1 Destinations of Irish exports

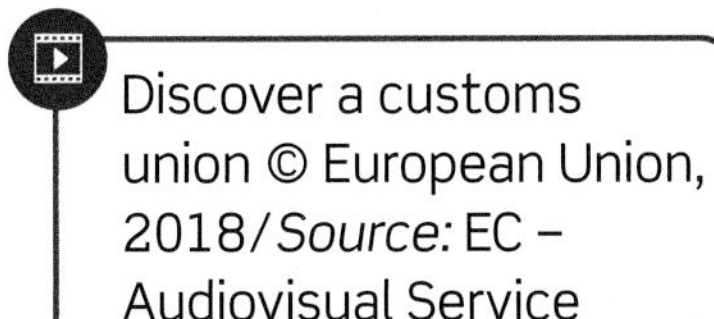
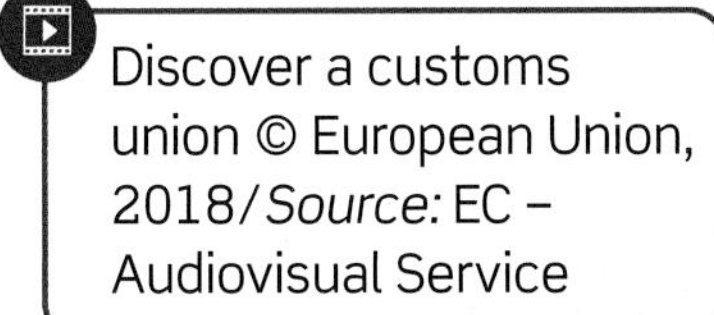
Discover a customs union © European Union, 2018/*Source:* EC – Audiovisual Service

- Ireland shares a common currency with 18 other member states in the euro area. This **eliminates exchange rate risk** when Irish businesses export to these countries. Exchange rate risk means that the relative value of two currencies may change over time, which makes the final cost of goods or services less certain.

Exchange rate risk

An Irish company signs an agreement to carry out work for a client in the UK. The work will take one month to complete and the agreed fee is £10,000. On the day the agreement is signed, this is worth €11,500.

In one month's time, when the £10,000 is actually paid, the relative values of the euro and sterling may have changed. As a result, the Irish company may get more or less when they convert their £10,000 fee into euros. If the euro strengthens against the pound, the £10,000 may only be worth €10,900 on the day it is exchanged. This means that the Irish company has lost €600 simply because the exchange rate has changed.

Exchange rate risk is a problem when working in different currencies. If both businesses are using the euro and the fee is agreed in that currency, there is no risk of its value changing, so the exchange rate risk is gone.

- Ireland receives huge amounts of **EU funding**, which has helped to develop our infrastructure and transformed our economy from one of the poorest in Europe to one of the wealthiest.
- The European Social Fund (ESF) funds projects to improve the skills of the unemployed and helps to reduce poverty, social exclusion and discrimination. Over €500 million was allocated to projects in Ireland between 2014 and 2020.

DID YOU KNOW...

Ireland has received over €6 billion from the EU's Social Cohesion Fund for investment in education and infrastructure. The Social Cohesion Fund aims to reduce economic differences between different regions of the EU.

- **Lower interest rates** have made it cheaper for Irish businesses to expand.

- Ireland is an attractive location for **foreign direct investment (FDI)**. Many foreign businesses have located their European headquarters in Ireland so that they can access the single European market (SEM).

Figure 40.3 Foreign direct investment in Ireland

DID YOU KNOW...

Even though Ireland has only 1% of Europe's population, we attract nearly 25% of all US greenfield industrial investment in the European Union. A greenfield investment is when a parent company starts a new venture in a foreign country. Overseas firms exported €250.5 billion from Ireland in 2016.

- The **Common Agricultural Policy (CAP)** is a major source of funding for the Irish agricultural sector. CAP invested €12.7 billion into Irish farms and rural economies between 2007 and 2020.
- Irish businesses can bid for government contracts worth over €50,000 in other member states. This is known as **public procurement**.

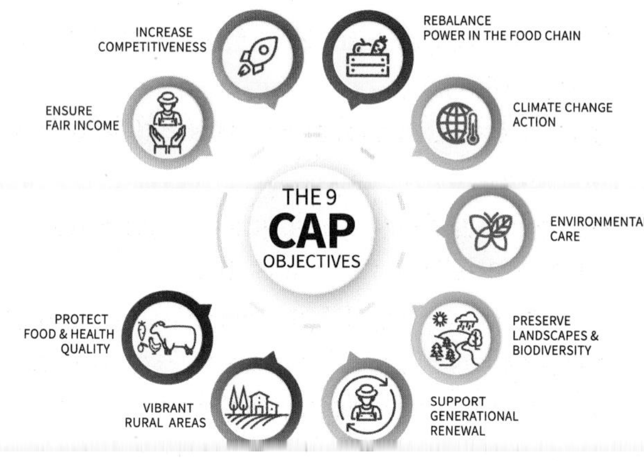

Figure 40.4 Europe's Common Agricultural Policy

Social benefits of EU membership

See Chapter 12 for consumer rights and responsiblities

- EU social policy has **strengthened the rights of Irish consumers**. For example, producers of processed food must provide consumers with nutrition and allergy information. Goods sold in the EU are subject to strict safety requirements and must have CE marking.

The letters CE are the abbreviation of the French phrase Conformité Européenne, which means 'European Conformity'. This is the manufacturer's proof that the product has been checked against EU safety criteria.

- EU social policy **has improved the rights of workers** by improving health and safety, setting minimum wage levels, ensuring better working conditions and providing holiday entitlements.
- Irish workers enjoy a **better standard of living** due to higher income levels.

DID YOU KNOW...

In 1973, Irish income levels (GDP per capita) were 65% of the EU average. By 2010, this had risen to 120% of the EU average.

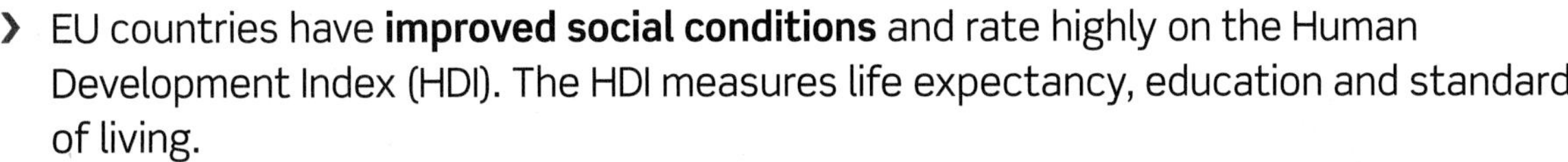

- EU countries have **improved social conditions** and rate highly on the Human Development Index (HDI). The HDI measures life expectancy, education and standard of living.
- EU laws on **workplace equality** have ensured that men and women are entitled to equal pay for equal work. Women are entitled to paid maternity leave and men are entitled to paid paternity leave. These measures have helped to increase the number of women in the Irish labour force.

DID YOU KNOW...

When Ireland joined the EU in 1973, women made up just 25% of the Irish workforce and married women were barred from working in public sector jobs such as teaching. In the second part of 2019, 56% of Irish women were employed outside the family home.

- **Consumers have greater choice**, as they can shop in any EU country without paying import duties.
- EU citizens can **travel and work freely** in all member states without visas or travel permits.
- EU roaming costs have greatly **reduced the costs of receiving and making calls** when travelling in EU countries.
- The European Health Insurance Card (EHIC) provides **healthcare access** to Irish citizens when travelling in the EU. The card entitles you to the same healthcare benefits as local citizens in EU member states.
- Almost 2 million young people have **studied in another EU member state** with the help of the Erasmus+ programme, an EU exchange programme for students.

KEY SKILLS: C, BC, BL

40.7 Study abroad

Research the Erasmus+ programme and create a presentation, poster or infographic explaining what it is, who can apply, which universities participate, and so on. Present your findings to the rest of the class. #Research #Presentation

KEY SKILLS: C, MIT, WO

40.8 The EU and you

(a) How do you think you personally have benefited from Ireland being in the EU? #WhatDoYouThink

(b) What do you think life would be like if Ireland was not a member of the EU? Write down your ideas and share them with the class. #WhatDoYouThink #Compare #Evaluate

(c) Does everyone in the class agree on the benefits? Why/why not? #Discussion

Challenges of EU membership for Ireland

Economic challenges of EU membership

- The single European market means that Irish businesses face **increased competition from lower-cost economies** in some other member states. This has resulted in job losses in some Irish industries.
- The ECB controls monetary policy for all euro area countries, including Ireland. This **removes our control of interest rates**, as we cannot reduce them independently to encourage economic growth or increase them to prevent inflation.
- **Ongoing reform of the CAP and Common Fisheries Policy (CFP)** will have consequences for Irish agricultural and fishing industries. Fishing boats from other EU member states can fish in Irish waters. These reforms may reduce income levels and the ability to create jobs in these industries.
- When the UK left the EU, it was no longer part of the customs union. This means that it will be **more difficult and expensive to trade with the UK**. As an EU member, Ireland is bound by EU rules on trade and cannot enter into a separate or individual agreement with the UK.
- As Ireland's wealth grows, we will need to make **larger contributions to the EU budget**.

Social challenges of EU membership

- Complying with EU laws on consumer and employee rights has **increased costs for Irish businesses**.
- Increasing the number of member states increases the diversity of the population of the EU, which creates **more language and cultural differences**. This can make it difficult to get agreement on policies, such as social policy.
- Protecting Irish culture in the European Union is a challenge. There needs to be a **balance between integration and independence**. Countries want to work together and share many things, but they also need to preserve their own identity and culture.
- Cutting turf is a traditional activity in rural Ireland and is a low-cost source of solid fuel in many Irish homes, but the **EU has banned turf cutting in some areas** to protect the bogland. Although this is an environmental benefit, it creates financial and social challenges for some people who have relied on it for fuel and employment.
- Europe is facing a **refugee crisis** on a scale not seen since the Second World War. Balancing human compassion with security and employment concerns is challenging.
- The EU has a **Common Security and Defence Policy (CSDP)**, which enables the EU to take a leading role in peacekeeping operations, preventing conflict and strengthening international security. Ireland's position as a neutral country may come under threat if this policy is expanded to provide for an EU army.
- Many **different languages are spoken** in the EU member states, which can make communication difficult. While English is one of the main languages of international trade, we need to learn other languages if we want to remain competitive.

KEY SKILLS

40.9 EU challenges

Listen to or watch the news on radio or TV or read it online once a day for the next two weeks. What EU challenges are being highlighted at the moment? #Investigate

KEY SKILLS

40.10 Up for debate

Now that you have learned about the benefits and challenges of EU membership for Ireland, hold a class debate evaluating Ireland's membership and what life would be like if we had not joined the EU in 1973. #Debate #Discussion #GroupWork #Evaluate

KEY SKILLS

40.11 Have you changed your mind?

Following the debate, have you changed your opinions on membership of the EU? Write down the main reasons why your views have changed or remained the same.

#Consider #Evaluate #Reflect

Impact of Brexit on Ireland

Ireland has a very close relationship with the UK for the following reasons:

- The UK is our closest trading partner – Ireland and Britain trade over €1 billion worth of goods and services each week.
- Overall, approximately 12% of Irish exports go to the UK, but this figure rises to over 40% for exports from indigenous businesses.
- The UK is the biggest export market for Irish food and drink products.
- UK citizens are the biggest customers for Ireland's tourism industry, with approximately 3.75 million UK visitors each year.

Possible economic consequences of Brexit for Ireland

Given the close relationship between the Irish and British economies, there are concerns about the impact of Brexit on Ireland in the coming years. The future is still uncertain, but you should monitor the following areas of concern:

- A fall in the value of sterling will make Irish exports more expensive in Britain and will make British imports cheaper in Ireland. This is likely to have a negative impact on Ireland's balance of payments since Irish-produced goods will be less affordable to UK customers and UK imports will provide increased competition for Irish businesses.
- Similarly, the tourism industry may suffer from a weaker pound, as British tourists will find it more expensive to visit Ireland.
- As a small open economy, Ireland is likely to feel the negative effects of any slowdown in the level of economic growth in Britain or the EU.
- Since the UK is outside the EU's free trade area, this will impact on the free movement of goods, services, capital and people. This is likely to increase business and travel costs and may see the reintroduction of tariffs and border controls.
- The UK may decide to cut its rate of corporation tax to enable it to compete more aggressively for foreign direct investment (FDI).
- As the only English-speaking member of the EU and the euro area, Ireland may be in a stronger position to attract FDI from businesses that want to locate their operations in the EU. For example, some financial services businesses may relocate from the City of London to the International Financial Services Centre in Dublin.

ASSESSMENT

Preparation for classroom-based assessments (CBAs)

In Junior Cycle Business Studies, you will carry out research and communicate your findings. These important skills will be assessed in Second and Third Year when you undertake two classroom-based assessments (CBAs).

Conducting research

Both of the CBAs will require you to conduct research and then evaluate and reflect on the information gathered. Media sources that may assist you in your research include:

- **Newspapers:** For example, the *Irish Independent*, *Irish Times*, *Irish Examiner*, *Business Post*, *Financial Times*, local newspapers, etc. You may access these in print, in your local library or online. If you access these in school you can do so for free through the Irish Newspaper Archive, which is available via the Scoilnet website.
- **Magazines:** For example, *Business Plus*, *Business and Finance*, *The Economist*, *Forbes*, etc. These may be available in your local library or online.
- **Radio programmes:** Local and national radio programmes, e.g. *The Last Word* and *The Sunday Business Show* (Today FM), *Morning Ireland* (RTÉ Radio 1) or the Newstalk radio station. Many of these radio programmes are available as podcasts, which you can listen to in your own time.
- **TV programmes:** Both Irish and international, e.g. *Prime Time*, *The Consumer Show*, *Watchdog*, *How to Be Good with Money*, etc. Nightly news programmes can also be good sources of information.
- **Online resources:** Try to avoid commonly used search engines and try some specialised business and economic websites instead, such as the Central Statistics Office (CSO), Economic and Social Research Institute (ESRI), Forbes, World Bank, World Economic Forum (WEF), International Monetary Fund (IMF) or the Organisation for Economic Co-operation and Development (OECD).

Other resources available to you include your teacher(s), family and friends. You could also follow economists, entrepreneurs, business newspapers and magazines on Twitter to keep up to date on current business and economic issues.

You should keep a research journal (scrapbook or folder), either actual or online (e.g. Padlet, Pinterest, Google Keep), to keep a record of all the sources of information that you use for research over the three years of the Junior Cycle. This will really help you when you are completing the CBAs in Second and Third Year.

When conducting research online, keep the following tips in mind.

Stay safe online	See the Webwise website for tips and information.
Think before you search	Don't type a question into a search engine – use key search terms.
Use special search functions	Using words like AND, OR, or NOT can narrow your search results, e.g. typing in 'budget AND 2020 AND Ireland NOT Europe' will provide you with results about the Irish budget in 2020, but not the European budget.
Try several search engines	Use several search engines for every search, as they may uncover different resources. SweetSearch and Bing are alternatives to Google.
Dig deep	The best results are often not on the first page of results. Try the second, third or fourth pages of results.
Don't believe everything you read	Searching for information online requires you to think like a detective – don't believe everything you read! Remember that anyone can publish anything online, so it's not always easy to tell if a website can be trusted. Compare the results on one site with those of several others.
Find primary sources	The best research sources you can use are primary sources, such as newspapers, magazines, films and photographs, as they are usually eyewitness accounts. If you search at school you will have free access to the Irish Times Digital Archive and the Irish Newspaper Archive via the Scoilnet website.
Consider who created the site or article and why	Information is only as good as its source. Always consider this when searching online. Visit the home page of a site and check the 'About Us' section. If there isn't an 'About Us' section, leave and find another source. If you find information on Wikipedia, remember that its contributors are anonymous and you don't know anything about them or how accurate their content is.
Check when the information was written	Always check the dates of your sources. Information often changes over time as more facts become available.
Record your sources	Keep track of the sources you use. Use web-based bookmarking tools, such as Pinterest, Symbaloo, OneNote or Google Keep, to keep a record of your sources on any device you use.

Communication

Communication is a two-way process that involves the transfer of ideas, information and messages from a sender (you) to a receiver (your teacher and other classmates). Communication plays an important role in business, work and life, so it's important that you develop your communication skills as early as possible.

Communication can take place:

- **In writing:** By preparing a letter, a memo, an email, a report or other business documents. For CBA1, you will present your work in a suitable written format.
- **Orally:** Occurs when people talk (and listen) to each other, either face to face, by telephone or by making a presentation. Body language and tone of voice can be used to reinforce a message as well as the words used. For CBA2, you will make an oral presentation on a business topic you have researched.

- **Visually:** Using slides, images, posters, charts or graphs (pie, bar, line/trend, etc.) or infographics. An infographic presents information and data graphically to enable it to be understood quickly, clearly and memorably. See page 9 in your Student Activity Book for an example. Infographics can be made online for free using tools like Piktochart, Easel.ly and Canva. Visual communication is an ideal way to communicate economic and financial information, the results of market research and to support oral and written communication.

CBA1

CBA1: Business in Action

You will complete a four-week CBA in Second Year. CBA1 is a group project (groups of three to five students), but you will have to carry out some individual research and reflection. Your teacher will provide you with research and reflection templates (sheets) that must be filled in and handed up along with the written group project. The templates contain a number of questions and your answers to these will be used to assess your individual contribution to the overall project. The templates you need to fill in can be found at the back of the NCCA *Junior Cycle Business Studies Guidelines for the Classroom-Based Assessments and Assessment Task*, which is available to download on the Curriculum Online website.

The group project can be completed in any written format of your choosing, such as a poster, report, information leaflet, slide presentation, etc. You will need to decide this as a group.

The guideline size for the group project is 1,200 to 1,500 words, but this may depend on the format you choose. Effective use of graphs and images may reduce the word count, so it's generally best to focus on quality rather than quantity.

Your CBA1 project will be based on **one** of the following areas:

- **Finance in Action:** Identify and research a financial challenge for a consumer or an organisation (profit or not-for-profit).
- **Enterprise in Action:** Engage in an enterprising activity. This will involve developing a product/service idea OR organising an enterprise event or activity.
- **Economics in Action:** Explore an economic trend, development, change or policy that is impacting positively or negatively on the Irish economy and society.

Your teacher will provide you with specific details about the chosen CBA before you begin the task.

Once the CBA is complete, your teacher will assess your work and award it one of the following descriptors:

- Exceptional
- Above expectations
- In line with expectations
- Yet to meet expectations

You will be assessed on the following aspects of your work:

1. **Your individual research:** Assessment will focus on the quality of your **individual** research; the effectiveness of your research method; your individual analysis of the research; and individual reflection on the research task.

2. **Your collective research:** Look at, share and evaluate all research collected by the **group**. Pick out the key findings and messages and use these to inform your group's action plan.
3. **Your action plan:** Based on all the (research) evidence available, your **group** needs to develop a plan of action. Try to be creative and ensure it's completed to a very high standard.
4. **The presentation of your group work:** The finished **group** project should be completed to a very high standard and include all relevant information. You should try to present information as clearly as possible using a variety of methods (words, images, graphs, etc.).
5. **Your individual reflection:** Assessment will focus on how **you** contributed to the project and what you have learned, not only about the topic but also about your ability to conduct research and work with others. Is there evidence in the group work to support what you have said about your individual research? This will be important, since teachers will need to verify your contribution. They will look for some proof that you have actually carried out the work that you say you have done.

The specific features of quality against which your work will be assessed are set out below.

Each feature is colour-coded so that it will be easier for you to see the difference between work at each descriptor level. For example, if you look at the green sections of text you should be able to see a clear difference between the standard of work and the quality of the reflection needed at each descriptor level. You should use these features of quality to guide your ongoing work and to self-assess your work before submitting it to your teacher.

Features of quality for CBA1: Business in Action

Descriptor: Exceptional

For work that is exceptional:

1. **The student uses a highly effective research method to collect data and demonstrates a high level of analysis of his/her data findings.**
2. **The evaluation of the collective research findings is of excellent quality, demonstrating a consideration of different points of view and the credibility of sources of information.**
3. **The action plan demonstrates ambition and creativity and is based on a sound, evidence-based judgment of all the information available to the student. It is completed to a very high standard.**
4. **The project is completed to a very high standard, is very comprehensive and represents information in a variety of different formats, e.g. visual, written, with little scope for improvement.**
5. **The individual Student Reflection describes clearly and in detail how the student engaged at an exceptional level in all stages of the project. It presents a meaningful reflection on his/her experience of group work.**

Descriptor: Above expectations

For work that is above expectations:

1. **The student uses an effective research method to collect data and demonstrates a good analysis of the data findings.**
2. **The evaluation of the collective research findings is of very good quality, demonstrating some consideration of other points of view and the credibility of sources of information.**
3. **The action plan demonstrates an evidence-based judgment of the information available to the student. It is completed to a high standard.**
4. **The project is complete and presented in a clear and organised manner, with some scope for improvement.**
5. **The individual Student Reflection demonstrates how the student engaged fully in all stages of the project. It presents some reflection on his/her experience of group work.**

Descriptor: In line with expectations

For work that is in line with expectations:

1. **The student uses an acceptable research method to collect data, although the analysis of the data findings lacks depth.**
2. **The evaluation of the collective research findings is sufficient, although there is limited consideration of other points of view and the credibility of sources of information.**
3. **The action plan is completed to a good standard, displaying a reasonably sound judgment of the evidence.**
4. **The project has some omissions, but overall is complete and is presented in an organised manner.**
5. **The individual Student Reflection provides some evidence of how the student engaged at some stages of the project. Reflections on his/her experience of group work are limited.**

Descriptor: Yet to meet expectations

For work that is yet to meet expectations:

1. **The student uses an ineffective research method to collect data and the analysis of the data findings is cursory.**
2. **The evaluation of the collective research findings is poor, demonstrating little consideration of other points of view or the credibility of the sources of information.**
3. **The action plan demonstrates a judgment of the evidence, though the evidence on which it is based is flawed in places.**
4. **The project provides a very basic summary of information, omits important elements and lacks clarity in its presentation.**
5. **The individual Student Reflection demonstrates limited engagement by the student in the project. The reflection on his/her experience of group work is very narrow.**

CBA2: Presentation

Your second CBA will take place over a three-week period in Third Year. The presentation is an individual project and involves three areas of activity:

- **Investigate:** You will carry out research related to your chosen topic.
- **Make an informed judgment:** You will reflect on your research findings and use them to develop an informed opinion about your chosen topic.
- **Communicate:** Communicate your findings to an audience during an oral presentation that will last for a maximum of 3 minutes.

CBA2 requires you to investigate and present on a business-related topic. Your chosen topic may be directly related to specific course content you have studied in class or you may decide to choose an issue of personal or local relevance, provided it is related to the business environment.

You will need to check with your teacher, but generally speaking, any topic that can be linked to one of the Business Studies learning outcomes will be suitable. You cannot present the same work you carried out for CBA1: Business in Action.

Some potential topics are:

- Field visit to a local enterprise
- Investigation of a business-related story in the media
- Leaders in the Irish business field
- Investigation of the impact of an organisation on a community
- Consumerism
- Investigation of a current economic issue
- Careers in business

We have included some other ideas that might inspire you in each chapter of your Student Activity Book.

It is probably best to choose a topic that you have a personal interest in. Your teacher can provide you with guidance to help you make sure it's related to Junior Cycle Business Studies.

You should avoid choosing a topic that is too broad, as this will make it more difficult to carry out the research and cover everything in a 3-minute presentation. It would be far better to choose one aspect or element of a broad topic and investigate it in greater detail. For example, rather than presenting on all four elements of the marketing mix for a chosen business, perhaps choose one element (e.g. promotion) and investigate it more thoroughly. You could then make a presentation on the effectiveness of their approach to promotion. Once you have decided on your topic, you will need to carry out some research to find out more about it. You can gather information from primary and/or secondary sources, for example interview someone and/or conduct online research. Make sure to record and cite your sources of information.

See Chapter 21 for more details about primary and secondary research. You will need to consider your research findings carefully and decide what is most relevant and valid for inclusion in your presentation.

It is very important that you take time to reflect on your research findings and include some of this reflection in your presentation (use the self-assessment and peer assessment template available on **www.edcolearning.ie** for this). For example:

- Has your research caused you to change your opinion about a topic or has it helped to confirm the view you already have?
- Are there aspects of the research that surprised you or made you think about the topic in a different way?
- Are there some questions you now have as a result of your research that might need further investigation?

You should not just present a list of facts about your chosen topic, as your teacher will need to see evidence of your reflection when they assess your work. It may be helpful to choose a title for your presentation that focuses on the 'value', 'importance', 'impact', 'effectiveness', etc. of something, as this will help you to reflect on your research and you will need to comment on this in your presentation.

Once you have analysed and reflected on your research, you will need to prepare and deliver a 3-minute presentation to communicate what you have learned. This presentation will enable your teacher to assess how your communication skills have developed across the three years of the Junior Cycle.

As part of this presentation you should give an overview of the topic and explain your interest in it. You should evaluate what you have learned about your chosen topic and reflect on your personal opinion.

When making your presentation, you may speak with or without notes. Reading a prepared script is allowed, but bear in mind that it is far better if you can avoid reading directly from a script. Confident communication and knowledge of the topic are aspects of the assessment, and reading from a script without engaging with the audience is unlikely to show strong evidence of communication skills or knowledge.

You should also have some support material that will help you to illustrate key elements of your presentation and make it more interesting for the audience. Possible examples of support material include (but are not limited to) PowerPoint or Google slides or Prezi presentations, posters, leaflets, digital billboards, props, etc. You have an opportunity to show some creativity here, but make sure the support material is relevant and will add something to your presentation rather than undermine it.

Make sure you practise your presentation at home before you have to do it in front of an audience.

Before making any presentation, you should:

- **Be prepared:** Know your key message and make it clear and simple for your audience to understand. Use the correct business terms associated with your topic, but avoid unnecessary jargon (language that is too technical and complicated). Remember, this is a chance for you to show your knowledge and understanding while also communicating effectively.
- **Rehearse what you plan to say in advance:** Write down what you intend to say and then *practise, practise, practise* until you can communicate your message without referring to your notes. Time yourself. Very often you will have a time limit for your presentation and you must stay within it (3 minutes for CBA2).
- **Consider creating an electronic presentation:** Use PowerPoint, Google Slides, Prezi, etc. or visual images to capture your audience's attention and support your oral communication.

During a presentation, you should:

- Begin in an interesting manner to capture the audience's attention.
- Remain on topic throughout.
- Present your information and ideas in a logical order.
- Make eye contact with the audience, not just one or two people.
- Speak clearly without rushing.
- Vary your tone of voice.

After making a presentation, you should:

- Seek feedback from the audience about what you did well and what you could improve.
- Reflect on what you did well and what you would change for future presentations.

Once the CBA is complete, your teacher will assess your work and award it one of the following descriptors:

- Exceptional
- Above expectations
- In line with expectations
- Yet to meet expectations

You will be assessed on the following aspects of your work:

1. **Your communication:** Have you communicated clearly and confidently? Did you show a clear understanding of the topic and have you presented your information in a logical order? Does your presentation have a definite start, middle and end?
2. **Your support materials:** Are they relevant and do they add value to your presentation? Are they used creatively to support your oral communication?
3. **Your reflection:** Can your audience clearly see/hear evidence that you have reflected on your research findings? Have you shown how this reflection has impacted on how you think or feel about your chosen topic? Has your opinion changed or stayed the same? How will this impact on your future actions and behaviour?

Features of quality of CBA2: Presentation

Descriptor: Exceptional

For work that is exceptional:

1. The student communicates eloquently and very confidently, displaying a very comprehensive knowledge of the topic, and the presentation is very well structured.
2. **The support material chosen displays creativity and is used very effectively to captivate the audience.**
3. The student's reflections on the topic are of excellent quality, demonstrating clearly how the student's point of view has developed or evolved over time.

Descriptor: Above expectations

For work that is above expectations:

1. The student communicates clearly, competently and with confidence, displaying a very good knowledge of the topic, and the presentation is well structured.
2. **The support material is well chosen to interest the audience, displaying some creativity.**
3. The student's reflections on the topic are of very good quality.

Descriptor: In line with expectations

For work that is in line with expectations:

1. The student communicates well, displaying a good knowledge of the topic, but lacks some confidence and the presentation is unclear in places.
2. **The support material chosen is appropriate but not used to its full potential.**
3. The student displays an ability to reflect on their own perspective of the topic.

Descriptor: Yet to meet expectations

For work that is yet to meet expectations:

1. The student does not communicate clearly or confidently, displaying a very limited knowledge of the topic, and the presentation lacks structure.
2. **The support material chosen is used in a basic manner.**
3. The student's reflections on the topic are narrow and of poor quality.

Assessment task

After you have completed CBA2, you will complete a written assessment task. This will be completed in your classroom but will be submitted to the State Examination Commission (SEC) for marking. It carries 10% of the marks when deciding your final SEC grade. The remaining 90% is decided by a final exam at the end of Third Year.

The assessment task is directly related to your CBA2 and requires you to carry out a focused reflection on your individual presentation and your experience of the CBA.

You will be asked to think and write about:

- The new knowledge, understanding or skills that you've developed as a result of carrying out the CBA
- How your perspectives/viewpoints/opinions have been changed or influenced by the experience of the CBA process.

How to reflect:

- You should think about what you did and what you have learned from **the experience**. This is likely to be about the process, the steps you took and the new knowledge you have learned.
- Consider what you liked and disliked about the experience and what parts you found challenging. Think about how you dealt with them and how this made you feel. Were you happy with your actions and with the outcome? Looking back on it now, are there things you could have done differently?
- You should also think about what you have learned about **yourself**.
- You should think about how your experience of the CBA has impacted on your thoughts and beliefs. Has your opinion of your topic or of yourself changed? Or have your existing views been reinforced by new information or by the CBA experience? Will this experience change your future thoughts or actions? If so, how and why?
- When completing the assessment task booklet you may have a choice of questions, so be sure to fill in the box to indicate which question you are answering.
- Your answer to each part of the assessment task should contain at least four separate points. Be careful not to simply repeat the same one or two points over and over again.

Final examination

Structure of the exam

The following is the structure of the final examination for Junior Cycle Business Studies.

Section A: 90 marks

- This section has 15 short questions.
- Questions are from all three strands (Personal Finance, Enterprise and Economics).
- Each question is worth 6 marks.
- Spend a maximum of 2½ to 3 minutes on each question.

Section B: 180 marks

- This section has three long questions.
- Questions are from all three strands. Parts of a question may be from different strands.
- Each question is worth 60 marks.
- Spend a maximum of 25 minutes on each question.

General tips for answering exam questions

- You will usually be supplied with some type of stimulus material for each question on the exam. This may take the form of a case study, a short news article or quote, an image, a graph, an account, etc. In some cases you may be able to use this information to support your answer – for example, you may need to highlight a trend in a graph or identify examples from an image or infographic.
- Always read the question fully before you attempt to answer any part of it. Carefully consider what you are being asked. Questions will be specific and you need to try to offer the most relevant information in your answer. You will not be asked to write all you know about a topic, so you need to think about your answer before you start writing. Unless told otherwise, you should try to give two relevant pieces of information for each answer. Use examples to support your explanations. In questions that refer to specific organisations or people, you should try to refer to these in your answer. For example, you may be given a case study about a consumer called David and asked about his rights in that situation, so your answer should say, 'David has a right to…'.
- You will write all your answers in the spaces provided on the exam paper, so this may limit the amount you can write for each answer. Do not write outside the answer boxes provided. If using extra pages for answers, make sure to show clearly which question you are answering. You should try to fill the space provided for each answer, but again, focus on giving the most relevant information based on the question you have been asked.
- Show your workings for all calculation questions.
- Look carefully at the action verbs in each question. This will help you to decide how much and what type of information is needed. For example, some action verbs ('name' and 'state') require you to provide key words, but do not require detailed answers. On the other hand, the action verb 'explain' requires a more detailed answer. A full list of action verbs for Junior Cycle Business Studies is set out below.

Be especially careful if you are asked to 'evaluate' something, as this requires you to make a judgment and explain how the evidence you present supports your judgment. For example, you may need to examine a household budget and make a judgment (or evaluation) about whether or not it is a good budget for the household. You will have to give reasons to support your judgment.

Information about previous exams along with marking schemes and suggested solutions can be found on the State Examination Commission's website.

Action verbs

Most exam questions will start with an action verb. Make sure you know what each of these terms means so that you can answer each question properly.

Analyse	Study or examine something in detail, break down in order to bring out the essential elements or structure; identify parts and relationships; interpret information to reach conclusions, e.g. *analyse* the financial performance of an organisation by taking a detailed look at their accounts.
Apply	Select and use information and/or knowledge and understanding to explain a given situation or real circumstances, e.g. *apply* your knowledge of consumer rights to a specific case and explain how the issue should be dealt with.
Appreciate	Recognise the meaning of, have a practical understanding of, e.g. *appreciate* that resources are scarce and choices have to be made about their use.
Assess	Judge, evaluate or estimate the nature, ability or quality of something, e.g. *assess* how an increase in interest rates might impact on borrowing in Ireland.
Calculate	Obtain a numerical answer showing the relevant stages in the working, e.g. *calculate* the difference between income and expenditure.
Classify	Group things based on common characteristics, e.g. *classify* items as needs or wants.
Compare	Give an account of the similarities and/or differences between two (or more) items or situations, referring to both/all of them throughout, e.g. *compare* standing orders and direct debits as payment methods.
Complete	Finish making or doing; bring to a successful conclusion, e.g. *complete* this sentence: 'The Consumer Price Index measures...'.
Conduct	Organise and carry out, e.g. *conduct* market research to assess a product idea.
Consider	Describe patterns in data; use knowledge and understanding to interpret patterns, make predictions and check reliability, e.g. *consider* how Brexit might impact on Irish exports.
Construct	Develop information in a diagrammatic or logical form, not by factual recall, but by analogy or by using and putting together information, e.g. *construct* a bar chart from information provided.
Convert	Change to another form, e.g. *convert* €400 to US$.
Debate	Argue about a subject, especially in a formal manner, e.g. *debate* the costs and benefits of taking out private health insurance.
Demonstrate	Prove or make clear by reasoning or evidence, illustrating with examples or practical application, e.g. *demonstrate* how knowledge of their rights can help a consumer who has bought faulty goods.
Describe	Develop a detailed picture or image of, for example, a structure or a process, using words or diagrams where appropriate; produce a plan, simulation or model, e.g. *describe* the stages involved in the product development process for a new good or service.
Determine	Ascertain or establish exactly by research or calculation, e.g. use the information provided to *determine* if the business has improved its profitability this year.

Develop	Progress or improve to become more mature, advanced, or elaborate, e.g. *develop* a business idea and produce a working prototype.
Devise	Plan, create or formulate a procedure or system by careful thought, e.g. *devise* a suitable promotional mix for a new gym.
Differentiate	Recognise or explain what makes something different, e.g. *differentiate* between volunteering and employment.
Discuss	Offer a considered, balanced view that includes a number of points, arguments or factors; opinions or conclusions should be presented clearly and supported by appropriate evidence, e.g. *discuss* the benefits of EU membership for Ireland.
Distinguish	Explain clearly the differences between two or more concepts or items, e.g. *distinguish* between debtors and creditors.
Evaluate (data)	Collect and examine data to make judgments about the value, importance or usefulness of something; describe how evidence supports or does not support a conclusion in an investigation; make judgments about ideas, solutions or methods, e.g. use the information provided to *evaluate* how well the household has planned their financial future and give reasons to support your viewpoint.
Evaluate (ethical judgment)	Collect and examine evidence to make judgments and appraisals; describe how evidence supports or does not support a judgment; identify the limitations of evidence in conclusions; make judgments about ideas, solutions or methods, e.g. *evaluate* how sustainable a particular organisation is.
Examine	Consider an argument or concept in a way that uncovers the assumptions or relationships of the issue, e.g. *examine* the relationship between price and demand for a normal good or service.
Explain	Give a detailed account, including reasons or causes, e.g. *explain* two factors that a business should consider when deciding on the selling price of a product.
Identify	Recognise patterns, facts or details; provide an answer from a number of possibilities; recognise and state briefly a distinguishing fact or feature, e.g. *identify* two benefits of membership of the EU for Ireland (note: this answer will require you to make two points and expand on each one).
Illustrate	Show clearly by means of diagrams, graphs or examples, e.g. *illustrate* your understanding of the term 'opportunity cost' (note: this answer requires an explanation and an example).
Indicate	Point out or show clearly, e.g. *indicate* whether the following statements are true or false.
Interpret	Use knowledge and understanding to recognise trends and draw conclusions from given information, e.g. *interpret* the data provided in a bar chart to answer questions about major trends.
Investigate	Observe, study or make a detailed and systematic examination in order to establish facts and reach new conclusions, e.g. *investigate* how an increase in the supply of new homes will impact on house prices.
Justify	Give valid reasons or evidence to support an answer or conclusion, e.g. *justify* the need for sustainable economic development in Ireland.
Monitor	Observe and check the progress of something over a period of time; keep under systematic review, e.g. *monitor* the ongoing impact of Brexit on Irish exports to UK.

Outline	Write a short summary with general details, e.g. *outline* one advantage to the consumer of contactless payments (note: this answer requires you to state and explain).
Predict	Give an expected result of an event; explain a new event based on observations or information using logical connections between pieces of information, e.g. *predict* how sales of a product may change if a new competitor enters the market.
Prepare	Make something ready for use or presentation, e.g. *prepare* a business plan in order to attract new investment for a start-up business.
Present	Promote or propose an idea; deliver or illustrate evidence; show something for others to examine, e.g. *present* two arguments to support the view that Ireland should remain in the EU.
Propose	Put forward a plan or suggestion for consideration, e.g. *propose* how a business may improve its liquidity.
Recognise	Identify facts, characteristics or concepts that are critical (relevant/ appropriate) to the understanding of a situation, event, process or phenomenon, e.g. how would you *recognise* if an organisation is having cash flow problems? (What information or data would you need to consider when making a judgment?)
Recommend	Put forward something with approval as being suitable for a particular purpose, e.g. *recommend* one suitable source of short-term finance for a household or business.
Relate	Associate, giving reasons, e.g. say if a particular business is profitable and *relate* your answer to the financial information provided (note: link your answer to figures).
State	Provide a concise statement with little or no supporting argument, e.g. *state* two reasons why a business should prepare a business plan.
Suggest	Propose a solution, hypothesis or other possible answer, e.g. *suggest* a suitable source of finance to make the following consumer purchases...
Understand	Have and apply a well-organised body of knowledge, e.g. use examples to show that you *understand* the difference between visible and invisible exports.
Use	Apply knowledge or rules to put theory into practice, e.g. *use* your knowledge of the principles of insurance to decide if a person making a claim for compensation is fully entitled to it.
Verify	Give evidence to support the truth of a statement, e.g. use the financial information provided to *verify* that an organisation is profitable.

 **PowerPoint Summary**

INDEX